JAPAN HANDBOOK

J.D. BISIGNANI

MOON PUBLICATIONS

JAPAN HANDBOOK

Send all corrections, additions
(enclose maps please), amend-
ments, comments, criticisms,
to Moon Publications,
P.O. Box 1696, Chico
CA 95927 USA

JAPAN HANDBOOK

Published by
Moon Publications
P.O. Box 1696
Chico CA 95927 USA
Tel: 916-345-5473

For single copies of either *Indonesia
Handbook, Japan Handbook or South
Pacific Handbook* airmailed anywhere in
the world send US$19 per book to:
Moon Publications, Box 1696, Chico CA
95927 USA.

Printed by
Colorcraft Ltd., Hong Kong

First Edition
January 1983

ISBN Number 0-9603322-2-7

© Hong Kong 1983 J.D. Bisignani

Library of Congress Cataloging in Publication Data

Bisignani, J. D., 1947–
    Japan handbook.

    Bibliography: p.
    Includes index.
    1. Japan—Description and travel—1945–   —Guide-
books. I. Title.
DS805.2.B57   1983   915.2'0448   82-20906
ISBN 0-9603322-2-7

this book available from: AUSTRALIA— Bookwise (Australia) Pty. Ltd., 101 Argus Street, Cheltenham,
Victoria 3192 (Box 204, Cheltenham, 3192), tel: (03) 584 4109/3507; NEW ZEALAND— Bookwise
(New Zealand) Pty. Ltd., 28 Fitzherbert St., Tetone, Wellington; SINGAPORE—MPH Distributors (S)
Pte. Ltd., 116-D JTC, Factory Building, Lorong 3, Geylang Square, Singapore 1438, tel: 4461088;
THAILAND— Chalermnit Bookshop, Erawan Arcade 1-2, Bangkok; HONG KONG—The Book Society,
16-18 Conduit Road, Flat 2 (G.P.O. Box 7804), tel: 5-241901; JAPAN—Charles E. Tuttle Co., Inc.,
2-6 Suido 1-Chome, Bunkyo-ku, Tokyo 112, tel: 811-7106/9; NETHERLANDS— Nilsson & Lamm BV,
Postbus 195, Pampuslaan 212, 1382 JS Weesp, tel: 02940-15044; WEST GERMANY— Nelles Verlag
GmbH, Schleissheimer St. 37lb, 8000 Munchen 45, tel: (089) 351 5786; UNITED KINGDOM—Roger
Lascelles, 3 Holland Park Mansions, 16 Holland Park Gardens, London W14 8DY, tel: 01-603 8489;
CANADA— Firefly Books, 3520 Pharmacy Ave., Unit 1-C, Scarborough, Ontario M1W 2T8, tel: (416)
499-8412; USA— Publishers Group West, 5855 Beaudry Street, Emeryville CA 94608, tel: (415) 658 3453;
Bookpeople, 2940 Seventh Street, Berkeley CA 94704, tel: (415) 549 3030; Pacific Pipeline, Box 3711,
Seattle WA 98124, tel: (206) 872 5523; or directly from Moon Publications, Box 1696, Chico CA 95927,
tel: (916) 345 5473.

ACKNOWLEDGEMENTS

I would like to offer a hearty *domo arigato gozaimashita* to the following people without whose contributions *Japan Handbook* would have been impossible: to John Redrup of Bookwise of Australia for having faith in this project from the beginning; to Bill Dalton for providing his publishing expertise and for hacksawing, ice picking and sandblasting the original manuscript so as to make it comply with the Moon format; to Keiko Saruwatari for teaching me my first words of Japanese and thereby making it possible to avoid making too much of a fool of myself when I first arrived in Japan; to John Nelson, Carl Parks and Wayne Stier for submitting and allowing me to publish their distinctive photographs; to Mr. Yamanaka of JNTO's San Francisco office for enabling me to peruse the photo files and to select the illuminating photos that appear throughout *Japan Handbook;* to Lorenzo Schilari for giving me tips on a bicycler's view of Japan; to Larry Taub, Vito Orlando, John Yoxall, Dave Cox and Bob Osmund for opening up their homes to me while in Japan and for sitting long hours while I soaked up their experiences of over 25 combined years of living in Japan; to Kaneda-san for leading me through the back country of Okinawa; to Moshe Matsuba for his long discussions of Hokkaido and the Japanese commune movement; to Masunobu Fukuoka for sharing his time and philosophy while at his commune in Shikoku; to Mayor Nishiyama for opening the doors of Yoshida town and to Tadachi Kikuchi for leading me through them; to David Castleman and Beth MacIntosh for taking a personal interest in *Japan Handbook* while typesetting it; to Dave Hurst for putting all the pieces of the mechanical jigsaw puzzle into place; to Clare Pryor for crossing t's, dotting i's and allowing no participles to dangle; to Linda Lang and Lori David for going cross-eyed stippling the maps in *Japan Handbook;* to Tour Companion for allowing me to publish their excellent maps of Tokyo; to Gordon Ohliger for his sensitivity and talent in creating the majority of illustrations that appear throughout the book; to Sarah Wiggett for typing at wages that only a friend would even consider; to Diana Hume for her herculean efforts at typing and editing and her spot-on insights that greatly improved the woman's point of view in *Japan Handbook:* to Yoshi Kuraishi for his translating and insightful talks and accuracy checks on the manuscript; to Frank Lavelle for his sharing of meditative beers when the spirit was willing but the flesh weak; finally, and most of all, to Marlene Marron Bisignani, my wife, my lady and my best friend, who supported me mentally, physically and spiritually through the three years of this assignment and who spent long, unsung hours typing her beautiful fingers to the bone.

photo credits: J.D. Bisignani — 43, 151, 158, 181, 182, 215, 220, 243, 248, 249, 267, 279, 282, 306, 320, 322, 356, 361, 362, 367, 371, 373, 374, 376, 380, 382, 387, 393, 394, 395, 397, 398, 404, 408, 414, 426, 437, 441, 449, 454, 464, 465; JNTO — 3, 26, 29, 73, 76, 107, 114, 159, 174, 189, 199, 201, 203, 204, 214, 223, 226, 238, 253, 258, 268, 269, 270, 271, 292, 294, 295, 299, 357, 391, 413, 420, 428, 430, 469; John Nelson — 30, 55, 257, 364, 386, 418; Wayne Stier — 25, 44, 52, 62, 152, 156, 173.

illustrations: Gordon Ohliger — 1, 9, 11, 13, 14, 18, 19, 22, 32, 33, 39, 40, 46, 47, 50, 61, 64, 67, 68, 71, 89, 111, 120, 122, 137, 140, 141, 165, 177, 186, 187, 200, 203, 207, 217, 218, 231, 254 (top), 259, 262, 278, 280, 301, 309, 315, 335, 339, 347, 352, 368, 383, 388, 389, 390, 405, 410, 415, 439, 448, 461, 471; note: Readers are invited to submit color photos and slides, or black and white prints, for consideration of publication in the next edition of *JAPAN HANDBOOK*. The publisher cannot be responsible for the return of this material to the submitter, so send only good quality prints or duplicate slides. The scenes depicted in all photos must be specifically identified if they are to be useable. If any photos are used, the photographer will receive an acknowledgement in the photo credits and a free copy of the book when it is published.

CONTENTS

INTRODUCTION

TRAVEL CHAPTERS

MAPS

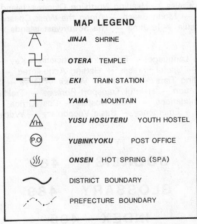

MAP LEGEND

⛩	**JINJA**	SHRINE
卍	**OTERA**	TEMPLE
-▭-	**EKI**	TRAIN STATION
+	**YAMA**	MOUNTAIN
Ⓨ︎H︎	**YUSU HOSUTERU**	YOUTH HOSTEL
Ⓟ︎O	**YUBINKYOKU**	POST OFFICE
♨	**ONSEN**	HOT SPRING (SPA)
～		DISTRICT BOUNDARY
⋰⋅⋰		PREFECTURE BOUNDARY

INTRODUCTION

THE LAND

The creation myths of Japan are found in the *Kojiki*, the oldest of the sacred Shinto scriptures. The accounts relate that two of the many gods of heaven decided to visit the then water covered earth. The 2 gods were brother and sister, Izanagi and Izanami. They descended to earth on the "floating bridge to heaven" (Amanohashidate), carrying the Jewelled Spear. They dipped the spear into the primordial waters and where the droplets fell, the first island, Onogoso, appeared. Izanagi and Izanami became lovers and their first offspring became the island, Futa-na. Many more island children were to follow and thus Japan was created.

GEOGRAPHY

The islands of Japan (*shima* or *jima*) rise in an irregular, jagged, elongated arc separated on the W from the Asian continent by the narrow Sea of Japan and facing the wide Pacific on the east. The archipelago stretches for almost 3000 km from Cape Soya, on the N tip of Hokkaido from where you can peer across the misty waters and see the USSR, to Yonaguni, a subtropical island S of Okinawa from whose sandy coast the mountains of Taipei are visible. An exact count is impossible, but more than 3000 islands make up the chain. The 4 main islands, according to size, are Honshu, Hokkaido, Kyushu and Shikoku. The remainder vary considerably in size with thousands being little more than a large rock along the coast supporting one lonely pine tree. The total land mass equals 380,000 sq km, which is less than .3% of the earth's total (slightly larger than Great Britain and slightly smaller than California); 80% of the land mass is mountainous with 60% of this total covered in dense forest. The Japanese live on only 3% of the land, farm 15% and the remainder is roads, pathways and river beds.

the coastline: There is approximately 27,000 km of extremely variable coastline in Japan. There are wild areas where mountains meet sea and foaming waves pound sea cliffs such as the San-In region of Chugoku and the western shores of Sado Island, the 5th largest in Japan. There are stony promontories surrounded by stepping stone islands as in the famous Matsushima area in E Tohoku, and countless gentle bays, peninsulas and beaches in the glassy calm Inland Sea. Sand dunes stretch along the shore at Tottori and further N in Niigata, while low, flat palm-treed beaches are found in the southern and far flung islands including Okinawa, and interspersed throughout the archipelago are rocky, pebbled beaches. The sea is ever-present in Japan, intermingled with the life of its people. Throughout the variegated coastal areas are fishing villages with nets being tended, the permeating odors of canneries and sea weed hanging like living drapes drying before the traditional houses on long racks.

mountains: The next most visible features of Japan are its mountains which include fuming volcanoes, snow covered alpine peaks, and

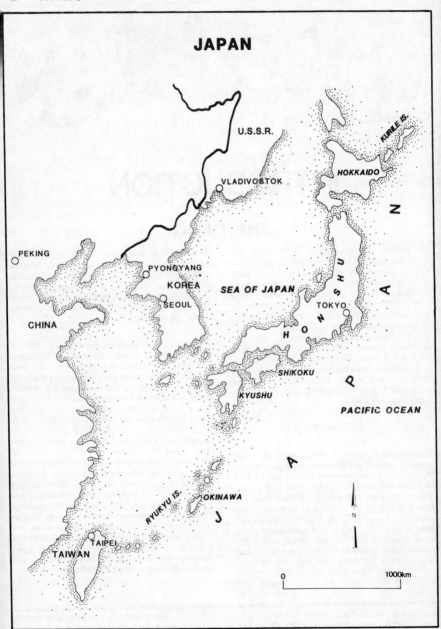

JAPAN

rolling hills of meadows and glens. Four fifths of the total land is taken up by these endless slopes. Mountain chains run from Hokkaido to the far flung Pacific Ogasawara Islands. The mountainous areas form the basis of most National Parks and offer mountaineering, trekking and skiing. The 2 main chains are the Hidaka Mountains (Japan Alps) and the Akaishi Range, including Mt. Fuji. The Central Highlands in the Chubu District of Honshu is the Roof of Japan, with dozens of climbable peaks over 3000 m. The mountains of Tohoku stretching from Bandai-san are frequented by the mystical mountain men of Japan known as the Yamabushi and are excellent for hiking and skiing. Hokkaido is a winter playland for skiers, and Rebun and Rishiri Islands off the N coast are mountainous, wide eyed, dazzling blankets of flowers in the spring. The 88 Sacred Temples of Shikoku are often located at the summit of mountains that yield extensive panoramas of the Pacific or the Inland Sea.

volcanoes: Geologically Japan is a youngster formed from the cooled lava of violent, cataclysmic volcanic upheavals, which now float restlessly on the Pacific Plate. The volcanoes are part of the Ring of Fire, a large geological circle in the Pacific which sweeps from the W coast of N and S America through Alaska and finally down the E Asian continent through Japan. Mt. St. Helens, recently awakened in N Washington, USA is one of these. There are about 70 volcanoes in Japan scattered irregularly over the islands. One of these is Mt. Aso in Kyushu, the largest and most active volcano in the world. Fuji-san, one of the 2 most perfectly formed volcanoes in the world, is the tallest mountain in Japan at 3776 m, and is the crowning glory of the benign side of this geological legacy. The volcanoes give rise to uncountable luxurious hot springs and mineral baths, deep rich soil supporting emerald green foliage, and breathtaking alpine vistas. They cause destruction as well as beauty. Minor eruptions are commonplace and the steaming geological sub-strata forces hot springs to surface which are tapped and give rise to numerous *onsen* (spas). Fumaroles, producing dank mists give an ephemeral, almost impressionistic veil along many mountain trails. Active volcanoes such as Mt. Sakurajima, standing like a brooding beacon in Kagoshima bay, are accepted as an ordinary part of life. At times tragedy occurs and villages are buried with a loss of life but the Japanese accept this as part of the darker side of the living nature that inhabits their islands. In the winter of

1982 a volcano suddenly erupted just S of Sapporo in Hokkaido. The momentary violence was regretable but life goes on.

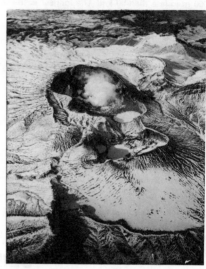

Nakadate Peak, Mt. Aso

earthquakes: The ancient myths say that a giant carp lies dozing under Japan. Every now and again he stirs and flicks his tail, sending rumblings through the land. The scientific explanation is that the Pacific Plate, afloat on the earth's mantle, slips toward the Asian continent under Japan. Not a day goes by in Japan without a tremor, the majority of which register only slightly on delicate, sophisticated equipment. The worst earthquake in modern times was on September 1, 1923 at 1158, centered around Tokyo and Yokohama. Tens of thousands of people were killed by the rubble and following conflagration, and the cities and surrounding countryside were virtually levelled in the hundreds of aftershocks. No one can predict when and if another killer quake will hit Japan. Only prayers and hopes can be offered against it. Another horrifying aspect of earthquakes are *tsunami*, tidal waves. If a quake's center is just off the coast, a giant wave can crash ashore, wreaking destruction. The Daibutsu (Giant Buddha) of Kamakura now sits in the open, but at one time was inside of a temple, that was over one km inland and was washed away by a *tsunami*.

rivers: The rivers of Japan (*kawa* or *gawa*), tumbling from the mountainous interior, are short, fast and mostly unnavigable. Many drop 1000 m in less than 50 km. The longest is the Shinano-gawa of Niigata that flows for 370 km. Many of the smaller, more rugged rivers are increasingly used for white water kayaking and canoeing, while tamer waters such as the Kumano-gawa on the Kii peninsula provide thrilling, yet safe descents through fantastic gorges. The Nagara of Gifu is known for pleasure boating to view cormorant fishing at close hand. Many rivers have been dammed to provide electricity for Japan's industrial furnaces, while lesser local streams are used for irrigation and even for traditional paper-making.

lakes: Lakes, ponds and streams are found in all areas of Japan, luring sightseers, trekkers and fishermen. Some are spring fed, others were formed by the natural collection of water in basins, and others are calderas of extinct volcanoes. Lakes and mountains seem to go together, forming a beautiful bond of a majestic mountain reflected in a glassy, tranquil pool. Biwa-ko just NE of Kyoto is the largest lake in Japan at 700 sq km. The Fuji Five Lakes of Hakone are picturesque backdrops in one of the loveliest areas of Japan. Hokkaido offers Lake Akan, known for the phenomenal barometric weed known as *marimo*, and Lake Mashu, also in Hokkaido, is the clearest lake in the world. Lake Chuzenji near Nikko feeds the lace-like Kegon Falls, while pleasure boats skirt its shores, stopping at lakeside temples and shrines. Many streams are fed by hot mineral springs. There is nothing more rewarding than a day of hiking and then coming across a natural, outdoor, hot spring bath. Most travelers arrive in Japan and are awe-struck by the richness of its 3000 year old culture. Its people are delightful, its rich folkways, temples, and shrines are endless. The tasteful riot of colors and shapes that are its cities and villages offer endless days of joy and excitement. All of these form the intricate design of an exotic tapestry, woven on nature's spectacular backdrop of a ruggedly sublime land afloat on a shimmering sea.

CLIMATE

One quick look at a world map will let you know that Japan is a long (3000 km), thin archipelago lying in the N Pacific just off the E coast of mainland China. Japan is in the N-Temperate Zone, making it a 4 seasons country with a temperature range similar to the eastern seaboard of the U.S., from Maine to Florida. The weather regions of Japan vary considerably depending mostly upon the mountainous topography of the interior and the ocean currents along the coasts. The mountainous backbone that splits the main island of Honshu down the center also divides the country into its 2 main climatic regions: the Pacific Coast Region and the Sea of Japan Coastal Region.

THE PACIFIC COAST REGION

This region embraces N Kyushu, Shikoku and all of eastern Honshu including Tokyo. For the most part, the summers in this region are hot and sticky in the coastal areas, which unfortunately include most of the largest of the Japanese cities, but in the small towns and villages of the mountainous interior, the temperature moderates a bit and there's much less humidity. The winters range from chilly in the S areas to cold in the north. Snow, except in the mountains, is not a major factor until approximately 150 km N of Tokyo. Here, the frigid Okhotsk current dropping out of Siberia hugs the coastline and can drop the thermometer drastically, but since the humidity is low, the snowfalls are, moderate. Spring and autumn, discussed later under "When to go," are superb as they are in all of Japan. An important factor in this region is rain. The least rainy period is during the winter and most rain falls in the early spring and autumn. It ranges throughout the region from 1000 mm to 2500 mm per year. Within the Pacific coast region are 2 special weather pockets: the Inland Sea Region and the Central Highlands Region.

the Central Highlands: Located in the Chubu (middle) District of Honshu, the Central Highlands Region is marked with a chain of tall mountains with a dozen or more topping 3000 m. This factor causes very changeable weather throughout the year. In the winter, the Central Highlands offer excellent skiing at many developed resorts along with isolated areas because of snowed—in mountain passes and roads. In the summer, the Highlands are a welcome escape from the dripping heat of the coastal cities and many fair weather resorts and spas have existed for centuries because of this reason. The general rule of thumb in this alpine region is that as the altitude climbs, the temperature goes down. You can be sunning yourself in shirt sleeves in a mountain valley while a blizzard rages high above in the peaks.

the Inland Sea region: Includes the N shores of Shikoku and the southern tail of Honshu from Okayama southwestward that borders the Inland Sea and makes up the majority of its shoreline. The Inland Sea Region gets the least amount of precipitation in all of Japan and can even experience drought which is a rarity in the remainder of the country. Since the Inland Sea is surrounded by land, it is seldom whipped to fury by storms and even escapes the typhoons that strike much of mainland Japan. In a nutshell, the year round weather can be considered Mediterranean with almost any time of year good for a visit.

THE JAPAN SEA CLIMATIC REGION

This region encompasses the entire length of Honshu bordering the Sea of Japan. The temperature gets markedly warmer as you head from N to South. This region has less rain than the Pacific Coast region, especially in summer, with the biggest difference occurring in winter when, amazingly, heavy snow falls amounting to 3 m and deeper are commonplace. What causes this are the winter winds that sweep across Siberia and Mongolia and then pick up water as they cross the Sea of Japan. When they strike mainland Japan, they are too heavy to cross the mountainous backbone and so they dump their staggering snow laden storms along the coast. Although there are heavy snows, temperature-wise the Sea of Japan Region can actually be a few degrees warmer than its counterpart on the leeward side of the mountains. This moderation is due to the Japanese current that runs along its shores, carrying warm waters from the South Pacific. Winter is generally too nasty of a time to visit, but the remaining 3 seasons are excellent.

THE NORTHERN AND SOUTHERN REGIONS

The region in the far N of Japan is made up almost entirely by the island of Hokkaido. It's chariacterized by bitter cold, snowy winters, superb but short springs and autumns, and just right summers. Hokkaido receives much less rain than most of Japan with the average yearly drop at about 1000 mm. This doesn't mean that you can leave your rain gear behind, but at least you can expect bright days although the temperature may be low. *the southern region:* stretches from Okinawa and its attendant island N to the S tip of Kyushu. It's the area of Japan that most closely falls into the category of subtropical. Winters at worst are cool and the summer heat is tempered by balmy sea breezes. Spring and autumn come very early, which adds up to good weather almost year around. The one drawback is that the southern region can be struck by fierce typhoons in season which will be discussed later.

PLUM RAINS AND TYPHOONS

the baiu (plum rains): In general, most rainfall occurs in the autumn throughout Japan, but along the entire Pacific coast of Japan, especially S of Sendai in Tohoku, a summer rain (*baiu*) occurs for about 6 weeks from early June to mid July. From time to time, the *baiu* is especially heavy and can even cause mudslides, but mostly it's a misty drizzle. City dwellers find this period particularly obnoxious when it seems that clothes are perpetually damp and green mildew waits to attack walls, closets and leather goods. The farmers, on the other hand, rejoice with the coming of the *baiu* which is extremely important to the raising of wet field rice. When the rains have been light, crop failures are commonplace. These rains aren't as depressing as they seem because there's a fair share of sunny days mixed in and the *baiu* departs almost as if on schedule at the end of 6 weeks. Another factor is that many Japanese gardens have been designed to be viewed when misty and wet and the panoramic views of coast and mountain have long been regarded by the Japanese to be at their loveliest when seen through a veil of rain and mist.

typhoons: These sea-going hurricanes, with their slashing rains, roaring winds and tumultuous seas, sweep out of the S Pacific and collide with the mainland of Japan in the fall, particularly during the month of September. The areas from Okinawa to the Kii peninsula SE of Osaka are particularly susceptible. There's nothing pleasant about these storms, but there's nothing outrageously dangerous either. It's true that over the years some typhoons have turned killer with an appalling loss of life and property, but most storms are short-lived and their fury dissipates as quickly as it appears. The typhoon season should be considered when planning your trip, but it shouldn't dissuade you from going.

WHEN TO GO

The safest way out for any guidebook giving advice on when to visit Japan would be to suggest spring and autumn. For anyone who has ever lived in a temperate region, the reasons are obvious. Simply, you have the best chance of experiencing the most temperate weather during these times. The drawback to visiting Japan during these seasons is that the Japanese, themselves, fully realize the weather benefits and Japan has one of the highest percentages of domestic tourism in the world. _spring:_ The spring in Japan is known for _sakura_ (cherry blossoms) that roll in a soft, fluttering wave of pink and white from Okinawa in February until they reach Hokkaido in May. They have a special place in the hearts of the Japanese and were even likened to the _kamikaze_ pilots of WWII who led a dazzling, but brief life. The _sakura_ are fickle and only last from area to area for about 2 weeks until their downy petals are driven to earth by wind and rain. _autumn:_ The highlight of autumn is the blazing foliage when the leaves of the trees of the abundant forests of Japan turn to crimson, saffron, scarlet and orange. The days between rains are crystal clear and brilliant. Mountain lakes offer a rippled mirror image of the surrounding natural ecstasy, but again, like cherry blossom time, for every sylvan vista there seems to be a tour bus full of hungry eyes ready to gobble it up. Accommodations at both times of the year are

AVERAGE TEMPERATURES IN JAPAN

LOCALITY NORTH TO SOUTH	WINTER (JAN)	SPRING (APR)	SUMMER (JULY)	AUTUMN (OCT)	ANNUAL AVERAGE
1. Wakkanai	-5.2	4.8	15.3	10.1	6.2
2. Sapporo	-5.1	6.1	20.2	10.1	7.8
3. Akita	-0.7	8.5	22.6	13.0	10.9
4. Sendai	0.6	9.6	22.1	14.0	11.6
5. Niigata	1.8	10.4	24.2	15.4	13.0
6. Kanazawa	2.6	11.5	24.8	15.8	13.7
7. Tokyo	4.1	13.5	25.2	16.9	15.0
8. Kyoto	3.5	13.1	26.1	16.7	14.8
9. Hiroshima	4.1	13.0	25.5	16.8	14.8
10. Shimoneseki	4.8	12.5	25.0	18.5	15.2
11. Kochi	5.2	14.9	25.9	18.2	16.1
12. Nagasaki	6.2	15.0	26.4	18.8	16.6
13. Kagoshima	6.7	15.6	26.9	26.9	17.0
14. Naha	16.0	20.8	28.2	24.1	22.3

RAINFALL AND HUMIDITY IN mm

LOCALITY	WINTER	SPRING	SUMMER	AUTUMN	TOTAL RAINFALL
1. Sapporo	104 (75)	118 (68)	64 (80)	90 (74)	1,141
4. Sendai	132 (71)	42 (67)	85 (86)	170 (77)	1,245
7. Tokyo	203 (57)	49 (66)	122 (79)	140 (74)	1,638
8. Kyoto	122 (72)	56 (67)	145 (76)	239 (74)	1,638
9. Hiroshima	111 (71)	51 (71)	156 (82)	276 (75)	1,644
10. Shimoneseki	100 (69)	77 (74)	134 (80)	252 (76)	1,705
14. Naha	149 (70)	122 (79)	142 (82)	174 (74)	2,118

(see map next page)

very tight, especially in the premier spots such as Kyoto and the mountain resort towns.

summer and winter: That leaves summer and winter, which are excellent seasons for visiting Japan, but you must be creative and flexible. Mid-January in Sapporo, Hokkaido can be magnificent. There are colorful festivals, world acclaimed ice sculptures, skiing, night life and few tourists. Remember that in Japan you have 3000 km to play with, all linked by efficient transportation. If skiing is your scene, leave Tokyo on a weekend for the resorts of the Central Highlands; if not, leave Tokyo by train, plane or ferry for the S regions. Head for Kyushu where you'll find a much more moderate climate or snow in its interior highlands. If you want warmth and beaches, island hop to Okinawa.

wintering and beating the heat Japanese style: Two conventions that make winters pleasant and particularly Japanese are the *kotatsu* and the *ofuro*. Since most homes don't have central heating, the *kotatsu* has been used for centuries to keep the cold at bay. Simply, it's a low table with a thick quilt draped over it. Traditionally, a *hibachi* (charcoal brazier) of burning coals was placed under it, but today this is replaced by an electric heating element. Sit around the table and hug the quilt around you. The Japanese believe that if the hands and feet are warm, then the entire body will be warm. Before retiring, immerse yourself in a steaming hot *ofuro* and then snuggle into your soft cocoon of thick quilts laid over a *futon*. In the summer, western style hotels and large buildings are always air conditioned. Most homes, *minshuku*, *ryokan* and YHs are not, but they're usually breezy with sliding doors and cool tree covered gardens. Don't let the weather stop your trip to Japan. Know what to expect and plan your itinerary accordingly.

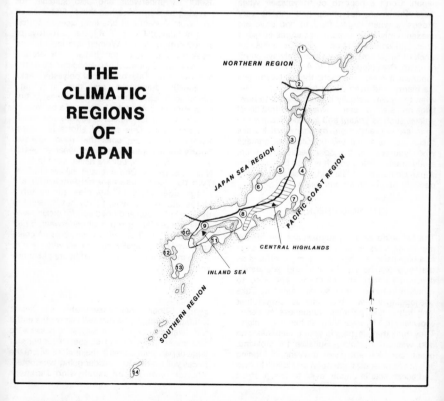

THE
CLIMATIC
REGIONS
OF
JAPAN

NORTHERN REGION

JAPAN SEA REGION

PACIFIC COAST REGION

CENTRAL HIGHLANDS

INLAND SEA

SOUTHERN REGION

N

WHAT TO TAKE

The type of clothing that you bring to Japan is, of course, determined by the seasons in which you visit, the places to which you go and activities in which you'll participate. You must remember that rain can occur at anytime. In mid summer you can be melting in Tokyo and in a few hrs. you can be freezing on the windy, stormy summits of 3000 m mountains. In January, you can be schussing the slopes of Hokkaido or Tohoku dressed like an Eskimo, and then board a ferry or plane S and in a matter of a few days or hours be scuba diving on a coral reef. The best rule is to use common sense, be prepared, and take a versatile range of clothing; this doesn't have to be bulky. Bring all the clothing that you think you'll need while in Japan. Don't expect to outfit yourself while there. Prices are not cheap and can be very expensive when larger, hard to find sizes are needed. Only large department stores in major cities and specialty shops will have a meager stock of larger sizes and you can't always count on them. Bras bigger than 34 A are a rarity. The Japanese live with the cliche that all westerners are giants, and even petite females, no matter what the reality actually is, are believed to have huge breasts. You can, however, find traditional articles such as *yukata* and *kimono* designed to wrap around, and more mundane articles like socks and hats that will fit. Clothiers grimace when you walk in the door because they are afraid of displeasing you. It is even believed that Japanese handkerchiefs and shoelaces couldn't possibly fit the enormous *gaijin*.

CLOTHING CHECK LIST

The following clothing suggestions are for the mid-range traveler taking one piece of luggage or a backpack. A range of clothing is offered so that you will be comfortable and adequately dressed to face the elements and also to function in more formal social situations. Take one jogging suit, which doubles as cold weather long johns and pajamas. (Japanese students, especially in YH, wear them to bed every night. They think that sleeping in your underwear is an odd western custom.) Suitable for trekking, beach combing and even traveling, a jogging suit needs no special attention and is well known and acceptable in Japan, even as casual street clothing. Also pack a down vest, less bulky and more versatile than an oftentimes too warm down jacket. Coupled with a windbreaker/raincoat, this is very warm and adequate in the mountains and in cold weather. A vest also makes a good pillow substitute for the rock hard miniatures used in Japan. A woolen sweater is fashionable and adequate for cool days and nights. A woolen sweater retains 40% of body heat, even when wet; synthetics and cottons will not. A lightweight windbreaker or raincoat may be used in combination with a woolen sweater and down vest for nasty weather. It's especially great for ferry rides. Try to find material that breathes, yet sheds water. The waxed cotton type from New Zealand, known as a *japara*, is one of the best. T-shirts (various colors) are useful as underwear and also suitable for traveling as warm weather shirts. Also include one short sleeved and one long sleeved cotton shirt or blouse; Two pair of jeans, corduroys or sturdy cotton slacks; Women can include one dress or skirt. The cotton, Indian wrap around types are good for most occasions and take little room and care. Take one pair of polyester slacks (optional); drawbacks are that they are inorganic, easily flammable and sweaty, but even after a month at the bottom of a backpack, they look neat for special occasions and wash and dry easily. One pair of shorts for warm weather; try to get ones that have pockets. Shorts are acceptable as street wear at beach areas and S islands, but are never worn in large N cities or towns. One swimsuit; bikinis are fine. Two bandanas: use as emergency first aid slings, scarves, small bundles, picnic table cloths, etc. A crushable, floppy hat is useful in the rain or hot sun and good also for picking wild fruits and berries. Five pair of underwear, 5 pair of cotton socks, 2 pair of woolen socks. Woolen socks will be especially appreciated when you're in the mountains or on the cold floors of shrines and temples.

shoes: Shoes present a few problems in Japan. Definitely bring a pair that will last for the entire trip. Western men find it almost impossible to find shoes to fit, except at special sections of large department stores in major cities where the prices will make you consider going barefooted. Western women can usually find Japanese men's shoes that will fit, but these are not always appropriate. *type of shoe:* For visiting shrines, temples, *ryokan, minshuku,* private homes or even restaurants you will be required to remove your shoes. It is not uncommon to do so as much as 10 times per day. Therefore, the heavy duty, lace-up hiking boot is a definite nuisance. On the other hand, if you plan to do extensive trekking, remember that mountains are great ankle-twisters and that volcanoes are strewn with sharp, jagged rocks. A good alternative is a sturdy pair of oxfords. Jogging shoes are usually OK, but trekking is really tough on them. If ankle support is a problem for you, bring a pair of rubberized ankle braces (like socks with the toes and heels cut out). They're available at most sport shops or pharmacies in the western world. If you can't bear to leave your hiking boots at home, remember the weight. You'll be lugging them most of the time. Bring a pair of rubber thongs, although you can find these to fit in Japan. They're used the same as anywhere. *Geta,* traditional Japanese wooden thongs, make great gifts and always bring a smile when worn by westerners in Japan. Most Japanese now only wear them to and from the *sento* (public baths) or when at a resort. It doesn't take long to get used to them and you can move along quite easily after a bit of practice. Take shorter steps and watch wet cobblestones. Even if they seem small, a proper fit, even for the Japanese, is to have your heel hang off just a bit.

note to women: The average Japanese woman dresses modestly in public. At the beach they are not body conscious and will wear bikinis, but on the streets of cities and towns, they tend to show less skin than western women. Tube tops, halter tops and short shorts are not worn. One annoyance in Japan is that you are always "center stage" and constantly being "checked out." Revealing too much only draws more attention. There is always the nagging, lingering problem caused by the belief of the uninformed sector of Japanese society that western women are "easy." The way in which you dress can either fuel or dampen these ideas.

TRAVELING KIT

Take a framed backpack or sturdy suitcase with you. A great alternative is the new style backpack that converts to a hand held suitcase. Japanese trains and subways, especially in large cities, are notoriously crowded and a large backpack is cumbersome in scurrying, pulsating crowds. *Daypack/flight bag:* Almost all train stations, ferry terminals and airports have coin lockers or temporary parcel service. Unburden yourself of your large pack and set out for the day with essentials only. Compartmentalize with plastic bags which keep things neater, easier to find, and dry.

necessary items: The following items are important ones to include in your pack: matches in a waterproof container, an all-purpose knife, nylon cord for clothesline, dental floss (can be used also for sewing and fishing line), a sewing kit, razor blade, flashlight (remove batteries when not in use), candle, mess kit, eating utensils, sleeping bag, sheet, tent (optional), extra passport size photos, pens and notebooks.

tiny items: In one empty film cannister, put in 4 nails with heads, a length of thin, bendable wire rolled up, safety pins, and a few fish hooks and line. These items have not been improved upon since the Industrial Revoltion; nothing else does what they do. Think geometrically. Safety pins can be used as quickie fasteners, cotter pins, instant tear repairers. Wire is easier than string for binding broken packs, handles, glasses, and doesn't burn. Nails come in handy as fasteners on walls or trees to string clotheslines or to improvise shelters. All combined, this miniscule "pack" should weigh just a few ounces.

toiletries: Mostly all toiletries are available in Japan. Brands may be different, but the results are the same. Naturally, take any specialty items with you. Toothbrushes, toothpaste, shampoos and other common toiletries are available from vending machines at travel terminals and other places. Tampax is available as well as local brands of sanitary napkins.

first aid kit: Over the counter medicines, lotions and salves are available, but not always when you need them, and sometimes, they're hard to describe to druggists. A good small kit should include aspirin, all-purpose antiseptic cream (for burns, rashes, cuts, insect bites), bandages and bandaids, pre-packaged alchohol swabs, sun tanning lotion, insect repellent, a small mirror to view private nooks and crannies, telfa pads, a razor blade, tourniquet string, cotton balls and an elastic bandage.   *prescription medicines:*

Bring a supply that will last. If impossible, prescriptions can be filled in large city pharmacies such as the American Pharmacy in Tokyo. Make sure that your doctor writes a very legible prescription.

contraceptives: The full range is available in Japan, with condoms ("condom" or "skin" in Japanese) being the usual. Contraception is usually considered the man's responsibility except in long term relationships or, of course, with "working girls." If you use the Pill, bring a supply. Getting them in Japan is a big rigamarole with lengthy and expensive physical examinations and other hassles. The Japanese manufacture boatloads of "The Pill" for export to other Asian countries. The side effects are considered to be "too dangerous" for Japanese women, but they're OK to sell to others. Abortion is legal and inexpensive in Japan.

HISTORY

About 20,000 years ago, massive natural upheavals separated the islands of Japan from the Asian mainland and generally outlined the present geography of Japan's islands. It is believed that 2 land bridges, one in the S connecting Japan to Korea and one in the N connecting it to Siberia, sank below the waves as the world's water levels increased at the end of the ice ages. The Sea of Japan was at one time an inland lake navigated by primitive sailors. These 2 land bridges accounted for the earliest migrations of pre-mongolian Asian peoples to Japan from northern China and S.E. Asia. Scholars also put faith in the idea that migrations of seafarers also landed in Japan at Kyushu from Polynesia and other South Sea islands. Legends and mythology common to both South Sea Islanders and the Japanese help to support this theory. Two other facts make this a supportable assumption. One obvious one is the general facial features of the Japanese. They are more refined than the flat featured neighboring Mongolians, pointing to an early infusion of other racial strains. The other fact, more open to conjecture, is found in Japanese architecture. Anthropologists feel that the basic style of Japanese houses, with thatched roofs and breezy air passages, points to an influence from a warm climate as found in the south seas. No one can ever pinpoint exactly where the people of Japan originated, but it is clear that for at least 2 millennia, they have maintained a racial purity second to none.

EARLIEST ARCHAELOGICAL FINDS

Stone implements such as knives, scrapers and spears have been found in Japan, placing the earliest inhabitants of Japan in the late Neolithic Age. Pot sherds of a type called *Jomon* (rope marked) show that a crude form of civilization existed in Japan at around 8000 B.C. This is early for any part of the globe. In approximately 300 B.C. rice began to be cultivated and, again, pot sherds from this period known as *Yayoi* (named after the area in which they were found in modern Tokyo) point to a more developed civilization. These *Yayoi* people also began to use metal. At first bronze articles were brought back from the Asian mainland, but quickly the *Yayoi* artisans caught on and began to manufacture their own. The bronze period was short lived and iron was quickly introduced and used. Iron implements were used mainly by farmers and the common man, while bronze was reserved for the aristocrats and for rituals.

early myths: The oldest myths held by the Japanese are that 3 divinities were spontaneously born in the "Plain of High Heaven." They were followed by 7 generations of gods until Izanagi and Izanami of this 7th generation decided to visit the celestial mud ball called earth. They descended on "The Floating Bridge to Heaven." The bridge can still be seen at Amano-hashidate in Hyogo prefecture about 70 km NW of Kyoto. This heavenly brother and sister pair could not decide if the mass below them was water or earth, so they dipped a spear far below to test the ground. When they pulled it back, a drip of brine fell off and formed Japan's first island. Izanagi and Izanami descended and gave birth to all the other islands of Japan as well as to numerous gods and goddesses. The last born was the God of Fire and being a bit more that his mother could handle, burned her to death. Izanagi then descended to the netherworld looking for his lost sister/wife, but could not retrieve her. On returning to earth he washed his face in the sea. While washing his left eye, he gave birth to Amaterasu, the Sun Goddess to whom all subsequent emperors of Japan traced their lineage. His right eye yielded the Moon God and while washing his nose, out popped Susawano, the Impetuous Male, better known as God of Storms. These 3 dieties are basic to primitive agricultural societies everywhere who rely on them for good crops and sustenance. Similar versions of a god giving birth to these deities after washing his face in the sea can be found in ancient myths of both China and South Sea Islanders.

Imperial Japan is born: The myths go on to tell that Susawano took great delight in tormenting his sibling Amaterasu. She finally became fed up with his pranks and decided to hide in a cave, thereby plunging the world into darkness. The other gods, finding the situation intolerable, devised a plan to lure her from her cave. They threw a party. They invited a number of cocks to crow whose clamor signalled the dawn. Ame-no-Uzume no Mikoto, a young goddess with a heavenly body, was asked to dance while the other gods drank *sake* and had a generally good time. One god positioned himself strategically with a mirror. Amaterasu, hearing the merry affair, was lured by curiosity from her cave. The god with the mirror reflected her beautiful image and she decided to once again light up the world. A rope was hurriedly stretched across the cave's entrance so that she could not change her mind. To this day, cocks are to be seen at Shinto shrines in remembrance of their past services, and the Sacred Mirror has since been a part of Imperial Regalia along with the Sacred Jewels and Sword prevalent in other myths. Susawano was expelled from heaven and descended to earth, landing at Silla, the then southern kingdom of Korea. From here he

headed for Japan and landed at Izumo. This myth gives credence to the fact that some of Japan's earliest settlers came from Korea.

the symbols of power: As time went on, Amaterasu and Susawano were reconciled and had 8 children. The eldest son, Ninagi, was commissioned by his mother to descend to "The Central Land of Reed Plains," Japan. He took the sacred mirror, jewels and sword along with him and alighted atop Mt. Takachiho in Kyushu. These regalia are still the symbol of Imperial Japan. After a series of worldly battles, Ninagi had a son who married the Sea Goddess. From this couple was born Jimmu Tenno, the first mythical emperor of Japan who moved in military campaigns northward and conquered the land of Yamato just south of present day Kyoto. A series of convoluted mathematics, based upon the Chinese notion of time cycles, cites the specific date of Jimmu Tenno's assumption to the Japanese throne as February 11, 660 B.C. This date is believed to be 800 years too early. A more accurate date of Jimmu's rule would be 100 A.D. He was probably an adventurer of Malaysian origin who used either the S tip of Korea or perhaps Okinawa as his power base. He did approach Japan from the S which supports the theory that a migration of people sweeping northward from the South Seas populated Japan in its early history. At first he allied himself with the sun goddess queens of Kyushu who did have direct ties with a city state (Karak, now Pusan) in S Korea. His main interest was conquest and he and his brigands moved on the main island of Honshu and set up their new kingdom between present day Nara and Kyoto.

THE YAMATO PERIOD
(100-600 A.D.)

During the heyday of the Roman empire, Japan was populated by hundreds of barbaric tribes who slowly fell under the influence of the new conquerors, the Yamato. Jimmu took with him a bronze mirror, a sword and a string of semi-precious stones. He brandished these before the barbarians, telling them that these were his source of leadership given to him directly by the gods. (Of the 3 original regalia, only a few scraps of the melted bronze mirror remain enshrined at the Imperial Shrine of Ise. Numerous shrine fires that occurred down through the centuries are the reason for its present condition. The beads were lost at sea with Emperor Antaku at the battle of Donnura about 1000 years after Jimmu reigned and the Imperial Sword housed at Atsuta Shrine in Nagoya was blown to bits by a B-29 during the final days of WW 11). Jimmu's empire soon became the most powerful in the land. He turned his attentions to driving back the *Ainu* who populated most of Honshu. Today, only a few of these original settlers can be found in far nothern Hokkaido. At first, the Yamato did not mix their blood with the conquered peoples. They sent back to Karak for wives and fathered enormous families, at times numbering more than 100 children. Their lives were that of consummate warriors. Other noble families, such as the Fujiwara, trace their lineage back to these times. They were the consuls of the emperors and remained in this exalted role for 1700 years with members of the Fujiwara advising Hirohito to the end of WW 11.

the early empire: The Yamato worshipped their ancestors and their beliefs merged with those of the newly conquered peoples blending easily into Shintoism. The Yamato were obsessed with maintaining purity. They initiated the Japanese bath which they used as a form of purification after battle, after sexual intercourse or after any act that they felt fouled their bodies. The greatest polluter was death. When a man died, his house was burned and when an emperor died, the capitol was moved. This practice lasted for almost 700 yrs until the bureaucracy became too large to uproot every time an emperor died. During these early times, the Japanese relied heavily upon the Empire of China and looked to them for advances in all cultural, scientific and practical fields. Chinese writing was adopted by scholars of the Yamato Imperial Clan in the 4th C and Buddhism was introduced in 552 A.D. Accounts of Japan previous to 400 A.D. must be gleaned from the writings of Chinese adventurers to the Land of Wa (Great Peace) their name for Japan. The Japanese called their homeland Yamato (mountainroad), a euphemism for conquest. There were many comings and goings by both people. One interesting account relates that the Japanese were ruled by queens in their early history, referring to those of Kyushu. One, Queen Pimiko, was said to be a sorceress who ruled by magic and divination. She was attended by 1000 women and only one man. Another, Empress

Jingo, was said to have led a military campaign against Korea in 200 A.D. Japan did hold political power in Korea until the 6th C at which time they were crushed by the Chinese empire. By the time the Yamato court began to take form just S of Nara in the 4th C, men were beginning to assume the roles of leaders and women began to be subservient. This social status of women became more codified with the introduction of Buddhism and Confucianism.

the sorceress, Queen Pimiko

fantastic "key hole" tombs: The greatest archaeological discoveries of this period are finds at a type of tomb called "key hole" tombs. There are thousands scattered throughout southern Japan. Some, although not as tall, are as massive as the Pyramids, and this points to the fact that the Yamato Emperors could summon huge labor forces along with the ability to organize them. The land barons of the times, known as *uji*, held direct control over vast areas of land. They, too, had tombs built and many have yielded armor, art works, jewelry and other accoutrements pointing to a privileged class. The greatest tomb of this period is found in Osaka and belongs to Emperor Nintoku. Archaeologists have never been allowed to excavate it because it is considered sacred. At first, court retainers were killed and buried with their liege lord. This practice was finally abolished by Suinin in the 3rd C when he used clay figurines instead of people. Even until Emperor Meiji, some retainers chose to die with their emperors. By the end of the Yamato Period, Chinese mariners began to refer to Japan as Zippon, "the Origin of the Sun." This later became Nippon or

Nihon which the Japanese call themselves and which translates as "the Land of the Rising Sun."

THE NARA PERIOD (600-784)

Before the age known as the Nara period, the Imperial Throne was moved with every succeeding emperor. Although the throne was moved a few times during the Nara Period, it was basically centered around Nara. Empress Gemyo established it permanently in Nara in 661 where it remained for almost 100 yrs. This entire age was marked by an enlightened culture. One of the most profound changes came to Japanese society during this period under Emperor Shotoku, who established Buddhism as the national religion. Shotoku was by all accounts an enlightened leader who encouraged culture and education and developed a code of behavior called the 17 articles. The 17 articles structured the government, placing it under the rule of the emperor. Shotoku also built Horyuji Temple near Nara and set the tone for emperors and aristocrats to follow a life of religion and learning. Later in the period, the powerful Soga clan who had risen in power were overthrown by the Emperor with the help of the house of Fujiwara, and Nara became firmly entrenched as the capital. After the death of Emperor Shomu in 756, his wife, Empress Komyo, completed the building of Taidoji and the casting of the Daibutsu (Great Buddha) that he had initiated. On the grounds of this famous temple, the Shosoin (Treasure House) still stands and holds accumulated relics from the then known world. Artifacts from throughout Asia, China, India, Greece and Persia point to a great deal of international intercourse that Japan enjoyed in its early history.

the Kojiki and Nihongi: During the Nara Period, the 2 greatest and classical Japanese epic histories were compiled: *The Kojiki* (Record of Ancient Matters) and *The Nihongi* (Chronicles of Japan). To these impressive works, Japanese of the following 12 centuries turned for history. Unlike many other peoples, the Japanese considered these 2 accounts of intermingled myths, legends and prehistoric accounts as historical fact, and based their lives on them. *The Kojiki* and *The Nihongi* were the prime sources of the notion of "We Japanese."

THE HEIAN PERIOD (794-1192)

The Heian Period began when Emperor Kammu decided to move the Imperial Court from Nara to a beautiful area called Heian Kyo (Capital of Peace and Ease). Heian Kyo developed into Kyoto (Western Capital). Here the Imperial Court remained for over 1000 years until the Meiji Restoration of the 19th C at which time the capital moved to Tokyo. The Heian Period in many ways was an age of enlightenment. China was still looked to as the great teacher, but Japanese masters of art, literature and religion began to come into their own. Buddhism was well-entrenched as the state religion and the emperors and royal officials began to spend more and more time studying it and leading a life of leisure. Eventually these practices turned into a type of Imperial rule called *In-sei*. *In-sei* meant that an emperor could abdicate the throne, pay most of his attention to scholarly pursuits and rule in a perfunctory manner only. This system gave rise to the ascendency of a noble family called Fujiwara. In effect, the Fujiwara ruled Japan. Also at this time, 2 great Japanese Buddhist priests spread the foreign teachings to

samurai warriors

the common man. They were Dengyo-Daishi and Kobo Daishi, the founder of the Shingon sect. Another religious step forward was taken when the ancient Shinto gods were merged with Buddhism. Teachings spread that the ancient gods were really manifestations of the Buddha, and the 2 religions were taught as being compatible. This made Buddhism acceptable to everyone.

the Samurai class: Internally the borders of Japan began to spread northward. In 794, Otomo Otomaro was sent to conquer the _Ainu_. He was given the title of _Sei-i-Tai Shogun_ (Barbarian Quelling Great General). By 820 the _Ainu_ were pacified and the borders of Imperial Japan stretched to the N tip of Honshu. At court, the Fujiwara became more and more powerful, holding the title of Regent with many of the daughters of this clan marrying into the Imperial Family. As the privileged class at court led a life of leisure, the farmers and peasants, especially on the frontiers, slipped further and further into a life of hardship. The court instigated a form of payment to officials called _shoen. Shoen_ were tax exempt lands, usually far from the center of government, ruled by military families (_buki_). The peasants in these areas often sought protection from thieves and civil strife, giving part of their farm production to these local rulers. This gave rise to the beginning of the _samurai_ class and feudalism, which was to last until the 19th C. At court, many literates, especially women, were encouraged in the arts. Two great achievements appeared by these literary, gifted women: The _Makura-no-Shoshi_ (_The Pillow Book_) and _Genji Monogatari_ (_The Tale of the Genji_). The rule of the Fujiwara became more and more corrupt until the situation became intolerable to other noble families. Finally, the Taira Clan (Heiki) challenged the Fujiwara and defeated them. The Taira were victorious, but were unfortunately just as corrupt as the Fujiwara. They ruled for approximately 20 yrs until the Minamoto Clan challenged and defeated them. The last decisive battle occurred in 1185 at Dannoura, just S of Shimonoseki, the southernmost point of Honshu. It is believed that the ancient Imperial Jewels were lost at sea in this battle. An epic narrative was written about the rise and fall of the Taira called, _Tales of the Heiki_. Yoritomo Minamoto, the general responsible for their defeat, became the first _shogun_ of Japan. In effect, the emperor gave Minamoto the reins of the government whose power came from a newly established warrior class called the

samurai. Minamoto moved his government to Kamakura and thus began Japan's rule by feudalism.

KAMAKURA PERIOD (1192-1333)

The Kamakura Period is primarily a militaristic period in Japanese history. The city of Kamakura, just S of Tokyo, was fortified and became the center of the _baku fu_ (camp office) or _Shogunate_ ruled under Yoritomo Minamoto. Subsequent shoguns divided Japan into territories with the help of _bushi_ (soldiers). The _bushi_ were all of the _samurai_ class and they evolved a code of ethics and behavior known as _bushido_ (The Way of the Warrior). The _samurai_ were similar to the Spartans of ancient Greece. Their lives were simple and straightforward. Loyalty was the greatest virtue. The arts took a masculine turn and war narratives began to be written. The greatest art of the period was the manufacture of fine swords and armor. The greatest swordsmith was Masamune and from that time to the present day, the Japanese became enamored with this symbol of class and masculinity. A fine cutting instrument passed down through the generations is still the most prized heirloom. Eventually, the Minamoto lost power and were replaced by a puppet _shogun_ from the Fujiwara family, whose strings were manipulated by the Hojo family.

threat from China: Late in the Kamakura period, Kublai Khan sent an expeditionary force to invade Japan. This first invasion occurred in 1274 and the Japanese warriors were victorious. Again in 1281 the Mongols invaded, sending 100,000 men in a great armada. The Japanese had built coastal fortifications at Hakata in Kyushu and in preparation, the priests of the Buddhist temples throughout the land fervently beseeched the gods for help. As the armada approached, a great typhoon swept down upon the invaders and the majority of the men were lost at sea. The Japanese named this heavenly intervention _Kami-Kaze_ (Divine Wind). It was from this aborted Mongol invasion of 1281 that the WW11 suicide pilots were given their name. A fascinating account of these battles was brought back to the western world by the great adventurer, Marco Polo. This battle also led to the subsequent downfall of the Kamakura shogunate. The warriors in effect were not paid for their services and the authority at Kamakura lost their support. Meanwhile, Emperor Godaigo saw his chance to reestablish the dominance of Imperial Rule and led a rebellion against the Shogunate. His first attempt was unsuccessful and he was exiled to Oki Island, 70 km from the coastal city of Matsue. He remained there for one year and returned to lead a successful rebellion aided by able generals. The short period of royal leadership became known as the Kammu Restoration. Again internal corruption led to its downfall when Emperor Godaigo refused to pay his warriors and rewarded the nobles, court officials and priests, instead. Takauji Ashikaga rebelled and restored the shogunate in 1338.

MUROMACHI PERIOD (1335-1572)

Takauji Ashikaga met Emperor Godiago's forces in Kyoto in 1338. The Imperial forces were routed and the defeated emperor took refuge in the Yoshino Mountains near Nara. The *shogun* then placed a new emperor on the throne and the Japanese royal house was split into the N (Kyoto) Court and the S (Yoshino) court. The royal court was not reconciled until 57 yrs later. Takauji lived a luxurious life. He built Kinkakuji, the Gold Pavilion, in Kyoto in which to pursue the finer pleasurers. When he died, no strong ruler rose to take his place and Japan slipped steadily into civil chaos. Finally, under Shogun

uchikake, an outer dress worn by ladies from the military class during the Muromachi Period. The *uchikake*, with some alterations, has survived to the present day and is worn as a wedding dress

Noh plays are dramatized by dialogue sung or chanted in varying tones. Their classic phase dates from the Muromachi Period

Yoshimasa, who built Ginkakuji (Silver Pavilion), the situation deteriorated to the point of open civil war. This was a political dark age for Japan that lasted over 100 years. *Daimyo* fortified themselves in their castles and constant power struggles raked the land as one tried to overthrow the power of his neighbors. Oddly enough, the arts did not suffer and actually flourished. The performing arts of *Noh* and its related farce plays, *Kyogen*, came into vogue. *Zen* (meditative) Buddhism occupied the spiritual leaders while *chanoyu* (the tea ceremony) and *ikebana* (flower arranging) were pursued by the privileged classes.

<u>*westerners arrive:*</u> To compound the internal turmoil even more, the western nations had discovered Japan and were sending traders and missionaries. The Portuguese, who were some of the first Europeans to arrive, introduced the Japanese to firearms in 1543 when a ship ran aground on Tanegashima Island S of Kagoshima. The military potential of the muskets that it carried was immediately recognized by the local Satsuma lords. A few years later, after these prototypes were purchased for a phenomenal amount of money, swordsmiths of Kagoshima were putting out well-made Japanese models. St. Francis Xavier landed in Kyushu in 1549 and began to convert the local citizenry and the ruling local *daimyo* to Christianity,

especially around Nagasaki. Japan was weakened internally and the time was ripe for conquest by the western barbarians. The Catholic Church vied for power and played the warring *daimyo* one against the other. The Christians were allowed to practice their new religions, especially because very strong Buddhist temples had gained a fair measure of political control and they were highly resented by the ruling class. Eventually, the Dutch sent trading ships and at the end of this stormy period were the only foreigners allowed to trade with the Japanese. They were given the tiny island of Dejima as their trading port in Nagasaki Harbor. This would be the only chink in the closed doors of Japan where foreign culture would seep in. First the country had to be reunited.

AZUCHI-MOMOYAMA PERIOD (1573-1600)

Although this period lasted a brief 17 years it would bear great influence upon Japanese history for the next 2½ centuries. It was a sink or swim period for Japan and from the very heart of its strongest samurai families, great leaders would emerge. Only the fittest would survive. The first was Nobunaga Oda. His domain was in the modern Aichi prefecture centered around Nagoya. He surrounded himself with able generals, conquered the surrounding *daimyo*, and moved on Kyoto with intentions of reestablishing the shogunate. He was the first to use firearms effectively in battle. He began to pave the long road of political hegemony. For 10 yrs he strove to this end, but before he completed his mission, he was assassinated by one of his guards in 1582. His most able general, Toyotomi Hideyoshi, took over and moved closer to completely dominating the country. Toyotomi was a brilliant military man but he was a commoner born to a peasant family. His legendary bad looks earned him the title, "Crowned Monkey." He partially overstepped his power when he sent a Japanese force to fight the Chinese in Korea in 1598. During this conflict, Hideyoshi died and the ill-fated campaign was broken off. His young son was placed in Osaka castle where he was surrounded by advisors until he reached a fitting age to rule. Hideyoshi's generals looked at each other with unmasked suspicion as the doors to total power lay wide open.

Japan fortifies: The Azuchi-Momoyama period brought castle architecture to grandiose propor-

tions. Everywhere the local rulers fortified themselves. Osaka Castle was the most stupendous. Some of the stones used in its walls were over 10 m long by 8 m high. Fifty thousand laborers toiled for 3 yrs in its completion, with *daimyo* sending materials from all over the land. It was because of this period that Japanese streets seem to be a purposely built maze. None leading to the castle went in a straight line. This feature was built in to slow up any would-be invaders who would be forced to march down very narrow roadways often ending in easily fortified dead ends. The castle grounds always sat high and gave an extensive view of the surrounding countryside. The arts of the period were infused with the feeling of grandeur. Paintings were done by such artists as Kano and Kaiho, who used vivid colors and bold strokes, paraphrasing the psyche of the leaders of the times. *Chanoyu* reached its greatest popularity, becoming a national art form, while *Kabuki* dazzled audiences with its magnificent scenery and grand productions.

EDO PERIOD (1603-1867)

This period is also known as the Tokugawa Period, named after the towering figure of the times, Ieyasu Tokugawa. When Toyotomi died, Tokugawa and Mitsunari Ishida rose to vie for the shogunate. It was a life and death struggle with Ieyasu Tokugawa defeating his opponent at the decisive battle of Sekigahara in the present Gifu prefecture. Three years later, Ieyasu was named *Sei-I-Taishogun*. Although there had been a *shogun* in previous Japanese history, none matched the complete control wielded by Tokugawa. His name has become synonymous with the title. He moved his *bakufu* government to a fortified town in the Kanto district known as Edo which later was renamed Tokyo. The beginnings of the Tokugawa period were ripe with intrigue and adventure.

the foreign menace: The western nations of Holland, England, Spain and Portugal sent merchant ships in ever-increasing numbers. During this period, and English pilot on a Dutch trading vessel came to Japan. His name was Will Adams. Anjin-san, the main character in James Clavell's popular and historically embellished novel, *Shogun*, was patterned after him. Adams was to become a naval advisor to Ieyasu. He was never again to leave Japan where he took a Japanese wife.

the *shogun*, Tokugawa Ieyasu

There is a momument to his memory at the small town of Ito on the Izu Peninsula. The Tokugawa government became aware of the fact that the Jesuit missionaries sent from Spain and Portugal were a real political threat. A growing number of *daimyo* had accepted the new faith, although it had been previously banned by Hideyoshi. Especially around Nagasaki, the *daimyo* had embraced Christianity (*Kirishitanshu*) and had sent envoys to Rome. One of the greatest sea-faring expeditions of all time was instigated by Date Masamune, a *daimyo* from modern day Sendai, who sent his retainer, Hasekura, to Rome. The adventure led the Japanese across the Pacific to Acapulco, Mexico and then on to Europe. What troubled the *Shogun* was the Spanish and Portuguese alliance to the Pope, who was seen as a temporal ruler interested in the conquering of Japan, itself. Particularly perplexing was a Papal Bull of which Ieyasu was aware. In effect, the Pope had divided the world down the middle between the Spanish and Portuguese, who had remained steadfast during the Reformation. The governing of Japan by a foreign nation was unthinkable. An excellent window into these times is given by Lafcadio Hearn in his historical work, *Japan: An Interpretation*.

shutting out foreign influences: Eventually, in 1637, the Christian *daimyo* supported by the Jesuits rose in rebellion in Shimabara near Nagasaki. Iemitsu, Ieyasu's son, was now *shogun* and his forces completely destroyed the insurrection. A number of foreign priests and faithful were crucified and Christianity was banned. It went underground and prevailed unassisted by clergy or a central church for 250 yrs. Since the Dutch were Protestants and owed no allegiance to the Pope, they were allowed to trade at Dejima Island, a small island in Nagasaki port. Only they, the Chinese and Koreans were allowed this privilege. Prostitutes and merchants were the only Japanese allowed to come into contact with them. During this period, Iemitsu built the greatest shrine in Japan, Toshogu in Nikko. These grand structures house the mausoleum of his renowned father, Ieyasu. The doors of Japan were closed, bolted and fortified, but not as tightly as most people assumed. Most importantly, the Japanese and westerners had learned a bit about each other's culture and it would be only a matter of time before the westerners returned in force. Japan did not realize it, but at that time its legions of disciplined soldiers armed with firearms were probably the 2nd strongest nation in the world. The population of Japan was equal to that of England, France, Holland, Spain and Portugal combined making a military conquest of Japan by the western powers pure folly. The spirit that prevailed throughout the land was one of peace and the peace was insured by the *samurai*. No citizen was allowed to leave Japan and any intruders were quickly put to death. The *bakufu* in Edo did, however, keep a watchful eye on the west. Japanese scholars studied western medicine and science, while the military progressed in gunnery and tactics. This knowledge was the guarded domain of the *shogun*.

ruling with an iron hand: The country was divided and placed in the hands of *diamyo*, who owed total allegiance to the *shogun*. For political reasons, they were kept constantly on the move between their home territories and Edo. Basically, they were held in a loose form as hostages. Every 2 yrs they were forced to make a journey from their feudal lands to the capital which in many instances took months. They would no sooner return home when preparations must begin for their return. No time was left to ferment political intrigue and the costs of such journeys was a constant monetary drain. The society was broken down into the nobility, who had no real power, the *daimyo* and their *samurai*, farmers, and lastly merchants. The

seppuku: During a *seppuku* ceremony the principal's best friend or a trusted comrade served as the second, ready with his sword to lop off the head if nerve or resolve waivered. A perfect ceremony called for the principal to thrust his sword into his belly just below the navel and then to draw upwards to the sternum. Then the sword is drawn in a horizontal line crosswise. The next gory step was for him to reach inside the gaping wound and eviscerate himself. Few achieved perfection

pursuit of money was below a samurai, who was borne up on the sagging shoulders of the peasantry. It was at this time that the peasants suffered great hardships. The system was top heavy with the *samurai* class, while the peasants paid the taxes. Gross crimes against them were rampant. Daughters were sold into prostitution, the mouths and noses of infant girls from overly large families were-pasted over with paper so that they suffocated, husbands and wives at times could not live together and were forced to stay in the homes or areas of their masters. Japan was, in effect, a police state. The *samurai* had no internal or external battles to fight. They also had unquestioned authority. Literally at their whim, they could draw one of the two swords, the symbol of their authority, and lop off the head of a peasant for the terrible crime of not bowing quickly enough. The offender's family would then apologize for the poor manners and the nuisance created by its errant member. These grisly scenes did not happen frequently, but once in a while was more than enough for everyone to get the message. There was almost no social mobility. What you were born into was generally what you remained. Your manner of clothing, food, and even sleeping postures were dictated. Given this seemingly depressing backdrop, all was not bleak. Life went on in relative peace. Generation after generation led a life of security free from hostility as long as they obeyed the rules.

lasting effects: This period had the most profound effect on the Japanese people, lasting to the present day. Residual customs, manners, beliefs and social etiquettes can be traced easily to these times. The arts also flourished and many art forms popularly enjoyed today trace their origins and highest points of development to this period. Basho, the most famous of the *haiku* poets, developed these ephemeral word images into an art. *Bunraku* puppet plays, raised to an art by the master Chikamatsu Monzae-mon, delighted the populace, and dramatic *ukiyo-e* painting came into vogue. The famous incident of the 47 *Ronin* (masterless *samurai*) occurred in 1703. Their heroic feats of undying loyalty, followed by their noble deaths by *seppuku,* have been immortalized in poetry and plays ever since.

the shogunate fails: By the 1800's, the system was beginning to fail. The *samurai* and peasants slipped further into poverty and the merchants, who were considered opportunist parasites, grew more powerful. A series of famines further weakened the people as political reforms began to erode the shogunate itself. The *samurai* had long since lost their taste for battle. They did follow a code of ethics, but skills in the tea ceremony were regarded as highly as the use of weapons. Many poorer *samurai* became monks as other families adopted the sons of merchants to bolster the family income. Many *ronin* roamed the countryside with little more possessions than their 2 swords, the last badges of their hollow rank. By the beginning of the 19th C, the system was weakening badly. Again, the westerners came. At first they were Russian traders in far off Hokkaido. Next came an American mercy ship to Uraga in 1837. Finally in 1853, the American Admiral Perry arrived with his "black ships" and the doors of Japan were pried open. A treaty of Friendship and Trade was signed with the U.S. and Townsend Harris became the first official diplomat. The British then came in 1863 and as a show of force bombarded Kagoshima. The next year a combined fleet of British, Dutch and French ships annihilated forces of the Choshu clan at Shimonoseki. It was then obvious that the shogunate was no longer able to effectively rule Japan. In 1867 the young Emperor Meiji ascended the throne. Silent and cloistered for 250 yrs, the Imperial family was now the only binding force effectively functioning in the nation. Meiji saw that Japan had only one course open to it and that was to enter once again into the world at large.

THE MEIJI RESTORATION (1867-1912)

Emperor Meiji, surrounded by able advisors, rose to squarely meet the times. In 1868, he officially moved the capital from Kyoto to Edo and renamed the new Imperial City, Tokyo (Eastern Capital). To get a firm grasp on the reins of power, the young Emperor effectively abolished Buddhism and instigated State Shinto. The basic tenets of State Shinto held the belief that the Emperor was of divine lineage, a living *kami*, and all allegiance and loyalty throughout the realm belonged to him. His decrees were unquestionable. In 1869, all fiefdoms were returned to the Emperor. In 1871, the class system was abolished. The *samurai* would be no more. Finally, the merchants, who had been accumulating wealth for centuries, were now legally equal and widespread human rights issues were faced and reforms instigated. The first few years were turbulent with political assassinations common on both sides. A few years before Meiji ascended the throne, there was an international incident concerning a British subject, Sir Rutherford, and the clan of Satsuma from Kagoshima. Rutherford was killed by Satsuma *samurai* and this resulted in the British bombarding of Kagoshima in 1863. The incident had far reaching effects. The Lord of Satsuma realized the military capabilities of the westerners and instead of holding a grudge, he began to adopt their ways and became a supporter of Meiji. A young naval officer by the name of Togo was sent from Satsuma to learn British naval maneuvers. Forty yrs later, this young officer would become the hero of the Battle of Tsushima where the Russian Baltic Fleet would be annihilated.

Emperor Meiji

the restoration survives: In 1876, the Satsuma Clan reversed its previous decision of support for the new Meiji government and an open, last gasp rebellion of the *samurai*, led by Saigo Takamori, known as the Satsuma rebellion, was launched. When it was quelled, the Meiji government was universally accepted as the unquestioned power and the *samurai* were gone forever. The Japanese then rushed headlong into the total acceptance of western ways. In the beginning, they pursued this goal with a passion. Misguided leaders avowed that Japanese ways be abolished. Peculiar fanaticism of the times gave rise to odd notions such as Japanese men marrying only western women to improve the basic stock; no thought was given to the fate of Japanese women. Dietary customs were seen as the cause of Japanese physical inferiority. The vegetarian diet of many hundreds of years was dropped in favor of meat eating. To this day, Japanese dieticians point to a lack of protein in the Japanese diet which they see as a main factor in the lack of the people's size and stamina.

early modern: It was during this period that the Japanese began their love affair with trains, and the first run was from Tokyo to Yokohama. The story goes that when the Japanese dignitaries took their first ride, on entering the train they customarily removed their shoes. When they arrived in Yokohama, they were dumbfounded when they stepped from the train and their shoes were not there. Great strides were also made at this time in medicine, science, engineering and manufacturing. Japanese scholars were encouraged to go abroad and study. The telegraph, telephone and electric lights were quickly adopted. In 1889, Prince Ito engineered the first Japanese constitution. It insured a measure of civil rights, granted limited suffrage to Japanese men and stated that the Emperor was both a theocratic and constitutional monarch. Japan flexed its international muscle for the first time in 1894-5 when it entered into the Sino-Japanese War. Japan soundly trounced China and it proved that it had learned its new military lessons well. As spoils of war, Japan acquired a part of Korea and the island of Formosa. A few military eyebrows were raised in the West, but generally the conflict was seen with the shameful racial belief that the 2 adversaries were merely inferior yellow men. In 1904-5, the Japanese entered the Russo-Japanese War. Again, it triumphed, but this time it had beaten a modern military western nation. Its worldwide prestige grew by leaps and bounds. Japan had come of age.

THE TAISHO PERIOD (1912-1925)

Emperor Meiji died in 1912 and his son Yoshihito, renamed Emperor Taisho, took command. There is a hush-hush about the later life of Taisho. It's not clear whether he had a physical breakdown or whether he suffered a mental breakdown later in life. His condition is usually euphemized as being of "weak health." Politically this made no difference. The new era was so firmly entrenched that no challenge was raised and able ministers ruled in Taisho's name. During Taisho's early reign, the first conflicts began to appear between Japan and the U.S. that would later be resolved only by WW11. Japan began to view itself as the leader of an emerging area, and like the west, began to think in "spheres of influence." Mainland Asia as well as the Pacific basin were viewed by the Japanese to be within their sphere.

relations become strained: After the war with Russia in 1905, the Japanese began building an immense and powerful naval fleet. The U.S. had newly acquired Hawaii and had doubled its naval power in the Pacific. The two opponents would not square off as adversaries for 30 yrs, but they began to look at each other coldly. Also, a more sinister psychological blow was leveled at Japan that they perceived as the ultimate insult. A growing number of Japanese had migrated to California and desired to purchase land. In effect, the U.S. passed a law discriminating against the Japanese ownership of land and disbarring the newly arrived Japanese from becoming naturalized American citizens. The Japanese could not believe that they were looked upon as being inferior. They, themselves, had looked upon other Asians as inferior and were amazed by the attitudes of westerners who they considered only one step above barbarians while they were, after all, the "children of the gods." They had fallen victim to their own deeply entrenched xenophobia. To this day, 3rd generation Koreans born in Japan are not allowed citizenship. Before the situation could deteriorate further, WW1 broke out and Japan entered on the side of the Allies. The bubbling pot of tension between the U.S. and Japan was for a time put on the back burner. In 1920, Japan joined the League of Nations and was an early proponent of international human rights.

the great kanto quake: September 1, 1923 saw the greatest natural disaster of modern times, the Great Kanto Earthquake. The mythical earthquake carp lying under the islands of Japan swished its tail furiously and Tokyo and Yokohama fell to rubble. For 3 days and nights, fires raged throughout the cities. In the end, 30% of the houses in the Kanto district were flattened and 100,000 people had perished. The saddest episode occured when 40,000 people, attempting to escape the flames, gathered in a field in downtown Tokyo at the Military Clothing Depot. The next morning all were dead. The world at large grieved. To make an already horrible scene worse, misguided Japanese hunted down and murdered hapless Koreans who were living in Tokyo. They blamed them for defiling the "lands of the gods" and causing the great disaster. In 1925, universal adult male suffrage was instituted, and in 1926 the present Emperor Hirohito ascended the throne.

THE SHOWA ERA (1926--)

Hirohito was a dashing young man. He had toured Europe and had become enamored of the carefree lifestyle of the West, especially that of the English monarchy. He returned home to take control of a government that was in the wild throes of nationalism. Unfortunately, the Japanese began to view themselves more and mroe as the distinct vanguard of Asia, calling it the Far Asia Co-Prosperity Scheme. The military had patterned themselves after Germany, and when the "Chinless Wonder" of Nazi Germany began spreading his insane concepts, the new military class in Japan accepted it whole hog. How exactly the Japanese fit into the Nazi view of the "master race" can only be answered by the lame-brained, convoluted thinking of demented racial fanatics. In 1931, Japan invaded Manchuria and began setting up the puppet regime of Manchuko. In 1933, Japan withdrew from the League of Nations and launched a full scale invasion of China in 1937. The greatest blemish on Japanese honor occurred with their raping of the prostrate city of Nanking, during this period. In 1940, Japan formally allied itself with Germany and Italy.

total war: On December 7, 1941, Pearl Harbor was bombed. The most intelligent and well-trained officers in the Japanese navy knew from the onset that a war with the U.S. would be in vain. For a number of years, a growing number of fanatics who viewed themselves as modern day _samurai_ had been creeping into the military higher echelons. Many of these men were of the traditional lower classes who were seizing what they saw as their opportunity to gain respect. Like in Nazi Germany, this was the heyday of misfits, psychopaths and dolts. The worst of the lot were usually placed in charge of POW camps and used as occupying forces. Most were worthless at the front. War atrocities can never be whitewashed or answered. The guilty remain guilty and those caught up in the situation by association must bear the humiliation. In 1945, for the first time in Japanese recorded history, the "lands of the gods" were conquered. In 1947, a new Constitution was formed and women were given the vote. The U.S. ended its occupation in 1952 and returned the Ogasawara Islands (Iwo Jima) in 1968 and Okinawa in 1972. The USSR still occupies northern islands off the coast of Hokkaido that they seized when

they entered the war against Japan during its final 10 days. This is still a sore point between the 2 countries. After the war, Japan normalized its relations with the international community of nations. It hosted the Olympics in 1964 and the Winter Olympics in Sapporo in 1972. Also in that year, it normalized relations with the People's Republic of China. Today, Japan is the second most powerful nation in the western world, second only to the U.S.

Japan repaired: At the end of WW11, Japan was prostrated. Its economy was in ruins along with most of its industrial cities. Famine was gnawing at the door. With vast amounts of U.S. aid matched by even vaster amounts of Japanese sweat, it put itself back together. Now it is the turn of much larger and richer western nations to be perplexed and ask the question, "How do they do it?" There are no simple answers, but there are some clues found in traditional Japanese attitudes. The west cut its economic teeth on the philosophies of the "robber barons" of the late 1800s. In effect, western business philosophy says, "Crush the opposition and take all the cookies." Such men as Rockerfeller and Carnegie built huge economic empires this way, and later generations of western businesses tried to follow the same philosophies that worked only when markets were seemingly infinite. This became the "sacred cow" of free enterprise, but it caused never ending life and death struggles between competitors. The Japanese, on the other hand, have the tradition of everyone in the same business splitting the market. Some corporations got enormously rich, but not at the expense of their fellow Japanese competitors. It is not OK in Japan to crush the competition. Most companies look towards long term gains (*rinban*) and this does not include making mortal business enemies. Many western corporations think of next year as long term. Japanese companies also look to each other for business advice. If one deals with a foreign company, the others are informed on how to negotiate in the future. In short, Japanese still see themselves as "We Japanese."

the present family: Emperor Hirohito was born on April 29, 1901 and ascended to the throne in 1926. As a young man he had toured Europe and had made friends with the nobility there and especially admired the freedom and personal openness of the English nobility. He was well versed in the ways of the West. The war came and he did what he was born to do. He led his country. After Japan's defeat, he did not go abroad for 25 years. Finally, the Empress and he visited Europe and met with President Nixon in Alaska in 1971. The Emperor has pursued a life-long passion for marine biology and has written a number of books on the subject. Empress Nagako, born in 1903, is an artist of classical Japanese painting. Her work is exhibited from time to time. The Crown Prince is Akihito, born December 23, 1933. Akihito and his wife, Michiko, met while playing tennis on a holiday and were married in 1956. They have 2 sons and a daughter. This gave rise to thousands of tennis courts popping up almost overnight and prospective brides including "tennis" in their marriage dosiers. The Imperial Family also includes Prince Hitachi, Emperor Hirohito's 2nd son and his wife Hanako Tsugaru, 2 brothers and the wife of a deceased brother. Hirohito also has 3 daughters, but all married commoners and are no longer part of the Imperial Family.

GOVERNMENT

Japan is governed by a parliamentary system based upon a constitutional democracy. The New Constitution was adopted after Japan's defeat in the Pacific War. It is a hybrid blending of principles similar to those of the U.S. and Great Britain. Along with basic human rights, the New Constitution states that Japan will never again make war, that atomic weaponry is expressly forbidden and that the Emperor is a state figurehead of unity devoid of political power. There is a Prime Minister elected from the ruling party of the National Diet, where all national laws must be ratified. All is overseen by a Judiciary Branch, a system including the Federal Supreme Court and lesser courts. Sovereignty rests in the majority vote. The voting age is 20. The New Consitution further prohibits an offensive professional army, but the ranks of Japan's Self Defense forces are beginning to swell. Given their position as a western aligned nation lying just off the coast of the 2 largest and most powerful communist nations in the world, many Japanese argue that in a time of real emergency that they can only really count upon themselves for protection.

POLITICAL PARTIES

The largest and strongest political party is the Liberal Democrats. They are semi-conservative, middle of the roaders with a very wide political base. The Socialist Party is 2nd and the Communist Part is a distant 3rd. May Day celebrations do, however, fill the streets with Red flags, but the average Japanese associates this not with staunch political communism, but as a display of the common bonds of the working class. On the far left is the Japanese Red Army. They made the headlines a few years back when they slaughtered a group of religious tourists at Tel Aviv Airport. Their counterparts are right wing, paramilitary groups that harangue the public on full volume booming loudspeakers in downtown Tokyo on any given weekend. The phenomenon of religious based political parties also occurs. They are small, but very influential. The best known is the *Komeito* (clean government) Party which is the political arm of the *Soka Gakkai* religion. Japan is based on a "law and order" government. It has the lowest crime rate of any industrialized nation. It is politically conservative but has a healthy anti-establishment movement fueled mostly by university students. Civil liberties are a prime issue and they are guaranteed in the New Constitution and would be about equal to those in Great Britain and the U.S. There are however minority groups in Japan that suffer from prejudice. For a full description see "General Introduction," "The People."

police at a demonstration

modern history: From the Meiji era until the end of WW11, full political power was in the hands of the Emperor who was considered a living god. Shintoism was the official state religion and the Emperor was its highest priest. All allegiance and loyalty belonged to him. These concepts were shattered with Japan's Unconditional Surrender at the end of WW11. The Occupational Government required Emperor Hirohito to denounce his divinity on national radio. The Japanese were dumbfounded, especially since this was only the 2nd time that the populace had ever heard his voice. The first was when he shockingly announced that Japan was defeated. The gods had spoken. No heavenly *kamikaze* had come this time to save Japan. Shintoism lost its official sanctions and monies began to dry up. Military men that had fought horrible battles against the Japanese argued that Emperor Hirohito should be placed on trial as a war criminal and the Imperial Family abolished. Others that knew Japan, concurring with General MacArthur, maintained that this step would have permanently mangled the collective Japanese psyche and irreparably traumatized the nation. Japan's recovery as a vibrant, respected nation since WW 11 points to the best alternative having been chosen.

ECONOMY

THE ECONOMIC MIRACLE

The Japanese economy can be expressed in the now common, anglicized words used to describe Japan itself: The Ecnomic Miracle. Economists and historians alike grapple with the profound question of how an agrarian, feudal nation could become the 3rd most important and powerful industrialized nation in the world today in only 100 years. Compounding the scholars' perplexity is the added weight that less than 40 yrs. ago, Japan was utterly destroyed in the Pacific War and that it lost nearly 50% of its pre-war territory and 40% of its real national wealth. Moreover, it is a country singularly poor in natural resources, importing virtually all of the oil necessary to keep its industrial furnaces roaring. Powerful, even world dominating, international corporations have had to look on in disgruntled amazement as they have been outstripped on many economic fronts by their Japanese counterparts in the last 2 decades. Now, these same corporations that at one time were egotistically complacent are sending teams of experts to Japan to find out the answers to one question: How do they do it?

after WW11: Fortunately from the Japanese standpoint, there is no one, simple answer. A great deal but not all of the mystery is answered by looking at the unique society which is Japan. Its people share and almost universally accept a common destiny that was forged and hardened by the disaster that they saw around them after WW11. This disaster unified, and gave direction like never before, to a people already known for their single-mindedness to rise out of and above the rubble that surrounded them. If there is any benefit to having a nation's heavy industry annihilated by bombs, it is that once they are rebuilt, they're the best that modern technology has to offer, and so it was with Japan in the early 1950s. Coupled with this fact, the US primarily poured huge sums of money into the Japanese economy that was matched step by step with hard work and sweat on the part of the Japanese. The mood after the war was to bind up the world's wounds and to let the past fade away with an eye to alliances and friendly relations in a much altered, changing world. Japan is perceived by the western powers to be a powerful presence in the Pacific and a check to the communist regimes of the USSR, China and SE Asia just off its eastern shores. This suited both sides perfectly and in an amazingly short time, the horrors of WW11 were put aside and Japan was welcomed into the free commerce of the West. Since it was considered no economic threat for 2 decades after the war, it was allowed to rebuild itself almost free of commercial sanctions and, with a US military presence, could divert all of its energies into industry without the enormous burden and drain of a national army. These situations provided the fertile ground in which the carefully tended Japanese economic garden could flourish. The factor of self-determination was also immensely important. After the war, the Occupation ruled by General MacArthur lasted approximately 5 years. During this period, the Japanese relinquished their former militaristic government and accepted wholeheartedly a deomocratic government. The Allies saw no reason not to withdraw and the Japanese felt not like an occupied and defeated nation, but like a free nation with self-determination that could work and prosper to its own ends. This was a far cry from the revengeful WW11 plans put forth by some Allied powers that wished to turn Japan into a perpetual, occupied, pastoral state, a fate that many Japanese thought would be a not too unreasonable retribution. New strength and vigor swelled the muscles of Japan's industry.

economic rebirth: Today, Japan produces as much steel more efficiently than the US itself. Its automobile industry is legendary and produces more exports than the US. Japan produces more watches than the Swiss, more cameras and optics than the Germans and more ships than North America and all of Europe put together. There is now a huge economic battle being waged between Japan and the US over the silicon micro-computer chips industry that at one time was dominate by the US and centered in California. In smaller industries such as those that produce pianos, stereo equipment, bicycles, skis, radios and tape recorders, Japan dominates the world. The Economic Miracle has now produced "sour grapes" in the west. Western union leaders try to mollify rank and file members who feel the economic pinch by touting that Japanese labor is cheap and that the workers are grossly underpaid. This is false. The average Japanese wage earner takes home as much money as his American counterpart and in many instances is offered much superior, comprehensive social benefits including retirement and medical plans. Recent polls also show that the Japanese per household have more luxury items such as TVs and electronic equipment than Americans. The one exception is housing. In most large Japanese cities, foreigners notice how small and how shoddy many Japanese homes are. This condition is not due to lack of funds, but to lack of space and too many people. Foreigners are also equally shocked to find out how much these little boxes actually cost.

he Japanese way: Another gripe often heard is that Japanese corporations are one large monopoly and work together. There is truth in this statement, but it's not as simple as it is put. There is no doubt that there are immense Japanese corporations, but it is not so well known that an enormous share of Japanese industry is made up of small, independent companies that are contracted by the large companies for components and partially manufactured goods. There is a very healthy sector of smallish private enterprise. What oils the smoothly running gears of the "economic miracle" is a healthy cooperation between management and labor. The main feature of this cooperation is an understanding that "once hired, never fired." This adds up to permanent job security and instead of causing haphazard production as western business experts might expect, it causes, instead, a sense of loyalty and a desire to produce the best quality of work in order to insure the survival of the all–important company. There is also no wide social gap or sense of worth between labor and management. Wages are oftentimes determined by length of service and not by job function. It is not rare to find an older man with 20 yrs. of experience, for example, working as a plant janitor and making more money than a young executive in the firm's advertising section. The Japanese have learned well the adage that a chain is only as strong as its weakest link. Managers and workers strive together in an attempt to advance and strengthen the whole, which will in turn secure a future for all concerned. Short-sighted profiteering at the expense of either group is definitely not the norm. For countless generations, the Japanese have felt that the worth of an individual is assessed by the quality of spirit and not by the bank account which may not be so equal. This one big happy family does have a fatal flaw which is especially distasteful to westerners. There is a decided lack of individuality and personal achievement that is so highly regarded in the west. This is vigorously undercut. Of course, there are bright young people, but they are not lauded or rewarded any more than the lowly loyal janitor; they are a part of the team and their best work, like everyone else's, is expected. Most westerners, if forced to assign a color to Japanese industrial society, would choose dark grey. There is a stifling sameness about the Japanese labor force. One day at a busy train station will show you that many Japanese dress the same, act the same, eat the same. Further observation will reveal that most live in indistinguishable housing, commute long hours to work, play and vacation with workmates and even have the same life goals. These situations are intolerable to westerners, but they forget that the Japanese are past masters at keeping up a private and public face. On the surface, they may appear to be all the same fish in a common barrel, but underneath and inside themselves, they are different and that's where it counts in the Japanese point of view.

the unseen economy: There is another side to the Japanese economy that takes in farmers, fishermen, craftsmen, artists and entertainers. These minor industries are vastly important within Japan, but have little weight outside of the country. For the most part, Japanese city dwellers look back to times when life was sdimpler and tied to the land. In the rural areas of Japan, smokestacks seem impossible where life goes on with ancient, unhurried rhythm. But relentlessly, the lure of wages and jobs is denuding the country areas of young farmers and the seas of young fishermen. The Japanese lament this loss, but seem unable to stem the tide. When visitors look over the spoilage created in the lands and seas surrounding the massive industrial complexes, they cannot believe that this is the land of simplicity and beauty. Neither can the Japanese who can only repeat the threadbare refrain, *"Shikata ga nai"* (It can't be helped). The cities abound in cultural riches and traffic jams, the coastline is a wonderland of diminutive misty islets, the interior is graced with majestic alpine peaks wherein nestle quiet villages, and the industrial complexes abound in smog, soot and industrial waste. The "economic miracle" is both magic and a nightmare for the Japanese.

THE PEOPLE

The countryside is awesome and beautiful; the art and architecture are perfection in simplicity; the customs are curious, amusing and intriguing; the cities present a riot of color, tradition, confusion and technology; and the aesthetic pursuits are the honed edge of the fine art of subtlety. All are Japan and all are secondary to the greatest curiosity, interest, anomaly and delight of them all: the people of Japan. Most senstive travelers take to the highway with a sense of wonder, and more than wanting to know what's on the other side of the mountain, they want to know who is on the other side of the mountain. Giant, scholarly tomes have been written about the infinitely involved topics of Japanese psychology and sociology with an attempt to draw clear conclusions about one of the most unique and self-admittedly different cultures in the world. Pearl S. Buck said in *The People of Japan*, "For if there is one single truth about Asia, it is that while each country there is totally different from every other country. Japan is the most different of them all." Some authors have tied the 130 million people of Japan into a neat tidy package, while others have bogged down in the quagmire of their own conclusions. The Japanese know very well who they are—sometimes even too well. The average Japanese is not a hothouse flower nurtured on aesthetic practices and deep religious sensitivities; most are fun-loving, gregarious, curious 20th-century people and they know as little about you as you know about them. The average knowledge about the west, unfor-tunately, has its roots in television and movies. It's up to you to make your visit real. Modern, perhaps more hip travelers have called Japan "the land of the talking bus" and "the plastic renaissance." Maybe so, but Japan, like anywhere else, enriches more by what you are willing to bring into the experience than by what you expect to take away.

PHYSICAL CHARACTERISTICS

"All Asians look alike"—HOGWASH. If anything, Japanese, Koreans, Chinese, Thais and other Asians can tell their nationalities apart much better than Europeans. "Japanese are small, thin, slant-eyed people with yellowish skin." Perhaps 100 yrs. ago when Japan was reopened to the West, the first part of that statement was true; the average height of men was only 160 cm (5'3") and women a mere 14? cm (4'10"), but these figures have been steadily growing with most authorities pointing to an increase of protein in the diet as the reason. The Japanese themselves have spread this belief. Modern thinkers just after Meiji ridiculed their race as being inferior in stamina and size to the recently arrived barbarians, and propagated the immediate acceptance of western-style nutrition.

today: Today in Japan you will still see small people, but you will also notice that men under 30 are now about 175 cm (5'9") and women about 160 cm (5'3") with the teenage generation even taller. A healthy proportion of the Japanese are slim with some recent plumpness due to a more western diet and most babies are butterballs with fat red cheeks. Teenagers and young adults are quite thin, but age seems to add pounds. Notice the paunches on business-men and the midriff bulges on maturer women. Weight-loss clinics, fad diets and fitness centers are doing a brisk business in sweating off pounds in the big cities of Japan. The Japanese are also guilty of seeing not with their eyes, but with preconceived beliefs. Foreign men are thought to be enormous with large noses, while all foreign women are thought to have giant breasts, even if the person standing in front of them is actually more petite than a Japanese. Myths go both ways. If you travel throughout Japan, you will notice that facial features vary to a great degree from region to region, and few Japanese seem to have the fabled yellow skin that westerners attribute to Orientals. Country folk are ruddy complected and much darker than most city dwellers, some of whom have such white skin that it seems almost transparent. At one time Japanese shunned the sun. The women, especially, kept covered because

tanned skin was the sign of being a farm worker or a person of low social class. Even today, most makeup for older women has a whitish cast. Today, like in the West, a rich tan is a sign of leisure for the younger set, and is sought after by those who can afford to lounge on the beach. Even the pencil-thin slanted eyes expected by most westerners are not as prevalent as you would think. Part of this stereotyped idea is due again to the Japanese themselves. Much of the art work of the feudal ages encouraged this convention because it was considered to be a sign of beauty. Eyes vary just like skin color, and some are as round as walnuts, although their color is invariably brown. The one physical feature that appears universal in Japan is raven-black hair. The women, especially, have thick black tresses, a source of pride and feminine vanity for countless ages. The Madame Butterfly hairdos that made the wearer look like a human cupcake are a thing of the past, now seen only occassionally at very auspicious occasions such as a marriage or in the dwindling *geisha* sector. Unfortunately, many Japanese women, especially school girls, have a penchant for the Buster-Brown straight-banged straight-cut hairdo, which is probably the least elegant way for a roundfaced woman to wear her hair, but to the Japanese it is *kawaii* (cute). Permanents and hair coloring have also made the scene, so expect all types. In general, most Japanese men under 40 would be considered in the West as being "medium" in stature, and the women as "petite." The biggest divergence is in shoe size. Most Japanese still have smallish hands and feet; buying shoes to fit a westerner in Japan is almost impossible.

preconceived notions: At one time, western observers said that Japanese had bowed legs from sitting crosslegged on the floor since childhood. Many still do have stumpy legs, but this is probably due more to genetics than to floor sitting. It's also believed that Japanese have slightly lower body temperatures than Westerners. Whatever causes this, it becomes particularly apparent on hot, stuffy trains in summertime. *Gaijin* sit there melting while the Japanese seem to remain cool and unperspiring. Japanese also believe that Westerners have strong body odor. Japanese, through long years of hot tubbing, can sit in amazingly hot baths and delight in watching westerners gingerly stick in a toe, yelp in surprise at the heat and beat a hasty retreat. The tables are turned, however, when the weather turns cold and the Japanese sit huddled and shivering while Westerners delight in the frosty nip. Japanese also look younger to foreigners (add 10 yrs. to your estimate), while foreigners appear older to Japanese. They can guess each other's ages, however, with uncanny accuracy.

GENERAL SOCIAL CHARACTERISTICS

Short-time travelers rate the Japanese as number one in the world in politeness, due to the extreme kindness and respect that they are shown. After some time has passed, the Japanese women maintain this high rating, while the men slip a bit. A good share of this is due to the fact that Japanese men get about more in society than women and hold a much larger percentage of jobs as bureaucrats—immigration officers, policemen, hotel managers, railroad clerks and the like. If a traveler is going to have a hassle, it will probably be with a person from one of these groups. In short, in non-social situations, you will deal more with Japanese men. All Japanese are taught politeness from day one, but the men are expected and trained to be a bit more outgoing and assertive than the women. Times are changing quickly, but Japanese women still lead a much more insular life and are trained to seem subservient, non-argumentative and generally soothing and

pleasing. Japanese simultaneously maintain 2 ways of dealing with the world, *tatemae* and *honne*. Simply stated, *tatemae* is surface behavior and *honne* is what they really think. Unless you know a Japanese for a very long time and have a strong friendship, you will never see *honne* and if you do, it will most likely be from a man. Both sexes in Japan feel that it is better to maintain harmony than to argue a point. With so many people cramped into such a small area, this is a good idea.

social attitudes: Japanese men fall into a wide range of groupings, from automaton "salary men" to punk rockers. How they will treat you is a matter of social roulette. If you are picked up hitchhiking, it will generally be by a man, and likewise for invitations to dinner and for drinks. Although both sexes experience "*gaigin* fever" (see later in chapter), men are a little less awestruck than the women, and if you need directions or travel advice, your best bet is to choose a young man to ask. Because of social training and very strong role modeling, Japanese women are reluctant to voice an opinion, even in a seemingly trivial matter, while men are slightly less so. This is not only because they don't want to offend, but also because group wishes and decisions are much more important than individual ones. The men can be coaxed into a deeper conversation, but with the women it's tough unless you are a woman. After a while, this can become boring. Both sexes are good-natured, sentimental and group-oriented. Men socialize with workmates and women with other women in their own social strata. It's not considered worthwhile to be an individual. Actually, the much admired rugged individual of the west is seen as somewhat sad and a bit absurd. The group dominates. Japanese are universally touchy about negative criticism. One of the worst insults to a Japanese is to suggest that neighbors may laugh at their behavior. Long discussions are still held about MacArthur's statement calling the Japanese a "nation of 12 year olds." Resentments still run high about the European belief in the "yellow peril" of the last century, and historians believe that "The Japanese Exclusion Act" passed by California in the early part of this century contributed to WW 11.

how the Japanese see themselves: Japanese view themselves as diplomats when dealing with foreigners. The objective is to create a good impression and to enhance the prestige of Japan throughout the world. Foreigners are usually afforded the highest courtesy. Even if a Japanese person is more knowledgeable on a subject, he will acquiesce to the foreigner and pay great attention to what is said. If you strike up an acquaintance with a Japanese, even merely asking directions on a street corner, you are temporarily their responsibility. They'll go to great lengths to please you, even to missing their own train and being late for work. Explaining to the boss that they were helping a *gaijin* will usually exonerate them. Also, it's not expected of foreigners to know all of the social rules and etiquette. You can bend many rules that would be unthinkable to the Japanese without worrying about creating bad feelings, with 2 exceptions. Never under any circumstances soap up in a communal bathtub (*ofuro*) or wear your shoes on a *tatami* mat. Besides these, you can bumble along to your heart's content. At times, however, the exaggerated politeness of the Japanese can become a nuisance, especially when you're in a hurry. Departing seems interminable, but once a Japanese does say, "Let's go!" they mean it. Up they jump, slip on their shoes and are out the door. There's also an attraction for anything

foreign. Even better-made domestic products won't be as highly prized as foreign ones of lesser workmanship. It's easier to hear rock n' roll in Tokyo than to hear traditional Japanese music. Also, the Japanese are faddish, especially with things western, and fads come and go with astonishing speed. The Japanese sense of group identity, coupled with their avid curiosity of things western, sometimes leads them to extremes. In themselves, individualism is not highly regarded, but it's much admired and even expected of a foreigner. In a way, all foreigners are seen as slightly eccentric. Abroad, the happy-go-lucky Japanese can cut a singularly forlorn figure. Massive western architecture becomes too much after a while and they long for the simplicity of Japan. Upon returning, they themselves feel estranged from their own society. Japan is one of the only countries where studying abroad, even at a prestigious university, can be a detriment in landing a good job. The returned traveler is just a little bit less Japanese. Abroad, Japanese are even known to be somewhat naughty because they're unfettered by customs and expectations. Many Japanese in their fantasies, and a few in reality, break loose, but in their innermost minds and hearts they never forget who and what they are.

LOVE, MARRIAGE AND ROLE MODELS

An *obasan* (grandmother type) was asked by her granddaughter if she had married for love or by *omiai* (arrangement). She replied, "Married for love? Don't talk dirty! What does love have to do with marriage?" This old-fashioned notion that love has nothing to do with marriage though fast disappearing in the larger cities, is still alive in the countryside and with old-fashioned families. *Omiai*, traditional marriages, were even contracted by the willing parents at the birth of their child. This doesn't happen anymore, but Japanese will still consult their parents if marriage is in the works, and a strong objection could end the romance. Frantic parents with older unmarried children will plague them with photographs of possible mates. Meetings are still arranged for young couples to get to know each other, but they're freer to chose their own partners and break off the relationship at any time. It's still the goal of most people to marry. The average age for marriage is higher in Japan than in the West, with the average age of men at about 26-28 and women 24. Before vows are exchanged, families will be asked to provide a genealogy, and if there's a flaw in the family line, this can terminate the relationship. In some rural areas, a marriage is not considered consummated until there is a child, and a childless marriage is still a good reason for a man to seek divorce. Divorces are also granted for various other reasons including infidelity, but usually only to a man if his wife is unfaithful. A woman usually sues for divorce on the grounds of infidelity only if her husband's sexual partner has been another married woman. In most cases, unlike the convention of the west, any children become the wards of the husband's family.

foreign marriages: Also when foreigners marry Japanese, only the western wife of a Japanese is automatically granted permanent living status in Japan. A western husband of a Japanese woman must apply through normal channels for a long-term visa on such grounds as cultural studies; marriage is not considered grounds for a permanent visa. Even if there are children involved, he and they may be forced to leave Japan. Japanese law says that nationality of the children passes through the father, not the mother. Recently, there has been a great deal of litigation attempting to change this law, but it currently still stands. Even so, there are 10 marriages of Japanese women to western men to every one of a Japanese man to a western woman.

women's roles: Once married, the greatest binding force in Japan, the family, reigns supreme. The father provides security and the mother binds the family with love, especially towards the children. The father is the

breadwinner and the mother is the homemaker and child raiser. Although many Japanese women work, they usually hold lesser and more menial jobs. In most cases, they give up any career upon marriage, and return to the work force only after the children have been raised. They're excluded from the "cradle to the grave" security pravalent in the Japanese company system, and aren't given retirement incomes or any of the other myriad benefits afforded to men. Men and women are given equal high-school education, but universities have only a 30% female population. Families still feel strongly that it's a waste of money to educate a woman when all she is going to be is a housewife. Naturally, like all situations, this too is changing, but slowly. A career woman is still hard-pressed to find a support group and many are lonely figures, unmarried and still generally unaccepted by the society at large. The first woman diplomat was appointed as ambassador to Denmark in 1982. The Women's Liberation Movement in Japan is gaining in prominence, but is still in its embryonic stage. Its central core is very radical. Most Japanese view a radical woman as an anomaly and a very radical one as a monstrosity. Women today have a greater amount of time to spend on leisure activities. Some take up aesthetic pursuits such as flower arranging and the tea ceremony. Most women that you'll encounter at these classes are married with school-age children. Another phenomenon is the *Kyoiku Mama*. These mothers pursue indefatigably the schooling of their children. They go to any length to get their children into the right preschool so they can attend the right kindergarten, grade school, high school and ultimately the right university. Naturally, this all leads to the right job with the right company and, of course, the right wife.

men's roles: Japanese men are expected to pursue their careers fully, but to turn over their pay checks to their wives who hold the purse strings. A husband is given an allowance by his wife. Although a man spends more time out in society, an inordinate amount of this time is spent at work or at work-related activities. The average Japanese city worker spends 2 hrs per day commuting to and from work. Once home, his wife will lavish him with attention, going so far as to bathe him at night and dress him in the morning. Much of this, no doubt, is out of love and duty, but also much is done to keep him on his feet and healthy so that he can bring home the *tofu*. A wife becomes almost like a surrogate

mother to her husband, treating him like a child. Japanese children's devotion to their mother is legendary, especially that of boys. Talking of childhood and remembering their heads cradled in their mother's arms will evoke tears from even the most hardened street merchant. It's not uncommon to see a man with an old mother riding him "piggy back" up the steep steps of a temple or shrine. While a man's love for his wife may be guarded, it's unbridled for his mother. A prevalent interpretation of Confucianism even goes so far as to state that a man's sexual desire for his own wife is immoral. These baser feelings should only be for mistresses and bar hostesses where they belong, not for the exalted bearer of his children. The Japanese sense of love also includes some pain. Lovers traditionally had to "prove" that their love was genuine. They even went so far as to write love letters in their own blood and to tear out their fingernails. Today, one partner of an arguing couple will seldom admit that he or she was wrong because of the fear that the other will throw this admission up to them forever. Again, most of these notions are dying a quiet death, but they do still have some sway on Japanese thinking.

<u>the family:</u> Unlike in the West, a Japanese family is an indivisible unit, not a collection of individuals. If a father dies, the eldest son takes his place. The mother then owes her allegiance to him, and younger brothers and sisters are bound more by tradition than any formal law to pay heed to his wishes. To be a family outcast is still one of the worst fates that can befall a Japanese.

children and oldsters: Japanese children are very much loved and pampered, as are old people. Both the beginning and end of life are considered closer to the spirit world and, thereby, are treated with more respect. The middle years in Japan, when people are obsessed with making a living, are the least respected. A man's thought and opinions aren't given much weight until he reaches the mystical age of 41. Japanese children until age 5 are spoiled rotten. They're free of almost all social restricitons and can do as they please. Seldom reprimanded and almost never spanked, they're free to terrorize the adult world with their childish pranks. All is forgiven. The Japanese grownups know the heavy restrictions which life has in store, and see childhood as a golden time to let loose. Consequently, Japanese children will appear misbehaved in public. They'll be gleefully loud, demanding of their parents, or either tearfully frightened or tickled by the sight of a foreigner. At school age, all this abruptly stops and they're thrown into the mainstream of society and must begin to follow the rules. The transition is lightning quick. *Obasan* and *ojisan* (old women and men) also have a special place. They've lived long enough to express their feelings openly. Unlike the cold treatment received by old people in the West, they remain snug and highly respected in the bosom of their families. Although the vast majority do not speak foreign languages, the ones that do offer the most glib and insightful conversations. After being in Japan for a time, politeness loses its initial impact, and you realize that it's a convention. Encounters with young kids and *obasan/ojisan* become more precious simply because you'll know just how they feel. There seem to be limitless numbers of both groups running or shuffling about everywhere. These are the only Japanese at large that will look you square in the eyes and more or less express what they think. If anyone is going to beat you to a seat on a subway, it will be a kid or an *obasan*. Most *obasan* are about as tall as the middle of your back, and all are armed with umbrellas or shopping bags. If you're going to be shoved, it'll be by a scurrying *obasan*. It will also be one of the only times in your life when you actually enjoy the experience; you better be quick to turn around to see who did it because these little old ladies can move. Much of the strict role modeling and strong family ties mentioned would seem smothering to a free wheeling westerner, but not so to the Japanes. These are the qualities that make Japan socially and culturally unique.

SEX

Sex, like gold, is where you find it, and it's not hard to pan a few nuggets in Japan. The Japanese in essence believe that human beings have 2 souls: one is the sublime, timeless and changeless and binds us spiritually to a higher reality; the other is earthbound, rowdy, bawdy and pleasure seeking. Both, they also believe, have their proper places and should be appropriately cultivated. Much ink and endless diatribes are focused on the Japanese male, attempting to harpoon him on his unabashed sexual curiosity and double standard. He is much maligned as a whoremonger and pleasure seeker, combing the streets as his humble wife sits home and darns his *tabi*. What makes this particular observation of the Japanese even more interesting is that it is often leveled by otherwise liberal foreigners who admire everything else in Japan's unique culture, but find this male chauvinistic aspect repulsive by western standards. The simple truth is that Japanese male sexuality and its practices are as old as the Grand Shrines of Ise and, until recently, just as accepted and approved of by society. What sets the Japanese man apart from the western man is his frontal approach, naivete and lack of hypocritical, puritanical hang-ups.

western women and sex: As far as western women are concerned, the average Japanese man will treat them with the utmost of respect. There are certain situations in which this will not be the case, but these generally focus around drinking, night clubs and hostess bars. If you're an unaccompanied woman out late on the town, chances are that sooner or later a Japanese man will make a pass at you. Japanese men looking at their own young women, feel that nice girls of any nationality aren't out on the town alone. This unwanted pass, sometimes accompanied by a lunging grab, can usually be stopped by an icy stare and a loud shrieking "No!," which all Japanese understand. That's usually the end of it and most would-be molesters will melt. Unfortunately, a great deal of the myths of western women's wanton sexuality are spread by porno books, magazines and the tall tales of returning traveling businessmen. Women have less of a chance of being raped in Japan than in any industrialized country in the world. Some western women have even complained that the opposite situation is closer to the truth. If a western woman is genuinely attracted to a

Japanese man, it's sometimes difficult to give him the message. After an evening out, don't be surprised if your Japanese male friend escorts you as far as your subway stop and then bows and smiles as you frustratedly slip away from the platform. Many western women have observed that the Japanese male's sex drive is actually very low. Women hitchhiking alone are generally safe and most times an invitation to dinner, even under these circumstances, is exactly that and nothing more.

carousing of Japanese men: In any large city or in a town of medium size, there will be rows of establishments catering to the drinking and carousing of Japanese men, many of whom spend a great deal of time after work and on weekends pursuing these baser pleasures. What westerners fail to see is that this is as much a part of Japanese custom as the social bow. Very few women accept infidelity in their husbands and Japanese wives are no exception. As long as the husband puts his family first, Japanese wives will turn a blind (but perhaps sad) eye to these episodes and even encourage their husbands to indulge. Most of these gatherings, however, are like middle-aged fraternity parties with much boasting and little action. Japanese men have kept mistresses and concubines since time immemorial. This is no longer the case in modern Japan, with most married couples opting for monogamy, but like all other dying traditions in Japan, there are some carry-overs among the wealthier who can afford the double existence a mistress entails. These male groups of Japanese revelers seen everywhere are invariably workmates blowing off steam. Their big night consists of getting drunk, fondling a bar hostess who tells them what handsome fellows they are, takes most of their weekly allowance and then sends them home to their wives who pound them into shape for work the next morning. A Japanese man who does have a sexual liaison is not considered immoral, but merely succumbing to his earthly soul. It's also the same for a Japanese woman, but if she's married, it gets sticky. More than anything else, her allegiance and first loyalty belong to her family. If caught being unfaithful, she upsets the social order, and is damned more for a breach in social decorum than for immorality. Plane loads of Japanese men travel to the fleshpots throughout SE Asia and the Philippines. They're like a benevolent plague descending on the locals. Many of these jaunts are actually subsidized by the companies they work for and they deplane with gleaming eyes and bulging...

camera bags. They're no longer in Japan, and to them and to their wives, they're not strictly accountable for their actions.

sex and the Japanese woman: Single Japanese dating westerners in Japan is commonplace and almost acceptable. Most middle-class Japanese parents prefer their children to marry other Japanese, but the younger generation doesn't worry much about this. If you're a westerner keeping company with a Japanese, his or her neighbors may asume that you're sleeping together. So what? Japanese girls will sometimes invite a friend along to quell these suspicions. If you date more than 2-3 times and she keeps inviting a friend, you can assume that your relationship will remain platonic. Japanese women relate to sex somewhat differently than western women. In a recent poll conducted in Japan, the women rated "boldness" as one of the highest qualities desirable in a man. Unbelievably, it even overshadowed a good job. Japanese women have also heard stories about the sexual prowess of western men and they, too, are curious. In the west, more or less, sex is agreed upon by both parties and with a woman of your own society, it's easier to pick up on the signs and proceed. In Japan, it's not so easy. A Japanese woman expects you to be the aggressor, and in the old-fashioned sense to "make" her. Obviously, this by no means includes force, but it does include directness. You lead and she responds. Ther's a bit of Scarlett O'hara in the Japanese woman. She wants Rhett Butler to sweep her off her feet and manfully carry her to the bedroom. This in a way exonerates her from responsibility because, after all, she couldn't refuse. Western travelers also remark at how bold Japanese women can be. If you're being too thick headed, she might take the lead. Japanese women enjoy sex and unlike westerners who didn't seem to discover the clitoris until the mid 1970s, they knew that it existed at least a thousand yrs. ago. They are orgasmic, warm and affectionate. Another difference from western women is that although Japanese women will engage in casual sex, they may also consider this a comittment to a deeper relationship. Western men have lamented that it has been very difficult and quite sad to leave a casual Japanese lover. Unlike other Asian women driven by financial necessity to mate and, therefore, find a way out of their dilemma, Japanese women genuinely care for their lovers. Their society is financially strong and they don't need a meal ticket at all. Japanese are still not demonstrative in public. They will almost never kiss and will only occasionally hold hands. Seeing a young Japanese couple holding hands looks more like a couple of kids playfully skipping down the street. Wives now walk abreast of their husbands and not behind as in days of yore. You'll now see young fathers pushing baby carriages and looking after tots—an unthinkable act only 20 yrs. ago.

how to feed the earthly soul: As far as prostitutes and play-for-pay are concerned, there's no problem. Technically prostitution was made illegal during the Occupation to cater to the misguided notion of the Japanese to American puritanism. There are still plenty of prostitutes around in any major city. Also there are turkish baths (turuko) offering "special treatment," topless and bottomless strip joints, burlesque and street hustlers. Any taxi driver can point the way. Lower-class bar hostesses will also double as "pros." As you sit sipping highly inflated drinks and playing footsy under the table, you can strike a bargain. If she leaves with you before closing, besides her charge you'll have to pay the owner a "ransom." Although many act like pros, they're not, and most likely their intentions are to get you to spend more money. At closing time, you'll be left with promises and nothing else as you're escorted out the door. Another establishment is the Pinku Saron. You can always tell these "all you can guzzle and grab joints" because they have barkers outside trying to get you in. Once inside, you're on the time clock. Prices vary, but Y3000 per 30 min. is about the norm, with prices escalating with the activities requested. Most of these places are geared for students who don't have much money. Basically, you drink as much as you can and fondle away until your time is up.

where to look: Any big city has turuko and Pinku Saron, usually around the train stations, but there are some areas especially known for prostitutes and their services. Just S of Tokyo, Kawasaki and Kisarazu on the Bozo Peninsula just opposite Kawasaki, reachable by frequent ferries, are high-class hotbeds of activity. It's best to go with a Japanese friend to keep the already unreasonable prices from getting astronomical. Gifu, known also for its cormorant fishing, is a well known play-for-pay area. Some onsen also provide women guaranteed to be as steamy as the baths, but since this is not at all the norm, it'll likely be too much trouble to arrange, mostly because of the language barrier. Another Japanese phenomenon is the Love

Hotel. It's sometimes difficult to find a place in Japan to make love, so these short-time hotels have been created. They're the epitome of discretion and rococo eroticism. You can easily tell them because most are surrounded by a high wall with a separate entrance and exit. Their by-the-hour costs are posted on signs outside. Walk through the garden and slip your money through a slot to the proprietor. You never meet face to face. The rooms are often red velvet affairs with satin-covered beds and plenty of mirrors. Some even have videotape machines so you can see what you've just done. Actually, after midnight rates are often affordable by budget travelers just looking to spend the night. Entire books have been written about getting it on in Japan, and almost every traveler has a tale or 2 to tell about sexual experiences while there, but like the world over, there are no surefire prescriptions. If a Japanese person is sexually attracted to you, he or she will let you know.

MIONORITIES, MISFITS AND COUNTER CULTURES

Perhaps at no other time is the concept of "We Japanese" so unattractive as when discussing minorities. Besides the cultural concept of "different," the Japanese also harbor racial prejudice. They look at white-skinned western-ers with grudging respect, even with a feeling of inferiority. In S Africa, Japanese businessmen are proud that they're considered "white" and separate themselves willingly from the blacks. Feelings, of course, are mixed, but Japanese generally look down upon other Asians who live in Japan, especially Koreans. Blacks (*kokujin*) are difficult for them to deal with as they've almost no experience and don't really under-stand them. Traditionally, the whiter a woman's skin was, the more attractive she was presumed to be.

Koreans: The single largest suffering minority in Japan are the Koreans. Their history goes back a long way, but in recent times the majority were taken to Japan as slave laborers during and just before WW11. Because of a quirk in the law during the topsy-turvy times of the Occupation, Koreans were stripped of their previously held naturalized status and were reverted to Korean citizenship. Although many families were well entrenched in Japan, they were required to register as aliens with long-term residency status that did not apply to their children. In fact today, a Korean born in Japan by parents who were also born in Japan must carry a passport like any other foreigner, and can be deported. Recent polls show that both Koreans and Japanese view each other as the least desirable people to emulate. The very beginnings of Japanese history are directly tied to Korea. Population movements, wars, cultural exchanges and arts bound the 2 nations from the earliest times. The 2 neighbors, in many ways including geographically, were so close and yet now so far away. Religious fanatics, goaded by political piranha, combed the streets of Tokyo after the Great Kanto Earthquake of 1923 and openly murdered thousands of Koreans as scapegoat defilers of the holy land who had angered the gods. Most Koreans hold menial jobs. Many are entertainers, night-club workers, prostitutes and criminals. They have very little chance to rise in Japanese society and because of discriminatory treatment, gravitate towards the seedier side of life. Many street gangs of Korean toughs are organized by the *yakuza* (Japanese Mafia) and run illicit busi-nesses including drug trafficking and prosti-tution. Korean families often live in ghettos and are shunned by the Japanese population at large. Traditionally, in movies and other public media, Koreans are always the heavies seeking to undermine the social order. Recently, laws enforcing civil rights are being applied with more pressure by some enlightened members of the judiciary. It's possible for a Korean to be naturalized, but they must officially relinquish their given names and take a Japanese one. Until they gain the right of citizenship and exercise the vote, their future in Japan will remain tentative.

eta and buraku-min: The most convoluted and twisted type of prejudice against any group of people in Japan is leveled against a social sub-strata called *eta* (much filth). What makes the bigotry against this group so strange is that they look like, act like, talk like, are named like and in fact *are* Japanese. The closest social phenomenon resembling this situation would be the Untouchables (*harijin*) in the caste system of India. It's extremely difficult to pinpoint in history exactly when and how the *eta* were distinguished as a group, but they, nontheless, exist. Traditionally, especially after the advent of Buddhism and bolstered by the ideas of purity inherent in Shinto, the *eta* performed tasks considered unfit by other Japanese. Mainly they worked as butchers, leather craftsmen and handlers of dead bodies. They made leather bindings for armor, sandals, *tabi* socks (at one time made of leather), and cleaned filth and dead animals from temple and shrine grounds. They could not marry outside of their caste (which was hereditary) and they were forced to live separately from the general populace. They were given family names that marked them as *eta* so there could be no future mobility. After Meiji, the *eta* caste was abolished by law (unofficially it still strongly exists) and the *eta* were renamed *buraku-min*. Supposedly this new group was socially equal to all other Japanese, but they were forced, sometimes even by open murder, to maintain the old status quo. If they tried to break out from these constrictions, they were hunted down by villagers afraid of the new job market competition. The bloody hunts were called *eta-gari*. Today, most young city Japanese are ignorant of the fact that *eta* even exist. The older generation is highly reluctant to talk about them since, after all, modern day Japan is a democracy. If the premarital prerequisites common to most Japanese families turn up even the slightest hint of *eta*, the liason is immediately terminated. *Buraku-min* euphemistically translates as "village dweller," but the full odious meanings still remain. Westerners can in no way distinguish *burakumin* from the average Japanese. The only way you can is to be sensitive to the occupation of the person and the task he performs. If it has to do with leather working or the butchering of animals, he could easily be a *buraku-min*. The most obvious are the shoeshine ladies gathered around the many train stations. Another less obvious way is to look at the housing. If you enter a small town and there seems to be a lttle community just on the outskirts or literally "on the other side of the tracks" separated by a field or 2 from the main community, they can possibly be *buraku-min*. Fortunately, this group has organized, and through the power of the ballot are slowly improving their lot. In the meantime, they must endure the stigma of being social outcasts.

the yakuza: This is the general name given to the Japanese underworld, a "Mafia" of organized crime. They run drugs, brothels and the rackets. Their legions are made up of non-persons—social misfits who could not deal with Japanese society. Yet they do enjoy a certain romantic mystique in Japan. Since they are anti-social and refuse to be crushed into oblivion or complacency by the system, they're seen by some as noble rogues. They view themselves as the last of the *samurai* and

pattern themselves superficially after the old and highly regarded codes of *bushido*. Hordes of lower-eschelon goons pay undying homage and loyalty to their bosses, who rule by a brass-knuckle paternalism. Politically, they are ultra-conservative, right wingers who long for yesterday when Japan was supposedly undefiled and right thinkers just like them ruled the land. *Yakuza* and their minions were frequently used in the political tornadoes that swept Japan prior to WW 11. They led riots and were willing assassins, for the right price. The average western traveler will never knowingly come in contact with a *yakuza*. Perhaps, if there's an altercation with a prostitute and she calls in her pimp, or if there's a bouncer called in to break up a fracas at a *Pinku Saron,* they may be lower eschelon *yakuza*. Besides these improbable occurrences, the *yakuza* stay hidden. Romanticism aside, they are really "low-lifers" living on the pain and misery of others. Goons trying to distinguish themselves in the eyes of their bosses will go to any length to prove their loyalty, even self-mutilation. One weirdness is to cut off a finger to show resolve, or as self-chastisement for a failed or bungled assignment. Their mangled hands become a form of twisted pride showing their macho nature. If you see a night hawk with no fingers left, he is either dripping with resolve or the worst con-man bungler in the world. *Yakuza* also love tattoos, although a portion of the Japanese public at large will also tattoo themselves. Considered an art form, tattoos are also considered anti-social. Japanese tattoos are, indeed, beautiful, created by artists with painstaking care. The fuzzy, blue-lined, uninspired fiascoes that westerners call tattoos pale to insignificance beside them. Japanese tattoos are vividly colorful, inspired, well-executed and classic. They often use spiritual or mythical motifs to tell a story on living flesh.

FOREVER GAIJIN

Arguments have raged for years in Japan over the use of the word *gaijin* (foreign person). Detractors maintain that it's an insult, like an icy curtain separating "We Japanese" from all others. Other less negative views say that *gaijin* is merely a convention of speech and has little, if any, negative connotations to the Japanese who often use impersonal pronouns when talking about each other. Whatever the case may be, only in Japan will all foreigners be addressed as *gaijin-san* (Mr./Ms. Foreigner). Don't be surprised if while you're walking, or in a train, a tiny tot points with startled eyes and blurts out "Gaijin Da!" ("It's a foreigner!") If young students get on a train or pass by, you'll hear multiple "*gaijin*" being whispered among the group as they turn around for a quick look and embarrassed giggle. You can be in Japan 2 min. as a visitor, or 20 yrs. as an expatriot, and you'll always be a *gaijin*. Even foreigners who eat, speak and live like Japanese after years of cultural study and residence in the country are *gaijin*. In truth, being a *gaijin* is both positive and negative. Your foreign appearance will evoke courtesy, understanding if you unwittingly commit a social faux-pas, minor celebrity status and, at least superficial friendship wherever you go. On the negative side, you'll always be scrutinized as being different, considered somewhat equivalent to a benevolent, amazing and somewhat unrefined oddity, and never accepted into the national family of Japan. People will stop you on the street just to practice English (all white-skinned *gaijin* speak English!). You'll be invited to weddings of acquaintances that you don't really know, out to dinner for no apparent reason, and molly-coddled by the authorities.and public at large like an overgrown baby. All this is done out of courtesy, because you are an honored guest. You'll never really know what your hosts think. All this attention can at times become a boring nuisance. If you visit a shrine or temple, for example, a bus load of recently disgorged Japanese tourists may find you even more interesting than the local art work. If you stop at a rural *ryokan* or *minshuku*, you may be refused admittance because the owners may be afraid that you don't understand the rules and that they can't please you. If you strike up a friendship, for example at a YH, the students may stick to you like glue. They can't imagine that you would actually desire to be alone on a mountaintop contemplating the sunset. There's really nothing you can do about all this attention, you just have to accept it in good spirits. The worst thing to do is to become angry. The Japanese smile in almost every situation, even if they're relating the death of a

loved realtive. They do this because they feel that they shouldn't burden or disturb anyone else's peace with their troubles. If they're running desperately through the rain to catch the last bus home and the door snaps shut in their face, they'll smile. You should learn this technique, too. Nowhere will a smile get you further than it will in Japan.

gaijin fever: This social malaise can strike any Japanese with ferocious speed. The majority of rural Japanese have never dealt with a *gaijin* before and they're the most susceptible, although even sophisticated city dwellers will become unnerved if the encounter is unexpected. Particularly bad cases of "*gaijin* fever" range from slack-jawed awe to startled hysteria. Sometimes it's funny, and sometimes it hurts your feelings. There are numerous instances where "*gaijin* fever" comes into play. The following are only a few examples: You may get on a train and sit down with the seat next to you obviously vacant. Even if the train is crowded, no one may sit there. Rural fishermen who risk their lives everyday out at sea may actually scream when they see you. People may find it impossible to understand you, even if you're using the proper Japanese word, not because the pronunciation is wrong, but because a Japanese word couldn't be coming out of a *gaijin*'s face. If you get into an argument or, heaven forbid, a fight, the police will assume that you're the guilty party. If you look back at a Japanese looking at you, they'll avert their eyes. If you're in a hurry to catch a train or bus, the ticket seller may stand there stupified as you desperately try to communicate before your train or bus pulls away. In almost any setting away from the cities, you're watched as if in spotlight on center stage. Japanese men delight in trying to get you drunk. The symptoms vary, but you'll soon become accustomed to "gaijin fever." Take it in stride. The only antidote is to remain calm and smile. Most of all, be yourself and the "fever" will pass.

RELIGION

SHINTO: THE WAY OF THE GODS

If any quality exists that sets the Japanese apart from other peoples of the world, it is their basic spiritual belief in nature defined as simple beauty. Look around you at anything that is natural and you will see the bedrock of Japan's indigenous spiritualism known as Shinto. The word *Shinto* is derived from the Chinese *Shin-Tao* by which it is universally known, but in Japan it is called *Kami-No-Machi*, the Way of the Gods. Shinto has its origins in pre-dawn Japanese civilization when tribal shaman beseeched the powers of nature (upon which the rudimentary agriculturalists were so dependent) to be benevolent. This spirit nature of *kami* (loosely defined as spirit-god) was seen to exist in everything in the physical world; including mountains, rocks, rivers, trees and even insects. The pre-civilized Japanese believed that their islands were the only inhabited areas on the flat earth and that they themselves were the

"children of the gods." Shinto as a philosophy never spread to any extent beyond the islands upon which is originated. Most primitive agricultural societies hold many common beliefs which deified nature and one akin to early *shinto* would be the rites and rituals of American Indians. Pure Shinto is not a religion because there is no dogma or moral principles except basic purity. Good and evil are not defined because nature has no good or evil. The main tenet says, "Stay pure and follow the true impulses of your heart."

basic beliefs: Shinto scorned lying, theft, adultery, incest and bestiality. Cleanliness was highly regarded for being unclean was disrespectful to the gods. Rituals to this day center around purification by water, fire and wind. The much loved Japanese bath (ofuro) is tied to this tradition which holds that it should be taken before the evening meal. Confucianism made its advent in Japan during the 5th C and Shintoism quickly absorbed its code of ethics. At the top of the list were filial loyalty and courage, and growing naturally out of these 2 concepts was ancestor worship. The rulers of Japan seized upon these concepts and the emperor was viewed as the head of the universal Japanese family. These concepts would be heavily abused when Shinto was bent into State Shinto for the 80 years leading up to and including WW11. All loyalty belonged to the Emperor-God and this would add greatly to the numerous useless human tragedies that Japan would bear. Ancestors are viewed as personal *kami* who take an interest in the lives of their living kinsmen. If they are kept alive in memory, then they can intercede from behind the veil of death. In many homes, there are 2 altars. One is for *kami* in general and the other is for departed relatives. Today, there is a thriving trade in bones of fallen WW11 Japanese soldiers on the remote islands of the Pacific. Family members scour old battlefields trying to locate a relic of a long dead soldier. These are brought back to Japan and enshrined in the family altar. The authenticity of most of these bones is questionable. Also, today at cremation ceremonies, the bereaved will use special chopsticks to retrieve bones from the ashes for this same purpose of enshrinement.

torii gate

the kami: In 712, the *Kojiki* (Records of Ancient Things) was written. It set down the pantheon of gods long revered as the creators of Japan. These are the main deities at Shinto shrines. The gods follow a hierarchy of power similar to the ancient Greek pantheon. At the top of the list is Amaterasu, the sun goddess, enshrined at the Imperial shrines of Ise and revered by the Japanese at large. Villages have their own *kami* as well as universal ones. Sometimes their power extends only to the village, and there are even gods that oversee only one farmer's field. These local gods provide the reasons for most festivals in Japan. There is often a portion of the festival where the local *kami* are carried around in portable shrines to see their earthly constituents at close quarters. There are gods for every manner of human situation possible. Some preside over old umbrellas, old hats and even broken sewing needles while others are more universal and govern the intangibles such as mercy, health, war and the elements. The pantheon of gods swelled even more after Buddhism came to Japan. The new religion was first embraced by the court of Emperor Shotoku in the 7th century and from there percolated down to the common folk. A schism began to occur between the ancient Shinto beliefs and the new religion. It was healed by the efforts of 2

Buddhist saints in the 9th century: Saicho, known as Dengyo-Daishi and Kukai, known as Kobo Daishi. These visionary evangelists held that Buddha was a manifestation of the old Shinto gods. This theory helped to defuse the situation, and, to this day, the Japanese have no trouble accepting both religions and see no paradoxes. Shinto appeals to basic nature and Buddhism appeals to the higher self. The 2 religions did not merge, but were not at odds. Many Japanese are born and married by Shinto priests and buried by Buddhists. Many times there are small shinto shrines on the very grounds of Buddhist temples. Both religions stress the subjugation of the ego. The primary aim is to bring oneself into a state of mind where this can occur without regard to the object of worship. Just feel it, never mind how. Between the 15th and 17th C, a revival of pure Shinto took place. It stressed the expunging of Buddhist and Confucian doctrine that had entered the religion and sought to return to the days of pure mythology without the intellectual concepts. This led to the system of State Shinto started by Emperor Meiji and carried to extremes during that of Taisho (Hirohito). Because of the loss of WW11, State Shinto was no longer subsidized by the government and fell to a low ebb in the minds of the people. Today, there are no longer great numbers of *ujiko* (shrine parishoners), but most Japanese still pay homage at the shrines in a sense of religious sentiment and a long, not easily forgotten tradition.

Shinto rites, shrines, etiquette and beliefs: A Shinto shrine is called a *jinja* and the entrance is always signalled by a *torii* gate (see description later). Unlike Buddhist temples, there is never a fee for entering although there is a donation box. *Jinja* are much less ornate than Buddhist temples (*otera*). They are usually made from unpainted wood and many have thatched roofs. Very rudimentary *jinja* are found throughout the countryside, many being no more than a cubbyhole covered by a piece of tin, but there is always a *torii*. The most well-known shrines in Japan are Meiji and Yasukuni Shrine (Tokyo), Ise Shrine (Ise), and Izumo Shrine (near Matsue). Yasukuni Shrine is the commoner's shrine. While the others house the gods from mythology and the spirit of the modern great Emperor Meiji. Yasukuni is dedicated to the souls of all the soldiers who were ever felled in battles, regardless of social rank. All of these shrines are excellent examples of the very early forms of shrine architecture. There are usually 3 *torii* leading to the main shrine with smaller shrines to lesser gods lining the main pathway. As you approach the shrine, there is a water fount or trough where you use the communal cup to rinse your mouth and wash your hands, another purification. When the devotee reaches the shrine, itself, he claps his hands 3 times and pulls a rope attached to a clapper in the ceiling. This calls the god's attention. A silent prayer from a bowing position is offered and sometimes money or a small offering, usually of rice or fruit, is made. Small strips of paper called *nusa* or *gohei* are also offered and at one time these were pieces of cloth. Great emphasis is placed upon proper formalities. The prayers are offered in the most polite form of archaic Japanese.

shinto today: After making their offerings, many modern families stroll about the shrine precincts with an air of merriment. Going to a shrine is more like a family outing than a religious ceremony. The services of the Shinto priests are sought for almost all occasions. They wear flowing robes and a tall, lacquered silk hat, the style unchanged since the 9th century. One of their main props is a *sakaki* (pine branch) that they wave as a sign of blessing and purification. Today, even, a new Toyota may be driven to the *jinja* for an official blessing. The doors of many shrines face the sunrise in memory of Amaterasu. This is considered a happy time of day and early morning prayers are considered the most potent. Sunset, on the other hand, is unhappy. There are approximately 100 million Japanese who follow the various sects of Shinto in one form or another. A minority take an active part as worshippers and pilgrims following closely the concepts of Shinto, but most Japanese follow out of habit and tradition and have no idea of the meaning behind many rituals and symbols. (Ask a westerner the "meaning" of a Christmas wreath hung on a door during Yuletide!) Shinto, in essence, says that life happens once, but the soul lives on in future generations. If the memory of it dims, the soul then merges with the universe like anything else that once existed. The merging of the soul is not a sad occasion; it's the unalterable and eventual end of earthly life.

Confucian concepts: Confucianism is a code of ethics. Only in the broadest terms may it be considered a religion. It was brought to Japan by Chinese merchants on Korean ships in 400 A.D. Its advent coincided with a change of social power to the Imperial Throne and Confucianism helped to pave the way for the transition. Confucius concerned himself with social order. The family is paramount. The father is the patriarchal head followed by the first born son and then down the line. The mother is revered and respected out of love and filial devotion. Loyalty is the highest virtue. Shinto had long accepted the Emperor as a son of the gods, and Confucianism supplied the philosophy and code necessary to put the concepts into action. It was an easy philosophical extension to owe all allegiance to the Emperor and to view Japan as one large family. The concepts exist to this day. Along with Confucianism's earthly concepts came the devotion to ancestors, both quickly and easily absorbed by Shinto. *Bushido* (the code of the samurai) built upon the now ingrained Confucian concepts evolved 1000 years later and accounted for undying devotion to leaders. The Japan of today, where workers view the company as an extension of the family and where men in general are dominant in the society, is the natural extension of the long held code of ethics taught by Confucianism.

the torii gate: The symbol of Shinto placed before every *jinja* is the *torii* gate (usually 3 in a row). The simplest constructions are of unpainted logs, but more elaborate ones are made of stone, copper, iron and even steel beams. Passing under the *torii* gate purifies the worshipper in heart and mind to go before the enshrined deity. The *torii* symbolizes the perch made for the mythical cock that heralded the dawn and brought Amaterasu, the sun goddess from her cave. There are various kinds of *torii* but they all follow the same general style. There are 2 staunch upright beams, and stretching across the top horizontally like a giant roost is a cross piece (*kasagi*] that extends out past the upright posts. Just below it is another horizontal brace called a *nuki* that usually stops at the uprights. When a worshipper passes under the *torii* and comes to the shrine itself, the first act is to clap the hands 3 times, called *kashi-wa-de* (young fowl hand). Roosters when crowing often flap their wings and this act commemorates the crowing cock that called Amaterasu from her cave. A common shrine throughout Japan is dedicated to the Fox God (*Inari*). A famous one is almost next door to the Grand Shrine of Ise. They are easily spotted by hundreds of *torii* leading to them that are positioned so close together that they almost form a tunnel. These are given by devotees as offerings to the Fox God. The Fox is a god messenger, and as in the west, is considered sly. He's a favorite with businessmen who seek his help in making deals. The Fox God is a tough taskmaster. Unless you please him completely, he will turn the tables and deliver a false message to the gods. To please him, further offerings of bean curd and rice are put before his shrine because it's a known fact that this is his favorite dish.

BUDDHISM

In 552 a Korean King, Kudara, hard-pressed by civil war, solicited the Japanese throne for military help. He sent Buddhist art works as gifts that were carried by priests and nuns. Officially, this marked the beginnings of Buddhism in Japan. The religion came ready made with rites and rituals and its esoteric principles appealed to the questioning minds of the educated Japanese. In the 7th C, Prince Shotoku, the Constantine of Buddhism was converted and the doctrines began quickly spreading through the nobility and intellectuals of the Imperial Court at Nara. The principle of *sessho kindan* (the prohibition of killing animals and eating their meat) and the *Bon* Festival came into being. Great temples and the giant *Daibutsu* at Nara were fashioned. The ruling class became infused with the new religion and the ranking princes became the abbots of the major temples. In the 8th C, Buddhist practices began to collide with long established Shinto rituals. Two priests emerged, Kobo-Daishi and Dengyo-Daishi, and between them devised the doctrine of *Honji-Suijaku*. Simply stated, it said that there was in essence no conflict. Buddhism filled the void left by Shinto whereby intellectuals could delve into the mysteries of life. From the nobility, its concepts spread down to the common man and became the guardian faith of the empire. For the next 4 centuries, Japan experienced relative peace both abroad and domestically and temples flourished throughout the countryside. They were, however, not only interested in the soul, but in politics as well and rivalries sprang up between different sects. Many ruled by princes and noblemen were involved in court intrigues. When Kublai Khan attempted to invade Japan in the 12th C, the Buddhist monks fervently prayed for intersession and the divine wind (*kami kaze*) saved the empire. This proved once and for all that the foreign, now completely Japonified religion, was the true religion of the land. The Kamakura shogunate that followed was dominated by the arts, architecture and esoteric pursuits inherent in the meditative, inward-turning philosophies of Buddhism. Flower arranging and the tea ceremony flowed from these introspective ideas. When the Tokugawas began their shogunate in the 16th C, they turned to the highly organized temples of Buddhism and incorporated them as organs of the state. All families were required to register at temples and thus began the idea of parishioners. The priests held wide authority, and many temples taught martial arts and kept civil order. Many samurai who had become masterless (*ronin*) became Buddhist priests. Obviously, there was no paradox seen between refusing to eat the flesh of a steer and at the same time beheading a peasant for a trifling social infraction. Today, before marriage ceremonies are performed, many families require the tracing of the family tree. These lineages often lead back to the records of temples begun in the Edo period. Before this time, families had no official names. Names were reserved only for samurai and nobility. The farmers and peasantry would be considered upstarts if they thought in terms of names. With the coming of the Meiji Restoration, the Buddhist temples, often firmly in the hands of the old clans, were considered a stumbling block to State Shinto. Their power was eroded and they quickly lost their former grandeur. The religion was not banned, but all "right thinking" people gave their allegiance to the emperor and it was socially unacceptable to believe too strongly in Buddhism. When WW 11 was lost, State Shinto was abolished and more importantly lost face in the hearts of the people. Buddhism, which had been languishing and biding its time just under the surface, re-emerged as Japan's leading religion. Its concepts and principles are deeply ingrained in the psyche of the people.

Buddhist monk

Buddhist sects: Buddhism, as practiced in Japan, is divided into varying sects whose beliefs and approaches to Buddhism are profoundly different. Tendai Buddhism, one of the oldest, was founded by Saicho who established the main temple at Mt. Hiei just NE of Kyoto. The proponents preached that the whole Buddha nature is discovered through meditation and prayer. *Shingon Buddhism:* Kobo-Daishi founded the Shingon sect and established many temples throughout Japan, with the main temple being located at Mt. Koya just S of Osaka. The Shingon sect busied itself with the study of esoteric principles. It instigated complex rituals complete with deep symbolism and mysticism that in its basic nature tended towards the magical. From these 2 mountain tops, Buddhism began its spread until newer sects began to emerge in the 13th century.

Jodo and Shinshu: Two of the most noteworthy new sects were the *Jodo* and *Shinshu* sects. The first was founded by Honen and the latter by his disciple Shinran. The *Jodo*

sect has its main monastery at Chion-in in Kyoto. Known as the Pure Land sect, it believes that meditation is unnecessary. Its main doctrine is *tariki-hongan:* absolute faith in the Buddha power. There are very few rituals and it renounced the idea that salvation can be attained by one's own efforts. Devotees are instructed to repetitiously recite the formula, *Namu Amida Butsu* (Glory to Amida Buddha), which is the mysterious key to salvation and coupled with faith and a religious life, will lead to the Pure Land of Buddha. The *Shinshu* sect (True Sect of the Pure Land) as interpreted by Shinran feels that faith in Amida is sufficient and that the chanting of the prayer is merely the offering of a contented heart. It has even less ritual and its priests are not required to remain celibate or follow ascetic practices. Its popular belief holds that all men are equal in the eyes of the *Amida* Buddha. *Shinshu* has few images except for that of its founder, which is accorded reverence more than devotion. This sect is one of the most popular in Japan today.

Nichiren Sect: Another important sect is Nichiren, named after its founder. There are many offshoots from this sect which maintains its primary temple at Kuonji Temple in Minobu, Yamanashi Prefecture. The parishioners of Nichiren are taught that the way to enlightenment is through repetition of the mantra, "Glory to the Sutra of the Lotus of Truth." The priests follow ascetic practices and lead their congregations in loud, boisterous chants punctuated by drums and gongs. This sect was also militaristic during times past and many of its priests were swashbuckling *samurai* schooled in the martial arts.

Buddhist rites, rituals and gods: Otera (Buddhist temples) are usually extremely ornate buildings in large compounds found throughout Japan. Many perch atop mountains, commanding a superb view of the countryside. Unlike *jinja* (Shinto shrines), *otera* often require an admission fee, but this can include tours of superb gardens with many temples offering museums in the bargain. *Otera* architecture is much more gaily decorated than *jinja*. Rafters are intricately carved and many panels are painted in bright colors of red, blue, green and gold. Highly stylized rituals go on day and night accompanied by chanting and music, especially by gongs and drums. Incense is often burning in large pots as offerings to Buddha. Sticks are purchased on entering. Also as you enter there is a cylindrical box that you rattle until a stick with a number attached pops through a hold in the top. The number corresponds to an *omikuji* (prayer paper) which is often written in the form of a fortune. You will see thousands of *omikuji* tied to the trees and bushes surrounding the *otera*. This is a way of offering a prayer so that the good luck fortune is granted.

rites and rituals: Most Japanese see no paradox in following both Shinto and Buddhism. Marriages and births are attended by Shinto priests, while funeral rites are held at a Buddhist temple. Many cemeteries are found surrounding these temples, although cremation is becoming more universal because of a lack of land space. Cemeteries are usually found on unusable land such as hillocks and knolls, even among rice paddies. They are never located at Shinto shrines. A Buddhist funeral service can easily be recognized. The house of the deceased is curtained in black and white. Often, on the doorway is hung a large picture of the deceased trimmed in black velvet. Men in the procession wear morning coats and striped trousers or substitute with a black kimono. Women wear dark shaded kimono.   *gods:* A favorite Buddhist deity easily seen and recognized is *Jizo*. *Jizo* is the Buddha of compassion, the patron of travelers and of pregnant women and children. The statuary representing *Jizo* sometimes differs but the classic pose looks like a shaven headed priest, holding a precious stone in one hand and a staff decorated with 3 metal rings in the other. There are often hundreds of tiny *Jizo* adorned with a red bib lining the pathways of temples. Heaped around *Jizo* will be piles of stone. Compassionate people place them there to aid the spirits of children who are doomed to pile stones along the banks of the river of hell (Sai-No-Kawara). The living gather stones to aid them and to secure their soul's release. Other Buddha manifestations include: *Hotei*, a jolly Buddha with a huge naked belly, who is the god of satisfaction and natural pleasures, and *Hachiman* (Japanese *Yawata*), the god of war whose empress mother, *Jingo*, carried him in her womb for 3 years during a Korean war of the 2nd century. *Ebisu* is the god of chance. He carries a fishing rod and a dolphin. *Kannon*, the goddess of mercy, can take many shapes. In one, she looks like a madonna with a babe in her arms. The hidden Japanese Christians during the Edo period revered her image as that of the Blessed Virgin. Sometimes she is given a horse's head and multiple arms. She is surrounded by traditional symbols such as the lotus, moon,

pagoda, skull, axe and thunderbolts. Often, one of her hands is offering alms. She ensures that prayers are answered.

Jizo, the patron of children, pregnant women and travelers

Pagoda (Japanese To): Another structure found on the grounds of *otera* is the pagoda. They were originally built in India to enshrine the bone relics of Buddha. It was believed that Buddha's bones were divided and fragments were sent throughout Asia. Later, pagodas were erected on holy spots, or as offerings to the dead and served as tombs. They can range from 1 to 13 stories and an important feature is the nine ringed spire placed on the top called a *sorin*. Some scholars feel that the pagoda structure was merely a base for the *sorin*. Inside the pagoda is a large beam suspended from the ceiling and almost touching the ground below. Some believe that this was devised as a pendulum and served as an anti-earthquake device for the building. Actually, records state that this beam was really a grave marker and was more important than the *sorin*. One of the finest pagodas, Goji-No-To, can be seen at Horyuji Temple in Nara. Another excellent one is at Itsukushima Shrine on Miyajima Island, just S of Hiroshima, while minor ones are found at many temples throughout Japan.

ZEN

The most Japanese form of Buddhism, however, is Zen. This is broken into many schools, but the most well-known are Rinzai and Soto. Zen teaches that *satori* (*nirvana* or enlightenment) is reached through the emptying of the self through strict ascetic practices and deep meditation. Although it was known in India and China, it really took off in Japan after it was introduced in the 12th C by Eisai and Dogen. It had the greatest appeal of all for the samurai caste and many principles of *bushido* (the way of the warrior) are based upon its teachings. Of all the Buddhist sects, it has the greatest following or at least interest in the west. Countless writers have tried to describe Zen and usually begin by saying that they are trying to describe the indescribable. Many of Japan's esoteric arts such as the tea ceremony, archery, flower arranging and even *Noh* plays are based on Zen. It is considered the highest form of Buddhism, passed on at the end of the Buddha's life when verbalization of his principles was considered redundant. It seeks to teach more by intuition and feeling than by intellectual or logical instruction.

Zen practices: Two of its most important techniques are the *mondo* and the *koan*. The *mondo* is a question and answer period between master (*roshi*) and pupil (*deshi*), but it is also much more than that. Actually, you are on your own to ferret out by feeling the mysteries of the oneness. The questions and answers appear vague with no clear logic designed to make the pupil stretch to his spiritual limits. The *koan* is offered as a point upon which the pupil meditates. The most famous of the thousands that exist is, "What is the sound of one hand clapping?" The *mondo* follow up to this *koan* could be, "I have no ears with which to hear. Can you make me hear the one hand clap?" Zen trainees are put through an almost torturous course of instruction. They leave all worldly matters behind when they enter a temple. Oftentimes, they live communally and are given only one '*tatami*' mat (1 m by 2 m) upon which to live and a tiny shelf to keep their very few personal belongings. The day usually starts at 0300 with many periods of meditation throughout. Westerners lured to Zen are often amazed that the spiritual path to *satori* is paved by so much actual physical pain. Besides deprivations such as meager diet and hard work (*samu*), the *seiza* (lotus position) held for long hours of meditation is excruciating. During the year, there are groups of days set aside (*sesshin*) when Zen monks literally meditate from morning to night. They assume the *seiza* position in which they remain for a fulll 60 min. with only a 5 min. break. Old stories tell of the abilities of the ancient Zen masters. One master once sat *seiza* in a cave for 9 consecutive years until his legs atrophied and simply fell off. Another master, crippled in youth, went through life with the bones in his hip, knee and ankle fused solid. He could meditate with only one leg in the *seiza* position. At the end of his life, when he had lived on this earthly plane long enough, he summoned his pupils. When they gathered around, he sat and proceeded to break the bones in his bad leg. He sat in the lotus position with the bones sticking through his skin, smiling and quietly bleeding to death. Today, Zen masters walk among their students sitting *seiza* and when they realize the discomfort is getting too great or the mind is wandering, they will thwack them on the back with a bamboo cane. This is not punishment, but kindness to alleviate the suffering. The pay off to these rigors is the belief that you will eventually experience *satori* (enlightenment) and break the chain of endless reincarnation whereby you will never be required to return to this earthly world of suffering and tears. Obviously, this route is not for everyone. Most must wait to pass through the turnstile of death and then get an onward going ticket. (See introduction: "Nirvana," "Getting there.")

Zen teachings: Zen does not seek to convert nor is it a religion. All people, regardless of their faith, can practice Zen and, perhaps, achieve a measure of enlightenment that can enhance their own personal beliefs. Zen strives to liberate the consciousness from the chains of words and to go past logic to the unconscious truth of oneness. Many Buddhist temples have opened their doors and function as YHs. A list of *Shukubo* (temple lodgings) is also available from TIC. Many Japanese go on retreats to temples to attune themselves to spiritual matters when the world is too much with them. The temples accept westerners also. These experiences can be some of the most memorable on your visit to Japan. Visitors are free to talk to the senior monks (many are well-educated and speak English). They are offered tea and the meals provided are *shojin ryori* (vegetarian macrobiotic). For more information on Zen temples and Zen study centers see "helpful addresses" at the end of this chapter and "accommodations" in the "General Introduction."

CHRISTIANITY

Christianity came to Japan in force just before the Edo period aboard ships of Portuguese merchants. St. Francis Xavier, on missionary tour of Asia, visited Japan in 1549 and his influence, supported by numerous missionaries, spread Christianity among the ruling *daimyo* (feudal lords). A series of political intrigues in the years that followed, and finally a Christian rebellion at Shimabara near Nagasaki, caused the new westrn religion to be banned in Japan and its followers mercilessly executed. (See "History," "General Introduction," for a further description.) It survived underground for the 250 years during the Tokugawa imposed isolation and reemerged in the 1860's with the coming of the Black Ships of Commodore Perry. There are sketchy earlier accounts of Christianity in Japanese folklore. A small village by the name of Shingo in Aomori prefecture lays claim to a legend relating that Jesus Christ came there to live and die at the venerable age of 106! The Shingo villagers say that Jesus' brother died on the cross in Galilee. Also, one report says that in the 7th C, Christians from India came to Japan and that an empress of Nara studied the new

religion for a brief period. Modern Christianity in Japan declined just before WW11, but after the war Christianity once again came into vogue as war torn Japan looked outward for leadership and heavenward to transcend the horror of subjugated Japan. The concept of a personal savior however is difficult for the Japanese spiritual mind to grasp, and most people still consider themselves as members of the singularly Japanese extended family first, and religious followers second. Christianity also implies that a convert must utterly renounce all pagan belief in Shinto and Buddist principles. These, as previously stated, are deeply ingrained as part of the general psychological makeup of a Japanese and even devout Christians have difficulty in abandoning them. Christian organizations in Japan are looked on favorably, however, because many function as self-help or charity groups and are admired for their desire to better the human condition. Neither Shinto nor Buddhism have a history for organized charitable organizations and so networks of broad social work are in the Christian domain. The various Christian sects are also powerful in the labor movement and maintain some of the best hospitals (foreign speaking) in Japan.

NEW RELIGIONS

Like anywhere else in this topsy-turvy world, when good sense seems to have abandoned ship, people cast about looking for a life raft upon which to climb. The Japanese are no exception. Japan has had more than its share of mind shattering change in the last 40 years and rapid industrial growth, coupled with the mass migrations to the cities, has caused a feeling of deep-seated alienation among the workers. This is a perfect environment for New Religions which preach earthly peace and salvation in which to grow and prosper. The Japanese, more than any other people, need a group to which they can belong, and the New Religions fill the bill. Most either revere or downright deify their central leader or founder. Many try to return to a simpler "natural time" and vilify the technical and scientific worlds. Many rely upon the graces of the master to relieve illness and return the world to a balance. Some are self-serving cults, a few are outright shams, while the majority honestly try to better the lot of mankind. Many have become politically active and have a strong voice in national affairs. The problem with New Religions, wherever they are found, is that they are bogged down in one-way theocratic dogma and, in essence, are close-minded. Peace and contentment are where you find them and many in Japan today look to the New Religions. The most important of these is the *Soka Gakkai* (Creative Education Society) founded in the 1930s by Tsunesaaburo Makiguchi and Josei Toda. It boasts 20 million Japanese adherents and includes international followers amounting to 500,000. The political branch of Soka Gakkai is the *Komeito* (Clean Government Party) founded in 1964. It has strong backing in Parliament and is often looked to, to tip the balance for one leading party or another. Other influential, legitimate New Religions are *Seicho No Ie* (The House of Growth), *P. L. Kyodan* (Perfect Liberty Organization) and *Sekai Kyuseiko* (Religion for World Salvation).

HELPFUL ADDRESSES

To study Zen or any other religion in Japan: It's best to have a cultural visa (4-1-8) or a student visa (4-1-6). This may be arranged before going to Japan, but is easier after you have arrived and enrolled in a school of your choice. TIC can provide some useful addresses. The list offered here in not-inclusive, but may help to get you started: Chiba Center, Naritasan, Shinsho-ji Danjikido, Narita Shi, tel: 22-2111. Inexpensive retreat, vegetarian meals; Kanagawa Center, Shintaido 34, Kasumigaoka, Nishi-ku, Yokohama, tel: (045) 241-5513. Odd bedfellows: Christianity and martial arts, Kumamoto Center, Tairyu Furukawa, Schweitzer Temple, Onsenku 584, Tamana-shi, Kumamoto Ken, Rinzai and Shinran Zen; Daitoku-ju, Ryoko-in, Kyoto. Tel: (075)491-0243. Large Zen temple that accepts foreigners; (Kyoto has the largest concentration of Zen training centers in Japan. Try the Kyoto TIC for info); Friends World College, 28 Gakooda-cho, Nishi-kujo, Minami ku, Kyoto. Good meeting place; Nagano Center, c/o Father Oshida, Takamori, Fujimi-cho, Suwa-gun. Tel: (07266) 64-172172. A Christian priest who follows Zen; Shizuoka Center, c/o Masahiro Oki, 777 Sawachi, Mishima-shi. Run by Oki the Yogi, Japan's most popular and worldly yogi. An old standby with foreigners; International Zen Dojo, Seitaji, 611 Tsurushima, Uenohara cho, Yamanashi ken (near Fuji). Westerners are welcome with nominal charges for students. *Sesshin* is the 1st week of each month at which time the students are completely absorbed in meditation and visitors should not interrupt.

ARTS AND CRAFTS

The islands of Japan glisten with cataclysmic beauty and its people, so tied to its natural wonders, have captured this beauty in art works for 2000 years. They have adorned their island nation with paintings, sculptures, architecture, handicrafts and folk art that mirrors every facet of their life. Fine arts are displayed in numerous museums and galleries. Ancient temples and shrines are not only religious centers, but also house countless intricate art works which are preserved and periodically displayed. Craftsmanship of all sorts is found in towns and cities, especially Kyoto, where jewelry, lacquerware, fine cloths, damascene, bamboo ware and paper products are made. Japan as a pottery and ceramics center is unparalleled in the world. Centers of pottery, such as Mashiko, Arita and Bizen, enjoy international acclaim and have thriving learning centers where foreigners are welcomed. Kilns deep in mountain villages trace their heritage to indentured Korean craftsmen, brought to Japan hundreds of years ago and sequestered so that their secrets remained inviolable. Folkcraft is the most easily attainable of all Japan's arts. Every section of the country has its specialty. Fine ironware is made in Tohoku; exquisite, naturally dyed cloths come from Okinawa; Japanese paper is made on the island of Shikoku as well as in other centers and is naturally bleached in mountain streams. There are folk toy cottage industries in uncountable villages. Many woodworkers and folk craftsmen specialize in a wide array of folk toys and items including *kokeshi* dolls, *temari* (embroidered balls), wooden boats, animals and papier mache masks. All of these wares are customarily shipped to cities where they are displayed in *depato*. Street stalls, shops and annual fairs are also major outlets. There is something for everyone with scores of items with manageable price tags. This chapter will give you a short synopsis of fine arts along with a list of museums and centers where they can be seen, but the main emphasis will be placed on handicrafts and folk arts. Throughout the travel chapters, there are sections called "Crafts" and "Shopping" that highlight the best items produced in the area and noting where they can be purchased.

FINE ARTS

The fine arts of Japan began to advance about 1500 yrs ago when masterly works were enthusiastically imported from China. At first, the influence of Chinese art dominated, but

CHRONOLOGY: JAPANESE FINE ARTS

Ancient Period

Jamon rope pattern pottery from 7000 B.C. and *Yayoi* wheeled pottery from 350 B.C. Tomb architecture of great nobles from 300 A.D., such as the royal tombs in Osaka. Ancient *Shinto* architecture displayed at Izumo and Ise Grand Imperial Shrines.

Asuka Period (552-645)

Horyuji at Nara, a great Buddhist temple that still stands. Mostly religious art of bronze and wooden sculptures of the Tori school.

Nara Period (645-794)

Building of impressive monasteries around Naha. The Daibutsu (Great Buddha) is cast and encased at Todaiji Temple at Nara and international art works are collected and placed in the Shosoin (Treasure House) on the temple grounds. Frescoes of Buddhist heaven adorn Horyuji Temple. Towards the end of the era, the *Kojiki* (Record of Ancient Matters) and *Nihon-Shoki* (Chronicles of Japan) are compiled.

Heian Period (975-1185)

Ho-Odo (Phoenix Hall) is built at Uji near Kyoto along with Nara's famous Kasuga shrine. Kobo-Daishi builds an impressive temple at Koya-san. Calligraphy begins as an art form and *Yamato-e*, narrative picture scrolls, are painted depicting Japanese topics such as the *Tale of the Genji*. The *Makura-No-Soshi* (Pillow Book) is written by Sei.

Kamakura Period (1185-1333)

Zen architecture dominates temple building, with excellent examples such as Daitokuji in Kyoto and Engakuji at Kamakura. Kokei ushers in the great age of sculpture with his Amida Buddha at Kamakura. Picture scrolls become more elaborate and *E-Makimono* (illustrated scrolls) depict warfare and lives of great Buddhist priests. Poetry becomes popular and an anthology is compiled by priest Saigyo known as the *Shinkokinshu* in a style called *waka*.

Muromachi Period (1333-1568)

The Kinkakuji and Ginkakuji elaborate pavillions are built at Kyoto. Zen inspired *Sumi-e* (black and white paintings) begin. Great *Noh* dramas are written by Kannami and *Kyogen* farces are portrayed between the *Noh* acts. *Chanoyu* (tea ceremony) is enjoyed by the nobility, and the pattern is established by Sen-No-Rikyu.

Azuchi-Momoyama Period (1565-1600)

Military unity of Japan gives rise to castle architecture and Shira-sage (White Heron) castle at Himeji sets the standards. Foreigners are painted on picture screens and exquisite tea houses are built.

Tokugawa (Edo) Period (1600-1868)

The elaborate shrines of Nikko are built as a mausoleum for the supreme shogun Tokugawa Ieyasu. The merchant class comes into prominence and the Genroku culture flourishes. Great Masters of *Ukiyo-e* depict scenes including commoners on their wood block prints. The greatest works of *Haiku* (17 syllable impressionistic poetry) is written by Matsuo Basho. *Bunraku* (puppet theater) and *Kabuki* dramas begin to thrill audiences.

Meiji to Modern (1868-present)

Art is heavily influenced by the West. Japan goes practical. Frank Lloyd Wright sets the tone for architecture with his construction of the Imperial Hotel (one of the only major structures to survive the great Tokyo earthquake of 1923). Hagiwara becomes the first poet to write in colloquial Japanese while Yosano Akiko, a woman poet, puts great emotion into her works. Great novelists such as Futabatei, Akutagawa and Mishimo emerge. Cinema and large theatrical productions with a western influence begin to dominate night life.

slowly the Japanese, graced with their own skills and insights, began creating personalized works. From the beginning, art was patronized by the nobility including the Imperial Household and great masters were supported in their endeavors. In its earliest stages, art was inspired solely by religion. By the end of the Heian Period (794-1185), a tradition of secular art began with the great literary chronicles of ancient Japanese tales such as the *Kojiki* and *Nihon-Shoki*, and art was no longer solely dominated by religion. This tradition exists to the present day and artists, alone among the rigid groupings of Japanese society, are free to follow their own inner voices and are even expected to be eccentric. *Ukiyo-e* prints, which came into vogue during the Edo Period (1615-1868) sometimes depicted bawdy scenes in the lives of ordinary men, and since then, Japanese art has become socially universal. Drawing on this tradition has freed the Japanese artist from social restraints and today excellent film makers, novelists, poets, sculptors and painters carry on giving insight into the unique qualities of Japanese society.

calligraphy, using *sumi* ink applied with brushes ranging from one hair's width to two-man giants, is a venerated art form in Japan. Many Japanese take classes in calligraphy, and there is a national tournament held in Tokyo around the New Year. Museums preserve ancient calligraphy by masters that are considered artistically equivalent to fine paintings

PAINTING

Except for contemporary works, the vast majority of traditional Japanese paintings were done in watercolors or in *sumi* (black ink), and sometimes the two media were combined. The artists dealt with their art subjectively, almost impressionistically, and the stress was placed more upon a free flowing action and movement and less on reality and form, the mainstays of the great western Renaissance masters. At first, painting was dominated by Buddhism and the masterpieces of most temples are painted screens, picture scrolls and frescoes.

Ukiyo-e: Color wood block prints, which are possibly the best known Japanese art form, are called *hanga*. The most famous type of *hanga* is ukiyo-e, which depicts scenes of everyday life along with portraits of actors and beautiful women. *Ukiyo-e* prints reached their hey-day in the Edo Period in the middle of the 18th century. At first, in Japan and later abroad, they were given little acclaim and considered on a par with comic book art. Such masters as Utamaro, Harunobu and especially Hiroshige, who painted and printed a masterful series of the 53 stages of the Tokaido (the ancient pilgrimage route that passed Mt. Fuji) were finally recognized for the great artists that they were. Today, takeoffs on these excellent prints grace inexpensive *kami-saifu* (paper wallets), notebooks, calendars and souvenirs of every description. A modern artist who has received international acclaim for his unique *ukiyo-e* is Masami Teraoka. All the well drawn and fantastic scenes of courtesans in traditional kimono are in his paintings along with modern additions like flying french fries, dilapidated hamburgers and cameras. Mr. Teraoka now resides in Los Angeles and has had a number of art shows in prominent galleries around the U.S.

HANDICRAFTS

The line that determines what handicrafts are and what fine arts are is thin and in Japan it's very thin. Handicraft items produced in Japan are crafted by artists who make their livelihood as artisans. A number of these artists are quite old and have preserved the traditions of their handicrafts from ancient times. What distinguishes their creations from fine arts is that they can often be used practically as well as being artistically admired. These masters are given great respect and are considered "Living Cultural Assets" and designated as "Possessors of Intangible Cultural Properties." One of these artists is Keisuke Serizawa who creates the most fantastic patterns on cloth through a fine and elaborate stencil dyeing process. Other "Living

Cultural Assets'' have gained prominence in many artistic media from papermaking to pottery and have become world famous. JNTO offices and TIC can help with information on the "Living Cultural Assets" of Japan and can help to arrange a visit to their studios where they sometimes hold "workshops" in their arts. Large *depato* will oftentimes feature an artist in residence where you can observe at close quarters their expertise. By far, the most prolific of Japan's handicrafts are pottery and cermics and excellent kilns are found throughout the archipelago. Besides the potters's art, Japan is highly regarded for its artisans who produce *makie* (lacquerware), *shippo* (cloisonne), metal work, damascene ware, handmade paper and various carvers of ivory, tortoise shell and glass makers.

pottery and ceramics: Of all the crafts available to a budget traveler, the best and most reasonably priced is the profusion of pottery and ceramics found throughout all quarters of Japan. Japanese skill at pottery is legendary and is admired by the Japanese, themselves, as well as being sought after by westerners ever since they were reintroduced to Japan in the 1860s. Like most cultures, the earliest traces of Japan's civilization are dated by potsherds. A type called *jamon*, which is dated at more than 9000 yrs old, is the earliest. The Japanese have perfected the potting art over the centuries and

elegance in technique was prodded on by demand for tea ceremony utensils since the 15th century. One of the spoils of many ancient conflicts between Japan and its neighbor Korea was the bringing to Japan of indentured Korean pottery masters who were highly regarded by the Japanese. Often, feudal lords considered these Korean masters their most valuable treasures and went to great lengths to hide them away in mountain villages where they produced their coveted art pieces in seclusion. One famous potting center, Arita, located in NW Kyushu, still maintains village potters whose ancestors were part of this tradition and ply their trade to this day. Since the 1930s, Mashiko, a small city N of Tokyo, has become Internationally famous as a pottery center. About 50 yrs ago, a master potter by the name of Shoji Hamada settled there and revived the finest traditions of Mashiko-Yaki (pottery). An Englishman, Bernard Teach, came to study and then returned home, spreading the fame of this small city around the western world. There are many kilns in Mashiko in operation and foreigners still flock there to study or buy. There is pottery available all over Japan at local fairs. The articles made are endless and there is something in everyone's price range. Tea cups, *sake* sets, bowls and vases of every shape and description are the favorites with foreigners. Special tea ceremony bowls are highly regarded for their beauty by the Japanese and often become treasured famly heirlooms. There are museums

FAMOUS POTTERY CENTERS		
Pottery	Location	Remarks
Arita-yaki	Arita, Mishi-Matsuura-gun, Saba Pref.	Designs include flowers and birds. *Arita-yaki* is especially noted for enameled porcelains.
Mashiko-yaki	Mashiko-Machi, Haga-gun, Tochigi Pref.	Folkart pottery. A thriving center of study with foreigners. Excellent as a side trip from Tokyo to Nikko.
Bizen-yaki	Bizen-Machi, Waki-gun, Okayama Pref.	One of the oldest kilns in Japan. Iron pigment in the local clay gives a unique color.
Kasama-yaki	Shimo Ichige, Kasama, Ibaraki Prefl	A distinctive earthy glaze made from wood ash and powdered rocks.
Mino-yaki	Toki City, Gifu Pref.	A profusion of kilns producing white pottery in a modern style.

and art galleries throughout the country that are dedicated totally to ceramics displays. Centers such as Bizen near Okayama go back over 1000 yrs in the production of their inspired wares. Villages such as Okamachi near Arita survive totally by the fruits of their kilns. Kagoshima in S Kyushu produces *satsuma-yaki* that has one of the oldest traditions for the manufacture of tea ceremony ware. Sado Island off shore from Niigata produces pottery with a unique reddish color only achieved by using local clay from a defunct gold mine and its wares are highly prized in the tea ceremony. The art helps to keep the island's economy alive.

tips for buying pottery: When looking for a piece of pottery, be aware that all works are not masterpieces. Ever increasing sales have caused the firing up of commercial kilns that put out uninspired, mass-produced works. The price tag usually tells the tale. Masters still produce pottery of great integrity. Hand thrown pottery usually has the name of the potter stamped into it. This stamp is small and usually found on an unglazed portion at the bottom of the article with the potter's name written in *kanji* and surrounded by a squared off border. It's also a good idea when contemplating a purchase to visit a local pottery museum where top notch works are displayed, just to get a feeling for quality. Before rushing off to a small kiln that looks authentic, go to a department store in the city or town if there is one and check out their displays to compare prices. Mingled among master potters, especially in centers known for their works, is always a smattering of johnny-come-latelys, trying to cash in on the pottery boom. Unfortunately, their prices do not always match their lesser skills.

pottery techniques: The most traditional way of firing pottery in Japan is by wood. Hand-made chambered kilns known as *noborigama* and single chambered kilns known as *anagama* are built, usually in step fashion, on the side of a hill. Some masters have modernized and use gas and oil fired kilns, but if you notice a traditional wood fired kiln, you're usually getting the genuine article. The glazes and slips used to decorate the pottery are the master potters' greatest secrets. The results are phenomenal. Glazes can be opaque, translucent, white, black and in every color imaginable. Sometimes they're splashed on so that the result is a dripping burst of color. Other times they're painted on to form intricate designs or are in motifs of birds, animals and flowers. Some of the finest pottery appears rough and obviously hand-made. Sometimes the glaze is on the inside. The Japanese put pottery to use in every conceivable way. Some elaborate articles that resemble little chests are actually burial pots to hold the ashes of the deceased. Gigantic vases are used as garden pots. One village near Bizen produced nothing but ceramic sewer pipes and is known as "sewer pipe village." Small human and animal figurines have been unearthed from tombs dating from the 3rd century. These clay facsimiles are believed to have replaced actual humans that were interred with thier liege lords. Sometimes ceramics is combined with other art forms to become faces on dolls and even miniature shinto shrines are fashioned out of pottery. Master potters of note usually have *deshi* (apprentices) so that their art will be

noborigama kilns

preserved for the future. Anyone interested in buying, looking or studying pottery techniques can gain information at JNTO and the TIC offices in Tokyo and Kyoto. Pottery centers and their wares have been given special attention throughout this book. They are listed with descriptive information given throughout the travel chapters under "arts and crafts." Wherever you travel iln Japan, you are likely to find pottery kilns in operation and most of the time you're welcome to inspect them. Pottery is one of man's oldest and most indestructible creations and you may purchase the beginnings of a family heirloom.

shippo-yaki (cloisonne): This art of enameling is believed to have originated in Egypt over 4000 yrs ago. It became popular in Japan during the 12th century, although its techniques did not become perfected until a modern master, Namikawa, began producing it in Tokyo during the 1880s. To begin the process, a metal base of gold, silver or copper is shaped. Over the base, thin ribbon-like strips of wire are carefully molded and connected to form the intricate patterns. These patterns are filled in with colored enamel pastes and fired. The glossy finish on the best pieces is achieved through hand rubbing, oftentimes employing more than 6 textured grindstones. Cloisonne is a featured article in many shops throughout Japan, although the main manufacturing centers are in Kyoto, Tokyo and Nagoya. Prices match the quality of the articles and these range from mass-produced trifles to exquisite, hand-crafted articles worth a king's ransom.

damascene: This art, whose name derives from Damascus, is believed to have been brought to Japan over 1800 yrs ago through Korea. Damascene has had a long tradition and was used by the samurai and upper classes to adorn sword handles, helmets and objects d'art that were often emblazoned with the family crest. Steel is the foundation of most articles. A pattern is etched into the steel with a fine chisel, and gold or silver threads as fine as spider web silk are hammered into the etchings. After many washings, the article is coated with muddy clay and baked. Finally, it is repeatedly rubbed by hand with oil and charcoal and the final carvings are made. The luster on good damascene ware can always be rejuvenated by rubbing with a cotton cloth dipped in olive oil. Prices on the best wares limit them to a one time special purchase, but reasonably priced articles of lesser craftsmanship can be found.

a 3 tiered lacquerware food container

makie (*lacquerware*): Lacquerware is one of the most sought after and fashionable souvenirs of Japan. Its sale in all kinds of shops and stores is prolific. The art originated in China and for the last 1500 yrs Japanese artisans have been making it. In the 15th C, Chinese artisans were sent to Japan to reclaim the secrets of the art from the Japanese! Today there are a handful of lacquerware artisans in Japan who have been distinguished as "Possessors of Intangible Cultural Properties." The process begins with a simple piece of wood that has been formed into an article. Repeated layers of a fine varnish are applied and then hand rubbed. Finally, a drawing of a design is made and stenciled onto the article. More varnish is applied and rubbed until the article has a smooth, shiny, hard finish. Excellent pieces often employ gold in the design and are extremely expensive, although fine but smaller articles can be had at a reasonable price. There are many souvenir shops that sell facsimiles of lacquerware done in plastic. Oddly enough, some of these facsimiles are tastefully done and, overlooking the materials used, are not bad purchases. The greatest centers for *makie* are Kyoto, and Tokyo, followed by Nagoya and Takamatsu. The least expensive ware comes from Fukushima and Wakayama prefectures. Okinawa is also known for its lacquerware. There the Japanese *deigo* tree is used as a base and considered one of the best media for creating lacquerware. It is also believed that the Okinawan climate helps in the creation of exceptionally beautiful ware. If you purchase a piece, keep it off windowsills and out of direct light in order to maintain the deep lustrous finish.

MINGEIHIN (FOLK CRAFT)

The most endearing of all art forms of a given culture is its folkart. These artistic expressions come from the hearts of the people. In days gone by, the Japanese peasantry, motivated by their own unsophisticated sense of beauty, began to create art, and this tradition thrives to the present day. Many of the articles that these craftsmen produce are utilitarian, while others are pure artistic displays. A good share of the folkart created are toys that mothers and fathers traditionally fashioned in their farmhouses just to delight their children. It's difficult to find an area of Japan that is not famous for something or other. Most folkart is made by hand in small, cottage industries. The media used in its creation are usually natural including iron, wood and cloth, and the articles are prized not only for their beauty, but also for their durability. Some folkart articles have their heritage deeply rooted in legends and myths and the toys, now more like display items, were at one time fully enjoyed by Japanese children. The folk artists range from ancient *obasan* (grandmothers) embroidering cloth for the finest *obi* (sashes) to masterly woodcarvers, kitemakers and doll makers.

folkart today: The machines of modern industrialization can mass produce wonders and marvels, but with most people, there's always a feeling that something is missing. What is missing is charm—the main and most abundant ingredient in folk art. Wherever possible, folkart has been highlighted in the travel chapters under "arts and crafts." Most items are inexpensive and represent the lion's share of souvenirs picked up for the folks back home. To get an idea of folkart in Japan, visit: Japan Folk Crafts Museum, 3-30-4, Komaba, Meguro-ku, Tokyo, tel: (03) 476-4527. Open daily 1000 to 1700, closed Mondays and from Jan 1 to Feb 28; Japan Handicraft Museum, 3-619, Shinkawa, Naniwa-ku, Osaka, tel: (06) 641-6309. Open daily 1000-1700, Closed Mondays; Hida Folklore Museum, Takayama City, Gifu Pref., tel: (0577) 33-4714. Open daily 0900 to 1600. In Tokyo, one of the best shops in the country in which to find folkart is Bingo-ya. The shop is like a warehouse with leisurely browsing as the norm. Its 6 floors are jammed to overflowing with the folkart of Japan. Prices start as low as Y100 and the prices charged for the items sold can be as inexpensive as they are in their native localities. The address is: 69 Wakamatsu-cho, Shinjuku, tel: (03) 202 8778. Open 1000 to 1900, Closed Mondays. There is an excellent book entitled, *Kites, Crackers and Craftsmen* by C. Condon and K. Nagasawa that lists the best craft shops in the Tokyo area. It's available at foreign language bookstores throughout Japan. The following list of items and folk toys is a mere sampling of what you can find in Japan. A full listing would simply be impossible.

daruma dolls

daruma: These curious little figures that come in all shapes and sizes from cones to round balls have one feature in common: they're round at the base and so designed that no matter how many times you knock them over, they'll right themselves. The Japanese take this feature to heart and view it as a maxim of daily life: you can never be successful unless you keep trying. Sometimes wood is carved into a *daruma*, but most likely the material will be papier mache. The history of these "tumbler" dolls is based on an Indian Buddhist priest, Bodhidharma, who is said to have assumed the *zazen* position for 9 years. When *daruma* came to Japan, they were likened to the sage Bodhidharma from whose name *daruma* is derived. Today, *daruma* are a favorite with the Japanese and fathers away on business trips will bring home these souvenirs to their families. Some *daruma* maintain the face of the old *zazen* poser, but the majority have childlike or humorous faces. There are animal *daruma* and female *daruma*. Sendai in Miyagi Pref. produces a jolly *daruma* believed to prevent fires. *Daruma* from Kochi are sold at temples as good health charms. Niigata produces ones that look like cones. Kofu in Yamanashi Pref. does not employ the usually bright colors of red and gold, but paint their *daruma* white. At New Year's, *daruma ichi* (fairs) are held throughout Japan. People scramble to purchase one for good luck for the coming year. Sometimes the *daruma* do not have eyes painted in. The custom is to make a wish and paint in one eye. When the wish is answered, the other eye is painted in. You can find *daruma* all over Japan and small ones are sold for as little as Y100.

toro-no-gangu (toy tigers): Although tigers have never inhabited Japan, the Japanese seem to admire them greatly. Many areas make *toro-no-gangu* and their design can be anything from a sitting warrior with a tiger's head to a realistic tiger, but the majority are fanciful shapes of this jungle cat that bobs up and down. A *hariko* is a *toro-no-gangu* that is made from papier mache plastered over a wooden mold. The mold is removed when the paper dries and a glue (*gofen*), made from crushed sea shells, is applied. Finally, the tiger is painted, usualy yellow with black stripes. The essence of the tiger, honored for his strength and courage, is captured in the *toro-no-gangu*. You can find them anywhere in Japan, but the prized ones come from Tottori, Izumo, Himeji and Fukushima.

temari (embroidered balls): The process for making these beautifully embroidered balls involves taking a natural stuffing such as rice chaff, cotton wadding or ferns and wrapping them in paper. White thread is then wrapped round and round until you have a firm ball. Sizes may vary from ones as big as a plum to giant ones like basketballs. Over the white thread, layers of different colored threads are wound to form geometric patterns. Finally, the ball is embroidered and sometimes a tassle is added. The workmanship on fine specimens is absolutely superb. The prototype of a *temari* was a *kemari*. This was a football that was kicked around in a circle in a game played by the nobility. Later, this crude deerskin ball was refined into a *temari*. The game went indoors and was played by bouncing the ball and singing a song (*temari-uta*) to count the bounces. Some areas still preserve the songs, but few children play with *temari*. Handmaidens of feudal lords began fashioning the balls as a pastime and created remarkable works. You can buy a simple *temari* for a few hundred yen, but there are other creations that come in their own wooden boxes and are very expensive. They would grace the sitting room of any home. Some of the best *temari* come from Arita, Ehime, Tsuruoka and Nagano prefectures. A remarkable one, the *benibana-goten-mari*, comes from Yamagata prefecture and is embroidered with silk threads that have been colored with natural dyes from safflowers.

kokeshi dolls: These simple, cylindrical dolls with round heads and no arms or legs are a favorite folk toy in Japan to this day. They are believed to have been originally made by *kijishi*, traveling woodcarvers, who roamed the forests of Tohoku in N Honshu looking for raw materials for their craft. (For a full description, see Tohoku "arts and crafts.") The *kijishi* made various household items and *kokeshi* were made for their children to play with. The Japanese fell in love with *kokeshi* and demand for them rose. Some families have *kokeshi* that are over 100 yrs old and cherish them as family heirlooms. Today, the dolls are made in various areas of Japan and collectors can pinpoint the locality of their origin because of the painted facial expressions that are distinctive to each area. Mostly, they're painted with concentric circles in reds and yellows, although other colors are applied. Some dolls are on wheels and are a pull-along toy for little children. Whether you

a *kokeshi* doll maker

purchase a *kokeshi* for a child back home or for yourself, it won't take long for its chubby, cherubic face to win your heart.

Japanese kites are an excellent folkart purchase. They come in a myriad of shapes and sizes ranging from diminutive aero-technics about the size of a postcard to huge fliers where a half dozen people are needed to manipulate the strings to keep them aloft. They are colorful, handmand, and inexpensive. Usually too fragile to be sent home through the mail as is, the painted paper can be easily removed from the wooden frame and make an excellent and distinctive wallhanging

folktoy potpourri: As previously mentioned, it would be impossible to list all of the folkart items made in Japan. The following is a whirlwind tour of items to keep an eye open for as you travel around. Most *depato* have a floor dedicated to folk art and you can find many items or innumerable shops and stalls as you wander through Japan. *Kijigangu* is the general name given to a variety of wooden toys. The best are diminutive tea sets that young Japanese girls love to play with. *Kijigangu* also include wooden toys such as tops, merry-go-rounds, fire trucks, animals, cork guns and piggy banks. *Omen* are masks usually made from papier mache. One favorite is a phallic-nosed goblin mask known as a *tengu*. Others look like kabuki masks, animals, demons, gods and simpletons. There's even a red mask with flaxen hair that comes from Tottori that is considered a work of art. *Omen* are light, tough, inexpensive and truly unique mememtos. *Fune no gangu* are wooden boats. Some are crude, simple designs that look like rowboats, but others can be elaborate, 2-masted junks such as the *yanbarubune* from Okinawa. The cheaper ones make great toys and the more elaborately carved and painted ones sitting on their display stands make excellent center pieces. *Ningyo* are Japanese dolls. Some *ningyo* are elaborate creations of lifelike dolls dressed in authentic, traditional kimono. These dolls are usually in glass or plastic cases and are designed more to look at than to play with. The prices vary, but a moderately priced one can easily be Y10,000. *Hina-ningyo* are dolls depicting ancient nobles and members of the royal family. There are 15 dolls in the full set and one per year is given to the daughters in a family on March 3, Girls' Day. Besides these, there are many clay figures made into dolls all over Japan. These true folk items are inexpensive, and at times exotic or hysterical. Osaka and Yokohama prefectures produce clay *ningyo* that are facsimiles of Europeans that came to trade in the earlier histories of Japan. They have preserved the tradition down through the years and many of the *ningyo* look like 15th C priests, sailors and soldiers. Most clay *ningyo* are brightly painted and with a Japanese motif can resemble everything from a *sumo* wrestler to a warrior in full armor.

nifty items: Everyone has his own ideas on what a gift or memento should be, but a budget traveler must consider not only the cost of an item but also its ability to weather the hazards of being lugged around during a trip. The weight and "packagability" of an item being sent home (most economically by sea mail) are also important factors. The following are suggestions of folk art and traditional items that fit all categories. One of the best, inexpensive, artistic items that you can buy is a *furoshiki*. This bolt of cloth (1m square) was traditionally used in the Japanese *ofuro* (bath) from where it gets its name. It served as a towel, bath mat and quick wrap around robe. Later, it became a giant handkerchief in which to wrap and carry bundles and today you can see countless Japanese carrying around all sorts of bundles wrapped in *furoshiki*. Some *furoshiki* are emblazoned with the family crest and are used to wrap special *giri* (''pay back the favor'') gifts, but most Japanese don't value the lowly *furoshiki*. Today in Japan, any piece of the right sized cloth will do, even polyester, but in all large *depato* and numerous shops you can find the genuine article. These are made of cotton and employ a dyeing method which is used to stencil elaborate and tasteful scenes on the *furoshiki*. Even good quality ones start at only Y2000 and make impressive table cloths or wall hangings. *Yukata* are Japanese lounging robes. They aren't nearly the magnificent articles that kimono are, but they cost much much less. You'll probably see people dressed in *yukata* from the first day you arrive in Japan, and you'll be given one to wear if you stay at a *ryokan*. These are one of the only items that westerners can easily find that will fit, because of their oversized sleeves and wrap around nature. All *depato* have them. They're comfortable, light weight, usually made of cotton and start at only Y2500. Their appeal is universal. To jazz up your *yukata*, you can buy a more elaborate sash to match separately,

although you'll be given an uninspired one with your purchase. The patterns are everything from floral to geometric, and the usual colors are blue on white. Other inexpensive items to look for are bamboo products from fruit bowls to hand luggage. They're inexpensive, well-made and available everywhere. You can even use them as incidental carrying bags on your trip. Another choice item that's a great purchase for a budget traveler is anything made from Japanese paper (*kami*). Japanese handmade paper has an earthy texture and a wide variety of items are made from it. *Kami saifu* (paper walets) are only Y200 and are colorfully stamped with patterns or *Ukiyo-e* prints. Although made of paper, they'll take a beating and last for an amazingly long time. There's also a profusion of posters, prints, notebook covers and memo pads that are made from gaily decorated Japanese paper. You can always pick up a stack of lacquered *hashi* chopsticks for little cost and the tiny leather cases made for carrying *hanko* (Japanese name seals used universally instead of signatures) are inexpensive. Finally, *naetsuke* (ivory carvings) are not too expensive and tortoise shell ware, often sold in kimono shops, are fashioned into elegant bracelets, barrettes and tiny boxes that are affordable.

MUSEUMS AND ART GALLERIES

HOKKAIDO AND NORTHERN JAPAN

Museum and Art Gallery	Address and Telephone	Remarks
Historical Museum of Hokkaido	Ko-Nopporo, Atsubetsucho, Sapporo (30 min. by bus from JNR Sapporo Station), tel: 011 (891) 0456	Folk arts and historical displays relating to the explorations of Hokkaido. Hours: 0930 to 1630, Tues. Through Saturday.
Chusonji Temple Treasure House	Hiraizumi-cho, Nishi-Iwai-gun, Iwate Pref. (5 min. by bus from JNR Hiraizumi Station), tel: 019146-2211	Historical and cultural relics. Buddist paintings and images of 800 yrs. ago. Hours: 0830 to 1630 daily.
Sendai City Museum	Sannomaru-ato, Kawauchi, Sendai City, Miyagi Pref. (15 min. by bus from JNR Sendai Station), tel: 0222 (25) 2557	Fine arts and crafts, historical documents, and cultural properties from the family of Date, a feudal lord. Hours: 0900 to 1600. Closed Monday.

TOKYO AND VICINITY

Tokyo National Museum	Ueno Park, Taito-ku. (5 min. walk from Ueno Station), tel: 822-1111	Largest museum in Japan; houses fine arts of Japan, China and India. Most are "National Treasures" or "Important Cultural Properties." Hours: 0900 to 1630. Closed on Monday.
National Museum of Modern Art, Tokyo	3, Kitanomaru Park, Chiyoda-ku. (5 min. walk from Takebashi Subway Station), tel: 214-2561	Fine arts and crafts of Japan since 1907. Hours: 1000 to 1700 daily.
National Museum of Western Art	Ueno Park, Taito-ku (3 min. walk from Ueno Station), tel: 828-5131	Sculpture and paintings by famous western artists. Hours: 0930 to 1630. Closed on Monday.
Bridgestone Museum of Art	1-1, Kyobashi, Chuo-ku (5 min. walk from Tokyo Station), tel: 563-0241	French Impressionists and contemporary western artists. Hours: 1000 to 1700. Closed Monday.
Idemitsu Art Gallery	1-1, 3-chome, Marunochi, Chiyoda-ku (3 min. walk from Yurakucho Station), tel: 213-3111	Fine arts and crafts of ancient Japan, China and W. Asia. Hours: 1000 to 1700. Closed on Monday.
Japan Folk Crafts Museum	3-30, 4-chome, Komaba, Meguro-ku (5 min. walk from Komaba-Todaimae Station on Keio-teito Inokashira Line), tel: 467-4527	Folkcraft of Japan and Korea. Hours: 1000 to 1700 daily. Closed on Mon. and from Jan. 1 to Feb. 28.
Nezu Institute of Fine Arts	6-5-36, Minami-Aoyama, Minato-ku, (10 min. walk from Omotesando Subway Station), tel: 400-2536	Ancient Oriental fine arts and crafts. Hours: 0930 to 1630. Closed on Mon. and days after national holidays.
Okura Shukokan Museum	3, Aoi-cho, Akasaka, Minato-ku, (10 min. walk from Toranomon Subway Station), tel: 583-0781	Fine arts and crafts of ancient Japan and Asia. Hours: 1000 to 1600. closed on Monday.
Riccar Art Museum	2-3-6, Ginza, Chuo-ku (5 min. walk from Ginza Subway Station), tel: 571-3254	*Ukiyo-e* woodblock prints and ancient Japanese fine arts. Hours: 1000 to 1800. Closed on Monday.

Suntory Museum of Art	2-3, Moto Akasaka 1-chome, Chiyoda-ku. (Near Akasaka-Mitsuke Subway Station), tel: 470-1073	Ancient Japanese fine arts and crafts. Hours: 1000 to 1700. Closed on Monday.
Tokyo Central Museum of Arts	Ginza-Boeki Bldg. 2-7-18, Ginza, Chuo-ku (3 min. walk from Ginza Subway Station), tel: 564-0711	Japanese and western style paintings. Hours: 1000 to 1800. Closed on Monday.
Tokyo Metropolitan Art Gallery	Ueno Park, Taito-ku (5 min. walk from Ueno Station), tel: 821-3726	Contemporary Japanese art. Hours: 0900 to 1600.
Yamatane Museum of Art	2-10, Kabuto-cho, Nihombashi, Chuo-ku (5 min. walk from Kayaba-cho Subway Station), tel: 669-3211	Modern Japanese painting from Meiji to Showa. Hours: 1100 to 1700. Closed on Mondays.
Kamakura Museum	2-1-1, Yukinoshita, Kamakura City, Kanagawa Pref. (10 min. walk from JNR Kamakura Station), tel: 0467 (22) 0753	Art works of 12th-16th centuries. Hours: 0900 to 1600. Closed on Mon. and national holidays.

CENTRAL HONSHU

Hida Folklore Museum	Kami-Okamoto-cho, Takayama City, Gifu Pref. (7 min. by bus from JNR Takayama Station), tel: 0577 (33) 4714	Folkarts and crafts. Hours: 0900 to 1700 daily.
Meiji-Mura	1, Oaza Uchiyama, Inuyama City, Aichi Pref. (1 hr. by bus from JNR Nagoya Station), tel: 0568 (67) 0314	Meiji Era structures (1868-1912), folk arts and crafts and architecture. Hours: 1000 to 1700, Mar.-Oct.; 1000 to 1600, Nov-February.
Tokugawa Art Museum	2-27, Tokugawa-cho, Higashi-ku, Nagoya City, Aichi Pref. (20 min. by bus from JNR Nagoya Station), tel: 052 (935) 6262	Swords, *Noh* costumes and art objects which belonged to feudal lords. Hours: 1000 to 1600. Closed on Monday.

KYOTO, NARA, OSAKA AND VICINITY

Kyoto National Museum	Yamato-oji, Shichijo-kita, Higashiyama-ku, Kyoto City (5 min. by bus from JNR Kyoto Station), tel: 075 (541) 1151	Treasures and works of art from Buddhist temples and shrines in Kyoto. Hours: 0900 to 1630. closed on Monday.
National Museum of Modern Art, Kyoto	Okazaki-Enshoji-cho, Sakyo-ku, Kyoto City (5 min. walk from Okazaki-koen Bus Stop), tel: 075 (761) 4111	Modern art works of Japan and other countries. Hours: 1000 to 1700. closed on Monday.

Kyoto Municipal Museum of Art	Okazaki Park, Sakyo-ku Kyoto City (5 min. walk from Okazaki-koen Bus Stop) tel: 075 (771) 4107	Japanese and foreign fine arts of Meiji-Showa eras (after 1868). Hours: 0900 to 1700 daily.
Nara National Museum	50, Tomino-oji-cho, Nara City (5 min. by bus from JNR Nara Station), tel: 0742 (22) 7771	Historical display of Buddhist works of art. Hours: 0900 to 1600. Closed on Monday.
Daihozoden Treasure Hall, Horyuji Temple	Ikaruga-machi, Ikoma-gun, Nara Pref. (5 min. by bus from JNR Horyuji Station), tel: 07457 (5) 2555	Buddhist art works related to Prince Shotoku (573-621) and Horyuji Temple.
The Museum Kofukuji Kokuhokan	48, Noborioji-cho, Nara City (5 min. walk from Kinki-Nippon Nara Station), tel: 0742 (22) 5370	Fine Buddhist statues and sculptures of Kamakura Period (1192-1333). Hours: 0900 to 1700 daily.
Japan Handicraft Museum	3-619, Shinkawa, Naniwa-ku, Osaka City (5 min. walk from Namba Subway Station), tel: 06 (641) 6309	Folk arts and crafts. Hours: 1000 to 1700. closed on Monday.
Osaka Municipal Art Museum	Tennoji Park, Tennoji-ku, Osaka City (3 min. walk from Tennoji Station), tel: 06 (771) 4111	Ancient and modern art objects. Hours: 0900 to 1700 daily.
Kobe Municipal Art Museum	1-35, Kumochi-cho, Fukiai-ku, Kobe City, Hyogo Pref. (10 min. by bus from JNR Sanno-miya Station), tel: 078 (221) 3043	Early western-style painting in Japan. Works depicting early western visitors. Hours: 0900 to 1630. Closed on Mon. and from Aug. 1-31.

WESTERN JAPAN

Ohara Museum of Art	1, Chuo, Kurashiki City, Oka-yama Pref. (10 min. walk from JNR Kurashiki Station), tel: 0864 (22) 0005	Western art at its finest. Hours: 0900 to 1600. Closed on Monday.
Okinawa Prefectural Museum	Onaka-cho, Shuri, Naha City, Okinawa Pref. (5 min. walk from Ikehata Bus Stop), tel: 0988 (32) 2243	Local painting, sculpture and calligraphy and other fine art objects. Hours: 0900 to 1600. Closed on Mon. and national holidays.

CULTURAL ARTS AND PURSUITS

The richness of the Japanese culture, fueled by the imagination of its people, have combined to create a vibrant legacy of art. This art legacy, today, is flourishing and surfaces in the performing, classical arts such as *Noh, Kabuki* and *Bunraku* and in the aesthetic pastimes of *ikebana, bonsai* and *chanoyu* (the tea ceremony). Besides these, there is a treasure trove of literature and poetry passed on by the famed *haiku* poet Basho down to the modern literary genius of the troubled Yukio Mishima. The Japanese film industry is strong and alive, and even personal-defense is raised to an art form in the martial arts such as *aikido, judo* and *karate*. A special place in art is also filled by the mammouth hulk of the *sumo* wrestler and the delicacy of Japan's dwindling *geisha*. Whether you want to stir your intellect at the semi-spiritual offerings of the classic arts or rouse your earthly soul at all-girl revues or at hotly contested baseball games, Japan generously offers all.

NOH

Although Japan had its own folk art forms that can be traced to prehistory and viewed today at numerous festivals, the performing arts as such began when Buddhism came to Japan in the 6th century. Along with the monks came sacred, courtly dances and music. The Japanese, as with everything, internalized these and made them their own. One of the first manifestations was *Noh* drama and its related *Kyogen* farces. This stately, ritualized drama traces its origins back to *dengaku* and *sangaku* performances which were rudimentary dances and songs offered at shrines during festivals. In the 13th C, troupes of actors were employed to stage these dances and songs and *Noh* began. During the Tokugawa shogunate, *Noh* reached its pinnacle and most of the classic plays have been handed down from that time. Then, *Noh* plays were an intricate part of life, especially to the *samurai* and upper classes, but today their portrayals are more a preserved art form. The main actor in a *Noh* play is called a *shite* and in many plays the *shite* will begin by playing one part and will then disappear to reemerge as another character. The stage is stark with few props, the main actors are gorgeously attired and wear masks, and music is provided by an orchestra of varying sized drums and a flute. Like in classical Greek theater, the plot is moved along by a chorus of 8 people. Since the movement of a *Noh* play is static and its main ideas are portrayed symbolically, it is necessary to study the art form before it can be truly appreciated. Most foreigners, and for that matter a large number of Japanese, find *Noh* a bit boring and difficult to understand. What is beautiful and easily understood is the almost zen-like quality of the spectacle. Foreigners can appreciate *Noh* if they look at it as a whole—a living still life.

Kyogen scene

Kyogen: These lively farces began as interludes between *Noh* plays and performed a type of social commentary by portraying real life situations and being allowed to poke fun at the establishment. In both *Noh* and *Kyogen*, the actors put on their characters whose movements, actions and dialogues have been minutely detailed. They do not "become" the characters. *Noh* plays are performed on weekends and admission costs between Y1500 and Y5000 depending upon seating and the performance. If you are interested, you can see *Noh* performed at one of the following: Ginza Noh Stage, 5-15 Ginza 6-chome, Chuo-ku, Tokyo. tel: (03) 571-0197; Kongo Noh Stage, Muromachi, Shijo-Agaru, Nakagyo-ku, Kyoto. tel: (075) 221-3049; Osaka Noh Kaikan, 12 Michimotocho, Kita-ku, Osaka. tel: (06) 373-1726

KABUKI

Above all the other performing arts, *Kabuki* is the most recognizable and enjoyable medium to foreigners. Like Shakespearian plays, it is the drama of the common man although this was not always so. The word *Kabuki* originally derived from an obscure word which meant "to slant." It connotated anything that was strange or out of the ordinary. Later, arbitrary Chinese characters were phonetically selected that read *Ka* (song), *bu* (dance) and *ki* (artistry).

Kabuki history: is believed to have its origin during the feudal days of the Tokugawa shogunate. In 1603, a priestess from the Izumo Taisho Shrine who was called Izumo-O-Kuni, began to dance in public, imitating warriors, courtesans and other recognizable figures of the day. It was her attempt to raise money for the shrine. O-Kuni's strange dances soon became popular and she was summoned to dance before high nobles and court officials. Her troupe grew and she added men to it. Soon the dances became flirtatious and downright bawdy, mimicking the intimacies of the patrons of the then in vogue tea houses. The new art form, which proved to be financially lucrative, was adopted by a growing number of troupes made up of *geisha* who began touring the country and were known as *onna-kabuki* (women *kabuki*). These wandering troupes of *geisha* went from town to town delighting audiences and later in the evening offering special delights to the men who could afford them. The Tokugawa government, outraged by the affront to public decency, banned women from performing *Kabuki* and called for all-male troupes with young boys playing the part of women. Soon, these all-male troupes began to tour, but the ribald scripts included sodomy as part of the performance...an even greater affront against public decency. Sodomy was a long accepted tradition in the *samuri* class and among temple priests, but was somehow considered degenerate when displayed before everyday society. Young boys were replaced by older men who perfected the art of female impersonation and became known to this day as *Onnagata*. This also changed the nature of *Kabuki* somewhat and the plays took on their pantomime nature.

modern Kabuki traditions: Down through the centuries, Kabuki came to be more and more appreciated by mass audiences. In the 18th C, 2

the *kabuki* actors Baiko, portraying a lady in waiting, and Kanzaburo as a young samurai in a dance scene. The scene is a "journey scene" which commonly takes place near a well-known scenic spot. See Mt. Fuji in the background

great actors, Danjuro known for his manly and romantic style and Tojuro known for his realistic portrayals, set the tone for *Kabuki* actors who followed. *Kabuki* performances are lively and elaborately staged with sword fighting scenes and *seppuku* (suicide) realistically portrayed. There are many comings and goings on and off stage and there is usually a traditional scene called a *michiyuki* where the action takes place near a very famous scenic spot. Many of the plots are weak melodramas, but with the artful settings, dazzling effects, magnificent costumes and inspired acting, they are easily overlooked. *Kabuki* plays are fully an actor's medium.

onnagata: The much publicized and often queried *onnagata* are amazingly convincing. They are more like women than women. At times they studied traditional female activities such as sewing and got the subtle art of female movement down perfectly. They wear a tremendous amount of makeup and at close quarters look grotesque. When *Kabuki* plays are televised, there is never a closeup of an onnagata. in recent years, *shimpa* (female screen actresses) have taken female roles, but their portrayals are frequently weak next to their overpowering male colleagues.

Kabuki today: In a *Kabuki* theater, there has always been audience participation. Don't expect the hushed silence of western theaters. People come and go, eat their lunch, call out loudly to the actors and generally behave in a casual manner. Western translations of *Kabuki* plots are available at the most famous theaters (Y600). Don't worry about following the plot. View the drama as a spectacle and get the meaning from watching the action. Performances take place at theaters periodically throughout the year (check with TIC and JNTO). There are usually 2 performances per day. The matinee runs from 0100 to 1600 with evening performances beginning at 1630 and ending at 2100. Full performance tickets, depending upon seating, range from Y5000 to Y10,000. Usually a 10% discount is offered to foreigners who present their passports. It is not necessary to buy a full performance ticket. You can see *Kabuki* by the act and a ticket of this sort is called a *tachi-mi-seki* (stand and see ticket). You'll be in the balcony, towards the rear. The main theaters in Japan at which to see *Kabuki* are: Kabuki-za, 4-3 Ginza-Higashi, Chuo-ku, Tokyo, tel: 541-3131. Nine performances per year are presented for 25 days with 2 performances per day. (see Tokyo chapter, Ginza, for more details.) Kokuritsu Gekijo (National Theater of Japan), 13 Hayabusacho, Chiyoda ku, Tokyo, tel: 255-7411; Shin Kabuki-za, 5-59, Namba Shinchi, Minami ku, Osaka, tel: 631-2121 (one seasonal performance per year in May is presented daily for 25 days). Minamiza Theater, Shijo-Ohashi Tamato, Higashiyama-ku, Kyoto, tel: 561-1155 (one seasonal performance per year in December is presented daily for 25 days).

BUNRAKU

One of the most fascinating forms of classical theater in Japan is *bunraku* (puppet plays). Today, 2 troupes, Chinami-kai and Mitsuwakai, perform their special brand of magic upon the stage about 50 times per year by expertly manipulating these ⅔ life-sized puppets. Most *bunraku* plays follow the same plot lines as *Kabuki* plays. The puppets are elaborately dressed and their manipulators standing behind them are dressed in black and concealed up to the waist by a special stage. Sometimes 3 men

bunraku puppet theatre

manipulate the main character puppet. Their puppet antics, complete with moveable heads and limbs, are truly lifelike. The plot is in ballad form called a *joruri* and it is recited accompanied primarily by the music of a *samisen*. *Bunraku* performances during the 18th C were the most popular performing art in Japan. Their classical scripts were written by the master dramatist, Monzaemon Chikamatsu, whose words are still given wide acclaim. Besides *bunraku* puppets, Japan also has a lively theater of string manipulated marionettes and hand puppets. *Bunraku* is believed to have originated on Awaji Is. and today local performers there still give impromptu village recitals with their particular type of *bunraku* puppet called *awa*. To see regularly scheduled performances of *bunraku* (check JNTO and TIC for scheduling) visit: Tokyo National Theater, 13 Hayabusacho, Chiyoda-ku, Tokyo, tel: 265-7511; Kyoto Gion Corner, Yasaka-Kaikan, Higashiyama-ku, Kyoto, tel: 561-1115; Asahi-za Theater, 1-1, Higashi-Yugar-acho, Minami-ku, Osaka, tel: 211-6431.

CULTURAL PURSUITS

From the aesthetic legacy of the past, that has been heavily influenced by zen like simplicity and Shinto's love of nature, come the purely Japanese cultural pastimes of *ikebana* (flower arranging), *chanoyu* (tea ceremony), *bonsai* (miniturized potted trees) and *bonkei* (tray landscaping). Besides these more well-known cultural arts, there is also incense burning and magnificent landscape gardening. Each has its

philosophy rooted in the Japanese psyche and each transmits a mirror image of aesthetic beauty as viewed by the Japanese.

IKEBANA

The history of flower arranging, known in Japan as *ikebana* or *kado*, is clouded but most historians agree that it came into prominence as a highlight for the tea ceremony as it was practiced at Ginkakuji Temple in Kyoto during the 15th C. One undisputed fact is that *ikebana* is purely Japanese and this masterly art form blossomed in Japan without outside influence. There are over 20 different styles (schools) of *ikebana* and each has its own particular philosophy of arrangement. One common thread is that the arranged flowers should represent *ten-chi-jin* (heaven-earth-man). The *ten-chi-jin* classical arrangement dictates that the main upward branch represents heaven, branches to the right are man, and the lowest branches on the left are the earth. Attention is also given to the kind of flower used, where it is placed and the shape of the vase that holds it. Most arrangements are very simple and not at all like floral bouquets prevalent in the west. Many women and a growing number of men practice *ikebana* and these arrangements can be seen everywhere. A favorite spot to display them is in the *takenoma* (alcove) of homes placed near, but not obscuring the *kakemono* (picture scroll). The arrangement always blends with and never competes with this place of honor. For any westerner interested in *ikebana*, contact *Ikebana* International, 2nd floor, Shufunotomo Building, Kanda-Surugudai, 1-chome, Chiyoda-ku, Tokyo, tel: (03) 293-8188. This institution can tell you where to find schools located around Japan, where you can pursue this art form and perhaps the location of a school where instruction is given in your native language.

CHANOYU

Although copious amounts of tea and even coffee are drunk daily in Japan, this custom is relegated to simple enjoyment. It's difficult to be in a Japanese home for even a minute without being offered a cup of *o-cha* (tea), but *chanoyu* (tea ceremony) has a significance high above this everyday pastime. *Chanoyu* is almost a religious rite and this strict discipline is seen as a medium for attaining enlightenment and composure.

tea history: Tea was first used as a medicine in Japan and it was a highly regarded trade item from the Tang court of China. The first seeds were believed to have been brought to Japan by a priest named Saicho in 805. At first this exhilirating brew was used exclusively by Zen monks who used it to stay awake while meditating and drank communal bowls of it as they postured themselves before Buddhist images. By the 15th C, *chanoyu* became a refinement of the upper classes who performed it in special dwellings called *sukiya* (tea house) and who find in its ritual, tangible purity. *Samurai* warriors were educated as strictly in *chanoyu* as they were in martial arts, and tea masters were as highly regarded as those who had mastered the sword. Every movement by a tea master has significance and the highly systematized etiquette that make up *chanoyu* is seen as an art of mental discipline.

chanoyu (tea ceremony) bowl and whisk

the ceremony: The average westerner, along with the average, untutored Japanese, finds *chanoyu* hopelessly slow and head bobbingly boring. The greatest difficulty is in trying to keep awake as the interminable ceremony creeps along in what seems to be the almost bare and noiseless main room of the *sukiya*. At first, the tea ceremony has some novel interest, but unless you are particularly interested in it, don't expect to be dazzled. You're expected to sit in the Japanese fashion (legs tucked under while you lean on your haunches) for a very long time which most westerners find tearfully excruciating, although Japanese will make allowances for you and suggest that you sit "Indian" fashion. A classical tea ceremony has 5 guests, the principal being called the *shokyaku* and the atmosphere is ultra dignified and solemn. There are a number of schools of *chanoyu* with varying philosophies and with differing ceremonies depending upon the occasion and the time of year. Basically, at a *sukiya*, you slowly walk along a garden path to begin your introspection and then you are led into a tiny anteroom where the tea ceremony utensils have been arranged. At this point, you are expected to go into rapture concerning the artistry of the arrangement. Anything less than ecstasy is considered a slight.

etiquette: Once the ceremony begins, the host will serve *gyokuru*, an excellent grade of powdered, pea green tea. This is placed in a bowl and whipped to a froth with a tiny whisk. When the bowl of tea is offered, take it in your right hand and lay the palm of your left hand flat under the bowl. Bow twice—once to the tea master and once to the Buddha in thanks. Before drinking, take the bowl with the right hand and turn it to the left so that the most beautiful side of the bowl is turned away. Raise it and sip noisily. Wipe the area where your lips have touched with your thumb and index finger. You will also be served a sweet cake on a tiny napkin. Eat the cake and use the napkin to further wipe the bowl. Rotate the bowl again to your left so that you see the most beautiful side and admire it. Place the bowl back on the table. If it all seems a bit much, it is that the subtle refinements of *chanoyu* can only be appreciated with years of study. Most westerners don't even like the taste of the tea. If you are interested in the tea ceremony, you can see it demonstrated in Tokyo at these major hotels: Hotel Okura, Imperial Hotel and Hotel New Otani. There are schools of *chanoyu* scattered all over Japan and JNTO and TIC can provide listings. At many temples, *chanoyu* is performed for visitors for a small fee.

BONSAI AND BONKEI

Both *bonsai* and *bonkei* deal with the art of miniaturizing nature. *Bonsai* is the dwarfing of trees that are grown in pots and *bonkei* is tray landscaping. *Bonsai enthusiasts either raise a sapling* or scour the countryside for a small tree. It is then placed in a pot and the branches and roots are pruned. This causes even normally giant specimens to become dwarfed. In *bonsai*, the trees are made to appear as naturally as they would if they were growing freely. *Bonsai* trees are often twisted, gnarled specimens that can easily be imagined growing on the sides of windswept mountains, deep forests or leaning over ravines. Many of these tiny oldsters attain great ages. Some specimens that have been handed down over the generations and lovingly nutured are over 200 yrs. old. They are wrapped in cold weather and the soil is painstakingly changed every so often so that they will get perfect nourishment.

Bonkei: This art attempts to recreate nature by fashioning a tiny, natural scene on a tray. Peat moss covered with watery clay becomes a mountain, sand represents the sea and plants (even artificial ones) become great forests. *Bonkei* probably began as an offshoot of the ancient Buddhist tradition of placing a stone on a lacquered tray to symbolize the sacred mountain of Buddha. Today, this art is perfected and it takes little imagination to feel that you are looking at a real scene from a great height. JNTO and TIC offices provide information on where these 2 arts can be studied. Large hotels also make arrangements and *bonsai/bonkei* works are displayed year round at large department stores. Anyone interested should visit Bonsai Village (about 30 min from Tokyo) at Bonsaimachi, Omiya City, Saitama Prefecture. Open 0800-1700 except 1st and 3rd Thurs. of the month.

JAPANESE GARDENS

Formal gardens in Japan have existed and have been greatly appreciated since as early as the 6th C. Until recently, there were no flower gardens as in the west, and instead of neat lawns and cropped shrubs, the Japanese saw beauty in their gardens as reflections of nature with no artificiality. Symmetry was not highly regarded and although they are meticulously cared for, Japanese gardens remained natural. Instead of sweeping grass lawns, most Japanese gardens are surfaced with rocks, pebbles and sand. There are no fountains or tiled pools, but streams and ponds are frequently used. All manner of natural and man-made accoutrements used are symbolic representations. A standing stone may suggest a waterfall, a rounded shrub a distant mountain, and raked sand the seashore.

types of gardens: There are 3 basic types of gardens: the hill garden, flat garden and tea garden. A hill garden has several hills and usually a pond or stream. Wherever there is water, there is an island and a bridge connecting it to the mainland. A stone lantern can represent a lighthouse. Two excellent gardens of this type are the Jojuin Gardens of the Kiyomizu Temple in Kyoto and Ritsurin Garden in Kumamoto. Flat gardens are usually built for Zen-like contemplation. Few trees and shrubs are used and the most common elements are sand and gravel. The most famous of this type is the Ryoanji Temple Garden in Kyoto. The 3rd type of garden, the tea garden, is always built around a teahouse. It usually takes the form of a natural path of stepping stones laid through a manicured, but naturally appointed garden area. There is always a stone basin filled with water so that guests can wash their hands and a stone lantern with a flickering flame at night to add subtlety. These beautiful gardens complement and contrast with the stark beauty and simplicity of the teahouse itself. The most famous tea garden is found at Kinkakuji Temple in Kyoto. Wherever there are teahouses, such as those found in the historical city of Takayama, there are resplendent gardens. *informal gardens:* The Japanese love to garden wherever there is space available. At homes and especially at *ryokan*, sliding screens will open to frame a perfect garden and it is considered an artistic appointment to the room like a favored landscape painting hanging on a wall in a western home. One of the added pleasures of strolling through a Japanese residential area is viewing family gardens through bamboo fences as you walk along. Gardens are found at many temples and around preserved castle areas. The following are the most famous in Japan and if you are in the area, they shouldn't be missed: Korakuen *Koen* (Park) in Okayama; Kairakuen in Mito; Kenrokuen in Kanazawa, and Ritsurin Park in Takamatsu.

SPORTS AND MARTIAL ARTS

Sports in Japan can basically be divided into traditional sports which are better described as martial arts and modern sports which have been introduced from the west. Most of the martial art tradition in Japan came from the self defense studies of the samurai class which were called *budo*. Many warriors studied martial arts that included swordsmanship, *jujitsu* (unarmed combat), horseback defense and even swimming as a martial art. The suffix *do* at the end of the names of most martial arts means "the way," ie., *ken-do*, the way of the sword (*ken*). The place of study is called a *dojo*. Most of these martial arts, especially *aikido* and *katate*, have world recognition, and *jujutsu*, which later became *judo*, is now a sport with full competition at the Olympic games. *Kendo*, (Japanese sword fighting) and *kyudo* (archery), are mainly practiced only in Japan, and their popularity is not worldwide. *Sumo* wrestling as an art is practiced only in Japan. Western sports entered and became popular in Japan only after the Meiji Restoration (1860). From these beginnings Japan has become a highly respected participant at the Olympic games. Tennis courts, golf links, bowling alleys and swimming pools are extremely popular and can be found throughout Japan, especially in large cities and resort areas. Spectator and gambling sports such as horse, automobile, boat and motorcycle racing are popular. There is even the Japan Bowl which features an American college level football game. All of these western sports combined cannot compete in popularity with Japan's greatest loved and most watched game: baseball.

SUMO

Of all the martial arts of Japan, the one with the greatest mystique and purely Japanese devotion is *sumo*. Historical records chronicle the first *sumo* bout as early as 200 A.D. It is believed that *sumo* was a religious rite to invoke the gods for a good harvest. Rudiments of this religious legacy are seen today. The roof over a *sumo* ring resembles a *Shinto* shrine and the wrestlers sprinkle salt about the ring in ritual purification. Many of these human mastodons tip the scales at over 160 kilograms.

the bout: The bout, overseen by the *gyoji* (referee), takes place on a packed clay, circular ring and is usually lightning fast, culminating abruptly after a series of false starts. The *gyoji* carries a type of fan as a symbol of his authority and in his belt he wears a dagger which he used at one time to disembowel himself if he made a mistake in judgment. The topknotted wrestlers, clad only in a large belt, limber up by stomping their feet. They squat and face each other like snorting boars, then clash. The bout, which takes so long to begin, is over when one contender touches the ground with any part of the body besides the soles of his feet, including one fingertip, or when one is hurled or pushed from the ring.

not all glamour: The life of a *sumo* wrestler is particularly spartan and very traditional. The wrestlers live in dormitory style dwellings (called stables) overseen by a former grand champion. Extremely reticent in public, they talk little and smile less, and a casual interview with one gains only a few noncommittal grunts. The wrestlers practice daily for the 6 annual tournaments and stuff themselves with rice gruel, beer and a stew (*hanko nabe*) which is designed to add pounds. Later in life, many suffer from heart disease, but a great number of *sumo* shed weight rapidly once their careers are over. Young boys enter the stables at the age of 15 and as apprentices are at the beck and call of the great wrestlers. Few westerners have ever attempted to become *sumo* and only one has ever become famous. He was Hawaiian-born Jesse Kuhaulua, known in Japan as Takamiyama. Part of *sumo* custom is for wrestlers to change their given names. Wrestlers move through the ranks and are rated by their win-loss record. The greatest champions become grand masters known as *yokozuma* and once attained can never be demoted.

kendo

tournaments: The tournaments enjoy great popularity and are usually televised, with almost every eye in Japan glued to the T.V. Tickets cost between Y500 for a faraway bench seat to Y6500 for a ringside, but almost impossible to book special seat. The audience is spellbound and many coquettish glances come from the eyes of Japanese ladies as they peek from behind fans as these great wrestlers grapple and change holds on the frail, silk bands that constitute their loin cloths. The following is a listing of the schedules of *sumo* tournaments: Tokyo—January 6-20, May 11-25, September 14-28 at Kukugikan Sumo Hall (near Kuramae Subway Station) tel: (03) 851-2201, tickets available at the door and at Tokyo Play Guides; Osaka—March 9-23 at Osaka Furitsu Taiikukan (near Namba Eki(tel: (06) 631-0120; Nagoya—July 6-20 at Aichi Kenritsu Taiikukan (15 min by taxi from Nagoya Eki) tel: (052) 971-0015; Fukuoka—November 9-23 at Kyuden Kinen Taiikukan (near Hakata Eki) tel: (092) 522-6366. For more information, contact the Japan Sumo Foundation, c/o Kokugikan Sumo Hall, 2-1-19, Kuramai, Taito-ku, Tokyo, tel:(03) 851-2201. Hours: 1000 to 1600, Mon through Sat.

SELF DEFENSE

Kendo: The way of the sword is the Japanese art of fencing. The *katana* (sword) has special, nostalgic significance to the Japanese and is often the most treasured family heirloom. In the sport today, a *shinai* (bamboo sword) measuring less that 118 cm is used. The fencers are protected by a face mask, breastplate, pleated skirt and gloves. The object of the match is to strike or jab the 3 principal parts of the body (head, trunk, wrist) or to touch the throat. This must be done with the top third of the blade and whoever gets 2 points first, wins the match. Matches and training are held all over Japan in city wards and outlying villages. Each December, the *Kendo* All Japan Championships are held in Tokyo. For information, contact Japan Kendo Foundation, 2-3, Kitanomura-Koen, Chiyoda-ku, Tokyo, tel: (03) 216-0781.

karate: This self-defense sport which stresses mental and spiritual discipline is not unique to Japan either in practice or origin. It developed in China and spread to Okinawa where it was refined. *Karate* came to Japan proper from Okinawa in 1922 and spread like wildfire. Many modifications and styles have developed and masters are found throughout the world. Although karate is very popular in Japan, it's not as highly regarded as a martial art as the more classical disciplines. For information, contact: World Union of Karate-Do Organization, 4th Floor, Sempaku Shinkokai Bldg., 1 1-15-16, Toranomon, Minato-ku, Tokyo, tel: (03) 503-6637.

Aikido: This traditional martial art puts equal emphasis on both the spiritual and the physical self. *Aikido* borrows from the disciplines of *judo, karate,* and *kendo.* The basis of form is the circle and the straight, upward line. Added to this, practitioners try to develop their *ki* (will) and use it to effortlessly disarm or reduce the fighting spirit of their opponents. Physical strength is seen as secondary to the power of the *ki*. *Aikido* was founded by Morihei Ueshiba (1883-1970) who began a *dojo* and introduced Japan and later the world to this spiritual martial art. Weapons are not used unless an opponent is armed and the greatest masters are believed to have the ability to throw their opponents by leading their *ki* without physically touching them. For information, contact: Aikido World Headquarters, 102, Wakamatsucho, Shinju-ku Station (west exit) or Ki Society Headquarters, Ushigome Heim No. 101, 2-30 Haramachi, Shinjuku Tokyo, tel: (03) 353-3461.

Judo: Judo, as practiced today, is more of a sport than martial art and has its origins in *jujutsu*. *Judo's* basic principle is to use the opponent's strength against him by unique techniques of throwing, grappling and strangling while remaining perfectly balanced yourself. Dr. Jigoro Kano (1860-1938) modernized *jututsu* and created *judo* which he infused with scientific principles and modern conditioning. For information, contact All Japan Judo Federation, c/o Kodokan, 1-16-30, Kasuga, Bunkyo-ku, Tokyo, tel: (03) 811-7151. It is possible to stay at the Kodokan Hostel; for particulars, consult the Judo Federation.

WESTERN SPORTS

tennis: Tennis received its biggest boost in popularity when it became known that the Crown Prince Akihito met his wife-to-be on a tennis court. Since that time, countless numbers of courts have sprung up around the nation. The young Japanese have taken up the sport not only for physical enjoyment, but also so that tennis can be listed as a desirable social interest in their marriage dosiers. Many courts are found at resort areas and also in cities wherever likely space can be found. *golf:* Golf is both popular and extremely expensive in Japan. Japanese tourists can't believe how cheap green fees are abroad, and many are seen alighting from their airplane already swinging a 4 iron in anticipation. In Japan, the courses are picturesquely laid out, but are somewhat narrow and more trap-laden than those in the west. There are over 900 courses nationwide, both public and private, but it's almost impossible to get a reservation. Green fees vary with the season, but expect to pay Y15,000 for a top course during the summer months. Caddy fees are usually fixed at approximately Y2500 per round. TIC and JNTO can provide particulars on location and requirements of courses. As in tennis, the Japanese are enamored with picture perfect form that they perfect with endless practice at numerous schools but actually get to play only a few times per year.

baseball: The Japanese love and watch baseball as much as the Americans do and they formed their first professional league in 1936. They are hot fielders, good base runners, and use the bunt quite often. Leagues run down to the grade school level and there are also high school, university and professional teams. The Inter-High Invitational Baseball Tournament, which began in 1924, dominates T.V. when it occurs. The 6 professional teams, which are divided into the Pacific and Western divisions, are allowed to have 2 American players per team. It's believed that U.S. players are a bit more powerful at bat than their Japanese counterparts. The record for greatest number of home runs hit by a professional ball player is held by the recently retird Japanese player, Mr. Oh, who played for the Tokyo Giants. A day at the ball park is complete with peanut, hot dog, and soft drink vendors. If you're watching a hotly contested game on television, don't be surprised if it goes off the air at the bottom of the 9th with a tie score, 2 outs and the bases loaded. The TV time slot is simply used up. So sorry. Read the results in tomorrow's paper. The professional season runs from April to October and the main stadiums are Korakuen and Jingu in Tokyo, Missei Stadium in Osaka, and Koshien Stadium in Kobe.

skiing: Besides seashores, mountains are Japan's greatest natural feature. Many of these rugged giants have been laced with ski grounds and lifts. There are always accommodations available for skiers in the vicinity and a rising flood of Japanese have been into the sport for the last 2 decades. The skiing is excellent, but is not a reason in and of itself to visit Japan. The slopes are amazingly crowded with skiers, ranging from flashy experts down to politely falling and apologizing beginners. An added attraction is that many ski grounds are in close proximity to *onsen* (spas) and after a day of frigid cold, their body and soul warming waters are inviting. Rental of ski equipment averages Y3000 per day. JNTO publishes and dispenses a pamphlet entitled, "Skiing in Japan" that lists all of the ski grounds, their fees, physical features and directions on getting there. Wherever the skiing is remarkable, it has been listed in the appropriate section of the "travel chapters" throughout this book. Some of the famous ski areas are Teine Olympia and Mt. Zoa ski grounds of Hokkaido, Kusatsu and Manza Onsen area 3 hrs N of Tokyo (on the Joetsu line towards Nagano), and a cluster of 5 grounds in the Shiga Heights area of the Japan Alps around Matsumoto.

swimming: If you can't get into the refreshing mountains to escape the sweltering, sticky heat of a Japanese summer (especially offensive in large cities), your best bet is to head for the seashore or a swimming pool. Many large hotels have private pools, but will open them to non-guests for a fee. You have to be pretty hot and miserable to pay the Y3500 for weekday use and the Y5000 for weekend use that they demand. Public inner city pools open daily from 1000 to 2100 and charge approximately Y150 per hour (see "Tokyo" for a listing of that city's pools). Summer doesn't arrive on its own warm wings in Japan. Like everything else, it must fit in properly and comes only like an invited visitor on June 1 and departs promptly on August 31, no matter what the thermometer reads. This means that Japanese don't swim at any other times *en masse*. There is always a reasonable renegade or two, but you can have the otherwise sardine-can-packed beaches to yourself. Beaches along the Pacific Ocean coast of Japan are warmer and less rugged than those on the Japan Sea side, but are much more crowded and heavily polluted with industrial wastes, especially around Tokyo and Osaka. The beaches on the Boso and Izu peninsulas, SE and SW of Tokyo, respectively, are much cleaner. Even the famous beaches at Kamakura just one hour S of Tokyo aren't too bad. Those of the Kii Peninsula and the ones spotted around the main islands of Shikoku and Kyushu are even better. Best of all are the numerous beaches surrounding the outlying islands, especially the semi subtropical isles leading to Okinawa. In Japan, you are never far from the sea and finding a beach is usually no problem, although it may not be secluded. Some famous beaches include Oarai in Ibaraki Prefecture, Tateyama and Hayama of Kanagawa Prefecture, Amanohashidate just 60 km N of Kyoto, Katsura and Shirahama on the Kii Peninsula, and Ibusuki near Kagoshima in southern Kyushu. If the sea, surf and islands fascinate you, take a leisurely island hopping ferry from Kagoshima to Naha and then to extremely remote islands beyond. Always check with the local people before taking a dip because many beaches have very strong under tows. There are a handful of Japanese "surfers" but only a few scattered beaches with even moderately good waves. Scuba, skin diving and spear fishing are especially good around most outlying islands S of Kyushu.

fishing: Japanese waters are alive with more than 150 species of fish, of which 40 or so are found in fresh water. A budget traveler can spend untold hours relaxing, creating fun and maybe even catching dinner just by carrying a collapsible mini rod and reel and dunking a line wherever possible. Today, pole, reel and tackle are small and light enough to be carried by anyone smitten by this gentleperson's sport. The cooks at *ryokan* and *minshuku* are more than happy to cook your catch for you and you'll be the envy of everyone if you smack a fat *ayu* (Japanese trout) into a frying pan at a YH. A shoreline campfire and a fresh fish being roasted on a spit is hard to beat anywhere. The fishing season on rivers and lakes runs year round, depending upon the fish. It's best to check at local city halls for regulations and a license, if necessary. No license is required for fishing in the sea, and a *gaijin* fishing on a mountain stream or lake will rarely, if ever, be bothered. The major game fish found in fresh water are imported rainbow trout, *ayu* (Japanese trout), *fuva* (carp), and bass. Any mountain stream and numerous lakes have their share. Hokkaido is especially alive with fresh water fish and its lakes, such as Akan and Nukabira, have an excellent reputation, for yeilding a day's limit. The major salt water fish are *tai* (sea bream), *kurodai* (gilt head), *aji* (horse mackerel), *buri* (yellow tail) and sea bass. Almost anywhere along the coastline will offer reasonable fishing, with the Inland Sea waters offering the largest number of species. Outlying islands are always great for fishing and you can combine snorkeling and spear fishing on any of the warm-watered, coral encircled islands of the south.

above, clockwise: woman in red (C. Parks); a contemporary couple in best kimono (C. Parks); Zen nun (C. Parks); artist at work (W. Stier); rice planting festival (C. Parks)

above, clockwise: a procession at Zenkoji Temple (J. Nelson); a blind *itoko* (J. Nelson); masked festival player (C. Parks); young festival dancers (C. Parks)

above, clockwise: the coast of Dogo Island (J.D. Bisignani); *sakura* time (J. Nelson); the mountains of Shikoku (J.D. Bisignani);

above, clockwise: Ura-Bandai (J.D. Bisignani); rococo garden of Dai Raku Ji (J.D. Bisignani); moody Matsushima (J.D. Bisignani); Moon Bridge of Kongoshoji Temple (J.D. Bisignani); sculptured ricefields (J. Nelson)

FESTIVALS AND EVENTS

Japan is a country rich in festivals and not a day goes by without some commemoration or other taking place somewhere in the country. The most interesting facet of most festivals is their antiquity. It is as if the pages of a living history book have been opened and the characters in traditional costumes have become reborn for a day. The majority of festivals have religious significance relating to the honoring of Buddhist or Shinto deities. Many include processions where *mikoshi* (portable shrines) are carried through the streets. Some are related to the arts and *kagura* (ancient sacred dances originally from India) are preserved and displayed now only in Japan. The musical accompaniment is always traditional. At other times the emphasis is on *Noh*, and often the performance seems more mystical and mysterious because it is displayed at night in the confines of an ancient temple with the stage lit only by torches. Sometimes the main participants are *bunraku* puppets portraying ancient tales. There are festivals honoring the sea, mountains, rivers, village gods, the dead, children, old people, broken umbrellas and even old hats. Anything that gives service or has a bearing on the affairs of men is remembered and revered. In almost every instance, these events are holly jolly with much *sake* drinking and active participation by

the spectators. There are times when only men take part, as in many *hadaka* (naked festivals) where the all-male participants, clad only in a *fundoshi* (loin cloth), gather at temples and perform ancient rites throughout the night. Other festivals are presided over by *yamabushi* (mystical, ascetic mountain priests) and include purification ceremonies such as fire walking and bathing in frigid waterfalls and icy streams. Women have their own festivals where the participants are *miko* (temple maidens) who perform dances or blind *itoko* who divine the future and communicate with departed relatives of spectators while in a trance. On other occasions, *geisha* or village women parade in their best kimono and in one festival they wear fancy paper lantern headresses. Whenever you visit Japan, try to observe at least one festival. Everyone is heartily invited and this is an excellent chance to see behind the cosmetic modern mask of Japan and into the hearts and spirits of its people. To get useful listings of festivals each month, contact the TICs in Tokyo or Kyoto who can provide you with photocopied sheets of the month's happenings. It's also important to remember that not all festivals and events have fixed dates. For example, they may fall within the third week of the month, so it's important to check up on them. If you intend to visit an area that is renowned for a particular event, be sure to reserve your transportation and especially your accommodations well in advance. Throughout the travel chapters there are sections, usually placed in boxes, that list all the main festivals and events in the area. The following lists include those festivals and events that are either universally observed in Japan, have special religious or mythical significance or are highly regarded as being spectacular and colorful. For a more complete description of a particular event, please turn to the respective chapter for more detailed information.

NATIONAL HOLIDAYS

There are 12 public holidays universally celebrated throughout Japan during the year. If they fall on a Sunday, the following Monday is also observed as part of the official holiday. The most important thing for the traveler to remember is that travel amenities such as banks, government offices and some YHs are often closed. Restaurants, hotels and large *depato* as well as shops remain open.

January 1 — *Ganjitsu* (New Year's Day)

January 15 — *Seijin-No-Hi* (Adults' Day)

February 11 — *Kenkoku Kinen-No-Hi* (National Foundation Day)

March 20 — *Shumbun-No-Hi* (Vernal Equinox Day)

April 29 — *Tenno Tanjo-Bi* (Emperor's Birthday)

May 3 — *Kempo Kinen-Bi* (Constitution Memorial Day)

May 5 — *Kodomo-No-Hi* (Children's Day)

September 15 — *Keiro-No-Hi* (Respect-for-the-Aged-Day)

September 23 — *Shubun-No-Hi* (Autumnal Equinox Day)

October 10 — *Taiiku-No-Hi* (Health-Sports Day)

November 3 — *Bunka-No-Hi* (Culture Day)

November 23 — *Kinro Kansha-No-Hi* (Labor Thanksgiving Day)

CALENDAR OF EVENTS

Jan. 1:   *Ganjitsu* (New Year's Day). This national festival is viewed by the Japanese as a day of renewal, rebirth and a fresh start for the coming year. The festivities go on in one form or another for about one week. Business is suspended as much as possible. Over the entrance way of each home is hung a *kado-matsu*, a type of wreath made up of pine, plum and bamboo boughs. These trees symbolize prosperity, purity, longevity and loyalty. Also, across the entranceway is hung a *shime-nawa*, a rope of twisted straw festooned with strips of paper. This is a *Shinto* talisman which purifies the home and bars all evil spirits. The entranceway to homes can also be adorned with ferns for prosperity, oranges which symbolize the passing generations, and lobsters with their bent backs suggesting ripe old age. There are a variety of foods eaten and each has its own special symbolism. They include *zoni* (a broth containing *mochi*), *kazunoko* (herring roe), *mame* (black beans), *kachiguri* (dried chestnuts), and *kombu* (seaweed). To complement the foods, *toso* (sweet *sake*) is served in the hopes that good health will prevail for the coming year. The first obligation of all Japanese is to visit their favorite shrine, *hatsumode* (first shrine visit), or Buddhist temple, *hatsumairi* (first temple visit). There are also special games played and everyone tries to repay debts owed from the previous year. On Jan. 2, the Imperial Family makes an appearance at the Imperial Palace in Tokyo and this is known as *Ippan Sanga*. The crowds attending are unbelievably large. The festivites come to an end on the 7th day called *nankusa* when a dish by the same name consisting of rice gruel and *nankusa* (7 herbs) is served.

Jan. 2-6:   *Daruma Ichi*. Stalls are set up at temples all over the country selling good luck *daruma* dolls. An especially good stall area is at Hajima Daishi Temple in Tokyo. The *daruma* dolls have no eyes painted in. The custom is to paint in one eye and make a wish. If it comes true, then the other eye is painted in.

Jan. 3:   *Tamaseseri* (Ball Catching Festival). Takes place at Hakozakigu Shrine in Fukuoka City. A group of young boys struggle to catch a sacred ball thrown by the shrine's priest which symbolizes good fortune for the coming year.

mame maki (bean throwing) at Asakusa Temple, Tokyo

On Jan. 5, at Tsurugaoka Hachimangu Shrine in Kamakura there is a demonstration of traditional archery.

Jan. 6: *Dezome-Shiki.* This is a New Year's parade of Tokyo's firemen along Harumi-Chuo Street. The main attraction is acrobatic stunts performed by the firemen on tall bamboo ladders.

Jan. 7: *Usokai,* at Dazaifu Temmangu Shrine in Daizufu City, Fukuoka Pref. The participants sit around glowing fires on the shrine grounds and pass around carved wooden bullfinches. The idea is to get the one that is decorated with gilt and hidden among the plain ones to bring a year of good luck.

Jan. 9-11: *Toka Ebisu* at Imamiya Ebisu Shrine, Osaka City and
Jan. 8-12: *Katsu Ebisu* at Ebisu Shrine in Kyoto at both shrines, merchants as well as townsfolk pay homage to *Ebisu,* the god of prosperity. In Osaka, the festivites are highlighted by a parade of women in traditional kimono who are carried through the streets in special palanquins.

Jan. 15: Adult's Day. This is when all young people who have turned 20 throughout the past year are honored. This date coincides with the "Grass Burning Festival" at Wakakusaka Yama Hill in Nara (see Nara: "festivals and events") which commenorates a fire that occurred there 1000 yrs ago.

Mid-Jan.: *Sumo Wrestling,* in Tokyo. This event lasts for 15 days and is repeated again in May and Sept. In March, *sumo* is held at Osaka, in July at Nagoya, and in Nov. at Fukuoka.

Feb. 1-5: *Yuki Matsuri* (Snow Festival) in Sapporo, Hokkaido. The entire city turns out to see the fantastic ice sculptures that have been fashioned in the preceding days. Smaller versions can also be seen in the Hokkaido cities of Asahikawa, Mombetsu, Abashiri and Obihoro.

early Feb.: *Setsubun.* Commenorating the last day of winter according to the lunar calendar, this festival is held at all major temples throughout the country. The main attraction is *mame-maki* (bean throwing) when the temple priests or luminaries such as actors and sumo wrestlers throw handfuls of beans to the crowd who chant in unison, "*Fuku wa uchi, oni wa soto*" (In with good luck, out with the devils). Some people go home and eat the number of beans that correspond with their age to insure their good luck. During this time, the *Mandoro* Festival also takes place where thousands of stone and bronze lanterns are lit at Kasuga Shrine in Nara.

mid-Feb.: *Kamakura Festival.* In the snowy districts of Tohoku in N. Japan, especially in Akita Pref., children build *kamakura* (igloos) in which they sit and receive guests. In the rear is a snowy alcove dedicated to *Suijin,* the god of water, whom they honor to insure good crops in the coming year. On the 3rd Saturday of Feb. the *Eyo Festival* takes place at Saidiji Temple in Saidiji, Okayama Pref. After loin-clothed young men purify themselves in the Yoshii River, they go to the temple grounds where a priest throws 2 special wands into the crowd. The jostling is ferocious and the ones who retrieve the wands are assured of a lifetime of happiness.

<u>Feb. 17-20:</u> Brings in the *Emburi* (Harvest Festival) at Hachinohe in Aomori Pref. More than 50 village groups assemble at Shiragi Shrine on Mt. Choja and then proceed to the city streets in a procession.

Mar. 1-14: *Omizutori* (Water Drawing Festival), at Todaiji Temple in Nara. During this time the temple priests go through a form of meditation that they have followed for 12 centuries. (For more details, see Nara "festivals and events.")

Mar 3-4: *Hina Matsuri* (Doll Festival). During this festival celebrated throughout Japan, young girls display special dolls called *hina* that depict 15 Imperial Court figures. The *hina* are very expensive and parents usually buy one per year which the young girls cherish but never play with. There's also an open air market with a fantastic array of wares at Jindaiji Temple at Chofu on the outskirts of Tokyo. Bargaining is acceptable here.

Mar. 13: *Kasuga Matsuri* at Kasuga Shrine in Nara. This festival dates back over 1000 years. (see Nara chapter for more information.)

Mar. 20 or 21: Vernal Equinox Day. A national holiday when temples throughout the country hold services for the dead.

Apr. 30: Cherry blossom time with festivities held all over Japan. The *Miyako Odori* is a special cherry blossom dance held during the entire month at Kobu Kaburenjo Theater in Kyoto.

Apr. 5-8: *Kagura-sai*, at the Ise Shrines in Ise. *Shinto* music and dances (*kagura*) as well as old court dances (*bugaku*) and *Noh* plays are performed at the Grand Shrines. Around Apr. 8, Buddha's birthday is celebrated throughout Japan with commemorative services at most temples.

Apr. 14-15: *Takayama Matsuri,* at Takayama City. Great crowds descend upon this historical city to see a parade of 12 enormous *yatai* (floats) that are wheeled throughout the city (see Takayama). A major event of the festival year.

Apr. 16-17: *Yayoi Matsuri* at Futaarasan Shrine in Nikko. A procession of 15 floats and thousands of participants parade around the shrine and then into Nikko (see Nikko).

late Apr.: Ancient martial arts displays, folk dancing, songs and *Noh* plays are performed at Yasukuni Shrine in Tokyo. Apr. 29 is the Emperor's Birthday when large throngs go to see him at the Imperial Palace. During this period, the festival of Meiji Shrine also takes place in Tokyo.

May 3-4: *Hakata Dontaku*, in Fukuoka. Large crowds turn out to see participants dressed as ancient gods riding horses through the streets.

May 5: *Kodomo-No-Hi* (Children's Day). This national holiday centers around all of the nation's children with a special emphasis on young-boys. At this time, families fly giant paper *koi* (carp) from atop their homes. The undaunted *koi* symbolizes the strength of manhood. The largest and uppermost *koi* on the pole is for the eldest son with the gradually smaller ones below for the other male children of the family.

May 3-5: *Oh-Take-Age*, at Odawara City in Kanagawa Pref. and at Hamamatsu in Shizuoka Prefecture. Giant kites, sometimes manned by more than a dozen people, wage an aerial battle. They try to maneuver so that they cut the strings of their opponents, thereby winning the event.

mid May: *Ukai* (Cormorant Fishing). This unique fishing season, lasting until October, commences in Gifu where these trained birds catch *ayu* from the waters of the Nagara River (see Gifu).

May 15-17: *Aoi Matsuri* (Hollyhock Festival). One of the grandest festivals held in Kyoto (see Kyoto). The *Kanda Matsuri* of Kanda Myojin shrine in Tokyo is held on odd numbered years.

May 17-20: *Toshogu Shrine Festival,* at Nikko. One of the grandest festivals at Nikko where over 1000 participants, dressed in feudal costumes, parade around the sacred shrines (see Nikko). The *Sanja Matsuri* takes place at Asakusa Shrine in Tokyo during the 3rd Saturday and Sunday of the month. It features a parade of town elders, dancers, *geisha* and 100 portable shrines. Also, on the 3rd Sunday, the *Mifune Matsuri* is held in Arashiyama on the banks of the Oi River in Kyoto (see Kyoto).

June 1-2: *Takigi Noh* at the Heian Shrine, Kyoto. Classical Noh plays are held after sunset on an open air stage in the shrine compound. Also, the annual *Ueki Ichi* (Poted Plant Fair) is held at Asakusa Temple in Tokyo and repeated again on June 30. Don't miss the *Hanashobu* (Iris Exhibition) held throughout the month at Meiji Shrine in Tokyo. Mid month is the best time to attend.

June 10-16: *Sanno Matsuri* at Hie Shrine, Tokyo. One of Tokyo's big yearly events. The festivites include open air tea cermonies, folk dancing, parades and priests on horseback. The event originated during the Edo period.

June 15: *Chagu-Chagu Umakko* (Horse Festival) at Morioka City, Iwate Prefecture. Colorfully decorated horses are paraded through the streets until they arrive at Sozen Shrine where prayers for longevity are offered (see Morioka).

Jul. 1-15: *Hakata Yamagasa* at Fukuoka City, Fukuoka Prefecture. The entire city is festive for 2 weeks. On the last day, a giant fleet of *yamagasa* floats representing castles and ancient buildings are hauled by young people through the streets.

Jul. 7: *Tanabata Festival*. Celebrated throughout Japan, this festival remembers 2 star-crossed lovers, a princess and a farm boy, who were forbidden to meet except for this one night a year. They are represented by the 2 stars, Vega and Altair, whose paths cross the Milky Way on this night. Large banners with streamers bearing love poems are hung throughout Japanese cities. The greatest *Tanabata Festival* takes place at Sendai city in Miyagi Pref. (see Sendai) one month later on Aug. 6-8. The entire city takes part and visitors from all over Japan go for the spectacle. Accommodations are booked solid in Sendai during *Tanabata*.

Jul. 13-16: *O-Bon Festival*. This is one of the most magical times of the year in Japan when Buddhist beliefs hold that all departed ancestors return to earth during this time. There are ceremonies held all over Japan and everyone makes an effort to return to their home villages. The most touching aspect of *O-Bon* are the lighted paper lanterns that are floated on rivers, bays and seas and symbolize the returning of the departed ones to the netherworld. Some exceptional festivals are held at Yasakuni Shrine in Tokyo, Tobata and Kita-Kyushu City in Fukuoka Pref., and at Nachi Shrine in Katsuura, Wakayama Pref. where white robed priests light 12 giant torches.

mid Jul.: *Kangensai* (Music Festival) at Itsukushima Shrine in Miyajima, just S of Hiroshima. Decorated sacred boats are sailed through the famous red *torii* of this shrine while classical and sacred dances are performed aboard them (see Miyajima).

Jul. 16-17: *Gion Matsuri* in Kyoto. This event ·dates back 1200 yrs and is one of the largest festivals in Kyoto (see Kyoto).

Jul. 23-25: *Warei Shrine Festival* in Uwajima City, Ehime Prefecture. This is one of the largest festivals on the island of Shikoku. It features bullfights, torch lit parades and fireworks.

Jul. 24: *Soma Nomaoi* (Wild Horse Festival) at Haranomachi in Fukushima Prefecture. One thousand riders in ancient costume try to catch 3 shrine flags shot into the air while men in white costumes try to catch the wild horses driven into a corral by the riders (see Fukushima Prefecture).

Aug. 1-7: *Nebuta Matsuri*, at Aomori and Hirosaki Cities, Aomori Prefecture. *Nebuta* are papier mache figures of warriors and animals that are placed on carriages and pulled through the streets during this festival. They commemorate a warlord's victory over his enemies by the use of a similar deception (see Aomori Prefecture).

Aug. 6: Peace Ceremony at Peace Memorial Park in Hiroshima. In remembrance of the A-bomb victims, this ceremony is one giant prayer by all men to all gods for peace on earth.

Aug. 15: _Kasuga Mandoro_ at Kasuga Shrine in Nara. All 1765 stone and metal lanterns are lit on this evening (see Nara).

Aug. 16: _Daimonji._ A giant bonfire is lit on the slopes of Mt. Nyoigadake near Kyoto. The giant fire takes the shape of the Chinese character _Dai_ (large) and is the closing festivity of the previous month's O-Bon Festival.

late Aug.: Lantern Festival of Suwa Shrine in Isshiki near Nagoya. On Aug. 26-27, huge paper lanterns with colorfully painted designs are lit in the shrine compound. On Aug. 26 at Fuji Yoshida in Yamanashi Pref., 40 giant torches are lit along the Old Tokaido Highway to mark the end of the Mt. Fuji climbing season.

Sept. 14-16: _Yabusame,_ at Tsuruguoka Hachimangu Shrine in Kamakura. _Yabusame_ (horseback archery) is the climax of the shrine festival and is reminiscent of the days of the _samurai_ (see Kamakura).

mid-Sept.: _Oyama-Mairi,_ at Iwaki Shrine at Iwaki, Aomori Prefecture. The local townspeople climb Mt. Iwaki, a Mt. Fuji look-alike, and offer prayers and lively music.

late Sept., early Oct.: The Annual Grand Tokyo Festival. The capital city of Japan comes alive with parades, dragon dancers and concerts of traditional music. Check with TIC for scheduled events.

Oct. 7-9: _Okunchi Festival,_ at Suwa Shrine in Nagasaki. the long tradition of Nagasaki's ties with China becomes evident. See dragon dances, parades and _kasboko_ carts, decked out with colorful ornamentation, wheeled through the streets (see Nagasaki).

Oct. 8-10: _Marimo Matsuri_ on Lake Akan in Hokkaido. This is a singular opportunity to see the last remnants of the _Ainu_ people gathered around the lake for a festival. _Ainu_ dances are featured while _marimo_ (a spherical weed with barometric abilities) is cast upon the lake (see Hokkaido, Lake Akan).

Oct. 9-10: _Takayama Matsuri,_ at Hachiman Shrine in Takayama. Many people from throughout Japan head for this historical city to participate in this festival, said to date back to

Toshogu Shrine Festival at Nikko

the 15th century. A procession of some of the most inspired floats in all of Japan is the highlight. Accommodations are very tight during this event. (see Takayama).

Oct. 11-13: _Oeshiki Festival,_ at Hommonji Temple in Tokyo. This event honors the great Buddhist teacher, Nichiren, who died at this temple in 1282. A parade of people carrying lanterns moves toward the temple, swaying to the rhythmic beating of drums.

Oct. 17: Grand Autumn Festival of Toshogu Shrine in Nikko. Thousands of people dressed in ancient costumes march through the city streets to the shrine. Many rites and ceremonies take place at this time (see Nikko). This is also the date of the Autumn Festival of Yasukuni Shrine in Tokyo, where traditional dances, music, _Noh_ and martial arts are displayed throughout the day.

Oct. 22: _Jidai Matsuri,_ at Heian Shrine in Kyoto. This festival celebrates the founding of the ancient capital in 794. A procession of over 2000 people dressed in costumes representing the various historical epochs takes place. This is a truly gala affair (see Kyoto). Another event on this date is the Fire Festival of Yuki Shrine in Kurama village near Kyoto. The village streets are ablaze with torches as a procession moves towards the shrine.

Oct. 31- Nov. 3: The Autumn Festival of Meiji Shrine in Tokyo. A seasonal affair in Tokyo, this festival features *Noh, Bugaku* court music and *sankyoku* traditional instrument concerts. There are also demonstrations of martial arts and *yabusame*. Check with TIC for the scheduling of events.

Nov. 3: *Daimyo Gyoretsu* at Hakone Town, Kanagawa Prefecture. The clock turns back to feudal days when participants, dressed like samurai, march along the Old Tokaido Highway. They depict the times when *daimyo* (feudal lords) made this pilgrimage to Edo (Tokyo). The starting point is Sounji Temple. This date also marks the *Karatsu Okunchi Festival* of Karatsu Shrine in Karatsu, Saga Prefecture.

mid-Nov.· *Tori-No-Ichi* (Cock Festival) throughout Tokyo. These festivals are held on Cock Days according to the Zodiacal calendar. Good luck bamboo rakes are sold at many shrine compounds. The event in times past was dedicated by the samurai to the god of war to whom they presented birds for good luck in battle. Otori Shrine at Asakusa in Tokyo is best known for its festivities. Contact TIC for more information (see Tokyo).

Nov. 15: *Shichi-Go-San* (7-5-3) or Children's Shrine Visiting Day. All over Japan children are dressed in their best attire and taken to shrines and temples where prayers are offered for good health. Those children who have reached the ages of 7, 5 and 3 are honored. In bygone days, it was the first time that the hair of 3 year old girls was put up. Boys of the age of 5 were dressed in their first pair of *hakama* (long, pleated skirts) and girls of the age of 7 were given their first *obi*. In Tokyo; Meiji, Hie and Kanda Myojin Shrines are popular.

Dec. 3: *Yomatsuri* at Chichibu City near Tokyo. This is a night festival complete with floats, *Kabuki* performances and fireworks. Most festivities take place at Hitsujiyama Park.

Dec. 8: *Harikuyo* at Horinjo Temple in Kyoto. Not even broken needles and pins are forgotten as housewives and seamstresses bring them to the temple to stick into a piece of *tofu*. This event also takes place at Asakusa Kannon Temple in Tokyo during early February.

Dec. 14: *Gishi Sai* at Ako City near Okayama. This event commemorates one of the best loved classical stories in all of Japan. In 1701, Lord Aki drew his sword in the preserve of the *shogun*, after being baited by an adversary, and was ordered to commit suicide for this impulsive act. His faithful *samurai*, who then became *ronin* (masterless *samurai*), swore an oath of vengeance and one year later, by stealth and daring, killed the offending adversary. They in turn were ordered to commit suicide. Their acts of bravery and loyalty have long been remembered and they are regarded as heroes by young boys. On this day, their loyal and courageous act is memorialized.

mid-Dec.: *Tosho-No-Ichi* (Year End Market) at Asakusa Kannon Temple in Tokyo. A year end open air market is held on the grounds of this temple and specializes in the sale of New Year's decorations. This is a very festive event and many good bargains are obtainable.

Dec. 17-18: *On Matsuri* at Kasuga Wakamiya Shrine in Nara. *Shinto* music, dancing and open air *Noh* performances are offered (see Nara).

Dec 31: *Joya-No-Kane*. Throughout Japan, people stay up until midnight to hear the temple bells peal 108 times to bring in the New Year. At Yasaka Shrine in Kyoto, a sacred fire is lit and throngs of people attempt to gather cinders to take home and use for the cooking of the New Year's meal. Also, *Namahage Festival* takes place on the Oga Peninsula in Akita Prefecture. At night, dressed as *namahage* (devils), the village men go from door to door to the joyful screeches of believing children and demand to know if there are any lazy people about. This is a night of festivity, magic and much *sake* drinking in this snow bound area of Japan.

GETTING THERE

It was at one time the specialized domain of a budget travel writer to inform the readers about all the nifty deals and money saving tips on how to get from point A to point B. Since it is practical in the vast majority of cases to reach Japan only by air, and since the air industry world-wide is topsy turvy fare-wise, this specialized domain is in shambles. Air fares at one time were stable for months at a time, but now they change even in a matter of days with fare hikes, cancelled flights and economy promotional deals being wedged in wherever there's an opening. An air traveler today must be willing to shop around and deal with an indispensable travel agent who is willing to ferret out a flight to match your travel aspirations and your pocketbook. With over 40 international carriers running regularly scheduled flights to Japan from every corner of the globe, it's well worth spending the time to choose the least expensive and most convenient one.

INFORMATION

If you're contemplating a trip to Japan, your first inquiry should be directed to Japan National Tourist Organization (JNTO). JNTO offices, which are found in countries throughout the world, are listed under "Facts, Figures and Practicalities" in this book. They dispense a useful pamphlet entitled, "Tours, Stopovers and Cruises" that will give you a general idea of what is being offered. Although they have information regarding all international carriers flying to Japan, they specialize in fares offered by Japan's own Japan Airlines (JAL). In the U.S., all airlines offer toll free numbers where you can inquire about prices. Just dial 1-800-555-1212 and ask the information operator for the toll free number of the airlines of your choice. You should do this to gain some basic information so that you can choose a worthwhile travel agent. Another alternative is to join a travel club that serves basically as a travel agent. There are many of these clubs operating and a good source of information regarding them can often be found at student services of major universities. One such club operating on the west coast of the U.S. and specializing in flights to Asia is OC Tours in Burlingame, California (toll free number available). For U.S. $15.00 membership fee, you're entitled to cut-rate group rates.

airline addresses: Internaional carriers maintain branch offices throughout Japan. For a complete listing inquire at TIC, any JTB or travel agent. The following is a partial list of international carriers along with their Tokyo phone numbers. Canadian Pacific (CP) 281-7426; Qantas (QF) 211-4481; JAL 213-1411; Cathay Pacific (CX) 504-1531; Continental Air (CO) 214-2621; Pan Am 216-6711; Korean Air Lines (KE) 211-3311; Philippine Air Lines (PR) 504-3791; Pakistan International (PK) 573-2494; Air India (AI) 214-7631; British Airways (BA) 214-4161; Lufthansa (LH) 580-2111; Air France (AF) 501-6331; Air New Zealand (TE) 213-0968.

domestic: All Nippon Airways (ANA) 580-4711; TOA Domestic 507-8111 also JAL.

FARES

There are 4 types of fares available to the general public with a few other specialty types such as Group Inclusive Tours (GIT) that are offered under special circumstances. In dealing with a travel agent, you should clarify which type of ticket you desire. They are in descending order from most expensive to least expensive: First class, economy class, special economy, and Advance Purchase Excursion (APEX). All have their benefits and drawbacks irrespective of costs. For example, an APEX fare, the least expensive, requires that you book and pay for your ticket 30 days in advance, stay in the visited country for a minimum of 14 and maximum of 180 days, and generally does not allow stopovers. Another factor to be considered is Peak and Off Peak prices. These vary from country to country, but usually run parallel with traditional vacation times. You can save a tidy sum by traveling Off Peak.

children: Fares for children between the ages of 2 and 12 are half the price of an adult fare. For children under 2 not occupying a seat, the fare is 10% of the adult fare. If you're traveling with an infant or active toddler, book your reservations well in advance and request the bulkhead seat or first row seat in each section of the plane and a crib if necessary and available. Many carriers are equipped with folding down cribs which have safety restraints for baby's protection and comfort. Toddlers also appreciate the leg room provided by the front row seats. Be sure to reconfirm this special request when confirming your reservations and arrive early on your departure date to assure getting this special seating. On long flights, you'll be glad you took these extra pains to obtain this helpful arrangement. Be sure to bring some small, special activities to keep your older children busy. Many airlines have specially tailored coloring books, puppets and other items to keep children happily occupied, but it's always a good idea to come prepared yourself. It can make the difference between a pleasant flight or a harried ordeal. Also remember to bring baby bottles, formula (if used), diapers, baby food and other necessities as many airlines may not be equipped with exactly what you need. It's always a good idea to inquire ahead of time so that you're not caught unprepared.

baggage: For flights originating in the US, Canada, Mexico and Brazil, baggage allowances are as follows: First class, 2 pieces of baggage with linear dimensions of each piece not exceeding 158 cm. Economy class, 2 pieces of baggage with a combined linear dimension not exceeding 270 cm. For flights originating in all other countries, the allowances are 30 kg for first class, 20 kg for 2nd class.

SUGGESTIONS

Travelers heading for Japan from Europe should keep in mind that it's oftentimes cheaper to arrange a flight with a stopover in a major Asian capital such as Bangkok, Singapore or Hong Kong with a connecting flight to Japan, rather than a direct flight. There's a cut rate market for tickets from London to Hong Kong. Carriers with good reputations for inexpensive tickets from Europe are Cathay Pacific (CX), Air India (AI) and Pakistan Airlines (PK). From Australia, you're basically limited to flying with Japan Air Lines (JAL) or Qantas (QF), but if you don't mind making a few fancy zigs and zags, there are other carriers available. You might try purchasing an APEX fare to Singapore, with a separate RT ticket to Japan. This is slightly more than the APEX fare, but you do get a stopover. From the U.S., the cheapest routine flights to Tokyo originate in Los Angeles and are operated by China Airlines (CI) and Korean Airlines (KE). If you keep a "weather eye" open, other major carriers offer special deals from time to time. From islands throughout the Pacific, the cheapest flights are offered by Air Nauru (ON)

and Continental Airlines (CO) and island hop throughout most of these far flung island nations. In short, the cheapest return fares from Europe, Australia and the U.S. are all about equal at U.S.$800.

JAPANESE AIRPORTS

There are 7 international airports in Japan. Tokyo (Narita and Haneda), Osaka, Nagoya and Niigata are on the main island of Honshu, Kagoshima, Kumamoto and Fukuoka are on the southernmost main island of Kyushu, and Naha is in Okinawa, the main island of the Ryukyu chain S of mainland Japan. Full details of all airports are given in the travel chapters of this book.

Tokyo: The lion's share of international flights land at Narita Airport about 60 km from city center. Haneda Airport, much more conveniently located to downtown Tokyo, services only China Airlines internationally, but is the main Tokyo airport for domestic flights.

Niigata: This industrialized city on the Japan Sea side of the country, almost directly N of Tokyo, serves as a main entry airport for travelers who have crossed the USSR on the Trans-Siberian Railway. Flights link it to Khabarovsk with a timetable to match the arrival and departure times of the Trans-Siberian train. Niigata is linked to Tokyo by numerous express trains that make the journey in 4½ hrs. Ferries are also available from Niigata heading S to Maizuru just 60 km N of Kyoto or N to Otaru in Hokkaido.

Osaka: Next to Narita, Osaka Airport is the busiest international airport in Japan. It's linked directly by *shinkansen* ("bullet train") to Tokyo in the N and to Kita-Kyushu on Kyushu Island. Most flights landing at Osaka have originated in Los Angeles and from most major cities throughout Asia.

Nagoya: This industrialized city is about midway along the Pacific coast between Osaka and Tokyo and is connected to both by *shinkansen*, highway bus and innumerable trains. It primarily connects with flights originating in Hong Kong, Seoul and Manila.

Fukuoka, Kumamoto and Kagoshima: These 3 airports on Kyushu primarily link with main

Asian cities and various island nations throughout the Pacific. Fukuoka does accommodate flights from Europe originating in Brussels and Antwerp, while Kumamoto specialized in flights from Korea. Kagoshima Airport services the cities of the Asian mainland, but also the flights of those that have island hopped across the Pacific with regularly scheduled services to the islands of Nauru and Ponape.

BY SEA

By and large, great ocean liners plying the seas to the exotic corners of the world are a thing of the past. Ocean going freighters willing to take passengers are even more scarce or virtually extinct. All but the most specialized travel agents cannot even help you find passage. Air travel, with its convenience and time saving qualities, have just about wiped out passenger liners, especially when you consider that traveling by ship can easily cost 3 to 4 times as much as taking a plane. If you do arrive in Japan by ship, you will invariably dock at either Yokohama or Kobe ports. Both are connected to Tokyo and greater Japan by numerous trains and special considerations for shore visitation visas are in effect as discussed in "Visas."

Kampu ferry to Korea: The Kampu Ferry Co. makes 3 regularly scheduled sailings (both ways) weekly between the port of Shimonoseki in Kyushu and Pusan, Korea. This is an old standby with both residents and travelers who wish to extend their visas for Japan. Full coverage is given in the travel section under "Shimonoseki."

USSR steamships: There is a steamship service between Nakhodka, a port of the E coast of the USSR and Yokohama just S or Tokyo. This ocean going connection is maintained for the convenience of travelers wishing to cross the vastness of the USSR on the Trans Siberian Railroad. Travelers have reported mixed feelings on this great, horizonless trek across the largest country in the world. Some report that it was a unique and exhilirating, never-to-be-forgotten experience, while others complain that it was the most horrible bore and waste of time that they had ever perpetrated upon themselves. Budget travelers should keep in mind that this train marathon is much more expensive than flying. Russian cruise ships, known for their excellent food, are also operated between Yokohama and Hong Kong. Reservations and information for the Far Eastern Steamship Co. (USSR) can be made by contacting their agent, United Orient Shipping Co., 4th Floor, Hazama Bldg., 5-8, 2-chome, Kita-Aoyama, Minato-ku, Tokyo 107, tel: (03) 478-7271. Information is also made available by contacting the Japan-Soviet Tourist Bureau in Tokyo at tel: (03) 432-6161 or in Osaka at (06) 531-7416. TIC in Tokyo also offers valuable information concerning these steamship services.

information: With so many freighter services disappearing, coupled with the difficulty in discovering the erratic schedules of those that remain, finding good information concerning them is left to groups of freighter enthusiasts who make a hobby of traveling the world in this exotic fashion. To get information, write to: Freighter Travel Club of America, P.O. Box 12693, Salem, Oregon, USA; Ford's Freighter Travel Guide, P.O. Box 505, 22151 Clarendon St., Woodland Hills, California, USA. The Norwegian Knutsen Line runs ships from Freemantle, Australia to Yokohama and upon returning to Freemantle docks at Keelung. For information in Australia, contact A.P.T. Shipping in Sydney at tel: 29-4352 and in Melbourne at tel: 679881; in Freemantle, tel: 335-5044. In Japan, for information on this same line contact: Interocean Shipping Corp., Tokyo, tel: (03) 506-2934.

VISAS AND OFFICIALDOM

Anyone desiring to enter Japan MUST either have a VISA or their home country must have reciprocal *visa exemption* with Japan. Entry (visas) to Japan must be arranged at Japanese consulates or embassies abroad before arriving in Japan. An exception is made for *travelers in transit*. A list of Japanese Consular offices is given at the end of this section. The most important thing to remember is that *all* entrants to Japan are in effect handled "case by case." The Immigration Officer at your point of entry has the final say in all entrance matters and is seldom, if ever, overruled. He also decides your status (see later) and your initial length of stay. If all of your documents are in order, there is no problem, but if the Immigration Officer suspects any shenanigans, you may be deprived of entry. Besides a passport and valid visa, tourists are required to have an onward going ticket and sufficient funds to cover their stay in Japan. In some cases, the Immigration Officer may request to *see* your money and tickets.

TEMPORARY LANDING VISAS

Temporary landing visas (72 hrs.) are granted upon entry into Japan to travelers on commericial air carriers provided that they have confirmed onward going reservations and the proper documentation. The area of travel while in Japan is restricted to the vicinity of the airport. Arrangements are made through the carrier. For travelers arriving by sea, a similar (72 hr.) visa is granted. Another type of visa (15 days) is granted for an overland tour for sightseeing between ports of call in Japan. Again, arrangements are made through the carrier. This 15 day visa does not apply to passengers on ships terminating their voyages in Japan.

CITIZENS OF COUNTRIES WHERE VISAS ARE REQUIRED

The 2 most notable countries where citizens are required to have visas are Australia and the United States. However, there is no fee for the issuance of the visa. On arrival in Japan, most tourists from these 2 countries will be granted a 60 day period of stay. Multiple visas can be issued to Australians (valid 12 months) and Americans (valid 4 years).

CITIZENS OF COUNTRIES WITH RECIPROCAL VISA EXEMPTIONS

The following is a list of the major countries that have reciprocal visa exemptions with Japan. If you are from one of these countries you need no visa to enter Japan. All of the countries with agreements are too long to list, so check with authorities at home. N.B., This visa free status only applies to *tourists* who do not engage in *any* remunerative activity in Japan. No one, regardless of their home country, is allowed to work in Japan without the proper visa. Although no visa is required, you will be given a landing status signifying your period of stay. *Visa Free Status for periods not to exceed 180 days are granted to the following:* Germany, France, Ireland, United Kingdom, Austria, Switzerland, Mexico. *Not to exceed 90 days:* Canada, Belgium, most Latin American and South American countries, Denmark, Finland, France, Greece, Israel, Italy, Netherlands, Norway, Singapore, Spain, Sweden and Yugoslavia. *Not to exceed 30 days:* New Zealand.

EXTENDING YOUR LENGTH OF STAY

Remember here, more than ever, that extensions are granted "case by case." The general rule of thumb is that landed statuses under normal circumstances are given 2 almost automatic extensions. Therefore, a 60 day 4-1-4 can be lengthened to 180 days. To extend your stay, you *must* apply at an Immigration Office 10 days prior to the expiration date stamped in your passport. At this time you may be asked for proof of an onward-going ticket and to show the funds necessary to extend your stay. The following is a list of Immigration Offices:

Tokyo Immigration Office, 3-20, Konan 3-chome, Minato-ku, Tokyo. Tel:471-5111.

Narita Immigration Office, New Tokyo International Airport, Marita. Tel: (0476) 32-6771.

VISA STATUS AND LENGTH OF STAY

Upon entering Japan, the Immigration Officer will stamp your visa with a 3 number code beginning with 4-1. The 3rd number in this 3 digit code, ranging from 1 through 16 will establish your status and length of stay. The following is a list of the categories and length of stay for each code. The most common is a 4-1-4, 60 day tourist visa.

Code	Status	Length of Stay
4-1-1	Diplomats	Indefinite
4-1-2	Government officials	Indefinite
4-1-3	Transits	15 days
4-1-4	Tourists	60 days
4-1-5	Commercial	3 years
4-1-6	Students	1 year
4-1-7	Professors or Educational entrants	3 years
4-1-8	Cultural entrants	1 year
4-1-9	Entertainers	60 days
4-1-10	Missionaries	3 years
4-1-11	Journalists, correspondents	3 years
4-1-12	Technicians	3 years
4-1-13	Skilled laborers laborers	1 year
4-1-14	Permanent residents	Permanent
4-1-15	Spouses and unmarried children (under age 20) for categories 4-1-5 to 4-1-13	Same as accompanying parent or spouse
4-1-16 (1)	Short term for statuses 4-1-5/10/11/12 including dependents	180 days
4-1-16 (3)	Special version of all statuses	3 years (case by case;

Yokohama Immigration Office, 37-9, Yamashita-cho, Maka-ku, Yokohama. Tel: 681-6801.

Nagoya Immigration Office 4-3-1, Sannomaru, Maka-ku. Tel: 951-2391.

Osaka Immigration Office, 2-31, Tanimachi, Higashi-ku, Osaka. Tel: 941-0771.

Kobe Immigration Office, Kaigan-dori, Ikuta-ku, Kobe. Tel: 391-6377.

Sapporo Immigration Office, 4, Nishi 12, Odori, Sapporo. Tel:261-9211.

Sendai Immigration Office, 3-20, Gorin 1-chome, Sendai. Tel: 56-6076.

Takamatsu Immigration Office, 1-11, Marunouchi, Takamatsu. Tel: 22-5851.

Hiroshima Immigration Office, 6-30, Kamihatchovori, Hiroshima. Tel: 21-4411.

Shimonoseki Immigration Office, 2-1, Kamitanaka-machi 8-chome, Shimonoseki. Tel: 23-1431.

Fukuoka Immigration Office, 1-22, Okihamacho, Fukuoka. Tel: 281-7431.

Kagoshima Immigration Office, 18-2-40, Izumicho, Kagoshima. Tel: 22-5658.

Naha Immigration Office, Aza Yogi 585, Maha. Tel: 32-9836.

Any specific questions regarding visas, including change of status while in Japan, should be directed to the Ministry of Foreign Affairs (Gaimusho), Visa Section, Tokyo. Tel: (03) 580-3311. The personnel here are helpful and will dispense all necessary information. Their function is to help the foreigner while in Japan, and they refrain from asking embarsssing questions.

useful visa booklets: Particularly helpful with visa questions is the booklet,"Immigration: A Guide to Alien Procedures in Japan" (Y300), published by the *Japan Times*. This booklet is available at most large bookstores in Tokyo and at the Tokyo Immigration Office. A copy can also be obtained by writing to: *The Japan Times,* 5-4 4-chome, Minato-ku, Tokyo 180. Include Y200 for mail within Japan and Y300 (surface mail) outside of Japan. Another excellent booklet is "Now You Live in Japan" (Y700) from Research Commitee for Bicultural Life in Japan, c/o *Japan Times*, Ltd., CPO Box 144, Tokyo 100-91. Include Y200 for domestic mail, Y300 (surface mail) overseas.

LEAVING AND REENTERING JAPAN

In most cases, 180 days is the magic number. After this length of time you will be required to leave Japan and start reentry procedures all over again. If you have a long term visa that has not expired and are leaving Japan with the intentions of returning, be sure to acquire a *reentry permit*. The reentry permit will facilitate matters upon your return and without it you are running the risk of losing your original status. The reentry permit is valid for one year. *Kampu Ferry to Korea:* The most common and economical route used by foreigners wishing to immediately return to Japan on a new tourist visa is to take the Kampu Ferry from Shimonoseki to Pusan, Korea. For complete details, see "Shimonoseki," Yamaguchi prefecture, Chugoku District.

alternatives: Next to taking the Kampu Ferry to Korea, most travelers wishing to acquire a new Japanese tourist visa opt for a brief visit to the Philippines. The Philippines are a very popular vacation area with the Japanese, themselves, and special excusion fares are almost constantly advertised in the leading newspapers. An excellent travel agent to try is John Bosworth of Ikon Travel, Tokyo, tel: (03) 400-9050. Before leaving, get your visa from the Philippine Embassy, 5-6-l5, Roppongi, Minato-ku, Tokyo, tel: (03) 583-4101. The Japanese Embassy in the Philippines is at 375 Buendia Ave., Makati, Metro Manila, tel: 818-9011. Another infrequently used alternative is to travel to Taiwan. You can fly directly from Tokyo or you can travel to Naha, Okinawa (many inexpensive ferries from mainland Japan—see *Okinawa,* "getting there") where you can connect with a ferry to Keelung, Taiwan. For a Taiwanese visa, contact the Association of E Asian Relations, Tokyo, tel: (03) 583-8030. Ever since Japan opened relations with the People's Republic of China, they have attempted to keep their diplomacy with Taiwan low keyed, and often resort to such ambiguous titles and diplomatic double talk. For a Japanese visa in Taiwan, visit the Interchange Assoc., 43 Tsinan Rd., Section 2, Taipei tel: (02) 351-7250.

ALIEN REGISTRATION CARDS (ARC)

All travelers who have been in Japan for 90 days must register with the authorities and apply for an ARC. Your visa status or length of stay, even if it is for more than 90 days, does not exclude you from getting an ARC. The law here is stringent and failure to comply will lead to deportation. Furthermore, Japanese law states that you must carry your passport or ARC (both is best) at all times. If a policeman stops you, he will ask to see them. If you don't have them on your person, he will be as embarassed as you are, but he will take you to jail. When you arrive there, you'll be lectured over and over again about the law until it's indelibly etched on your soul. It's not uncommon to be detained all day or even overnight. The police *will not* allow you to go to your accommodations and retrieve your ARC. A friend or acquiantance must bring it to the station. No one knows what happens to the hapless soul who doesn't have someone to bring their papers.

getting an ARC: This is no problem. You must go to the municipal office/city hall in the town or city in which you're residing. Bring three (3) passport size photos. The registration procedure takes about one hour and there's no fee. If you are a traveler, the address of your current accommodations (hotel/YH, etc.) is acceptable. The Japanese simply want you to check in and know precisely where you are. If you haven't realized it after 90 days, the ARC will remind you that you are a *gaijin*.

WORKING IN JAPAN

Unless you have been hired from abroad or transferred by your company and have the proper credentials, it is illegal to work in Japan or to change your status from a 4-1-4, for example, if you do land a job while there. However, both procedures are regularly accomplished although the process is full of bureaucratic pitfalls and smothered in red tape. The Japanese government does not want foreigners coming to Japan and filling jobs that can be done by nationals. Usually only highly skilled technicians, academics and specialty tradesmen are given working visas.

teaching English: The one outstanding exception are foreign language teachers, primarily English teachers (*Eigo no sensei*), followed with much less demand for German and French. The situation is ludicrous and both the foreigner and the Japanese bureaucracy enter into a type of undeclared pact of transparent fraud. The *gaijin* pretend that they

are not teaching English and the bureaucracy pretends that they don't know what's gong on. What creates this unique situation is Japan's huge international trade dealings, where foreign language is a must and the total deficiency of Japan's educational system in producing competent English teachers. After 10 years of rigorous study, Japanese foreign language teachers can diagram sentences *ad infinitum*, spot the difference between a gerund and a gerundive from 100 paces, but can't order lunch. Enter the illegal *gaijin*.

getting a teaching job: Foreign language schools (2 pages of classified ads in the Monday edition of the *Japan Times*) and large Japanese corporations constantly clamor for teachers. The word "teacher" is also very loosely applied. Anyone, even illiterates, are included just as long as they can mumble a few sentences of English. All foreigners are usualy considered American and, therefore, native English speakers. Frenchmen with English accents as thick as 2 day old hollandaise sauce teach English to undifferentiating Japanese. The results are a unique language understandable to a mass audience of about 3 people. The normal procedure is to follow up on an advertisement and to be hired by a foreign language school to teach illegally and risk immediate and final deportation if you are caught. The owner or director of the language school then writes you an offical LETTER OF GUARANTEE stating your name and vital statistics along with a promise to insure your conduct, expenses and housing while in Japan. The guarantor then signs it, listing his or her vital statistics and, oftentimes, is required to show a tax statement from the previous year insuring that they can provide the guarantees promised. Most Japanese don't like to do this. You then write an official letter of apology for even looking for work. To some this may sound ridiculous, but the Japanese take it seriously. You then leave Japan for a neighboring country (Korea) and apply for a working visa. This process is lengthy, taking up to 2 months, but you can return to Japan on a tourist visa while your working visa is being processed. You must check on the progress of your visa at the Ministry of Foreign Affairs (Gaimusho), Tokyo. Tel: (03) 580-3311. Since this process is so mired in bureaucracy and your case number is different in Korea than in Japan, it is much better to have a Japanese friend perform the inquiries. The going rate at most schools is Y2000-Y3000 per hour. This sounds good, but sometimes you are starved for hours or you are worked to death. Forty hours a week constantly repeating, "Hello, how are you?" is more than most people can take. The school owner also knows your situation and is in a powerful position, especially if he's your guarantor, to rip you off. Most schools are on the "up and up," but hundreds open for business and close within a month. Be careful of your choice. After you know the scene and have made good contacts, private students are the best, both for money and satisfaction.

other work: Other work opportunities in Japan include translating and entertainment (modeling, acting in television and film roles, and bar hostessing). Translating is a legitimate reason for applying for a working visa and is preferred by some to teaching. It involves translating all kinds of books, manuals and brochures and a knowledge of Japanese is not necessary. The material has already been translated into the foreign language, but the word usage, grammar and syntax are sub-standard. Your job is to make it readable. Naturally, a command of the written foreign language is essential. Visas for entertainment, except the 60 day 4-1-9, are not usually given. There's good money to be made by modeling (both men and women), but you can't count on it for a steady income. Jobs can include modeling in magazines, newspapers or at large *departos*. There is also a steady need for actors for TV and film productions. Again, work here only comes in dribs and drabs and contacts provide most leads.

bar hostessing: Foreign women and a growing number of foreign men are sought after to work as bar hosts or hostesses. You should not go into these occupations blindly. The best course is to contact other foreigners that have worked in bars and find out first hand their experiences. (In Tokyo, try the western hangouts in the Roppongi area.) The bars employing such workers range from all you can grab dives to elegant cabarets where you will be treated with respect. The *gaijin* taking these jobs must have the right temperament and understanding of Japanese culture. Basically, Japanese men go to hostess bars to have their egos salved by understanding women. They are looking for, and are willing to pay for an illusion. Women can find it hopelessly boring trying to please a man with whom she cannot communicate. Western women also find many of the tasks required in hostessing demeaning. In short, you are a sex object. Your patrons will be Japanese business-

men who are looking for "fun" completely acceptable by Japanese standards. Also, you must look the part. Legs and underarms must be shaved. Stylish hairdos and makeup are required and a fashionable wardrobe is expected. Traveling clothes are unacceptable. Some foreign women have landed good jobs in respectable bars where a high standard of behavior is the norm, but you can't always count on it. Recently, similar institutions for hosts are coming into fashion. Usually older Japanese women or disgruntled married ones seek the companionship of hosts, but these bars are a new phenomenon. Cross-cultural differences and the circumstances usually leave most women with a distorted, negative view of Japanese men and mars their Japanese experience. These jobs are also totally illegal and if caught, you will be deported.

cultural visa: While in Japan you may wish to enroll in a Japanese language school, take up pottery, flower arranging (*ikebana*), the martial arts, *sumo* or any one of a long list of cultural or artistic pursuits. The process for a cultural visa (4-1-7) is the same as one for a working visa; find the school and then apply. You may even legally arrange to work part time while studying in Japan.

JAPANESE EMBASSIES AND CONSULATES ABROAD

U.S.A.

Washington, D.C.:	2520 Massachusetts Ave., NW Washington, D.C. 20008 tel: 202-234-2266
Boston:	Federal Reserve Plaza, 14th Floor, 600 Atlantic Ave., Boston MA 02210. tel: 617-973-9772
Chicago:	625 N Michigan Ave., Chicago, IL 60611 tel: 312-280-0400
Atlanta:	Ste. 1501, 400 Colony Sq. Bldg. Peachtree St. Atlanta, GA 30361. tel: 404-892-2700
New York:	280 Park Ave., New York, N.Y. 10017 tel: 212-986-1600
Los Angeles:	Ste. 1507, 250 E 1st St., Los Angeles, CA 90012 tel: 213-624-8305

San Francisco: 1601 Post St.
San Francisco, CA 94115
tel: 415-921-8000

Other Japanese consulates in the U.S.A. are found in Guam, Anchorage, Honolulu, Houston, Kansas City, New Orleans, Portland and Seattle.

CANADA

Ottawa: 255 Sussex Drive, Ottawa Ontario, KIN 9E6
tel: 613-236-8541

Toronto: Toronto Dominion Ctr., Ste. 1803, Toronto, Ontario, M5K 1A1. tel: 416-363-7038

Other Canadian cities where consulates are found are: Edmonton, Montreal, Vancouver, and Winnipeg.

CENTRAL AND SOUTH AMERICA

Buenos Aires, Argentina Azucenaga 1035, Buenos Aires tel: 83-1031

Rio de Janeiro, Brazil Praia do Flamento, 200, 10, ander 2210 Rio de Janeiro, RJ. tel: 021-265-5252

Other Japanese consulates in Brazil : Belem, Brasilia, Manaus, Porto Alegre, Recife and Sao Paulo.

Santiago, Chile Huerfanos 757, 8 Piso, Casilla 2877, Santiago. tel: 31163

Mexico City, Mexico Paseo de la Reforma 395, Col. Cuauhtemoc, Mexico 5, D.E. Mexico. tel: 553-67-44

Panama City, Calle 50 y Calle 61, Edificio Don Camilo, Apartado No. 1411, Panama 1. tel: 23-9750

Lima, Peru Avenida San Felipe 356, Jesus Maria, Lima. tel: 61-4041

EUROPE

Vienna, Austria 1040 Wien, Argentinierstrasse 21. tel: 65-97-71

Bruxelles, Belgium Avenue des Arts 58, 1040 Bruxelles. tel: 513-9200

Copenhagen, Denmark Oslo Plads 14,2100, Copenhagen. tel: 0126-33-11

Paris, France 7, Avenue Hoche, 75008-Paris. tel: 766-02-22

Marseille, France 352, Avenue du prado 13008-Marseille. tel: 9171-61-67

Bonn, Germany Bundeskanzlerplatz, Bonn Center HL-701, 5300 Bonn 1. tel: 0228-5001

Berlin, Germany Wachtelstrasse 8, 10000 Berlin 33. tel: 030-832-70-26

Frankfurt, Germany Hamburger Allee 2-10, im Plaza, 6000 Frankfurt am Main 90. tel: 0611-770351

Other Japanese consulates in Germany are in: Hamburg, Dusseldorf, and Munchen.

Dublin, Ireland 22, Ailesburry Road, Dublin 4. tel: 69-40-33

Rome, Italy Via Quintino Sella 60,00187 Roma. tel: 475-7151

Milan, Italy Piazza Diaz 7, 20123 Milano. tel: 867559

Hague, Netherlands Tobias Asserlaan 2, 2517 KC The Hague. tel: 070-469544

Lisboa, Portugal Av. Fontes Pereira de Melo 14-13°, 1098 Lisboa, CODEX. tel: 562177

Madrid, Spain Calle de Joaquin Cosaa, 29. Madrid-6. tel: 262-55-46

Las Palmas, Spain Calle Santiago Rusinol 12, Las Palmas de Gran Canaria. tel: 24-4012

Stockholm, Sweden Gardesgatan 10, 115-27 Stockholm. tel: 08-63-04-40

Geneve, Switzerland 10, Avenue de Bude, 1202 Geneve. tel: 34-84-00

Berne, *Switzerland*	Engestrosse, 43, 3012 Berne. tel: 03124-08-11
London, *United* *Kingdom*	43-46, Grosvenor Street, London, WIX OBA. tel: 01-493-6030

MIDDLE AND NEAR EAST

Teheran, *Iran*	Bucharest Avenue, Corner of 5th Street, Teheran. tel: 623396
Baghdad, *Iraq*	365/716 Masbah, Baghdad. tel: 95156
Tel Aviv, *Israel*	Asia House, 4, Weizman Street, Tel-Aviv. tel: 257292
Beirut, *Lebanon*	Immeuble Oflat Salha, Corniche Chouran, Beyrouth. tel: 810408
Jeddah, *Saudi Arabia*	Palestine Road, Jeddah. tel: 02-6652402

AFRICA

Alger, *Algeria*	1, Chemin Macklay, El-Biar, Alger. tel: 79-13-00
Pretoria, *South Africa*	1st Fl., Prudential Assurance Bldg., 28, Church Square, Pretoria. tel: 21-9561

ASIA

Rangoon, *Burma*	100 Natmauk Road, Rangoon. tel: 52288
Peking, *PRC*	7. Ri Tan Road, Jian Guo Men Wai, Beijin. tel: 52-2361
Shanghai, *PRC*	1517 Huai hai Road Central Shanghai. tel: 372073
Hong Kong, *Hong Kong*	Gammon House, 25th floor 12, Harcourt Road, Central. tel: 5-221184
New Delhi, *India*	Plot. No. 4 & 50-G, Chanakya- puri, New Delhi. tel: 694271
Bombay, *India*	No. 1 Babasaheb Dahanukar Marg, Cumballa Hill, Bombay 400-026. tel: 363853
Calcutta, *India*	12, Pretoria Street Calcutta 700071. tel: 44-2241

Djakarta, *Indonesia*	Jalan M.H. Thamrin 24, Jakarta tel: 324308
Medan, *Indonesia*	No. 12, Jalan Suryo, Medan, North Sumatra. tel: 321533
Surabaja, *Indonesia*	Jalan Sumatra 93, Surabaya. tel: 44677
Seoul, *Korea*	18-11, Chunghak-Dong, Chon- gro-ku, Seoul. tel: 73-5626
Pusan, *Korea*	No. 1147-11, Choryang-Dong, Dong-ku, Busan. tel: 43-9221
Kuala Lumpur, *Malaysia*	AIA Bldg., Jalan Ampang, Kuala Lumpur. tel: 22400
Islamabad, *Pakistan*	Plot No. 53-70, Ramna 5/4, Diplomatic Enclave 1, Islama- bad. tel: 20181
Karachi, *Pakistan*	233, Sommerset Street, E.I. Line, Karachi. tel: 511331
Manila, *Philippines*	375 Buendia Avenue Extension, Makati, Metro Manila. tel: 818-9011
Singapore, *Singapore*	16, Nassim Road, Singapore 1025. tel: 2358855
Colombo, *Sri Lanka*	No 20, Gregory's Road, Colombo 7. tel: 93831
Bangkok, *Thailand*	1674, New Petchburi Road, Bangkok 10. tel: 252-6151
Taipei, *Taiwan*	Interchange Association 43 Tsinan Road, Section 2, Taipei, tel: (02) 351-7250

OCEANIA

Canberra, *Australia*	112 Empire Circuit Yarralomla, Canberra A.C.T. 2600. tel: 733244
Melbourne, *Australia*	3rd floor, "Holland House," 492, St. Kilda Road, Melbourne, 3004. Victoria. tel: 267-3244
Perth, *Australia*	8th Fl., Commonwealth Bank Bldg., 150 St., George's Ter- race, Perth, W.A. 6000. tel: 09-321-7816

Sydney, *Australia*	36th Floor, CAGA Centre, 8-18 Bent St., Sydney, N.S.W. 2000. tel: 02231-3455	*Wellington,* *New Zealand*	Norwich Insurance House, 3-11 Hunter St., Wellington, 1. tel: 859-020
Brisbane, *Australia*	26th Level, Brisband Plaza, 68 Queen Street, Brisbane, Queenland 4000. tel: 0731-1438	*Auckland,* *New Zealand*	6th Flr., National Mutual Centre Bldg., 37-45, Shortland Street, Auckland, 1. tel: 34-106

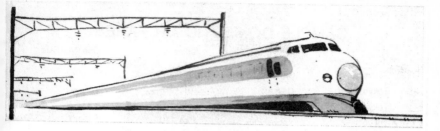

GETTING AROUND

Japan boasts one of the finest networks of public transportation in the industrialized world. Three domestic airlines have regularly scheduled flights to all areas of the country, while trains operated by the Japan National Railroad (JNR), supplemented with privately operated lines, connect virtually every city, town and village in the nation. Where train lines end, highway buses pick up and take you to even the remotest areas that Japan has to offer. Port cities are serviced by a flourishing number of coastal ferries that link all of the far flung islands with the mainland, while taxis, subways, commuter trains, buses and archaic richshaws in tourist areas move you about the great cities and prefectural towns. The general rule of thumb in Japan is that if there is a road leading anywhere, there is always a form of public transportation to take you down it. Bicycling around Japan's archipelago is an intimate and exhilirating experience for bike enthusiasts, and hitchhiking is a workable alternative for getting around and meeting the Japanese people at close hand. Other travel options include renting or buying motorcycles or cars . Whatever your choice of transportation, Japan provides much to see and convenient and enjoyable ways to get around its varied countryside.

DOMESTIC AIR SERVICE

The convenience and speed of air travel is well known and needs no lengthy description. Japan has air travel to every major city, most prefectural capitals, and to a wide array of major and monor islands scattered throughout the archipelago. Unless time is of the essence, or if an emergency arises or if you wish to take great leaps across Japan, the budget traveler can forget about air travel. For one, it's expensive and the excellent rail system, which includes the *shinkansen* (bullet train) and numerous express trains, get you to wherever you wish to go cheaper and with computer efficiency.

domestic airlines: There are 3 major ailines that offer regularly scheduled service throughout Japan. Reservations can be made and tickets can be purchased from any travel agency including JTB. The airlines are: Japan Air Lines (JAL) Headquarters, 5-37-8, Shiba, Minato-ku, Tokyo, tel: (03) 456-2111; All Nippon Airlines (ANA), 3-6-3, Irifunecho, Chuo-ku, Tokyo, tel: (03) 552-6311; TOA Domestic Airlines (at Haneda Airport), 2-2, Haneda Kuko, Ota-ku, Tokyo, tel: (03) 747-8111. Besides these main offices, there are regional offices maintained in cities throughout the country. There are also minor airlines such as Southwest Airlines (SWAL) that operate flights throughout Okinawa and small locally owned firms that fly to islands and cities in their immediate areas.

RAILWAYS

Ever since the first Japanese dignitaries warmed the seat of their *kimono* by straddling a miniature locomotive brought to Japan by the first U.S. ambassadors in the 1860s, the Japanese have had a love affair with trains. Stories circulate that when the first Japanese train made its maiden voyage between Tokyo and Yokohama a few yrs later, the Japanese luninaries riding it were aghast to find that when the doors opened, their *geta* (Japanese clogs) which they had diligently removed in Tokyo were not lined up and waiting for them to step into at Yokohama. From these humorous beginnings, the Japanese have built a rail system that is unsurpassed by any in Asia and is probably the best in the world. Every day, tens of millions of travelers, including everyone from high powered businessmen in Italian silk suits to

SAMPLE DOMESTIC AIR FARES

From	To	Airline	One Way Fare
Tokyo	Sapporo	JAL,ANA,TOA	Y23,400
Tokyo	Osaka	JAL,ANA	Y14,100
Tokyo	Sendai	ANA	Y10,600
Tokyo	Kagoshima	ANA,TOA	Y27,800
Tokyo	Naha	JAL,ANA	Y34,600
Tokyo	Nagoya	ANA	Y10,700
Osaka	Sapporo	JAL,ANA	Y34,100
Osaka	Tottori	ANA	Y 7,100
Osaka	Oita	ANA	Y12,000
Osaka	Naha	JAL,ANA	Y28,700
Nagoya	Fukuoka	ANA	Y16,300
Nagoya	Kumamoto	ANA	Y18,600
Nagoya	Miyazaki	ANA	Y18,900
Nagoya	Naha	ANA	Y31,200

farm workers carrying their bundles of tools, board over 25,000 regularly scheduled trains. These trains include everything from the *shinkasen* (bullet train) that zips along at 210 km per hr to the *Enoden*, a diminutive commuter train that services Kamakura and that time has forgotten. Trains rumble across the countryside to the farthest reaches of the nation and also whiz through the hearts of major cities. All run to the minute when the system is operating properly, which is almost all of the time, and are hopelessly late when there's a breakdown. Custom even infiltrates the train system. There's a yearly strike by train workers in the early spring that usually lasts a few days. Be aware of it and make your plans around it. Notice that the strike is usually politely announced in advance through the communications media. The rail system functioning in Japan is both nationally and privately operated.

the Japanese National Railroad (JNR):

Because of its efficient and economic services, the JNR is the most frequently used means of transportation in Japan. This governmentally operated network, known as the *Kokutetsu*, operates and maintains service throughout the entire nation, including lines to the most out-of-the way regions. The JNR network is slightly more expensive than privately owned rail service which seems to limit its lines to either well-known tourist areas or large commercial cities.

fares and types of trains: Both the JNTO and TIC offer pamphlets and hand out sheets that summarize the fares between major cities. Besides fares for the *shinkansen*, there are 3 types of fares levied by the JNR along with extra charges for berths, Green cars and reserved seats, which will be discussed separately. These basic fares relate directly to the type of trains used. They are: *futsu*, *kyuko*, and *tokkyu*. The *futsu* is a local train that stops at every rail siding and town along its course. These trains routinely operate within 100 km of a major city, servicing all of its suburbs and attendant towns and they're also found deep in the countryside where they stop at every village along their route. They're slow, folksy and the cheapest train travel in Japan. Usually their rolling stock is older, being hand-me-downs from the flashier types of train service, and inside are local people moving with the beat of everyday Japan. The *kyuko* is an ordinary express that stops at only a limited number of towns and cities between 2

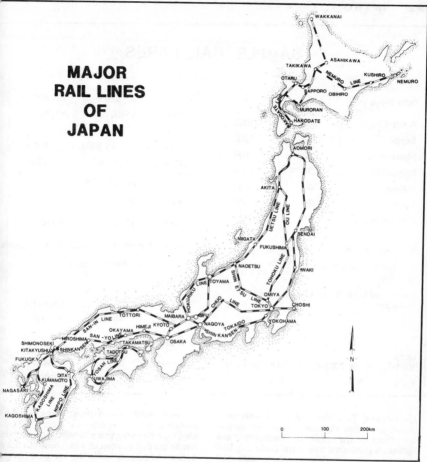

MAJOR RAIL LINES OF JAPAN

Labels on map: WAKKANAI, TAKIKAWA, ASAHIKAWA, OTARU, KUSHIRO, NEMURO, NEMURO LINE, SAPPORO, OBIHIRO, MURORAN, HAKODATE, AOMORI, AKITA, OU LINE, UETSU LINE, SENDAI, NIIGATA, FUKUSHIMA, TOHOKU LINE, NAOETSU, IWAKI, HOKURIKU LINE, TOYAMA, SHIN ETSU LINE, OMIYA, CHOSHI, CHUO LINE, GIFU, NAGOYA, TOKYO, YOKOHAMA, MAIBARA, TOKAIDO, SHIN KANSEN, TOTTORI, SAN-IN LINE, KYOTO, HIMEJI, OKAYAMA, OSAKA, SAN-YO LINE, HIROSHIMA, SHINKANSEN, TAKAMATSU, TADOTSU, SHIMONOSEKI, KITAKYUSHU, FUKUOKA, UWAJIMA, YOSAN LINE, OITA, KUMAMOTO, NAGASAKI, KAGOSHIMA LINE, NIPPO LINE, KAGOSHIMA

0   100   200km

N

points. An extra charge is added for *kyuko* (see chart) according to the km traveled. The *kyuko* is the workhorse of the budget traveler. Although more expensive than the *futsu*, it is also more efficient timewise. Sometimes it takes so long to travel on a *futsu* that the extra *kyuko* charge is worth it. On some runs, the time saved is negligible, so when buying a ticket, you should ask the price of both tickets and let the differing time factor make the decision for you. *Tokkyu* and the even speedier *Cho-Tokyu* are limited expresses or "through" trains. They either have direct runs between 2 points or stop at only one or 2 main stations. There is also a surcharge levied on the use of the *tokkyu* which is governed by the amount of km traveled (see

chart). On both the *kyuko* and *tokkyu*, there is the added service of a Green Car which is basically first class and offers more comfortable seats, service attendants and minor niceties such as hot or cold towels for the comfort of the travelers. Some long distance trains also offer overnight berths. Seats can be reserved on all trains up to a week in advance of departure, and if obtained from a travel agent, up to one month in advance. Reserved seating charges range from Y300 to Y500. The following charts represent the fares that are charged for the *kyuko* and *tokkyu* over and above the basic fare. Tickets are available at all JNR stations, JTBs and travel agents.

SAMPLE RAIL FARES

Basic futsu Charges

from Tokyo to:	km	Y
Aomori	740	Y6800
Beppu	1230	Y9200
Matsumoto	252	Y2800
Nagasaki	1331	Y9800
Niigata	330	Y3700
†Sapporo	1026	Y9500
†Takamatsu	766	Y7340

† includes JNR ferry charges, *tatami* mat accommodations.

note: add *kyuko* and *tokkyu* charges when necessary.

Kyuko Charge

up to 100 km	101-200 km	201 km and over
Y500	Y700	Y900

Tokkyu Charge

100 km	101-200 km	201-400 km
Y1000	Y1400	Y1800

401-600 km	601-800 km	800 +
Y2200	Y2600	Y3000

Green Car Charges

Y1000	Y2000	Y3000
Y4000	Y5000	Y6000

Available at green windows at all JNR stations

Berth Charges

A Class:

Upper	Lower	Roomette
Y7000	Y8000	Y10,000

B Class:

Upper	Middle	Lower
Y3500-4500	Y3500-4000	Y3500-Y4500

special fares: Excursion type tickets available in Japan are called *shuyuken*. There are certain variations on *shuyuken*, but basically these tickets give unlimited train travel (including JNR ferries, ropeways, buses etc. where applicable) from a starting point through a designated area and back to the starting point during a designated period of time. The fare is fixed and savings will depend upon how much you avail yourself of the transportation facilities. Unless a traveler has a basically fixed itinerary, a *shuyuken* will give only limited savings. Most times it's better to buy a *kyuko* or *tokkyu* ticket for the long hops and then use *futsu* in the immediate area. The glaring exception to this rule is a 20 day *shuyuken* that's offered for traveling in Hokkaido. Since there are no private rail lines in Hokkaido, the JNR has a monopoly on service, and because of this, it calls almost every train a *kyuko* which saddles you with the extra charge. The distances in Hokkaido are relatively large, so train travel can be expensive. The Hokkaido *shuyuken* can save you a bundle, but you must remember that you can only purchase this ticket *before* you arrive in Hokkaido, not once you get there as is the case with all *shuyuken*. If you intend to purchase a *shuyuken* for Hokkaido, the most common starting points are Sendai and Aomori. Both TIC and JNTO will be able to give you additional information.   JNR *rail pass:* There is also an unlimited travel JNR Rail Pass offered. These passes, similar to the Eurailpass, are good for 7, 15, or 30 days. So far they can only be purchased from Japan Airlines Offices abroad. Some say that you can get around this stipulation and purchase them in Japan, but there will be a great deal of rigamarole involved. If you intend to purchase a JNR Rail Pass, it's best to make arrangements at any JAL office in your home country and purchase it before you arrive.

the Shinkansen: The shinkansen, as it's called in Japan, is known to the English-speaking world as the "Bullet." This name was derived because it was the fastest public land transport in the world, being topped only recently by a faster train in the French National rail system. The shinkansen whips along at 210 km per hr on a continuously welded track imbedded in concrete and because of its smooth ride, the speed at which you're actually traveling is deceptive. Today, this engineering marvel stretches for about 800 km along the Pacific coast from Tokyo to Hakata on Kyushu island. Its main stations heading W from Tokyo are located at Nagoya, Kyoto, Osaka, Kobe, Okayama, Hiroshima and Hakata and are designated by the prefix shin, i.e. shin-Osaka. Along its course, it passes by the foot of Mt. Fuji and a view of these radically different symbols juxtaposed side by side capsulizes the paradoxical spirit of modern Japan. Shinkansen lines are now being constructed to expand the system to, Sapporo in Hokkaido and Niigata on the Japan Sea side. The Hokkaido branch will include the longest undersea tunnel in the world (55 km) as the train slips below the waters of the Tsugaru Straits separating Honshu from Hokkaido. There are 2 services on the Shinkansen: The Hikari and the Kodama. They both travel at the same speeds, but the Kodama makes more stops along its route and runs only through the heavily built up areas between Tokyo and Osaka. One Hikari run is between Tokyo and Hakata stopping only at Nagoya and Kyoto along the way. You could ride the Kodama to Nagoya and then switch there to the Hikari if you intend to travel past Kyoto. Other Hikari arrive at Shin-Osaka Eki, where there are an additional 4 services for onward going travel. Two go straight to Hakata while the other 2 terminate at Okayama or Hiroshima. Although reserved seats are not absolutely necessary, except during peak seasons, you should book one. Tickets are available at any Green Window in JNR stations and through the JTB and travel agents. The fares charged are definitely not within the budget spectrum. They're about the same as internal flights, so you can expect to ride the shinkansen more as a one-time joy ride and not as your normal means of transportation. There are numerous trains throughout the day with one leaving the major stations about once every 15 minutes. They start running at 0600 and the last train from Tokyo to Shin-Osaka leaves at 2100, although there are a few later trains leaving from Hakata. There are meals served on the shinkansen, but they are notorious for their mediocrity, so purchase a tasty bento at a train

station before you leave. Shinkansen tickets are also available from JAL offices in the U.S. and Canada. JNTO and TIC provide a useful pamphlet of schedules and fares entitled, "Condensed Railway Timetables." Besides containing information on the shinkansen, this pamphlet also gives the schedules and rates of the most commonly used kyuko and tokkyu runs.

FERRIES

Since Japan is an island nation with many far flung islands as part of its archipelago, public ferry service is very well developed. For any budget traveler wishing to take long hops down the coast of Honshu, or especially if you wish to visit Hokkaido, Shikoku, Kyushu and the Ryukyu Islands including Okinawa, ferries are the most economical and fun way of doing so. There are many types of ferries and some are just large launches traveling for an hour or so between the main islands of the mini-archipelagoes of Japan, but others are very large ocean going crafts that may be at sea for 30 hrs or more. Part of this ferry system includes zippy hydrofoils for short jaunts and car carrying boats as well. The JNR usually have ferries where their rail lines end at the coast, while other companies are privately owned. There are varying accommodations aboard these boats and they include everything from expensive private cabins to economical tatami mat class (actually carpet) which house a number of people in one large state room all sleeping on a claimed portion of the floor. There is usually a 20% student discount offered for tatami class with proper identification, and if the trip is long, a night's lodging fee is saved.

ferry travel: The boats that make long voyages often have restaurants, snack bars and junk food machines. Boiling water is always at hand so you may consider taking your own supply of easily prepared foods and beverages to further offset costs. The boats, especially in tatami class, are very folksy and offer one of the best windows into the lives and social attitudes of the common Japanese. People, especially the Japanese, in such close proximity become friendly quickly and it's almost a matter of course to be offered food and sake, and to be included in the good-natured frivolity that accompanies most Japanese groups when on vacation. Although the ferries are comfortable and modern, they're a far cry from luxury liners.

SAMPLE FERRY FARES

Route	Ferry Company	Cheapest fare to furthest point	Time
1. Tokyo-Tomakomai (Hokkaido)	Nippn Enkai Ferry Co. Tokyo tel: (03) 574-9561 Tomakomai tel: (0144) 34-3121	Y11,500	32 hrs
2. Tokyo-Kushiro (Hokkaido)	Kinkai Yusen Co. Tokyo tel: (03) 447-6551 Kushiro tel: (0154) 24-5134	Y13,500	33 hrs
3. Tokyo-Kochi (Shikoku)	Nihon Kosoku Ferry Co. Tokyo tel: (03) 274-1801 Kochi tel: (0888) 31-0520	Y14,500	21 hrs
4. Tokyo-Kokura (Kyushu) via Tokushima (Shikoku)	Ocean Tokyo Ferry Co. Tokyo tel: (03)567-0971 Kokura tel: (093) 582-6761 Tokushima tel: (0886) 62-0489	Y12,000	36 hrs
5. Tokyo (Kawasaki)-Hyuga (Kyushu)	Nippon Car Ferry Co. Tokyo tel:)03) 563-3991	Y15,500	20 hrs
6. Osaka (Kobe)-Beppu	Kansai Steamship Co. Tokyo tel: (03) 274-4271 Osaka tel: (06) 572-5181 OR Hiroshima Green Ferry Co. Osaka tel: (06) 532-3121 Hiroshima tel: (0822) 28-1665	Y 6500 Y 4500	15 hrs 11 hrs
7. Osaka-Hyuga (Kyushu)	Nippon Car Ferry Co. Osaka tel: (06) 345-6771 Hyuga tel: (09825) 2811	Y 7500	14 hrs
9. Hiroshima-Beppu	Hiroshima tel: (0822) 48-2678 Beppu tel: (0977) 21-2364	Y 3100	9 hrs
10. Tokyo-Naha via Kagoshima	Ryukyu Kaiun Co. Tokyo tel: (03) 281-1831 Naha tel: (0988) 68-1126 OR: Oshima Unyu Co. Tokyo tel: (03) 273-8911 Naha tel: (0988) 68-7783	Y18,000	60 hrs

There are usually few, if any, deck chairs provided and no organized social activities. You must make your own fun. One boat, an oddity, plies between Tokyo and Kushiro in Hokkaido and does offer a swimming pool. If you're traveling through Japan by bicycle, it can accompany you on board at no extra charge. Some of the longest ferry routes include: Tokyo to Tomakomai or Kushiro in Hokkaido; Maizuru and Tsuruga on the Japan Sea side to Otaru in Hokkaido via Niigata; Tokyo to Osaka and then from Osaka over veritable ferry super highway through the Inland Sea, stopping at various ports on Shikoku and Kyushu; from Kagoshima heading S, island hopping all the way t Okinawa. TIC and JNTO offices hand ou numerous mimeographed sheets on ferr service and tickets can be purchased at an JTB, travel agency or directly from the ferr companies, who usually have offices at th departing piers.

BUSES, PRIVATE TRANSPORTATION AND MAPS

In every travel section throughout this book, an effort has been made to give you adequate alternatives for touring the sights and getting around the major cities. Full listings under "Getting Around" include buses, subways, ferries, taxis and hitchhiking. You should refer to the travel sections for precise information and the following is offered to give you a general idea of what to expect. Every Japanese city and town has an urban bus system. Far flung villages are also connected by bus. There are always plenty of taxis available and a few cities, namely Tokyo, Sapporo, Yokohama, Nagoya and Osaka, offer a subway system. Hitchhicking, especially for foreigners, is always good and there are car rental agencies, motorcycle sales and bicycle sales and rentals all over Japan.

buses: Wherever train travel leaves off, usually in remote areas, buses are your best travel alternative, and you can safely assume that there is always at least one going in your direction. For the most part, rural bus terminals are either adjacent to or in very close proximity to train stations, and their schedules usually are made to conincide with incoming trains. Using buses to travel between cities is not a good idea because they're usually slower and more expensive than trains. The biggest exception is in Okinawa where there's no train service and well maintained and efficiently run highway buses are your only choice of public transport. Within cities, buses go everywhere, but the major drawback is that their oftentimes convoluted routes are marked only in Japanese. If you do use city buses, save yourself much time and grief by inquiring beforehand which bus to take and jotting down all the *norikae* (changes). Upon entering, it's usually sufficient to inform the driver where you are going merely by saying the name and he'll inform you when to get off and where to wait for your connecting bus, if there is one. Often, Japanese passengers will do their utmost to guide you along in the right direction, and some will even take you under tow to your destination. While waiting at *basu noriba* (bus stops), just give any waiting passenger the name of your destination and they'll set you straight.

fares: Bus fares are usually a simple matter. If you intend to use a highway bus between cities, this involves a straightforward ticket purchased at the bus station. For most bus travel within a city, there's a flat fare clearly marked that is charged and paid upon entering. There's always a little box upon entering that will change Y100 coins, and some have changers for Y500 notes. The other method most commonly used on rural runs is the "pay as you go" method. Upon entering the bus, usually through the side doors, there will be a little machine dispensing numbered tickets. Take one. As the bus moves along, a meter above the driver's head will start clicking and this will indicate the fare. Simply match the fare indicated on the meter with your numbered ticket and pay it as you leave through the front doors. Except for a few city runs, there are no transfer tickets. JNR does operate convenient inter city runs between Tokyo-Nagoya-Kyoto and Osaka. These buses leave at various times throughout the day, but the best ones to take are the night buses, although a reservation will be necessary. Pertinent information on these JNR highway buses is given in the corresponding travel chapters and TIC and JNTO have hand-out sheets of these and buses in general that can be useful.

taxis: Taxis are found in every city, town and even village throughout Japan. They cruise the streets and can be hailed by a wave (don't whistle), but there are always some in designated taxi stands, usually around train stations. They are no bargain and should be used only in an emergency, when other public transportaiton has stopped running for the night or if you are hopelessly lost. Taxis charge Y380 minimum for the first 2 km and then Y70 for every 405 m thereafter. In heavy traffic, which is common, they charge Y50 for every 2 min, 20 seconds in which they are moving less than 10 km/hr and when you really need them, which is at night, they charge an extra 20% between 2300 and 0500 and an additional 20% if they're summoned by phone. You will sometimes see people holding up more than one finger when hailing a taxi. This usually happens late at night or during a rain storm. The number of fingers that they hold up indicates how much they're willing to multiply the actual fare by to get a ride (3 fingers = 3 times the fare, etc.). The only good note is that there is NO TIPPING in Japan unless the driver performs an extra service such as helping you with your luggage which they normally don't do. *taxi tips:* When a taxi stops or when getting out, do not attempt to open the door. The driver has a remote control and he will open and close the door for you. Unless you are going to a well known landmark, hotel or train station, don't be surprised if the driver cannot find the address and stops many times to ask directions at police boxes. This is common practice. You're not being ripped off or charged extra. Whenever possible, have a Japanese friend or your hotel clerk write the address of your destination in Japanese to facilitate matters. Wherever you're staying, try to take a book of matches which are common to almost every establishment. Most matchbook covers list the name, phone number and address, and oftentimes inlcude a tiny map giving directions back to the establishment. They're very handy to save you from getting lost.

automobiles: The first thing to remember for those foreigners not accustomed to it, is that the Japanese drive on the left. If you're a pedestrian, make sure to look in the opposite direction before you cross a street or you could be in for a nasty surprise. If you're a traveler who has either purchased or rented a car, it doesn't take long to acquaint yourself with driving on the opposite side of the road. Straightaways are easy and when making a turn, just remember to keep the driver's side to the center of the road, not to the curb side. Unless a traveler intends to live in Japan or to be there for at least a year, it's simply not worth buying or even renting a car. A business person, however may have limited use for one. Automobiles are expensive to begin with, redundant because of the excellent public transportation available, and of dubious convenience because of the almost impossible situation of finding a parking space. Some city areas require proof of a parking space before you can even bring an automobile there, and these car parks in congested city areas can cost almost as much per month as apartments.

costs, laws and requirements: If you do decide to operate an automobile while in Japan, you can drive on an International Driver's License or convert your home country's license to a Japanese one. Have a license before you arrive or you must complete an exhaustive training course to get a Japanese one. You should also consider that gasoline costs approximately Y100 per litre and oil is Y1200 per litre. The speed limit will make most Europeans and Americans squirm. The fastest limit on the largest expressways is 60 km/hr; most roads are posted at only 40 km/hr and in cities you crawl along sucking exhaust at a pokey 30 km/hour. Why torture yourself? If you stil must have a car,

rental charges are comparable to those in most western countries and the purchase price of a new or used vehicle is also comparable. Here, like everywhere else, you are in the realm of car dealers and used car salesmen who are the same world over. Besides the initial price, you should be aware of a Japanese regulation called a *shaken* (this sounds ominously like a "shake down" which it very much resembles). A *shaken* is a combination of inspection, licensing fee, road tax and insurance. It is levied upon the initial purchase of a new car and every 2 yrs thereafter, which includes used cars. The rate you pay is proportional to the size and horsepower of the vehicle. When looking at used cars, and especially at cheap ones, make sure to find out when the *shaken* comes due, because in some instances it can be as much as the purchase price, itself, although with higher priced cars, this is not the case. An average *shaken* is Y100,000. For any information regarding motor vehicles in Japan, contact the Japan Automobile Federation, 3-5-8, Shiba-koen, Minato-ku, Tokyo, tel: (03) 436-2811. There are branch offices throughout Japan and the Federation has reciprocal service agreements with most automobile associations throughout the world. Rental cars are available at most airports. The following are only 2 of many companies: Japaren Co., 12-7, Shinjuku, 2-chome, Tokyo, tel: (03) 352-7635; Nipon Rent-A-Car (Hertz), Jinnan Bldg., 4-3 Udagawa-cho, Shibuya-ku, Tokyo, tel: (03) 463-8881.

motorcycles: Touring Japan on a motorcycle gives you as much freedom of movement as owning a car with a lot less hassle. Motorcyles are cheaper to buy and run and are much easier to park. Because of the slow speed limits enforced in Japan, the danger of an accident is also greatly reduced, and so a single traveler or a couple could consider this means of transpor tation. You must remember, however, that i you must take a ferry, you will be charged extra (about ½ the normal fare) to take you motorcycle along, and on some very small, oute island ferries you will not be able to take it at all. The same considerations apply if you find yourself in a position where you must take the train. The motorcycle will be charged separately and will be placed in a baggage car. The bes way to purchase a motorcycle is through a private owner and optimally through a foreign owner. Oftentimes, ads appear in the *Japan Times* with excellent listings also in the *Tokyo Weekender*. The Japanese tend to use motorbikes less as pleasure vehicles and more for practical purposes. Therefore, many of the used bikes, although generally well-maintained, have been used hard. Foreigners are accustomed to big machines over 750cc being exported from Japan. In the "Land of Motorcycles" these big honkers are a rarity. It is increasingly difficult for Japanese to get licenses for big bikes, so the majority that you'll find are in the 250cc range. This means that big bikes are often better financial deals than the smaller ones. You should not consider purchasing a motorcycle unless you intend to tour Japan extensively for at least 2 months. Any time touring less than this will not offset the purchase price. You must also consider resale unless you intend to export the vehicle, which is a headache. All pertinent information for exporting is also available from the Japan Automobile Association. To resell the bike, allow plenty of time (2 weeks) and place an ad in the *Tokyo Weekender* as well as the *Japan Times*. If you get no bites, then you can try taking your bike to a motorcycle dealer (many are located around Ueno Eki in Tokyo). If at last resort you go to a dealer, they may refuse to buy your bikes at any cost regardless of condition if it's an old model (a 10 yr old bike is a dinosaur).

hitchhiking: Japan for foreigners is a hitchhiker's paradise (you won't need the thumbs of Sissy Hankshaw). The Japanese, themselves, except for a few students, are not into hitchhiking, but they all recognize it and know what's going on. Hitching is especially OK for a *gaijin* because Japanese realize that you don't have your own means of transportation and many are more than happy to give you a lift. There are a few rules of etiquette which you should know. If a Japanese person stops for you, in their mind you become their temporary responsibility. They will go to all lengths to please you, even driving out of their way to get you to where you're going. There are many tales spread by hitchhikers who have reported that drivers have gone hours out of their way for the hitchhiker, buying meals and offering snacks as they go. At times, it is advisable to carry cardboard on which to write in *kanji* your destination, but the good old thumb is sufficient. Sometimes writing on a sign backfires since most drivers take them literally. For instance, if your sign says, "Tokyo," a driver heading towards Tokyo won't pick you up because they're not going exactly to Tokyo. The same thing happens when you get into a car or when one pulls up. They may ask where (*doko*) you are going and if they're not going exactly there,

although they may be going close by, they may say, "Sorry" and drive off. To avoid this, carry a map and beat them to the punch by asking them where they're going. Offer the map so that they can point to their destination. Learn one phrase: "*Kono kokudo massugu*" (Straight ahead on this highway) and by saying this, you can avoid destination problems. Just follow your map and when you get to a crossroads where you must turn off, say: "Stop please" (*Tomatte kudasai*). For long hops, it's best to get a ride from a truck driver. These "knights of the road" are friendly and folksy. They'll also make an effort to get another truck driver to take you along once they've arrived at their destination. This also happens with car drivers who might ask around or even flag down a car for you! Many drivers will often stop and buy you something to eat or a *bento* for the road. They will never allow you to buy for them. Any gift is appreciated, so if you're intending to hitchhike, stock up on munchies, chewing gum or cigarettes to offer to your driver. Communications are difficult, so to break the ice you might try the universal language of music. Sing them a folk song and they'll probably reciprocate by singing a Japanese one, which most Japanese love to do. In this way, you can pass the time and fill the long pauses between halting communications. You should also know that many Japanese will be convinced that you want to be taken to the nearest train station no matter what you've previously said. Don't be surprised if many rides end up there. Female hitchhikers should note that although drivers may seem overly friendly by buying lunch or other meals or snacks, this is just what it appears to be with no sexual overtones intended. You have less of a chance of being hassled in Japan than in most countries. Since most Japanese cities have so many maze-like intersecting roads, it's best to take either a bus or a train out of town to the first stop where the road you need to take is most easily followed. You are not allowed to hitchhike on expressways. To get a ride, stand by the toll gate. If your driver is going to be turning off, ask to be let out at the *tsugi no kyukeijo* (Rest Area) and you can carry on safely from there. Politely approach a truck or car with map in hand and it's usually no problem getting a ride.

cycling: If you have the stamina and time, there is no better way of getting an intimate view of Japan than by *jitensha* (bicycle). There are bicycle shops everywhere in Japan and it's no problem to get a bike that will fit both your body

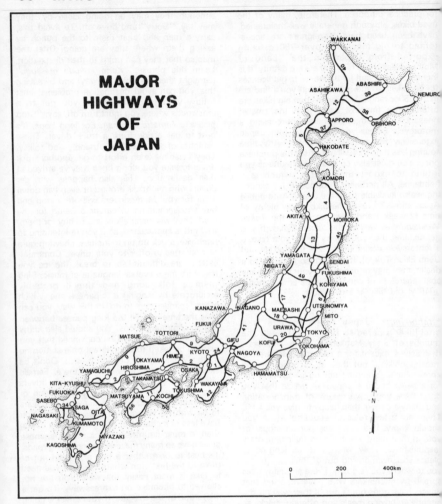

MAJOR HIGHWAYS OF JAPAN

WAKKANAI

ABASHIRI

ASAHIKAWA

NEMURO

SAPPORO

OBIHORO

HAKODATE

AOMORI

AKITA

MORIOKA

YAMAGATA

NIIGATA

SENDAI

FUKUSHIMA

KORIYAMA

KANAZAWA   NAGANO   MAEBASHI   UTSUNOMIYA

FUKUI

URAWA   MITO

MATSUE   TOTTORI   GIFU   KOFU   TOKYO

KYOTO   NAGOYA   YOKOHAMA

OKAYAMA   HIMEJI

YAMAGUCHI   HIROSHIMA   OSAKA   HAMAMATSU

KITA-KYUSHU   TAKAMATSU   WAKAYAMA

FUKUOKA   MATSUYAMA   TOKUSHIMA

SASEBO   SAGA   KOCHI

NAGASAKI   OITA

KUMAMOTO

MIYAZAKI

KAGOSHIMA

0   200   400km

and your pocketbook. For a new touring bike, expect to spend about Y40,000 although used ones go for much less. If you don't wish to travel by bicycle exclusively, it's an easy matter to rent a bike for the day. Rental shops are usually found close to train stations. You will see many Japanese touring by bicycle and they usually have a *rinko* (collapsible model) that easily disassembles and fits into a carrying case that can be taken aboard trains. If you plan to do this, it's best to belong to the Japan Cycling Association which dispenses a membership card for an initial joining fee of Y600 and a yearly fee of Y1500. This entitles you to take the bike aboard trains for a charge of Y150. The Japan Cycling Association has its main office in Tokyo at: 3-8-1 Ueno, Taito Ku, Tokyo, tel: (03) 833-3967. For more information from English speaking personnel, you can also contact: Japan Bicycle Promotion Institute, Nihon Jitensha Kaikan Bldg., 9-3 Akasaka, 1-chome, Minato-ku, Tokyo, tel (03) 583-5444.

<u>maps:</u> Every effort has been made throughout this book to provide useful travel maps of the areas described. To supplement these maps, you should also get free maps of Japan offered by TIC and JNTO. The most useful one is called, "Tourist Map of Japan" and highlights the entire country with insert maps of the major cities on the back. JNTO and TIC also offer city maps, ie. Tokyo, Kyoto, etc. If you intend to purchase detailed maps in foreign languages, these are available from any bookstore mentioned in "Facts, Figures and Practicalities." A good choice is *Teikoku's Complete Atlas of Japan.* Don't let the title scare you. This atlas is a rugged paperback about the same size and weight as a magazine. It offers details of roads, train lines and ferry routes through all of the areas of Japan. Its index is comprehensive and it's very easy to use. Another excellent series of maps is foldup types offered by Nippon Kokuseisha Co., Ltd. These are also available in bookstores for about Y500 each. The best and most useful choices in this series are "Road Map of Japan, Detailed" and "Japan Railroad Map." The one drawback with these maps is that although the paper used appears sturdy, it will tear on the seams after repeaated use. The Nippon Kokuseisha co. is located at 18-24 Kohinata, 1-chome, Bunkyo-ku, Tokyo, tel: (03) 947-4611.

<u>travel agents:</u> There are charter members of Japan Association of Travel Agents (JATA) located in almost every city of Japan, with a number to choose from in the larger cities. For an excellent travel agent in Tokyo, try Mr. Bosworth at Ikon Travel, tel: (03) 400-9050. A long term resident of Tokyo, Mr. Bosworth knows the ins and outs of budget travel and can arrange low priced fares throughout Asia and the rest of the world, and can help with almost any travel problem that arises. Another travel agency in Tokyo with a good reputation for low fares is Air Voyages, tel:(03) 467-3795. The following list is only a sampling of JATA approved agencies. JNTO offices as well as TIC can provide you with comprehensive lists and information so that you can choose an appropriate one.

TRAVEL AGENTS

Japan Travel Bureau, Inc.
1-6-4, Marunouchi, Chiyoda-ku, Tokyo, 100
tel: 284-7026. telex: 24418

American Express International Inc.
3-16-26 Roppongi, Minato-ku, Tokyo, 106
tel: 586-4321. cable: AMEXTRAN.
telex: J 25497

Japan Tours International, Inc.
Dai-Ichi Taisho Bldg., 1-9-12, Nishi-Shinjuku,
Shinjuku-ku, Tokyo, 160
tel: 342-1911. telex: J28408

Sotetsu Kanko Co., Ltd.
1-3-23, Kitasaiwai, Nishi-ku, Yokohama, 220
tel: 045-319-2301

Jusvel Co., Ltd.
200, 1-3-1, Umeda, Kita-ku, Osaka, 530
tel: 06-345-0701

Showa Travel Service Co., Ltd.
1277-3 Aza-Ishidohminami, Oaza-Minami-
Nagano, Nagano, 380. tel: 0262-27-2145

Meiho Tourist Co., Ltd.
1-23-36, Izumi, Higashi-ku, Nagoya, 461
tel: 052-951-0111. telex: 444-3656

North Japan Overseas Travel Co., Ltd.
Kahoku Bldg., 1-14-35, Ichibancho, Sendai,
980. tel: 0222-27-6106. telex: 852814

Hiroden Kanko Co., Ltd.
1-2-23, Kamiya-cho, Hiroshima City, 730
tel: 0822-47-9868

Sanden Koku Travel Service
1-12, Hayamacho, Shimonoseki City, 750
tel: 0832-31-1000. telex: 6822-97

Kyushu Sangyo Kotsu Co., Ltd.
3-35, Sakuracho, Kumamoto City, 860
tel: 0963-25-1111. telex: 762770

Nangoku Traffic Co., Ltd.
11-5, Chuo-chu, Kagoshima, 890
tel: 0992-54-8111

Tosaden Travel Service Co., Ltd.
1-5-35, Harimayacho, Kochi, 780
tel: 0888-82-0111. telex: 5882-530

Mitsuwa Travel Service Co., Ltd.
Mitsui Bldg., Nishi 4-chome, Kita Nijo,
Chuo-ku, Sapporo, 060. cable: MITSUWA
KOKU SAPPORO. tel: 011-241-1586.
telex: 932-523

'Okinawa Tourist Service Inc.
1-2-3, Matsuo, Naha, 900
tel: 0988-62-1111. tele: 795-220

DISTRICTS AND PREFECTURES OF JAPAN

DISTRICT	PREFECTURES	CAPITALS
Hokkaido	Hokkaido	1. Sapporo
Tohoku	Aomori	2. Aomori
	Akita	3. Akita
	Iwate	4. Morioka
	Yamagata	5. Yamagata
	Miyagi	6. Sendai
	Fukushima	7. Fukushima
Kanto	Ibaraki	8. Mito
	Tochigi	9. Utsunomiya
	Gunma	10. Maebashi
	Saitama	11. Urawa
	Chiba	12. Chiba
	Tokyo	13. Tokyo
	Kanagawa	14. Yokohama
Chubu	Niigata	15. Niigata
	Nagano	16. Nagano
	Toyama	17. Toyama
	Ishikawa	18. Kanazawa
	Fukui	19. Fukui
	Gifu	20. Gifu
	Yamanashi	21. Kofu
	Aichi	22. Nagoya
	Shizuoka	23. Shizuoka
Kinki	Shiga	24. Otsu
	Mie	25. Tsu
	Kyoto	26. Kyoto
	Nara	27. Nara
	Osaka	28. Osaka
	Hyogo	29. Kobe
	Wakayama	30. Wakayama
Chugoku	Tottori	31. Tottori
	Okayama	32. Okayama
	Shimane	33. Matsue
	Hiroshima	34. Hiroshima
	Yamaguchi	35. Yamaguchi
Shikoku	Kagawa	36. Takamatsu
	Tokushima	37. Tokushima
	Ehime	38. Matsuyama
	Kochi	39. Kochi
Kyushu	Fukuoka	40. Fukuoka
	Oita	44. Oita
	Saga	42. Saga
	Nagasaki	43. Nagasaki
	Kumamoto	44. Kumamoto
	Miyazaki	45. Miyazaki
	Kagoshima	46. Kagoshima
Okinawa	Okinawa	47. Naha

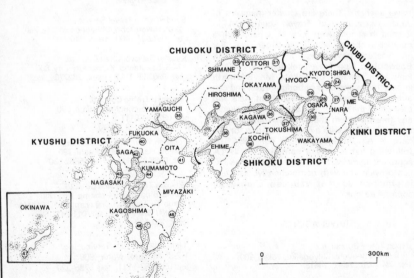

0   300km

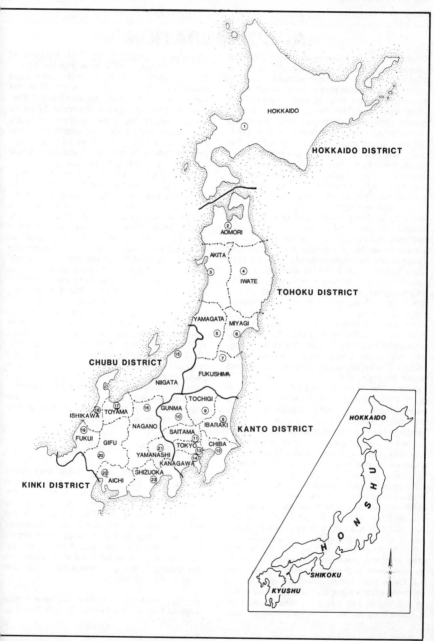

ACCOMMODATION

One of the major considerations facing a budget traveler once they've arrived in Japan is the price for nightly accommodations. Luckily, Japan has an exceptionally wide spectrum of accommodations with varying prices from which to choose. They include western hotels, *ryokan* (traditional Japanese inns), *minshuku* (guest homes), *yusu hosuteru* (youth hostels), *kokumin kyuka mura* (national vacation villages), *kokumin shukusha* (people's lodges), business hotels, *shukubo* (temple lodgings) and camping. After costs, most travelers are concerned with the quality of the accommodations, especially the cleanliness. In 99% of the cases, Japanese accommodations are meticulously clean. The proprietors of even the most meager *minshuku* take pride in their establishments and the Japanese people, themselves, are on the whole the cleanest in the world and attach an almost religious significance to a daily *ofuro* (scalding hot bath). In short, you don't have to worry about any creepy crawlers. The only exception is that in western hotels or any other type of accommodation that features carpeting, you'll notice that it's not looked after as well as it normally is in western nations. This is probably due to the fact that the Japanese have a short tradition in dealing with carpeting, and any place where shoes can be worn, carpeting included, is not generally considered to be an area where spotless cleanliness is required. The range of prices *between* types of accommodations mentioned is significant with a much smaller price range *within* the types themselves, except for *ryokan*. It is almost an unofficial rule of thumb that prices are fixed nationwide, especially with youth hostels and government run accommodations. If you stop in a small town and inquire the price at an average *minshuku*, you can bet that the prices of the other *minshuku* in town will vary less than Y100. This reduces your ability to ferret out cheaper places to stay as in the remainder of Asia, but you do know what to expect in advance and you can rest assured that you're not paying any more than the going rate. Bargaining is not the norm when looking for a place to stay, and may even be considered an insult by the owners. However, many proprietors will lower their prices during off season and may even offer a slight discount out of kindness to a foreigner, but you can't always count on it. Leave it up to them to make the suggestion.

choosing accommodations: All foreign and domestic offices of JNTO as well as the TICs in Tokyo, Narita and Kyoto offer numerous brochures and hand out sheets on all of the accommodations mentioned. These are broken down by areas and give rudimentary directions and an idea of costs. In the travel section of this book, after each area, city, island or village mentioned, there is, in most instances, a section entitled "accommodations." Naturally, it would have been impossible to give every accommodation available, but these lists do give a range from which to choose and a good idea of costs. The prices given are based on *single occupancy*. Like all other prices, they are susceptible to change without notice, but should be accurate to within Y500. Wherever there is a positive deviation from the norm (which can include an exceptionally inexpensive price, outstanding food or magnificent surroundings), the accommodation is handled in the travel section almost as if it were a "sight" as well as being mentioned under "accommodations." These exceptions are rare in Japan. During peak seasons, which vary depending upon area but is usually during the summer months, it's wise to make reservations. This can be easily done without charge at any JTB or private travel agency. JNTO and the Tokyo TIC will not make reservations, but the Kyoto TIC will, if the accommodations fall within the greater Kyoto area. The following descriptions of accommodations will deal with what to expect in the nature of quality, services, etiquette, price and helpful offices and organizations.

WESTERN HOTELS

These facilities are exactly what their name implies and they range in quality from internationally famous luxury hotels, usually found in major Japanese cities, down to delapidated, but clean flop houses. On the positive side, western hotels are convenient because of their familiar services and facilities, but they offer the least value for your money. Although some offer Japanese style rooms, the experience of staying in them is not unique and is distinctly unJapanese.

services: Even the smallest of these hotels normally have central heating, air conditioning, western beds and furniture, western toilets, parking lots, TVs, restaurants and bars. The larger ones will often include swimming pools, sauna baths, tennis courts, westernized doctors on call, convention facilities, money changers and interpreters. At the largest hotels in the big metropolitan areas there are always foreign speaking staff and travel arrangement facilities. Many also include boutiques and shopping arcades. Besides these services, the hotels may also offer shuttle buses to and from airports and railway stations, baggage handling and organized tours. For the timid traveler or preoccupied businessman, western hotels are the best bet, and even budget travelers may wish to use these facilities during their first night in Japan until they get their bearings. After that, try to avoid them in most instances in order to get a richer Japanese experience and to keep costs within reasonable limits.

rates: The rates given throughout this book are for single occupancy and the average price for a moderate hotel is Y5000 and up. Many hotels will accept international credit cards and have facilities for converting foreign currency to *yen*. If your room costs less than Y4000 per person per night, there is no tax. If it exceeds Y4000, Y2000 will be subtracted and a 10% tax will be levied on the remainder. This includes any meals or drinks that you have while at the hotel. There is no custom for individual tipping to doormen, bell hops and others, and it is only done if you ask for special, individual services. However, a 15% service charge is customarily added to all bills. Keep these 2 extra charges in mind when deciding on a place to stay. Sometimes there are discounts offered to groups, for long stays and during the slack season. Inquire at your travel agency. Eating at hotel restaurants is also an expensive proposition. If the menu offered includes international cuisine and especially if it's in a foreign language (primarily English), know that the price will be 3 to 4 times higher than normal. Prices charged at hotel bars for drinks are also high, but you don't risk the price gouging that can easily befall any unknowing foreigner who haplessly falls into a hostess bar. Observe normal western etiquette in all circumstances, except if you're staying in a Japanese style room where you must remove your shoes on all *tatami* mat areas and douse away all traces of soap before getting into the Japanese bath.

information: At JNTO and TIC, pick up a copy of *Hotels and Ryokan in Japan* and a handout

sheet entitled, *Reasonable Accommodations in Japan.* For reservations, contact any JTB office or JTB National Headquarters (see "Facts, Figures and Practicalities" for address). Any member of the Japan Association of Travel Agents (JATA) (there are over 100) can make reservations and give advice. Two are: American Express International, 3-16-26, Roppongi, Minato-ku, Tokyo 106, tel: (03) 586-4321 and Fujita Travel Service Co., Ltd., 7-2-22 Ginza, Chuo-ku, Tokyo 104, tel: (03) 573-1040. A list of nationwide travel agents is also given in "Facts, Figures and Practicalities."

a *ryokan* (traditional Japanese inn)

RYOKAN

To immerse yourself fully in the Japanese experience, you should try to spend at least one night in a traditional Japanese hotel called a *ryokan*. The history of *ryokan* dates back thousands of years and they maintain some of the finest cultural traditions to the present day. The highest standards at *ryokan* dictate that they are not only geared to the physical comfort of their guests, but that they also appeal to their aesthetic side. Many of the rooms open out into exquisite gardens in which you may walk or merely contemplate. Two meals (breakfast and dinner) are also included in the price and these are usually of Japanese gourmet quality. If you make arrangements, the *ryokan* staff will prepare western foods, but these, in most instances, will be merely adequate. The average price of a *ryokan*, Y10,000, is unfortunately not geared to a budget traveler, but if used sporadically, especially when you consider that 2 meals are included, they are not financially crippling. Sometimes a foreigner turning up unexpectedly at a *ryokan* will not be admitted. This is usually due to a misunderstanding by the *ryokan* owners who feel that they will not be able to please you and the etiquette required of you will be "too foreign." Also, some *ryokan* are almost private and will admit guests only if they have been properly introduced by former respected clientele. In most cases, this is not a problem.

rates: A typical *ryokan* stay costs approximately Y10,000 which includes two sumptuous meals. A 10% tax and 15% service charge are levied in the same way as for a western hotel. *Ryokan* vary greatly in service and atmosphere and you must develop a good eye for choosing them. At the pinnacle, they offer the absolute best that Japan has in ways of accommodation, and staying in them is a totally enjoyable experience. At worst, some are bland, uninspired establishments and are only *ryokan* because their owners call them *ryokan*. Although the atmosphere and services vary greatly, the prices charged do not. Choose carefully and the Y10,000 will be the best you ever spend (or if you make a mistake, the most aggravating).

services, food and etiquette: When you arrive at the entranceway for a *ryokan*, you will be met by a maid who will bow you a welcome and invite you inside. After removing your shoes and slipping into house slippers (remove even house slippers before stepping onto *tatami* matting of rooms and use special toilet slippers found at the door to the toilet, only in the toilet) follow her to your room where she will set about making you comfortable. You will be given a *yukata* (Japanese robe) used for lounging, and sometimes a pair of *geta* (Japanese wooden clogs). It's quite acceptable to walk outside in the area of a *ryokan* with *yukata* and *geta* and this is one of the only times that the Japanese routinely wear this immensely comfortable

garment and these not so comfortable clogs. It's a sign that they're "on vacation," but a foreigner who is already an oddity will create a minor spectacle complete with tittering if seen walking around wearing them. Inside the room, the furnishings will be Japanese and the flooring will be *tatami* matting. Often, there will be elegant scrolls upon the walls, perhaps a flower arrangement, and the maid will slide open the *shoji* screens to offer a view of the soothing garden. By day, the room is designed for lounging and eating, and at night it will be transformed for you into a sleeping room. Throughout the day your maid will provide *ocha* (green tea) and maybe a few sweets. Your meals will be served on a low, lacquer table in your room, although some *ryokan* do have a communal dining hall. The food will be exemplary with special care taken for the foreigner, but if you're foolish enough to order western food, this can also be arranged in advance. In this case, expect cold eggs, tepid coffee and greasy bacon. If you choose, you can also arrange to have your meals "out." Approximately 20% will be deducted from your bill, but the few hundred yen that you'll save won't be worth the nuisance. In the evening or upon request, a hot *ofuro* will be drawn for you. Some *ryokan* offer private baths while others have semi-communal facilities. In any case, wash thoroughly before entering, douse away every trace of soap, and then soak away. When you return to your room, a thick *futon* (sleeping mat) covered in snow white, crisp sheets and quilted blankets will be ready and waiting. The only uncomfortable feature might be the ridiculous Japanese excuse for a pillow, which is about the same size and hardness as a cement building block. These torturous, tiny monsters, routinely covered in leatherette, deserve to be expunged from the face of the earth. If they don't repeatedly slide from under your head throughout the night, then in the morning they're stuck fast to the side of your face like a giant wad of bubble gum.

information: Again TIC and JNTO offer a booklet entitled *Ryokan Guide* that lists *ryokan* by area and includes prices. There are over 80,000 *ryokan* operating in Japan and reservations can be made through JTB or other travel agency. Many *ryokan* are found around train stations and oftentimes there's a window at the train station that will direct you to one and make reservations. The staffs, however, do not normally speak foreign languages. Check out time is 1000 to 1100.

geta (Japanese wooden clogs)

MINSHUKU

Far and away the best lodging for a budget traveler is a *minshuku*. Official definitions say that a *minshuku* is a family run, overnight boarding house where the guest is made to feel like one of the family. Just as in a *ryokan*, a *minshuku* offers a purely Japanese experience including a private *tatami* mat room and 2 sumptuous meals. Basically, a *minshuku* is a budget traveler's *ryokan*. There are some differences between the 2, but to the budget-minded traveler, they are negligible. It comes down to the finer points of elegance and style. In a *minshuku* you cannot always expect a manicured garden, individualized maid service, a *yukata*, a private bath or meals served in your room, but sometimes you get them none the less. *Minshuku* also vary widely in services with some being lovely little places while others again are just bland. Experience will show you that the services of a fine *minshuku* will outshine those of a mediocre *ryokan*. So if you don't mind making your own bed at night and putting it away in the morning, eating with the family and sharing a non-private bath, you can stay in a *minshuku* for less than half the price of a *ryokan*. The meals served will not be as visually elegant

as those at a *ryokan*, but they will be as delicious. The average price of a *minshuku* including 2 meals is Y3800. You could also arrange to have your meals "out" and receive a deduction, but you would be mad to do so. Follow the same etiquette as at a *ryokan*.

information: There are about 30,000 *minshuku* scattered throughout Japan with about 200 routinely accustomed to accommodate foreign guests. JNTO and TIC provide brochures, but the best information is obtainable from: Japan *Minshuku* Assoc., New Pearl Bldg., 2-10-8 Hyakunincho, Shinjuku, Tokyo, tel: :03; 371-8120. They offer an excellent booklet describing the etiquette required at a *minshuku* along with a list of *minshuku* and directions to them. It's always best to be on the safe side and make reservations, but you can usually find an accommodating *minshuku* near a train station, especially in country towns.

YOUTH HOSTELS

Japan has an exceptionally good network of YHs encompassing the entire country including some of the remotest islands. There are approximately 550 government subsidized YHs operated by Japan Youth Hostels, Inc. (JYH) with another 75 under private management, but associated with the national organization. On the whole, these are the least expensive accommodations available in Japan and using them as your nightly "mainstay" will keep travel costs down. Intersperse your nightly lodgings by staying at a variety of accommodations mentioned so as not to limit your experiences. YHs come in all shapes and sizes and are found in hot spot tourist areas and at the top of remote mountains. The physical characteristics vary and include everything from box-like buildings to ancient, converted temples or one time *minshuku* or *ryokan*. There are 2 drawbacks of sorts involved in staying at YHs. Although there is no age limit imposed at YHs, and now and again you'll find maturer Japanese travelers, families, businessmen and a sprinkling of western travelers, the vast majority of hostelers are Japanese university students. Because of societal restrictions and lack of worldly experience, most Japanese students are immature and unsophisticated. Their activities and conversations would be more like western junior high school students as opposed to university students. They're friendly, open and energetic, but after being bombarded by them with the same questions and reactions time and again, most westerners are happy for some private space. Most of this is due to the language barrier, but another part is due to real naivete. The other drawback is that in a YH, the *parento-san* (YH owner or operator) reigns supreme and, in short, you are not your own master.

rules and regulations: To stay at a YH you must have a membership card from your home country or an International Guest Card which can be obtained from the JYH Assoc. (see address later) for Y1800. The YHs in Japan follow the worldwide accepted codes for YHs and maintain separate dormitories for men and women. Eating times are generally from 0600 to 0800 and 1700 to 1900. Bathing can only be done at specified times during the evenings. You should make all effort to arrive no later than 2000 and all activities cease and lights go out promptly at 2200. It's obvious why these rules must be maintained under the vast majority of circumstances, but some *parento-san* rule with an iron glove and are inflexible regardless of the circumstances. For example, you may be the only guest, especially if you're in a remote area off season, and you may be sitting quietly in your bunk writing a letter. Suddenly, the door will open, and at exactly 2200 the *parento-san* will command, "Go to sleep" and the lights will be turned out. Complaining will get you nowhere. On the other hand, some *parento-san* are quite simpatico and if you're the more mature type, they'll enjoy sitting and talking with you later than usual and may even offer you a cup of *sake*, but this is not the norm and you can't expect it. There are other very reasonable rules that are easily complied with such as smoking only in designated areas, no alcoholic beverages permitted and generally cleaning up after yourself. In the morning, most Japanese wake up loudly. They clump around, talk, play radios and generally have no respect for the sleeping man. They're not being rude; this is their way. In YHs, people are always rousing loudly at different hours to make train connections. The other Japanese in the room will sleep like babies until their internal alarm clock tells them to get up. Most hapless *gaijin* will spend the early morning hours grumpily pounding their pillows and swearing, "Never again!" Don't complain. In days of yore, farmers would awaken their sleeping household which used one long, thin log as a communal pillow, by rapping upon it with a mallet. *Ohayo gozamiasu!* (Good morning). If you break any of the major rules, and this is left totally up to the discretion of the *parento-san,* your membership card can and will be lifted *on the spot.*

reservations: Most foreign travelers are at a disadvantage as far as advanced bookings are concerned, although the procedure is simple. Just send a note with a return prepaid postcard enclosed giving your name, address, occupation, sex, kind of membership card held and number, your arrival and departure dates, and your meal requirements for the day you intend to arrive. This system assumes that you'll know exactly where you're going to be on a specific date and that you have a return address to which the prepaid confirmation post card can be sent. If you're a free spirited traveler in Japan for any length of time, both requirements can be difficult. Japanese hostelers know months in advance where they're going for vacation and can comply with advanced bookings accordingly. Travelers on a more open itinerary generally do not. If you're letting fancy be your guide while touring Japan, don't be shocked if after a hard day of traveling, you're turned away at a YH because you have no reservations. Sometimes this can't be helped because the YH *is* booked solid, but some *parento-san* will turn you away even if there's room simply because you have been a naughty *gaijin* and not reserved your space. By all means, if your itinerary is strict, and especially if you are visiting during traditional vacation periods at places of high tourist interest, book in advance (2 weeks, no problem—one week, generally OK). To save on being disappointed, one method is to have the YH where you have spent the night call the YH where you're heading that day to inform them that you're on the way. That way, you'll know in advance if you can stay there and if not, you can make alternative arrangements accordingly. It's definitely worth the Y100 or so for the phone call to do this. Also, always carry a supply of food because if you arrive later than meal time, you won't get any, but there are generally soft drink and junk food machines available.

<u>rates:</u>   There are some minor variations in charges, but they are generally as follows:

	Public YHs	JHY YHs
Bed	to Y1300	to Y1150
Breakfast	to Y 400	to Y 450
Dinner	to Y 700	to Y 650
Sleeping sheet (†)	Y50-Y150	to Y 150
Self cooking charge	to Y 60	to Y 30
Heating (private unit)	Y50-Y200	Y50-Y150
Air Conditioning (private unit)		Y 150

†To save on sleeping sheet charges, carry your own. One about the size used for a single bed is perfect. Sleeping bags *do not* fulfill this requirement.

<u>information:</u>   For all information about YHs, contact Japan Youth Hostel, Inc., 2nd Floor, Hoken Kaidan Bldg., 1-2 Ichigaya-Sadoharacho, Shinju-ku, Tokyo, tel: (03) 269-5831. This national headquarters is only a few minutes walking distance from Ichigaya YH in Tokyo. TIC and JNTO hand out current foreign language booklets entitled, "Youth Hostels in Japan." They list all the YHs in Japan and give rudimentary directions. It's also imperative to combine the use of this booklet with the Japanese "Youth Hostel Handbook" available from JYH Inc, or at many YH front desks (Y350). This rather large (400+ pages) and infintely useful book lists the available YH according to geographic locations. Although mostly in Japanese, it's easy to follow. In front of the Hostel Handbook are regional maps with city place names written in Roman print. Surrounding these are the corresponding numbers of the YHs in the area which can easily be cross referenced in the text. The name of the YH in the text is also given in Roman print and the directions following it complete with a pin pointing map can easily be followed or shown to any Japanese passerby who can then read them and direct you to your destination.

USEFUL ALTERNATIVE ACCOMMODATIONS

<u>business hotels:</u>   These pragmatic accommodations are no frills, western style hotels. They're found everywhere in Japan and there's

a typical business hotel

usually a row of them near major train stations. Traveling businessmen do indeed use them, but they cater to all sorts of people. They're almost universally clean and offer smallish private rooms with private toilet and bathing facilities. Many are convenient to downtown areas and are also common at resort areas. On the average, they cost Y3800 per night. This is reasonable and below Y4000, the cut off point over which a 10% tax is levied. Some business hotels have restaurants, but none of the wider services that western style hotels offer. TIC and JNTO hand out pamphlets entitled "Business Hotels" and "Reasonable Accommodations in Japan." Advanced bookings are not generally needed.

<u>*Kokumin Kyuka Mura*</u> (*National Vacation Villages*):   These are government sponsored resort facilities found throughout Japan in vacation areas and especially in National and quasi-National Parks. There are currently 31 in operation. There is no membership system so they are open to everyone, but because they're considered a bargain, reservations are tight. They offer a combination of *ryokan* and western hotel type facilities. Most rooms are private, but toilets and bathing facilities are often communal.

Their average price is Y6000 per night including 2 meals. For information, contact: Kokumin Kyuka Mura Assoc., Tokyo Kaikan Bldg., 1st Floor, 10-1, Yurakucho, 2-chome, Chiyokda-ku, Tokyo, tel: (03) 216-2085. Osaka Office tel: (06) 343-0131. Nagoya Office tel: (052) 261-8536. Reservations can be made either through the Association or at any travel agent.

Kokumin Shukusha (People's Lodges): These lodges are about the same as Vacation Villages, but do not offer as wide a range of facilities on the premises, limiting themselves to pleasant accommodations in scenic areas. There are over 300 operating in Japan with an average nightly cost of Y3900 including 2 meals. Foreigners are a rarity, but are welcomed. It is best to book through JTB who will collect the money and present you with a receipt called a Green Coupon. *Kokumin Shukusha* are extremely popular during the summer months when reservations are not always assured and can take up to a week to confirm. Inquire at TIC or JNTO for further information and booking procedures.

shukubo (temple lodgings): There are Buddhist temples throughout Japan that open their doors to overnight guests. Over 70 function as YHs and are listed in the YH booklets followed by a left to right swastika symbolizing a temple (卍). They can be spotted also by the last syllable in their name which is *ji*, ie. Onshon *ji*-YH. Other temples, especially those around Kyoto and Nara where there are over 50, are not YH affiliated, but provide overnight lodgings in communal *tatami* rooms along with *shojin yori* (vegetarian food). These are known as *shukubo*. The island of Shikoku, famous for its 88 Sacred Temples, has clusters of temples functioning as *shukubo* and lists for all can be obtained from TIC and JNTO. Many of the temples are ancient and follow deep religious ceremonies every day. Some offer *zazen* meditation where guests are invited to participate or to observe, while other temples offer merely a room for the night on temple grounds with no religious participation involved. The experience at a *shukubo* is genuine and, because of its nature, gives insight into the Japanese mind. Many priests are well educated and can speak various foreign languages. It is possible to arrange periods of longer stay where you can study Buddhism and Zen. The average price per night, including 2 meals, is Y3500. Addresses of *shukubo* and helpful organizations are given throughout the travel sections of this book in the areas where they can be found. For *shukubo* that are accustomed to dealing with foreigners, see "Koya San" in the Nara chapter.

communes: Japan has a very lively commune movement with communes found in all parts of the country. The life philosophies at each one vary: some are vegetarian, others are religiously based, some are back-to-nature farms, while others are inner city homesteads. The commune movement publishes an English version of a 240 page book listing all of the communes in Japan and their philosophies. For a copy, send your request to: Japanese Commune Movement, c/o Moshe Matsuba, Kibbutz Akan, Shin Skizen Juku, Nakasetsuri, Tsuruimura, Akan gun, Hokkaido 085-12, Japan. Include the equivalent of U.S $7.00 (includes sea mail postage, allow 6 weeks). Moshe Matsube is an expatriot Englishman who has spent years on Israeli *kibbutzim* and is an active member of Akan Kibbutz. If you're in Akan National Park in Hokkaido, it's well worth it to look him up and spend some enjoyable time at Akan Kibbutz. Depending upon your inclinations and the particular commune's philosophy, you can stay there only overnight or for long periods of time as an active commune member.

sauna baths: It is possible to spend a very comfortable and inexpensive night in many hotel sauna baths, but these in no way should be confused with *turuko* (turkish baths) which are basically "play for pay" cat houses. Since sauna baths are unofficial lodgings, there is no organization representing them, and costs vary from one to the other. It's also a hit and miss proposition finding one that will accommodate you. Many western style hotels have an entire floor dedicated to their sauna bath facilities, so you could wind up staying at the best place in town for only a fraction of the normal cost. When you enter a hotel, ask for the sauna. When you arrive at the appropriate floor, make your overnight intentions clear and agree on the price. It varies, but expect to pay between Y1500 to Y2000. Once inside, deposit your clothing and luggage in a locker, and you'll be given a *yukata* and a small bag of toilet articles, including soap, shampoo, toothpaste, a brush and a razor. Besides the sauna, there is usually a whirlpool and showers. There is also a large lounging room that usually has overstuffed chairs and a small food concession. Orange juice and cigarettes are oftentimes free. When you wish to sleep, there is very often a separate rest room. You will be provided with blankets and a pillow. There are some slight drawbacks. Once inside the sauna's facilities, you are not permitted to go out for the evening and then come in again later. You must stay put. Obviously, to make this situation more convenient, enter the sauna when you intend to stay in for the night. The other colorful clientele are oftentimes businessmen who have been out drinking, night club workers rolling in at the wee hours of the morning, and a smattering of homosexuals looking for liaisons. All of these people present no real hassles. You must leave the sauna in the morning by a specified time, usually 0900, or you'll be charged extra. Unfortunately, sauna baths are for men only. There are those catering to women, but they close at about midnight because, "you see, no nice Japanese girls stay out all night."

camping: The Japanese are enamored with the outdoors, but have not gotten into camping as much as westerners. Most stay in YHs or other facilities in the area visited, especially because there's usually no camping allowed in some national parks. This does not mean that there is any shortage of campgrounds. On the contrary, TIC in Tokyo can provide a list that runs to 20 typewritten pages. Japanese campground range from primitive, with only pit toilets, to luxurious with hot showers, tennis courts, swimming pools and even cabins. In the countryside you can put up a tent wherever you can find a likely spot, but if it's anywhere near a farm house, you should ask permission first. Camping on beaches, especially on outlying islands, is usually OK and a pleasure, but the average traveler will not get full value from lugging around camping gear because much of the best that Japan has to offer is either in cities or well built up areas. If you're heading for Hokkaido, the outback areas of Tohoku, the Japan Alps or the beaches of Okinawa, it may be worth it to take a tent. Otherwise, leave it at home.

cycling inns: A new phenomenon catching on in Japan are cycling inns that are designed for the growing number of people touring Japan by bicycle. They are about the same in cost and facilities as youth hostels. The aim is to have at least one facility every 100 km or so, but so far there are only about 20 in all of Japan. You can either take your *jitensha* (bicycle) with you to Japan or buy or rent one while there. It's best to have a model that can fold into a carrying bag because oftentimes you must combine train travel with cycling in order to get around efficiently, and these folding types are accepted as baggage on passenger trains. If your bicycle doesn't fold, you might have to ship it separately on a freight train and this can be a problem. For information concerning all facts of cycling in Japan, contact: Japan Bicycle Promotion Institute, Nihon Jitensha Kaikan Bldg., 9-3 Akasaka 1-chome, Minato-ku, Tokyo, tel: (03) 583-5444.

love hotels: Yes, believe it or not, budget travelers in Japan can cut costs by staying at "love hotels." These unbelievable hotels are found in all metro areas of Japan and are used by privacy-starved Japanese lovers for a few hours of erotic frolicking. The rooms are by the hour and the peak hours are in the late afternoon to early evening. Signs at the entranceways give the hourly rate, and if you arrive around 2200, you can get a room for the night for about the price of one hour. Although the activities that take place in the rooms do not fall into everyone's definition of "good clean fun," like all other accommodations in Japan these hotels are very clean. You can spot a love hotel first by its garish architecture or by its neon signs that can be shaped like hearts and colored in pastel shades. The hotel will be surrounded by a wall and will have a separate entrance and exit. Because they're designed to be discreet, you may have a problem communicating your needs to the owners, who oftentimes stay demurely behind a window and out of sight with only a slot to exchange money for a key. When they see that the hour is late and you are alone, they'll understand that you would like to spend the night. Agree on the time that you must leave in the morning because over-staying can result in having the hourly charge tacked on. Once inside the rooms, you will be pleasantly or shockingly amazed by their design. If you like red velvet wall paper along with fluffy pink furniture and mirrors everywhere you'll feel right at home. There is always an *ofuro* for bathing, and sometimes there are vibrating beds and even videotape equipment for those who want an "instant replay." As you sink down into your satin sheets and look at yourself in the mirrors on the ceiling, you'll have a good chuckle at these alternative accommodations fit for a "porno" king or queen.

pensions: The name and style of these accommodations are borrowed from their

European counterpart. Pensions are a recent phenomenon in Japan, dating back only about 10 years. They are usually found in rural areas and their accommodations are a mixture of *ryokan* and hotel. What makes a pension particularly attractive is that they are somewhat cosmopolitan, offering a generally wide array of foods and services that are particularly convenient for traveling families. Most pensions offer either a single room or a suite of rooms that are furnished in western style. The owners often act as tour guides for the area and will go to any reasonable length to make their clientele comfortalbe. Fishing, hiking and skiing equipment are frequently available for guests who wish to avail themselves of these local recreational opportunities. Many pensions offer common rooms that convert to entertain-yourself type beds at night, and oftentimes there are activites especially for children along with babysitting services during the evening. One remarkable pension is Shirakaba, located in the Ura-Bandai area of Tohoku (see travel chapter). Costs at most pensions start at Y5000 and include 2 meals. For more information, contact: Pension System Development, 4th Floor Inuzuka Bldg., 4-11, 2-Chome, Suragaku-cho, Tokyo, tel: (03) 295-6333; Odaka, tel: (06) 448-2641; Sendai, tel: (0222) 65-0534; Fukuoka, tel: (092) 271-7555.

long term housing: If any item causes head shaking disbelief among foreigners in Japan, it's the exorbitant cost and usually low quality of Japanese housing. With so many people clamoring for a place to live, especially in the metro areas, housing is most definitely at a premium. Besides the high prices, the living space in Japanese homes and apartments is miniscule compared to most western standards. This is somewhat offset by the fact that rooms can be transformed in a matter of seconds by sliding open a *shoji* screen or tucking away the *futon* (sleeping mat) in its cubby hole. Rooms in Japan are measured by the number of *tatami* mats that cover the floor. Although the official size of a mat has been shrinking in the last few yrs, the traditional measurement is 1 m by 2 meters. Japanese students, traditionally known for their lack of funds, may attend 4 yrs of university while living in a three mat room about

the size of a large closet in the west. The average Japanese room is 4½ mats in size (3 m x 3 m) and the average Tokyo apartment contains 3 rooms of this size which includes the bath and a food preparation area. For an apartment of this size in the Tokyo area, you can expect to pay Y50,000 per month. Unfortunately, this does not include all of the costs that you may incur. It is common upon moving in to be charged the first and last months' rent plus a damage deposit and even a monthly maintenance charge for services that seem nonexistent. To rub salt further into the wound, the Japanese maintain a customary rip off called *reikin* (key money). This sum of money, which can range from one to 3 months rent, is pocketed by the landlord, never to be returned. Basically, it comes down to "Thank you very much for politely allowing me to rip you off." To find an apartment, check the listings on the back pages of the Tokyo Weekender (see Tokyo chapter) and the *Japan Times,* especially the Friday edition. When looking at the classified ads, apartments will often appear with abbreviations such as 3 LDK. This means: living room, dining room and kitchen. You can also try running an ad in a local Japanese newspaper (all suburbs of Tokyo and major cities have them). For this, you'll need a Japanese friend to compose the ad for you. Offer foreign language lessons in exchange for all or partial rent. Sometimes it works out that you can share an apartment with a Japanese looking for language lessons. The best method of all is to bide your time until you have become settled and made a few friends. Often, the word of mouth technique can save on key money and turn up a few bargains. Many foreigners who have settled in Japan and are going abroad on trips will employ house sitters. These are the best and cheapest deals, but they lack permanancy. If all else fails, you can employ the services of a *fudoya* (rental agency), but you'll feel as though you're in a swimming pool filled with sharks who are in a frenzy to dine on your pocket book. Two rental agencies in Tokyo that have good reputations and are accustomed to dealing with froeigners (although most of their clientele come from the non-budget oriented business sector) are Eastern Real Estate Co., tel: (03) 583-2181 and Tokyo House Bureau, tel: (03) 501-2496.

FOOD AND DRINK

One of the greatest joys of visiting a foreign country is sampling the local cuisine and the ethnic foods offered. The universality of sharing a meal with someone is also one of the best ways of getting to know them and their country. Japanese food, perhaps more than any other item, is cloaked in misconceptions. The most common misconceptions are that food prices are astronomical and that the ingredients used are bizarre. The myth of high prices arises from the tales of trapped tourists who never ventured past the western style restaurants in their luxury hotels. Compounding this problem is that many of these same tourists order giant slabs of prime ribs that cover their entire plate. A wide strata of Japanese society eats out all the time. Businessmen, families and the working class all manage to have hearty, inexpensive meals. You can, too, by merely eating where and how the Japanese eat. You can have 3 filling restaurant meals for under Y1500 per day. The assortment of foods and restaurants in Japan is amazing and the typical diet is changing rapidly. Sometimes it seems that every second shop sells food of some sort. Larger cities offer cuisine ranging from French to Vietnamese. Pizza parlors, chain hamburger restaurants, donut shops and ice cream stands are commonplace. Chinese restaurants are so well established that they hardly seem foreign to the Japanese anymore. Traditional Japanese food is a delight in every sense of the word. It is designed to be not only nutritious and delicious, but aesthetically pleasing as well. Lovely ceramic dishes and bowls hold foods that are arranged, shaped and sculptured to please the eye. In traditional restaurants, you are served in *tatami* rooms that often look out onto soothing gardens. Sometimes foreigners feel that the ingredients used in traditional foods are strange. This problem is in the mind and not in the palate. To be sure, many ingredients are exotic, but they are wholesome. Staples such as *tofu, miso* and various sea weeds are becoming well known in western kitchens and hardly even raise an eyebrow. If you desire to be a successful budget traveler or, at least, a well-nourished one, you cannot have a rigid concept of what food "should" be. Rejecting Japanese food off hand or turning your nose up before even sampling it is depriving yourself of one of the most savory cuisines available in the world today. The Japanese prior to the Meiji Restoration of the last century did not routinely kill animals and never ate them. Imagine the horror of the first Japanese farmer who was summoned to bring his plough animal to the quarters of the new American Consul, Townsend Harris. The foreigners were not only going to slaughter the animal, but they were also going to eat its hind leg. All foods can be considered weird if you look at them weirdly. The Japanese today routinely eat beef, pork and chicken, and the portions, although smaller than western standards, are not miniscule. Fish cooked in a thousand-and-one savory ways is still the main protein staple. Fruits, vegtables, roots and a wide variety of sea weeds garnish and enhance most dishes. Milk products are popular and available (although it is said that 70% of all Asian population have trouble digesting them), but Japanese ice cream and cheese still have a long way to go. Travelers returning home from Japan carry tales not only of the intricate shrines and temples that they have visited, or the remarkable countryside and culture they have witnessed, but also of the moutwatering array of exotic foods that they have sampled.

HELPFUL HINTS

There is an excellent restaurant custom in Japan that is extremely helpful to visitors. In the windows of most restaurants are remarkably true to life wax or plastic facsimiles of the dishes offered. There is no need to read the menu. Just beckon a waitress outside and point to what looks good. This custom of wax facsimiles started in Japan after the Meiji Restoration. It was designed to help the Japanese in selecting from the new foods that were flooding into their previously closed country. Thankfully, this preserved custom helps the traveler in much the same way today. If the replica shows food in a bowl, it is usually of Japanese origin. If it's in a dish, then it's considered western. You get what you see. If one green pea sits atop a hamburger in the facsimile, you will get that one (no more, no less) green pea. *noren:* These are slitted curtains that hang to the middle of the doorway over restaurants. If they are tucked inside, the restaurant is closed. If they are out, it is open. *oshibori:* These napkin size damp cloths are served hot in winter and cold in summer. The idea is to wipe your hands and mouth before eating and to use them as a napkin during meals. Don't overdo it. Save scrubbing your neck for your evening bath. *ohashi:* These are Japanese chopsticks. They're smaller, lighter and more pointed at the ends than Chinese chopsticks. There are 2 types. The first and most common are disposable unpainted sticks that have been only partially split. Take them from their wrappers and split them. The Japanese then usually rub them together to remove any splinters. These are always found in *soba-ya, ramen-ya* and other inexpensive restaurants. The more elegant type of chopstick is called *warabashi.* These are lacquered and reusable and are found in better restaurants and in Japanese homes. Close to one billion pair of *ohashi* are discarded in Japan each year. Japan imports a tremendous volume of wood each year and it's curious to note that the conservation-minded Japanese haven't conceived of a way to recycle them. The Japanese would balk at the idea of using them to eat with again since they are unpainted, but they could easily be ground into pulp for paper. Proper etiquette dictates that you turn the chopsticks and use the end not placed in the mouth to take portions from the communal bowls.

noodle slurping: Japanese slurp noodles and make loud sucking noises. The sucking is usually followed by a deep, contented *aahh.* It doesn't take westerners long to catch on. The slurping helps to cool the noodles and gourmets say that the extra intake of air excites the palate and delivers the full taste of the food. Lean over your bowl, tuck a few strands of noodles into your mouth and suck away. Be careful of the whipping ends staining your shirt. Spoons are usually not provided for soup and broth . Lift the bowl and drink from it. The hot soup may make your nose run but never blow your nose in a Japanese restaurant. They consider it horrifyingly disgusting. You'll clear the place out. Use the bathroom to blow your nose if you must.

WHERE TO EAT

The following is a partial list of where to eat and what services and foods to expect. Western style restaurants and expensive Japanese restaurants really need no description and for the most part have been omitted. They are easily found in large expensive hotels in major cities that usually offer both. These restaurants have their place, but should not be used as a means of daily fare, especially if maintaining a budget is a priority. Save them for that "big night out."

Japanese eateries: The Japanese restaurants in this category provide rich cultural experience. *shokudo:* This is your general, all purpose restaurant. It's the most common type in Japan. Their menu offers a limited, yet adequate selection of Japanese, Chinese and western foods. They are easily spotted by the array of replicas of the differing cuisines in the windows. Look for hamburger dinners displayed next to *donburi* dinners. These restaurants are frequented by students and downtown city workers. Expect to spend Y500 to Y1000. *chuka ryori ya:* This is a basic family style Chinese restaurant, usually where dad takes mom and the kids for a night out just to break the routine. Certain dishes have been Japanified, but most look like typical Chinese food anywhere. Most window replicas will be in bowls. Look for a dish of *cha-han* (fried rice with bits of meat and vegetables) to spot one of these restaurants. *koryori ya:* These are traditional Japanese restaurants (not expensive) that serve a limited menu of the most popular Japanese dishes. They are small and intimate. Look inside. If there are tiny, partitioned *tatami* rooms, it's probably a *koryori-ya.* A *shokuji dokoro* is the same type of restaurant but is even smaller, perhaps seating less than 8 people.

soba-ya: This is also a very common type of restaurant in Japan as well as being one of the cheapest. Even in the smallest towns and villages, there's usually a *soba-ya*. They sell noodles, usually in soup. Japanese eat as many noodles as they do rice. They're a staple in the diet and there are literally 100s of varieties. Eating in a *soba-ya* at least once a day is a mainstay of keeping on a budget. The portions are large by any standards and the prices are cheap (Y300). There are 3 basic noodles used: *soba*, *udon* and *ramen* (Japanese: *lamen*). *Soba* is a Japanese noodle made from buckwheat. They are long with squared corners and the colors vary from brown to grey. *Udon* is another type of Japanese noodle. They are longer and whiter and made from wheat. Both *soba* and *udon* noodles are used in a variety of dishes interchangeably, so be sure to specify if you have a preference. *Ramen* is the familiar Chinese noodle. It's longer than either of the Japanese noodles and usually thinner, with a yellowish tint due to its egg content. It's usually served in a pork broth and can also be served fried. Many shops have posters depicting the types of soups sold, and sometimes they are labelled in English. The 3 following suggestions should get you started until you discover your own favorite. The simplest order is to just say *ramen*. In this soup you will get *ramen* noodles in a pork and *shoyu* (soy sauce) stock. A few bits of pork, bamboo shoots, leeks and an egg float on top. *Go moku soba* comes with your choice of noodles in a pork broth. Atop are a hard boiled egg, ham slices, shrimp, fish cakes and a few peas. *Miso udon* has a fish stock. Along with a few pieces of beef, there are leeks, a large mushroom and sometimes *fu*. *Miso udon* is usually served in an earthenware pot and eaten as a hearty dish in winter. In summertime, noodles are served cold. A basic example is *mori soba*. The noodles come in a lacquered box sitting atop a rack. The idea is to mix the accompanying condiments along with sweetened *shoyu* in the broth. Dunk the noodles and slurp away. If you are in a new town and don't know what to order in the local *soba-ya*, just say the name of the town followed by *soba* (ie. *Nagoya-soba*). The counterman might laugh, but he'll get the idea. You'll be served the local specialty which is usually the most savory and the least expensive. *Soba* is also sold at small booths in most train stations. Eat it standing up. If it's a bit plain, ask for *tomago* (egg) to thicken it up. Just stir it into the hot broth.

nomi-ya: No frills, intimate, neighborhood drinkeries. They are colloquially called *akachochin* (red lantern) because of the large red paper lanterns that mark their doorways. This is where the Japanese go for a quiet beer or a cup of sake. Small portions of food are served such as nuts, roasted baby prawns and usually a more substantial dish or two. There are no hostesses and with the price of one drink you can sit and relax for hours. These shops usually do not display replicas of their menu since all Japanese know what to expect. It's best to go with a Japanese friend and let them order. Memorize names of your favorite dishes for the future when you may be on your own. If you must order on your own, try *tempura teishoku*. (See *teishoku* later in this section for a full explanation).

snack: A "snaku" is the modern, westernized variation of a *nomi-ya*. What sets them apart is the atmosphere. A *nomi-ya* is quieter and more traditional. A snack usually has a juke box and a fancier bar. In some, the custom is to play a pop song (music only) while a patron sings the words. Everyone takes a turn. Feeling is much more important than talent. Foreigners are usually asked to join in. A *snack* is allowed to stay open and serve drinks longer than a bar and has a slight neighborhood pub atmosphere.

kissaten: This is a very civilized Japanese institution. Basically, they are a coffee (*kohi*) shop. Often the word "coffee" appears at the doorway. Light snacks and desserts are sold also. The Japanese people, especially students and businessmen, sit in them for hours. A great percentage of corporate deals are signed in *kissaten*. The price of a cup of coffee is usually a costly Y300, but don't be put off by the price. Once you buy a cup, you can sit there all day. They're great places for reading or catching up on letter writing. *Kissaten* offer an atmosphere. The insides are usually plush and large overstuffed chairs surround low coffee tables. Each *kissaten* also specializes in different forms of music. Jazz, easy listening, pop and classical are all offered. The sound systems are A plus. *Kissaten* also offer *morningu serbisu* (morning service) until 1000. This means that for the price of a cup of coffee (Y300), you also get toast, salad, fruit juice and an egg. This makes for a cheap, yet reasonable breakfast. The breakfast offerings may differ slightly from place to place. Ask first.

department stores: Larger department stores (*depato*) are like mini villages. They have a section for almost everything and food is included. The underground floors usually have a supermarket, where salespeople offer samples of what they're selling. Long term residents have perfected this sampling to an art. Making the rounds not only gives you first hand experience of Japanese foods, but by the time you're through, you usually won't want lunch. The top floors of most *depato* are restaurants. Most are inexpensive and offer a variety of standard dishes. Sometimes you take a number before you're seated. All offer plastic facsimiles.

chain restaurants and fast foods: Large international fast food chains do a thriving business throughout Japan. There are a large number of them, but the most common are MacDonald's (*Mackodonaldo*), Shakey's Pizza (all you can eat from 1000 to 14000 weekdays), Lotteria, Mister Donut, and A&W Rootbeer. Mister Donut sells reasonably priced coffee at Y50. Naturally, they are not as swank as a *kissaten,* but for a quick cup of coffee, they're the best buy.

sushi maker

sushi-ya: Sushi-ya are just what their name implies. They sell *sushi* and *sashimi*. Westerners often have the mistaken belief that *sushi* is raw fish. However, *sashimi* are the thin slices of raw fish, while *sushi* is the general term referring to the seasoned, packed rice upon which toppings such as egg omelette, various vegetables, sea weed and raw fish are presented. There are 2 basic types of *sushi* served in Japan: *nigiri* and *oshi zushi*. Nigiri sushi originated in the Tokyo area and is made by packing the rice in the hand and then placing the toppings on it. *Oshi zushi,*

from the Osaka region, is made by forming the rice in wooden containers with marinated or boiled fish squeezed inside. No trip to Japan is complete without dining in a *sushi-ya*. The chefs, amazingly adept at their art, are a side show of excitement and fanfare. They can keep an elbow to elbow counterful of customers supplied with a tremendous assortment of *sushi*, keeping track of everyone's orders and bills in their heads. It's said that an apprentice *sushi* maker is only allowed to cook rice for the first 5 years of his employment. *Sushi* shops are judged by the *sushi* maker's ability to make a fantastically thin egg crepe designed to enfold the rice. The state of the art of egg crepe making by a local *sushi* maker provides hours of friendly, yet serious argument for the loyal patrons of different shops. The best fun in a *sushi* shop takes place at the counter. If you sit here, you're expected to pick and choose different *sushi*. (The table or *tatami* mat area usually means a fixed plate.) Just look into the case and point to what looks good. The cleanliness of *sushi-ya* is beyond reproach. Start off with tiny *ebi* (cooked prawns) and then try *maguro* (raw tuna) which has the reputation of being the foreigner's favorite. *Hamaguri* are raw clams, familiar to many westerners, and *chakin zushi* is the rice wrapped in the egg crepe. A point to remember is that raw fish is surprisingly much more delicate in flavor than cooked fish. Even people that don't like fish are surprised at how good raw fish tastes. Be brave. Thrill seekers should order *fugu*. This blowfish is served raw and has potentially deadly poisonous glands. Death can occur in minutes. *Sushi* makers specializing in *fugu* are specially licensed by the government and are masters *par excellence* in their craft. Only amateurs kill themselves with *fugu*. Sushi bars have their own specialized language. Some examples are: *agari*, Japanese green tea (multiple cups are served without charge): *wasabi,* hot green mustard with the consistency of horseradish: *murasaki* is the name given to *shoyo* (soy sauce) in *sushi-ya*. Remember also, that eating *sushi* does not usually constitute a full meal. They're more like snacks to accompany beer or *sake*. For about Y1000 you can have a good sampling of the morsels offered.

street vendors: Tangy, tasty and inexpensive morsels can be easily bought from vendors at temples and on most downtown city streets. Chestnut vendors and *yakitori* (skewered, marinated, charcoaled chicken) stands are some of the most common. *Oden* stalls, specializing in a variety of boiled foods such as eggs, tofu and fish balls, set up shop around busy train stations at night. Little stools attached to the cart overlook the boiling pots of goodies. Just pick and choose. **Bento.** This Japanese favorite is a boxed lunch that contains bits of fish, perhaps some salad, a cup of tea, and always *o-nigiri* (thick triangular rice cakes surrounding fish or an *umeboshi*, pickled plum, wrapped in seaweed). *Bento* are a favorite with Japanese on picnics or train rides. They can be purchased anywhere, but the most colorful way is to hail a *bento* seller who is walking up and down the platforms at train stations yelling, "*o bento.*" They'll hand it to you through the window. *Bento* containers are usually neatly wrapped wooden boxes, but they can sometimes be reusable clay pots. The Japanese eat the contents and then very neatly rewrap the boxes. Unfortunately, they then throw them on the train floor or on the slopes of beautiful mountains, even Fuji.

WHAT TO EAT

The following are some inexpensive food suggestions — tips and dishes to get you started: *teishoku:* This is a general term that roughly means "fixed plate." These are available in all general purpose restaurants. They vary in content and price, but adequate dinners should cost around Y600. This will include tea, bottomless bowls of rice and *miso shiru* (soup), salad, the main dish and, perhaps, fruit. A blase one is hamburger *teishoku.* A very tasty one is *yakini ku teishoku*, which is savory strips of marinated meat (beef or pork) fried in vegetables. A nightly choice from an assortment of 10 favorite teishoku supplies enough diversity to serve as the main daily fare for budget traveling.

curry rice: Just what the name implies. This is usually the cheapest meal at most restaurants and is a favorite with students. It comes on a flat plate (western) and the curry either comes poured over it or in a side gravy boat. Adequate, but redundant. A once or twice a week staple for the really budget minded. *don buri:* This is a basic standby, like a *teishoku*, and is eaten often to keep prices down. There are many *don buri*, which means "something atop rice in a bowl." Some favorites are *ten don* (*buri*), battered shrimp; *kotsu don*, fried pork cutlet; *oyako-don*, chicken and egg (*oyako* means parent and child); *gyu don*, beef; and *tomago don*, egg. All come with tea and a bowl of pickles and sell for less than Y500.

other suggestions: a few more hints should complete the list. Many establishments, especially *soba-ya*, offer *o-mori* for bigger appetites. *O-more* means a larger portion. The extra price for the 30% larger helpings is usually Y100. *Gyoza* are little dough balls of wonder sold in *chuka ryoriya* (Chinese restaurants). They're

most restaurants have a display case at the doorways exhibiting exact plastic or wax replicas of the dishes offered along with their prices. Language in ordering a meal is never a barrier. Just summon the waitress outside and point to what looks good

inexpensive and appeal to just about everyone. Dough is wrapped around a mixture of vegetalbes, including cabbage spiced with garlic, and then fried. Dip the *gyoza* into the accompanying sauce and munch away. Most westerners and a good many of non-Tokyoites are repulsed by *natto*. These are fermented, bitter, sticky beans whose admirers claim lead to good health. They taste so bad that even starving hyenas won't eat them. The story goes that a 19th C Tokyo wholesaler forgot about a batch of beans in the dark recesses of his warehouse. When he found them under the leaky roof months later, they had partially fermented and formed a sticky substance. He then forced one of his downrodden workers to eat them. The worker didn't die, although he wished that he had. The wholesaler pawned them off as health food and *natto* was born.

standards and cliches: There are a few standbys that appeal to almost everyone's taste. They are delicious, but are such a common order of *gaijin* that they have become a cliche. Some are also served in specialty restaurants and are expensive. One of these standards is *tempura*. *Tempura* consists of bits of vegtables and fish that have been dipped into an egg and flour mixture and then deep fried. They are delicious and there are no surprises. *Tempura* is available at most restaurants and at *tempura-ya*. Another common *gaijin* request is *teppan yaki*, which means "iron plate grilling." In this process, the raw food is brought to your table and you cook it yourself. You place bits of fish, meat, or vegtables on the grill. When they are cooked, you then dip the morsels into a mixture of soy sauce and sweet sake (*mirin*). Another table top cooked food is *shabu-shabu* (onomatopoetic name given to this dish because of the sound of the boiling water). *Shabu-shabu* arrives as a plate of thinly sliced, uncooked beef, vegetables and tofu. A pot of boiling water sits in the middle of the table, kept hot by an electric element or gas flame. You submerge the ingredients in the hot water and pick them out when cooked. Dip them into the specially prepared sauce before eating. *Sukiyaki* (pronounced *ski'yaki*) is probably the most internationally known Japanese food. Again, vegtalbes and meat are brought to your table along with mushrooms, tofu and vermicelli. You boil the vegetables and meat in a prepared stock. When cooked, you then dip the pieces into a mixture of raw egg and *shoyu* before eating. An exception to the above mentiuoned pricey dishes is *okonomi yaki*. Basically this is a "build your own omelette." A variety of ingredients such as bits of meat, fish and vegetable are added to the egg mixture. The cheapest version is simply the eggs with seasonings. *Okonimi yaki* is often sold at street stalls, especially during festivals.

TEA AND SOFT DRINKS

O cha, co cha and water: O cha is Japanese green tea, available in all restaurants free of charge. Co-cha is dark tea, sometimes called English tea. It is also readily available, but a nominal charge may be added. *Mizu* means water, but *o-hiya* is used when asking for a glass of cold water. *Oyu* is hot water.   *grades of tea:* There are three grades of tea served in Japan. *Gyokuro* is the smallest, most tender leaved tea, usually served with cakes and at the tea ceremony. *Sencha* is made from slightly larger, less tender leaves, but the tea is still considered good enough to be served to honored guests. *Bancha* is the "everyday" tea, made from the larger leaves and stems after the two better grades have been picked. *Matcha* is the powdered green tea used in the tea ceremony (*chano-yu*). Japanese say that the water used for steeping decides the tea.

soft drinks and vending machines: Japan is 2nd only to the U.S. in numbers of vending machines and all seem to work even though they may look rusty and are found in unlikely spots such as secluded mountain temples. They sell a variety of soft drinks and foods. Cuppa Ramen (ramen noodles in a cup needing only boiling water) is a favorite with students. It's cheap, and tastes it. If you want a soft drink (Coca Cola, etc.) never order it in a restaurant. You may be charged Y250, even though there's a machine at the doorway selling it for Y70. Fruit juices in cans and bottles are also readily available. The two most common types are *ringo* (apple) juice and *orenji* (orange) juice.

DINING IN THE JAPANESE STYLE

To truly enjoy Japanese food, the right setting is all important. This is observed both in elegant restaurants and in private homes. A perfect eating area looks out onto a delightful garden framed by sliding doors and soothing to look at in any season. The place of honor in a Japanese home is before the *tokonoma* (an artfully arranged alcove). The place of least honor is closest to the door, a subtle way of saying, "Please be the first to leave." The eating room is covered in *tatami* mat and there are no chairs. Instead, flat cushions (*zabuton*) surround a low table. Sometimes, on very special occasions, individual legged, lacquered trays are used. You are first given an oshibori (hot or cold, sometimes scented, damp towel). Then you may be offered sake. Your host will pour for you. Never pour your own, as it is considered bad manners to serve yourself. Sake is not drunk after the rice is served. When the meal arrives, it all comes at once, not in courses. It is considered vulgar to show hunger. Take small portions of the many courses. A great deal of time and effort is placed into choosing the perfect dish or ceramic bowl to complement the color or consistency of the food inside. Bowls are lifted when eating from them, and soup is drunk directly since no spoons are provided. The freshness of the food is as highly prized as the actual taste. Each food is prepared not only to bring out its flavor, but to bring out its visual beauty as well. Food is not merely put into bowls and dishes. It is carefully placed and artfully arranged. The actual consuming of the food is almost secondary to the esoteric qualities of its appearance. The eyes are as important to the gastronomic experience as the mouth. The Japanese revel in esoteric mysteries and the preparation of food is no exception. Much is surrounded by folklore and ritual. Excellent cooks gauge the time for cooking rice not only by the area in which it was grown, but also by the weather during the particular growing season. Remember most importantly that a Japanese meal is not only food for the body, but also food for the soul.

ALCOHOLIC BEVERAGES

When people are first introduced to the refined aspects of Japanese culture, they are often amazed to learn that Japanese drink and drink heavily. Somehow this seems incongruous, but Japanese from all social levels hit the bars with their workmates almost as a ritual to cement friendship. Public drunkenness is overlooked and almost any act done while intoxicated is forgiven. The one exception is drunk driving and the Japanese don't do it. They'll call a taxi, walk or use the subways instead. The last subway in Tokyo at 2400 is notorious, especially on Friday and Saturday nights. It's not unusual to see a well dressed businessman standing on a railway

platform and depositing a "golden arc" on the tracks below. Legions of bleary-eyed office workers with disheveled suits, hands deep in trouser pockets to the elbows and seemingly standing on well-greased ball bearings descend on subway platforms. An attitudinal difference is that westerners drink in what will be called the "English style." The idea is to consume a vast amount of booze, but never show it. The Japanese, on the other hand, drink with the idea of getting drunk and then show it badly. If they become sick to their stomachs, even on a railway car, look out, partner, because they'll let it fly. A favorite Japanese pastime is trying to get a *gaijin* drunk. Maybe, because of body weight, Japanese just can't keep the pace and what usually happens is a mildly tipsy *gaijin* sitting at an empty table with his Japanese friends scattered in rumpled heaps. When going drinking with Japanese acquaintances, unless they are well-known friends or poorer students, it is almost impossible to pay your own tab. They will insist on paying. It is the custom. Don't expect it as a matter of course, but when it happens, accept it graciously. When drinking with someone, male or female, they will fill your glass for you. Don't pour your own. Take the bottle and fill their glass. Another Japanese drinking oddity is the bottomless glass. Westerners will drink beer, for example, to the bottom of the glass and then refill it. Japanese top it up after every sip. The same happens with sake. If you don't want this to happen, either don't set your glass down on the table or hold your hand over it. If you absolutely want no more, turn your empty glass upside down.

beer: The Japanese brew excellent beer. The story goes that a German in the late 1800s observed wild hops growing and started the first brewery in Japan. There are innumerable small breweries, but the most famous names in Japan are Suntory, Asahi, Kirin and Sapporo. The most common type is a light lager. The Japanese drink beer in conjunction with food. Beer rivals sake when eating *sushi*. Vending machines sell it (Y200) as well as most restaurants. The average price is Y250 for a 633 ml (19 oz) bottle. The price can go as high as Y1000 per bottle in a hostess bar. Even in a lowly establishment, there is the ubiquitous nuisance of *otsunami* (tiny portions of snack food — may only be pickles) that is tacked onto the bill and served wether you want it or not usually when drinking beer. Forget about leaning over a meditative cold beer. If you are determined, the best places for this, however, are Suntory

Standup Bars (*Ba*) and converted rooftops of *depato* that serve as beer gardens in the summer. Also *kissaten* and snack bars are OK for a quiet beer.

hard liquor: All manner of alcoholic beverages are available in Japan. Imported alcohol, as in any country, is more expensive than the domestic varieties. At one time it was a money making proposition to bring in hard-to-get foreign labels, but the import system has opened up and this is no longer profitable. The Japanese have a taste for the full range of liquor, but seem to prefer whiskey and scotch. Again, you can get most world wide famous labels, but the domestic brand, Suntory, is rated very highly and is much cheaper. The Japanese have a distinct dislike for sweet or mixed drinks and most order *mizu-wari* (whiskey with water). Prices vary too much to give an accurate estimate, but except to pay Y250 for a glass of whiskey. A good place to find most spirits is in the basement of *depatos*.

compa: A special category of bar-restaurant is a *compa*. This is a type of nightclub where a Japanese with a few yen to spend will most likely take a date or a friend. You are expected to order food along with drinks, and if you're drinking *mizu wari*, you'll be charged for the set-ups, ice and water. The water is supposedly mineral water, but if you look closely, you can ovserve the bottle being filled from the tap. Waiters and waitresses, usually in skimpy outfits, are in attendance. If you're going to be ripped off, it will most likely happen in a lower class *compa*. The people working here are "night people." They address their boss, "*ohayo gozaimasu*" (Good morning) when they start in the evening for an all night stint. Most night workers do not fit the mold of the average Japanese company man and are treated with little respect and are considered renegades outside of society. They may be rougher than the average Japanese, but obviously they are more spirited and infinitely more interesting. Many *compa* are owned by the *yakuza* (Japanese organized crime — see "The People" in the Introduction for a lengthier discussion). A *compa* is often a piano bar where the player, who may be competent, is forced to play uninspired renditions of "Moon River" over and over again as an accompaniment to the slurred howls of drunken businessmen. Frequently, the waitresses must double as barkers, standing in front of the clubs handing out handbills as a part of their nightly duties. Although there is a darker side to *compa* behind the scenes, most people congregate here for carefree fun.

sake: This fermented rice wine began in Japan's early history as a thick gruel made from the excess rice of an abundant harvest. Its socially lubricating qualities were instantly appreciated and the process was refined. Today, sake is a clear rice wine with a delicate bouquet and a not so delicate kick (it's about 16% alcohol by volume). The fermentation process is more like beer making than wine making, but the results are more like a wine. Sake is used as a sacred wine at religious rituals and festivals as well as being a daily drink. Sold everywhere, it comes in containers ranging from distinctive clay pots to the common large glass bottle of 1800 ml called *issho*. In restaurants and bars, sake is served in a small clay vessel called a *tokkuri* containing 180 ml commonly called *ichi go*. The average price is Y250 and the *tokkuri* holds multiple servings that are drunk from thimble sized cups called *sakazuki*. These sake sets are one of the most common, yet delightful souvenirs of Japan. *Tokkuri* are often confused with bud vases. *Sake drinking etiquette:* Sake drinking, like most meaningful activities in Japan, has set etiquette. You never drink sake and eat rice at the same time. When you're with company, never fill your own glass. This will be done for you. Then take the bottle and fill the other person's glass. One who fills his own glass and then drinks is a *toku shaku*. This term implies a person who can't get enough, fast enough or simply an alcoholic. Sake comes in 3 grades, determined yearly by the government. They are from top to bottom: *tokkyu, ikkyu* and *nikkyu*. Pocketbook as well as the occasion usually determine the grade. Most bars have them all, but *nikkyu* is the everyday drink. Sake has no vintage years and is not considered to improve with age. The best sake is said to come from the colder northern areas, but all districts lay claim to the best. It's usually served warm, but sake coolers are becoming popular summer drinks. Many unsuspecting amateurs think that the warming process makes sake impotent and that the thimble sized glasses could never get you drunk. Wrong! The glasses are tiny, but they are kept constantly full. The warming process makes the alcohol more easily assimilated into the blood stream. You can easily get a terrible case of "stray foot" (that is, the right foot proceeds due north, while the left foot determined to go southwest) if you underestimate the potency of numerous tiny cups of sake.

sake in an old fashioned bottle

<u>shochu:</u> This is a sake type drink, but since it's distilled, it's much more potent. Sometimes sweet potatoes are used in its manufacture. At one time, when it was mostly bootlegged, *shochu* was considered a low class drink, but is now quite acceptable. Don't confuse it with sake, although it may seem very similar. The difference is like drinking gin as compared to wine. The best *shochu* is said to come from the warmer regions: *awamori*. This distilled spirit was at one time made from *awa* (millet). *Awamori* entered Japan from trade with Thailand and is amazingly potent. The manufacturers have corked a typhoon in every bottle. (See "Drinking," Okinawa chapter).

TOBACCO

The Japanese are heavy smokers. Notice the billowing cauldrons where half smoked butts are deposited at train platforms. These are almost like vast incense burners to Japan's newest gods—modernization and industrialization. Domestic brands of cigarettes are available on almost every street corner from vending machines or from thousands of shops. Foreign brands are available in most shops and always in big cities. The Japanese often ask if their cigarettes are as good as foreign made ones. They must be—the Japanese are dying from lung cancer at about the same rate as the rest of the smoking world. The most common brands are Hi-lite, Mild 7 and Seven Stars. Golden Bat is the cheapest and tastes like the ingredients have been gathered from the floor of the bat cave. Tobacco, as well as alcohol, is subsidezed by the federal government. They're considered necessary to keep the populace happy.

DRUGS

In the spring of 1980, Paul McCartney, his family and a large entourage of world class musicians and technicians arrived in Japan to do a national tour. Their coming was wildly heralded and tickets had been "sold out" for months. During a routine customs search, a small amount of marijuana was found in the ex-Beatle's possession. The tour was cancelled. Paul McCartney was put in jail. He was kept there for weeks of nerve jangling hassle where he was politely, but firmly informed that his crime could get him several years in prison. Finally, after the Japanese government had made their statement loudly and clearly, Paul McCartney was released from prison and promptly deported. Chances of his ever being allowed to return to Japan are slim. Paul McCartney has fantastic personal charisma, international clout, top notch lawyers and a great deal more money to spend on his defense than the average traveler. He did not make out well at all.

SAMPLE FOOD LIST AND COMMON INGREDIENTS

Aisu Kurimu - ice cream

beer *biru*

Bread *pan*. Japanese pastry shops sell exquisite looking pastries. Sometimes emphasis is put upon looks and not taste. Japanese bread comes in enormous slices. Toasters have been made larger to accommodate it. In most shops they give away *pan-no-mi-mi* ("ears of bread"), the ends of the loaf. It's good and fresh, but Japanese won't eat it and feed it to the birds.

Cake—*keiki*

Cheese--*chizu*

Cola--*cora*

Daikon--enormous Japanese white radish (30 cm x 20 cm). Used grated as a garnish and in dipping sauces. A favorite with the Japanese as a pickle. Every town claims to make the most delicious.

Gobo—Burdock root cut into slivers and often served as a salad.

Gohan—rice has almost a mystical quality to the Japanese. It is often referred to as "honorable food" and is considered one of life's essentials. It is offered to the gods and is always found in one form or another at felicitous occasions. *Gemmai* is brown rice. It is not commonly eaten in Japan as many health food people think. The Japanese admit that it may be better for you, but most simply say that they don't like it. Most restaurants don't serve it. Commonly, the ill or the old eat *gemmai*, almost like a medicine. Even if you buy it at a rice store, you may be disappointed. Japanese rice is grown with the idea in mind of processing. Therefore, Japanese brown rice has very tough hulls and overcooking almost to a mush is the only way of making it palatable.

Hot dog—*hotto doggo*

Kamaboko—processed, mashed fish combined with flour and rice wine. Dyed bright pink and found floating atop many soup or broth dishes.

Katsuobushi—dried bonito, hard enough to be used as a club. Used grated on many dishes and is the basic ingredient in *dashi* used to make soup stocks.

Konyaku—a starchy root made into a translucent cake or into plastic looking noodles. A basic ingredient in *sukiyaki*.

Mirin—sweetened sake used in cooking.

Miso—fermented, mashed, salted soybeans used like bouillon. Basic to many dishes. *Miso*

shiru (soup) is part of the traditional Japanese breakfast. Most Japanese can't face the day without it. A wide range of differing types of *miso* are used from *shiro miso* (white, sweet and lightly salted) to *hatcho miso* (pure, unadulterated bean paste).

Mochi--glutinous rice formed into a doughy ball, can be baked or broiled. Used as an ultra sweet dessert.

Mushrooms—*shiitake* is a large, flat, dark mushroom with a strong flavor. It is used in *soba* and most dishes calling for mushrooms. *Matsutake* (pine mushrooms) are highly prized and expensive, even in season.

Raisu—rice served on a flat plate. Called *gohan* in a bowl (white rice) and *gemmai* (brown rice). If you order *gemmai*, most restaurants won't have it and they'll think that you're ill.

Salad—*sa ra da*

Sandwich—*san do ichi*

Seaweeds—*Nori* is black seaweed in paper thin sheets. Eaten with a Japanese Breakfast and wrapped around *sushi*. *Kombu* (kelp) is a basic ingredient in soup stocks. *Wakame* is large, flat seaweed sold either fresh or dried. Used in salads and soups.

Shungiku—Chrysanthemum leaves used in casseroles and soups.

Soy sauce—*shoyu*. A bottle is found on every table and used to complement most foods. *Koikuchi* is darker, stronger *shoyu* used in cooking.

Tofu--a custard-like molded soy bean curd. Almost pure protein. A universal food of the future. Used in many dishes. *Yakidofu* is grilled *tofu*. *Aburage* is deep fried *tofu*.

Umeboshi—a very sour pickled plum served with many dishes as a condiment.

HEALTH

HEALTH CARE

Hospitals are found on every level in major cities and large towns, and clinics for minor illnesses are commonplace. Japanese doctors are well-trained professionals who could practice medicine in any country. If a serious medical problem arises, handle it as you would at home. No operation should occur anywhere without a second or even third opinion. Incompetent doctors can slip into the profession in any country. Make sure that you know to whom you are entrusting your well being. Prices for medical services in Japan are sky high, due mostly to National Medical Insurance. Doctors there, unfortunately, like everywhere else, are becoming increasingly concerned with their bank statements. Only children of very rich families willing to pay a gratuity to medical colleges become doctors in Japan. They want the money back and in a hurry. Recent scandals have exposed price gouging by some unscrupulous doctors who have kept patients well past the necessary time required. You can cut costs if you visit a hospital clinic as an outpatient. Your doctor will be chosen by chance, but an effort will be made to find a foreign speaking doctor. An excellent idea is to get Traveler's Insurance with a "medical rider" if your personal health plan does not cover you abroad. Most are quite reasonable and can be purchased on a short term basis. Any good travel agent in your home country can give you details. For foreign speaking doctors, the Tokyo and Kyoto TIC have an up-to-date list including foreign doctors practicing in Japan. The major English speaking hospitals (byoin) in Japan are: Tokyo: St. Luke's (03) 951-1111. Yokohama: Bluff Hospital Yamate Byoin), (045) 641-6961. Kyoto: Japan Baptist, (075) 781-5194. Osaka: Yodogawa Catholic, (06) 322-2250. Kobe: Kaisei Hospital, (078) 871-5201 and International, (078) 331-5697. Emergency numbers in Japan are: Police—110, Ambulance— 119. Expect only Japanese speaking personnel. JNTO puts out a small booklet entitled, "The Tourist's Handbook" which basically works on a "point to what you want" system with Japanese next to English phrases. The last few pages deal with parts of the body and medical emergencies. If you don't want to carry the entire booklet, tear out the necessary pages.

special note: If you have an illness that requires special care and you would like to contact a doctor in Japan before you arrive, you can get a list of appropriate doctors who speak foreign languages from: International Association for Medical Assistance to Travelers, IAMAT, Suite 5620, 350 5th Avenue, New York, New York 10001, USA. You should carry a supply of prescription drugs that will last for your entire trip. If this is impossible, have your doctor write a complete and *legible* prescription. These can be filled at the hospitals previously mentioned and at the American Pharmacy, Hibiya Park Bldg., 1-8-1, Yurakucho, Chiyoda-ku, tel: 271-4035. Other Tokyo pharmacies include, Fuji Pharmacy, Sankei Bldg., 1-7-2, Otemachi, Chiyoda-ku, tel: 231-0745: Hibiya Pharmacy, Mitsui Bldg., 1-1-2, Yurakucho, Chiyoda-ku, tel: 501-6377. In Kyoto, try Sasanami Pharmacy, Shioya-cho, Shijo-Kawaracho-Agaru, Nakagyo-ku, tel: 221-3373; or in Osaka, try Shin-Asahi Pharmacy, Shin-Asahi Bldg., 2-3-18, Nakano-shima, Kita-ku, tel: 202-6800.

dental services: Adequate professional dental care is available; but it's very expensive. TIC in Tokyo and Kyoto can provide you with dental contacts.

SELF-HELP

Sometimes while traveling you just need someone to talk to, someone who speaks your own language and to whom you can relate. Don't be embarassed; even seasoned travelers experience loneliness and culture shock. One method for alleviating this problem is to prearrange times to call home. Even a spontaneous call can work wonders. Damn the costs. If you're feeling unsettled, you can try the following phone numbers in the Tokyo area: Tokyo English Life Line (TELL), (03) 264-4347. All calls are anonymous and confidential. If they can't help, they can refer you to an agency that can. Another useful service of TELL is Tokyo Tapes (03) 262-0224. Tapes lasting 5-8 min. are available on every subject from Pre-menstrual Blues to How to Write a Term Paper. Ask for Directory Tape No. 302 for a full listing. TELL and Tokyo Tapes offer services every day from 0900 to 1300 and 1900 to 2300. Another excellent organization that offers counseling and referral services is Tokyo Community Counseling Service (03) 403-7106.

HEALTH TIPS AND ALTERNATIVE HEALTH CARE

Increasingly, people throughout the world are turning to alternative health care in the form of special diets, homeopathic medicines, acupuncture, massage, and various folk remedies. The Japanese have placed a great deal of confidence in Chinese medicine (*Kampo-Yaku*), since its introduction in the 8th C., and shops dealing in these remedies can be found in almost any town or city throughout Japan. The following is a partial list of where a wide variety of alternative services may be found. More are listed under "Services" in each chapter. Also contact TIC in Tokyo at 502-1461 and TELL at 264-4347 for more suggestions. For an exhaustive list of alternative restaurants, lodgings, clinics and temples throughout Japan, try the excellent *A Pilgrim's Guide to Planet Earth*, Spiritual Community Publications, Box 1080, San Rafael, California, 94915.

macrobiotics and health foods (*shizenshoku*): INTERMAC, 11-5 Oyama Cho, Shibuya-ku, T 151 Tokyo, tel: (03) 469-7631. Kenko Kaikan (Foods and clinic), 425 Kurihara-cho, Adachi-ku, Tokyo, tel: 869-0015. Shizenshoku Center (health foods), Shibuya, Tokyo, tel: 461-5188. Various temples throughout Japan offer lodgings (*shukubo*) and macrobiotic foods. A list is available from TIC.

acupuncture (*hari kyu*): Dr. Hiroshi Motoyama, 4-11-7 Inokashira, Mitaki shi, Tokyo. tel: (0422) 43-5558. Clinics and lectures are offered in English. Lima Ohsawa (macrobiotics and acupuncture), c/o Star Height, 1-12-13- Naka-Ochiai, Shinjuku, Tokyo. Dr. Kumiko Inoue (speaks English), Tokyo. tel: 872-6494. Some acupuncturists specialize in *Okyu* which is the burning of dried moss on the energy points throughout the body.

chiropractic: Sumida Shinzen-shoku, 2-1-2 Oshiage, Sumida-ku, Tokyo. tel: (03) 623-0573. *alternative health clinic:* Shinzen Igaku-kai, Karaki Building, 1-17-3 Hongo, Bunkyo-ku, Tokyo. tel: (03) 815-3088. *shiatsu* (*Japanese acupressure massage*): First class hotels and *ryokan* can arrange for you to be visited by a

master of *shiatsu*. Traditionally, these masters were blind, but sighted people also practice shiatsu now. Don't be surprised if it is administered through your clothing with the practioner working away from the heart. If you wish to study shiatsu contact Masunaga-san, Iokai Clinic, Okachimachi (near Ueno), Tokyo. tel: (03) 832-2983. Y3000 per week of study.

an *onsen* (mineral spa) can always be recognized by the symbol of a couldron with 3 flames rising from it. Although *onsen* are found in many varying types of buildings and settings, this symbol is always used

mineral baths (*onsen*): The most common gateway to good health used by foreigners in Japan are the mineral baths (*onsen*). Wherever these volcanic springs bubble up laden with minerals, an *onsen* has probably been built. Many go back for centuries and each claims curative powers for everything from rheumatism to hair loss. Most contain common elements such as iron, but many have unique components such as radioactive materials. A good hot soak in a congenial atmosphere helps everyone to relax and feel rejuvenated.

home remedies: Eat *umeboshi* (very salty pickled plums) for dehydration caused by perspiring during the summer. For burns, apply egg white mixed with *shoyu* (soy sauce). Ease hangovers by drinking a tea of boiled cloves. For headaches, mix equal amounts of sesame oil and ginger juice and apply to the head. For rashes, rub with cucumber. Alleviate sore throats by roasting and eating orange seeds.

Use charred, ground bamboo and water to cure stomach aches. For diarrhea, drink peony tree root tea. To get rid of toothaches, apply burned pine needles or charred eggplant and for intestinal parasites, chew (100 times) a handful of raw brown rice (*gemmai*). For fever, take one tb. grated *daikon*, 2 tb. *shoyu* and one tsp. grated ginger. Brew in one liter water. Drink, cover up and go to bed. For the common cold, try sake and a beaten egg or a charred mandarin orange. The Japanese "cure all" is tea. *Sencha* green tea is the most widely used, but explain your complaint and an appropriate tea will be offered. Also, seaweed of all types is offered for everything from high blood pressure to radiation poisoning.

kampo yaku (*Chinese medicine*): Try some of the following remedies to cure what ails you: Shrunken monkey's head for headache, baked bat to grow hair, toasted hawk for skin diseases, sparrow's claws for coughs, owl ashes for sore throats, dragon flies and goldfish for fevers, ground monkey brains for madness, and finally, charred lizards as a love potion.

common drugs and potions: For those inclined, Oranimin C is liquid synthetic vitamins in small brown bottles, sold everywhere. Japanese businessmen start the day by slugging one down. *Akamashi* (red snake) is a readily available sex potion, again in a small brown bottle with a dragon on the label. Oftentimes, it's found in hallway refrigerators at *ryokan* for

that needed boost. Snakes, in general, are believed to promote sexual prowess. Look in bars for sake bottles with a pickled snake at the bottom. *Shin Seirogan* is an over-the-counter drug used for diarrhea.

gauze masks: Gauze masks and eyepatches are a common sight during the cold season. The mask was adopted during a flu epidemic at the turn of the century. Japanese consider it impolite to blow their noses in public (*never* in a restaurant) and the gauze mask saves embarassment while helping to control spread of infection. Unfortunately, raucous spitting almost anywhere in public is OK.

food and drink: You have as much of a chance of getting sick from the food in Japan as you would in any modern westernized country. Water is safe to drink anywhere, milk is pasteurized and the vast majority of restaurants are clean. Street vendors probably have been selling their snacks at the same corner for years. They have built a clientele by serving good food. Their establishments may be meager, but their standards are high. *Sushi* is made form only the freshest fish; *ramen, soba* and various dishes are cooked before your eyes, and *yakitori* is charcoaled. Stomach distress is likely to be more psychological than physical, given the admitted strangeness of some Japanese food to westerners. For a full description of "food and drink" refer to "Food and Drink" in the "General Introcution."

FACTS, FIGURES AND PRACTICALITIES

The following pages are full of lists, charts, graphs and addresses designed to help you with your day to day living while visiting Japan, and to assist in ironing out any problems and queries while there. Of course, there will be exceptions and oversights, but the following compendium of "How to..." should at least give you a general direction in which to proceed. Good luck!

INFORMATION

Japan National Tourist Organization (JNTO): This is a semi-governmental agency whose primary function is to aid and inform any foreign traveler bound for Japan. Good and accurate information is your best ally while traveling. It's in your own best interest to fortify yourself with enough useful facts to make your trip run smoothly, and JNTO will prove to be one of the most accurate and available sources. JNTO provides an exemplary international and domestic network of facilities to aid you. Their services are indispensable. They readily dispense brochures, pamphlets, films, slides and up to the minute travel information. They also assist travel agents in preparing tours to Japan and they hand out well-done posters. *brochures:* The most useful items to travelers are the brochures that JNTO freely hands out. All of their offices have racks of these excellent publications from which to choose. The most important ones are available in English, French, German, Spanish, Italian, Chinese, Thai and Malay. The choice is up to you, but some good ones are: "Your Guide to Japan," "The Tourist Handbook," and "Japan Traveler's Companion." These 3 offer practical tips, maps, places of interest, travel information and basic communication skills. They're accurate and useful, but only skin deep. Other especially useful publications offered are maps. JNTO covers the entire archipelago of Japan and offers maps of all regions free of charge. They also offer quite useful maps of the major cities and primary tourist spots. The best course is to visit one of the foreign JNTO offices listed below and to stock up before arriving in Japan. In Japan, JNTO main office is at Tokyo Kotsu Kaikan Building 10-1, 2-chome Yuraku-cho, Chiyoda-ku, Tokyo, tel: (03) 216-1901. Besides the offices listed above, most Japan Airlines (JAL) offices also offer most of the brochures and maps.

JNTO OFFICES ABROAD

U.S.A.	Rockefeller Plaza, 630 Fifth Ave., New York, N.Y. 10111. tel: 212-757-5640	*England:*	167 Regent St., London W 1. tel: 734-9638
	333 N Michigan Ave., Chicago, IL 60601. tel: 312-332-3975	*Australia:*	115 Pitt St., Sydney, N.S.W. 2000. tel: 232-4522
	1519 Main St., Suite 200, Dallas, TX 75201. tel: 214-741-4931	*Hong Kong:*	Peter Bldg., 58 Queen's Road Central. tel: 5-227913
	1737 Post St., San Francisco, CA 94115. tel: 415-931-0700	*Thailand:*	56 Suriwong Road, Bangkok. tel:233-5108
	624 S Grand Ave., Los Angeles, CA 90017. tel: 213-623-1952	*France:*	4-8, rue Sainte-Anne, 75001 Paris. tel: 296-2029
	2270 Kalakaua Ave., Honolulu, HI 9681. tel: 808-923-7631	*Switzerland:*	Rue de Berne 13, Geneve. tel: 292792
Canada:	165 University Ave., Toronto, Ont. M5H3B8. tel: 416-366-7140	*Mexico:*	Reforma 122, †Piso, B-2, Mexico 6, D.F. tel: 535-85-83

Tourist Information Centers (TIC): JNTO also maintains 3 TICs in Japan. They can help to resolve almost any question or problem while in Japan. Their staff speaks most foreign languages and hands out up to the minute, detailed information about traveling and functioning in Japan. When you arrive in Japan, you should go to one of the following TICs as soon as possible. They'll freely photocopy any information that you may request. Neither JNTO nor TIC make reservations, either for travel or accommodations. For that, you'll have to visit a travel agent. The 3 TICs in Japan are: Tokyo Office, 6-6 Yurakucho 1-chome, Chiyoda-ku, Tokyo. tel: (03) 502-1461/2; Tokyo Airport Office (Narita), Airport Terminal Building, Ota-ku, Tokyo. tel: (03) 502-1461/2; Kyoto Ofice, Kyoto Tower Building, Higashi-Shiokojicho, Shimogyo-ku, Kyoto. tel: (075) 371-5649. Refer to these areas in the travel chapters for maps directing you to the TICs.

other information offices: Each prefecture and most major cities throughout Japan offer tourist information organizations. Usually there's a branch office at main train stations in the major cities. These prefectural tourist information centers are primarily geared toward domestic travelers, but sometimes offer information useful to foreigners. The staffs usually don't speak any foreign languages.

MONEY AND FINANCES

Japan's universal currency is the *yen* (Y). The coins used are 1, 5, 10, 50 and 100 *yen*. The banknotes are in denominations of 500, 1000, 5000, and 10,000 *yen*. Everyone is aware of the rapid fluctuations in exchange rates so common in the world money market today. It's no longer possible to give an exact exchange rate. What might be true today could easily be misleading tomorrow. For a general average, expect about Y200 per U.S. \$1.00. The Japanese big business community rarely lets the Y drop below Y200 per U.S. \$1.00. This makes exports, Japan's financial life blood, cost too much on the world market. The wisest choice in the long run is to exchange your currency as you need it while keeping an eye on the exchange rate. This is prominently displayed in foreign exchange banks and in the English language newspapers. Another important consideration is the actual buying power of your *yen*. This largely depends upon prices in your home country and Japan's domestic economy at the moment. Again, there are no major rules of computation as prices vary with the items and services sought. In general, for most manufactured goods, especially cameras and electronic equipment, you get slightly more than what you would get for the U.S. equivalent.

currency exchange: It's illegal to use anything but *yen* in Japan, so you must exchange your foreign currency for *yen* when you arrive. U.S. dollars, like all others, are not recognized, and shop keepers and hotel clerks cannot be coaxed into accepting them. Foreign currencies can only be exchanged at Foreign Exchange Banks and at a handful of big, well-known shops dealing in the tourist trade in only the largest cities. The currencies of most major European nations can be exchanged plus those of the U.S., Canada, Australia and Hong Kong. The currencies of Taiwan and Korea are worthless in Japan and will not be exchanged. Change these before you arrive!

traveler's checks (TCs): These are the easiest and safest way to carry your money. Like actual currency, they will be exchanged by the proper designated facilities, although many major hotels and a few shops might be willing to accept them. There's no black money market in Japan, so whatever the official exchange rate is that day is exactly what you'll scrupulously receive. The most accepted traveler's checks are those drawn on currency from the U.S., Switzerland, W. Germany, Canada, France, the U.K., Italy, India and Australia. To exchange foreign traveler's checks is simple, but time consuming. Don't expect to walk into a foreign exchange bank and plop them down and be handed your *yen*. Most banks maintain a separate exchange department and if the bank has more than one floor, it will invariably be upstairs. You must show your passport and fill out the proper forms. You'll be given a number by which you'll be summoned once the transaction has been recorded. Expect a delay of 30 minutes. There's usually no handling charge. Large hotels also often have a traveler's check and currency exchange window. Always keep a reasonable supply of *yen* handy. Outside of main cities and prefectural capitals, it's difficult to find a Foreign Exchange Bank. If you do run short, try any bank. This isn't normal proceedure, but if you flash your empty wallet and wave your TCs, the manager may get the message and accommodate you out of kindness and because you're a foreigner. This will involve interminable conferences of the bank personnel and long distance calls to the head office. It just isn't worth it so try not to let it happen. Another positive thought to remember is that there's very little theft in Japan, so don't be worried about carrying cash. If you're the fretful type, you can always buy Japanese TCs, but you must bear in mind that unlike other countries, they're not always universally accepted in Japan. They're drawn on a particular bank, Fuji Bank for example, and other banks and many business establishments won't readily take them. If you do purchase Japanese TCs, make sure there's a branch bank in the area where you intend to visit to avoid unnecessary hassles. You may also be charged a small service charge.

foreign exchange banks.: You are entitled, without documentation, to exchange foreign currency up to Y3,000,000. You can also take this amount of *yen* out of Japan. Most major banks can also supply you with foreign currency

in exchange for your *yen* before you return home or move on to another country. Although totally trustworthy, Japanese banks are extremely slow and bogged down by red tape. If you run out of funds and must send home for a money transfer, you're in bad shape because there's no quick way to do it. The fastest and surest way is to seek out a representative branch of your home bank operating in Japan and go through them. Don't use a Japanese bank— you'll die of starvation before the money arrives. TIC or JNTO can supply you with a complete list of foreign banks operating in Japan. The following is merely a partial list of the major foreign and domestic banks in Japan where you can carry out foreign exchange transactions. The Japanese banks, as well as a few of the foreign banks listed have branches throughout Japan. Only the Tokyo addresses are given here. Banking hours are: weekdays, 0900-1500; Saturday, 0900-1200; closed Sunday and holidays.

FOREIGN EXCHANGE BANKS

JAPANESE BANKS

Bank of Japan
2-1, Nihombashi Hongokucho, 2-chome, Chuo-ku. tel: 279-1111

Dai-ichi Kangyo Bank
1-1, Uchisaiwaicho, Chiyoda-ku. tel: 596-1111

Daiwa Bank
Nomura Bldg., 1-1, Otemachi, 2-chome, Chiyoda-ku. tel: 231-1231

Fuji Bank
5-5, Otemachi 1-chome, Chiyoda-ku.
tel: 216-2211

Hokkaido Takushoku Bank
Hokkai Bldg., 1-3-13, Nihombashi 1-chome, Chuo-ku. tel: 276-6611

Mitsubishi Bank
7-3, Marunochi 2-chome, Chiyoda-ku.
tel: 211-8111

FOREIGN BANKS

American Express
Toranomon Mitsui Bldg., 3-8-1, Kasumigaseki, Chiyoda-ku. tel: 504-3341

Banca Commerciale Italiana
Nippon Bldg., 2-1, Marunochi 1-chome, Chiyoda-ku. tel: 242-3521

Bank of America
Tokyo Kaijo Bldg., 2-1, Marunouchi 1-chome, Chiyoda-ku. tel: 214-0241

Banque National de Paris
Yusen Bldg., 2-3-2, Marunouchi, Chiyoda-ku.

Commercial Bank of Australia Ltd.,
Shin Tokyo Bldg., 3-3-1, Marunouchi, Chiyoda-ku. tel: 214-2456

Deutsche Bank
Yarakucho Denki Bldg., 1-7-1, Yutaku-cho, Chiyoda-ku. tel: 214-0035

First National City Bank
Time Life Bldg., 2-3-6, Otemachi 2-chome, Chiyoda-ku. tel: 279-5411

Hong Kong & Shanghai Banking Corp.
Chiyoda Bldg., 1-2, Marunouchi 2-chome, Chiyoda-ku. tel: 211-6461

Lloyds Bank International, Ltd., Tokyo Branch
Yurakucho Denki Bldg., 1-7-1, Yuraku-cho, Chiyoda-ku. tel: 212-0958/9

Swiss Bank Corp.
Furukawa Sogo Bldg., 2-6-1, Marunouchi, Chiyoda-ku. tel: 214-1731

Thomas Cook Bankers Ltd.
No. 24 Mori Bldg., 3-23-5, Nishi Shimbashi, Minato-ku. tel: 436-4946

JAPANESE MONEY

100 yen: silver color

10 yen: copper color

One yen: aluminum

5 yen: bronze color

50 yen: silver color

Coins shown here are actual size

10,000 yen

1,000 yen

500 yen

5,000 yen

FROM "TOUR COMPANION"

other accounts: Another obviously safe method is to open an account at any bank and carry your passbook. The obvious drawback is that you can only draw from that one bank which may not have offices everywhere you wish to go. You can also open a Postal Account at any major post office. These are more convenient because you can draw at any P.O., but to employ either method will mean exchanging your foreign currency in one lump sum and you may lose out in the long run with fluctuating currency rates.

credit cards: Most major credit cards such as Master Charge, Visa, American Express, Carte Blanche and Diners Club are accepted, but usually only at high priced, no discount, flashy tourist trade shops in major cities. The best bet is to use them only in an emergency.

COMMUNICATIONS

To travel reasonalby and wisely, you must be well informed and know what's going on around you. The following information is designed to help. The media of television, radio and movies along with newspapers, bookstores, telephones and the post office (P.O.) are covered in the following.

print media: The most readily available and informative source of information to travelers are Japan's daily English language newspapers (*shimbun*). Unfortunately, newspapers in other languages aren't easily available. Only the following are regularly sold at newstands at almost every central train station and at numerous street stands throughout the larger cities and in hotels. In smaller towns, if you see an English language daily, grab it. It's not uncommon for rural communities to receive only 1 or 2 copies, if any. The most useful newspaper is *The Japan Times* (Y100). The Monday and Wednesday editions are particularly helpful if you're seeking employment or housing. The 2 other main dailies are the *Asahi Evening News* (Y100) and the *Mainichi Daily* (Y100). There's also the *Daily Yomiuri* (Y40), but it's not as helpful as the other three. In the largest cities you can also find international magazines with a few being offered in major foreign languages.

special publications: Three of the most useful publications for visitors are the weekly *Tour Companion* and *The Weekender* along with the bimonthly *Japan Visitor's Guide.* They're available free at all TICs and in most international hotels. Although each focus is somewhat different, collectively they tell you what's going on and where to find it. For more information, see "Tokyo—Information Please" in the Tokyo chapter.

bookstores: Since the Japanese are voracious readers, themselves, with many studying foreign languages, a good number of the larger bookstores feature sections of foreign language books along with road maps, atlases and periodicals. Unfortunately, Tokyo is the only city where there's a reasonable number of shops from which to choose. The other major cities also offer some bookshops and their addresses and locations have been given in the "Service" section following their descriptions in the travel section of this book. The following list includes only Tokyo: Kinokunia (5th floor) near Shinjuku Eki, tel: 354-0131; Jena, not far from TIC near Ginza subway station, tel: 571-2980; Maruzen, near Nihombashi subway station, tel: 272-7211; Yaesu, near Tokyo Eki, tel: 281-1811; Charles E. Tuttle Bookstore in Kanda. Charles E. Tuttle bookstores specialize in books about the East. They have many bookstores throughout Japan and are the most worthwhile if you intend to be traveling. For a complete list of their bookstores, call their main office in Tokyo at tel: 811-7106/9.

telephone (denwa):   The telephone system throughout Japan is modern and technically advanced. Phones are readily available and are color coded according to their functions. Pay phones in Japan are equipped to receive Y10 and Y100 coins, allowing you to speak for a designated amount of time. When your time is just about up, there will be a chime, a click or a ding. Whenever you hear one, feed the phone or you'll be disconnected. When you're going to place a call, it's best to fortify yourself with a pocket full of Y10 and Y100 coins. Just keep feeding. Don't worry. If you put too many coins in, the unused portion will be returned. It's better than an abrupt dead line.   *red phones* (*normal desk size*):   These are for local calls. One Y10 coin cuts off after 3 minutes.   *red phones* (*very large bodies*):   The most common phones in Japan, these are used for local and intercity calls. They'll accept six Y10 coins at a time.   *pink phones:*   These are the same as large red ones, only less public. They're found sometimes in private homes, and in smal restaurants. *blue phones* (*in booths*): Used for local and intercity calls, they'll accept ten Y10 coins. *yellow phones*: Local and best for intercity calls, these phones will accept ten Y10 and nine Y100 coins at a time. Best choice for lengthy, intercity, direct dialed calls.

telephone numbers (*denwa bongo*): Japanese phone numbers have 9 or 10 digits. The first 3 or 4 (in brackets) are area codes and are used only if you're outside of the area. Area codes of major cities are: Tokyo (03), Kyoto (075), Nara (0742), Hiroshima (0822), Yokohama (045), Sendai (0222), Sapporo (011), Osaka (06), and Naha, Okinawa (0288). Japanese answer the phone by saying *moshi-moshi*.

international calls: Overseas calls can be dialed direct or through your hotel desk if you're familiar with the system. However, for most travelers it's best to call the international operator and have him/her place the call for you, especially if you want the charges reversed. For international operators, dial: Tokyo 0051, Okinawa (0988) 54-0011, all other cities (03) 211-4211 for Asian countries excluding Hong Kong or (03) 211-5111 for North/South America, Europe and Hong Kong. International information is (03) 270-5111. Rates are based on 3 min with discounts available on weekends. Approximate costs (3 min) are: North/South America, Australia Y2430; Europe Y2700, Hong Kong Y1980.

English telephone directories: The *Japan Telephone Book* (Y2000) from Japan Yellow Pages (tel: 239-3501) lists frequently called numbers of Japanese businesses, hotels, restaurants, hospitals and others. The *Japan Times Directory* (Y4000, tel: 453-5311) includes numbers of foreign residents, businesses, organizations and more.

emergency numbers: For emergencies, dial 110 for police or 119 for fire and ambulance. The person taking your call may not speak a foreign language, so it's best to get the assistance of a Japanese passerby if possible.

overseas telegrams: These are sent from telephone offices, some post offices and some larger hotels. The rates vary according to the country telegrammed. The minimum is 7 words ordinary telegram, 22 words letter telegram (half price, but slower). Urgent telegrams are double

the rate. For information, contact: KDD offices, tel: Tokyo (03) 270-5111.

radio and television: The vast majority of radio and TV programming is obviously in Japanese, but there are a few opportunities to hear broadcasts in English. The major English radio programming is presented by the Far East Network and is geared towards U.S. military personnel stationed in Japan. You can pick up their programs on the AM dial: Tokyo (810), Kyushu (1575), Okinawa (650) and northern Honshu (1575). Since music is an international language, you can tune to any AM station that strikes your fancy. It's much easier finding pop music than traditional Japanese music. Japan also has FM stations, but the frequencies used, by international standards, are very low (76-90 MHZ compared to 88-108 MHZ for the majority of the world). You can buy most radio equipment to pick up radio frequencies used in your home country. While in Japan, buy an inexpensive converter to pick up Japanese FM. Television programming is also in Japanese and you can have hours of pleasure watching the Japanese depict themselves, even if you can't understand a word. Soap operas are a well-known bore and intellectual anesthetic while at home, but they give an unpretentious, exaggerated birds' eye view of Japanese society and their outlooks. Check them out. Television cable broadcasting of English programming is available at larger hotels. Broadcast times are from 0700 to 0945 and from 1750 to 2400. Entertainment as well as news programs are offered.

post office symbol

post offices (*yubinkyoku*): The P.O. for the average traveler is his or her lifeline. It's services are indespensable and the P.O. system in Japan is modern and reasonably efficient. You can find P.O.s in even the smallest of towns. The rates are also some of the highest in the world. Although there are local P.O.s in suburbs of large cities and in some medium sized towns, it's always best to do your business with the Central P.O. (usually closest to the main train station) because they'll be the most familiar with foreigners, posterestante, overseas mail and packages. Sometimes neighborhood P.O.s do

POSTAL RATES

	LETTERS		POSTCARDS	
Destination	Air mail 10 grams	Ordinary 20 grams	Air Mail	Ordinary
North America and Canada	Y120	Y90	Y80	Y60
Asia	Y100	Y90	Y70	Y60
Oceania	Y100	Y60	Y70	Y40
Europe	Y140	Y90	Y90	Y60
Domestic		Y60, 25 gr.		Y40

International aerogrammes, the best for the traveler, are universally mailed for Y100.

PARCEL POST RATES

	SURFACE		AIR MAIL	
Destination	1kg	each additional kg	.5kg	each additional kg
U.S.A. and Canada	Y1300	Y400	Y1800	Y750
Europe	Y1650	Y300	Y2200	Y700
Oceania	Y1500	Y250	Y2100	Y700
S.E. Asia	Y1450	Y250	Y2000	Y600
S. America	Y1750	Y250	Y2600	Y1200

note: There are restrictions on sizes of packages. For accurate information, check at the Post Office. A general rule is that packages should be no larger than 1 m by .5 m and weigh no more than 10 kg. Only Central P.O.s handle international parcels. A customs declaration, available at the P.O., must be filled out and must accompany all packages.

not handle foreign mail or services. *hours:* The Central P.O. in Tokyo and Kyoto are open 24 hrs every day of the year. Main P.O.s are open 0800 to 2000 Mon-Sat and 0800 to 1200 on Sundays and holidays. Local P.O.s are open 0800 to 1700 Mon-Fri and 0800 to 1200 Sat and are closed Sundays and holidays. In Tokyo there's a special International Post Office (*Koksai Yubinkyoku*) near Otemachi that can be used if you foresee a problem, but the Central P.O. near Tokyo Station is also excellent for the majority of overseas mail. Use Red Boxes for domestic correspondence, Blue Boxes for special delivery and overseas mail.

Hisoka Maejima, the father of Japan's modern postal service

receiving mail: Japanese can read *romanji* (Roman alphabet), but it's much safer to *print* neatly than to write in script. Unless you have a friend or permanent address, you'll be dealing with posterestante/general delivery. In addressing a letter to Japan, write: Name, c/o Poste Restante, Central Post Office, Japanese City, Japan. All poste restante will go to the Central P.O. where there is a special window, usually downstairs if there's a downstairs. The clerks are reasonably efficient, but expect to spend a half hour to get your mail. You must show your passport or ARC as identification. The Japanese P.O. will hold your mail for only 30 days and then will return it to sender. This is their most efficient service. For poste restante, ask for *kyoku dome* or *tome oki*. These phrases should be sufficient. Youth hostels and hotels will also hold mail if you're a guest, but this can be a bit more risky than P.O.s, expecially at youth hostels. Embassies of the U.S., Canada, Australia and most European nations except the U.K. will also receive and hold mail for 30 days. Another good mail pick up is at American Express. Address letters: c/o American Express, Halifax Building, 16-26 Roppongi 3-chome, Minato ku, Tokyo 106. tel: (03) 586-4321. For addresses of American Express offices throughout Japan, contact your local office or the Tokyo office above. Ask for the American Express travel office booklet. A small fee may be charged for services for non-American Express credit card holders.

ELECTRICITY, WEIGHTS AND MEASURES AND TIME

Electric current in Japan is generated at 100 volts at 50 cycles in eastern Japan (Tokyo to Hokkaido) and 100 volts at 60 cycles in western Japan (Nagoya to Kyushu). North American made electrical goods that operate on 110 volts, 60 cycle will function well with no major problems. European made electronics which run on 220 volts can generally be used only at larger hotels that have outlets to accommodate them. Many travelers desire to purchase the superb electronic marvels for which Japan is so internationally famous. In most cases, this presents no problem whatsoever as the Japanese have long built models to accommodate foreign electrical currents. For more information, see "Shopping—Electrical Equipment."

time: All of the islands of Japan are in the same time zone, so domestically there's no time differences. The following is a representative time table (+ or - hrs) showing time lags between Japan and major cities throughout the world. (For telling time, hours and minutes, see "Language.") *Europe:* Amsterdam - 8, Geneva - 7, London - 9, Moscow - 6, Paris - 8, Rome - 8. *S. America:* Buenos Aires - 13, Mexico City - 15. *N. America:* Anchorage - 19, Chicago - 15, Los Angeles - 17, New York - 14, Vancouver - 17. *Oceania:* Sydney + 1, Wellington + 3. *Asia:* Bangkok - 2, Hong Kong - 1, Jakarta - 2, Singapore - 30.

weights and measures: Japan employs the metric system in all weights and measures. The following chart presents the most common conversions used by the average traveler. The figures given have been "rounded off" to the closest decimal point.

distances: The basic unit of measure is the meter (m). In one m there are 1000 mm or 100 cm. There are 1000 m in 1 kilometer (km).

1 millimeter (mm(	= .04 inch
1 centimeter (cm)	= .4 inch
1 meter	= 3.3 feet or 1.1 yards
1 kilometer	= .62 miles

to convert:

km to miles	— km x .62 = miles
miles to km	— miles x 1.6 = km
meters to yds	— m x 1.1 = yds
hectares to acres	— Hectare x 2.5 = acres
sq. km to sq. miles	— sq. km x .38 = sq. miles

weight: The basic unit of weight is the kilogram (kg). There are 1000 grams (gm) in a kilogram.

to convert:

gm to ounces	— gm x .035 = ounce
kg to ounces	— kg x 35.3 = ounce
kg to pounds	— kg x 2.2 = pounds

temperatures: Centrigrade to Fahrenheit — the simplest approximation for the conversion is to double the C and add 30. For example, 30 C = 60 + 30 = 90 F.

volume: The basic unit is the liter (1). Units given are based on the U.S. system.

to convert:

liters to fluid ounces	— L x 16.6 = fluid ounces
liters to quarts	— liters x 1.04 = qt.
liters to gallons	— liters x .26 = gallons U.S.

TOILETS

There are 3 easy ways of saying "toilet" in Japanese. They are *otearai, benjo* and *toilet* (Japanese "*toiret*). The first two are universally recognized by all Japanese except that *benjo* is a male word and seldom considered dignified enough to be used by Japanese women. Telling the men's from the women's room is not difficult. Many toilets are marked with a figure of a man or woman. If this is lacking, it's sometimes easy to tell by the color of the paint used. Blue will be for men and pink for women. Sometimes small restaurants, hotels and even train stations will not have separate facilities for men and women, so don't be shocked if a member of the oppoxite sex walks in. There are usually partitions or doors, and Japanese maintain the highest decorum in such situations. Japanese toilets are primarily of the Asian (squatting) type. Most large department stores, banks and hotels do have western toilets, so if you can't bridge this gap, it's up to you to make a mental note of where they can be found. Sooner or later you must use the Japanese type. There are 2 kinds of Japanese toilets. One is a flush type and the other is a pit type over a septic tank. They're usually made of porcelain and resemble a small, western men's urinal which has been imbedded lengthwise in the ground. There's a raised cup end at one side and that's the direction in which you point. The idea is to straddle the fixture, squat down and do your business. There are 2 schools of western thought on Asian toilets. One group feels that their use presents the most natural position and is actually beneficial to the workings of the bowels. The other group balks and insists that the position necessary is the most undignified and uncomfortable imaginable. Japanese toilets are not always kept hygienically clean, and the pit toilet type can be smelly. Toilet paper is not always provided, so it's best to always carry a supply. Also, some Japanese toilet paper could be easily used to scrape barnacles off submarines, so bring your own.

etiquette: In private homes, minshuku, ryokan, YHs and generally where there are non-public toilets provided, there's a basic etiquette to follow. If you have already removed your street shoes and are padding around in house slippers, then this is a cue that the following procedure should be used. Just inside the toilet door, there may be another pair of slippers. Remove your house slippers, leave them outside the door, and use the toilet slippers while inside the toilet area. Never wear them outside of this area as the Japanese consider this unhygienic. Japanese men are known to urinate in public. They'll usually turn their backs and face a wall or a tree if one is handy. This is usually seen in the countryside, but late at night, even in cities and especially if the man has been drinking, he'll relieve himself in this manner. The otherwise extremely formal and clean Japanese feel that it's OK to soil public ground and they have little, if any, regard for it. Women, on the other hand, always use toilets.

SHOPPING HINTS

Shopping in Japan, even if you're only browsing, is an excellent way to learn about the country and culture while spending delightful hours almost buried in the overflowing cornucopia of Japanese manufactured goods.

Basically, shopping falls into two categories: electronic marvels and traditional Japanese folkcrafts. Most of its other goods can be purchased anywhere in the world. For a complete listing of suggested items and where they're sold, refer to the travel section of this book. Also for a description of traditional arts and folkart see "Arts and Crafts." This section will deal primarily with "Tips" and should be referred to as merely a general buyer's guide. The following tips are designed to steer the discriminating shopper to Japan's best bargains and highest quality items:

bargains The most important item when looking for bargains in manufactured goods is to know prices before you arrive in Japan. There are, of course, great deals to be had in cliche goods like cameras, calculators and stereo equipment, but it's also true that you can sometimes find these items cheaper at home. The simple reason for this enigma is that Japan is export oriented and domestic goods carry a hefty (10-35%) tax. Hong Kong and Singapore can almost always be relied upon to offer cheaper prices on these items and if either is part of your itinerary, wait until you arrive there. The shops of Japan do, however, offer up to the minute, state of the art articles. Don't be dissuaded because if you're willing to look around, you can come up with excellent bargains.

customs: JNTO and TIC offices hand out brochures on tax free items and tax free shops. It's also wise to know your home country's limitations on such goods and custom taxes that can be levied drive the price up. The U.S., as well as most other countries, offer brochures dealing with "Customs" to its citizens contemplating a trip abroad. Foreign embassies in Japan can also be helpful.

tax free shops: Japan has almost 1000 retail outlets that have been designated as tax free shops. Usually, as part of their services, they maintain a foreign language speaking staff, double as authorized money changers and readily accept credit cards. If you purchase here, you'll be required to fill out a "Record of Purchase Commodities Tax Free Form." This is painless and the clerks know all about it. Simply, it's a record of your purchases that will be attached to your passport and checked by a customs official before you leave Japan. This prevents anyone from buying tax free for a Japanese friend. You can expect a discount from 5-40%, but this will only cover the tax on the item. It's not a reduction on the suggested retail price.

discount stores: Becoming more and more popular in Japan are new outlets that offer even better deals than the tax free shops. These discount stores cut their prices 10-40% below the suggested retail price. That adds up to real savings even if you include the tax. Bargain stores are only available in the largest cities, especially Tokyo, and they have been listed throughout this book. Remember that in these stores, the price tags are already set at rock bottom, so don't expect much more of a reduction. It's always worth a look around, but if you visit a number of bargain stores, you'll quickly realize that the price tags for items are almost exactly the same. Japanese retail practices usually work on fixed prices. The shops know their competition much better than you do and adjust the prices accordingly. Haggling for lower prices is not the norm and will only bring hard feelings, not a reduction. Just say, "*besto price*" and leave it up to the sales clerk. They might take off 5% or so to sweeten the deal or more likely they'll offer an extra gadget to clinch it.

where to buy: Large department stores (*depato*) in western countries are usually synonymous with inflated prices. This is not necessarily so in Japan. *Depato* here are worlds unto themselves. Big ones literally carry everything under the rising sun. If you're after a specialty item, it saves time to check out the big *depato* first. Their prices are competitive and it saves a lot on shoe leather. Besides the normal dry goods of western department stores, Japanese ones often include super markets (basement), restaurants (top floor), child care rooms, folk art, aesthetic arts classes, lumber, gardening shops and even family shrines. Browsing from floor to floor is like watching Japanese manufacturing history unfold. No one can take a steady diet of *depato*, but everyone should include at least one on sightseeing itineraries.

shopping arcades: These malls can be found everywhere, but a favorite spot is in the sub-basements of large train stations. Most establishments included are former street corner specialty shops that have gone underground. Many offer good bargains, traditional goods such as *kimono, tabi,* and *geta,* and all have a few inexpensive coffee shops and restaurants. If you're on the go and in a city waiting for the next train departure, these arcades are the most convenient way to pick up a few needed items.

choice items: As previously mentioned, traditional goods will appear under "Arts and Crafts." This section will deal with Japan's electronic renaissance, namely computers, calculators, stereos, recorders and cameras. Japan leads the world in the production of these quality items and fortunately for the traveler, the domestic price competition is stiff. Perhaps you can save a few Y in Hong Kong and Singapore, but you can never match the mind-boggling array of these goods offered in Japan. The 2 best areas for purchases and choices are Akihabara and Shinjuku, both in Tokyo. They've been covered in detail under "Tokyo's Main Areas."

cameras: The ascendancy of Japan in the field of optics is one of the prime components of the "economic miracle." They have eclipsed all other nations in the production of excellent, reasonably priced 35 mm cameras and lenses. If you're a photography buff or just an enthusiastic novice, Japan is camera heaven. If you intend to buy a camera in Japan, you best bet is to make it your first purchase. Don't wait until you're leaving Japan to buy. In this way, you can use your camera on the spot and appraise your results. If it's faulty or somehow unsatisfactory, you can get good guaranteed service at the place of purchase and avoid the hassles of international haggling. Check out the comparative prices of the discount stores first. Make sure that "the models" are the same and then buy it. The Canon, Nikon and Yashica companies offer guided tours of their factories and show rooms. You can see first hand the newest and most remarkable innovations. Applications should be made 2 wks in advance with information being offered at JNTO and TIC.

film and film processing: The 3 name brand films readily available in Japan are Kodak, Fuji and Sakura. Both Kodak and Fuji can be easily processed world wide, while Sakura is much less known. The prices of Kodak and Fuji are comparable, with Sakura slightly cheaper. *slide film:* The Japanese use very little slide film. Consequently, it's often difficult to find outside of large metropolitan areas. Since it's much cheaper than print film to buy and process, this is a paradox considering the usually cost

conscious Japanese. To avoid being disappointed, always carry enough slide film to see you through your trip, especially if you intend to venture into outback Japan.

Kodak vs. Fuji: There has been a long debated battle between photographers on the comparative qualities of Fuji and Kodak films. It will probably never be resolved. The Japanese, themselves, seem to prefer Kodak, but this could be just because it's foreign. Beauty is in the eye of the shutter snapper. There's full choice of all ASAs manufactured by Kodak and Fuji. Film prices vary considerably so you'll have to look for bargains in discount stores. An approximation of film cost for both Kodachrome and Fujichrome is Y900 (36 exposures). You can often do better bringing your film supply from home.

processing: The most invaluable and irreplaceable items to many travelers are the films and slides of their trip. Japanese processing is satisfactory, but not cheap, so you may consider stockpiling your exposed film until you can get it processed at home. This method incorporates the creeping paranoia that perhaps your camera isn't working properly and all you film is ruined. There's no easy answer. Any camera shop in Japan offers processing. The normal time is 4-8 days, but 24 hr service is common and you can often have same day service if you arrive early enough in the morning. This is only possible at large, metropolitan camera stores. Again, prices vary but expect to pay Y800 (Fujichrome—36) and Y1200 (Kodachrome—36). To save on the anxiety of films being lost, save them until you arrive in a large city where you expect to spend at least 2 days. This can also save on processing costs as you'll be able to shop around for the best deal. Prepaid mailers common to Kodachrome film are unattainable in Japan. You can bring them from home and use them in Japan, but you must have a Japanese address where the slides can be sent. Poste restante may cause too much paranoia. Send Kodachrome prepaid mailers to: Far East Laboratories, Ltd., 14-1, 2 chome, Higashi-Gotanda, Shinagawa ku, Tokyo. Kodak also has a "fast service" booth in the Ginza (Tokyo). They normally have your film back in 48 hrs, but your best bet is to deal with a discount camera shop in Shinjuku (Tokyo) for one day reliable, inexpensive processing.

electronic gizmos: If you are after electronic wizardry, you have found the right place Calculators, watches, stereos, TVs, radios and

above, clockwise: Emma, defending the temple from demons (J.D. Bisignani); bronze bull of Daisenji Temple (J.D. Bisignani); Seki Butsu of Usuki (J.D. Bisignani)

above, clockwise: roadside Okinawan Buddha (W. Stier); temple at dusk (C. Parks); Kirishima Jinja (J.D. Bisignani); Kokuzo Bosatsu, the dispenser of wisdom and happiness (J.D. Bisignani); fancy roofwork at Kirishima Jinja (J.D. Bisignani)

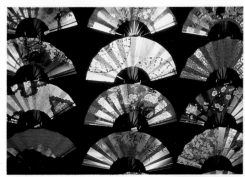

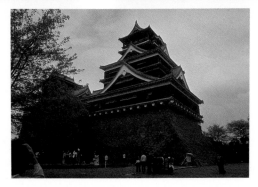

above, clockwise: Kumamoto-Jo Castle (J.D. Bisignani); a *Kyogen* farce (W. Steir); Ainu woodcarvings (J.D. Bisignani); fans of many colors (C. Parks); temple statuary (W. Steir);

above, clockwise: food for the eye and palate (J. Nelson); the realism of plastic window food (W. Stier); art nouveau of downtown Tokyo (J.D. Bisignani); ''Please accept this worthless gift.'' (C. Parks); a Tokyo fish market (J.D. Bisignani)

computers literally overflow their shelves and are packed, stacked and displayed on the streets in front of inumerable shops. They're not necessarily cheaper in Japan, but the best place to purchase them is at tax free shops and discount stores. There's one major pitfall — Japanese electrical current. The 100 v 50 cycle oddball Japanese current is what most electronic devices that you'll see on the shelves are designed to run on. The majority of these items will work satisfactorily on 117 v U.S. current, but the extra power boost could cut down on their longevity. The 220 v used in Europe and Australia will fry them. (A converter is available in most electronic shops at about Y4000). All tax free shops and many discount stores have models suitable for use in foreign countries, but they are limited. Also remember that domestic Japanese TV and FM are channeled differently than European and American bands. The Japanese are aware of this dilemma and many shops have technicians that will make the necessary adjustments usually free of charge. It's up to you to specify where the item will be used. Before you burden yourself with one of these bulky items, remember that extra baggage costs dearly and that shipping costs can easily offset any savings. If you still can't resist, go to Akihabara where the very streets look like one large console.

watches and calculators: A small pocket calculator is no longer a luxury item to a traveler — it's almost a necessity. Everyone is obsessed with knowing how much those *yen* are in his or her own currency and they really help to keep that tight traveling budget balanced. The models available in Japan are almost endless. They'll also help with computations of metric to miles, kgs to lbs, C to F, and many are also clocks with built in alarms that can get you to the train staion on time. Another handy item for travelers is an electronic watch, especially one that has an alarm. Japanese trains roll on the minute with some busy train stations having departures only a minute or so apart. Nowhere in the world is the exact time more useful than in Japan. The International brands include Seiko and Citizen. They're excellent timepieces, but are hardly inexpensive. Many smaller companies offer watches that are just as reliable without the big price for the big name. The best inexpensive, electronic watch made in Japan is a Casio. (Swiss watches, unless they're made of gold, no longer have an exotic mystique in Japan. They're even featured as little more than cereal box top prizes).

HELPFUL SERVICES AND MISCELLANEOUS

While in Japan you may require one or more of the following special services. These are listed below for your convenience.

housing: The daily newspapers, as well as the *Weekender* magazine, run classified ads for housing. If they can't provide a lead, you may wish to try:

Eastern Real Estate Co. Sankaido Bldg., 1-9-13, Akasaka, Minato-ku	583-2181
Plaza Homes, Ltd. Chuo-Likura Bldg., 3-4-11, Azabu-dai, Minato-ku	583-6941
Tokyo House Bureau Ishizuka Bldg., 1-4-8, Toranomon Minato-ku	501-2496

babysitters: If you need a night out free from the kids, many hotels offer baby sitting services. If not, try:

Tokyo Domestic Service
Tameiki, Tokyo
tel: 584-4769

Tokyo Maid Service
Suidobashi, Tokyo
tel: 291-3595

Hote New Otani's Baby Room
Kioicho, Tokyo
tel: 265-1111

lost and found: If you lose or misplace an article in Japan, you have an excellent chance of having it returned. Many tourists have told incredible stories of how they've left their camera on the back seat of a taxi and had it returned to their hotel by the driver. Bus, railroad, subway and taxi companies all maintain a lost and found department. In Tokyo, all lost items are given over to the Central Lost and Found Office of the Metro Police force after 5 days. To check, go to 1-9-11, Koraku, Bunkyo ku, Tokyo. tel: 814-4151.

for the businessman: Many services are offered to foreign businessmen by the Japanese in their effort to improve international business relations. A wide range of booklets is distributed by any JNTO and this organization is also helpful with any specific questions that a businessman may have. *business/calling cards:* Everyone, including itinerant travelers, would be wise to carry a calling/business card (*meshi*) while in Japan. All Japanese seem to have them and exchange them readily. They're not only a social lubricant but also you're almost a nonentity without one. The Japanese also consider them a memento from foreign friends and acquaintances. If you already have cards from home, just bring them along with you. It's a simple matter to have the Japanese equivalent printed on the back. Another alternative to printing is to have a rubber stamp made of your particulars and stamp the cards as you need them. Always hand a Japanese your card with the foreign printing up. Japanese up assumes that he can't read the foreign language, and even if true, is slightly insulting. Shops in all major cities of Japan offer this printing service. Hotels can also

arrange it or if you're flying JAL, they can also provide the service for you. While in Tokyo try: Nagashima Assoc., 1st Floor, Imperial Hotel. tel:591-5733 or Itoya, 2-7-15, Ginza. tel: 561-8311. *business directories:* If you require a business directory, the largest and most complete is Japan Business Directory. This is available from: Diamond Lead Co., 4-2 Kasumigaseki, 1-chome, Chiyoda ku. tel: 504-6790. The directory costs Y50,000.

INTERPRETERS AND SECRETARIAL SERVICE

Japan Convention Service
Nippon Press Center Bldg., 508-1211
2-2-1 Uchisaiwai-cho, Chiyoda-ku, Tokyo

Japan Guide Association
Shin-Kokusan Bldg., 4-1, 213-2706
Marunouchi, 3-chome, Chiyoda-ku, Tokyo

Japan Lingua Service
2-9-13, Ginza, chuo-ku, Tokyo 567-3814

MAJOR DIPLOMATIC DELEGATIONS

Almost every country in the world is represented with a diplomatic delegation in Japan. These are found in many major Japanese cities from Sapporo to Naha, but the largest concentration of embassies and consulates is found in Tokyo. The following is merely a partial listing of the major delegations found in Tokyo. For a complete listing of delegations from other countries as well as a listing of other Japanese cities where foreign diplomatic delegations can be found contact any JNTO office or TIC.

American Embassy
1-10-5 Akasaka, Minato-ku. tel: 583-7141

Australian Embassy
2-1-14 Mita, Minato-ku. tel: 453-0251

British Embassy
1 Ichibansho, Chiyoda-ku. tel: 265-5511

Canadian Embassy
7-3-38 Akasaka, Minato-ku. tel: 408-2101

Danish Embassy
Denmark House, 4-17-35 Minami Aoyama, Minato-ku. tel: 404-2331

French Embassy (Consulate)
4-11-44 Minami-Azabu, Minato-ku. tel: 473-0171

German Embassy
(Federal Republic of Germany)
4-5-10 Minami-Azabu, Minato-ku. tel: 473-0151

Indonesian Embassy
5-2-9 Higashi-Gotanda, Shinagawa-ku. tel: 441-4201

Italian Embassy
2-5-4 Mita, Minato-ku. tel: 452-7611

Korean Embassy
1-2-5 Minami-Azabu, Minato-ku. tel: 452-7611

Malaysian Embassy
20-16 Nampeidaimachi, Shibuya-ku. tel: 463-0241

New Zealand Embassy
20-40 Kamiyamacho, Shibuya-ku. tel: 460-8711

Norweigian Embassy
5-12-2 Minami-Azabu, Minato-ku. tel: 446-4711

Philippine Embassy
5-6-15 Roppongi, Minato-ku. tel: 583-4101

Soviet Embassy
2-1-1 Asabudai, Minato-ku. tel: 583-4224

Spanish Embassy
1-3-29 Roppongi, Minato-ku. tel: 583-8531

Swedish Embassy
1-10-3 Roppongi, Minato-ku. tel: 582-6961

Swiss Embassy
5-9-12 Minami-Azabu, Minato-ku. tel: 473-0121

ETIQUETTE AND CONDUCT

All travelers with even a modicum of sensitivity for an intriguing foreign culture want to know how to act when visiting that culture. The answer to this query is simple: act naturally and with common sense. People, no matter where they're from, have an innate sense of what is acceptable behavior; simply follow that sense. The classic film, "Harvey," featuring a philosophical 6 foot rabbit, summed it up: "Life is so much easier when we are pleasant." A foreigner, especially one with western features, is given a lot of space socially when traveling through Japan. When the Japanese see that you're a *gaijin*, they will not expect you to know all of the intricacies of acceptable Japanese behavior. You'll be given a great deal of latitude and if you make a mistake, as long as it is unwittingly, it will cause humor instead of anger, with no harm done. The Japanese are not tough taskmasters or foreigners visiting their country; actually, the obverse is true. If you can display even rudimentary skills in handling a purely Japanese situation, your hosts will be amazed. Most Japanese assume that westerners have absolutely no idea of Japanese norms of behavior, so making an honest attempt to act correctly will endear you to your hosts, even if your actions are somewhat askew. The Japanese will know that your heart is in the right place and their culture is much more geared to teach by positive rather than negative criticism. You also don't have to feel as though you're walking on "social eggs" when traveling in Japan. Some countries, like the island nations of the S Pacific, are isolated and the actions of visitors can have a heavy bearing on setting the future tone of interactions. Some travelers are condescending, usually in the form of being too free with their money, and they view everything that the "natives" do as quaint. If you need to be reminded, Japan has an exceptionally strong culture which is over 2000 years old. They are also the 3rd richest, industrialized nation in the world and they have assimilated, used and discarded foreign cultures since their beginning. If anything, the Japanese "natives" might view *you* as quaint. The following section is in no way intended to be a behavioral "straight jacket." Most of the advice given below will also be found in other sections that correspond to the particular topics throughout the book, but they're important enough to be repeated here again. The intention is to clue you in, so that you

won't make any major *faux pas* while visiting. Actually, there are surprisingly only a handful of instances where you *must* conform to the Japanese way; for the rest, turn your attentions to having a good time.

OFURO

An *ofuro* is the general name given to a Japanese bath. The Japanese people love them and try to take one every day. The *ofuro* is a Japanese birthright with heavy religious overtones, although many people don't realize it. Shinto regards purity and cleanliness both in body and soul with paramount importance. It is disrespectful to the gods to be unclean. Communal (usually sexually segregated) *ofuro* are found at *onsen* (spas), *sento* (public baths), and at most *ryokan, minshuku* and youth hostels. The rules regarding taking an *ofuro* are simple and never change. When you walk into the *ofuro* room, wherever it might be, there will be a large tub usually designed for more than one person. This tub is the *ofuro* proper. It can be a modern, plastic affair or a beautiful stone pool surrounded by mosaic, which is the case at most *onsen* and some *sento*. You do not bathe in the *ofuro* in the western sense; it is for soaking and relaxing *after* you have washed yourself. In the *ofuro* room will be a series of hot and cold water taps lining the walls and, perhaps, a western style shower. In the corner will be a stack of buckets and tiny stools for your use. Sometimes they will be made from wood, but most likely they'll be plastic. Take one of each and find a space away from the *ofuro* near the taps. Here is where the soaping and washing is done. Notice that the little stool has a hole in the middle. This is so your truly private parts will not touch where other's private parts have been. Sit on the stool and fill your bucket with water and repeatedly douse yourself. Then soap and shampoo yourself with gusto. Refill the bucket numerous times and wash away every single trace of soap. Once you're squeaky clean, then sit in the *ofuro*. The water is usually hot enough to boil a lobster. The Japanese like it that way, but there is usually a cold water tap at one end that you can turn on and sit under. Another technique that helps is to remain motionless. Don't stir a muscle and you'll be surprised at the temperature that your body can withstand. Don't duck your head under the water; this is considered unclean. Many Japanese will place their wet and cool towels on their heads. Once you have soaked enough, get out and rinse off at the taps again. You can go in and out of the *ofuro* as many times as you please. When walking around the *ofuro* area, notice that most Japanese hold their towels in front of their genitals. If you get into an *ofuro* with soap on and get soap into it, you'll shut down the establishment for the day. Bathers will leave the tub and the management will close the doors so that they can drain the tub and meticulously wash it. Even an unknowing *gaijin* in Japan that does this will cause hard feelings. So remember to rinse that soap off before gingerly immersing yourself in these traditional Japanese baths!

TATAMI MATTING AND SHOES

Whenever you see *tatami* matting, do *not* under any circumstances walk on it with your shoes. *Tatami* matting, like the *ofuro*, is tied in with basic religious concepts. Shoes touch the earth and are made unclean; unclean things do not belong in a house. When you enter a *ryokan*, *minshuku*, YH, or temple, you will usually see a pile of shoes. Simply use this as a cue to take yours off. Oftentimes, plastic slippers await at the doorway to be used when walking in the building on non-*tatami* areas like wooden floored hallways. If a doorway leads to a *tatami* matted room, take off the plastic slippers. A separate pair of slippers is always provided in toilet areas. Don't wear your house slippers into toilets or your toilet slippers outside of the toilet. It doesn't take long to get the hang of shoe changing, and after a while it seems to be a very reasonable idea. For more infor-

mation on the subject, see "Accommodations" (ryokan) and "Facts, Figures and Practicalities" (Toilet).

EATING

If you are invited to a Japanese home or even as a guest to a restaurant, don't wait for your host and especially your hostess to begin eating first or you'll never eat. You, as the guest, are expected to thank your host profusely and then to delicately, but deliberately dig in. Just say, "*ita dake masu*" (I'm about to eat) then go ahead. If you're drinking *sake*, you must finish it before the rice is served. This is usually the go ahead for the entire meal to be served. Rice and *sake* are generally not consumed together, but if you're at a bar and eating snacks, it's not the same as a formal dinner and is generally OK. Strict etiquette says that rice is eaten separately as the last course, but you'll notice that even the Japanese don't always observe this. Don't cross your *hashi* (chopsticks) in your empty bowl. This is a bad omen and signifies death. If you are picking morsels from a communal bowl, turn you *hashi* around and take your food with the non-eating end. Reverse them to eat. Don't eat while walking down the street. It's sign of ill breeding. For more information see "General Introduction," "Food."

GENERAL DOS AND DON'TS

The following are not earth shattering social errors, but you should try not to commit them whenever possible. Don't blow your nose in public, especially when dining or at a restaurant of you'll clear the place out. Japanese consider nose blowing disgusting and an act that should be done in private, if possible. If they're with and no toilet is available, the Japanese will turn away from a group or hunker down behind a pillar at a train station to blow their nose. They also usually use tissues and not handkerchiefs. Many feel that blowing your nose into a hanky and then stowing it and its contents in your pocket is...oooooh! Unfortunately, they don't have the same regard for spitting. Men and women, too, will hack it up and let it fly. Watch your step! It is OK for men to urinate in public areas usually against a wall. This is usually done only in villages, but night time carousers in cities who have rented some beer for an hour or two will relieve themselves in this way. Your job is not to look at them. Again, another rule

apanese traditionally wrap money in fancy paper when ffering it as a gift and it is usually tied with red and hite paper string

pertaining to feet is that if you find yourself sitting around in a group on the floor, which will be common, don't call people's attention by touching them with your feet. This is insulting, especially if a woman does it. Japanese men don't whistle at girls. It is rude and whistling while walking down a street after dark is almost an admission of being a thief. The Japanese throw away perfectly good, hardly used articles into the trash. Many foreigners in Japan just about furnish their apartments by picking through these throw aways. This is a difficult area. In one way it's okay, but in another it's an admission of poverty which is not only a slur against the poverty stricken one, but against any good responsible Japanese whose attention it comes to. You even have to be a bit careful when offering someone a used article. This doesn't carry over into giving a memento of your visit, which is always greatly appreciated. One rule, however, is never to poke around in the trash after dark. When shopping, generally don't haggle over prices. The feeling is that the goods or services offered are set at the fair price and haggling means that you think that they're not worth it or you feel that you're being ripped off. When you pay someone for something, they won't count your change into your hand. They'll simply count it out to themselves and hand you the notes and coins in a lump. Don't recount your change in front of them. Have faith—you won't be short changed. There are even certain circumstances when you should place the money in an envelope, like when tipping a maid at a *ryokan* or paying for lodgings at a *shukubo* (temple lodging). This comes from an old sense that money is a distasteful subject and no cultured person should give it a second thought. Don't kiss or be huggy in public. The Japanese are very discreet about public displays of intimacy. Only recently in Japan have Japanese young people even begun to hold hands in public. Kissing a Japanese girl in public, even if she's only a friend, will mean to all concerned that you're sleeping with her and that she has little self-respect. When talking with someone while sitting down, don't let your legs swing like rocking chairs or fidget around. This is somehow a sign of poverty and the low breeding of uncultured, backwoods folks. When a Japanese person meets or says goodbye to a *gaijin* they may or may not bow. You are not expected to bow. Just shake hands as you normally would. All Japanese know and use this custom which they expect as normal behavior from a westerner. Remember most of all to always thank any Japanese who has been kind or helpful. Nowhere else in the world does a hearty, "*Domo arigato gozaimasu*" (Thank you very much), go so far or mean so much.

THEFT

Under the best of circumstances being "ripped off" is a terrible nuisance and while traveling it can be disastrous. Having your sleeping bag, camera or even your pocket knife lifted can cause a traveler misery and sabotage your spirits. Japan fortunately is 99% theft free. The Japanese as a people simply don't steal. It is a matter of honor and a deeply ingrained social morlaity. A thief in Japan is a disgrace both to himself, his family and even his ancestors. Many times when the few thieves in Japan are cought and brought to justice they are required to make a personal appearance at the home of the person that they robbed and to offer an apology. They are also required to make restitution for the stolen items. A traveler should always be weary of losing his/her possessions but in Japan it is not a constant worry. In large cities or busy train stations take normal precautions. There are always coin lockers and temporary parcel storage rooms available and it is best to check your baggage if you plan to be separated from them for any length of time. In small villages and towns you can leave your pack or bags leaning against a pillar at the train station all day long and the chance of finding something missing when you return will be minimal. Notice in YHs that Japanese students will even leave their camera and watch lying on top of their bunk when they go for a bath or even for an evening stroll. Unfortunately other western travelers can not be trusted nearly as much as the Japanese. Long term western residents in Japan report that there are Japanese sneak thieves who will break into their apartments. They are usually after cash or jewelry. Unlike western countries they don't normally take stereos, cameras or tvs. Most of these thieves "case" their targets for a time and a traveler has little to worry about from them. If you happen to lose something say, for example, your camera on a bus stop bench, don't assume that it's gone forever. Go back for

it and if it isn't sitting where you left it check at the closest *koban* (police box) and it will probably be there. If in a big city check at the central police stations "lost and found." There are only 2 items that are regularly lifted in Japan: umbrellas and bicycles. On a rainy day don't leave your umbrella lying around. A Japanese person might take it more for their own convenience than out of malice but you'll get wet none-the-less. Bicycles are a prime target for city thieves who sell them easily but they're usually only after expensive touring or racing bikes. An old clunker or a rental bike is probably immune from theft but don't tempt fate. If you are traveling in the country and can't shake the paranoia of being ripped off just ask a ticket seller at the train station or a shop keeper to watch your gear. If you are lodging at a *minshuku* or *ryokan* don't worry at all. The best export item that the Japanese have to offer the world is their honesty and integrity.

TOKYO

INTRODUCTION

The city is a dainty lady with pink cherry blossoms in velvet black hair, a sweaty workman in cement-covered shoes, a quick bow and a sincere desire to help by any hailed stranger, along with rude shoves by the half-million commuters scurrying gracefully at rush hours. Then suddenly there's a quiet temple where Buddha is praised with sweet-smelling incense next to a reeking harbor with waters thick enough to walk on. The resounding plunk of a *samisen* played by delicate geisha fingers competes with the bumps and grinds of topless bar girls with red lips and even redder bottled hair. Scrubbed and starched apple-cheeked laughing children contrast with the older fake punk rockers in look-alike Elvis apparel and *takenoko,* teens in bright-colored ancient Chinese costumes gyrating in orderly, polite anti-social groups. Public drunken horror shows on the last midnight suburban trains are condoned, while a joint of marijuana will send you to jail. A vast array of eateries beckon to the hungry: *sushi* bars, hole-in-the-wall drinkeries, street stalls, hot chestnuts, food to go, elegant French revolving restaurants, chrome-deco musical coffee shops. The sublime *kabuki, noh* and tea ceremony coexist with flashy vaudeville, strip tease and amiable (now illegal) prostitutes. Endless throbbing lines of commuters surge grey faced in grey business-suit uniforms while ancient hunched *obasan* (grandmothers) in old-age-dark kimono shuffle along with sparkling, knowing eyes. Cramped streets house the National Diet, the Imperial Household, oasis gardens and fresh-air parks, all intersected and connected by slicing, screeching rail lines. Telephone lines everywhere! Neon, harsh and garish. Neon softly reflected in puddles on misty rainy nights soothes. Such noise, such clamor, industry! A half million farmers—where? The spirit of a nation crammed over 12,000,000 strong between ocean and mountain, international city, giant village, bombed, repaired, growing, growing Tokyo.

GETTING THERE

Narita International Airport, 60 km from Tokyo Eki, is one of Asia's busiest airports, as well as being one of the most inconveniently situated. International flights from throughout the world land here, except for those of China Airlines. The building of the new airport caused great civil turmoil in Japan for 10 years, complete with demonstrators and riot police. The issues were environmental, as land had been taken from the farmers, but now that the initial fervor has died

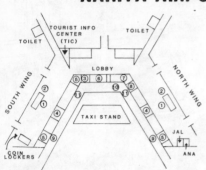

NARITA AIRPORT TERMINAL

NARITA AIRPORT TERMINAL

1. Information Counter
2. Money Changers
3. Rent-A-Car Counter
4. Hotel Reservation Counter
5. Limousine Bus & Hire-Car Counter
6. JNR Ticket Counter
7. Keisei Line's Ticket Counter
8. Baggage Delivery Service
9. Limousine Bus
10. Shuttle Bus (to Keisei Airport Sta.)
11. Shuttle Bus (to JNR Narita Sta.)

down, although there is very strict security. The airport has 24-hr money changers, lockers, and numerous means of travel to Tokyo. Change your money into yen at the customs hall before proceeding into the main concourse. If you fail to do so, you must trudge to the 4th floor where more changers are located. The 1st stop for any traveler should be the TIC (Tourist Information Center), located in the main lobby. Personnel speak English and can provide you with invaluable information, including maps, accommodation prices, onward-going timetables, and more. They don't make reservations, however. Narita TIC (see map) is open Mon.-Fri., 0900-1200, and again from 1300-2000, Sat. 0900-1200, closed Sunday. There is another TIC in Tokyo at Yura-

kucho, but don't leave the airport until you have received free copies of the *Tourist Map of Japan, Tourist Map of Tokyo, Tokyo and Vicinity,* and *Tokyo.* There are other information booths located in the main concourse, but they are of limited use because the personnel do not usually speak foreign languages. Details for commuting to Tokyo are given in the following map and chart and more information concerning Narita is given later under "Vicinity of Tokyo." Once you have decided upon a course suitable to your needs for reaching the city, tickets for the appropriate bus, skyliner, JNR train or Keisei Rail Line are available from vendors in the airport's main lobby.

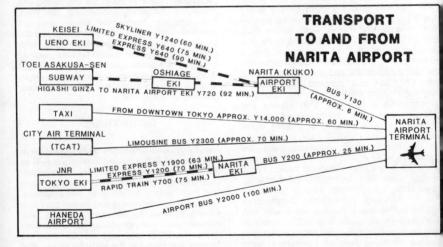

TRANSPORT TO AND FROM NARITA AIRPORT

Haneda Airport: This much more conveniently placed airport handles the lion's share of domestic air traffic to Tokyo as well as the international flights of Taiwan's China Airlines. Haneda borders E Tokyo Bay and is only 30 min from downtown Tokyo by bus although the best means of reaching Tokyo is by monorail (clearly marked) in 15 min to Hamamatsucho Eki near Tokyo Eki. Because of the convoluted political reasoning that accompanied Japan's diplomatic recognition of the People's Republic of China, Taiwan's China Airlines was relegated to using Haneda Airport. This "arrangement" quickly became a financial boon. Because of Haneda's convenience to Tokyo, many international travelers in the know opt for China Airlines who offer reasonably priced air fares from Taiwan and the W coast of the U.S. For those with connecting flights from either Haneda or Narita, buses shuttle between the 2 airports from 1840-2030, making the run (depending upon traffic conditions) in about 3 ½ hrs, Y2500.

by steamer: The last of the ocean-going steamers still making for Japan drop anchor either at Yokohama or Kobe. From Yokohama's S pier, taxi to Yokohama Eki in 10 min, then rail to Tokyo Eki in 15 minutes. From Kobe Pier No. 1, taxi to Kobe Eki in 15 min, then train to Tokyo. The *shinkansen* connects the 2 cities in 3 hrs 30 minutes. *by ferry:* Ferries from throughout the archipelago dock at Tokyo Harbor, utilizing the Tokyo Ferry Terminal that is connected by bus to various points throughout the city. The main ferries heading N are those operated by the Nippon Enkai Ferry Co. to Tomakomai in Hokkaido. Tokyo tel: (03) 574-9561, Tomakomai tel: (0144) 34-3121; or by the Kinkai Yusen Co. to Kushiro in Hokkaido, Tokyo tel: (03) 447-6551, Kushiro tel: (0154) 24-5134. The main ferries heading S are those operated by Nihon Kosoku Ferry Co. to Shikoku, Tokyo tel: (03) 274-1801, and by the Ocean Tokyu Ferry Co. also to Shikoku, Tokyo tel: (03) 567-0971. Ferries are also operated further S to Kyusu by the Nippon Car Ferry Co., Tokyo tel: (03) 563-3911. Numerous ports of call along the Inland Sea with connecting ferry schedules allow you to travel the length of the archipelago and to island hop all the way to Okinawa. The Tokai Steamship Co. services the Oshima and far-flung Ogasawaka Is. scattered deep in the Pacific, S of Tokyo. Full information, including mimeographed lists of ferry routes and prices, is available from JNTO and TIC. Reservations and tickets are available from most travel agents and any JTB.

by bus: Buses leave the capital for destinations in every direction, but the main artery is S to Nagoya with connections for Kyoto and Osaka. The JNR Highway Bus Terminal is at the S-side of the Yaesu exit at Tokyo Station. JNR Highway (daytime) buses from Tokyo to Nagoya (6 hrs) have daily departures at 0630, 0930, 1330, Y4000 with connections from Nagoya to Kyoto, (2 hrs 30 min) leaving every 1 ½ hrs from 0700-1000, then every 2 hrs from 1250-1550, Y2000. From Nagoya to Osaka (3 hrs 20 min) buses depart every 2 hrs from 0750-1630, Y2500. JNR also operates "night buses" to these destinations. This saves the daytime for sightseeing, but seats must be reserved (Y1500 extra) at "green" windows of JNR stations. These night buses leave Tokyo at 2300, arrive Kyoto at 0745, Y6800; leave Tokyo at 2220, arrive Osaka at 0740, Y7000; leave Tokyo at 2320, arrive Nagoya at 0740, Y5500. For complete details, check with JNTO, JTB or TIC in Tokyo.

by rail: All branch and feeder lines connect one way or another to the main rail arteries servicing Tokyo. Not only the JNR, but also numerous private lines converge on the city. The main trunk lines are the *shinkansen* to Fukuoka (Hakata) in Kyushu, which runs W along the southern shores of Honshu. The Sanyo Main Line and the Tokaido Main Line parallel the *shinkansen* and join at Osaka. The Shin-Etsu Main Line runs due N to Naoetsu where it connects with the San-In Main Line servicing the coast along the Sea of Japan. The Tohoku Main Line cuts NE through Tohoku, with connections to Hokkaido.

GETTING AROUND

Taxis: Tokyo taxi drivers are hard—pressed working men out to make a living. They know the city well and drive like banshees. Taxis cruise the streets looking for fares; just hail them. Remember—the back doors open and close automatically. On rainy days taxis are particularly hard to come by. Late at night in the entertainment areas, particularly at Ginza, they're at a premium, and so they price gouge. It's expected that you'll pay more than the normal fare. The number of fingers that you hold up while hailing them is your offer. Three fingers triple the fare, etc. From 2200-0100, taxis don't cruise in the Ginza area, but are found only at designated taxi stands. Yellow cabs go only to and from JNR railway stations. Except when you must be somewhere at a particular time, or

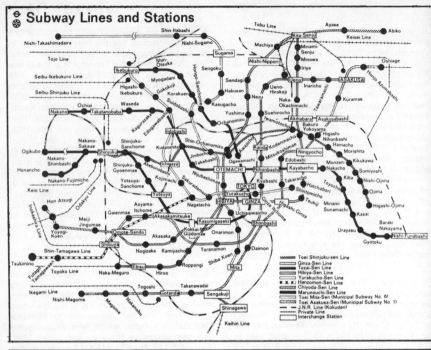

Subway Lines and Stations

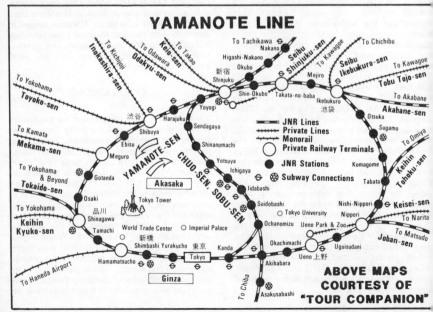

YAMANOTE LINE

ABOVE MAPS
COURTESY OF
"TOUR COMPANION"

when you're hopelessly lost, you can avoid taxis altogether.

buses: It's estimated that 2,000,000 Tokyoites ride buses daily. They go everywhere, but unfortunately, there are no bus signs in English. Unlike trains, there's no way for you to know their routes in advance, so when you want to "zig," they might "zag." Unless you have detailed instructions about which bus to take and where to change (*norikae*), your chances of getting to where you want to go are slim. Buses, at one time or another along their routes, stop at a subway or railroad station, so if you're kidnapped by one, just bide your time.

trains and subways: Trains and subways are by far the best means by which to get around Tokyo. Inter-urban trains and subways run every few minutes from 0500-2400. Tickets are available at windows or from vending machines in the stations. Until you know the exact fare, buy the cheapest ticket. If you owe money, the ticket taker at the end of your run will charge you accordingly. If you've overpaid, go to the fare adjustment window at all stations. The main interchange stations running counter-clockwise from Tokyo Eki are: Akihabara, Ueno, Ikebukuro, Shinjuku, Shibuya and Yurakucho. All trains and subways are color coded, so just follow the correct color when walking through stations. Remember that the easiest of all lines to follow is the JNR Yamanote Line, and its color code is green. All of the 10 subways and 11

private rail lines operating in Tokyo connect with it at least once along their routes. Again, your color-coded maps will be indispensable. In most cases, transferring from one line to another requires an extra fare. Sometimes many lines converge on one station and are connected by passageways. Simply, if your ticket is taken along the route, you'll need another to carry on. Both rail lines (JNR and private) and subways show maps of their routes above ticket-dispensing machines. Use your maps to count the stations and compute your exact fare, or use the "cheapest ticket" system. Once you become familiar with the system you'll be able to improvise by using combinations of trains and subways. To make matters easier, the names of all major and most minor stations are written in *romaji* (roman letters) along with the name of the previous station and the one coming up. You'll soon acquire an eagle eye for this. These names, as you peer from the train window, are sometimes neatly and obviously displayed on hanging placards, other times they are small faded little signs on dirty pillars. Most times just count the number of stops shown on your map, and get off at the right one. For insurance, say the name of the station you want to any commuter and they'll let you know when you've arrived. Another important item to remember is that the last trains stop operating at about midnight. After that you're at the mercy of taxi drivers. Commuter and station-to-station discount passes are available, but these are useful only if you intend to spend a long period of time in Tokyo. Information is available at TIC. The saving for short-time usage is minimal.

TOKYO – INFORMATION PLEASE

1) Tokyo, if you relax and plot your course, despite the vast numbers of people, is one of the easiest cities in the world in which to get around. Your worst enemy is anxiety; to combat it you'll need some invaluable tools. If you have not stopped at TIC (Tourist Information Center) at Narita, your 1st stop should be Tokyo TIC at 6-6-1 Yurakucho, Tokyo, tel: (03) 502-1461, open daily 0900 to 1200, 1300 to 1700, half-day Sat., closed Sun. and holidays. Yurakucho is one stop S of Tokyo Eki. Many trains and subways take you there, but the easiest is the Yamanote Line. Although TIC doesn't make reservations, the foreign-speaking staff dispenses invaluable information including maps, available accommodations, directions, shopping hints, eating spots, guided tour schedules, etc. Their services are A+. Make sure to pick up a copy of *Tokyo Railway and Subway* map available from TIC, JNTO or JTB. All lines are color

TOKYO TIC

(cont.)

coded, so just plot your course and follow the colors through the stations. JNTO is the parent of TIC, its most useful branch office, and is located nearby on the 10th floor, Tokyo Kotsu Kaikan Bldg., (adjacent to Yurakucho Eki), 10-1-2 Yurakucho, Chiyoda-ku, Tokyo, tel: (03 216-1901. Another indispensable aid is the semi governmental travel agency of Japan Travel Bureau (JTB), located at cities throughout Japan. They are invaluable for making all types of reservations and purchasing tickets. The main office is located at Nihon Bldg., Annex 2-7-1, Otemachi, Chiyoda-ku, Tokyo, tel: (03) 270-0372.

2) Become familiar with the Yamanote Line, the green, slow-moving, always coming, great looping Tokyo train helping you to not get lost. In the spaghetti tangle in which Tokyo subways and trains exist, the Yamanote Line is the easiest to understand. This welcome friend at least always gets you back to where you started from. The main stops along its lumpy, egg-shaped loop are in one way or another the best that Tokyo has to offer, presenting more local colorful life than you could absorb in a lifetime of trips to Japan. For an excellent, handy guide to central Tokyo featuring all of the stops on the Yamanote Line, buy *Footloose in Tokyo* by Jean Pearce, published by Weatherhill, and available at most large book stores. Its pages are crammed with history, shopping and eating tips, insights, maps and generally useful information gleaned by this witty and sensitive columnist of the Japan Times from her years of experience living in Japan.

3) Pick up a copy of *Tour Companion,* a weekly newspaper, available free at large hotels, department stores and tourist agencies. Years of experience concerning what the *gaijin* needs to know fill its pages. Area maps, money rates, tax-free shopping, calendar of events, restaurants, movies, telephone, postal rates, tours, TV and radio channels and more are included. Excellent and a "must" for any visitor to Japan. To receive copies of *Tour Companion* overseas, direct inquiries to:

Tour Companion Mail Service
Tokyo News Service, Ltd.
Tsukiji Hamarikyu Building
3-3-5 Tsukiji
Chuo-ku, Tokyo 104

(U.S. rate for 3 months is $15.00 sea mail, $32.00 air mail. Mail your checks to *Tour Companion*.)

4) Pick up a copy of *Weekender*, another weekly newspaper available free at large hotels, shops, department stores and travel agencies. Excellent information on what's happening in and around Tokyo. Specializes in lists of theaters featuring foreign language films. Includes a "Community Bulletin Board," jobs, autos, room-and-board and other helpful information.

Tokyo Weekender
Oriental Building
55-11-1 Yayoicho
Nakano-ku, Tokyo, 164
tel: 374-2631

5) Purchase a copy Y200 (sometimes free at large downtown hotels) of *Tokyo Journal,* the newest monthly newspaper geared toward the foreign visitor. Insightful editorials, book and film reviews, seasonal travel itineraries and the most comprehensive calendar of events and address directory of all the Tokyo monthly guides. Subscriptions available from Intercontinental Marketing Corp., No. 5 Wako Bldg., 1-9-8 Kakigaracho, Nihonbashi, Chuo-ku, Tokyo 103.

6) It's impossible to travel in Japan, especially Tokyo, without relying on the Japanese, The naming of streets in Tokyo was an afterthought following WW11. Only major thoroughfares are named, and street addresses do not follow numerically. The numbers on buildings represent the order in which they were built and not their relationship to each other on the city block. Therefore, what you'll need is hand-drawn maps using large, well-known buildings and train stations as landmarks to place you, at least, in the general vicinity of your destination. Don't be embarrassed to ask the hotel staff, hostel houseparent, Japanese student, shopkeeper or passerby to draw you a map. The Japanese do this also. If possible, include directions in Japanese, phone numbers, your point of origin and your destination. Most Tokyoites will politely point you in the right direction and, if time permits, might even escort you there. Policemen are particularly helpful, and the police boxes (*koban*) in each area have detailed information on all places and people in their area. Don't overlook the lowly matchbook cover; even inexpensive soba shops print matchbook covers with area maps and phone numbers. Big hotels always have them. If all else fails, simply show your matchbook or address to a likely person in a train station or a taxi driver and say simply, "*koko*" (here) or "*koko wa doko?*" (Where is here?)

TOKYO'S MAIN AREAS

The most fascinating and intriguing sight in Tokyo is Tokyo itself. A handful of cities throughout the world, although part of a nation, have a quality, a sense of beingness that molds a distinctive personality. Tokyo is one of these and its personality, although complex, makes a composite whole. By day it is all business and purposeful movement. Things must get done, the affairs of Japan are demanding and will not wait. Hand in hand, superimposed, squeezed within the busy city is the historical and artistic city. Shrines, temples, museums, zoos, parks, theaters, somehow they exist also. A visit to Tokyo needs no plan. The city is vibrant enough without a plan. A walk through the streets, a simple lunch, an odyssey in a large *depato*, perhaps a garden or 2; these are enough to fill any day's itinerary. At night the city changes. The business suit comes off, the endless clack of ticker tape stops, the roar becomes a hum, the neon is lit. It's playtime, but only until midnight. Bars, cabarets, hostesses, and rabbit-hole eateries are everywhere. Each section of the city is a variation on the theme, from refined to "hot and nasty." Ginza is an expensive, classy night-club area, Shinjuku is more "pop," with a heavy influx of students and businessmen patronizing the bars at night. Shibuya is colorful and a bit hard, while the Akasaka-Roppongi area is the *gaijin* hangout. There are certain sights that have become institutions and are easily available

through a number of regularly scheduled sight-seeing tours, complete with English-speaking guides and pick-up service. Reservations can be made at hotels, travel agencies, JTB and other places throughout the city. The itinerary usually includes the Imperial Palace, Meiji Shrine, the Akasaka Palace, Tokyo Tower, a handful of temples, and shopping in Ginza. The names of the tours are self-explanatory. For example, there are the Tokyo Uptown Tour, Tokyo Morning Tour, Tokyo Golden Night Tour, Industrial Tokyo, and Geisha Party Tours. For a full list, call TIC at 502-1461 or JTB at 211-3211. For the most part, however, Tokyo is most enjoyable on your own.

MARUNOUCHI

If any area deserves to be called downtown Tokyo, it's Marunouchi. Here are Tokyo Eki, Tokyo Central Post Office, the JTB Bldg., large hotels such as the Palace and Marunouchi, the Japan Guide Association, Tokyo Metro Government Offices and the eastern entrances to the imperial Palace compound.

the Imperial Palace: The Imperial Palace is surrounded by moats and gardens. The outer gardens, especially the East Garden (Higashi-

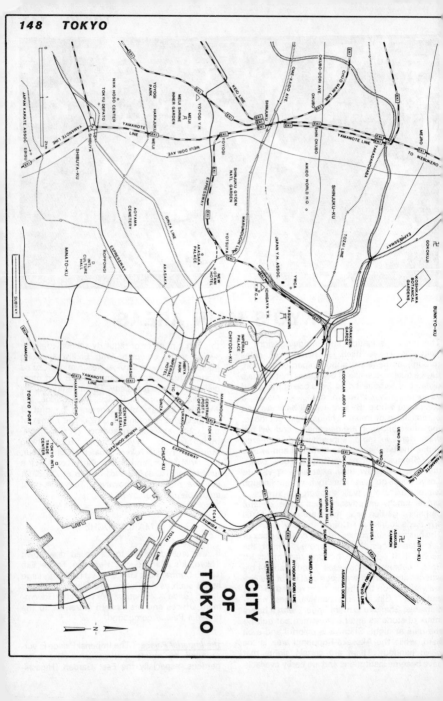

CITY
OF
TOKYO

Gyoen) are perfect for strolling and a feeling of being away from the city. The garden is open daily (except Mon. and Fri.) from 0900-1600. You must enter by 1500. On Sun., there's also a 7.5 km cycling track around the garden with 500 bicycles available free of charge. The original castle grounds were occupied by the Tokugawa Shogunate until Emperor Meiji moved the court there. Most buildings on the grounds were firebombed during WW 11 and rebuilt in the late 1960s. Although the materials are modern, the architecture is purely Japanese. The general public can only visit the inner Palace twice yearly, on Jan. 2 (New Years), and April 29, the Emperor's birthday. People have been trampled to death during these times. Special permission to visit the palace can be arranged at other times. A request (passport necessary) should be directed to the Imperial Household Agency (tel: 213-1111, extension 485) located on the grounds just outside the Sakashitamon Gate. You can have a 90 min tour in Japanese on weekdays from 0900-1630 and on Sat. from 0900-1200.

Tokyo Eki: A period piece dating from the turn of the century. Its red-brick construction has survived the devastating earthquake of 1923, the firebombings of WW 11, and countless attempts to tear it down by city planners. On levels beneath the station is a shopping arcade housing over 400 business establishments, a mirror image of the streets above. You can buy anything there, including folk products from all over Japan. It's a perfect spot to watch Japanese life go by, but with scant public areas to sit down and rest weary feet. A few blocks NE of Tokyo Eki is Nohonobashi Bridge. The bridge itself, an iron span dating from 1911, is uninteresting, but during the Tokugawa Era it served as the starting point from which distances were measured to all parts of Japan. Here, also, is a monument to Will Adams, the English navigator who was shipwrecked in 1600 and became a principle advisor to Tokugawa Ieyasu on matters military and Western. Will Adams is drawn upon as the central character in James Clavell's *Shogun.*

YURAKUCHO

This area, one stop S of Tokyo Eki on the Yamanote Line, is an extremely important stop for the traveler because the TIC is located here. Directly across the street from the TIC are foreign exchange banks. Go 100 m W on Harumi Dori (the main street running E-W) and you come to Hibiya Park. This is the best way to enter the Imperial Gardens. Just before the entrance to the park is the Imperial Hotel, a landmark which overlooks the park. The Original Imperial Hotel, designed by Frank Lloyd Wright, has been replaced, because of age, but its ferroconcrete design is still seen in modern Japanese architecture. The lobby of the original hotel can be seen at Meiji Mura Museum just N of Nagoya. On the R side of the hotel (look for the sign) is an institution called the American Pharmacy. It's just what its name implies. Here you can get all of the sprays, lotions medications that you've become accustomed to. Prescriptions written overseas can be filled here also. Surrounding Yurakucho Eki is Sogo Depato; though not one of the more well-known, it's stocked with everything from garden rocks to designer jeans. Also in the vicinity are the Nichigeki and Takarazuka Theaters, where all-girl revues prance about performing Japanese burlesque. The headquarters of JNTO is also located near Yurakucho Eki. The station area overflows with tiny, inexpensive restaurant stalls mainly selling *yakitori, sushi* and *sake.* If you've been longing to try these delicacies, this is a good opportunity to do so. Head E a few hundred meters down Harumi Dori to the intersection of Chuo Dori and you're in the heart of the Ginza.

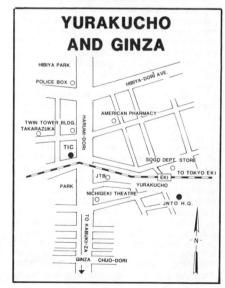

YURAKUCHO AND GINZA

HIBIYA PARK

POLICE BOX

HIBIYA-DORI AVE.

AMERICAN PHARMACY

TWIN TOWER BLDG.
TAKARAZUKA

HARUMI-DORI

TIC

SOGO DEPT. STORE

JTB

EKI

TO TOKYO EKI

PARK

YURAKUCHO

NICHIGEKI THEATRE

JNTO H.Q.

TO KABUKI-ZA

-N-

GINZA   CHUO-DORI

GINZA

Gin means silver, so the name is reminiscent of the days when a mint was located here. Vast sums of money still change hands in this super expensive fashionable area, but it costs nothing to browse and see what's offered. Numerous boutiques in the area offer world-known designer products including high fashions, jewelry and art works, all with staggering price tags. Wako Department Store is one of the best known in Ginza, especially for its architecture, and Seiko watches, and the main Mitsukoshi Depato across the street is an old-style department store where artisans are often brought in to display their crafts and put on demonstrations. It's said that even the Emperor buys his underwear here. Arrive just as the store opens and be treated to all of the staff bowing to you, the honored guest, as you move from floor to floor. Japanese businessmen and foreign executives on bottomless expense accounts frequent the nightclubs of Ginza. The hostesses in them are beautiful, elegantly dressed, punctiliously mannered and demand more tribute than the Queen of Sheba for their services. Actually, the expensive nightclub scene is mildly boring and forced, expecially when the clientele feel almost honor bound to have a good time. It's impossible to tell from the outside which establishments are expensive. None in this area are cheap, so whatever amount you expect to spend, add another zero at the end, and that will be more like it. From the Ginza spring the stories of horrifying Japanese prices. What returning visitors fail to tell slack-jawed listeners is that it's supposed to be this way. Large Japanese corporations heftily budget entertainment as part of their yearly business expenses and go out of their way to spend vast sums of money to impress prospective business clients (it also helps greatly for generous tax deductions). There are smaller bars on the side streets and alleys where prices are closer to normal. Check first before entering. Most policemen in this area are hand-picked to deal with foreigners, so don't be afraid to ask questions and solicit advice. Proceed E on Harumi Dori to the intersection of Showa Dori, and on the L you'll come to the Kabuki-za Theater, tel: 541-3131, where classical kabuki is alive and well. The TV broadcasts of kabuki even vie with the honored sport of baseball for ratings. Matinees run from 1100-1600, evening performances from 1630-2100. Full-performance tickets range from Y5000 to Y10,000. A 10% discount is given to foreigners presenting their passports. Tickets can be purchased from your hotel and picked up at the "will call" desk. Although the plots are as intriguing and intertwined as the most difficult of Shakespeare's, they still can be followed and enjoyed, with their fluctuating rhythm of tragic and comic, winsome and sober, genteel and violent. The costumes, posturing and voicing alone are worth an afternoon or evening. English programs, available for Y600, add greatly to the enjoyment of the plays. If you don't wish to chance an entire performance, you can buy a ticket for only one act called a tachi-mi-seki (stand-and-see seat), but you'll be in the rear of the theater in the far balcony. The dim, hushed silence encountered in Western theaters is entirely lacking. The audience comes and goes, eats their lunch and calls out the actors' names with appropriate remarks during the performance. True audience participation is expected. The kabuki season lasts for 9 mo. with about 25 performing days per month.

eating in Ginza: To have a good time in Ginza while keeping prices down, you must explore and avoid the obvious ultra-expensive establishments. The large department stores, such as Mitsukoshi, have supermarkets and food stalls in the basements and sub-basements. Often, there are exotic morsels to sample as you wander around. You can literally eat at bargain-basement prices from numerous stalls selling skewered and charcoaled chicken, pork and beef for only Y100 each or so. There's also the cafeteria-style, inexpensive restaurants at the top floor. Across from the Kabuki-za in the heart of Higashi-Ginza is Nair's Indian Restaurant. Most of the chefs are from India and serve savory curries and various Indian delights for less than Y1000. The owner, Mr. Nair, sits on a stool in the corner and greets his guests, often with humorous comments heavily spiced with Indian mind games. Almost like a breath of fresh air in over-polite Tokyo, Mr. Nair's is one of the only places where you can come to be mildly and playfully insulted. shopping: For a truly colorful scene, proceed to SE Ginza (Shinbashi), near Tokyo Bay, where you'll find the Central Wholesale Market in the Tsukiji area. It's best around 0600 when cooks, housewives and chefs come from all over the city, converging to buy fresh fish, meats and vegetables. Fish is by far the major item. Uncountable stalls sell purely Japanese foods for ridiculously low prices. You can eat until you burst for Y1000. A new phenomenon for Japan is discount stores. Many line the side streets around Ginza where you can buy clothing, electronics and cameras even cheaper than at the official tax-free shops. A rule of thumb is to promenade and look at the flashy joints in Ginza, but to buy and dine on the side streets where prices are more reasonable.

SHINJUKU

This bustling area possesses the busiest railway station in all of Japan, with more than 2,000,000 passengers going through its turnstiles on an average day. It's located almost directly W from Tokyo Eki on the far loop of the Yamanote Line. Shinjuku is where Tokyo flexes its 21st C. muscles. Here the skyline is filled with skyscrapers, many 60 stories high, defying the tail of the mythical earthquake carp lying under the islands of Japan. Shinjuku, at that time a mere rice-paddy village, was one of the only areas of Tokyo left functioning normally after the earthquake of 1923, when it began to enjoy a brisk business and an accelerated rise in commerce. It now offers more action than any single area of Tokyo, being overfilled with hotels, bars, bath houses, *depato* and constantly humming streets. Per sq m, it's the world's most expensive real estate. A Y10,000 note laid down on the sidewalk won't pay for the ground it covers. Under Shinjuku Eki are vast underground

shopping centers such as the Subnade with more than 130 stores and numerous restaurants selling all manner of food, from traditional Japanese to pizza and hamburgers, and the prices are right. The large department stores in Shinjuku such as Isetan, Mitsukoshi and Keio, from their bargain basements and supermarkets to their rooftop museums and restaurants, sandwich everything else conceivable in between, and are mini-Japans in themselves. For an excellent overview of the city, ride the elevator to the 51st floor of the Sumitomo Bldg., just W of the *eki*. On a clear day you can even see Fuji-san from here as well as a grand view of Tokyo.

on Sundays the streets surrounding Shinjuku eki are closed to traffic and form a gigantic outdoor shopping mall

food and shopping: The streets are a neon-lit maze of tiny eateries. Nearby, on the street-side Nishi-guchi (W exit) of Shinjuku Eki (to the R as you go out), is Smokey Alley, a twisting rabbit warren of cozy bars with smoking grills sending delightful odors into the streets. Though it has an unsavory reputation, Japanese businessmen and shoppers frequent this cheap, totally ethnic area until midnight, drinking beer and unwinding. Two blocks NE of the _eki_ (Kabukicho section) along the alleys behind Meiji Dori is a down-trodden area of doorways filled with night ladies and young boys displaying their wares. This area is tough. Browsing is safer than buying. Just outside Higashi-guchi (E exit) of Shinjuku Eki is a shoppers' paradise, especially for camera equipment. A number of stores offer discounts even lower than the tax-free shops. Two prominent ones are Yodobashi and Sakuraya Camera, almost next door to each other. Just listen for the advertisement ditty played over and over on the loudspeaker to find your way. Mr. Hiroto Ohta, manager of Sakuraya Camera, speaks English well and is ready to deal. There are also excellent camera shops one block W from the W exit, towards Keio Hotel. East from the _eki_ along Shinjuku Dori is Kinokuniya Bookstore, where an entire floor specializes in foreign language books; the array is quite impressive. In the basement is a small-but-good assortment of reasonable restaurants and coffee shops, where you can eat, sip, and read your new books. Down the back stairs and across the street is an annex, where one floor is devoted to maps and language tapes. Other floors offer all kinds of European and American goods, and a very good art supply shop. Another excellent and varied restaurant is on the 6th floor of Takano Depato. Here food from all the corners of the world is offered by Japanese waiters in appropriate ethnic costume. The Indian curries served by the waiters in orange turbans is a good choice. Check the plastic display window for prices from Y700 for generous portions. The best aspect of Shinjuku, however, is the atmosphere. It's a Japanese mixture of bohemian, hippy, politely radical and pop, all standing in a purely Japanese substructure. One phenomenon seen, and especially heard, are neo-fascist groups in military attire riding flatbed trucks haranguing the populace with ultra-booming loudspeakers. These displays occur at many of the larger stations, and people go about their business without raising an eyebrow for, after all, these radical groups have registered with the police and _do_ have an official permit to demonstrate. Amidst the never-ending bustle is Shinjuku Gyoen

National Gardens, a short walk E of the _eki_ or take the Maranouchi Subway 2 stops E to Shinjuku Gyoen Mae. The gardens are a haven of pastoral peace. The cherry blossoms in spring and the chrysanthemums in fall are especially beautiful.

night life: At night, the Shinjuku area is alive with businessmen and young people out on the town. Many movie theaters are located in and around Shinjuku (Check _Tour Companion_ and _Weekender_) offering first to fifteenth-run foreign movies. They cost only Y400 and are open all night. For anyone completely stuck for a place to stay, they're uncomfortable, but at least out of the rain. Besides the theaters offering foreign and legitimate films, there are scores of dingy places offering porno films as well (Japanese-style, with air-brushed genitals). They look like what they are. For those inclined there are also numerous clip joints with barkers outside, some elegantly dressed in tuxedos. Don't be fooled; inside the hostesses smile and wait for the flock to be brought in for fleecing.

YOTSUYA

If you continue on the Marunouchi Line for more stops past Shinjuku Gyoen-mae, you'll come to Yotsuya. The greatest landmark here the New Otani Hotel. Even if big hotels are not your style, you should wander through the canyon-like halls of its many buildings to see Japanese-style luxury at close hand. It's a good place to change TCs at the foreign exchange window, especially when banks are closed. Or

minute from Yotsuya Eki heading back toward Shinjuku is an excellent bar, both for relaxing and gaining information. It's the Rising Sun, owned by Jerry Hegarty, a large, amiable, blond rugby player and long-time Tokyo resident. He knows the ins and outs of Tokyo and freely dispenses information. He draws the best beers in town and boasts one of Tokyo's few British-run pubs. The address is: Shinsei Bldg., 2nd Floor, 1-9-3 Yotsuya, Shunjuku-ku, tel: 353-8842. Many foreigners gather here. Here also in Yotsuya is the Meiji Shrine Outer Garden. If you take the Chuo Line from Yoyogi, you can go 2 stops to Shinanomachi, or one more stop to Yotsuya. The Meiji Outer Garden is mostly dedicated to housing foreign dignitaries at the Akasaka Palace. On the grounds, however, is the National Stadium, and there are some quiet spots to walk through. Near the New

Otani is the Japan Foundation, 3rd Floor, Park Bldg., 3-6 Kioi-cho, Chiyoda-ku, tel: (03) 263-4491. It's a good place to meet foreign scholars interested in Japan and there's also a small, but well-stocked lending library. Between Yotsuya and Shinjuku is the famous Bingo-ya, a multi-floored shop that specializes in folk art, toys and gifts. They feature everything in traditional Japanese art from *kabuki* masks to pilgrims' straw sandals. The building itself is set up like an old-fashioned Japanese storehouse. It is not close to any major station and the owners like it that way. They feel that the real enthusiasts will search them out. The norm is pressureless browsing and the atmosphere is half shop and half living museum. Bingo-ya is at 69 Wakamatsu-cho, Shinjuku (E from Shinjuku towards Yotsuya near the Dai-Ichi Hospital), tel: (03) 202-8778.

IKEBUKURO

Again, using Shinjuku as a western point of reference, Ikebukuro is 4 stops N on the Yamanote Line. Although extremely busy, Ikebukuro lives up to Tokyo's reputation of being a series of villages. The atmosphere is down-home and earthy. Working people, students and executives with modest expense accounts come here to relax. The bars are as varied as in any other section of Tokyo, but are homier and much less costly. Accommodations in the area are cheaper and, once again, there are all-night movies. Ikebukuro at first appears a bit run down, but for the traveler without pretentions, it's comfortable. At night, around the station, there's a thriving, unofficial street market with vendors spreading out their wares on blankets. _food:_ Oden carts with their steaming pots and multi-colored *takoyaki* tents are on almost every corner, filling the air with savory smells. *Oden* is boiled food, such as eggs, fish and vegetables in a tangy slightly sweet, light soy soup, and *takoyaki* are fried balls of dough mixed with octopus and flavorings. Just pick and choose for a hearty, filling meal under Y500. These traditional foods are very rarely sampled by foreigners visiting Japan.

sights: Notice the fortunetellers along the side streets. They sit at little tables with magnifying glasses illuminated by flashlights. Some Japanese put great stock in fortunetellers, often consulting them in important decisions. Some English is spoken by a few, and for Y1500, these oriental masters of the occult will offer a reading. Even if there's a language barrier, perhaps sign language and facial expressions will suffice. Ikebukuro Onsen, 5 min from the *eki,* is an excellent institution in which to be initiated into the Japanese ritual of bathing. You not only get to have a bath, but the 3rd floor of the *onsen* is dedicated to delicious, home-style foods and entertainment. Many people from throughout Tokyo come to share in the camaraderie. There's professional entertainment in the form of singers, balladeers, and story tellers, but there are also amateur performances. People from the audience will sing, dance and perform bits of plays. Everyone is a star. At the *onsen* you can immerse yourself in scalding-but-soothing waters as well as in delightful Japanese customs.

shopping: Ikebukuro has a number of department stores including Tobu, Seibu and Parco, but the most amazing complex is 5 min E of the *eki* at the Sunshine 60 Building. This ultramodern complex of 4 connecting buildings is built over the old Sagama Prison where Tojo was executed as a war criminal. The decor is unrestrained 21st century. White marble, circles and cubes, long streamers of shiny steel wire, pink-winged female centaurs hanging in the main entrance all blend, collide and entangle themselves in this Mulligan's stew decor. The establishments within are also an odd blend, and include a culture center, aerobics center, Sunshine apartments, trade center, kiddyville circus, aquarium, planetarium, museums, travel agents and restaurants featuring food from around the world. These restaurants include The Tropical Hut (Hawaiian, 9th floor), reasonably priced steak dinners; Bambi (3rd floor, Alpha Bldg.), pizza, hamburgers, light lunches, reasonable; Baikal (Russian, 3rd floor), medium price range, and the Brazilian which adds a S. American flavor. Denny's is here with Y200 coffee (infinite refills) and outside of the Sunshine Bldg., on the main street back to Ikebukuro Eki, is an all-night Mr. Donut. Once outside of Sunshine, Ikebukuro becomes a village again, the contrast of ultramodern and traditional is remarkable.

HARAJUKU

Meiji Shrine (Inner Garden) is 2 stops S of Shinjuku on the Yamanote. Get off at Harajuku on the JNR, or Meiji Jingumae on the subway, just at the entrance. The shrine, dedicated to Emperor Meiji, is an excellent example of pure, refined *shinto* architecture. The craftsmanship and materials are of the very best, a testament to Meiji's leadership into the 20th century. Near the shrine is the Iris Garden, resplendent with flowers in June, and behind is a treasure house with numerous artifacts from the Emperor's Household. The beautiful gardens and tree-lined expanses have always been a favorite with foreigners in Tokyo and a haven when the crowds just get too much. Within the confines is Yoyogi Park, which was built up for the 1964 Olympic Games. Two ferro-concrete buildings of the complex, built by Kenzo Tange to house swimming and basketball events, are still considered to be among the most beautiful architecture that Tokyo has to offer. In keeping with Japanese taste, they are simple, graceful and elegant (from a distance). (See their sculpted rooftops from the walking bridge leading to the park.) Many athletes still come to the park to train, and the pool (check schedule) is open to the public. Just S of the Sports Center is the NHK Center, which houses Japan's public broadcasting system. Tours are available daily through this overwhelming communications network. The stage settings are like taking a time trip through Japanese history. You can be entertained for an entire afternoon. Just ask for the Ken-Ga-Ku Tour and let your imagination loose as you tour fantastic sets, see programs in operation and, perhaps, bump into some budding Japanese stars.

shopping: After WW 11, the occupation forces lived in Harajuku in an area called Washington Heights. Because of this, many shops in the area along Meiji Dori and Omotesando Dori catered to foreign tastes, and still do. A variety of shops are available, from street vendors to Parisian-high-fashion boutiques. Antiques, not really appreciated as such by the Japanese, are also available. The area smacks of money, and admidst the bargains are gaspingly high prices. Many young promenading Japanese come here to see and be seen. The *takenokozoku* (bamboo-sprout gangs), and the *bosozoku* (hot-rod gangs) are two groups that use the Harajuku area as a weekend playground. You can see the *takenokozoku* in brilliant costume dancing in orderly formation just outside Harajuku Eki (100 of them!), while the *bosozoku*, with slicked-back hair or *paama* (permanent waves) blast through on flashy motorcycles in close-packed formation, doing wheelies and blaring their claxon horns. Money seems to be no object; some of the most exclusive shops in town are located here. But there are bargains too. If you go out the rear Harajuku Eki exit and hit the alleyway next to the 31 Flavors ice-cream store you'll find a maze of shops selling the latest fads and fashions at backstreet prices. Back onto

Omotesando, stroll down to Playland (R side from Harajuku Eki) for a multi-stories look at any toy you could imagine, then go a little further to the Oriental Bazaar. If you must purchase Japanese gifts and are in a last-minute panic, quell your anxiety; this shop carries everything from pocket calculators to *katana* (Japanese swords) to *kanji*-emblazoned T-shirts. Nearly all are reasonably priced, and may be shipped home from here. Look for some especially good buys in everyman's *mokuhanga* (woodblock prints) on the 2nd floor, then go have a coffee or Italian ice in a Europeanized street-view *kissaten*, and watch the latest in kitch pass by.

SHIBUYA

Three stops S of Shinjuku on the Yamanote, and the terminus of the Ginza Subway Line is Shibuya. If anyone in Tokyo suggests to meet you at Shibuya, they have only one place in mind. That is at the statue of a dog named Hachiko, the best known, casual meeting place in all of Tokyo. Already, Hachiko has become Japanese legend. His story is based on undying faithfulness. For years he accompanied his master to the station. One day his master died and never returned to meet Hachiko. The dog refused to leave. He was fed by passersby for years until he finally died. This so touched the Japanese that they sent contributions for his statue from all over Japan. During WW 11, Hachiko was melted down to make growling bombs, but he was replaced in 1948. He's such an institution of "waiting" that it's rumored that even Godot came there 3 times.

Food and shopping: Surrounding the *eki*, as usual, are a number of large *depato* and an excellent one, especially for the *gaijin*, is the Tokyu Depato. Actually there are 2 *depato* of this name. One is virtually connected to the *eki*, but the most interesting one is about 4 blocks W and is caled the Tokyu Hoten (free bus service from the *eki*). The upper floors are given to a Japanese section selling clothing such as *obi, yukata, kimono* and *hori*. Untypically, they stock sizes that will fit foreigners. If you desire any traditional clothing, this is a good spot to pick it up. Surrounding the *eki* are numerous restaurants and specialty shops, all part of Tokyo, where you can sample food and get a good glimpse of traditional folk art. West of the *eki*, in numerous alleyways, are massage parlors that feature "special" services at expensive competitive prices. Hordes of Japanese workers dine at the numerous inexpensive restaurants in the area. One, known as Kujiraya, specializes in whale meat. East of the *eki* at the first street L of Meiji Dori is Ryuodo, a Chinese-type pharmacy specializing in snake medicines. Japanese men put great stock in the potency of snake medicines that they believe heighten their virility. (A nation of over 130,000,000 must know a few tricks.) Two hundred m SW of Shibuya (the opposite side of Hachiko, walk along the street that parallels the tracks past the JTB) is Ten Me, an organic macrobiotic restaurant (a supposed favorite of John Lennon and Yoko Ono), tel: 496-7100. In the land of Zen Buddhism, it's astonishing that macrobiotic food is sometimes difficult to find. The 1st room of Ten Me is a market where many macro items can be found; behind is the restaurant. The prices range from Y500 up for a well-done, but small-portioned meal. Open 1130-1430, 1630-1930.

ROPPONGI

One stop S of Shibuya on the Yamanote is Ebisu, a terminal for the Hibiya Subway Line that cuts across town to Ginza and then goes north. Two stops E from Ebisu on the Hibiya Line is Roppongi. Roppongi is a famous *gaijin* night spot. No one knows exactly why foreigners began coming here, but one theory states that Roppongi is where the occupation forces' tanks ran out of gas. More realistically, the nearby San-no Hotel, still in operation, housed the majority of servicemen who came to take in the sights of Tokyo. Regardless, it's one of the best spots in town to meet foreigners and to pick up on information about what's happening in Tokyo. Most Westerners know some of the problems that you are facing and willingly

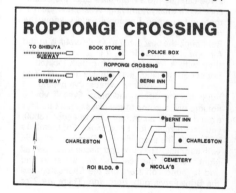

ROPPONGI CROSSING

Gaijin still fascinate the Japanese who insist on portraying them in bizarre rolls and off beat life styles. To the Japanese, preconceptions of westerners are often made into reality

will give you tips on how to find a job, an apartment or even how to extend a visa. Many Western women take jobs as bar hostesses, and if you can get into a high-class club, the experience is not totally horrifying. Western women at the night spots in Roppongi usually know the ropes. If you're going to meet someone in Roppongi, the best place to rendezvous is at the Almond ("Arumondo"). It's a confectionary shop with a front of shocking pink located at Roppongi crossing, just outside the *eki*. You can't miss it. Mainly what's happening in Roppongi are discos and pubs. Even if you're not into disco, some of the places aren't bad for a night out. For an entrance fee of about Y3000, you get unlimited food and drinks. For members with cards, it's even cheaper. Combat the music with earplugs. The pubs and discos stay open all night. Two of the best known, easiest to find and to launch off from are the Charleston and the British-style pub, Berni Inn. There are 2 of

each in the immediate area. At the Charleston, you will be "eyeballed" by the doorman and you must be reasonably dressed or you'll be turned away. Drinks are from Y500, and there's a varied menu with the cheapest item, fish and chips, at Y1200. The Berni Inn's decor is red velvet from the curtains to the stools. British favorites like kidney pie, pork sausages, and fried potatoes under Y800. The well-stocked bar serves imported scotch and Guinness. Henry Africa is another well-known watering hole in Roppongi. Nearby is Nicola's, an Italian restaurant. It has a cozy atmosphere and well-prepared Italian food. Large pizza Y1400, chicken parmesan Y1000. Turn R at the 1st main intersection past the Almond and ask for the very well-known Roi Building. Almost next door is The Zen Bookshop. Don't be fooled. The 1st floor of this establishment sells kitchen appliances. The bookshop, run by Mr. Kato, is on the 2nd floor. The Zen Bookshop has a good collection of

Western books and reasonably priced art works. One bargain is classical Japanese prints. At the front of the bookstore overlooking the street below is a coffee shop and light snack section. During the day, it's a good place to relax. _Akasaka:_ Just N of Roppongi, reached by the Ginza or Chiyoda Subway. You can even walk from Roppongi. Akasaka is a night-time area, costlier and a bit more fashionable than Roppongi, yet cheaper than the Ginza. Many foreigners frequent the local bars and discos. For Mexican food, try Mexico Lindo, 2nd fl. Saikai Bldg., 12-12-2 Akasaka, tel: 583-2095, 2 min from the Green Hotel.

UENO

To arrive at Ueno, go 4 stops N of Tokyo Eki on the Yamanote or Sobu RR, or take the Hibiya or Ginza Subway. Ueno Park was the last stand of the devastated shogunate armies, falling to the Imperial forces in 1868. Shortly thereafter, it became Tokyo's 1st city park. Trees, flowers and shrubs were sent from all over Japan to be planted at Ueno, and its manicured walks and tree-lined lanes have been a favorite for rousing family and school excursions ever since. Ueno is also noted for perverts lurking in the manicured bushes who generally are no hassle. On the grounds is Kaneji Temple, built to protect Edo Castle from the malevolent winds of the northeast. Ueno is a treasure house of museums. On its grounds are Tokyo National Museum, National Museum of Western Art, Tokyo Fine Arts Gallery, Ueno Library and also Ueno Zoological Gardens. All are open from 0900 1630, except on holidays.

shopping: Outside of Ueno Park's E entrance, turn L about 200 m down Asakusa Dori onto a side street and you will discover a semi-black market open-air bazaar, a holdover from the military occupation after WW 11. The sellers line the streets and many of the clientele are Korean and various minority groups from throughout Asia. Goods, such as larger-sized clothing, leather, and even blocks of cheese (a delight after Velveeta, offered as gourmet food in _depato_), can be had. Bargaining is possible.

ASAKUSA

Official travel brochures always lead visitors to Asakusa Kannon Temple, a showpiece of Tokyo, well worth a visit. Take the Ginza or Asakusa Subway, or Tobu RR. The entrance way is marked by amazingly huge paper lanterns, giant straw sandals and two ferocious and exquisitely carved _enma_, the guardians against evil. The temple is the main headquarters of the Sho-Kannon sect. If you're a short-time visitor not intending to go to Kyoto or Nara, Asakusa Kannon should not be missed. The Kannon Festival is held yearly in March.

shopping: Leading to the main building is a covered promenade called Nakamise. It features elbow-to-elbow souvenir shops, with merchandise ranging from junk to works of art. The entire Asakusa area is dedicated to entertainment. It was one of the 1st areas to show motion pictures and from this seed, theaters, cabarets, and bars sprang up like wildflowers. It was a traditional red light district, but among all the gaiety are some of Tokyo's finest arts and traditional crafts shops. If you're interested in "things Japanese" such as swords, geta, geish accouterments, instruments and dolls, then the small, long-established Asakusa shops are the place. The goods are genuine and the prices are set to match. Here also is the Kokusai Theater, famous for its all-girl opera. Asakusa Eki is the starting point for the Tobu-Nikko Line, the best and cheapest means of getting to Nikko. One stop S at Kuramae on the Asakusa Line is the Sumo Museum and Kokugikan Hall, where _sumo_ tournaments are held.

AKIHABARA

Akihabara, in one word, is electronics. Go 2 stops N of Tokyo Eki on the Yamanote, or by the Sobu Line or Hibiya Subway Line. Stereos, televisions, calculators, washing machines, tape recorders and gizmos of every description literally tumble out of the jam-packed stores into the street. Salesmen stand hawking their goods. Speakers attached to fabulous sound systems play everything from the Beatles to Beethoven to attract your attention. The foreigners come looking for a deal and the shopowners know it. There are 2 types of stores: Official tax-free shops and discount stores. Often, the discount stores are cheaper than the tax free. A transaction goes something like this: You name the item. The clerk will whip out his calculator and after playing over the keys with fingers like the wind, he will give you the "best price." This really is the best price, usually about 20% less than the price tag. If you doubt, go to another

a traditional wedding at Kanda Myojin

store and name the same item. Again, the pocket computer is whipped out and lo and behold, after many machinations, the same price is arrived at. Why? Because all of the stores work on very slim mark ups and they know what the going price is. You can doubtlessly find better deals in Singapore and Hong Kong, but not much better. What you should go by is how much an item costs at home, and then you'll really appreciate the lowered prices. Remember that domestic Japanese electronic items operate on 100 volts, North America 120 volts and

Europe 240 volts. Specify where you're from and there should be no problem. The same applies to different frequency bands on TVs and FM radios. The Japanese are fully aware of this and will give you the correct equipment or make the modifications accordingly. They may offer to sell you a converter for approx. Y4000. Akihabara is absolutely worth a visit just to see the state of electronic art, even if you have no intention of buying.

sights: To clear your head of the competing musical din and to escape this electronic jungle, head for Kanda Myojin, a _shinto_ shrine, or Yushima Seido, a shrine dedicated to Confucius. Walk 3 blocks down Chuo Dori away from the Kanda River, turn L and walk up the hill to Kanda Myojin. From Kanda Myojin you can see the walls of Yushima Seido surrounding this park-like shrine. Kanda Myojin is a bustling shrine almost with a picnic atmosphere, frequented by families. Sundays are a good time to see weddings, with the brides dressed in traditional clothing. Inside, on a stone lantern, is an inscription written in English. "May peace prevail on earth." Yushima Seido is much more tranquil. The main building is fronted by a park and laced with quiet walking paths. There's a large statue of Confucius, and carved into the grass in front of it is an inscription in _kanji_. The main building is austere, with many older Japanese offering prayers and burning incense. The grounds are a good place to relax before taking on the city again.

TOKYO FESTIVALS AND EVENTS

Jan. 1-4: _New Year's Celebration_. The best time of year to see both men and women in their most exquisite kimono. This is a family-oriented holiday as people return to their towns and villages to be together with their kin, so many Tokyo streets may seem empty. After paying respects at Meiji Shrine, most families gather at the Imperial Palace to gain a glimpse of the Emperor. On Jan. 6, there's a huge parade of Tokyo Fire Brigades (_Dezomeshiki_) who perform aerial tricks perched high on bamboo ladders. See this sight at Chuo-Dori, Harumi.

mid-Jan.: The 1st _Sumo_ Tournament of the year is held for 15 days at Kokugikan Hall, Kuramae.

Feb. 3-4: _Setsubun_. This festival is held at a number of temples throughout the city, but the best festivities are at Asakusa Kannon and

Gokokuji. Luminaries gather to cast dried beans to the crowd shouting, "Out with bad luck, in with good!" The dried beans (_fuku mame_) symbolize good luck.

Apr.: _Tokyo International Trade Fair_. This event alternates yearly with Osaka, occuring in Tokyo on odd-numbered years. The fair attracts exhibitions from throughout the world and presents the state of the art of manufacturing. There are various exhibits to see throughout the city. Information is available from TIC.

Apr. 21-23: _Yasukuni_ Shrine Festival. This is a spring celebration of rebirth and remembrance for all of the warriors who have fallen in battle. The festivities include processions, and craftsmen and souvenir vendors set up innumerable stalls. See these events just N of the Imperial Palace grounds along Yasukuni Dori.

Apr. 29: *The Emperor's Birthday.* The populace is admitted to the Imperial Palace Grounds. The royal family makes frequent appearances. The enormous, jostling crowds make this event unenjoyable for most westerners.

May 12-15: *Kanda Matsuri* at Kanda Myojin, Akihabara. This festival features 2 huge main palanquins followed by scores of neighborhood shrines balancing precariously on the shoulders of the heavily partying participants. There's fun and gaiety lasting into the night.

May 3-5: *Meiji Shrine Festival.* Traditional arts of *Noh*, archery and sacred court dances are offered.

mid-May: *Sumo* Tournament at Kokugikan Hall; takes place for 15 days.

May 17-19: *Sanja Matsuri* at Asakusa Shrine near the Kannon Temple. Highlighted at this festival, along with processional floats, are *dengaku* court dances.

Jun. 14-15: *Sanno* Festival of Hie Shrine (near Tokyo Hilton Hotel). The highlights of this festival include martial arts demonstrations, Shinto music and rituals, and court dancing. The Sanno Festival is a light-hearted, gay affair.

Jul. 9-10 (dates may vary): *Hozuki-Ichi,* a fair at Asakusa Kannon temple, where Chinese lantern plants plus potted plants of every variety are displayed and sold by swarms of Tokyo gardeners. Around the same date at the temple, huge crowds gather to buy charms against lightning.

July 13-16: *Mitami Matsuri,* at Yasukuni Shrine. Traditional arts and crafts are featured and can be seen at close hand. Go early in the morning to escape the heat and the crowds.

Early August: *Hanabi Matsuri.* Gigantic, colorful fireworks displays at various spots along the Sumida River in the Asakusa area.

August: *Tsukimi.* Full-moon viewing at Hyakka-en Gardens at Sumida Park (2km N of Asakusa). This genteel activity is enhanced by music of the *koto* and *shakuhachi* wafting on the night breezes.

Mid-September: *Sumo* Tournament at Kokugikan Hall for 15 days.

October: *Gagaku* (courtly dances and music) are held at the Imperial Palace. Although open to the public, they're not publicized in order to hold down the crowds. There's limited admission available through the Imperial Household Agency. Contact TIC for up-to-the-minute information.

Early November: *Meiji Shrine Festival.* This is another display of martial arts, archery, folk music and dance, and is an excellent opportunity to view and appreciate traditional arts.

Nov. 15: *Shichi-go-san* (7-5-3 Festival). Parents with daughters aged 3 and 7 and sons aged 5 go to the shrines for special blessings. The best shrines at which to view the special costumes and ceremonies are Meiji, Kanda Myojin and the Hie Shrine.

November: *Cock Fair* at Otori Shrine and other main shrines on "cock" days according to the oriental calendar. Celebrants go to buy *kumade* (bamboo rakes), a symbol of good fortune, to be hung in shops and homes for a year, then brought back to the shrine to be burned, and a new one bargained for. When a rake has been purchased it is accompanied by a rousing hand-clapping ceremony.

Dec. 17-19: *Toshi-No-Ichi.* A fair at Asakusa Kannon Temple. Stalls are set up to sell New Year's decorations on Dec. 29. Decorations are also sold at nearby Torikoe Shrine.

ACCOMMODATIONS

There is no problem for anyone to find suitable accomodations in Tokyo. The range is awesome and includes everything from luxury ultra-modern hotels to bed and basics. The following listings should be supplemented by the handout sheets and brochures readily available at TIC. *Western-style/luxury hotels:* Internationally famous, with exquisite restaurants and many special features such as babysitting, business-men's information, guided tours, swimming pools, money changers, shopping arcades and museums. Obviously the prices are not for budget travelers, but the staffs are accustomed to foreigners and even if you are not a guest you can gain valuable information and avail yourself of some of the services offered. The New Otani, 4 Kioi-cho, Chiyoda-ku, Tokyo 102, tel: (03) 265-1111, 15 min by car from Tokyo Sta., from Y11,000; Palace Hotel, 1-1-1 Marunouchi, Chiyoda-ku, Tokyo 100, tel: (03) 211-5211, 3 min by car from Tokyo Sta., from Y10,000; Tokyo Hilton Hotel, 2-10-3 Nagata-cho, Chiyoda-ku, Tokyo 100, tel: (03) 581-4511, 10 min by car from Tokyo Sta., from Y18,000; Hotel Okura, 10-4-2 Toranomon, Minato-ku, Tokyo 107, tel: (03) 582-0111, 10 min by car from Tokyo Sta., from Y10,000; and Imperial Hotel, 1-1-1 Uchisaiwai-cho, Chiyoda-ku, Tokyo 100, tel: (03) 504-1111, 5 min by car from Tokyo Sta., from Y15,000. *moderate western-style:* Ginza Nikko Hotel, 8-4-21 Ginza, Chuo-ku, Tokyo 104, tel: (03) 571-4911, 10 min by car from Tokyo Sta., from Y7000; Hotel Tokyo, 2-17-8 Takanawa, Minato-ku, Tokyo 108, tel: (03) 447-5771, 10 min by car from Tokyo Sta., from Y7500; and Haneda Tokyo Hotel, 2-8-6 Haneda-kuko, Ota-ku, Tokyo 144, tel: (03) 747-0311, 2 min by car from Haneda Airport, from Y9000.

old standbys: The following is a list of inexpensive lodgings where you can stay for an extended period of time. They have been frequently used by budget travelers and are old standbys when conserving money in Tokyo. Their residents provide a wealth of information on jobs, housing, visas, cheap flights, etc. Okubo House, 11-32-1 Hyakunin-cho, Shinjuku-ku, tel: 361-2348, by JNR to Shin-Okubo, dormitory Y1150 (for men only), 2 bedded room Y1250, Japanese style rooms (for men and women) Y2600 for one person, Y3200-3400 for 2 persons. Although the price is right, Okubo House is a little worse for wear. The staff has seen and heard it all and perhaps at 1st might seem stand-offish, but they'll help with any problems. Okubo House is cold in winter, hot in summer and by all means don't be the last to use the tub. Train on the Yamanote Line to Shin-Okubo Eki. Turn L at the exit and L again at the 1st sidestreet. Located on the R towards the end of street. Closed 0900-1200, curfew is midnight. Ryokan Yashima, 15-5-2 Hyakunin-cho, Shinjuku-ku, tel: 364-2534, Y3500 single, Y4500 double. Although more expensive than Okubo House, Yashima is much more comfortable and good value for a *ryokan*. It is only a 3 min walk from Shin-Okubo Eki (same as Okubo House) Ask directions at the police box on the corner outside of the station. Kimi Ryokan, 1034-2 Ikebukuro, Toshima-ku, tel: 971-3766, JNR or subway: Ikebukuro, from Y2500. Because of the inexpensive prices and the more-than-adequate atmosphere, Kimi might be the best of the lot, especially for couples or long-term stay. Next door to the *ryokan* is Kimi Business Hotel at Y2200, with discounts offered for longer stays. Take the Yamanote Line to Ikebukuro Eki and leave by the W exit. Proceed for 100 m down the main street turn right at the large, red Marui OIOI sign and walk 100 m to the Post Office. Turn L for another 100 m and R at the 3rd side-street for 10 m, and then L again. Kimi is on the L of this small street. A coin laundry is around the corner. Reclaim Center, 2-6-2 Nishitaka, Bunkyo-ku, tel: 815-6749, or 649-7659, ask for Mr. Aizawa. The Reclaim Center offers housing and language conversation among residents. An initiation fee of Y10,000 is good for one yr, and rooms go for Y20,000 per month. Kitchen, laundry and bathing facilities are provided. Take the Marunouchi Subway to Korakuen Eki. Turn R at the exit, then L down Hakusan Dori past the Taiyo-Kobe Bank. The Reclaim Center is the blue house on the right. Natural Stone House, 210 Kuriyama, Matsudo City, tel: (0473) 68-0802. Natural Stone House is about one hr from downtown Tokyo and very convenient to Narita Airport. Opened in 1982, it is operated by a collective group of young Japanese world travelers who are in the know about a traveler's needs. There is no curfew and at Y1200 per night the deal, including cooking facilities, can't be beat. Take the Keisei Line From Ueno Eki for about one hr to Konodai Eki and call from there. Often-times the co-op members will come to Konodai and escort you to Stone House. Its location makes it perfect while in transit from

Tokyo to Narita Airport or for an extended period of stay if you've had enough of the city's frenetic pace.

youth hostels: There are 2 large and busy YHs in Tokyo. The busiest is Ichigaya YH, 1-6 Goban-cho, Chiyoda-ku, Tokyo 102, tel: (03) 262-5950, 1 min on foot from Ichigaya Sta. (on the Sobu Line), 128 beds, closed Dec. 28-Jan. 3. Just down the street from Ichigaya YH is the National Headquarters of Japan's Youth Hostels. You can make arrangements here for YH cards and pick up a copy of the complete Youth Hostel Handbook (in Japanese, but invaluable for finding YHs by using the easy-to-follow cross-reference maps). The other less crowded hostel is Tokyo Yoyogi YH, 3-1 Yoyogi-kamizono, Shibuya-ku, Tokyo 151, tel: (03) 467-9136, 10 min from Sangubashi Sta., 150 beds, closed 2nd Mon. of Mar., 1st Mon. of June, 3rd Mon. of Sept., Nov. 10-15, Dec. 27-Jan. 5. Yoyogi YH is one of the dormitories from the Tokyo Olympics and is located in the N section of the grounds housing the Meiji Shrine (Inner Garden).

potpourri: The following list is a potpourri of reasonably priced lodgings throughout Tokyo. It is a mixture of business hotels, Western hotels, *minshuku, ryokan* and private homes. If the previously mentioned accommodations are booked out or inconvenient, you should be able to find suitable lodgings in this list. Tokyo YMCA Hotel, 7 Kanda Mitoshiro-cho, Chiyoda-ka, tel: 293-1911, 3 min walk from Awajicho Sta. (Marunouchi Subway Sta.), from Y4000, men only; Japan YWCA Hostel, 4-8-8 Kudan-Minami, Chiyoda-ku, tel: 264-0661, 10 min walk from JNR Ichigaya Sta., from Y3600, women only; Tokyo YWCA Hostel, 1-8 Kanda Surugadai, Chiyoda-ku, tel: 293-5421, 5 min walk from JNR Ochanomizu Sta., from Y3500, women only; Tokyo YWCA Sadohara Hostel, 3-1-1 Ichigaya Sadohara-cho, Chiyoda-ku, tel: 268-7313, 10 min walk from JNR Ichigaya Sta. or 2 min walk from Ichigaya Sta (Yurakucho Subway Line), married couples room from Y7500 includes private bath and kitchen; Asia Center of Japan, 8-10-32 Akasaka, Minato-ku, tel: 402-6111, 5 min walk from Aoyama Itchome Sta. (Ginza Subway Line), from Y3000; English House, 23-8-2 Nishi-Ikebukuro, Toshima-ku, tel: 988-1743, JNR: Mejiro Eki on the Yamanote Line from Y1700, long-term O.K.; Shin-Nakano Lodge, 1-1-1 Honcho, Nakano-ku, tel: 381-4886, 5 min walk from Shin-Nakano Sta., Marunouchi Line Subway, from Y2000; Mr. Yotaro Sugii's Home, 5-32-2 Shimo-Meguro, Meguro-ku, tel: 712-4406, take a bus for Shibuya Sta. (Eki) from JNR Gotanda Sta. and get off at Iriyabashi bus Stop, from Y2500; Mr. Oshidari's Home, 5-29-5 Shimo-Meguro, Meguro-ku, tel: 712-6064, take a bus for Shibuya Sta. (Eki) from JNR Gotanda Sta. and get off at Iriyabashi Bus Stop, from Y2500; Tokyo Sta. Hotel, 1-9-1 Marunouchi, Chiyoda-ku, Tokyo, tel: (03) 231-2511, in Tokyo Central Sta. Bldg., from Y6000; Shibuya Business Hotel, 1-12-5 Shibuya, Shibuya-ku, tel: 409-9300, 2 min walk from JNR Shibuya Sta., from Y5000; Shibuya Tokyo Inn, 1-24-10 Shibuya, Shibuya-ku, tel: 462-0109, 5 min walk from JNR Shibuya Sta., from Y7000; Yayoi Kaikan, 1-14-2 Nezu, Bunkyo-ku, tel: 823-0841, subway: Nezu (Chiyoda Line), from Y4000; Hotel Sun Route Tokyo, 2-3-1 Yoyogi, Shibuya-ku, Tokyo, tel: (03) 375-3211, 3 min walk from Shinjuku Sta., from Y7000; Ueno Sta. Hotel, 2-14-3 Ueno, Taito-ku, tel: 833-5111, 5 min walk from JNR Ueno Sta. (Shinobazu exit), from Y7000; Central Hotel, 3-17-9 Uchi-Kanda, Chiyoda-ku, tel: 256-6251, one min walk from JNR Kanda Sta., from Y4500; Tokyo Green Hotel, Awajicho, 2-6 Kanda Awajicho, Chiyoda-ku, tel: 255-4161, 2 min walk from Awajicho Sta. (Marunouchi Subway Sta.), from Y4500; and Hokke Club Tokyo-Ten, 2-1-4 Ikenohata, Taito-ku, tel: 822-3111, 3 min walk from Yushima Sta. (Chiyoda Subway Line) or JNR Ochanomizu Sta., from Y4000. For a listing of accommodations at Narita City and around Narita Airport, see "Narita" in the following chapter "Tokyo Vicinity."

PRACTICALITIES

food: First go to the "General Introduction" "food" and familiarize yourself with the type of eating establishments available. All are found in Tokyo. Expensive, international quality restaurants are always found in the luxury hotels, with many also located in Ginza. Remember that in any restaurant where the bill comes to more than Y1700, a 10% tax will be added. Tipping in the vast majority of restaurants is not necessary. Budget travelers can find vast numbers of low-cost restaurants around main train stations. Westernized fast-food chains such as McDonalds are popular, and pizza parlors such as Shakey's and Pizza Hut offer all you can eat for Y500 from 1000-1400. For those that have been traveling in Japan for any length of time and eating exclusively Japanese fare, remember that this long-awaited munch feast can easily turn into a case of monumental indigestion. The restaurants in large department stores, usually located on the top floor, are always reasonable and like most restaurants present plastic facsimiles of their dishes in large display windows. You can easily see what you are getting and how much it will cost. Soba or ramen at thousands of shops is always a good, light budget lunch. For breakfasts, try the _moningu sabisu_ (morning service) at _kissaten_ (coffee shops), and eat _teishoku_ (fixed menu) at almost any restaurant for dinner. A reasonable regimen of variations on these types of food will keep eating costs below Y1500 per day. Many restaurants close at around 2100, but the ones in Roppongi and Akasaka stay open until the wee hours of the morning.

cultural and aesthetic events: TIC provides pamphlets and brochures about cultural events and aesthetic studies offered in Tokyo and throughout Japan. The 2 free newspapers, _Tokyo Tour Companion_ and _Tokyo Weekender,_ are indispensable in finding out about what's going on in Tokyo. Tokyo is a thriving center for studies and pursuits of "things Japanese." Flower arranging, the tea ceremony, _sumo, kabuki, noh,_ martial arts, and _bunraku_ puppet performances can be easily seen and studied at many centers throughout the city. Addresses, along with a description of these arts and pursuits, are listed in the "General Introduction" under "Cultural Arts, Entertainments and Sports." Please refer there for any necessary information. The following is a partial list of associations from where you can get necessary information. _Cha-no-yu_ (the tea ceremony): make inquiries at Cha-no-yu International, tel: (075) 441-2452, Sado Kaikan Bldg., Ogawa Teranouchi-agaru, Kamigyo-ku, Kyoto. The tea ceremony is also offered at facilities of the Imperial, Okura and New Otani Hotels. _Ikebana_ (flower arranging): there are at least a dozen _ikebana_ schools in Tokyo which follow a varied philosophy of this aesthetic art. TIC provides information, or contact: Ikebana International, 2nd fl., Shufu-no-tomo Bldg., 1-6 Kanda Surugadai, tel: (03) 293-8188; or World Flower Assoc., 7th fl., Kano Bldg., 18-1 Shibuya 3-chome, Shibuya-ku, tel: 400-9109. The Asahi Culture Center offers classes in hundreds of Japanese arts and crafts. Prices for study vary considerably depending upon the class taken. For information, go to the Asahi Center at Shinjuku Sumitomo Bldg., (Box 22), 2-6-7 Nishi-Shinjuku, Shinjuku, tel: (03) 344-1941.

martial arts: Where observers are welcome: Aikido World Headquarters, 102 Wakamatsu cho, Shinjuku-ku, Tokyo, tel: 203-9236, 10 min by bus from W exit of Shinjuku Sta., Kodokan Judo (Kokusai-bu or Intl. Division), 16-30-1, Kasuga, Bunkyo-ku, Tokyo, tel: 811-7154, near Kasuga Sta. on Toei Rokugo-sen Line, Korakuen Sta. on subway Marunouchi Line or JNR's Suidobashi Sta., Mon.-Sat. 0400-1930; and Federation of All Japan Karate-do Organizations, 6th floor of Senpaku Shinko-kai Bldg., 35 Shiba, Kotohira, Minato-ku, Tokyo, tel: 503-6637, near Toranomon Sta. on subway Ginza Line. Karate training is not given here; information on karate will be obtainable from Mr. Tsuchiya (1300-1700) in English by contacting the organization. Nippon Budokan Kendo School, 2-3 Kitanomaru-koen, Chiyoda ku, tel: (03) 216-0781, near Kudanshita Subway Sta., visitors welcome 1700-1900; All Japan Kyudo (archery) Federation, Kishi Memorial Hall, 4th Floor, 1-1-1 Jinnan, Shibuya-ku, tel: (03) 467-7649; Tai 'Chi at Tokyo Taiikukan, (near Sendagaya Sta.), tel: 408-6191, or at Do Sports Plaza, Sumitomo Sankaku Bldg. Annex at Nishi-Shinjuku, tel: 344-1971; Yoga at the Ghosh Yoga Institute, tel: 352-1307; or with the world-renowned master Masahiro Oki, tel: 344-1941; Nihon Sumo Kyokai (Japan Sumo Wrestling Assoc.), c/o Kokugikan (Sumo) Hall, 1-9-2 Kuramae, Taito-ku, Tokyo, tel: 851-2201, near Kuramae Sta. on subway Toei Ichigo-sen Line, Mon.-Sat. 1000-1600, closed Sun. and holidays. There are 3, 15-day *sumo* tournaments held in Tokyo during Jan., May and September. The Japanese adore *sumo* wrestlers and flock to the tournaments. Tickets are difficult to come by. Purchase them well in advance at any Tokyo "Play Guide." (Addresses for Play Guides are located under "practicalities").

sports: There are 2 tracks that run horse races year round. They are Tokyo Race Course about 32 km W of the city, and Oi Race Course about 9.5 km south. Betting is government controlled. *baseball:* The Japanese are avid baseball enthusiasts. Next to *sumo* it is the most-watched sport. Major league games take place at Korakuen Stadium, Bunkyo ku. Many games are televised, but don't be shocked if at the bottom of the 9th with the score tied the game suddenly goes off the air. The time allotment is up. So sorry. *cycling:* For information on rentals and bike trails, contact the Tokyo cycling Assoc., tel: (03) 832-6895. Also, 500 bicycles are available free of charge for the cycle course surrounding the Imperial Palace, Sun. only. *swimming:* Many large hotels have private pools open to non-guests but charge a whopping Y2000-3000 for the privilege. Public-but-crowded pools include: Tokyo National Gymnasium, near Harajuku JNR Sta., tel: (03) 468-1171, open all year round; Tokyo Gymnasium Indoor Swimming Pool, near Sendagaya JNR Sta., tel: (03) 403-3456, open early June-early Sept.; Korakuen Jumbo Pool (outdoor), near Korakuen Subway Sta., tel: (03) 811-2111, open late June-early Sept.; and Ikebukuro Mammoth Pool, near Ikebukuro JNR Sta., tel: (03) 916-7171, open all year round.

shopping: The general rule for large stores is that they are open at around 1000 and close at 1900. Most are open 6 days per week and always on weekends, with days closed falling usually on Mon. or Thursday. Small shops are open 7 days per week. For more shopping hints see the sections under "Tokyo's Main Areas" this chapter. An excellent book detailing the *mingei* (folkart) shops in and around Tokyo is *Kites, Crackers and Craftsmen* by Camy Condon and Kimiko Nagasawa. This handy book provides shopping tips and highlights some of the most traditional shops in Tokyo, including some history on the proprietors' crafts, along with easy-to-follow maps. A good place to see a wide display of folk art is at Amita Handicraft Center located in the Yashica Bldg. on Meiji Dori near Harajuku Eki and at Bingo-ya, an exemplary folkart shop, highlighted in the "General Introduction" under "arts and crafts—folkart." For flea markets and antique sales try: Ari-Yakushi Antique Charity Fair at Arai-Yakushi Shrine, held the 1st Sun. and Mon. of the month; Tokyo Flea Market at Nogi Shrine, held on the 2nd Sun. of the month; Roppongi Antique Fair, near Roppongi Eki (Roi Bldg. sidewalk) on the 3rd Fri. and Sat. of the month. To really tickle your fancy and to see the state of the art in every conceivable "gizmo," visit the housewares sections of large *depato* or one of the chain stores of Osama-no-aidea (King's Idea) that specialize in new patent ideas by budding inventors. They sell everything from glass eyeballs to miniature folding clotheslines. The stores are found at many major train stations. *bookstores:* Some bookstores carrying foreign language titles as well as maps and periodicals are: Kinokuniya, (6th floor) near Shinjuku Eki, tel: (03) 345-0131, or at the Toho Tower Bldg.

a tub maker on a Kichijoji side street

near Hibiya Subway Sta., tel: (03) 504-0821; Jena, near Ginza Subway Sta., tel: (03) 561-8446; Maruzen, near Nihonbashi Subway Sta., tel: (03) 272-7211; Kyo Bunkan, near Ginza Subway Sta., tel: (03) 561-8446, and Biblos, located near the Big Box at Takadanobaba Eki.

visas and immigration: Tokyo Immigration Office, 3-20-3, Konan, Minato-ku, tel: (03) 471-5111. *health care:* The following hospitals and pharmacies are accustomed to dealing with foreigners and have foreign-speaking staff. St. Luke's Hospital (near Tsukiji Subway Sta.), tel: (03) 541-5151; International Catholic Hospital, tel: (03) 951-1111; Tokyo Medical and Surgical Clinic, tel: (03) 436-3028. The American Pharmacy (near TIC in Yurakucho) fills foreign prescriptions and has a full line of foreign health aids, tel: (03) 271-4034. *general information:* Tokyo Tapes is a self-help service providing information on day-to-day problems. Tel: (03) 252-0224. Tokyo Hot Line is operated by the English-Speaking Society and offers recorded tapes dealing with general tourist information. The main number is (03) 375-4331. Tokyo TIC is the best place to find information. The number again is (03) 502-1461. TIC also provides handout sheets on museums, galleries, parks, gardens and amusement centers. The lights on the top of the Asahi Shinbun Bldg. (newspaper) flash a summary of world news in both Japanese and English. For a taped message on current events happening in Tokyo, call: (03) 503-2911. Tourist help is also available from JNTO and JTB (addresses and numbers see "Tokyo Information Please" in this chapter). JAL offers information at tel: 747-1200. For information regarding tours to Imperial Shrines, etc. contact the Imperial Household Agency at 213-1111, ext. 485. *child and home care:* For babysitters, contact Tokyo Domestic Service Center, tel: (03) 584-4769; Tokyo Maid Service, tel: (03) 291-3595; Hotel New Otani Baby Room, tel: (03) 265-1111.

guides and interpreters: There are a number of organizations based in Tokyo that will provide interpreters free of charge or have regular meetings where foreigners are invited to attend and socialize with foreign-speaking Japanese. Some are: Tescort (free guide service), tel: Mr. Araki at (03) 478-6577; International 3F Club (regular weekly meetings), tel: 812-7700; Tesco English-Speaking Society (get togethers), tel: 479-6577. Professional guide and interpreter service is available from Japan Guide Association, tel: (03) 213-2706. A variety of languages are spoken, Y15,000 per day. The Home Visit Program is also available in Tokyo. For information and applications contact TIC. *for the business person:* Business and commerce information is available from JAL Executive Service Lounge at the Imperial Hotel, tel: (03) 580-0727; Japan External Trade Organization (JETRO), tel: (03) 582-5511. A full range of secretarial service is available from Simul International, tel: (03) 582-4224; I.S.S. at the Tokyo Hilton, tel: (03) 581-7591; and Japan Convention Service, tel: (03) 401-1111. *emergencies:* (The staff may not speak foreign languages). Fire and ambulance 119; police 110. *entertainment:* The most convenient places to purchase tickets for almost any cultural or sporting event is at Tokyo Play Guides. They have offices scattered around the city but the easiest to locate are: Play Guide Center, Ginza, tel: 561-8821; Kyukyodo Playguide, also in Ginza, tel: 571-0401; and Akagiya Play Guide, in Nihonbashi across from Tokyu Depato, tel: 273-5481. *travel agents:* The best budget travel agent in Tokyo is Mr. Bozworth of Ikon Travel, tel: (03) 400-9050. This long-time Tokyo resident can arrange low fare tickets throughout Asia and is especially adept at helping with almost any travel problem that arises. Another travel agency with a good reputation for budget fares is Air Voyages, tel: (03) 476-3795. Other government approved travel agencies are listed in the "General Introduction" under "Getting Around." *study:* For those wishing to study Japanese and various courses at the university level contact: Intermediate College for Foreign Students, Instruction Section, Tokyo University of Foreign Studies, 4-51-21, Nishigahara, Kita-ku, Tokyo. Lists of language schools are available from TIC. A good one offering reasonable rates is Interworld, Sampo Bldg., 3-4-20, Minato-ku, Mita, tel: (03) 453-0343. Ask for Mike Galbreith.

KANTO

INTRODUCTION

The Kanto district, located in S-Central Honshu, gained national prominence rather late since the thrust of Japanese civilization filtered eastward from the western regions through Kyoto, the traditional capital. In 1603, a small muddy military post in Kanto known as Edo was chosen by the Shogun to be his main fortress. Since then, this tiny village has metamorphosed into Tokyo, a gigantic global metropolis, and the heart of the Japanese nation. There's much more to Kanto than Tokyo, but since this benevolent, immature colossus dominates the nation, it dominates its immediate surroundings even more so. It's a fact that the bulk of international visitors will receive their first painless, yet overwhelming impression of Japan on the streets of Tokyo. Keep in mind that this is only the first tangy sip of the seemingly bottomless cup of the entire Japanese experience. Under no circumstances should you avoid Tokyo, because in this cornucopia of buzzing streets, you'll find Japan's finest foods, arts, theater, classical pursuits, museums, religious centers and every manner of hedonistic pleasure that you can desire or, more importantly, handle. Depending upon your length of stay, let your first visit to Tokyo be one of orientation. Don't get stuck; move on, knowing full well that you'll return

even a number of times during your trip. The main transportation arteries that keep the life blood flowing into and out of this powerfully beating "heart" are all easily traveled. A few hours in almost any direction will slow the beat to a relaxed rhythm. Ferries, trains, buses and planes, unerringly computerized, go everywhere. In one hour southward by train, you can be strolling the village-like classical streets of Kamakura, an historical city and one-time capital during the first shogunate of the 1100s. Kamakura is now a religious and tourist center, featuring the Daibutsu (Great Buddha), fascinating shops, open air restaurants and restful *ryokan*. Two hours NW by bus or rail and you can be in Saitama or Gunma Prefectures, leaving a spa town on a mountain trail with Tokyo only a faint illumination on the eastern horizon. Two hours NE will take you to Mashiko, renowned for its folk pottery, where foreigners are welcomed to buy or even to study it. In approximately the same direction is Nikko, if not the most beautiful, at least the greatest attempt towards beauty of all of the religious shrines of Japan. Appreciated or not, Nikko is a fascinating exposition of Japan's religious art. Another 2 hr ride and you can be in Tohoku, a mountainous, underdeveloped region of mainland Japan. If your time is extremely limited, the Kanto District is like a tray of hors d'oeuvres where you can sample almost everything that Japan has to offer. If you have more time, it's the first course of a delightful feast.

the land: The Kanto District is comprised of the 7 prefectures of Ibaraki, Tochigi, Gunma, Saitama, Chiba, Tokyo and Kanagawa. Like all of the districts of Japan, Kanto is made up of mountains and seacoast, but untypically, it contains the flatlands of the Kanto Plain, the largest in the country. A number of rivers drain the plain into the delta surrounding Tokyo Bay; the largest is Arakawa, but the most important is Tonegawa. The Kanto Plain is primarily upland and not easily irrigated; therefore, there are a few wet rice paddies, the majority of crops being fruits and vegetables. The coastline of the Kanto area is fairly regular, with long, straight stretches, except for Tokyo Bay. On the western border are the Kanto Mountains, including the Fuji Volcanic Chain with numerous peaks over 2000 meters. Part of these are the 7 volcanic Isles of Izu and the far flung Ogasawara Islands (See "Fuji-Hakone-Izu National Park"). In the N is the Mikuni Range, tall and rugged, saving Kanto and Tokyo from the howling winter winds off the Japan Sea. Running N-S along the seaboard are the Abukuma Mountains and further inland are the minor ranges of Yamizu and Ashida. These mountains contain the passes used to head northward into Tohoku. In Ibaraki Prefecture NE of Tokyo is Lake Kasumigaura, the 2nd largest in Japan next to Lake Biwa.

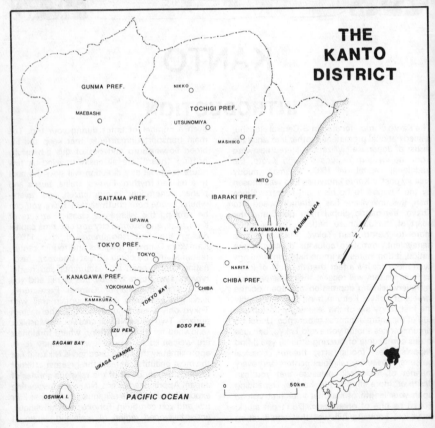

THE KANTO DISTRICT

GUNMA PREF.

NIKKO

MAEBASHI

TOCHIGI PREF.

UTSUNOMIYA

MASHIKO

MITO

SAITAMA PREF.

IBARAKI PREF.

URAWA

KASHIMA NADA

L. KASUMIGAURA

N

TOKYO PREF.

TOKYO

KANAGAWA PREF.

NARITA

YOKOHAMA

CHIBA

CHIBA PREF.

KAMAKURA

TOKYO BAY

IZU PEN.

BOSO PEN.

SAGAMI BAY

URAGA CHANNEL

OSHIMA I.

PACIFIC OCEAN

0   50km

climate: Summers in Kanto are sticky and humid, almost unbearably so in Tokyo. Green mold grows on leather in dark closets and clothes hang like wet rags. Westerners seem even more affected, and those that know better head for the sea or mountains whenever possible. Fall brings typhoons and heavy rains that cause flood damage. Winter is crisp and clear, saved from savage arctic storms by the mountains in the N and west. Snowfalls sometimes occur in Tokyo, but they don't last long; however, you can expect cold, howling winds. South of Yokohama and the southern part of the Boso Peninsula are warmed by the sea in winter and have milder, balmy weather. Spring is lovely and blossoms are everywhere.

history: The history of Kanto is actually the history of the shogunate and the adaptation of its particular form of rule, the *bakufu* (camp office). In 1192, Minamoto Yoritomo is appointed by the emperor as Sei-I-Taishogun (General-in-Chief for the Subjugation of the Eastern Barbarians). Thus began the Kamakura Period lasting from 1192 to 1333, which firmly established a new military class known as the samurai, and spread their code of conduct known as *bushido*. The new *shogun* established his fortress at Kamakura, 30 km S of Edo. With Kamakura as capital, Kanto saw a rise in prosperity and enjoyed national influence for 140 years until the shogunate was abolished in the 14th century. Two-and-a-half centuries of strife and civil war followed until Toyotomi Hideyoshi militarily unified the nation once again, though he never became *shogun*. His most able general, Tokugawa Ieyasu, was given a fiefdom which included Edo, and after Hideyoshi's death and a determined military struggle, Ieyasu Tokugawa became *shogun*. Edo, the small mosquito-infested outpost, now became the capital because of intricate military and political considerations. The new government's retainers and courtesans moved in, and the population of Edo swelled. To keep a tight reign on his domain, the *shogun* required all of the *daimyo* throughout the empire to make yearly visits to the new, distant capital. The constant coming and going left little time to ferment political intrigue among the generals, and the large numbers of retainers required for these regal caravans kept the coffers of the *daimyo* empty. In the intervals, the families of the *daimyo* had to remain in Edo as hostages. Finally, after 250 years, with the coming of the Meiji Restoration and the abolishing of the shogunate, the Imperial capital moved from Kyoto (Western capital) to Edo, now renamed Tokyo (Eastern capital). The history of Tokyo is marred also by a series of natural catastrophes. The first occurred in 1657 when virtually the entire city burned down. Then in 1923, Tokyo was completely destroyed by the worst disaster in modern times when an earthquake-fire leveled it and left hundreds of thousands of dead and homeless. The latest heavy blows came to the city during WW 11 when ceaseless bombings turned the proud city into a mangled, smoking heap of rubble. By 1951, most of the scars had at least been cosmetically covered and the city was on the rise once again. Today, because of this period of hasty reconstructions, many buildings are lifeless, grey boxes. Since the late 1960s, however, the architecture has improved, with an eye more towards beauty and design. Today Kanto is one of the most vibrant areas on the face of the earth, and the history of the ups and downs of its whirring center, Tokyo, is really the history of modern Japan.

economy: The business of Kanto, centered around Tokyo, is big business. Since the 1920s when heavy industry began to grow by geometrical proportions, Tokyo has felt a land squeeze. Like the hub at the center of a wheel, Tokyo remained, while the spokes branched out in many directions and became the Tokyo-Yokohama Industrial Zone. This industrial zone is the core of the massive "Pacific Coast Industrial Belt" stretching from Kashima N of Tokyo in Ibaraki Prefecture, through Osaka, the Inland Sea and into northern Kyushu. Textiles, foods, heavy equipment, oil refining, automotive manufacturing and chemicals, each with thousands of spin-off industries, are located in the belt. Tokyo is the commercial and administrative center where the decisions are made and from where the directions are sent. Unbelievably, amidst this 21st C. high technology, over 500,000 Tokyoites on the outskirts and on postage stamp lots within the city limits are farmers. On the Boso Peninsula, the warm year-round climate makes for excellent truck farming, and the upland regions of Ibaraki produce a multitude of fruits and vegetables as well as animal husbandry and silkworm raising. Though Tokyo Bay is too polluted to produce fish that are fit for consumption, tiny villages from throughout the archipelago nevertheless send their catches to Tokyo Central Fish market at Tsukiji. This constantly moving wave of industry, labor and commerce drives the Kanto District, and the Kanto District drives the nation.

special note: Due to the fact that Tokyo, located in Kanto, is the dynamic center of Japan, it warrants in-depth coverage of its own. The normal chapter breakdown of this book will be altered accordingly. "Arts and crafts" and "Events and public holidays" will appear separately under the prefectures and cities of Kanto. Except for the following brief description concerning transport in and around Kanto, the same alteration will occur with this category and complete information will be offered under the corresponding areas in the travel chapters.

getting there: The cliche applies: all roads, flights and ferry routes either lead to Tokyo or connect with it. Narita, Tokyo's new International Airport 60 km from city center, is the main disembarkation point for the majority of international travelers. Haneda Airport, only minutes from city center, primarily services internal flights. The last remaining passenger steamers bound for Japan usually dock at Yokohama, from where passengers are conducted to Tokyo by train or bus. Ferries ploughing throughout the archipelago from Hokkaido to Okinawa either originate from Tokyo or dock there in passing.

by bus and train: Internally, numerous buses depart from Tokyo to major cities and Japan's extensive rail system is particularly advanced throughout Kanto. The Joban Line heads NE along the Pacific coast through Ibaraki Prefecture and on to Sendai and points north. The Tohoku Main Line heads NE roughly through central Honshu, servicing Tochigi and on to Sendai. The *shinkansen* and Tokaido Main Line skirt along the southern coast through Kanagawa, with branch lines to the Izu Peninsula. Completing the system is the Takasaki Main Line, heading due N from Tokyo through Saitama and Gunma, terminating at the Sea of Japan.

TOKYO VICINITY

NARITA

Narita (pop. 60,000) is an historical city primarily famous for Naritasan (Shinshoji Temple), a main temple of the Shingon sect. Pilgrimages to the holy temple are made by more than 8,000,000 devotees yearly, including 2,000,000 during the New Year's festival. Naritasan enshrines Fudo, the god of fire, whose image was carved by the renowned priest Kobo-Daishi. The temple was first erected in 940 at nearby Kozugahara, where special prayers were offered to crush the rebellion raised by one Taira Masakado. In 1705, the buildings were removed to the present site. Naritasan is considered one of the holiest temples in Japan where pilgrims converge to humble themselves through asceticism. Close to the Main Hall is a sacred well where the devotees douse themselves with ice-cold waters in the early mornings of winter. They also walk around the Main Hall 100 times, praying and chanting while keeping tally on 100 white strings. Because of the reverence accorded to Naritasan, there's no smoking, photos are prohibited inside the buildings, and shoes are removed before entering any building. In the 20 ha precincts are also included the Niomon Gate, the Belfry and a Three-Storied Pagoda. Adjacent to Naritasan is a manicured 16 ha park, whose cherry-lined paths lead past ponds, waterfalls, fountains and numerous flower beds.

Also in the park is an historical museum which is open daily from 0830-1600, except Monday. Admission is Y100. *getting there:* From Narita Airport, go by JNR bus or take the Chiba Kotsu Line from the 1st floor of the Terminal Bldg. to Narita Eki in 20 min, Y300. (See map Tokyo Chapter, "Getting There.")

accommodations: If you are in transit or wish to be closer to Narita Airport because of an imminent departure, try the following lodgings in Narita. The following Western-style hotels, although expensive (Y9000), offer free limosine service to and from the airport. Their staffs also speak foreign languages and there are often foreign money exchange services provided. They are: Holiday Inn Narita, tel: (0476) 32-1234; Narita View Hotel, tel: 32-1111; Narita Prince Hotel, tel: 33-1111; Hotel Nikko Narita, tel: 32-0032; Narita International Hotel, tel: 32-1234; and Narita Airport Rest House, tel: 32-1212. For more reasonably priced lodgings try: Business Hotel Tsukuba, 847 Hanazaki, Narita-shi, Chiba-ken, tel: (0476) 24-1234, a few min walk from JNR Narita Sta., and about 20 min by taxi from Narita Airport, single w/b Y5000, Y7000 w/2 meals; or Business Inn Kinoshita, tel: (0476) 22-0800, Y4000. *Ryokan* in the area include Ohgiya, 474 Saiwaicho, Narita-shi, Chiba-ken, tel: (0476) 22-1161, about 15 min by taxi from Narita Airport located behind Naritasan Shinshoji Temple, from Y4500; and Wakamatsu

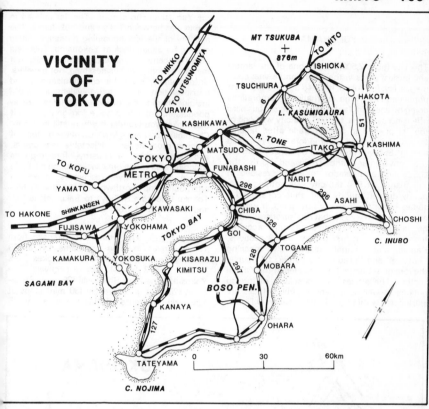

VICINITY OF TOKYO

Honten, 355 Honcho, Narita-shi, Chiba-ken, tel: (0476) 22-1136, 15 min by taxi from Narita Airport (about Y1500), in front of the approach to the Naritasan Shinshoji Temple, from Y10,000. For a unique lodging experience try Natural Stone House (see "Tokyo" "accommodations") located in nearby Matsudo City. The world-traveled staff here is very tuned into the needs of a budget traveler and offers great lodgings and other services for only Y1200, tel: (0473) 68-0802.

POINTS SOUTH: KAWASAKI,YOKOHAMA

Directly S of Tokyo (approx. 20 km) and actually part of the giant metropolis, are the 2 cities of Kawasaki and Yokohama. Kawasaki (pop. 972,000), is one giant industrial complex housing some of the largest corporations engaged in heavy manufacturing in all of Japan. Kawasaki also has the dubious distinction of being one of Japan's largest red-light cities. To soothe aching muscles, fragile egos and to lubricate business deals, the city abounds in turkish baths and love hotels. Businessmen, executives and office workers slip off from Tokyo to the night spots of Kawasaki to gain anonymity and to let their hair down. Helping with the overflow of clientele is the town of Kisarazu across the bay on the Boso Peninsula. No less than 30 ferries per day make the 1 hr 10 min crossing. Business is lively and there's no shortage of "raw materials." Foreigners wishing to try their hands at the night spots should go with a Japanese friend to bridge the communications barrier and to keep the prices within reason. For "getting there" see "Yokohama."

YOKOHAMA

This city (pop. 2,500,000), is one of the largest and busiest ports in the Orient and a vital commercial link for Tokyo. It's also Japan's 3rd most populated city. Huge international corporations doing business in Japan usually have a business office in Yokohama. In 1859, the city was one of the 1st opened to foreign trade after Japan's forced dormancy. Commodore Perry landed here in 1854 with his letter of diplomacy from the U.S. government, and Townsend Harris, the U.S.'s first ambassador to Japan, resided in Yokohama. At first the city was nothing but a poorly drained muddy field, thus considered a suitable area for the new foreigners. It was far enough from Tokyo so that no "surprises" could be launched by Japan's recently acquired friends. It was at first divided into 2 sections, Kangai and Kannai, respectively meaning "outside" and "inside" the barrier. Of course, the foreign settlement was located in the Kannai section. The offices and consulates of foreign nations as well as Japanese public offices are still located within Kannai along Nihon-O Dori in the Yamashita-cho section. The 1st railroad in Japan was between Tokyo and Yokohama. The majority of the few remaining passenger liners making for Japan dock at Yokohama. There's a heavy concentration of foreigners in the city, but the vast majority are businessmen, not travelers. Unfortunately, signs for communications and transportation aren't as prevalent as you'd imagine them to be, owing to the large foreign population. Yokohama has a foreign flavor to it that makes you wonder if you're still in Japan. Chukagai, a neon-glow Chinatown full of Chinese products and delectable restaurants, and Motomachi, a nearby foreign-goods shopping area with a great walk around a hillside of old European-style residences, make an afternoon's trip worthwhile. Take the Keihin-Tohoku Line from Shibuya to Sakuragicho Eki, and bus (10 min) from there.

getting there: The Kodama *shinkansen* from Tokyo arrives in Shin-Yokohama Eki in 19 minutes. From Kyoto and Osaka, it takes 3 hrs 34 min, and 3 hrs 51 min respectively. The Yokosuka Line from Shinbashi (26 min), Shinagawa (20 min) or Tokyo Eki (30 min) stops at Kawasaki en route. Trains leave every 15

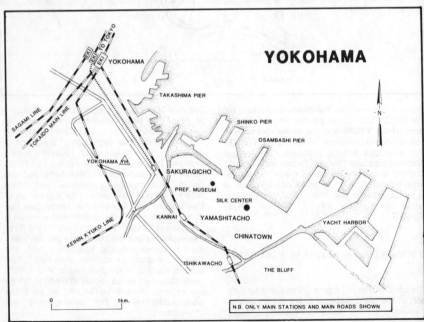

YOKOHAMA

EKI TO TOKYO
EKI TO TOKYO
YOKOHAMA
SAGAMI LINE
TOKAIDO MAIN LINE
TAKASHIMA PIER
SHINKO PIER
OSAMBASHI PIER
YOKOHAMA YH
SAKURAGICHO
PREF. MUSEUM
SILK CENTER
KEIHIN KYUKO LINE
KANNAI
YAMASHITACHO
YACHT HARBOR
CHINATOWN
ISHIKAWACHO
THE BLUFF
0   1km.
N.B. ONLY MAIN STATIONS AND MAIN ROADS SHOWN

minutes. The Tokyo Line from Shibuya Eki runs trains every 15 min which arrive in Yokohama in 30 minutes. The ordinary (*futsu*) trains run every 2-4 min and take 40 minutes. The Keihin Tohoku Line from Yurakucho (Tokyo) takes 40 min and leave every 2-5 minutes. They also stop at Kawasaki and go on to Kamakura. Note: Kannai Eki in Yokohama (2 stops from Yokohama Eki) is the closest to the Silk Center on the South Pier which is the commercial heart of the city. *by ferry:* Ferries bound for Hyuga in Miyazaki Prefecture on the E coast of Kyushu depart daily from Kawasaki. The trip takes 20 hrs, lowest fare is Y12,000. Check at TIC for current information. *getting around:* Yokohama has extensive bus service throughout the city as well as a subway line. If Yokohama City Air Terminal (YCAT) is your destination, take the shuttle bus from the E exit of Yokohama Eki Bus Stop 1, Y150. To the Silk Center from Yokohama Eki, take bus 26 from the bus terminal next to the Sky Bldg. outside of the

E exit. Buses 8 and 56 pass near the Silk Center. Say "Silk Center" when you get on and you'll be told when to get off. Maps and accommodation information are available at the Silk Center.

accommodations: Yokohama YMCA is located near Kannai Eki at 225 Yamashita-cho, Naku-ku, tel: (045) 681-2903. Kanagawa YH is 10 min by bus from Sakuragicho Eki. Its address is 1 Momijigaoka, Nishi-ku, Yokohama, tel: (045) 241-6503. *services:* The following offices provide information for travel, accommodations and the Home Visit System. Their services are indispensable for a rewarding tour through Yokohama: Kanagawa Prefectural Tourist Information Center, Silk Center Annex No. 1, Yamashita-cho, Naku-ku, Yokohama, tel: (045) 681-0506. Yokohama International Welcome Association, 1st Floor Silk Center Bldg. No. 1, tel: (045) 641-5824. The Yokohama Immigration Office is at 37-9 Yamashita-cho, Naka-ku, Yokohama, tel: 681-6801.

KAMAKURA

A green valley surrounded by rolling hills and balmy, sandy beaches fronting Sagami Bay, was chosen by Minamoto Yoritomo in 1192 as the seat of his newly formed shogunate. Until 1333, Kamakura was the political center of Japan, populated by the new military class, the samurai. At this time in Japanese history, Zen Buddhism was the dominant religion and its philosophies of loyalty and fealty became an intricate part of the samurai code of ethics known as *bushido*. Because of this, Kamakura was not only the seat of political power, but also blossomed as a center of religion and culture. Due to this spiritual legacy, Kamakura offers 65 temples and 19 shrines with more than a dozen temples as well as 2 shrines within a 20 min walking radius of the main *eki*. The back lanes are lined with exquisite Japanese homes surrounded by bamboo fences. A peek through any of these fences offers a view of lovely manicured, miniature gardens. Kamakura is only 50 km S of Tokyo, but the surrounding seas keep it balmier throughout the year. Excellent rail systems make the trip from Tokyo in less than one hour. Its beaches and religious centers attract multitudes of visitors throughout the year, but especially in the summer. This is the one drawback in visiting this enchanting, magical town whose main attraction is a giant bronze Buddha known as the Daibutsu; trainload after trainload of visitors is disgorged at the *eki* on almost any weekend. In summer, if one sun bather rolls over on the

beach, then everyone else must. But remember that summer officially ends on Sept. 1 and although the weather is still very warm, the Japanese no longer go to the beaches. Kamakura is as close as you can get to Old Japan in the Tokyo area. If your visit to Japan is very short and you can visit only one place, Kamakura would be an excellent choice.

getting there: From Tokyo Eki, travel one hr on the JNR Yokusuka Line (Track 9 or 10) to Kita-Kamakura Eki for Y600, or to Kamakura Eki for Y650. From Yokohama Eki, go 30 min on the Yokosuka Line to Kita-Kamakura Eki for Y250, or to Kamakura Eki for Y300. You can also take direct trains from Kawasaki. Note: Trains are available every 10-15 minutes. Either *eki* in Kamakura is a good place to start your tour. Only a 20 min walk separates the two. *getting around:* Buses are available to all of the sights from the bus stop at Kamakura Eki. They are actually unnecessary as the best way to see and enjoy Kamakura is by a leisurely stroll. Viewing the homes and actual life style of the Japanese in the residential areas as you walk along makes the visit to Kamakura more complete. Signs in English point the way, maps are available from any small tobacco shop for a modest price.

sights: The Enoden is a little old, slow-moving local train from times past. Its 3 wooden cars painted light green bounce along on narrow gauge tracks from Kamakura to Fujisawa about ½ hr away, where connections for Tokyo are easily made. The Enoden literally goes through and over the backyards of the area, giving you a close-up glimpse of daily life. A trip on the Enoden is a unique delight. On the weekends it's crowded, but during the week only housewives and students use it. It makes frequent stops along the way and the best is at the resort island of Enoshima. (Enoshima "sights" are covered later in this chapter.) You can continue on the Enoden to Fujisawa, or at Enoshima you can try the monorail to Ofuna, another major train link to Tokyo. By riding the Enoden, you not only get to see the sights, but you also get a joy ride on one of the quaintest trains left functioning in Japan. Enoden Eki is just outside Kamakura Eki and at its terminus in Fujisawa, there's a large modern *depato* surrounding the Enoden Eki where you can shop.

The Daibutsu (Giant Buddha): A pilgrimage site in Kamakura ever since its bronze figure was cast in 1252 by one of 2 famous masters, Ono Goroemon or Hisatomo Tanji. At one time it was enclosed in a massive wooden temple, but this was destroyed in 1494 when a colossal tidal wave swept inland, flattening Kamakura and sweeping away the temple. The Daibutsu has braved the elements ever since, sitting in peaceful repose on the grounds of Kotokuin Temple. Over 11 m tall and 29 m at the base, the bronze used in its casting is estimated at 90 tons. The inside is hollow, with a staircase leading to shoulder level. Nara's Daibutsu at Todaiji Temple is larger, but the rendition is not as elegant. *getting there:* Bus from Kamakura Eki or ride the Enoden 3 stops to Hase Eki, then walk 300 m to the Daibutsu. Hase Kannon Temple (just S of the Daibutsu, 200 m from Hase Eki), like the Daibutsu, has an image with a counterpart in Nara. At this Jodo-sect Buddhist Temple

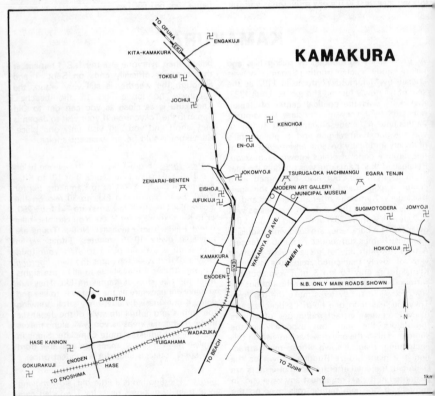

KAMAKURA

TO OFUNA
EKI
ENGAKUJI
KITA-KAMAKURA
TOKEIJI
JOCHIJI
EN-OJI
KENCHOJI
JOKOMYOJI
ZENIARAI-BENTEN
EISHOJI
JUFUKUJI
TSURUGAOKA HACHIMANGU
EGARA TENJIN
MODERN ART GALLERY
MUNICIPAL MUSEUM
SUGIMOTODERA
JOMYOJI
HOKOKUJI
KAMAKURA
EKI
ENODEN
WAKAMIYA OJI AVE.
NAMERI R.
DAIBUTSU
N.B. ONLY MAIN ROADS SHOWN
HASE KANNON
YUIGAHAMA
WADAZUKA
GOKURAKUJI
ENODEN
HASE
TO ENOSHIMA
TO BEACH
TO ZUSHI
N
0   1 km

the Daibutsu's hands lying in his lap form two symetrical circles. With fingers bent upward and thumbs touching, this symbolizes the Buddhist concept of unshakable faith

is a 9 m tall, carved wooden image of Kannon, the goddess of mercy. The image was carved by Priest Tokudo in 721 out of one-half of a giant camphor log. The other half was carved by the same priest into a statue of Kannon that reposes at Hase Temple, just S of Nara. Like most of the temples of Kamakura, a stroll through the grounds here offers a wide range of religious art. The small stone or concrete statues with red bibs are *jizo*, the Buddhist patron of children, pregnant women and travelers.

around Kita-Kamakura Eki: The closest temple is Engakuji (2 min E of Kita-Kamakura), built in 1285. At one time this was one of the most beautiful temples of the Rinzai sect, and one of the Five Great Temples of Kamakura along with Kenchoji, Jufukuji, Jochiji and Jomyoji. Unfortunately, it was almost completely destroyed in the earthquake of 1923, and concrete buildings were used to replace the originals. Fortunately, its intricately carved main gate remains as well as the temple bell, the largest in Kamakura, which is at the belfry on the hill to the R of the main gate. The Shariden Hall on the grounds is reputed to hold a tooth of Buddha, brought from China. Along the main road leading S to Kamakura Eki are scores of temples. Tokeiji (on the R) was unique in times past, affording sanctuary to ill-treated wives. Divorce and refuge were granted to the desperate women who were able to reach its confines. A few min further S is Jochiji, another victim of the 1923 earthquake. Its tall cypress trees still provide shade during the summer. All of the temples along this route are famous for one treasure or another, but it's close to impossible to visit them all. There are so many splendid temples and shrines in Kamakura

to visit that the minor ones can be given little more than a perfunctory look. The larger and more well-known temples, however, are crowded, so if solitude or quietude is your aim, try any of the lesser ones. Kenchoji (15 min S of Kita-Kamakura, to the L of the main road) is renowned as the most beautiful of the Five Great Temples of Kamakura. The temple grounds sit among truly impressive Japanese cedars. Founded in 1253 by dissident Chinese priests, the temple is the headquarters of the Rinzai sect. The buildings were destroyed in the mid-17th century. The main building is a superb example of traditional Japanese temple architecture and design.

around Kamakura Eki: Proceed N along the main street, Wakamiya Oji leading from Kamakura Eki, for about 10 min (buses also available) and you will come to a trio of sights offering the old and the new. They are Kamakura Art Gallery, The Municipal Museum and Tsurugaoka Hachimangu Shrine, all within a 5 min walk of each other. Both the art gallery and the museum offer a number of treasures related to Kamakura's history. A feeling for the times is achieved through displays of armor, swords, statues and numerous paintings. Here, again, the design of the Municipal Museum is related to Nara. Its inspiration, although done in ferro-concrete, comes from the Shosoin Treasure House at the Todaiji Temple in Nara. Open daily except Mon. from 0900-1600. Tsurugaoka Hachimangu Shrine, except for the Daibutsu, is the most visited attraction in Kamakura. Sitting atop a rolling hill, it commands a sweeping panorama of Kamakura and the sea beyond. The shrine was originally founded on a different site in

1063, but was moved to its present site in 1191 by the *Shogun*, Minamoto Yoritomo. The main deity of the shrine, Hachiman, is the god of war, a fitting patron for the newly formed shogunate. The vermillion buildings and tree-lined walkways are excellent examples of shrine architecture and landscaping. Hachimangu Shrine also has a dramatic history. On the grounds is a gigantic ginkgo tree where Kugyo, the head priest and nephew of Shogun Sanetomo, waited in ambush to murder his uncle in 1219. The shrine gounds are also the scene of a favorite artistic Japanese theme. Here Shizuka, the lover of a banished *samurai*, was made to dance for her captors, Shogun Yoritomo and his wife. Her tragedy is recounted in many stories. The main colonnade of the shrine is resplendent with art objects. The shrine festival is held on Sept. 15 and 16 when ornate palanquins are carried through the streets and demonstrations of *yabusame* (horseback archery) take place on the grounds. Also, on the nights of Sept. 21 and 22, Takigi Noh is performed by torchlight at the *noh* stage at the foot of the staircase leading to the main shrine. In the close vicinity, E of Hachi-mangu, are Egara Tenjin Shrine, Kamakura Shrine (with its treasure house open daily from 0900-1700), as well as Jomyoji, Sugimotodera and Zuisenji Temples. Just S of Jomyoji, across the main road, is Hokukuji Temple, which offers classes in Zen Meditation every Sun. beginning at about 0600. Across the main road heading W from Hachimangu is another cluster of temples. These include Jokomyoji, Eishoji, Jufukuji and Zeniarai Benten Shrine. Zeniarai Benten is known for its curious ceremony of "money washing." Numerous *torii*, so close as to form a tunnel, have been donated by merchants and businessmen in hopes that the gods in the shrine will smile on their enterprises. A steep walkway leads to a cave with a spring where money is placed in wicker baskets and swooshed around. The belief is that whatever is placed in the basket will be returned 3-fold. The bank-teller gods even work on national holidays.

events: Apr. 7-14: *Kamakura* Festival. This is the largest and most festive occasion held at Kamakura throughout the year. On Sun. during this time, an enormous procession of partici-pants wearing traditional costumes makes its way from Yuigahama Beach to Tsurugaoka Hachimangu Shrine. Other notable highlights during this festival are numerous open-air tea ceremonies and *yabusame* (horseback archery) events. *Mid-August:* fireworks at Yuigahama Beach. Huge crowds gather on this beach in late summer to watch this dazzling aerial display. *Sept. 14-16:* *Tsurugaoka Hachimangu* Shrine

yabasume (horseback archery)

Festival. This festive occasion centered around the shrine offers a parade of *mikoshi* (portable shrines) carried through the streets. On the 15th, *yabasume* is displayed in the shrine compound. <u>*Sept. 18:*</u> *Haramitto* at Gongoro Shrine. A large group of male participants depart from the shrine wearing grotesque masks. An all-out effort is made to portray the most comical figure. *Sept. 22:* *Takigi-Noh* at Tsurugaoka Hachimangu Shrine. Nature provides the background and torches provide the stage lighting as this ancient *noh* is performed outdoors at the shrine's *noh* stage. <u>*December:*</u> *Zeniarai* (money cleansing) at Zeniarai Benten Shrine. Held on the last "snake" day of Dec., people, especially merchants, flock to this shrine to wash their money at a special pool. The hopes are that it will multiply in the coming year.

arts and crafts: Wakamiya Oji, the main street, as well as many smaller streets branching from it, are lined with shops selling traditional Japanese arts and crafts. *Kamakura-bori* is the specialty of the area. This craft is finely chiselled wood, painted and lacquered to a glossy finish, most often red on black. Many small items, such as jewelry boxes, trays and pins, are made. Classes are offered at the Kamakura-bori Kaikan Hall, tel: (0407) 25-1500. Many of these shops also sell toys, pottery and antiques. They line the walkways to the temples and shrines, reminiscent of the Asakusa area in Tokyo. Almost any coffee or tobacco shop sells maps and colorful prints of Kamakura. Directly outside Kamakura Eki, to the L as you leave, is one of the best shopping areas for *mingei-hin* (folkart objects) that you will find anywhere. The shops lining this narrow street are a delight to wander in and out of. Even if you don't plan to buy, it will give you a good idea of the variety of arts that are available. Try a traditional sweet and a cup of green tea here at the end of a long day of walking through temple grounds.

swimming beaches: The 2 beaches of Zaimokuza and Yuigahama (follow Wakamiya-Oji Street S, 1.5 km to the sea) are the main swimming beaches of Kamakura and, as previously mentioned, are outrageously crowded during the summer (until Sept. 1). The Shonan Highway parallels the Enoden Railway heading W to Enoshima, and various swimming spots dot the route. You won't find any all to yourself, but they do get a little less crowded until you reach Enoshima, where they're packed once again. If you go to any of these in the early morning, however, you'll have them mostly to yourself.

accommodations: It is difficult to find budget accommodations in Kamakura. The western-style Tsurugaoka Kaikan Hotel offers lodgings and 2 meals at Y12,000. It is a 5 min walk from Kamakura Eki, tel: (0467) 25-5121. Kaihin-so Ryokan located near Yuigahama Eki on the Enoden Railway offers lodgings plus 2 meals at Y9000, tel: (0467) 22-0960. The Nihon Gakusei Kaikan YH is 5 min from Hase Eki on the Enoden. It is often booked out, so make reservations, tel: (0467) 25-1234.

KAMAKURA VICINITY

Enoshima is a tiny island in Sagami Bay, connected by a bridge to the mainland. The island itself, as well as the surrounding area (Katase), is extremely popular with vacationing Tokyoites. The main point to head for on the island is the Benten Cave in the southwest. It was believed to be the home of a dragon. The cave has 2 branches; at the far end of the L-hand branch is an image of Benten, the only female among the 7 Gods of Good Luck, often represented in the *Takara-Bune* (Treasure Ship). There are a number of historical temples at the exit of Enoshima Eki and on the hill behind it. The 1st temple, Ryukoji, just at the crossroads, is renowned for an execution that almost took place there. As the executioner raised his sword to behead the outspoken priest, Nichiren, in 1271, the sword was struck by lightning. The gods had spoken; Nichiren was spared to start one of the most popular modern sects of Bud-

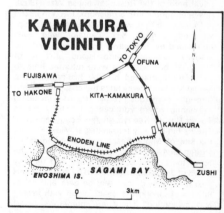

KAMAKURA VICINITY

dhism extant in Japan today. Later in this immediate area, the Emperor of Japan gave his answer to the envoys of Kublai Khan, who were sent to demand tribute. The executioner's sword was again raised; the sky remained clear, and their tombs are nearby. If you wind your way up the hill past this temple, on many of the branch paths you will find tiny temples populated by hermit-style priests and nuns. The top of the hill offers an extensive view of the bay, the Miura Peninsula, and even Mt. Fuji. Sunset is the best time. From Enoshima, you can continue on the Enoden to Fujisawa to make connections either for Tokyo or to the Mt. Fuji area. You can also go to Ofuna by monorail to make the same connections. If you go to Ofuna by monorail, you'll see a 25 m high statue of Kannon. For once, ferro-concrete has been used to make something of beauty. Although the materials used are modern, this snow-white statue is rendered in classical form, towering visible for miles on top of a rounded hill.

MIURA-HANTO PENINSULA

The diminutive (16 km) peninsula jutting into Tokyo Wan (Bay) SE of Kamakura. The NE coast is a built-up industrial area. The largest city, Yokosuka, pop. 370,000 is the site of a strategic U.S. Naval Base, a concession since WW 11. Most of the military personnel head for the bright lights of Tokyo or Yokohama, and overlook the bright sandy beaches in the SE and the less built up and populated W coast of the peninsula. At Yokosuka is Mikasa Park where the *Mikasa*, the flagship of Admiral Togo, the naval hero of the Russo-Japanese War (1905), has been turned into a museum. Two km inland is Tsukayama Park where Will Adams, the shipwrecked English sea captain who was befriended by Tokugawa Ieyasu, is buried. He actually died at Hirado Island, just N of Nagasaki, but his ashes were returned here to the fiefdom granted him by his patron. The Keihin-Kyuko Railway hugs the coast southward through numerous resort towns, including Kurihama, where you can get a ferry across Tokyo Bay to Kanaya on the Boso Peninsula. The Keihin Railway terminates at Miura-Kaigan, the site of Miura Beach, whose white sands stretch for 4 km. From here you must bus to the tip of the peninsula, where you'll find the tiny island of Jogashima connected by a bridge. This area is preserved as a seaside park and offers quiet walks along the beach along with fishing and swimming. There are numerous resort accommodations as well as Jogashima YH, 121, Jogashima, Misaki, Miura City, tel: (0468) 81-3893.

Zushi: The main town on the NW coast. It is only 4 km from Kamakura on the Yokosuka Line. Buses are available S along the coast. As you proceed southward to Hayama, Mt. Fuji becomes more visible in the distance. This area is extremely wealthy, with seaside villas and accompanying yachts. The length of the W coast is dotted with quiet bays and wide, undisturbed seascapes. On the extreme SW coast, only 4 km N of Miura and Jogashima, is Aburatsubo Marine Park with its superb displays of aquatic animals, complemented by a nearby botanical garden. The Miura Peninsula is a restful escape from the cities, providing a tiny taste of Japan's outdoors. *getting there:* From Tokyo via Yokohama on the Keihin-Kyuko Railway. At Kanazawa-Hakkei, a branch goes either to Zushi in the NW or Yokosuka in the NE. From Kamakura to Yokosuka, go via Zushi by bus or on the Yokosuka Main Line. *note:* For a visit to Mt. Fuji and the spectacular sights nearby, see the mini chapter "Fuji-Hakone-Izu National Park."

MIURA-HANTO PENINSULA

NIKKO

Nikko is the site of the most extravagant display of religious architecture in all of Japan. This treasure trove of shrines, mausoleums and temples, all richly gilded, intricately carved and painstakingly rendered, are unsurpassed in design or craftsmanship anywhere in the world. The word simple, often used as the cornerstone in descriptions of Japanese art and taste, is just not applicable. Nikko transcends personal taste. You cannot merely like it or dislike it. There is too much involved. Its detractors say that it is too gaudy, too rococo, too rich, and that it causes an artistic stomach ache. Its admirers say that Nikko's shrines are the pinnacle, the crescendo of Japanese religious art. Everywhere you look, your visual senses are bombarded. The roofs, pillars, and the very walls of the temples are carved. Delicate inlays and reliefs depicting animals, mythical beasts and fowls, dragons and flowers adorn every edifice. Statues of gods with blazing red and green faces, draped in indigo robes, raise golden swords. Enough gold leaf was used on the shrines at Nikko to cover the fields of a small farm. Stone lanterns of every conceivable size and shape line the pathways. Serpents with human faces, growling lions, sleeping cats and the 3 famous monkeys peer from rooftops and eaves at the dazzled visitors. Just when you have gasped your last artistic gasp, when you think you can take no more, look around and realize that the setting for these wonders is a pristine forest. The shrines of Nikko are set in Nikko National Park, where giant cedars planted 400 years ago provide a towering green canopy, their soothing quiet descending to the mossy forest floor. The National Park of Greater Nikko covers 140,700 ha, touching Tochigi, Gumma, Fukushima and Niigata prefectures. In its confines along with the shrines, are spas, lakes, rivers, mountains, and walking trails. Nikko offers both sides of the coin: natural timeless Japan and artistic timeless Japan.

getting there: JNR offers train service from Ueno (in Tokyo) to Nikko. The fare is expensive, the trains are slow and you must change trains. (Y1900 for a 4 ½ hr ride.) The Tobu-Nikko Line (private) offers direct service from Matsuya Department Store in Tokyo, just outside of Asakusa Eki, on the Ginza Subway Line. There are twice as many trains per day than on the JNR. They are faster, no changes are involved and they are cheaper (from Y900 for a 4 ½ hr ride to Y1900 for a 1 ¾ hr ride, reservations necessary). A wide range of information, including travel, accommodations and maps of Nikko are offered at the Tokyo TIC and at both the JNR and Tobu stations in Nikko. *getting around:* Both JNR and the Tobu Railway offer buses throughout Nikko, especially to the natural areas of Lake Chuzenji and nearby Kegon Waterfalls. Buses are available just

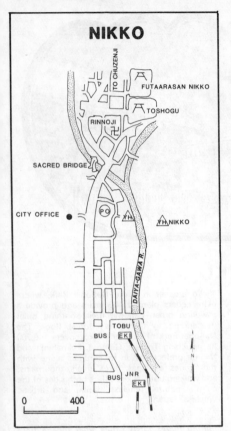

NIKKO

TO CHUZENJI

FUTAARASAN NIKKO

TOSHOGU

RINNOJI

SACRED BRIDGE

CITY OFFICE

P.O.

NIKKO

DAIYA-GAWA R.

TOBU
EKI

BUS

BUS

JNR
EKI

N

0   400

outside the train stations in Nikko. The Tobu buses are more frequent (about every 20 min starting from 0800); the fares are about equal (Y650 one way). Tobu Eki has a well-stocked information booth of the area with some English spoken.

NIKKO'S SACRED SHRINES AND TEMPLES

The Sacred Bridge, *Shinkyo:* The 1st sight that you come to just before you enter the shrine and temple precincts proper marked by the giant cryptomeria (Japanese cedars) on the hill behind you as you approach up the main boulevard. It is obvious at first glance that this vermillion span sitting on 2 stone *torii* girders was intended for ceremonial purposes only. On one side is a

steep, overgrown bank and on the other is the busy main highway. The bridge dates back 1200 yrs to Priest Shodo, and is steeped in legend concerning 2 magical snakes sent by the gods to span the Daiya River. Shinkyo's present architecture dates from 1636 and was used only by the *shogun* and messengers from the Imperial Household. This graceful, colorful crescent, rebuilt in the exact same style after a flood in 1907, is 28 m long and 7.2 m wide. It is now open to the public, but only during special shrine festivals. Opposite the bridge is a monument to Matsudaira Masatsuna, one of the *daimyo* responsible for the building of Toshogu Shrine. He was also responsible for the planting of the now-giant trees that line the shrine precincts and extend for over 40 km to small villages housing centuries-old thatch-roofed farm houses. At the Matsudaira Monument, flights of stone steps lead up the hill to the shrines.

Rinnoji Temple: The large temple compound on the R side of Omotesando before you reach the Toshogu *torii*. It is a temple of the Tendai sect, and the main sanctuary, Sanbutsu-do (Three Buddhas), erected in 1648, is the largest wooden building in Nikko. Inside Sanbutsudo are 3 Buddhas over 3 m tall, sitting on giant lotus petals. The one on the R is the 1000-handed Kannon (only 40 hands, but each can dispense 25 wishes), in the center is Amida-Nyorai, and on the L is the Bato Kannon, with a horse's head carved into the forehead, representing the deity of animals. Other sights on the grounds include the Gohotendo, housing 3 more deities and a 13 m tall, bronze pillar known as the Sorinto, which encases 10,000 volumes of holy sutra. The 2 large bronze lanterns sitting outside of the Sanbutsudo were donated by silk merchants in the 1600s. Because merchants were held in such low esteem during this period (even below farmers), their gifts were not worthy of a more dignified spot on the grounds. In times past, princes of the Imperial Family served as the abbots of Rinnoji. The abbots' private garden is superb, but special permission must be granted in advance to view it.

along Omotesando: The main pathway that leads to the giant *torii* that marks the entrance to Toshogu Shrine. Here numerous vendors sell food and trinkets. One tent-covered stall sells fresh, blender-whipped fruit juices (melon, orange, lemon and others) for Y200 per large glass. A carnival-type attraction along this walkway is a man with his trained birds, Y100.

SHRINES AND TEMPLES OF NIKKO

Customers pay the birds for a prayer paper. The birds take a 1Y coin in their beaks, proceed along a tiny pathway, deposit the coin in a prayer box, ring a bell, flap their wings 3 times, then open the doors on a tiny shrine to retreive the prayer paper. The birds are great, but the master is a "Step back, son, you bother me" type. He doesn't like photographers.

admission to the shrines: The shrines are open daily from 0800-1700 from April to Oct., and from 0800-1600 from Nov.-March. Tickets are available at booths near the 5-Storied Pagoda located at the end of the main pathway just at the entrance of Toshogu Shrine. At the R-hand window, tickets (Y550) entitle you to enter all of the shrines and temples, including Ieyasu Tokugawa's tomb. On the L, tickets cost Y230, but access is limited to most buildings but does not include the tomb. You can buy tickets to supplement the Y230 ticket but then you save nothing. Don't miss Ieyasu's Tomb. Plenty of information on the shrines is available from the shrine office.

TOSHOGU SHRINE

The recipient of most of the superlatives used to describe the sacred precincts of Nikko. Toshogu is the final resting place of Tokugawa Ieyasu, the 1st Tokugawa Shogun. Before his death, Ieyasu commanded that this immensely ornate and expensive shrine be built in his memory. His wishes were carried out by his grandson, Iemitsu, in 1636, who employed 15,000 workers over a period of 20 years. Iemitsu is enshrined at Daiyuinbyo, 400 m to the L of his grandfather. Ieyasu did not commission Toshogu purely out of egotism. He was primarily a warrior-politician, with immense personal power and a visionary's eye for the future. A keystone of his rule, that helped it to endure for 250 years, was to keep the *daimyo* from building large personal fortunes so that a coup against his household would be impossible. Even his own death was used as a political tool and, therefore, Toshogu was built with the financial burden being carried by the *daimyo*.

the entrance: Toshogu is marked by 10 stone steps leading to an immense stone *torii*, 8.4 m high, that spans the entranceway. As you enter, to the L is the 5-Storied Pagoda (buy your tickets at the booths here). The pagoda, standing 35 m high, is emblazoned with the crest of Tokugawa, the 3-petalled hollyhock and the 12 signs of the zodiac. The stories, from top to bottom, represent sky, fire, earth, water and wind as well as the 5 Buddhas of wisdom. The 3rd story contains a large wooden beam designed to sway to maintain equilibrium in case of an earthquake. Proceed up the main pathway to the stone steps to Omotemon (Deva) Gate, which is the official entrance to Toshogu. The

paintings on the ceiling of the Sacred Palanquin House

Omotemon is richly carved with flowers and lions, and standing guard on each side are 2 ferocious Dewa Kings (*Niosama*) that protect the shrine from evil spirits. The crescendo that is Toshogu hits its first harmonious chord at Omotemon. Passing through the gate, the 2 buildings to the R are the lower and middle storehouses. The unpainted building to the L, the only unlacquered building of Toshogu, might be a surprise after all the promises of artistic splendor. Realize that, in effect, it is only a barn, the Sacred Stables. Around the lintels are carvings of the monkey life cycle, beginning with a pregnant mother. The 2nd panel on the L offers the 3 famous monkeys which "hear, speak and see no evil." Monkeys were believed to protect horses from illness. The next stop past the Sacred Stables on the L is a covered cistern. Here, Japanese visitors wash their mouths and spill water over their hands to purify themselves before proceeding. Pass under the bronze *torii* and on the L is the Kyozo, a revolving library of 7000 sutras. The area is adorned with numerous stone lanterns. Across from it is the Upper Storehouse. Under the eaves are carvings of elephants (that had never been actually seen in Japan). The artist, Tanyu Kano, drew them from imagination after reading accounts about them. Except for slight miscalculations in the ears and tails, they are remarkably exact. Ascend the next series of steps flanked by protective lions and to the L and R

are the Drum Tower and Belfry. Surrounding the Drum Tower are a number of bells and lanterns presented by foreign nations such as Korea and the Netherlands. The lantern in front of the Drum Tower was presented by the Dutch traders of Nagasaki in 1636. Unfortunately, the Tokugawa crest imprinted upon it is upside down. Even then the *gaijin* made mistakes.

Yomeinon: Now in front of you, Yomeinon looms. This is the magnificent structure, the Gate of Sunlight, the promised superlative. The materials used were the finest, the artists were the best in the land and their dedication was bottomless. You cannot take in the lavishness of the entire structure in one staring gulp. You must take it in small sips. Yomeinon is literally art work piled upon art work to form the whole 2-storied structure. You can spend an entire day inspecting it. There are mythical *kirin* (somewhat like blazing giraffe-horses) from China, dragons, clouds, lions, flowers, children, immortal sages, tigers and innumerable geometric patterns. Two dragons dance on the ceiling, one ascending and one descending. Yomeimon was considered so magnificent that one of the main columns was carved upside down so that the gods themselves would not become jealous. The main structure is flanked by lesser buildings and fences running E-W for over 200 m.

Yakushido: The symphony goes on. Before passing under Yomeimon, the pathway to the L takes you to Yakushido, a structure with a strong Buddhist flavor. Its main attraction is the Naki Ryu (Crying Dragon), a pen−and−ink drawing on the ceiling. Visitors stand on a marked spot and clap their hands. The reverberating sound produced, heavily spiced with imagination and wishful thinking, sounds like a weeping dragon. The original drawing by Yasunobu Kano was destroyed in a roof fire in 1961. The present one, crafted by Nampu Katayama, dates from 1968. _The Honden (Main Hall):_ Pass under Yomeimon and on the L is Mikoshigura (Sacred Palanquin House), where the portable shrines used in the shrine festival are kept. To the R is Kagaruden (Sacred Dance Stage) and the Upper Shrine Offices. Straight ahead is Karamon (Chinese Gate), the entrance to the innermost shrine. Over the front portal is Tsutsuga, a bronze figure of a mystical animal that protects all buildings. Here again, dragons cling to the pillars and flowers adorn the panels. REMOVE YOUR SHOES HERE* NO PHOTOS ALLOWED. Proceed down the 5 copper steps. Nuns dressed in snow−white blouses and billowing orange pants are in full attendance and will direct you. Pass through a small chamber, Ishi-no-Ma (Stone Passageway), down 3 more copper steps. Climb the 5 copper steps on the other side and you are in the Honden (Main Hall). The inner sanctuary is usually closed to visitors. Inside the innermost chamber (Nai-Naijin) is the golden shrine, Gokuden (Sacred Place), where reside the deified spirits of Tokugawa Ieyasu, Toyotomi Hideyoshi and Minamoto Yoritomo. Upon leaving, follow the covered, red-lacquered passageway on your R to a gateway over which Nemuri-Neko, the famous sleeping cat, lies among blooming peonies, symbolizing the sleepy time of the year. Although asleep, he performs his function so well that mice are never found in the shrines. Half legend, half fact says the Nemuri-Neko was carved by the artist Jingoro Hidari (Hidari means left), whose superb talent was so coveted by a rival artist that he chopped off Hidari's R hand. Hidari, undaunted, used his L to carve the cat.

Ieyasu Tokugawa's Tomb: Passing under Nemuri-Neko, a pathway leads through Sakashitamon (Gate), the entranceway to Ieyasu's Tomb. Follow the stone steps (200) along the pathway lined with giant cedars which form a natural cathedral. The pathway leads to the Akaganegura (Copper Storehouse) with a rest area on the left. Smoking is permitted here, but you must purify yourself with water before proceeding. Another flight of steps leads to the Hall of Worship, completely covered in bronze. Next comes Inukimon, a solid bronze gate, and finally the Hodo, a small bronze pagoda sitting on an octagonal pedestal, where the ashes of Tokugawa Ieyasu are entombed. Notice that although the Hodo and the pathway leading to it are impeccable, they are, however, much less ornate than the Gokuden, where the _shogun's_ spirit is deified. The spirit becomes a _kami_, while the ashes remain, the remnants or a mortal.

the _shogun_, Tokugawa Ieyasu

Futaarasan Shrine: Lies 300 m W of Toshogu Shrine (take the pathway to the L before ascending the steps to Omotemon Gate). It enshrines 3 deities: a father, his consort and their son. These deities are revered for bringing prosperity to the country. Futaarasan dates back to Priest Shodo who founded the Okumiya (Inner Shrine) on the summit of nearby Mt. Nantai. Two others, Chugushi (Middle Shrine) on the shores of Lake Chuzenji, and the Honsha (Head Shrine), are all part of Futaarasan although quite distant from each other. The entrance to the shrine is marked by a bronze _torii_ (6.6 m) and on the R is the Oratory. Karamon

rest area near Futaarasan

(Chinese Gate), ornately decorated and lacquered, is at the entrance to the Honden (Main Shrine). Futaarasan offers *kagura* (sacred dancing) during the shrine festival held Apr. 13-17. Another important function of Futaarasan, rarely mentioned, is escape from the crowds at Toshogu. It's amazing how few of the Japanese tourists visit the shrine. It is set in a magnificent grove of Japanese cedars and there are even large, rustic picnic tables and benches perfect for a rest. After the explosive colors of Toshogu, the natural browns and greens surrounding Futaarasan are a welcome relief. If you really want to be alone and would enjoy a lengthy walk, follow the pathways up the hill along the fence surrounding the shrine. There is a circular course (marked) going up into the foothills that passes many small and unvisited shrines and takes about 2 hrs to complete.

Daiyuinbyo (Iemitsu's Mausoleum): Is on a smaller scale than Toshogu, but is also superbly appointed. It is 400 m W or Toshogu. Follow the main path L from Omotesando, just before the steps at the giant, granite *torii*, or take a side path S from Futaarasan about 150 m. Here, Iemitsu, the 3rd Tokugawa Shogun, after fulfilling his obligation to his grandfather, was in turn entombed at Daiyuinbyo. Enter the shrine precincts under Niomon Gate, protected again by the 2 guardian Dewa Kings. A walkway leads through a small garden, and then a flight of 21 steps takes you up to Nitenmon. This gate is flanked by Komokuten and Jikokuten, the gods of wind and thunder. Komokuten holds a bag enclosing the damaging winds. After 2 more flights of steps, you pass under Yashamon, decorated with 4 Buddhist gods, before you enter an inner courtyard with a belfry and drum tower. The next gate is Karamon (Chinese Gate), overlaid with gold and numerous bas reliefs, which leads to the Oratory. In the center of the Oratory is a gilt canopy and the walls and ceiling are ornately carved. Pass through the connecting chamber, Ai-no-Ma; the gold lacquered boxes lining the hall are prayer desks. Finally you enter the Honden (Main Hall). The feeling here, like at Toshogu, is appropriately reverent, but photos are allowed. Again, the motifs are of *kirin*, dragons, lions and flowers. The main object is a Buddhist shrine in which sits a wooden figure of Iemitsu. Proceed from there under Kokamon, a white plastered Chinese gate, modeled after the architecture of the Ming Dynasty. A flight of stone steps leads under Inukimon, a solid bronze gate, and finally to Iemitsu's Tomb, which is in a similar style to that of Ieyasu.

Nikko Botanical Garden: At Hanaishicho Bus Stop, 10 min from Nikko Eki on the way to Chuzenji. If you are templed out, a stroll over the 10.5 ha gardens is revitalizing. There are over 3000 varieties of plants, including wildflowers. Part of the complex is Jamozawa, a former Imperial Villa now housing a museum, which is a fine example of Japanese architecture.

EVENTS

<u>April 13-17:</u> Ya Yoi Matsuri at Futaarasan Shrine. This festival is the annual celebration of this protectorate shrine of Nikko. There is a palanquin procession along with singing and dancing.

<u>May 2:</u> Gohan-Shiki at Rinnoji Temple. In effect this is a rice planting ceremony that takes place at the Sanbutsudo on the temple grounds. Today the priests throw small gifts of food and toys to the people assembled on the temple grounds. In times past, *daimyo* from all over the country assembled here. They were given huge bowls of rice that they were forced to consume. The temple priests could even strike them to hurry them along. The rice symbolized the bounty provided by the gods. At night during the *Gohan-Shiki* the temple priests light a sacred fire called *goma* and perform sacred dances to the accompaniment of chanting.

<u>May 17-18:</u> Toshogu Shrine Grand Festival. This is one of the grandest festivals in all of Japan. The festivities begin with a procession of 1000 people (*sennin gyoretsu*) dressed in costumes from the Tokugawa Period. They represent samurai, falconers, priests, child monkeys and even fairies. On the morning of the 2nd day, the spirits of Ieyasu, Yoritomo and Hideyoshi are carried in *mikoshi* (portable shrines) to the Ota Baisho (Sojourn Hall). Here they are paid homage with sacred music and special dances called *azuma-asobi-surugamai,* performed by the temple priests. Finally the portable shrines are taken to the Mikoshigura (Sacred Palanquin House). At about 1400, a demonstration of horseback archery is performed on the pathway leading from Toshogu to Futaarasan Shrine.

<u>October 17:</u> Toshogu Shrine Fall Festival. Basically the same events held at spring festival in May, except there is no display of horseback archery.

<u>Festivals in the nearby areas:</u> The Lantern Floating Festival held at Lake Chuzenji on the nights of July 31 to Aug. 2; the Pilgrim's Festival on Aug. 1-7 when participants climb Mt. Nantai walking through the night carrying lanterns (repeated on Sept. 20-22).

PRACTICALITIES

<u>accommodations:</u> For the full range of accommodations offered in the Nikko area, inquire at the Nikko Tourist Assoc. located at Nikko City Office, tel: (0288) 4-2496. Nikko is very popular, so if you are contemplating a tour here, it's important to make reservations before arriving. Contact any JNTO or TIC for information and make reservations through any JTB or any travel agent. For a Western-style hotel in Nikko, try Nikko Kanaya Hotel, Kami-Hatsuishicho, Nikko 321-14, tel: (0288) 4-0001, 5 min by car from Nikko Sta., from Y6000. Many more hotels and *ryokan* are found at nearby Lake Chuzenji (see "Nikko Vicinity") and the surrounding spa towns. YHs in Nikko include Nikko Daiyagawa YH, 1076 Naka-Hatsuishimachi, Nikko 321-14, tel: (0288) 4-1974, 5 min by bus from Nikko Sta. and 3 min on foot, 29 beds. Daiyagawa YH has a better reputation for friendliness than Nikko YH, 1140 Tokorono, Nikko 324-14, tel: (0288) 4-1013, 24 min on foot from Nikko Sta., 50 beds.

<u>food and shopping:</u> The town of Nikko centers around one broad avenue heading NW (2 km) from the train stations to the shrines. Shops and restaurants line both sides of the street. The restaurants range from the basic *soba* shop at Y500, to exquisite, but super-expensive Japanese full-course feasts. The shops sell souvenirs of lacquerware and woodcarvings along with the usual junk, overusing the redundant motif of Nikko's famous sleeping cat and the 3 monkeys. There are several choice shops to head for which are stuck away in the alleyways off the main street. One of these is Mr. S. Kobayashi's Art Gallery and Antique Shop. Look for a sign that reads THIS WAY on the E side of the street, about midway between the Sacred Bridge and the Post Office. Follow the signs over a series of stepping stones through a quiet garden leading to the shop. Mr. Kobayashi speaks English and his family history as art dealers is fascinating, going back to his grandfather, Shohei, who started the business in 1873. Ask to read the newspaper articles about his family, and then check out the visitor's book, dating back to 1898, with signatures from all over the world. The museum-like antique shop has everything from 100 yr old woodblock prints to well done, but inexpensive coasters with motifs from classical *shoji* screens. You can spend from Y100 to Y2,000,000, or just enjoy browsing.

NIKKO VICINITY

Chuzenji is a spa town 19 km W of Nikko, lying on the NE shore of a 12 sq km lake of the same name. A famous attraction in the town limits is Kegon Falls, known for producing an almost constant rainbow effect. The area around Chuzenji offers mountain trails, relaxing mineral spas and unique high-plateau swampland, resplendent with wildflowers. *getting there:* JNR Bus, available from Nikko Eki, or Tobu Bus, available from Tobu-Nikko Eki, are the main means of transportation. Tobu buses are more frequent, leaving about every 20 min starting at 0800 from Bus Stop 2, Y650 one way. The bus from Nikko passes through Umageshi (10 km), where the road splits into No. 1 and No. 2. Irohazaka Drive. Number 1 is a one-way drive leading to Chuzenji from Nikko that completely lives up to its reputation for having 22 white-knuckled, hairpin turns. (Number 2 returns to Nikko). The bus wheedles its way through the mountains, stopping at Akechidara, a commanding overview about midway. There is a cable car here to the mountain summit that provides an even more extensive view, taking in Lake Chuzenji, Mt. Nantai (2848 m) to the N, and Kegon Falls. For those inclined, you can walk a trail from this point along the mountain rim (45 min) to Chanokidaira and then from there take another cable car to Kegon Falls.

CHUZENJI

This resort spa town has long been popular with foreigners, many of whom have built homes along its shores. The main street through the center of town runs from Lake Chuzenji on one end to Kegon Falls on the other. It's lined with shops selling all manner of souvenirs and handmade folk crafts. Artists sit in front of their shops, manufacturing their wares. Two noteworthy places are a calligraphy shop where the artisan uses a hammer and chisel to gouge out *kanji* on a flat piece of wood, instead of working with the usual ink and brush. Another is a shop specializing in gourd masks. The masks, used in festivals, are easily visible, hanging in front of the shop to dry after being brightly painted. They range from Y800 upwards.

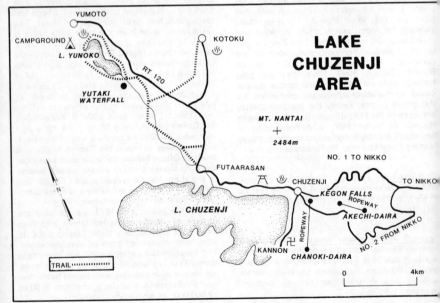

hand crafted gourd masks

constant rainbow effect. Over the chasm, 1000s of sparrows dart, chirping and dipping into the froth. The overall effect is very soothing.

temples and shrines: If you have any desire to visit more temples and shrines after Nikko, Chuzenji offers two. Chugushi is the middle shrine of the main Futaarasan Shrine. It's on the S slope of Mt. Nantai, facing the lake. The Honden (Main Hall), lined with copper, is heavily ornate. The shrine festival occurs from Aug. 1-7, with pilgrims stopping here for purification before ascending Mt. Nantai. Chuzenji Temple, belonging to the Rinnoji sect, offers a 1000-handed Kannon carved by Prince Shodo as the main object of worship. Chuzenji Temple is reachable by excursion boat from the dock area, or by a 2 km access road along the E shore of the lake. The temple also offers a museum. The main interest of Chuzenji is its superb setting, especially after the heavy doses of religious art from Nikko.

heading north: Route 120 heads N from Chuzenji for 13 km to the spa town of Yumoto and its nearby Lake Yunoko. (Bus from Chuzenji or Nikko). En route, it passes some intriguing natural spots. Included is Ryuzu-no-Taki (Dragon's Head Cascades), and a highland swamp known as Senjogahara Plain. Although wet and marshy, Senjogahara has wooden elevated walkways into its interior. The wild flora of the area is worth a look. Yumoto Spa lies at 1800 m and is surrounded by mountains. Numerous relaxing baths are available. In winter, this area is a favorite of ice skaters and skiers. Lake Yunoko, nearby, houses a trout hatchery. The waters are teeming with fish. Purchase an inexpensive permit in town during the fishing season from May 15 to Sept. 15.

Lake Chuzenji: A lovely lake surrounded by mountains. Along the shore near town are choice spots to relax and eat lunch. Tour boats holding 50-100 people circumnavigate the lake, but are pricey at Y500 for the 45 min ride. They leave from the main dock. There are rowboats for hire, some are even made to look like sharks, but again they are expensive at Y400 per half-hour. At one time the lake was devoid of fish, but it's been stocked with trout and other fish for the past 100 years.

Kegon Falls: Fronted by a small park. Follow the paths to the booth where you can buy a ticket, Y300, for an elevator that descends to the bottom of the falls. The pathway to the R leads to a walkway and stairway leading down the side of the mountain where you can also get a free, bird's-eye view of the falls. The stream originates at Lake Chuzenji and then cascades over a huge, horseshoe-shaped chasm. The falls are delicate rivulets, whipped by the winds into foam. This misty quality produces an almost

accommodations: Western-style hotels in the Chuzenji area include Chuzenji Kanaya Hotel, 2482 Chugushi, Nikko 321-16, tel: (0288) 5-0356, 40 min by car from Nikko Sta., from Y8000; and Nikko Lakeside Hotel, 2482 Chugushi, Nikko 321-16, tel: (0288) 5-0321, 30 min by car from Nikko Sta., from Y14,000. Some _ryokan_ in these areas are Oku Nikko Onsen Hotel, Yumoto Onsen, Nikko City 321-16, tel: (0288) 62-2441, from Y8000; Izumiya Ryokan, Chuzenji Onsen, Nikko 321-16, tel: (0288) 5-0340, from Y8000; and Chuzenji Hotel, Chuzenji Onsen, Nikko 321-16, tel: (0288) 5-0333, from Y3000. Yumoto Yama-Noie YH is 10 min from Yumoto Bus Stop, tel: (0288) 62-2421.

MASHIKO

Mashiko has become synonymous with folk pottery ever since Hamada Shoji, an Intangible Cultural Property, established his kiln there in 1930 and, with encouragement from the British potter Bernard Leach, dedicated his life to preserving and passing on traditional pottery techniques. The village, on the border of Ibaraki and Tochigi Prefectures, is located approximately 95 km NE of Tokyo. The most desirable *Mashiko-yaki* is produced from local clays fired in the traditional *noborigama* (a multi-chambered kiln often-times stepped on the side of a hill and fired by wood). Soft-hued, subtle glazes, with a simple design on irregularly shaped pottery are the distinctive features of Mashiko ware. Hamada-san desired that the potters who came to Mashiko would preserve these simple traditions. So sorry. As Mashiko's reputation grew, the quality, for the most part, declined. There are still potters tucked away in the surrounding hills that keep the faith, but most shops in town sell mass-produced, gas or oil-fired, uninspired works. For those with the time and a keen eye to ferret out the exemplary works, masterpieces are still to be had. The local people are accustomed to dealing with foreigners, and it's not difficult to find a kiln at which to study this art. *sights:* To see examples of what Mashiko has to offer, visit the Hamada Home. This is a collection of thatch-roofed houses gathered and moved from the surrounding areas. There are a few works by the master himself, as well as treasures that he collected from around the world. Unfortunately, the main building cannot be entered and must be viewed from the outside. Visits to nearby working kilns are no problem. Unless you are deeply interested in pottery, Mashiko is best visited as a side trip on your way to Nikko. The village offers 2 yearly pottery fairs, one from May 3-6, and another from Oct. 10-13. Approximately 50,000 people attend.

getting there: Mashiko is not difficult to reach from Tokyo, but it does involve 2 *norikae* (transfers). Train from Tokyo to Oyama by JNR. Change here for Shimodate (10 km E) on the Mito Line. In Shimodate, change to the Moka Line to Mashiko (15 km N). From Mashiko to Nikko, in order to avoid backtracking to Oyama, bus directly to Utsunomiya, and then go by the JNR Nikko Line.

potter at a traditional sunken wheel

FUJI-HAKONE-IZU

INTRODUCTION

As in any nation, there are certain areas that are exceptionally famous, and Fuji-Hakone-Izu is one of these. Although technically spilling over into 3 prefectures in 2 separate districts, this park must be considered as a whole. Concentrated in the park is the grand peak of Mt. Fuji and the mirroring backdrops of Fuji's Five Lakes. Here is Hakone, packed with bubbling mineral spas, very welcomed after days of tramping over dozens of lofty peaks. In Hakone is Lake Ashi, a sparkling jewel encircled by verdant volcanic mountains and deep green forests, with cone-shaped Mt. Fuji perfectly framed in the background, perhaps the most well-known and photographed panorama in all of Japan. The park dips southward into the Izu Peninsula, with its sunny seaside resorts, and includes the 7 islands of Izu along with the Ogasawara Is., lying 1200 km out into the Pacific. Oshima, one of the Izu Is., is easily visible from Fuji's summit, and often silhouetted as the shimmering red sun lifts out of the Pacific at dawn. Because of this, Oshima is considered one of the most romantic places in Japan on which to die. Hakone, at the center of the National Park, is the most accessible area from Tokyo. This also means that city-weary Japanese flow by endless trainload into Hakone to boil their cares away in the hot springs, shed their Western business suits for the far more comfortable *yukata,* and bask in the sunshine, absorbing their birthright of mountains, coast and blossoming pastures.

getting there: From Tokyo Eki, take the Kodama Shinkansen for 42 min from Tokyo to Odawara, Y2500. Or you can travel on the JNR Tokaido Line for one hr 30 min, Y1000. From Shinjuku Eki in Tokyo, take the Odakyu Electric Railway to Odawara in one hr 15 min, Y850, then travel on to Hakone Yumoto in 15 min for Y200. Odakyu Electric Railway offers a "Hakone Free Pass" which includes the train trip from Shinjuku Eki (limited express fare is extra) and all transportation in the Hakone area, including the Hakone Tozen operated railway, bus, ropeway, cruise boat and cable car. Cost is Y4000 from Shinjuku, Y3000 from Odawara; good for 4 days. _getting around:_ All points of interest in the area are serviced by the Hakone Tozan Railway and railway bus. Where the roads and rail lines give out, a cable car and ropeway service are available to the summits of most mountains and across deep ravines. A cruise boat is available to tour Lake Ashi. An excellent pamphlet describing the park and transportation within it is available from JNTO and TIC offices.

SIGHTS

Odawara: The main city (pop. 170,000) and transportation center of the area. Odawara faces Sagami Bay and has numerous, but overly crowded, beaches. In traveling to Hakone, you'll pass through Odawara. Use it only as a stopover on your way into the park where older spas,

ryokan and _minshuku_ await, all with an excellent view of Fuji. Heading W on the Hakone Tozan Railway, the 1st stop is Hakone-Yumoto, the oldest spa in the area. The streets are lined with souvenir shops and dozens of hotels and _ryokan_. Dogashima and Miyanoshita further W offer the greatest cluster of spas. These towns sit at an altitude of 400 m and offer cool nights, even in mid-summer. The train dips to Kowakudani (Valley of Lesser Boiling), named after a cave emitting sulfurous fumes. The train turns N again and just before entering Gora, the end of the line and beginning of the Hakone Ropeway, it passes Chokoku-no-Mori, an open-air museum of sculptures and paintings by renowned Japanese and international artists; open 0900-1800. The ropeway from Gora to Togendai costs Y1500, with cars leaving every 15 minutes. Enroute, you pass Mt. Sounzan and Owakudani (Valley of Greater Boiling). Owakudani features numerous fumaroles emitting steam and gases. There's also a Natural Science Museum in Owakudani containing special exhibits pertaining to the Hakone area; open from 0900-1700, Y500. The ropeway passes

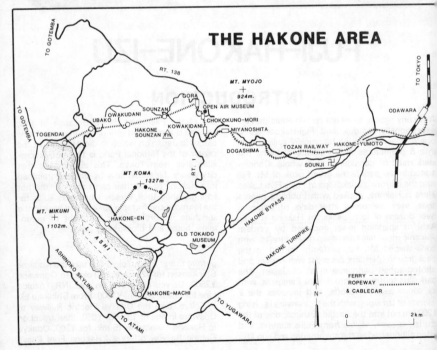

THE HAKONE AREA

the Hakone Ropeway

through Ubako, a secluded but fascinating spa with some of the best mountain views in the area. Togendai is the end of the line. Here buses are available down the E or W shore of Lake Ashi. Tour boats also cruise S, disembarking at Hakone-en or Hakone Shrine. Buses are available from either point going back to Odawara, or from Togendai on to Mt. Fuji.

EVENTS

The Hakone area has numerous festivals, with most occurring from April to August. The central theme is nature as artist. Flowers, blooming trees and mountains are the focal points. In April, the mountains are pink with cherry blossoms, in May and June adorned with delicate azaleas, and in Oct.-Nov. blazing in red and yellow maples. A few of the most colorful festivals of this area are:

Aug. 5: *Torii Matsuri*. At night along the shores of Lake Ashi, a wooden *torii* is set afire, and 1000 glowing lanterns are set adrift.

Aug. 16: *Daimon-ji Yaki*. Seen from Gora, the Chinese character *Dai* (great) is formed by burning torches on Mt. Myojo. Folk songs and dances highlight the evening festivities.

Nov. 3: *Daimyo Gyoretsu* at Hakone-Yumoto along the old Tokaido Road. A re-creation of the endless journeys of *daimyo* to the capital at Edo (now Tokyo) during the Tokugawa Period. A realistic display by hundreds of participants in full costume.

PRACTICALITIES

arts and crafts: The craftsmen of Hakone specialize in delicate and intricate inlay work using small pieces of cherry and camphor wood to create a wide range of items, from delicate, tiny jewelry boxes to lavish pieces of furniture. Their handiwork is available at hundreds of shops centered in all of the spa towns. There's also a thriving cottage industry of folkcraft (*hakone-zaiku*), focusing on wooden toys and dolls.

accommodations: Hakone has it all, from high-rise luxury hotels to charming and intimate family-operated *minshuku*. For Western-style, try Fujiya Hotel, 359 Miyanoshita, Hakone-machi 250-04, tel: (0460) 2-2211, 20 min by car from Odawara Sta., from Y5000; Hakone Hotel, 65 Hakone-machi 250-05, tel: (0460) 3-6311, 30 min by car from Odawara Sta., from Y7500; Gora Hotel, 1300 Gora, Hakone-machi 250-04, tel: (0460) 2-3111, 20 min by car from Hakone Yumoto Sta. of Odakyu Railway, from Y7000; and Hakone Kanko Hotel, 1245 Sengokuhara, Hakone-machi 250-06, tel: (0460) 4-8501, 30 min by car from Hakone-Yumoto Sta. of Odakyu Railway, from Y8000. All of these hotels offer Japanese-style rooms as well. There are many *ryokan* in the mountains and valleys of Hakone. Here are a few: Hakone Kowakien, Ninodaira, Hakone-machi 250-04, tel: (0460) 2-4111, Y8000-20,000; Ichinoyu, Tonosawa, Hakone-machi 250-03, tel: (0460) 5-5331, Y9000-10,000; and Naraya Ryokan, Miyanoshita, Hakone-machi 250-04, tel: (0460) 2-2411, Y15,000-25,000. For *minshuku*, there are Matsuzakaya, 64 Motohakone, Hakone-machi, tel: (0460) 3-6315, 50 min by bus from Odawara Sta., Y4000-5000 per person w/o meals, Y9000-10,000 per person

w/2 meals; and Yugiri-so, 138 Hakone, Hakone machi, tel: (0460) 3-6377, 50 min by bus from Odawara Sta., Japanese-style, 8 rooms, Y6000 7000 per person w/o meals, Y9000-10,000 pe person w/2 meals. The 2 closest YHs to Hakon are Manazuru YH, 1842-9 Manazuru, Manazuru machi 259-02, tel: (0465) 68-3580, 4 min on foo from Manazuru Sta., 23 beds; and Hakone sounzan YH, 1320 Gora, Hakone-machi 250-04 tel: (0460) 2-3827, 10 min by cable car from Gor Sta., and 2 min on foot, 27 beds.

services: TIC and JNTO publish very usefu brochures on this entire area that contain maps brief descriptions of sights and railroad time tables. For more information, contact th Tourist Division of Hakone Town Office, 256 Yumoto, Hakone, Kanagawa, tel: (0460) 5-7111 Tokyo, tel: (03) 231-3902; Osaka, tel: (06 341-9427.

MT. FUJI

No other feature of Japan, whether man-made or naturally occurring, is as ingrained into the Japanese psyche as Fuji-san. Revered from ancient times as a sacred peak, its motif appears time and again in paintings, murals and sculptures, and the most sublime Japanese poetry has sung its praises. Its perfect shape, blanketed in fog or regally purple and majestic in full sunlight, adorns everything from tiled bath houses to cheap plastic souvenirs. The fascination that Mt. Fuji holds for the Japanese is many faceted, inexorably tied to ancient Shinto, unconscious basic spiritualism, a sense of beauty and nationalistic pride. Fuji-san, along with the ensign of the Red Rising Sun on a field of white, is the national emblem, the symbol of Nippon. If Japanese could travel to only one place in their lifetime, most would choose Mt. Fuji. Almost a caricature of what a volcano should be, it rises 3776 m in a snow-capped symmetrical cone with an almost perfectly round base. Most scholars agree that Mt. Fuji is an ancient Ainu word for fire. Now quietly dormant, Fuji was at one time very active. The last eruption occurred in 1707 and covered Tokyo, 100 km away, in a thick blanket of ash. Until the Meiji Era, no Japanese woman was allowed to climb the mountain. Now, nearly half of the 400,000 climbers per year are women. The 1st foreigner to climb Mt. Fuji was Sir Rutherford Alcock, the British consul, in July of

1860. Lady Parkes, an Englishwoman, firs scaled Fuji-san in 1867. Another Wester notable who loved Fuji and climbed it man times was Dr. Frederick Starr, an anthropologis from Chicago University. A monument has bee erected to his memory near Sengen Shrine Subashiri in the Mt. Fuji vicinity.

the climb: The climbing season is officially ope for only 2 months in mid-summer, from July 1 Aug. 31. The mountain is climbed in "expeditio style" throughout the year but this is unadvi sable for the casual climber. All mountain hut and services are closed except during th "official season." The climbing on the trails i not overly difficult, but is steady. The trails tak from 5-9 hrs for the ascent and 3 hrs for th descent. Clothing should be appropriate for th cool, brisk winds of high altitude (5 C is th average summer temperature at the summit and raingear is always advisable. The foo offered at stalls and from vending machines a the summit is atrocious and expensive. Brin your own to save money and to avoid indi gestion. Japanese climbers, often-times dressed in pilgrim white with straw sandals t cover their shoes, carry walking sticks that ar branded at the summit as proof of the conquest. If you wish to do the same, thes articles are readily available at numerous shop

MT. FUJI
CLIMBING TRAILS

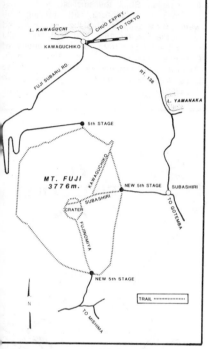

throughout the area. They're more for show than necessity. The goal of most climbers is to experience *goraiko*, the sunrise. *Goraiko* is a genuine, guaranteed starry-eyed, spiritual experience, but the timing and weather must be perfect. Climbers either set out late in the afternoon and climb all night to reach the summit, or lodge at the 7th or 8th station along the way and rise very early (0400) to push on to the top. At dawn, the sky turns a misty purple, then slowly and steadily the blood-red sun floats to the surface of the Pacific, the colors changing from red to bronze to pale dawn-blue, then *goraiko*. As the long shadows give way to dawn, you look around and have another jolting, utterly inspiritual experience. The summit and trails of Fuji are filthy with garbage. Hundreds of thousands of *bento* boxes, rotting oranges, butts, papers and scraps carried up for that extra

boost of energy have been discarded. How can the Japanese love Fuji so much and treat it so shabbily? After the sunrise, there isn't much to do on the summit of Fuji. Savor *goraiko* as long as possible, and with your eye on the horizon, head down.

the trails: The 5 trails up Fuji-san are equally divided into 10 stages, called *go*. These trails are named Kawaguchiko, Subashiri, Fujinomiya, Fuji-Yoshida and Gotemba. Most Tokyoites ascend by way of Kawaguchiko and descend on Subashiri. Kyotoites seem to prefer Fujinomiya. For an interesting descent, try sand-skiing (*sunabashiri*) from the 7th station of Gotemba Trail. Sliding these 7 km to Sta. 2 takes only one hour. Kawaguchiko and Fuji-Yoshida lead up the northern face of Fuji, offering a view of the Japan Alps and Fuji Five Lakes. Gotemba and Subashiri approach from the E and Fujinomiya from the S, with a panorama of the Pacific in the background. There's no remarkable difference in difficulty between the trails. Bus service is available to the 5th stations of Kawaguchiko, Subashiri and Fujinomiya. Both the Fuji-Yoshida and Gotemba trails begin lower on the mountain, leading through forests and the approaching foothills. The walk is enjoyable, but longer, and the scenery is not overly remarkable.

getting there: The Kawaguchiko 5th station can be reached by direct bus service from Hamamatsucho Bus Terminal in Tokyo at the World Trade Center Building, 3 hrs, Y2000, or from Shinjuku Bus Terminal in 2½ hrs, Y1800. Reservations are available from any JTB. By train from Shinjuku (Tokyo) to Kawaguchiko, 2 hrs via Otsuki where the train splits. Be sure you're on the correct car; Y2000. Then by bus to the 5th Stage, Y1000. To the Subashiri trail, take a train from Shinjuku to Gotemba, 2 hrs, Y1500, then bus to Subashiri. To the Fujinomiya trail, take a train from Osaka, Kyoto and other points on the Tokaido Main Line to Fuji Town, then to Fujinomiya, or take the *shinkansen* to Mishima, then bus to Fujinomiya. Bus: Y2000.

mountain accommodations: Lodgings are available at mountain huts, located above the 5th stage of all trails. They are open from July 1 to Aug. 31. They charge Y4500 w/meals, Y3000 without. There is NO CAMPING allowed on Mt. Fuji. The full range of accommodations in the area is listed after the following "Fuji Five Lakes."

FUJI FIVE LAKES

To the N of Mt. Fuji, in a gentle arc on the S boundary of Yamanashi Prefecture, are the Fuji Five Lakes. From E to W, they are Lake Yamanaka, Lake Kawaguchi, Lake Saiko, Lake Shoji and Lake Motosu. The Five Lake area is a year-round vacation spot. Fishing, hunting, camping, trekking and spas are its features. Each lake has its own claim to fame. Yamanaka is the largest at 646 m; Kawaguchi offers the best reflection of Fuji; Saiko has the best fishing

and offers nearby Jukai (Sea of Trees), a vast forest region; Shoji, the smallest, is the most picturesque; and Motosu, with dazzling blue waters, is the deepest. The lakes are connected by excellent roads (Rt. 139) and are easily accessible by bus from the main centers of Gotemba, Fuji-Yoshida and Kawaguchiko. There are campgrounds available at all of the lakes, as well as hotels, *ryokan* and youth hostels.

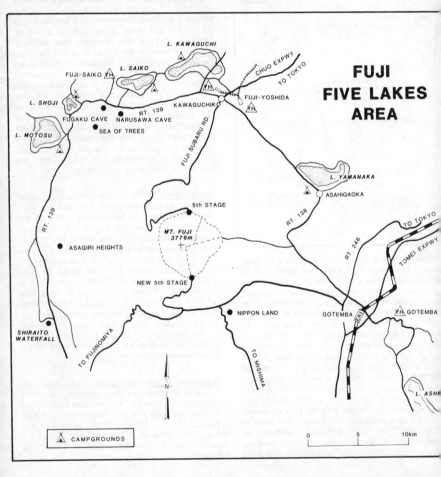

sights: The best sights in this area include the primeval forests of Jukai and Aokigahara surrounding Lakes Motosu, Shoji and Saiko. Kilometer after kilometer of tall, stately trees line the hillsides of this golden plateau country and have been assigned as a "National Natural Monument." On Rt. 139 S of Lake Saiko is Narusawa Ice Cave, and a little further W is the Fugaku Wind Cave. Both caves were formed by inner pressure forcing back the lava of one of Fuji's ancient eruptions. Living up to their names, both caves are strewn with icicles—a natural ice box, even in mid-summer. There are 2 museums a short walk from Kawaguchiko Eki. Yamanashi Visitor's Center Museum highlights the natural history of the area, while Fuji Museum focuses on the lives of the people of the area and offers a collection of phalluses and other fertility items. Shiraito Waterfalls, the most distant attraction of the area lying S of Lake Motosu on Rt. 139 leading to Fujinomiya, shouldn't be missed. Shiraito is considered a feminine waterfall and it's one of the most delicate and dainty in Japan. Instead of the usual gush of water cascading over a cliff, Shiraito drops only 26 m, but is 130 m wide. The falls fan out into tiny, white trickles, bubbling and murmuring, making their sinuous way to the bottom. Camping, boating and relaxing around the shores of Fuji Five Lakes is the best way to slowly end a visit to Mt. Fuji and to savor the natural beauty of the area before moving on.

accommodations: A great variety of accommodations throughout the area. Western-style/luxury accommodations include the Fuji-View Hotel, 511 Katsuyama-mura 401-04, tel: (05558) 3-2211, on the shore of Lake Kawaguchi, from Y10,000; Hotel Mt. Fuji, 1360-82 Yamanakako-mura 401-05, tel: (05556) 2-2111, 15 min by car from Fuji-Yoshida Sta. of Fujikyu Railway, at Lake Yamanaka. This hotel offers free rooms from Jan. 6-31, if Mt. Fuji is not visible. From Y7000. New Yamanakako Hotel, 352-1 Yamanakako-mura 401-05, tel: (05556) 2-2311, 15 min by car from Fuji-Yoshida Sta. of Fujikyu Railway, from Y8000. For more moderately priced lodgings try Hotel Grand Fuji, 8-1 Heigaki-Honcho, Fuji 416, tel: (0545) 61-0360, 3 min by car from Fuji Sta., from Y4000; or these *minshuku:* Minshuku Nogi, Konohana-cho 4-chome, Kanazawa, tel: (0762) 21-8579, 5 min walk from Kanazawa Sta., Y5000-6000 w/2 meals; and Fuji-so, 735 Kodachi, Kawaguchiko-machi, tel: (05557) 2-1869, 10 min by bus from Fujikyuko Kawaguchiko Sta., Y5000-6000 w/2 meals. Hostelers should seek out the Fuji-Yoshida YH, tel: (0555) 2-0533, 7 min walk from Fuji-Yoshida Sta.; Kawaguchiko YH, tel: (05557) 2-1415, 5 min walk from Kawaguchiko Sta.; Fuji-Saiko YH, tel: (05558) 2-2616, 35 min by bus from Kawaguchiko Sta. to Saiko Minshuku; and Gotemba YH, tel: (0550) 2-3045, 20 min by bus from Gotemba Sta. to Higashiyamako Stop, 10 min walk.

services: JNTOs and TIC offer brochures of the area. Reservations for travel or accommodations can be made through any travel agent or JTB. A full range of guided tours is offered, and arrangements can also be made at any JTB. Many of these tours originate at large Tokyo hotels and include all costs for transportation, lodging and dining. They are expensive.

THE IZU PENINSULA

Stretching luxuriously into the Pacific is a thin, 60 km spit of land known as the Izu Peninsula, and off its shores to the S are the 7 Isles of Izu. This sun-drenched coast is inundated with countless bays and beaches, endlessly massaged by rolling breakers. Two remarkable Westerners that changed the history of Japan made their temporary homes on Izu. The first was William Adams, a shipwrecked Englishman who lived at Ito village while attempting to build a ship for the Tokugawa Shogun in the early 1600s. Known as Anjin-san, this amazing seaman and his exploits became the pattern for James Clavell's central character in his popular book, *Shogun*. Two-and-a-half centuries later, in the early 1850s, Townsend Harris, the 1st American consul to Japan, came to live on the SE tip of Izu at Shimoda. Later, in 1857, Harris concluded the 1st treaty of Japan with a foreign nation. Izu has been a famous spa and relaxation area for generations. Almost every town nestled along its serpentine coastline offers a spa, swimming and general sunny relaxation.

getting there: The 2 main transportation centers to Izu are Atami in the NE and Mishima in the NW of the peninsula. Both are stops on the *shinkansen,* and both are regularly serviced by numerous trains on the Tokaido Main Line: Tokyo-Atami, 55 minutes. Tokyo-Mishima, 67 min by *shinkansen*. *getting around:* Only the E coast from Atami to Shimoda, a stretch of 48 km, and a small section of the central interior from Mishima to Shuzenji (18 km) are serviced by local trains. For travel to the interior and along the W coast, the Tokai Bus Co. provides service from Atami or Mishima, while small local ferries make short hops between main towns along the W coast. Hitchhiking is also excellent.

SIGHTS

the spa towns: Atami was the traditional hot-springs resort with a picture-perfect fan-shaped beach immortalized in a woodblock print by Toyokuni. At one time known for its quiet walks in the surrounding mountains, it has now become too touristy, with row upon row of souvenir shops and amusement parks. For the real charm of the peninsula, quickly head S to Ito, Atagawa, Inatori and Shimoda, the main spa towns from N-S along the E coast. Each offers

restful spas and evening mountain treks after days of lolling on the fine beaches. The Ikeda Art Museum, 30 min by bus from Ito Eki, offers contemporary and historical paintings, sculptures and woodblock prints by well-known Western and Japanese artists. Open daily from 0830-1700. Another interesting afternoon can be spent at Atagawa Banana and Crocodile Gardens, not far from Atagawa Eki, open 0800-1700. Shimoda is the most interesting spa town, offering a park, a lovely seashore, aquarium and Ryosenji and Hofukuji Temples, later associated with the American "Black Ships" of Commodore Perry. Townsend Harris, the American consul for the period, lived for 18 months at Gyokusenji Temple. Here a few of his personal articles are exhibited. (Notice a hole cut in a wall surrounded by tin for his stovepipe.)

THE IZU PENINSULA

On July 8, 1853 Commodore Perry and his American fleet, which became known as the "Black Ships," anchored in Suruga Bay. The Commodore carried a letter from President Fillmore addressed to the *shogun*. The letter asked for a normalization of trade relations between the 2 countries and requested that American clipper ships be allowed to anchor in Japanese ports, so as to re-supply. Perry's arrival breeched a steadfast law that had been enforced for the previous 2½ centuries which stated that NO foreign visitor was welcome in Japan and that Japan would enter into no treaty whatsoever with a foreign nation. The *daimyo* of Uraga immediately passed on the news of Perry's arrival to the Edo Government and the entire nation was informed to prepare for war, which fortunately never occured. The Commodore came ashore on July 14, escorted by 300 heavily-armed marines. The Daimyo of Uraga received him and accepted the letter. Perry informed him that he would return in one year to receive an answer. This brief and guarded mission paved the way for the arrival of Townsend Harris, the first American Consul to Japan, in July of 1856. After much negotiation and court intrigue, Harris was finally allowed to travel to the capital, Edo, in 1857, to meet with the *shogun* and negotiate a treaty. At last in July of 1858 the first treaty of Japan with a foreign nation was signed at Kanagawa and within one year was ratified by the U.S. Senate.

Here is also a monument to Harris, along with the Butchered-Cow Tree, marking the spot where the first animal was slaughtered to become food for the strange visitor. This incident caused great consternation among the then non-meat eating Japanese. Local farmers feared for their cattle, which were used only as draft animals, and began to hide them lest they disgustingly became food for the obviously uncivilized, hairy barbarians. Nearby, at Ryosenji, personal articles of Okichi-san, Harris' hapless geisha attendant are preserved. Many stories circulate about their love affair and closeby is the grave where she was laid to rest after her suicide. It was her duty to attend to Harris' needs. After he returned to America, she took the only honorable alternative after having been forced into such an unacceptable relationship and "purified" her soul by throwing herself in the sea.

the interior towns: Shuzenji and Nirayama are surrounded by rugged mountains where wild boar still roam. Their savory meat is often-times skewered and charcoaled as a special food of local *ryokan* and *minshuku*. Shuzenji Temple was founded by Kobo Daishi, and its main hall, open from 0830-1700, houses many treasures and a famous *noh* mask. Nearby, is also Cycle Sports Center, offering trails and numerous styles of bikes for rent. At Nirayama, there's Egawa Old House, preserved intact from the Edo Period, the oldest private dwelling in Japan. On the southern tip is Cape Iro with the tumultuous sea far below, pummeling the coast. The W coast includes, from N to S, the spa towns of Takasagoya, Dogashima and Matsuzaki. Less visited, the accommodations here are limited to the homestyle, unpretentious *minshuku*, which offer the finest in down-home hospitality and traditional, home-cooked meals. Route 136 links the entire area, and small ferries pass up and down the W coastline. To enjoy Izu and to get away from the crowds, this coast is best. The views of Fuji-san are startlingly close, and the fishing villages that come into sight around snakey turns on the narrow coast road beckon the traveler to join in for a day of simple joys and magnificent walks.

accommodations: The entire Izu Peninsula, especially in the larger resort towns, has an excellent network of lodging facilities. The following are only a few. Western-style places to stay include the New Fujiya Hotel, 1-16 Ginzacho, Atami 413, tel: (0557) 81-0111, 5 min by car from Atami Sta., from Y7500; Atami Fujiya Hotel, 13-8 Ginza-cho, Atami 413, tel: (0557) 81-7111, 5 min by car from Atami Sta., from Y8500; and Kawana Hotel, 1459 Kawana, Ito 414, tel: (0557) 45-1111, 20 min by car from Ito Sta., from Y10,000. *ryokan at Atami:* Many *ryokan* on Izu offer a special dish made from wild boar hunted in the interior mountains. They also feature *ayu* (Japanese trout) caught in the Kano River. Tsuruya Hotel, Higashi-Kaigan-cho,

Atami 413, tel: (0557) 82-1212, from Y11,000; and Happoen, Minaguchi-cho, Atami 413, tel: (0557) 81-6125, from Y12,000. *at Ito:* New Tokai, 1-8 Takara-cho, Ito 414, tel: (0557) 37-0114, from Y12,000; and Yokikan, Suehiro-cho, Ito 414, tel: (0557) 37-2101, from Y11,000. *at Inatori:* Hotel Ginsuiso, Higashi-Izumachi, Inatori 413-04, tel: (0557) 95-2211. *at Shimoda:* Shimoda Onsen Hotel, Takegahama, Shimoda 415, tel: (05582) 2-3111, from Y11,000; and Shimoda Yamatokan, Kisami, Shimoda 415, tel: (05582) 2-2935, from Y11,000. *at Suizenji:* Asaba Ryokan Kansuikaku, Shuzenji-machi, Suizenji 410-24, tel: (0558) 72-0700, from Y11,000; and Kikuya Ryokan, Shuzenji-machi, Suizenji 410-24, tel: (0558) 72-2000, from Y11,000. *YHs:* There are 10 YHs on the Izu Peninsula. The main ones are Ito YH, Komuroyama-koen, 1260-125 Kawana, Ito 414, tel: (0557) 45-0224, 15 min by bus from Ito Sta. and 8 min on foot, 96 beds; Shuzenji YH, 4279-152 Shuzenji, Shuzenji-machi 410-24, tel: (0558) 72-1222, 15 min by bus from Shuzenji Sta. and 10 min on foot, 120 beds; Gensu YH, 289 Shimokamo, Minami-izu-machi 415-03, tel: (05586) 2-0035, 25 min by bus from Shimoda Sta., 34 beds; and Sanyo-so YH, 73 Naka, Matsuzaki-machi, 410-36, tel: (05584) 2-0408, 50 min by bus from Shimoda Sta., 80 beds. For the location of other YHs, see Izu Peninsula map. *kokumin shukusha (peoples' lodges):* There are 6 of these special lodges on Izu, perhaps the most reasonable accommodations, offering rooms and 2 meals for Y4000. Reservations are a must, and can be made at JTB and through other travel agents: they are Izu Matsuzaki-so, tel: (05584) 2-0450, Shimoda area; Toi Fujimi-so, tel: (05589) 9-0511, Matsuzaki area; Kidachi-so, tel: (05588) 5-1035, Mishima area; Naka-Izu-so, tel: (05588) 3-1155, Shuzunji area; Kawazu, tel: (05583) 5-7111, Kawazu area; and Izu-Heda-so, tel: (05589) 4-2301, Shuzenji area.

THE SEVEN ISLES OF IZU AND BEYOND

These diminutive islands are part of the Fuji Volcanic Chain, stretching southward from the tip of the Izu Peninsula for 300 km. From N to S They are Oshima, Toshima, Niijima, Kozushima, Miyakejima, Mikurajima and Hachijojima. Oshima (90 sq km), the largest and closest to the mainland, is the most touristed, usually by young Japanese looking to meet a girlfriend or boyfriend. This is also true to lesser degree on the remainder of the islands, but only during the summer vacation. The remainder of the year the islands are left to sun, surf, snorkeling and camping. Offshore fishing is excellent around any of the Isles of Izu, and deep-sea fishing boats can be easily arranged. Toshima, a tiny dot of an island (4 sq km) is one large, natural hothouse, completely covered in camellias. The balmy flowers bloom in Feb. and the few families on the island make their living from camellia oil. Niijima (24 sq km) is also popular with the young Japanese, and has plenty of accommodations. Besides the usual sun, surf and hiking, it offers unique architecture. The houses are built from the light, porous, volcanic stone found in the area and are different from those of any other area in Japan. Shikinejima, just offshore, was at one time connected to Niijima, but they were separated by a tidal wave. This 4 sq km island offers natural hotsprings at the shoreline of 2 of the beaches on the island; a very popular attraction. The steamy water mixes with the tide and creates a soothing free hot bath. Kozushima is renowned for the best fishing, and although all of the islands have excellent beaches, Mikurajima is special, with coal-black sand spewed long ago from its central volcano. Mikurajima is the most unspoiled of the islands, with infrequent ferry service, no public transportation and less than 200 permanent residents. There's no camping allowed on the island. Hachijojima is the most distant, and along with regular ferry service, offers a direct flight to Tokyo. Hachijojima was at one time a place of exile, with a few elegant ruins of villas remaining. It's now famous for *ki-hachijo,* a woven silk fabric naturally dyed by plant extracts found only on the island.

getting there by ferry: Oshima from Tokyo, overnight out, day-evening return, 7 hrs 20 min; from Atami and Ito (Izu Peninsula) in 2 hrs 30 min, and one hr 30 minutes. From Yokohama in 7 hours. Toshima from Oshima in one hr 30 minutes. Niijima from Tokyo in 11 hrs, 3 times per week. From Oshima in 3 hours. Kozushima from Tokyo in 14 hrs via Oshima. Direct service in 9 hrs during July and August. Miyakejima from Tokyo in 7 hours. Mikurajima from Miyakejima in one hour. Hachijojima from Tokyo in 11 hours. *by air:* Oshima from Tokyo daily by ANA, 25 minutes. Hachijojima from Tokyo and Nagoya daily by ANA, one hr 10 minutes. Miyakejima from Tokyo, daily by ANA, 50 minutes. *getting around:* Bus service is adequate on all islands, usually making a loop around the coastline. The smaller islands are perfect for hiking. Bicycle rental, the best way to tour the islands, is available on most.

accommodations: All islands have numerous *minshuku* and *ryokan,* but they can become crowded during July-August. Reservations are recommended. Oshima and Miyakejima also have YH accommodations. Camping sites are no problem, except on Mikurajima where it's not allowed.

THE SEVEN ISLES OF IZU

OGASAWARA ISLANDS

The outlying Islands are tiny volcanic dots located deep in the Pacific, the most remote of all the Japan islands, inhabited by the Japanese only in 1593. The Ogasawaras lie S of the Izu Is., almost 1200 km from Tokyo. The 2 main islands are Chichijima (Father I.) and Hahajima (Mother I.). The most famous of the Kazan (Volcano) Group-part of the Ogasawaras is Iwo Jima, the site of one of WW 11's most desperately fought battles. The island is still closed to tourists since live ammunition is still found in many areas. The caves on the island are natural tombs for the remains of the soldiers who fought and died there. This group of islands was occupied by the US and returned to Japan in 1968. Many Western-style buildings from this period are still found, and large numbers of islanders speak English. The islands are sub-tropical, balmy and as far off the beaten track as you can get. Get there by steamer to Chichijima from Tokyo in 38 hrs, one boat per week. To Hahajima from Chichijima in 3 hours.

THE BATTLE OF IWO JIMA

In the closing months of WW11 General Tadamichi Kurnbayashi and his army of 21,000 Japanese soldiers dug into the black volcanic ash of Iwo Jima and prepared to desperately defend it against the American invasion that they knew would come. They also knew that they would never survive. The Japanese general had repeatedly written home before the battle and in every letter had said, "Do not plan for my return." His battle plan was to dig bunkers into the volcanic soil and to heavily fortify the natural caves with mortars and machine guns, allowing the U.S. marines to land on the beaches and then later to engage them in battle. For weeks Iwo Jima was pulverized by long-range American bombers and, remained secure. On the morning of Feb. 9, 1945, 30,000 American marines waded ashore. The black ash turned red with blood as 566 marines died on the 1st day of the assault. Slowly the Americans pushed the Japanese back to the natural barrier of Mt. Suribachi (in photo above). The fighting, at most times hand to hand, was a nightmare of brutality. On Feb. 23, 5 marines and one Navy corpsman raised the American flag atop Mt. Suribachi. Joe Rosenthal, a photographer and correspondent for the Associated Press, captured the flag-raising ceremony during WW 11. Some people claim that Rosenthal staged the photo but others testify that it was completely impromptu. Three of the five marines who raised the flag died in the following days of fighting. Another, an American Indian, was found frozen to death on his reservation 10 years later, and the last marine is still alive in Manchester, New Hampshire while the Navy Corpsman lives in Wisconsin. Before the battle finally ended only 216 of the 21,000 Japanese defenders were still alive. The Americans sustained 21,000 casualties and 4,500 fatalities. Iwo Jima has now returned to the jungle, and is inhabited by two teams, one Japanese and one American, who report on weather and tide conditions. Because of its volcanic activity Iwo has risen over 11 m form the sea since WW 11. Atop Mt. Suribachi are 2 weathered memorials; the American one depicts the flag raising and the Japanese one is a simple black marble stone

TOHOKU

INTRODUCTION

Tohoku was once known as Michinoku (The Interior Road), in effect the end of the line. Its vastness and inacessibility were immortalized by Basho in his work "The Narrow Road to the Deep North." It gained its reputation of inaccessibility because of the rugged mountains that form its spine, its deep snowy winters, and its resistance to being tamed. What more adventurous place to head for than Tohoku? Tohoku is the northern section of the main island of Honshu and its boundaries are the 6 prefectures of Aomori, Iwate, Akita, Miyagi, Yamagata and Fukushima. The total land area is 66,900 sq km and it is home to only 9,500,000 people. Tohoku and the island of Shikoku in the S vie as the least touristed areas of Japan. It lags behind the rest of Honshu in industrialization and modernity. Tohoku combines the temples, shrines and culture of classical Japan with natural unblemished scenic areas. There are 3 exceptional National Parks: Bandai-Asahi (S Central), Rikuchu Kaian (E coast), and Towada-Hachimantai (N Central). Matsushima, a miniature archipelago of pine covered islands lying E of Sendai, has been a tourist haunt for Japanese seeking a communion with nature ever since the mid-1600s. The area also abounds with temples and shrines. Hirosaki, a small inland city, once a far northern castle town, is legendary for having the most beautiful women in Japan. Whenever the climate is at odds with the population, the festivals are made to be more impressive, serving as a psychological softening against the realities of nature. Tohoku is no exception. The festivals of this N country, especially the Nebuta, Tanabata and Kanto are some of the most spectacular in Japan. Folk art in these rural communities is thriving; the cottage industries of lacquerware, and copper and iron utensils are a way of life. Tohoku is the best place to view the older profile of Japan: the Japanese as farmers immersed in centuries of tradition in tiny villages. Those employed in the larger cities, nostalgically thinking of a simpler time, have come from regions such as Tohoku. Today some even call Tokyo a village, trying to capture in words the feeling of a fading memory. A traveler in Tohoku's tiny villages, nestled deep in rugged mountains, can still glimpse the idealized Japan of simplicity and unpretentious beauty. Here, faintly but firmly, beats the heart of Japan of times past.

the land: Tohoku is like the spiny back of a mythical dragon risen from the sea. Gnarled volcanic mountains run N and S along its entire length. The Ou Mountains, the most extensive, run along the center from Shimokita Peninsula in the N to below Lake Inawashiro in the south. They virtually cut Tohoku in half, dividing it into the Pacific and Japan Sea sides. The Kitakami Basin in the NE is sandwiched between the Ou and Kitakami Mountains that face the Pacific along the NE coast. There is a gap of 150 km along the E coast between the Katakamis and the Abukama Mountains in the SE wherein lies Sendai Bay and the relatively expansive Sendai Basin. The Abukama Mountains form the head-waters of the Abukama River which flows inland and northward until it meets the sea at Sendai Bay. Along the W coast, the pattern is repeated. The Dewa Mountains lie in the NW with a gap of 50 km between them and the Ou Mts. of the interior. The Noshiro and Akita plains lie at the foot of the western slopes of the Dewa Mts., and face the Japan Sea. On the SW are the Echigo Mountains that stretch southward into the Chubu distict. Nasu and Chokai are two active volcanic zones along the central and western mountain ranges. Their activity is responsible for the beautiful caldera lakes such as Towada and Tazawa. A trip to Japan would be incomplete without climbing one active volcano. Mt. Bandai in the S, Mt. Gassen (1980 m) in the

central W, and Mt. Iwate (2041 m) in the NW should provide all the challenge necessary. The volcanic areas abound in hot springs and mineral baths. Small, rustic resorts are everywhere. The Sanriku Coast along the Pacific is punctuated with numerous bays and tiny fishing villages and harbors. The Japan Sea side is more tame, with long, sandy beaches and shifting sand dunes.

the climate: The climate of Tohoku is similar to that of Vermont or Northern Germany. The winters are long, snowy and cold. The summers are about 3 degrees C. cooler than southern Honshu, and spring and autumn are superb. The Japan Sea side measures its snow in meters, while the Pacific coast is more moderated with usually light dustings. The E coast of Tohoku can experience *tsunami,* which are tidal waves caused by submarine earthquakes. The mountainous interiors have frequent heavy snowfalls; if you enjoy flying down mountains instead of grunting up them, try skiing the slopes of Hachimantai even as late as early June. The small basins between the mountains have varied and unique climates of their own and can provide an oasis of warmth and sunshine, even while blinding snow rages in the mountains above. Be prepared for cool mountainous traveling, rapid changes in temperature because of altitude, and a fair amount of rain. There is no central heating in winter, so if you plan to visit at that time, bring those thermal underwear.

HISTORY

Tohoku as an indigenous area is infrequently cited in Japanese history. The ancient Japanese occupied the southern islands and areas of Honshu, and as the population fanned out, they slowly moved to the more hostile environments of Tohoku. At one time, the Ainu controlled this area, as evidenced by numerous place names. The Taigajo Monument, erected in 762 at the site of Taga Castle a few km from Sendai, proclaimed that the frontier controlled by the Ainu was only 78 km north. Tohoku was a series of garrison towns marking the northern limits of the Japanese empire. It was home to soldiers, warlords, a few farmers, and religious sects seeking seclusion. For example, Zuiganji Temple, noted for its 2-storied caves used for meditation by priests of the Rinzai sect of Buddhism, was established in 828 near Matsushima. In short, Tohoku was a forgotten backwater. It did not come into prominence until Masamune Date built his castle (Aobajo) at Sendai in 1602. Date secured his territory from

samurai warriors ride again at the *Chagu-Chagu* horse festival at Morioka

Hideyoshi Ieyasu, and built the largest fiefdom N of Edo (Tokyo) under the Tokugawa Shogunate. With Date, a man of vision sitting at court, Japanese culture flowed into Tohoku and flourished. Date instructed the rebuilding of Zuiganji, which initiated an infusion of art and architecture in the region. Basho, the haiku poet, chose Matsushima as a subject for his immortal works, distinguishing it as a place of beauty and serenity, and firmly establishing at least southern Tohoku as a place of unsurpassed beauty. The flow of tourists has not ceased since.

<u>feudal times:</u> Also under Date, one of the most amazing seafaring adventures of all time was initiated. For reasons that still remain unclear, Date procured the release of a Franciscan missionary, Padre Sotelo, from Ieyasu Hideyoshi. Some historians speculate that Date was a secret Christian, while others feel that his patronage of

Sotelo came from the more secular desire to master advanced European manufacturing techniques and warfare. Date allowed Sotelo to preach Christianity openly for awhile, and then devised to send Sotelo and Tsunenaga Hasegura, a close court advisor, on an expedition to Rome. A violent storm had washed a British ship ashore at Uraga, and using it as a model, Date built the first Japanese open-sea craft. It was appropriately named *Date Mura*, and with Sotelo and Hasegura aboard, it set sail with a ship's company of 150 in Sept. 1613. Cruising across the Pacific, and stopping in the Philippines, it arrived in Acapulco, Mexico in Jan. 1614, marking the first recorded voyage of the Japanese across the Pacific. Sotelo and Hasegura continued their voyage from there to Europe on a Spanish ship. Hasegura was welcomed at the court of Philip III of Spain, and continued on to be received by Pope Paul V in Rome. He was converted to Christianity, toured Europe for a time, and returned to Mexico in

1618. The *Date Mura*, awaiting him, carried him back across the Pacific. He arrived in Japan in August 1620, successfully completing the first Japanese return voyage across the Pacific. Little is known of the Japanese crew making the voyage, but taking into consideration that Japan had no historical tradition of deep water sailing, a voyage of this magnitude was truly monumental.

modern age: Tohoku prospered under the Date clan for 270 years, becoming one of the country's largest producers of rice. The Meiji Restoration brought an end to the Date clan rule, and Tohoku once again slipped into obscurity. With Tohoku now as an established region of Japan, the Meiji government neglected it. They turned their attention to newly acquired lands in Formosa and Korea and the taming of Hokkaido, leaving Tohoku to fend for itself. In 1907, Tohoku University was founded at Sendai, providing a long-awaited higher education for the populace. Sendai came under American bombardment in WW11, and was virtually destroyed. Finally, after the war, the Japanese paid increasing attention to the development of Tohoku, and vast land reclamation projects, industrial complexes and a sorely needed transportation system was gotten underway. Today, Tohoku is slowly catching up to modern, industrialized Japan. Japanese businessmen and

office workers are "imported" from Tokyo and the larger cities to develop the urban areas. The faces of Tohoku's larger cities are changing, becoming more scarred and stained by industrial growth, but the mountains and deep inland villages remain as quiet enclaves of tradition populated by easy-going people.

ECONOMY

Tohoku has virtually no large industrial areas or major shipping ports. The economy is based upon rice farming, cattle raising and forestry, with an emphasis in recent years on tourism. One-third of the population once earned its livelihood from farming and forestry, but with the turn towards mechanization, fewer and fewer farm hands are needed, so many young people make the one-way trip to the cities of the more southern areas. Rice fields account for the largest portion of arable land. Tohoku produces only one rice crop per year, but the yield is so extensive that it accounts for 20% of the national total, supplying the bulk of the rice needed in the industrial areas of Tokyo, Osaka and Kyoto. Cold, wet summers can turn against the farmers and cause crop failures, especially in the mountains and the northeast. Until recent years, little emphasis was placed upon the economic growth of Tohoku. Since the mid '50s, a number of schemes have been initiated to raise the productivity of the area. The Hachirogata land reclamation project just N of Akita is the most extensive. This lagoon, at one time the second largest inland body of water in Japan, has been reclaimed and is divided into neat 10 ha. mechanized farms. The mountainous backbone of Tohoku may be bent, but it will never be broken. Tohoku will exist in its natural splendor for many generations.

THE PEOPLE

The present population of Tohoku accounts for only 9% of the national total, with fewer people per ha. than any other district in Honshu. In fact, there has been a decline in population in recent years. Traditionally, Tohoku farmers migrated to warmer areas of Japan to work as itinerant laborers during the winter, or ventured out to sea to supplement their incomes through fishing. Today, they are attracted to the large city factories and very seldom ever return home. Many of the slick urban dwellers that you will encounter were rice paddy farmers only a few short years ago. The air of sophistication is a

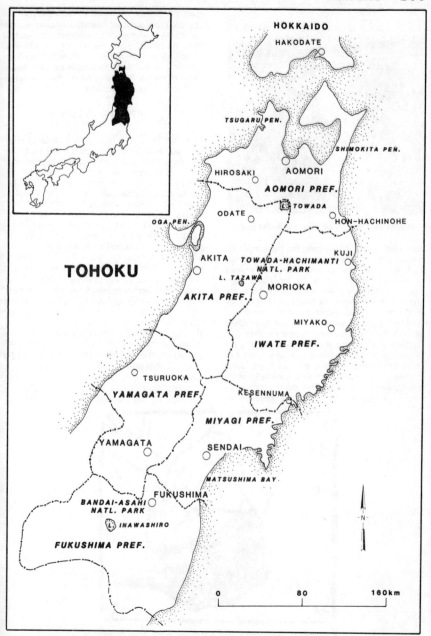

the ancient rhythm of rural life in Tohoku

very thin facade. Many long for the simple life that is now irretrievably lost as they nostalgically sip beers in city hostess bars. Many new arrivals to the cities seeking work are more and more frequently disappointed. Ashamed to go home empty-handed they drink heavily to forget their problems and their numbers fill the legions of the urban poor. Subway stations and back alleys of large cities become their transient homes. The people remaining in the district and running the farms are in many instances women, adolescents too young to leave, and old folks. Open curiosity, naivete and friendliness are delightfully widespread in Tohoku. This district offers an elusive antiquity not found in temples or gardens. If you are sensitive enough, you will glimpse the spirit of Japan captured in the venerable customs and traditions, and etched into the psyche of the people of Tohoku. Tohoku-*ben,* the dialect of these earthy northerners, is a delight to people all over Japan, who in hearing the folksy tones, feel the breath of fresh, crisp countryness.

ARTS AMD CRAFTS

Although Tohoku is becoming inundated with more and more industrialization, it still produces handmade, age-old crafts. Some outstanding examples are *kogin,* embroidery in white cotton thread on lengths of cloth from Hirosaki; *nambutetsu,* substantial ironware from Morioka, including kettles produced from hand-fired forges used to heat water for tea; and *kaba-zaiku,* (lunch boxes) and *chabitsu* (tea chests) fashioned from cherry bark, a special product from Kakunodate in Akita Prefecture. All of the handicrafts from Tohoku carry a wealth of tradition, simple but unique design, painstaking craftsmanship and authenticity born of age and custom passed from one generation to the next. Other of Tohoku's fine folk crafts include: simple wooden toys called *kijigangu* made by craftsmen in the villages and spas throughout Tohoku. *Kiji* originally referred to the wood used to make the toys, and *kijishi* were the craftsmen who roamed the countryside carrying their portable lathes (*rokuro*) over their shoulders. They moved from one area to another, carving their wares from oak, maple and camellia. At the beginning of the Edo Period,

a traditional *nambutetsu* (iron ware) tea kettle from Morioka

a display of handmade *kokeshi* dolls

these craftsmen began to settle down, many establishing themselves in the spa towns of Tohoku where they sold their wares to travelers, a tradition that continues to this day. Some noteworthy examples of *kijigangu* are: *kokeshi*, simple wooden dolls with a cylindrical body and round head; these are the most famous type of *kijingangu*, although numerous variations are also made. *Kokeshi* head the list as the most sentimental souvenir for the Japanese. Farmers would traditionally carve them for their children who would then paint in the faces. The results were touchingly individual renditions. Today *kokeshi* are made all over Japan but the best and most valued come from Tohoku. *Izumeko-guruma* is a small *kokeshi* doll suspended between 2 large wheels; the doll sways as the toy is pulled along. This toy recounts the time when farmers carried their children into the fields in large straw baskets (*izumeko*). Other toys include wooden merry-go-rounds; *ken-dama*, a stick with cups at one end designed to catch a ball secured to it with a string; and various *koma* (tops): a rounded one called *zuguri goma* is designed to be spun on snow. These colorful and fascinating toys, usually cylindrical or spherical, are painted with concentric circles of yellow, red, purple, green and black. *Kijigangu* are found throughout Tohoku, but Naruko in Miyagi Prefecture is the largest center, housing more than 60 families of *kijishi*, selling their wares in numerous shops. Another excellent example of woodwork is the *miharu-goma*, a wooden toy horse made at

Miharu-machi, Tamaru-gun, Fukushima Prefecture. In an age when toys have become miniature electronic marvels made of plastic, these earthy toys carved by hand from wood become more and more desirable.

temari: Delightfully colored handmade balls created from cloth and paper, and exquisitely wound and embroidered with thread. Many areas of Japan produce *temari,* but Tohoku has an especially lively and thriving tradition. The balls were at one time used in children's games, but today they make colorful decorative objects in many Japanese homes. This art was at one time considered a pastime for courtesans of feudal lords, but today they are made by rural women in cottage industries. *Temari* of various designs come from these main centers in Tohoku: the *kukemari* from Hachinohe in Aomori Prefecture; the *goten-mari* from Honjo in Akita Prefecture; and *gote-hana-mari* from Tsuruoka. Each ball is a distinctively handmade piece of art.

dolls: Tsuchi ningyo (earth dolls) are colorful unglazed clay dolls, one of the oldest traditional toys is Japan. *Tsuchi ningyo* originated in Fushima in Kyoto, and were sought after as health talismens by pilgrims. This demand spread their manufacture all over Japan, and exquisite specimens began to be made by many artisans in the Tohoku region. Today, only one surviving family makes the dolls, the Haga family living in Sendai, Miyagi Prefecture. *daruma:* These papier mache good luck dolls are manufactured throughout Japan. Sendai produces the *Matsukawa daruma,* which protects dwellings against fire. This unusual *daruma* has a face framed in blue, and is speckled with plum blossoms. It depicts the God of Good Fortune.

omen: Masks made of wood, or more commonly, of papier mache. One of the most common is a mask representing a *tengu,* a long phallic-nosed goblin. In Takashiba, a small village on the outskirts of Koriyama in Fukushima Prefecture, a group of 5 families specializes in their manufacture. They carry on a 400-year-old tradition, passing on their cultural legacy from one generation to the next.

tako: Strikingly colorful Japanese kites. Tohoku, buffeted by strong winds, has a long, venerable history of kite making. Some of the most picturesque and excellently done kites are the *tsugaru-dako* made in Hirosaki. This is a rectangular kite depicting a samurai and a dragon. The frame is made of cedar and the corners are secured by nails. Akita Prefecture produces 3 famous kites: the *yuzawa-dako* and *managū-dako* are both produced in Yuzawa. The first is a long slender kite and the second features a face with disproportionately large eyes. The third kite, *noshiro-dako* is a fantastically painted face of a *kabuki* actor. The kite has a special string attached that produces a humming sound when the kite is airborne.

TOHOKU FESTIVALS AND EVENTS

Tohoku, buttressed by mountains and lying in the most inaccessible region of Honshu, has been the slowest area in Japan to change. Here modernity is known, but has made the least impact. Tohoku's ancient beliefs are best preserved in its wealth of festivals and still-practiced ancient customs. The large cities with their neon lights, bustling streets and computerized communications networks make a strange and awkward setting for the natural and earthy qualities of the living, watchful gods, the *kami.* Natural catastrophes and the whims of nature with its penchant for violent storms are softened by numerous festivals of color, flowers and lights. Simple customs performed by farmers beseech the benevolent, but awesome *kami* living deep in the stark mountainous terrain for fertility and abundant crops. Candles and sweetmeats are offered to the gods for blessings. Dancing, singing and frivolity ward off evil spirits lurking in the night. Here the *kami* live intertwined with the affairs of the living. The ancient Shinto beliefs of spirits inhabiting the land and administering to all aspects of life is accepted and heartily believed. Immortal in Tohoku is the ancient, mystical face of Japan. Here are only a few of the many customs, festivals and events.

January: Hadaka Matsuri (Naked Festival). Found throughout Japan, the participants of this festival wear no flower garlands, ceremonial robes or masks. The all-male participants are au natural, wearing only a traditional Japanese loincloth (*fundoshi*). They are naked to show the *kami* that their bodies have been purified. The first *Hadaka* Festival is performed on Jan. 15 in Akita City and at the Hachiman Shrine in Morioka. On Jan. 16, there is one at Honjo in Akita Prefecture.

Feb. 1-2: Kurokawa Noh. A highly ritualized religious theater put on by the Kurokawa Settlement in the village of Kushiki-machi at Higashitagawa-gun, Yamagata Prefecture, before the sacred shrine of Kasuga. This combination of folk theater and religion is perhaps the oldest form of worship known to man. The *Kurokawa Noh* is a preservation of the sacred origins of folk theater where the undisputed deified presence of the *kami* is acknowledged. The performance begins late at night when the winds are quiet and sounds are muffled by the deep snow. The villagers are extremely reverent and sincere during this time because they believe that they are under the watchful eye of the village gods, *ujigami,* which are present at Kasuga Shrine. Because of these religious beliefs, the performances are not popularized, although guests are welcomed but expected to keep a very low profile and act with proper dignity. The participants are ritually purified by water and fire and remain untainted by avoiding all contact with recent births and deaths. The village elders oversee the performers, usually children and young adults, and ensure that the rituals are carried out in minute detail. Records are strictly kept of the participants taking part in the performances from year to year. On festival day, the village is divided into 2 parts, the mountain section—*kamiza,* and the river section—*shimoza.* The emblem of the *kami* is a large fan made of white cloth which is transported to the village center. After the performance, men from each section race to the Kasuga Shrine to return their emblems, in reverence to the *kami.* The *Noh* is ended after a second performance is held facing the shrine for the benefit of the *kami* enshrined. The *kami,* it is hoped, hear and see the devotion of the villagers and favor them with blessings for the coming year.

Feb. 15-17: *Bonten* or *Kamakura* Festival. Held in Yakote city and other areas of Tohoku, this festival, dedicated to Suijin (the Water Deity), is performed in the hopes that this god will bless the area with abundant water so necessary for the spring rice crop. The children build igloos in which they sit upon *tatami* mats. They warm themselves all night around charcoal *hibachi* and prepare sweet, hot *sake* (*ama-zake*) for their families and the townspeople that visit them. To the rear of the igloo set in a snowy alcove dedicated to Suijin are offerings of a lighted candle, some sweet cakes and fruit.

June 15: Horse Festivals. There are 2 festivals dealing with horses held in Tohoku. The *Chagu-Chagu* Horse Festival takes place on June 15 in Morioka. At this festival, dozens of horses laden with ornamentation are paraded through the streets until they reach the Sozen Shrine. The prayers offered to the gods are for a long, prosperous life. On July 23, the *Soma Nomaoi* is held at Haramachi, Hibarigahara, Fukushima Prefecture. This is the Japanese rendition of a wild west show. Thousands of riders dressed as medieval knights gallop over a wide plain. Other participants dressed in white try to capture yellow flags shot into the air by firecrackers. If they get one, it represents that they "walk in the path of the *kami*." This festival is not only exciting and colorful, but gives a glimpse of history and pageantry of the time when *daimyo* ruled.

Aug.: The *Nebuta Matsuri* historical pageants take place at Aomori from Aug. 3-7 and at Hirosaki from Aug. 1-7. Here, *nebuta*, huge papier mache dummies representing men and animals, are carried through the streets. Legend says that Sakanoue, the *daimyo* of the region in the 700s, subjugated the local rebels by fashioning these *nebuta* to make his forces look larger, thereby carrying the day. Today the prayers are offered for a plentiful harvest. The *nebuta* are particularly delightful at night. The translucent paper dummies carrying lighted candles on the inside glow eerily as they bob up and down carried on the shoulders of the participants.

Aug. 6-8: *Tanabata* Star Festival. *Tanabata* is one of the gayest, most enjoyable festivals of the year, and Sendai attracts many tourists as it goes all out for this festival. The festival is dedicated to love. The theme is familiar in many cultures; 2 star-crossed young lovers, one a beautiful princess and the other a lowly farm boy, are kept apart by social restrictions. At this time of year, the stars are particularly brilliant, especially 2 that shine very brightly in the heavens representing the 2 lovers that meet once a year if the clouds do not obscure their chances for a rendezvous. Young Japanese lovers are permitted to spend this evening unchaperoned.

Banners with streamers carrying love poems fly from doorways and colorfully decorated bamboo branches are everywhere. *Tanabata* are actually large, colorful balls hung in the doorway to drive away evil spirits. At one time they were heavily scented with herbs and spices, but this practice is dying out. It is the one night in Japan when you are permitted, even encouraged, to speak the feelings of your heart.

Dec.-New Year: *Kagura* festivals entwined with the performing arts. A blend of ritual and improvisational theater that is still very popular in the mountain villages of Tohoku. The village rendition of *Kagura* is called *Sato-kagura*. Although the influence of *Noh* can be recognized in the symbolic stage settings, *Kagura* is much more straightforward and easier to understand by simple country folk. The actors, in many cases, are farmers earning some money during the slack season. They travel to villages on appointed days and as *Kagura* represent *kami* coming to visit and frolic. The townspeople, bogged down by snow and harsh weather, eagerly await them. The masks employed in the performance are made by the farmers themselves and are priceless renditions of simple country humor. One character in particular is *Hyottoko*, a simpleton with twisted, puffy lips, who must carry out all requests made of him. The *Kagura* is teeming with folk dances enthusiastically performed by the villages. One old standby is the lion dance. Village *Kabuki* is also performed in Tohoku, usually out of doors in midwinter. Once again, the actors are farmers and their stylized renditions bring culture and aesthetics to their villages.

others: Tohoku, being a farming area, also has numerous festivals dedicated to harvests and fertility. Local customs are steeped in tradition imploring the gods to favor the efforts of the farmers. In Jan., on barren fields covered in snow, farmers gather to plant rice straw. The ritual, which imitates rice planting, asks the *kami* for help in the coming spring season. At New Year, the emphasis of other festivals is placed on rebirth and renewal. Farmers place white paper banners in their doorways inviting the *kami* to visit. Even the farm tools used are not forgotten. *Mochi* and lighted candles are placed before them to celebrate the passing of a year and their coming use in the spring. In Tohoku, Shinto runs very deeply in the hearts of the people. They clearly feel the unity of all things and the common spirit that binds one to the other. Some may scoff that these customs are useless superstition, but they are the binding force in the lives of the people that have endured and sustained them for unending centuries.

mystical mountain men: A special flavor is added to *kagura* when it is performed by the *yamabushi*, the mystical mountain men that still haunt the deep mountains of Tohoku. In isolated villages, nestled between snowy crags, the *yamabushi* will appear heralded by flutes and drums. Their ascetic, solitary religion makes them appear more authentic as visiting *kami*. With audience participation welcomed, they become a true delight to the snow-bound farmers. The *yamabushi* can be seen at Haguro-cho, Yamagata Prefecture from Dec. 31 to Jan. 1, and at Ohazama-cho, Iwate Prefecture on March 3

blind soothsayers of Tohoku: Itoko are women who are children of the gods and serve as oracles to the spirit world through telepathy performed under trance. In most of Japan, professional *itoko* are diminishing and the custom is performed by women only on festival days. In Tohoku, a number of blind *itoko* still roam the countryside and serve as a link to the netherworld. They carry a wooden doll made of mulberry and use it as a familiar to transmit their messages. The belief in the *itoko's* power is still widely held and on festival days, worshippers at shrines will employ an *itoko* to speak to relatives in the spirit world

TRAVELING IN TOHOKU

The prefectural capitals and major cities in Tohoku are, for the most part, the least interesting places to visit. Of course there are beautiful sights such as the castles of Sendai and Hirosaki and jubilant festivals to be enjoyed in other cities, but to savor the unique cultural heritage preserved in Tohoku you must head for the outlying villages. The main cities do serve a practical purpose. All are serviced by the JNR and are good jumping off points from which to visit the remoter regions. Foreign exchange banks are available along with full-service P.O.s, and you can find a wide range of shopping in the numerous city arcades.

by air: Internal flights into Tohoku, as in other areas throughout Japan, are only necessary when time saving is of the first importance. The majority of internal flights to Tohoku originate in Tokyo. They are quick, adequate and expensive. The airports in Tohoku are linked to the cities they serve by efficient, readily available buses, taxis and trains. JAL, ANA and TOA all service the Tohoku area. Sendai, Yamagata, Aomori and Akita are the principal airports linked with Tokyo. Flights can also be obtained to Morioka (Hanamaki Airport) and to Hachinohe on a daily basis. The longest flight, Tokyo-Aomori, takes less than 2 hours. Internal routes and fares are constantly changing. For reservations and the most up-to-date information on fares and schedules, contact any JTB office.

by rail: The main rail line servicing Tohoku is the Tohoku Line originating in Tokyo and running through Fukushima, Sendai, Morioka, Hachinohe and connecting Tohoku to Hokkaido at Aomori by JNR ferry. This line has the greatest frequency of limited expresses and the furthest point from Tokyo, Aomori, can be reached in 8½ hrs. At Fukushima, the Ou Line splits from the Tohoku Line and runs through the center of Tohoku, stopping at Yamagata, Shinjo, Yokote and joining the Uetsu Line at Akita. The Uetsu Line begins at Niigata (from points S), and runs along the Japan Sea side through Sakata, Akita, Noshiro, Hirosaki and terminates at Aomori. These 3 lines constitute the bulk of the train service through Tohoku. They basically run N-S; the lines running E-W are scanty and slow. For example, it is possible to travel from Sakata on the W coast to Ishinomaki near Matsushima on the Pacific side, but you must make many changes (_norikae_). Along the E coast, there are a few minor lines that suddenly stop in a small town with a gap of perhaps 50 km before you can board another train. Fortunately, the main artery, Hwy. 45, meanders along the Rikuchu Coast, allowing the traveler to see this particular side of Tohoku.

by bus: Because of the lack of train service in the mountainous interior and on the E coast of Tohoku, buses are an important alternative. It is safe to assume that all small towns and even minor villages have a bus service. The schedules vary greatly, but buses always link up to a major town from where onward-going connections can be made. The primary drawback of using buses is that they are expensive, especially in those instances where there is little or no competition. They do, however, pass through seldom-seen remote areas, and you get a more intimate view of the people's lifestyle and the natural simplicity of the villages. A good example of one of these convoluted outback bus routes is the one from Nikko to Urabandai National Park. From Nikko train (0855) to Shimoimachi, only a 7 km ride, change and train to Kinugawa (Y140). Bus from Kinugawa (1500) to Izu Tajima (1200) Y1550. There is a train from Izu Tajima to Wakamatsu, but the bus company has it well timed; the bus arrives at 1200 and the train departs at 1156. Bus from Tajima (1300) to Wakamatsu (1430) Y1050. From Wakamatsu (1440), bus to Goshikinuma Iriguchi (1630) in Bandai National Park (Y980). What makes this run superior to taking the train is that you go from national park to national park right up the center of Tohoku. The bus crests Sanno Pass and the leisurely pace takes you through the essence of Tohoku.

FUKUSHIMA PREFECTURE

Fukushima is the most southerly prefecture of Tohoku, and therefore, the most readily accessible to Tokyo and points south. A scant quarter million people live in this ruggedly beautiful area. The most outstanding attraction of Fukushima is the enormous Bandai Asahi National Park, which spills over from Niigata Prefecture on the Japan Sea side across Fukushima and adjoins the Nikko area in the south. The choicest spot is volcanic Mt. Bandai (1819 m) with its extensive plateau encompassing over 100 lakes formed by the great eruption of 1888. Lake Inawashiro, the fourth largest lake in Japan, lies on the S of this plateau 500 m above sea level. The curative mineral waters common to this area are piped into numerous spas where it is believed that they have a calming effect on nervous disorders. The area surrounding Mt. Bandai is collectively known as Ura Bandai.

URA BANDAI

This area is a treasure trove of lakes and mountains that are laced with a network of hiking trails. The largest lake is Inawashiro, followed by Hibara and Akimoto. They are all overseen by the ragged, looming summit of Mt. Bandai which lies roughly in the center of other extant peaks. In 1888 Bandai-san exploded after lying dormant for 1000 yrs and changed the topography of the area. Besides burying 11 villages and killing 500 people, its falling rocks dammed rivers and streams causing the formation of dozens of lakes and ponds over a 70 sq km area. Each, because of mineral content, took on a different color. They range from emerald green to royal blue. Goshikimuna, a main stop in the area, translates unromantically as 5-colored swamp. Since there was no lava flow, the original devastation is vivid and remains hauntingly beautiful. The remaining peaks form a semicircled crater with the N face blown off.

getting there: Aizu-Wakamatsu is the largest town in the Ura Bandai area. It lies 50 km W of Koriyama and is serviced by both rail and bus. Here the rail line branches N and south. The N branch passes through Kitakata and then proceeds due W to Niigata. The S branch leads to Nagano and points south. Unless you are intending to proceed in these directions, it is not necessary to go as far as Aizu Wakamatsu. In fact there is very little to see here or at Kitakata. Their only claims are a reconstructed castle in Aizu featuring a samurai residence compound

that was a last holdout for the Tokugawa Shogunate during the time of Meiji, and a few preserved rice graneries in Kitakata. To save time and money, you can stop at the small town of Inawashiro, 20 km E on the N shore of Lake Inawashiro through which the train from Koriyama passes. _bus service:_ The Aizu Bus Co. provides extensive service throughout the area with connections to all major towns. Frequent buses head N from either Aizu-Wakamatsu or Inawashiro to the cental Bandai area stopping at the 2 main bus terminals of Goshikinuma Iriguchi on the E side of the mountain and Bandai Kogen on the W side. Bandai Kogen is the more built-up area of the 2 and offers shops and restaurants. The bus from Inawashiro to Bandai Kogen takes 50 min (Y500). Bus service from either of these two heads N out of the area to either Fukushima or Yonezawa from where train connections are easily made to Sendai. These routes are over specially built toll roads that lead through spectacular country. The route to Fukushima passes Mt. Azuma (2035 m), a favorite for climbers, but the fares are unreasonably expensive at Y2000. Many Japanese take these sightseeing toll roads, so the hitchhiking is good.

Inawashiro: While waiting for bus connections, check out the small town of Inawashiro. There are some fine old shops here selling local arts. An excellent one is Shioya-gura, specializing in the traditional arts of _aizu-momen_ (handwoven cotton), rattan work, lacquerware, as well as _sake_ and _soba_. It's a small, old traditional shop

Shioya-gura, a
minghei (folkcraft)
shop

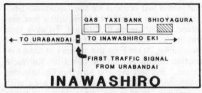

with something for everyone on a wide price range. An amusing oddity at Inawashiro Eki is a bronze nude. It's done in Renaissance style, but with an intriguing posture. She stands there heroically gazing at the distant mountains with her hands cupped under her breasts. Only you can provide the artistic interpretation.

Goshikinuma Hiking Trail: A well-marked, easy walking trail leading for approx. one hr (6 km) from Goshikinuma Iriguchi to Bandai Kogen. The trail passes through a dense green forest of pines, maples, ferns and wild flowers. A profusion of tiny lakes, miniature waterfalls and amazingly colored swamps are everywhere. Little trails branch off and lead to lakesides with open patches ideal for camping. Mt. Bandai looms in the distance and its reflection, colored by the multi-hued waters of the lakes, is truly impressive. As you walk along, on one side of the trail is a foamy mountain stream blasting down from the mountain. It courses through a tiny gorge, then flattens out as it passes through a marshy area. To your amazement, you'll see that the water in the marsh is not stagnant but crystal clear. In summertime the forest is alive with the sounds of cicadas (*semi*) and the songs of many species of birds, yet the bent trees reveal that they have only recently shaken off the burden of heavy snow. If you started the trail from Goshikinuma Iriguchi, after an easy walk of about one hr you'll arrive at Bandai Kogen on the southern shores of Lake Hibara. This is a major bus stop. There are numerous shops selling refreshments; *soba,* light meals and camping supplies are all available.

the lake country: From Bandai Kogen head S (away from Lake Hibara) on the main road. After 100 m, there is a simple little shrine on the ridge to your right. Go up and take a look. On your L you will pass the modern, well-furnished and expensive Ura Bandai Hotel. Here they'll cash foreign TCs—the only place in the Bandai area that will. Walk past the hotel until you see a sign stretching across the road that says TOLL ROAD. Turn L here and you'll find signs to Mt.

Bandai. If you prefer to take the low ground and head for Lake Oguninuma, continue past this sign for 100 m. On your R, you'll see Lake Hibara. Continue walking until the lake ends and there will be a group of rundown buildings that look like they were once a lodge. Turn R here and follow the trail which crosses low, flat, swampy country for about 10 km, finally arriving at Lake Oguninuma and an excellent camping spot. In the morning, if you decide to camp, follow the trail a little further (one km) to the village of Omuni where you can make a bus connection to Kitakata. If you want to see it all, follow the trail SW around the lake and you will crest 3 mountains. After a walk of about 5 hrs, you'll once again hit the main road at Bandai Kogen and the trail leading to Mt. Bandai.

Mt. Bandai Trail: If you prefer to head directly for the mountain, after turning L from the main road at Bandai Kogen (as mentioned) you'll be on a dirt road leading to the Bandai ski lodge. Keep bearing to the R and go up the mountain. After 30 min on this nondescript road you'll come to the ski lodge. Continue straight up the ski run until you reach the top of the lift. From here you have a magnificent sight. Lake Hibara lies at your feet, and the alluring, steaming, orange-cratered Mt. Bandai is at your back. The mountain rumbles. There are small avalanches every 20 min with boulders tumbling down the precipices. Here and there are spouts of steam. The ground is covered in very rugged, reddish-brown lava and ash that has blown off the mountain, and scarred, jagged peaks form a huge, semicircled cauldron. The trail is very well marked and leads over a number of rises until it reaches the foot of Mt. Bandai's highest peak. The climb from here is tough and dangerous and not recommended unless you are in excellent physical condition. If you decide to head back from this point, take the easy-to-follow trail through an area of large boulders and volcanic ash. Rocks are painted with red and white and there are red ribbons tied to trees. In 10 min you'll come to a forest area heading down to the foothills. Keep going until you arrive at the main road and Kawakami Onsen. Stop here and soak away your aches and pains. This road is the main bus route between Inawashiro and Ura Bandai, with Goshikinuma Iriguchi just a few km to the north.

accommodations: Pitching a tent is acceptable throughout the entire area. A good idea is to spend your first night at local lodgings until you become accustomed to the logistics. Spend the

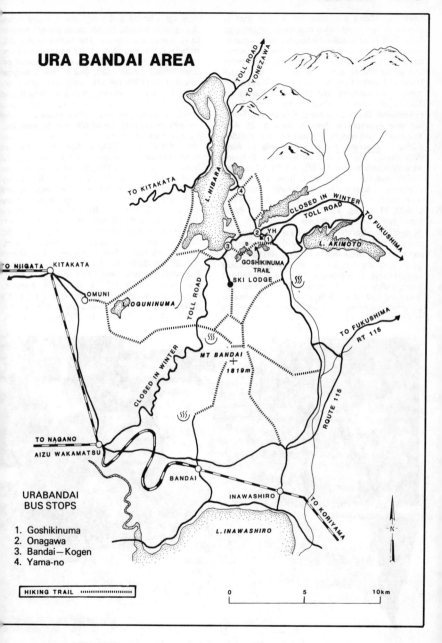

URA BANDAI AREA

TO YONEZAWA

TOLL ROAD

TO KITAKATA

L. HIBARA

④

TO NIIGATA   KITAKATA

OMUNI

OGUNINUMA

TOLL ROAD

CLOSED IN WINTER

② YH
①

③

GOSHIKINUMA TRAIL

SKI LODGE

CLOSED IN WINTER   TOLL ROAD   TO FUKUSHIMA

L. AKIMOTO

MT BANDAI
+
1819m

TO FUKUSHIMA
RT 115

ROUTE 115

TO NAGANO
AIZU WAKAMATSU

BANDAI

INAWASHIRO

TO KORIYAMA

L. INAWASHIRO

-N-

URABANDAI
BUS STOPS

1. Goshikinuma
2. Onagawa
3. Bandai—Kogen
4. Yama-no

| HIKING TRAIL ·················· |

0   5   10km

next day hiking and look for a spot that is secluded, yet handy to a bus route or built-up area. This is an excellent opportunity to economize on accommodation costs. For a modern but expensive (Y7000 up) Japanese-style hotel in the Ura Bandai area, stay at the Ura Bandai Hotel at Bandai Kogen. *ryokan:* A number of *ryokan* are available just N of Ura Bandai at Tsuchiyu Onsen serviced by train from Fukushima. There are a handful to choose from, but one example is Ryokan Nakaya, 25 Aza Yuzawa, Iizaka-machi, Fukushima, tel: (02454) 2-2582. *business hotels:* Available in Aizu Wakamatsu are: Green Hotel Aizu, Ekimae, Aizu-Wakamatsu, tel: (02422) 4-5181, 57 rooms, Y3410 and up, 2 min walk from JNR Aizu-Wakamatsu Station; and Fuji Grand Hotel, 1-12 Nakamachi, Aizu-Wakamatsu, tel: (02422) 6-1500, 71 rooms, Y3500 and up, 3 min drive from JNR Aizu-Wakamatsu Station. *youth hostels:* Ura Bandai YH, run by a young congenial couple, is a pleasure to stay at. The parento-san are more interested in helping you to have a good time than in blindly imposing restrictive regulations. Ura Bandai YH offers excellent food, a slide show of Ura Bandai in the evening, and hard-to-find washing machines. The house parents also make a natural mosquito repellent from local mountain grasses called *otogoriso.*

Pick up a bottle and you'll use it many times during your travels. To get there, get off the bus at Goshikinuma Iriguchi. The hostel is only 200 m behind the bus stop at the beginning of the hiking trail. As you walk toward the hostel on the narrow, paved road, you'll pass a bicycle rental shop (Y200 per hr). Daily rates are available. There is a camping area just outside the doors of the YH, but it is very popular and crowded with campers. Other hostels in the immediate countryside of Mt. Bandai include: Bandai Yuai-sanso YH, 7105 Hayama, Inawashiro 969-31, tel: (02426) 2-3424, 15 min by bus from Inawashiro Station, and 3 min on foot, 70 beds; and Bandai-so YH, Yokomuki-onsen, Inawashiro 969-27, tel: (02427) 2-2911, 40 min by bus from Inawashiro Station, 200 beds. Others may be found in the surrounding towns. They include: Azuma YH, 3984 Seki, Yonezawa 992-14, tel: (0238) 55-2002, 50 min by bus from Yonezawa Station and 15 min on foot, 50 beds; Azuma-Kogen Fukushima YH, Takayu-onsen, 1-49 Jin-no-mori, Machiniwasaka, Fukushima 960-22, tel: (0245) 91-1412, 40 min by bus from Fukushima Station, and 8 min on foot, 96 beds; and Aizu-no-sato YH, 36 Hatakeda, Kofune, Aizu-shiokawa 969-35, tel: (02412) 2-2054, 10 min on foot from Shiokawa Station, Aizu-Wakamatsu, 14 beds. Closed Dec. 25 through Jan. 5.

cottage industry shoemakers producing *geta* in Aizu Wakamatsu

<u>*Urabandai Pension village:*</u> Most of the 31 pensions of this village have been in operation for about 5 years. Yet this "new idea" of accommodations is perfect for a single traveler and even better suited for a family or group. They differ from a traditional *ryokan* in that the rooms are Western-style, the food is cosmopolitan, and the pensione owner and his family provide a congenial atmosphere for fun and entertainment. Most pensiones have a bar designed to be used for recreation in the evenings. A piano and a few instruments are available for creating your own musical concoctions. The pensione owners will also serve as guides for mountain walks, make travel reservations, do laundry and help with child care, bike rental and ski equipment—anything to make your stay relaxing and enjoyable. One outstanding example is Mr. Shiro Nakamura's Shirakaba (White Birch) Pension. He learned Russian as a POW in WW11, and during the U.S. occupation of Japan became proficient in English and later Spanish. An avid outdoorsman, photographer and mountain climber, he is a wealth of information for the Ura Bandai area. He kindly offers information to any traveler in the area, regardless of whether you stay at his pension or not. Shirakaba Pension is fashioned from pine; the architecture is similar to a Swiss chalet. Its comfortable 18 rooms are designed for single occupancy, but adjoining doors can be opened to form a little suite for a family or group. The smallest and least expensive room is no. 301. The pension provides a small bus to take skiers to the nearby slopes; they also rent crosscountry skis for Y2000 per day, and bicycles for Y600 for 2 hours. There is fishing gear available for the nearby lakes. The food is cosmopolitan—French, German, American and Japanese. The main foyer at Shirakaba transforms into a small piano bar at night. As well as the piano, there are a few guitars, a balalaika and some bongo drums. Mr. Nakamura can be contacted at tel: (02413) 2-2746, Shirakaba Pension. Tariff: room w/o bath Y3500, breakfast Y500, supper Y1500, tax Y350; total: Y5850. A Western family visiting Japan and interested in the culture and tradition found in less traveled areas would be advised to head for the Urabandai Pension Village. In Tokyo, call the Pension Association at (03) 295-6333, or write to: Pension System Development, 4F Inuzuka Building, 2-4-11 Saragakucho, Tokyo. One may also contact the Ura Bandai Pension Association directly at Urabandai Highlands, Fukushima-ken 969-27, Japan, tel: (02413) 2-2004. The Pension Village is just a few km N of Bandai Kogen on the well-serviced bus route leading to Yonezawa.

MIYAGI PREFECTURE

SENDAI

With a population of 600,000, Sendai is the pre-fectural capital of Miyagi Prefecture, and is the cultural and industrial center of Tohoku. Called the "metropolis of the woods," it has wide, tree-lined avenues and numerous parks. Large num-bers of Tokyoites have settled in Sendai, mostly employed as office workers with large firms, or working for a multitude of government agencies. This influx of city dwellers lends an air of sophistication to Sendai. Luxury items and up-to-date fashions are readily available in the thriving, downtown department stores. Farmers from the rural districts flock to the city on the weekends. There are 8 universities in Sendai with many students from abroad. *getting there:* Sendai is connected to Tokyo by express train in just 4 hours. When the new Tohoku Bullet Train (*shinkansen*) is completed, the journey will be cut in half. It is a main stop on the Tohoku Line, with many branch lines connecting it to all parts of Tohoku. Sendai's airport at Natori (30 min by bus) links it to Tokyo in less than one hour.

sights: There's no reason to spend a lenthy amount of time in Sendai, but if you are there for an afternoon or overnight between trains, there are some sights worth exploring. Aoba Hill is 15 min by bus from city center, the site of Aobajo (Green Leaf Castle) built by Masamune Date in 1602. The main residence of the Date clan for 250 yrs, it now offers little more than a sweeping view of the city. At Komyoji Temple there is a small monument to the memory of Tsunenaga Hasegura, Date's ambassador to Spain on the famous sea journey (see "history" in Tohoku "Introduction"). Nishi Park within the city was another residential quarter for the Date

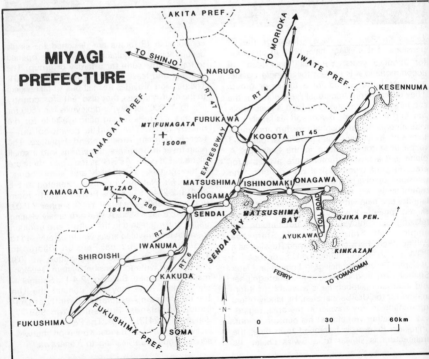

clansmen. It now houses an astronomical observatory open to the public. The Tomb of Shihei Hayashi at Ryun-in Temple, located 5 km NW of Sendai Station, is also worth a visit. The Osaki Hachimangu Shrine 4 km NW of Sendai Eki is known for the beauty of its main building, built in 1607, now a National Treasure. This is also the sight of the burning of New Year's decorations on Jan. 14. For a general overview of the Date clan's influence and the history of the Sendai area, visit Sendai City Museum, Sannomaruato, Kawachi, Sendai 980, tel: (0222) 25-2557, 10 min by bus from Sendai Station. Hours: 0900-1600; closed Mon., day after national holiday, end of each month. Admission: Y150. Its well-appointed displays include art objects, old costumes and samurai armor.

accommodations: Western-style hotels include: Sendai Hotel, 1-10-25 Chuo, Sendai 980, tel: (0222) 25-5171, 2 min walk from Sendai Station, from Y6000; Grand Hotel Sendai, 3-7-1 Ichiban-cho, Sendai 980, tel: (0222) 25-2101, 3 min by car from Sendai Station, single from Y5500; and Sendai Central Hotel, 2-1-7 Chuo, Sendai 980, tel: (0222) 22-4161, 3 min walk from Sendai Station, single from Y4000. These hotels also offer Japanese-style rooms. One good _ryokan_ is the Miyako Hotel Bekkan, 2-9-14 Honcho, Sendai 980, tel: (0222) 21-3311, Y4000-10,000. There are also several business hotels: Sendai Washington Hotel, 2-3-1 Omachi, Sendai, tel: (0222) 62-1171, from Y4300, Tokyo reservations (03) 433-5151; Sendai Royal Hotel, 4-10-1 Chuo, Sendai, tel: (0222) 27-6131, from Y3900; and Sendai Business Hotel, 1-4-25 Uesugi, Sendai, tel: (0222) 21-5711, from Y3300. There are 5 YHs in and around the Sendai area. Three of the most centrally located are: Chitose YH, 6-3-8 Oda-wara, Sendai 983, tel: (0222) 22-6329, 6 min by bus from Sendai Station and 3 min on foot, 70 beds, closed Dec. 31 through Jan. 3; Sendai Akamon YH, 61 Kawauchi-kawamae-cho, Sendai 980, tel: (0222) 64-1405, 10 min by bus from Sendai Station and 5 min on foot, 51 beds, closed Dec. 30 through Jan. 3; and Sendai Onnai YH, 1-9-35 Kashiwagi, Sendai 980, tel: (0222) 34-3922, 15 min by bus from Sendai Station and 2 min on foot, 25 beds.

MATSUSHIMA

Long regarded as one of the most scenic spots in all of Japan, Matsushima certainly lives up to its reputation. Many Japanese homes have tiny gardens fashioned from stones and bonsai trees that imitate much larger scenes in nature. It is as if Matsushima is nature's miniature garden

archipelago. Scores of tiny islands lie in a misty bay, large rocks resemble mountain peaks, and the few pine trees atop them a forest. The scene gives the impression of looking over a vast area from a great height, when in actual fact it is a view of a nature closeup. Matsushima fits the Japanese sense of aesthetics perfectly if you politely overlook a few modern touristy monstrosities that threaten to deface the natural

Tanabata decorations

Matsushima Bay

artistic still-life. As well as the natural beauty, there is some fine architecture evident in surrounding temples and shrines. Interlacing trails for scenic walks, secluded camping areas and clean, relatively vast stretches of swimming and fishing beaches complete this near-perfect picture. _getting there:_ The Senseki Line branches from the Tohoku Main Line in Sendai and arrives at Matsushima-Kaigan in 40 minutes. You can also train as far as Shigoama and then bus along the coast for a more close-up view. Shiogama to Matsushima takes 20 minutes.

sights: Matsushima Shi-daikan (the Four Grand Sights of Matsushima) are 4 beautiful but overly crowded vantage points from which Matsushima Bay has been traditionally viewed. In fact you can view Matsushima Bay from many excellent overlooks merely by walking along the numerous less-traveled hiking trails. Going specifically to these 4 is more tradition than necessity. They include: Otakamori, located on Miyato Island (Oku Matsushima), one hour by boat or 20 min by rail from Matsushima-Kaigan; Mt. Ogidani, 25 min on foot from Matsushima-Kaigan; Tamonzan, a hill on Cape Yogasaki, 30 min by boat from Shiogama; and Tomiyama, a short walk from Rikuzen-Tomiyama Station. _Shiogama Shrine:_ Located on a wooded hill in the middle of Shiogama, Masamune Date had this shrine rebuilt in 1607 in an attempt to bring culture to Tohoku. He succeeded admirably. The shrine is a National Treasure and an excellent example of classical renaissance Japanese architecture. The shrine houses the guardian deities of sailors and expectant mothers. There is also a museum with the usual artifacts, including swords and armor, but more informative is the exhibit of salt making and fishing techniques employed from very early times. _Kanrentei:_ A few minutes from Matsushima-Kaigan Pier, this is a 2-room wooden tea house presented to the Lord of Date by Hideyoshi Toyotomi at the turn of the 17th century. The tea house was moved in toto from Fushimi-Momoyama castle in Kyoto to its present site. The beautifully painted _shoji_ screens of the tea house are attributed to Sanraku Kano, a foremost artist of the 17th century. _Zuigangi Temple:_ Accessible in 5 min from Matsushima-Kaigan Station. Again, Date, in his efforts to bring art and religion into the region, had this perfect example of a Zen temple reconstructed. He imported noted artists for its construction and it is said that they labored on it for over 4 years. There is also a small treasure hall (Seiryuoen) on the grounds which is open daily from 0730 to 1700.

festivals: Travel could be difficult during festivals as many city dwellers head home to their vilages at festival time. _Aug. 4-5:_ The Shiogama Harbor Festival is dedicated to the deities of the sea. Portable shrines are escorted by hundreds of gaily bedecked ships through the bay. _Aug. 15:_ Matsushima Toro Nagashi features fireworks and the floating of thousands of lanterns out to sea as a part of the Bon Festival. _Aug. 6-8:_ The Matsushima and Sendai areas are a madhouse during the *Tanabata* Festival when over 2 million people converge on the area. Any type of accommodation is impossible to get without an advance reservation of 6 months, and prices are inflated. The tourists clear out quickly, however, so plan your visit accordingly. *accommodations:* To save money, it is advisable to stay in a less expensive hotel in Sendai and then day trip to Matsushima, but for an authentic *ryokan* stay in Matsushima, try Matsushima Daiichi Hotel, Matsushima-cho 981-02, tel: (02235) 4-2151, Y7000-12,000; or the larger Hotel Tainkanso, Matsushima-cho 981-02, tel: (02235) 4-2161, Y8000-18,000.

small islands off Matsushima: Oshima is a picturesque little island only 5 min from Matsushima-Kaigan Station. An ornate, red-lacquered little bridge (Togetsukyo) links it to the mainland. In times past, no women were allowed on the island as it was used as a place of meditation for local priests. *Kinkazan Island:* Accessible from Ishinomaki or Onagawa in one hr by ferry, or in 30 min from Ayukawa. The island lies off the tip of Ojika Peninsula. It has one peak, Mt. Kinkazan (445 m) in the center which is home to wild monkeys and deer. Natural formations of white, flat rocks forming spires (Senjojiki) provide a pleasant afternoon of hiking. *accommodations:* Kinkazan Jinja YH is a converted temple YH on the island. It's a good chance to combine a night's lodging with a close-up view of Buddhism. The address is: 5 Kinkazan, Ayukawahama, Oshika-machi, Oshika-gun, Miyagi-ken 986-25, tel: (02254) 5-2264, 15 min on foot from Kinkazan Port, 50 beds, closed Dec. 28 through Jan. 3.

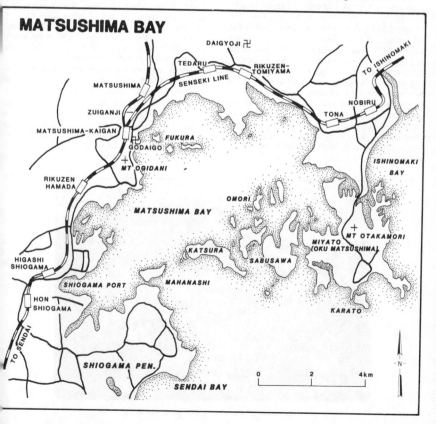

MATSUSHIMA BAY

OKU MATSUSHIMA (MIYATO ISLAND)

One of the most favorable places to view Matsu-shima. Take the local Senseki Line from Sendai to Nobiru (8 stops, about one hr.). A mountainous island laden with beaches, tiny villages and criss-crossing hiking trails, Oku Matsushima provides all of the natural beauty of the area, yet has fewer tourists. There are a few small hotels, a smattering of *minshuku* and an excellent youth hostel. There are also secluded but readily accessible camping spots. *accommodations:* Matsushima YH, about a 20 min walk from the train station, is excellent. The house parents are friendly and they provide better-than-average meals. Bicycles for rent at only Y400 per day are perfect for visiting the area. The address is: Matsushima YH, 94-1 Minami-Akazaki, Nobiru, Naruse-machi, Mono-gun, Miyagi-ken, tel: (02258) 8-2220, 20 min on foot from Nobiru Eki, 124 beds. *sights:* Take the main road from Nobiru Eki S onto the island. Don't worry about getting lost. There are only a few branching roads and they all lead back to one main road. Bus service is available with stops at each of the islands handful of villages, where the local enterprise is fishing and the gathering of flat shells as large as tea saucers. The shells are strung on wire and resemble giant necklaces. They can be seen in great heaps on the many beaches of the area. High on a hill in the center of the island is the local temple, Kanonji. It is

worth a visit and provides an excellent vantage point from which to see the surrounding seascape. About 30 min pedaling from the YH on the W side of the island is Otakamori village where there are a few places to eat lunch and rent wooden rowboats for Y500 per hour. The price is high but it's the only game in town. There is also an expensive ferry that circumnavigates the island from here though it's better to stay on land and bike and hike. The 2 best places to pick up the hiking trail are Satohama on the W coast, and Ohama in the southeast. Either will lead to secluded camping beaches: Hamagu-Murihama and Otomega-hama respectively. Pick up water and supplies at a village before you head out.

plate sized shells strung like giant necklaces

Ohama: This larger of the 2 villages is on the bus route and has a few hotels and inexpensive _soba_ shops. Okumatsushima is a small _minshuku_-type hotel right on the beach that also has a restaurant and a bar; Y6000 including 2 meals. It is passable and a bit expensive, but it offers a relaxing stay in a secluded village. If you plan to take the hiking trail, this is your last chance for water and a few supplies. If you have come by bicycle, ask any small shopkeeper to watch for it for you. As usual, your belongings will be very safe.

Ohama Hiking Course: When you get to Ohama, ask anyone where the "Hikingu Kosu" is and you'll be directed. Basically, face the sea with town at your back and go left. Follow the road for about 200 m until it becomes a dead end. Look to your R for stone steps going up the mountain; this is the trail. The paved walkway lasts for only 150 m and then it turns into a dirt track. In a few min you'll come to a fork in the trail: L leads to a high spot with a little monument giving you a good view; R bends along the coast. The R trail leads through a pine forest; many of Japan's conifers are dying and it is evident here. Continue walking for about ½ hour. The trail forks again: one path leads directly down to the beach and the other keeps to the high ground until it also dips down to the beach as the 2 trails meet. This is Otomegahama, an excellent camping spot. There is a grassy knoll overlooking the beach which is perfectly suited for pitching a tent. There is plenty of driftwood for a fire, but _no drinking water,_ so bring some. Don't camp on the beach; high tide can flood you out. Watermarks on the rock walls of the cove tell you how high the water gets. This is a fine area for sunning and fishing. Spend a night or 2 here while looking around Oku Matsushima.

IWATE PREFECTURE

After visiting Matsushima, the bulk of the travelers in Tohoku breeze through Iwate Prefecture heading for Aomori and the ferry to Hokkaido or to Tokyo and points south. This deprives them of seeing some of the most unvisited areas of Tohoku and perhaps some of the most intriguing coastline in Japan. If time permits, it's much more rewarding to follow a zig-zag course bouncing from quiet coastal villages to the wild mountainous areas of the interior. _getting there:_ To head N to Iwate from Sendai, the Tohoku Line runs through the center of Tohoku to Morioka for a distance of 184 km, taking 2 hrs by limited express. This is a good rapid way to travel, but the drawback is that you miss the Rikuchu Kaigan National Park along the Pacific coast. You can catch the park, however, if you change midway at Hanamaki and take the Kamaishi Line to Kamaishi and then to Miyako (56 km, one hr 10 min). If you choose this route, stop over at Hiraizumi, a small village 35 km S of Kitakami and visit Chusonji Temple. It was originally built by the Fujiwara clan in the 11th century. A fine museum here (also 2 others in Hiraizumi) is laden with exquisite robes, fans and personal belongings of the ruling lords. Open 0800 to 1700 (Y500), tel: (019146) 2211. Two mummies were also found after WW11 beneath the Konjiki-do (Golden Pavilion) on the temple grounds. The bodies were returned to rest after plaster casts were made. Jewelry taken from their bodies is on display. The museum is open 0900 to 1700 and is an excellent afternoon stopover on the long ride north. If you enjoy the old mountain atmosphere of this town, put up at Ozawa-Onsen, a short bus ride away. The original _ryokan_ here, though showing its age, exudes a folksy feeling of backcountry Japan and a breathtaking view of a foamy tumbling river just outside its doors. _Momiji_ (Japanese maples) make the already lovely scene even more dramatic as they blaze transparent scarlet in the fall. The natural hot spa and the sincere kindness of the owners make this stop even at _ryokan_ prices a bargain for the foot sore and travel weary. Retrain at Hiraizumi and continue N to Morioka. Then catch the park, go E on the Yamada Line to Miyako (102 km, 2 hr 20 min by express). This route is acceptable, but it leaves a great gap of beautiful coastline unseen. A more interesting, but slightly more difficult route, is to board the train at Nobiru after visiting Oku Matsushima and follow the coast N to Kesen-Numa. The slow-moving _futsu_ takes 3½ hrs, but the ride is very enjoyable and costs only Y1200. Leave Nobiru at 0834 and arrive in Kesen-Numa at 1150. Here the connections become difficult because of the uncompleted rail service along the coast. The next train N from Kesen-Numa is at 1500, a wait of 3 hrs, and it goes for only a few km. Forget the train and bus directly to Kamaishi from Kesen-Numa and then train to Miyako. _hitchhiking:_ Highway 45 (_Kokudo yon-ju go_) runs along the coast from Kesen-Numa and the hitchhiking is easy. Combine rail, bus and thumb to get to Miyako through very beautiful and virtually unvisited countryside.

sights: Along this route you'll pass through the extensive Kitakami Plain, one of the largest in

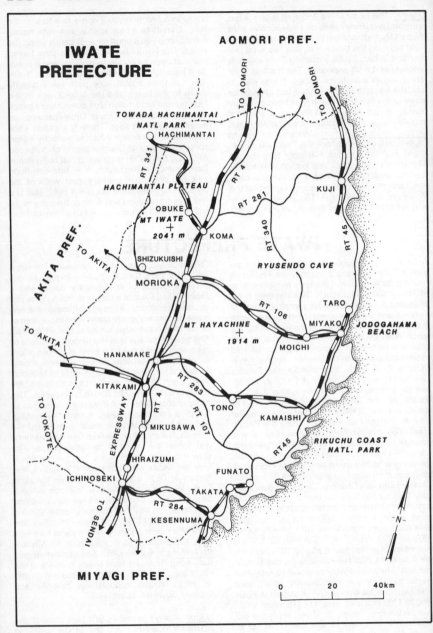

IWATE PREFECTURE

AOMORI PREF.

TOWADA HACHIMANTAI NATL PARK
HACHIMANTAI

TO AOMORI

TO AOMORI

RT 341

RT 4

RT 281

KUJI

HACHIMANTAI PLATEAU

OBUKE

MT IWATE
+
2041 m

KOMA

RT 340

RT 45

SHIZUKUISHI

TO AKITA

RYUSENDO CAVE

MORIOKA

TARO

RT 106

MIYAKO

JODOGAHAMA BEACH

MT HAYACHINE
+
1914 m

MOICHI

TO AKITA

HANAMAKE

RT 283

KITAKAMI

RT 4

TONO

RT 107

KAMAISHI

MIKUSAWA

RT 45

EXPRESSWAY

HIRAIZUMI

RIKUCHU COAST NATL. PARK

FUNATO

ICHINOSEKI

TO YOKOTE

TAKATA

RT 284

KESENNUMA

TO SENDAI

-N-

MIYAGI PREF.

0   20   40km

AKITA PREF.

Japan—a sea of rice fields. The coast is punctuated by small villages huddling in rocky coves, the mountains jutting out to sea surrounding them like pincers of a lobster. The coastline is rugged, a mixture of sandy and rocky beaches. When you enter Kamaishi from the S, you'll see a gigantic Buddha sitting on a lonely promontory. He watchfully protects the fishermen by bringing good luck and a safe journey. This sight, so idyllic, is soon destroyed. As the road banks deeply around Kamaishi, you are faced with the noxiously fuming steel plant that dominates the town. It refines the iron ore found nearby. Unfortunately, Japanese businessmen consider this progress for Tohoku. Try to disregard this eyesore. The next spot along the way worth a stop is the village of Namieta. At one time, whales sought out the nearby sheltering coves to feed. Now all that remains is Whale Mountain, named posthumously in their honor, a sad reminder of a lesson that Japan has still failed to learn. A few more km along Rt. 45 and you'll come to Yamida Bay sentineled by mountains. The profusion of colorful fishing boats bobbing in the harbor is lovely. This route to Miyako is suggested as a leisurely visual followup, designed as a day of travel and relaxation after the camping and hiking at Oku Matsushima.

MIYAKO

A thriving town, a good spot for an overnight stay. The main attraction in Miyako is Jodogahama, a beach area featuring walking trails, sea cliffs, a bayside ferry ride, coves, plus the world's smartest and fattest seagull. Before

heading for Morioka and points N, first take an interesting mini-tour of Jodogahama. A few hrs in the morning should do it. *getting there:* Go to Miyako Eki and deposit your belongings at the parcel storage for Y200. From Bus Stop No. 1, take the bus to Jodogahama at 0855 (Y150, 17 min). The bus arrives at 0912 and a tour boat for the bay departs at 0930, taking only 35 min for a whopping Y600. The boat ride is very touristy, but nonetheless interesting. The boat zig-zags its way through a maze of small islands, some nothing more than a jagged rock protruding from the sea. Every now and again there's a relatively large one about 400 sq m or so, such as Hideshima, located in the mouth of the harbor. It looks like the top of a flat mountain. Another sizable rock island is Anagasaki. You do get a chance to see spellbinding seascapes and hidden ocean caves. Another hilarious attraction is the seagull, you can't miss him. He has a green ribbon tied to his foot and performs amazing aerobatics as he follows the boat, snatching bread crumbs from the air. He's got his job down to a science. Long after the other seagulls have given up in squawking disgust, he perseveres. His size and girth are outward signs of his accomplishment. It's amazing that such a fat gull can still fly! The one detraction to this otherwise enjoyablle cruise is the obnoxiously loud bleating of the loudspeaker which the Japanese suffer in polite silence. Or you can rent a rowboat for Y400 per hr, more private and enjoyable than taking the ferry. At the beach front at Jodogahama there are a number of paved hiking trails which skirt the coastline, affording some fine vantage points. As you walk along, notice the stony beach with small fishing boats pulled ashore. The fishermen and their families are harvesting *wakame* (edible seaweed). After having a short look around, board the return bus to Miyako Eki at 1035. The train leaves for Morioka at 1110. If you wish to spend more time, there is another train later in the afternoon. Be sure to get on the first 2 cars (2-toned) in Miyako for Morioka, as this train splits and the 2 cars at the rear go to Iwaizumi! *accommodations:* There is a YH at Miyako called Miyako Kimura, a converted, deliciously seedy *ryokan* at 1-28 Kuroda-machi, Miyako 027, tel: (01936) 2-2888, 7 min on foot from Miyako Station, 70 beds. Another handy YH in a modern but boxy building is the Suehiro-kan YH at 7-27 Suehiro-machi, Miyako 027, tel: (01936) 1-1555, 3 min on foot from Miyako Station, 70 beds, closed Dec. 31 through Jan. 7. There are also inexpensive business hotels for Y3500 and a number of *minshuku* for Y3500 including 2 meals.

akame (seaweed) drying along Jodogahama Beach

MORIOKA

This small, mountain-ringed city (pop. 206,000) began as a castle town of the Nambu family and is now the capital of Iwate Prefecture. A special craft of Morioka is *nambutetsu* (ironware). These heavy, well-cast articles range from *furin* (small wind bells) to elaborate statuary and filligreed wall hangings whose patterns are copied from ancient designs. Substantial garden lanterns are also part of this iron casting tradition. An especially fine article of this craft is *nambutetsubin,* heavy iron kettles used to heat tea water that come in a multitude of shapes and sizes and colors ranging from brown to green. The town is also the sight of the *Chagu-Chagu* Horse Festival (see "festivals" in Tohoku "Introduction"). Although Morioka possesses some provincial charm and an interesting castle, there is little else to recommend it for an extensive visit. It serves mainly as a way station for much more intriguing vistas just up the road, namely Hachimantai. *getting there:* As previously mentioned, Morioka is serviced by the Tohoku Main Line and Hwy. 4; the 2 main arteries running N-S between Aomori and Tokyo. If you have come from Miyako on the 1110 train, it arrives in Morioka at 1354. After a ride of almost 3 hrs, the stop is welcome. On the lower level of Morioka Eki is a department store complex offering a wide range of consumer articles. The town also offers a full service P.O., and foreign exchange banks just outside of the *eki.* For a quick lunch, the *soba* in the *eki* at the small shop in the main walkway is exceptionally tasty (Y300). There are a few stools and a booth or 2 where you can eat and relax between trains. *accommodations:* Morioka YH is located at 1-9-41 Takamatsu, Morioka 020-01, tel: (0196) 62-2220, 15 min by bus from Morioka Station, and 3 min on foot, 96 beds.

HACHIMANTAI AND VICINITY

This tract of great mountain vastness is one of the few remaining untamed areas that you encounter in Japan. The mountains are tall, peaked and rugged. Above the foothills, the mountains are wind-swept and ice fog predominates the upper reaches. *getting there:* The afternoon train for Obuke, the S entrance to Hachimantai, leaves from Morioka from Platform 5 at 1503 and arrives at 1542 (Y1500). The bus station for Hachimantai is just in front of Obuke Eki. The bus arrives at 1701 and there is a

ride of about 50 min (Y560) before you arrive at Hachimantai YH, the gateway to the upper reaches of the mountains. There is excellent bus service throughout the mountains. On severe turns and wind-swept plains, the road has been covered with artificial tunnels to make traveling possible. The 2 hottest tourist seasons are late summer (July-Aug.) and winter for skiing.

sights: Even in June there are large patches of snow, and skiing is still possible although no lifts are working at the area's lodges at this time of year. There are many mountain gorges and valleys that crease the faces of the mountains, and lying deep in them are lakes fed from melting snow. The trees are predominantly evergreen, and with all their boughs bent downward by winter's great weight of snow, testify to the harshness of the weather. Interspersed among the live evergreens are dead, gnarled trunks of old trees that form whole forests of gray trunks that stand like sentinels proclaiming the rigorous climate. The changes in temperature are quick and drastic. Down in the foothills the temperature may be 25 degrees C and a few kms into the mountains it can dip to 5 degrees C. Dress accordingly. Rain gear is necessary to cut the wind and keep off the thick fog.

accommodations: Take the bus from Obuke to Hachimantai YH, 5-2 Midorigaoka, Matsuomura 028-73, tel: (019578) 2031, 50 min by bus from Obuke Station and 2 min on foot, 150 beds. This YH is enormous and geared towards parties of skiers, and is virtually empty in June. Another YH on the bus route is Matsukawa-so YH, Matsukawa-onsen, Matsuo-mura 028-72, tel: (019578) 2255, one hr. by bus from Obuke Station and 5 min on foot, 77 beds. This hostel is located at a hot spring resort where you are allowed to use the baths at no extra charge. Make sure to emphasize to the bus driver which YH you prefer as the road forks N to the first and S to the latter. Next door to the Hachimantai YH is a fashionable hotel with rooms from Y5000. The area here is laced with mountain trails and ski slopes, but the best itinerary is to take the bus from in front of the YH to Hachimantai Chonjo (Y330) deep in the mountains.

Hachimantai Chonjo: The ride to Hachimantai Chonjo takes about ½ hr from the Hachimantai YH, an absolutely beautiful ride. Take the first bus at 0745. There are plains of mountain laurel and wildflowers, and every turn presents an awsome panorama. Anyone with a yearning to explore and lose themselves from the crowds should come to Hachimantai Chonjo. Again, don't be fooled by the temperature in the lower areas. To spend a night camping here even in summer you need a tent and a good down-filled bag. At Hachimantai Chonjo Resthouse there is a restaurant, and in the basement skis are rented for Y800 per hour. The bus for Lake Towada and points N does not leave until 1155, so if you take the first bus to Hachimantai Chonjo, you will have about 4 hours to hike, explore or ski. Remember there are no lifts operating in the late season, May-June, so what skis down must walk up. The area is perfectly suited for cross-country skiing, but this type of ski is unavailable, a definite oversight. A hiking trail starts at the resthouse; go through the little tunnel and take the stairs up the hill. The trail is well maintained and quickly gives way to an extensive snowfield. Bamboo poles sticking out of the snow mark the trail. After a walk of ½ hr, you will come to a pristine mountain lake nestled high in a hidden valley. This would be an excellent spot for overnight camping, or just a good 2 hr hiking experience if you continue hiking around it. From Hachimantai Chonjo, bus to Fukenoyu Onsen, 20 min, Y290. The hot springs here at Y200 are an excellent place to relax and evaporate the mountain chill.

Yuki-no-Koya: A special accommodation 40 min by bus (Y290) from Hachimantai Chonjo on Rt. 341, or 20 min from the *onsen*. Just ask the bus driver to drop you off at Yuki-no-Koya, most know where it is. You can also ask to be dropped off at Toroko, the established bus stop, but then you must walk about one km. Yuki's Koya (cottage) is on the way to the town of Hachimantai (you can also bus from Hachimantai; just ask for Yuki-no-Koya). Yuki's place is unique, restful and inexpensive, only Y2600 with

Yuki's Cottage

2 meals! When you get off the bus, there will be a red metal *torii* gate. Follow the road underneath it for 100 m until you come to the cottage, a combination of *minshuku*, resthouse and alternative youth hostel. Yuki herself is very unique in Japan. She has decided to create alternative accommodations in one of the most remote and beautiful areas of Japan. The cottage itself is small, but adequate. It is in a little valley surrounded by streams. In summer many waterfalls and pools provide great places to swim. In the area are also many established hot springs. Yuki's food is not only homemade, but homegrown. She raises a garden, and these fresh vegetables go into her delicious meals along with local fish caught from the streams, as well as natural herbs and bamboo shoots picked from the surrounding mountains. Staying here is an excellent cultural exchange. Yuki has many friends living on communes in northern Japan and Hokkaido, and she will give you advice on where to go and may even provide a letter of introduction. She speaks only a few words of English, but communicating is no problem. Yuki-no-Koya is a perfect base for touring Hachimantai National Park.

AOMORI PREFECTURE

An old castle town renowned for its beautiful women only one hour from Aomori and about 4½ hrs from Hachimantai. From Hachimantai National Park or Yuki's Koya, first take a bus (Y350) to the town of Hachimantai, then train from Hachimantai to Odate. Change trains in Odate and head N for Hirosaki (Y980 plus Y500 *kyuko*). Hirosaki is a good town to spend the night in before heading to Hokkaido. It is much smaller and easier to get around than Aomori, yet it provides travel amenities and a beautiful castle especially famous during cherry blossom season. _accommodations:_ Hirosaki YH is run by a young family, and is modern and friendly. The address is: 11 Mori Machi, Hirosaki 036, tel: (0172) 32-5833, 10 min on foot from Daigaku Byoin Mae bus stop, 40 beds. Just down the street from the YH (follow the neon lights) is a night quarter full of discos, hostess bars and restaurants. The prices are expensive, as usual, but it's a good place to have a night on the town before heading to Hokkaido.

AOMORI

Aomori is a coastal city and the prefectural capital. It is best used as a stop along the way; there's no particular reason for spending any length of time there. _getting there:_ From Hirosaki, catch the train at 0751 (Y440), arriving in Aomori at 0900. The next ferry to Hakodate on Hokkaido leaves at 0950 arriving at 1340. What lies ahead is beautiful, untamed Hokkaido. Aomori is the N terminus of the Tohoku and Ou Main Lines. It is also connected to Tokyo by domestic flight in 2 hours. Its main function is that of ferry port to Hokkaido (see "combination rail and ferry" under "getting there" in Hokkaido "Introduction").

sights: There is too much excitement lying ahead in Hokkaido and quainter provincial towns in the Aomori area to dally in this port town long, except if you have come to see the *Nebuta* Festival (see "festivals" box under Tohoku "Introduction"). Spend a few enjoyable hrs between onward-going transport by visiting Munakata Shiko Art Museum. This museum houses works by Munakata Shiko, Aomori's best known contemporary artist. It is located at 2-1-1 Matsubara, Aomori, tel: (0177) 77-4567. Bus from Aomori Eki in 15 minutes. Open 0939 to 1630 (Y2000).

the eerie glow of a giant lantern, lit by candlelight, during the Nebuta Festival of Hirosaki

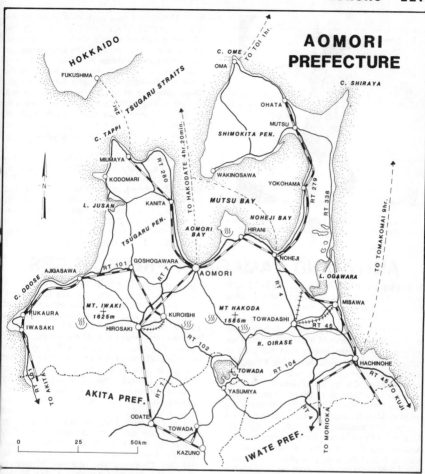

AOMORI PREFECTURE

accommodations: Except for the *Nebuta* Festival (Aug. 3-7), accommodations are no problem in Aomori. Western-style include: Aomori Grand Hotel, 1-1-23 Shin-machi, Aomori 030, tel: (0177) 23-1011, one min walk from Aomori Station, from Y5000; and Hotel Aomori, 1-1-23 Tsutsumi-machi, Aomori 030, tel: (0177) 75-4141, 5 min by car from Aomori Station, from Y4500. For business hotels, go to the Aomori Green Hotel, 1-11-22 Shin-machi, Aomori, tel: (0177) 23-2001, 89 rooms, from Y3900, 3 min walk from Aomori Station; and Hotel Universe Aomori, 1-4-7 Honcho, Aomori, tel: (0177) 76-7711, 114 rooms, from Y3800, 10 min walk from Aomori Station. There are 2 youth hostels: Uto YH, 13-9 Chaya-machi, Aomori 030, tel: (0177) 41-7416, 13 min by bus from Aomori Station, and 3 min on foot, 160 beds; and Asamushi-Koyasan YH, 203-6 Yamashita, Asamushi, Aomori 039-04, tel: (0177) 52-2865, 15 min on foot from Asamushi Station, 160 beds.

Lake Towada: An alternative to heading directly N to Hirosaki or Aomori from Hachimantai is to make a tour of Lake Towada. It is a crater lake renowned for its crystal clear water, pine-clad most hesitant visitor to raptures of 17 syllable *haiku* poetry. _getting there:_ Buses are available

the true warrior is always poised and ready, be it rain, sleet, or deepest snow. (Attrib. to L. Hearn)

from Aomori, Hirosaki, or from Kazuno on the islands, and lovely scenery. The shores of the lake are dotted with rustic shrines and temples and numerous hot springs. The lake forms the headwaters of the Oirase River, and the fishing is excellent. Tour boats are available from ports along the S shore for an up-close inspection. Many Japanese in the throes of romanticized autumn introspection journey to Lake Towada in the fall. The serene blue waters of the lake reflecting the fiery autumn foliage moves even the train line from Hachimantai. _accommodations:_ The spas in the area double as _ryokan,_ but as usual they are pricey. Two YHs available at Lake Towada are: Nishi-Towada YH, 18 Nagasakashita, Itadome, Kuroishi 036-04, tel: (01725) 4-8265, 25 min by bus from Kuroishi Station and 4 min on foot, 60 beds; and Hakubutsukan YH, Yasumiya, Towadakohan, Towada-machi 018-55, tel: (01767) 5-2002, 75 min by bus from Aomori Station and 2 min on foot, 200 beds, closed Nov. 11 through Apr. 14.

AKITA AND YAMAGATA PREFECTURES

Akita (pop 250,000) is the major city in Tohoku facing the Japan Sea, and the capital of Akita Prefecture. Like all of the major cities here, it is passably interesting, but the small villages surrounding it and the Oga Peninsula jutting out to sea a few km north of it are much more so. _getting there:_ From Tokyo, take the train to Fukushima on the Tohoku Main Line. Change at Fukushima to the Ou Line, and take it to its terminus at Akita, 4½ hrs from Fukushima, or 8 hrs from the Ueno Station in Tokyo. From Niigata, take the Uetsu Main Line directly N along the coast to Akita for about 5 hours. There is also a 1½ hr flight available from Tokyo. _festivals:_ Aug. 5-7. Akita is known for the _Kanto_ Festival. A _kanto_ is a 10 m long bamboo pole to which approx. 8 bamboo poles are attached horizontally. Forty to 50 paper lanterns are hung on the horizontal poles, and young men endeavor to balance them in their hands, hips and heads as they waddle down the street. Prayers are offered to the gods for a good rice harvest in the fall. _accommodations:_ If you intend to stay in Akita, try the following accommodations: for Western-style business hotels, there is Hotel Hawaii Ekimae, 2-2 Senshu Kubotacho, Akita Station; and Hotel Hawaii Kawabata, 1-1 Senshuyadomemachi, Akita, tel: (0188) 33-1141, 132 rooms from Y4000, 4 min drive from Akita Station. Youth hostelers may stay at Yabase Seinen-no-Ie, 86 Yabase, Akita 010, tel: (0188) 23-0008, 15 min by bus from Akita Stations and 3 min on foot, 92 beds, closed Dec. 29-Jan. 3.

Oga Peninsula: One hr by train N of Akita, this peninsula projects into the sea for 20 km. Hachiro-gata, at one time the second largest inland body of water in Japan, is a lagoon in its eastern sector. It is now a massive land reclamation project that has been divided into 10 ha. farms. The Oga Peninsula itself is perfectly suited for outdoor recreation. Tourism is highest during the time of the _Kanto_ Festival. Sheer cliffs, sea grottos, caves and rugged, rocky coastline form the tortured western shores. _accommodations:_ On the Oga Peninsula, you have a choice of 2 YHs. One on the N coast and one on the south. They are respectively: Oga YH, 85-1 Nakazato, Kitaura-yumoto, Oga City 010-06, tel: (01853) 3-3125, 50 min by bus from Hadachi Station and 3 min on foot, 120 beds; and Oga Chorakuji YH, Monzen, Funakawaminato, Oga 010-05, tel: (01852) 7-2611, 50 min by bus from Oga Station, and 5 min on foot, 80 beds.

heading south: The small villages along the coast between Akita and Niigata are very rarely visited as there are few attractions or any particular reason for going there. And this is what makes them fascinating. They are unassuming, unpretentious small towns where life goes on as it always has. Just check the map and pick your spot. Each will have a temple, a shrine and a local marketplace. Any artifact you find will be authentic and a personal discovery. All the

AKITA AND YAMAGATA PREFECTURES

towns have accommodations of one form or another—a business hotel or a *minshuku*. If you are hard up for a place to stay, camp on the beach or check into the local temple where the priest will most likely put you up for the night.

YAMAGATA PREFECTURE

Tsuruoka: A small city and a gateway to the Dewa Mountains located about halfway between Niigata and Akita on the Uetsu Line. The 3 mountain peaks in the area are Mt. Gassen (1980 m), Mt. Yudono (1500 m) and Mt. Hagurao (420 m), each offering a mountain shrine. Mt. Gassen is an excellent skiing area attracting a multitude of skiers each year. Diehards can ski the SW slope of the mountain even as late as August. If you are not there for the skiing, the primary attraction is climbing. *getting there:* Bus from Tsuruoka to the base of Mr. Yudono (1½ hrs). An 8 km hike (approx. 3 hrs) will take you over Mt. Yudono and to the summit of Mt. Gassen.

sights: This area is held sacred by the *yamabushi,* the mystical mountain men of the Shugendo sect, a combination of Shinto and Buddhism. They gather here every year on July 15 to pay homage to the mountain deities (*kami*)

enshrined on the 3 mountains, to pray, and to gain strength. With a view of the sea to the W and the rugged peaks rising in the distance, this area of Tohoku embodies the heart and spirit of old Japan.

accommodations: While passing through this area, you may prefer to stay at one of the following business hotels: in Yamagata City, Yamagata Business Hotel, 5-12-17 Nanokamachi, Yamagata, tel: (0236) 23-7300, 40 rooms from Y3000, 6 min drive from Yamagata Station; or Hotel Sakaiya, 1-14-10 Kasumicho, Yamagata, tel: (0236) 32-2311, 51 rooms from Y4000, 2 min walk from Yamagata Station. YHs in the area include: Tsuruoka YH, 1-1 Miya-no-mae, Sanze Station, 96 beds. Along the coast about 25 km N of Tsuruoka is the town of Sakata. From here you can take a ferry to the diminutive unvisited Tobishima Island where you can stay at Sawaguchi Ryokan YH, 73 Ko-Katsuura, Tobishima, Sakata 998-02, tel: (02344) 5-16, 7 min on foot from Katsuura Port, 30 beds. Ten km further N along the coast from Sakata is Fukura Village and Fukura Kaihin Shukusha YH, 2 Nishi-hama, Fukura, Yaza-machi 999-85, tel: (02347) 7-2069, and Fukura Kaihin Shukusha YH, 2 Nishi-hama, Fukura, Yaza-machi 999-85, tel: (02347) 7-2069, 20 min on foot from Fukura Station, 17 beds.

CHUBU

INTRODUCTION

The Chubu (Middle) District is exactly what its name implies. It encompasses the 9 prefectures in the center of the main island of Honshu. This large district is further divided into 3 regions. Hokuriku, made up of the 4 prefectures of Niigata, Ishikawa, Toyama and Fukui, borders Tohoku in the N and stretches SW along the Japan Sea, taking in the Noto Peninsula. South of Hokuriku is the Central Highlands region of Gifu, Nagano and Yamanashi, the 3 prefectures creased by the Japan Alps and collectively known as the Roof of Japan. In the S along the Pacific is the Tokai region with Aichi Prefecture bordering Ise Bay and Shizuoka Prefecture, famous for the great, mystical Mt. Fuji. The regions of Hokuriku, Tokai and the Central Highlands, although grouped into the one district of Chubu, are vastly diverse in climate, geography, historical background and folkways. In Hokuriku is Niigata, the premier port city along the northern reaches of the Japan Sea. Opened to foreign trade in 1869 and laced with canals and intersecting RR lines, it's the transportation hub for coastal and northward travel in the region. The villages in the hills surrounding Niigata are quiet, backward and insulated like those in nearby undeveloped Tohoku. At the E and W base of the Noto Peninsula are the two historical

cities of Toyama and Kanazawa. Toyama has a long tradition of folk medicine with remedies available at centuries-old apothecaries throughout the city. Kanazawa is a culturally rich oasis, a legacy handed down by the Maeda Clan, its rulers during the Tokugawa Shogunate. Its artistic traditions include *noh* and comic recitals often performed by the townsfolk. Many classical samurai homes dot the main streets and Kenrokuen, a prime example of landscape gardening, is part of an easy and rewarding walking tour. Kanazawa is also the main gateway to the luxuriant, wild Noto Peninsula, which beckons like a crooked finger in the turbulent Japan Sea. Sandwiched between Hokuriku and Tokai are the Central Highlands. Here the spectacular Japan Alps reach their greatest heights and slice Honshu from N to south. Gifu in the SW has been known for its *ukai* (cormorant fishing) for 1200 years. Also, deep inland in this prefecture is Takayama, a town singularly dedicated to museums and the preservation of ancient folkways and arts. Here is Koshokan, one large building bursting with artisans where you can observe various folk arts being created and purchase directly from the artist. Nagano, the hilly capital of Nagano Prefecture, offers harmonious Zenkoji Temple where worshippers

CHUBU DISTRICT

N

NIIGATA

NIIGATA PREF.

ISHIKAWA PREF.

TOYAMA

KANAZAWA   TOYAMA PREF. NAGANO

FUKUI   NAGANO PREF.

FUKUI PREF.

GIFU PREF.   YAMANASHI PREF.

GIFU   KOFU

NAGOYA   SHIZUOKA PREF.

AICHI PREF. / SHIZUOKA

numerous peaks at 3000 m plus. Two other ranges, the Kanto and the more northward Mikuni, comprise the eastern border separating Chubu from the Kanto district. They are slightly less rugged and massive, with the average peak at 1700 meters. On the SE border, in Yamanashi and Shizuoka Prefectures, is Mt. Fuji (3776 m), the stately colossus and its attendant fuming volcanos of the Fuji Volcanic Zone. The plains of the interior are quite small, alluvial fans in the valleys between the tall mountains. The largest is the Ina Basin in the eastern foothills of the Kiso range. The Nobi plain surrounding Nagoya is the largest in the Tokai regions of Chubu. Where there was once rich farm country producing tea and rice, now only skyscrapers and transmitting towers grow. In Hokuriku on the Japan Sea, the Fukui, Kanazawa, Toyoma and Niigata plains are the largest, still producing quality rice harvests. Numerous foaming rivers cascade from the Central Highlands. The Tenryu and Kiso empty into the Pacific while the Shinano, the longest river in Japan at 370 km, drains the Niigata basin on the Japan Sea. Combined, these rivers produce a hefty amount of the hydroelectric power needed to fuel Japan's industrial furnace. The land of Chubu is a combination of floral alpine meadows, towering snowcapped peaks, rugged river valleys and industrial wasteland, spoiled waterways and polluted beaches. Head to the mountains where the sun shines and the air is crystal clear.

climate: The climate of this district varies considerably due to the fact that Chubu stretches from the Japan Sea to the Pacific, with the weather-buffeting mountains in between. The Hokuriku region has deep snowy winters with accumulations of up to 3 m, aided by the winter typhoons sweeping out of the Japan Sea. The summers are humid, with spring and autumn by far the best weather. The Central Highlands are frigid in winter, with many peaks snowbound even during the summer months. Here the altitude is the determining factor. The valleys surrounded by the stupendous mountains have a varying climate, much warmer and sunnier than the surrounding peaks. Bring mountaineering clothing whenever you visit, although the summers in the lowlands can be hot and sticky. In winter, Eskimo drivers and a dog sled are recommended. Along the shores of the Tokai, the weather is the mildest. The winters are clear and bright. This Pacific coast climate suffers the annual Sept. typhoon season and heavy, sporadic summer rains.

grope through a dark tunnel, hoping to touch the Key of Paradise which they feel will assure their passage into heaven. Nagano is also the gateway to Matsumoto and Kamikochi deep in the Japan Alps. From here, trekking and mountaineering to Japan's rooftop offer breathtaking panoramas and the crisp, clear days of high-mountain trails. Yamanashi in the SW Highlands is slashed by the Fuji Volcanic Chain. In Yamanashi's S are the Fuji Five Lakes and on its border with Shizuoka is stately Mt. Fuji itself, overlooking Tokyo and the Kanto plain. (See the mini-chapter "Fuji, Hakone-Izu National Park".) Nagoya in Aichi Prefecture, Japan's 4th largest city, is the slightly drooping "flower" of post-WW11 city planning. Although heavily industrialized and known for its massive weaving mills, the back streets of the Arimatsu section house the fascinating cottage industry of _shibori_ (tie-dyed cloth). The Middle District, Chubu, like a large delta, has sifted the ebb and flow of Japan's 2500 years of recorded history and deposited here are the thick layers of past, present and future Japan.

the land: Chubu is criss-crossed from N to S by tall, rugged peaks, especially in the Central Highlands. The Japan Alps are actually a combination of the Akashi, Kiso and Hida ranges with

CHUBU EVENTS

<u>2nd week of Feb.</u>: Snow Festival at Toka-machi, Niigata Prefecture. Huge snow sculptures and ice carvings are executed with great artistry, although this festival is not as spectacular as the one in Sapporo, Hokkaido. Snow caves are built for children to sit in, and food is offered to the neighbors who come to visit them during their all night vigil.

<u>Apr. - May</u>: The *Om Bashira Matsuri* at Suwa Shrine, Suwashi, Nagano, takes place every 7 years. A 10 m spruce tree is cut from nearby Mt. Happo. The trunk is hauled down the mountain and across a river while the men sing the *Kiyarai*, a sacred festival song. Finally, the trunk is erected with a number of participants precariously clinging to it while thousands pull on ropes.

<u>Apr. 14-15</u>: *Takayama Matsuri* at Takayama, Gifu Prefecture. One of the grandest festivals in all of Japan, held at the Hie Shrine. The entire town takes part in pulling the festival's centerpiece, 23 wagon floats (*yatai*), through the streets. Some *yatai* are 300 yrs old.

<u>Jun. 5</u>: Sumo and judo matches are featured at Atasuta Shrine, Nagoya, during the day. At night, a flotilla of boats burning multi-colored lanterns on poles float past the shrine.

<u>Jul. 10</u>: *Mushi Okuri.* An ancient farmers' festival takes place at Sofue Machi, Aichi Prefecture. Pine torches are lit in the evening and the smoke, accompanied by the dancing of the participants, drives away the insects, hopefully for the entire growing season.

<u>Jul. 20-21</u>: Fireworks, music, acrobatics and general gaiety of raftsmen in Nagoya port, Nagoya. A water festival to invoke good fortune on the high seas.

<u>Aug. 28,31</u>: *Tomobata Matsuri* at Ogi-Machi, Niigata. A water festival featuring the fishing fleet who raise tall colorful banners on the masts of their boats. This invites the good spirits to come and insure a good haul.

<u>Sept. 16, 17</u>: Ceramics Fair at Seto, Aichi Prefecture, with more than 200 potters who set up stalls selling their famous wares along the main street. Discount prices and friendly bargaining.

<u>mid-Oct.</u>: *Nagoya* Festival. Originally a thanksgiving of good fortune held by the Nagoya merchants. Highlighted by processions, floats, traditional costuming of feudal times, and martial arts displays.

history: Japanese have wandered through Chubu for many centuries on the Tokaido, the main highway leading from Tokyo to Kyoto. White-clad pilgrims have stopped to contemplate or climb (men only until the Meiji Era) the holy beacon of Mt. Fuji on their way to the grand shrines of Ise further south. The way stations at which they stopped soon developed into stagecoach towns known as *shukuba machi*. Artists have immortalized the meandering ancient Tokaido in poetry and paintings. Victorious feudal armies, vanquished samurai, merchants and humble farmers have all trudged through Chubu on the Tokaido. Today, the *shinkansen* streaks along this ancient trail. At Gifu, on the banks of the Nagara River, the fishermen, documented from as early as the 700s, use their trained cormorants to bob for fish like apples in a barrel. The Hokurikudo, another time-worn trail, wound from Nagoya through the forbidding mountains of the interior to Niigata on the Japan Sea, and then northward to Tohoku. The newest in ceramics, cloth, manufacturing, concepts and customs were all, in one way or another, bundled along this course. Fallen statesmen and even emperors were sent into exile on Sado Island off the coast of Niigata. Along the Japan Sea, the city of Toyama pursued the science of medicine; its secret home remedies spreading throughout the Empire and later to China, Korea and SE Asia. Kanazawa, under the Maeda Clan, advanced the performing arts and lured many scholars to take up residence there, earning that city the title of "Library of the Nation." By this peaceful tactic, the Maedas preserved their ancestral lands when more ambitious and militaristic *daimyo* were scattered like rice hulls under the ever-watchful Tokugawas. Chubu leapt into modernization with the rest of Japan after the Meiji Era. During WW11, the industrial complexes of Tokai were obliterated. Nagoya was flattened, then rebuilt. The prewar twisting streets and alleyways were straightened, and the city followed a grid plan that almost keeps abreast of this era's phenomenal growth. The interior mountains remain unchanged and the people on the coast of the Sea of Japan still earn their living through agriculture.

economy: Tokai around Nagoya is industrialized, producing cars at the city of Toyota, and heavy equipment, chemicals and textile machines. Even the area around Mt. Fuji is not spared, its forests being turned into pulp. The human and ecological pollution is devastating. Workers crammed into hastily constructed company towns suffer chronic respiratory problems. The ground water is being pumped at such a furious rate that the land has subsided. Specially constructed villages called *waju* are surrounded by dikes and canals that will prayerfully keep back the floods when they come. The farmlands, for the most part, are cemented over. A few isolated areas hold on. Shizuoka manages to produce Japan's finest tea, and hothouses on the Atsumi Peninsula S of Nagoya yield fresh fruit and chrysanthemums. The Central Highlands are resisting taming. Farmers scratch out a living from the fertile but scanty mountain soil. Apples, grapes and peaches come from the isolated Nagano Basin, but for the most part, these rural dwellers of Japan are lured to the factory jobs of the city, either supplementing their income during the winter or becoming permanently displaced. Throughout Ishikawa and Toyama, and even more so along the banks of the Shinano in Niigata, the Hokuriku region remains Japan's rice granery, where millions of bushels are produced and sent to feed Japan. Industrial development is moving in slowly. Planners are busily drawing, but more precious than ever, the snowy winter, frigid temperatures and wild mountains remain the true gifts from the gods to their people.

ARTS AND CRAFTS

shibori (*tie-dyed cloth*)*:* A tradition dating back from 1607 in Arimatsu, a one-time village, now a suburb of Nagoya in Aichi Prefecture. Mostly women, but sometimes men, tie tiny knots on the base cloth and then dip it into boiling vats of dye to produce intricate, rich patterns. A well-done piece takes over 300 hrs to produce, and the price matches the effort. Most artists work out of their own homes, but the process can be seen at Arimatsu Shibori Industrial Cooperative Association, in the Arimatsu section of Nagoya.

pottery: The collective name for the ceramics produced around Nagoya is *seto-yaki.* This art dates back to the Edo period and these wares, as those from the Nagoya area, have undergone many changes. Kilns that at one time produced delicate tea ceremony sets now produce industrial pottery. One village is even called Dokan Machi or Village of Sewer Pipes. Fortunately, a small but thriving number of traditional kilns survived, producing handmade and artistically conceived ware. The clay of *seto-yaki* is fine grained and an excellent medium for producing pots. Three types, well known and distinguished for their craftsmanship, are *ki-seto* (yellow *seto*) with a faint yellow glaze highlighted with greens and browns; *gin-yuteki,* a splash of silver speckles on dark underglazes; and *ofuke,* blue-tinged, blurred glazes on a heavy underglaze. For another distinctive pottery produced in Chubu, see "Sado Island," later in this chapter.

other art centers of Chubu: At the western base of the Noto Peninsula is Kanawaza, with its long dedication to art. The city has a renowned theater where *noh* classics are performed. Local artists called *hanashi-ka* participate in these productions as well as in traditional comic monologues known as *rakugo.* The stories are in the oral traditions, with the plots drawn from daily events. A fan is the only prop, metamorphosing into a pipe, sword, tea tray, etc. as the story dictates. The tales can be of a bawdy nature and usually have a surprise ending. Kanazawa also has a long tradition of ceramics, dyeing and lacquerware. The colorful *kutani* pottery of the area is prized, and *kaga-yuzen,* a dyeing technique used in the manufacture of kimono patterns, is a colorful and age-old art form.

GETTING THERE

by air: Nagoya is the main city in southern Chubu, serviced domestically by TOA and ANA (flight from Tokyo one hr). JAL, Cathay Pacific and Korean Airlines also service Nagoya, internationally linking it to Seoul, Hong Kong and Manila; from the airport there are frequent buses to Nagoya Station (30 min). Kanazawa and Niigata on the Japan Sea receive regularly scheduled ANA and TOA flights. A small airline called Nippon Kinkyori Airways flies 5 round trips daily from Niigata to Sado Island, though unavailable Jan.-Mar. because of bad weather.

by rail: The entire Chubu district is criss-crossed by reliable, advanced and well-maintained railways. The *shinkansen* links Nagoya to Tokyo and Kyoto in a few hours. The Tokaido Main Line services the same area along the coast of Tokai, with uncountable limited and ordinary expresses. The Chuo Line heads inland from

Tokyo to the center of Chubu in the Japan Alps. It departs from Shinjuku Eki in Tokyo and proceeds NW to Kofu and on to Matsumoto, then turns SW and terminates in Nagoya. The Joetsu Line runs directly N from Ueno Station in Tokyo to Niigata, making the trip in 5 hours. The Shinetsu, also from Ueno, (Tokyo), runs a special express, the Asama 1, through Karuizawa and then into Nagano. From Nagano it proceeds directly N to the small town of Joetsu on the Japan Sea, linking there with the Hokuriku Line. The Hokuriku is the main line running along the Sea of Japan in Chubu. It links Niigata in the far N to Fukui in the SW with numerous trains for Toyama and Kanazawa along the way. Another main line is the Takayama, passing from Nagoya and Gifu in the S directly N to Takayama and on to a link-up with the Hokuriku in Toyama. Virtually every valley town and village in the interior and most certainly along the coasts are serviced by railways.

by ferry: Nagoya and Shimizu on the Pacific and Toyama and Niigata on the Japan Sea are important international ports. Regular ferries run northward from Nagoya to Tokyo in 12 hrs, and then on to Sendai in Tohoku in 23 hours. You can take a ferry from Nagoya southward to Katsuura in Wakayama Prefecture (8 hrs 30 min) where connections can be made for Tokushima on Shikoku, and points south. On the Japan Sea, a ferry plies from Otaru, near Sapporo in Hokkaido, to Niigata in 18 hrs 3 min (see "leaving Hokkaido"). Proceed on the same ferry to Maizuru, 60 km N of Kyoto in Hyogo Prefecture. Regular routes connect Niigata, Joetsu and Suzu on the tip of the Noto Peninsula to various ports on Sado Island. Bad weather disrupts this service and leaves Sado cut off from the mainland for much of the winter.

by road: Roads and bus services are well developed throughout Chubu, especially once train travel leaves off. The most heavily trafficked routes are the Nagoya-Kobe and Tokyo-Nagoya Expressways servicing the Tokai region. JNR highway buses run numerous daily routes connecting Tokyo/ Nagoya/ Kyoto/ Osaka. (Tokyo-Nagoya, Y4000.) Nights buses on this system are also available but reserved seats (Y1500 extra) are a must. Reservations can be made at travel agencies or at green windows at JNR stations. TIC in Tokyo provides a schedule of these service.

THE TOKAI REGION

The protruding coastal bulge between Nagoya and Tokyo primarily consists of the Tokai region. For countless centuries the Japanese have trudged through Nagoya, strategically placed between Osaka and Tokyo. Ever present in the background, drawing wayfarers like an adventurous, spiritual magnet, is the soaring sacred peak of Fuji. (For Fuji and environs see "Fuji-Hakone-Izu National Park".) To the W of Fujisan (Mt. Fuji), in the area surrounding Shizuoka city, are large plantations producing Japan's finest teas. Row upon row of neatly tended bushes line the sides of hills like giant furry green caterpillars. Here also, amidst this heavily industrialized zone, are the last remnants of unspoiled coastline. Smaller towns and villages earn a good proportion of their livelihood from the sea. Many canneries, some specializing in tuna (*maguro*) dot the coastline. Heading westward, the coastline gradually turns from sand to cement until you enter Nagoya (pop. 2,000,000) in Aichi Prefecture. Nagoya is Japan's 4th largest city and, either to its glory or chagrin, the huge industrial zones of Osaka and Tokyo lean on it commercially from both directions.

NAGOYA AND VICINITY

For a city as large and important as Nagoya, very few travelers are drawn to it. Most are dissuaded because of its commercialism, but there is a beauty and an unexpected whiff of cosmopolitan air hidden among its smokestacks. The city is a leading international port and travelers will pass through Nagoya making connections for Kyoto or E to Tokyo; as a way station or overnight stop, it serves the traveler well. Its central area, obliterated in WW11, is the best-planned mainland city of Japan, featuring regularly laid out wide boulevards. It follows a grid plan, making it unexpectedly easy to get around.

getting there: From Tokyo, it's only a 45 min flight to Kamaki, Nagoya's international airport, 14 km N of Nagoya Eki, connected by frequent buses. By rail from Tokyo (2 hrs) and from Osaka (one hr 6 min) on the *shinkansen*. A major

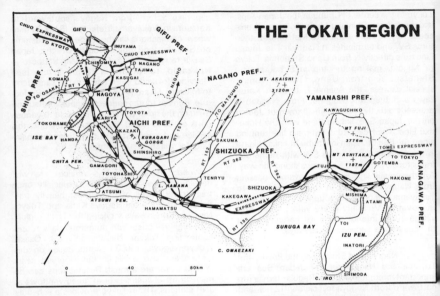

THE TOKAI REGION

stop along the Tokaido Main Line with branch lines going throughout Japan. There are also regularly scheduled ferries to and from Tokyo and to major ports S on Honshu, Shikoku and Kyushu. Bus service is available throughout the Chubu District, including the interior Japan Alps, Kanazawa on the Japan Sea, and to Tokyo, Kyoto and Osaka. The Nagoya bus center is 100 m E of Nagoya Eki. *getting around:* Because of the city's street grid system, bus travel, the primary intra-city transport, is not as difficult as in other Japanese cities. Ask for routing and timetables to specific spots at the City Information Office at Nagoya Eki; the base fare is Y50. There is also a partially developed subway system in Nagoya. Its main station is at Nagoya Eki, and the main routes run from the *eki* to Nakamura Park, and from the *shiyakusho* (City Hall) to Nagoya Port. Trains leave every 3-5 min beginning at 0530 and ending at 2330.

sights: Nagoya Castle (subway or bus from Nagoya Eki, 10 min) was built by Tokugawa Ieyasu in 1610 to deplete the coffers of the local *daimyo*, making them easier to control, and later served as the residence of his son Iemitsu. This act initiated Nagoya's rise to prominence. The castle is a faithful reconstruction of the original, which was destroyed in WW 11, and features 2 golden *shachi* (dolphins) on the roof. They were at one time so heavily covered in gold that wire nets were fastened to ward off temptation. One was featured at the Vienna Expo of 1873 and on its return to Japan the ship carrying it sunk in Nagoya Harbor. It was retrieved a few years later. In the *donjon* there are exhibits of toys, armor, portraits and implements. The grounds form Nino-maru Garden, where a quiet tea ceremony can be enjoyed. Castle hours are 0930-1630, Y250 entrance. *Nagoya T.V. Tower:* One km directly S of Nagoya Castle on the subway line. It's 175 m tall and difficult to miss. Visiting the tower is almost obligatory and from its giddy height you get an excellent view, including tree-lined Tsuruma Park, the harbor, and the outstanding red profile of Osu Kannon Temple. Open 1000-1700, Y400. *Atusuta Jingu Shrine:* Two km further S of Nagoya T.V. Tower on the same subway line. It is second in importance only to the Grand Shrines of Ise. On its tranquil grounds, complete with pecking chickens, is the repository for Kusangi-No-Tsurugi (grass-mowing sword). Legend says that Prince Yamato-Kakeru was given the sword from Ise Shrine and carried it in a war against rebels. After vanquishing the rebels, he hung the sword from a tree from where it was carried away by Princess Miyazu-Hime. It then began to shine so brightly that it set fire to a Japanese cedar that fell into a field. From here the name Atsuta (Hot Field) was derived. Like all revered Shinto shrines of Japan, Atsuta is serene and mossy quiet, a combination rare in Nagoya.

Nagoya Port: Among the world's ten busiest ports. To see it at close hand, take the bus from Nagoya Eki or the subway from Nagoya castle to the end of the line. Excursion boats are available between 0930 and 1700; Y600 for a 45 min tour.

others: Other noteworthy sights include Higashiyama Park at the E end of the city, covering 82 hectares. It features a Botanical Garden, museum, observatory and Culture Center. Nearby is Nagoya University, and one km to the N is Heiwa Park and its famous ceme-

tery. Nakamura Park, known as the birthplace of Toyotomi Hideyoshi, is 2 km W of the station. Some notable temples to visit are Osu Kannon, Higashi-Honganji and Nanatsu. *museums:* The Municipal Science Museum is located 10 min by bus, 2 km E of Nagoya Eki. It features a planetarium and the newest in scientific technology. Hours: 0930-1700, closed Mon., Y200. The Tokugawa Museum, 5 km NE of Nagoya Eki, is surrounded by Aoi Park. More than 10,000 artifacts, documents and paintings make up its displays. Picture scrolls of the Tale of the Genji housed here are considered National Treasures. Open 1000-1600 (except Mon.), Y200.

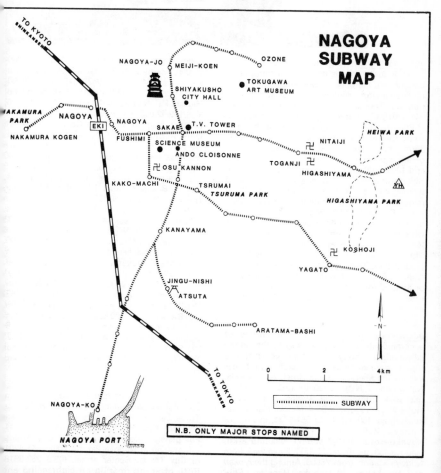

NAGOYA SUBWAY MAP

N.B. ONLY MAJOR STOPS NAMED

Nagoya-Jo
(castle)

industrial tours: Nagoya, being a center of heavy industry, opens its doors to tours of its ultramodern factories as well as to some of its traditional crafts centers. Find out about tours from City Tourist Information at Nagoya Eki (tel: 541-4301). Most, free of charge, are conducted in English. The following are some of the best. Ando Cloisonne Factory, one of the largest in Japan, has English-speaking guides and pamphlets explaining the process; open 1000-1200 and 1300-1600 daily, except Sundays. Arimatsu Shibori Industrial Co-op employs hundreds of women who sit bent over, tying thousands of miniscule knots to produce the tie-dyed *shibori* cloth. Exquisite but expensive articles can be bought in the immediate vicinity. At Noritake Chinaware Co., commercial china is made. Honda Motor Co. is at Harata, Mie Prefecture. The Industrial Bus Tour Co. specializes in this type of tour. They depart only on Fri. from the Nagoya T.V. Tower at 0900 for an all-day tour, or at 1200 for a half day. For information and reservations (a must), contact City Tourist Information or JTB.

accommodations: Since your choice of accommodations is larger in Nagoya than in the surrounding vicinity, you might consider day trips to the nearby sights. Western-style hotels include the Meitetsu Grand Hotel, 2-4-1 Meieki, Nakamura-ku, Nagoya 450, tel: (052) 582-2211, 3 min walk from Nagoya Station, from Y5500; Hotel New Nagoya, 7-35-4 Meieki, Nakamura-ku, Nagoya 450, tel: (052) 551-5131, in front of Nagoya Station, from Y5000; and Nagoya Miyako Hotel, 9-10-4 Meieki, Nakamura-ku, Nagoya 450, tel: (052) 571-3211, 5 min walk from Nagoya Station, from Y5500. Among the *ryokan* are: Hasshokan, 29 Ishizaka, Hirojicho, Sho-

waku, Nagoya 466, tel: (052) 831-1585, Y10,000-20,000; Maizurukan, 8 Kitanegicho, Nakamura-ku, Nagoya 450, tel: (052) 541-1346, Y9000-12,000; and Kamame Ryokan, 2-7 Shirakabecho, Higashi-ku, Nagoya 461, tel: (052) 931-8506, Y38,100-42,000. For *minshuku* accommodations contact: Nagoya Minshuku Center, Shirakawa Dai-san Bldg., 4-8-10 Meleki, Nakamura-ku, Nagoya City, Aichi Pref. The following are business hotels: Nagoya Roren Hotel, 1-8-40 Nishiki, Naka-ku, Nagoya, tel: (052) 211-4581, 10 min walk from Nagoya Station, 140 rooms, Y3700; Business Hotel Kiyoshi, 1-3-1 Heiwa, Naka-ku, Nagoya, tel: (052) 321-5663, one min walk from Tobetsuin Subway Sta., 56 rooms, Y2500; and Businessman's Hotel Koyo, 3-23-33 Sakae, Naka-ku, Nagoya, tel: (052) 261-4401, 6 min drive from Nagoya Sta., 23 rooms, Y2700. For youth hostellers try YH Miyoshi Ryokan, 5-8-3 Mieki, Nakamura-ku, Nagoya 450, tel: (052) 583-0758, 10 min on foot from Nagoya Sta., 18 beds; Nagoya YH, 1-50 Kameiri, Tashiro-cho, Chikusa-ku, Nagoya 464, tel: (052) 781-9845, 16 min by subway from Nagoya Sta. and 8 min on foot, 100 beds, closed Dec. 29-Jan. 3; and Aichi-Ken Seinin-Kaikan YH, 1-18-8, Sakae, Naka-ku, Nagoya 460, tel: (052) 221-6001, 10 min by bus from Nagoya Bus Terminal and 3 min on foot, 50 beds, closed Dec. 29-Jan. 4.

services: Nagoya offers the Home Visit System for information contact the Tourist & Foreign Trade Section, Nagoya City Office, 3-1-1 San-no-Maru, Naka-ku, Nagoya, tel: (052) 961-1111 For general information, contact City Tourist Information at Nagoya Eki, tel: (052) 541-4301 or City Tourist Center at tel: (052) 262-8918 Both offer information on sightseeing and industrial tourism. JTB has a few offices scattered around the city; the most convenient is at Nagoya Eki, tel: (052) 582-1201. For reading material, try Maruzen Bookstore, 3-2-7 Sakae-cho, Naka-ku, Nagoya.

VICINITY OF NAGOYA

Inuyama: Pop. 57,000; 25 min N by train from Shin-Nagoya Eki on the Inuyama Line, or one hr 10 min by bus from Nagoya Eki. The city is industrial, producing textiles and cars, but it also has worthwhile attractions, such as Inuyama Castle. This is the oldest surviving fortress in Japan, built in 1440 and preserved in its original state. Although privately owned, it is open to the public. After so many ferro-concrete reconstructions, Inuyama Castle is the real article. Nearby is Inuyama Zoo and Garden which affords an excellent view of the tumultuous Kiso River where nightly displays of cormorant fishing are held from June to October. *the rapids:* An exhilarating, but safe descent can be made down the rapids of the Kiso River from Inuyama. The journey takes about 2 hrs by tour or privately hired boats (Y2500). Train directly from Shin-Nagoya Eki to Imawatari on the Meitetsu Line, and float back to Inuyama. For this boat trip, trains are also available to Imawatari and Rhine Yuen from Inuyama, or to Sakahogi, another starting point if you approach from Gifu. The boats used for the descent are flat-bottomed, with two oarsmen to guide them. Motorized boats are also available, but the noise is a distraction. Since a number of small companies offer this service you'll have your choice. The spray from the white water laps over the side of the boat at times so you should be prepared. Either shorts or raingear are recommended, depending upon temperature. *ukai:* This unique form of fishing using trained cormorants can be viewed at Inuyama (for more information see "Gifu"). The tour boats leave their slips at about 1900 and arrange themselves before the fishing boats arrive. To save the Y1800 charged for a seat on the boat, you can often times see quite well from the banks on the Unuma side of the river. Most large hotels or any travel agency in town can make reservations.

Meiji Mura: This is a reconstructed open-air village museum representative of the lifestyle and architecture ushered into Japan by the Meiji Era. Located 25 min from Inuyama Rhine Park or one hr from Nagoya by bus. The village is complete with gas lamps, steam-powered locomotives, trolleys (housing the first ever in Japan from Kyoto) and numerous turn of the

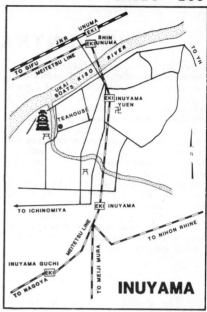

century memorabilia. (Open 1000-1700, Y700). In keeping with the heavy Western influence of the times, the houses are 19th C. American and European. The Japanese are more impressed by them than most foreigners, except for the preserved lobby of the Imperial Hotel designed by Frank Lloyd Wright. The combination of Inuyama Castle, the Kiso Rapids and Meiji Mura makes for an excellent family outing, but taking in all 3 will definitely be an all-day affair.

accommodations: If you have not day-tripped from Nagoya or Gifu to Inuyama, you can stay at one of Inuyama's many hotels. A cluster of Western-style hotels line the river banks between the castle and Inuyama-Yuen Eki. Most offer Japanese-style rooms, although these are more expensive. One example is Meitetsu Inuyama Hotel, 107 Kita Koken, Inuyama 484, tel: (0568) 61-2211, 3 min by car from Inuyamayuen Sta. of Nagoya Railway, from Y5500. *Ryokan* are also easily available throughout the city. The following should give you an idea of price: Geihanro, Inuyama, Inuyama 484, tel: (0568) 61-2205, Y7500-12,000, and Meitetsu Inuyama Hotel Bekkan Hakuteikaku, Inuyama, Inuyama 484, tel: (0568) 61-2211, Y9000-19,000. Finally, the Inuyama Youth Hostel, 162-1 Himuro, Tsugao, Inuyama 484, tel: (0568) 61-1111, is 25 min on foot from Inuyama-Yuen Sta.; 96 beds, closed Dec. 29-Jan. 3.

THE CENTRAL HIGHLANDS

Japan has 2 geographical features in abundance: seacoast and mountains. Over 80% of its land mass is mountainous, and the Central Highlands are the most spectacular of all. The 3 primary ranges of Hida, Mikumi and Kanto, stretching across Gifu, Nagano and Yamanashi Prefectures, provide a full range of mountaineering, from sheer rock climbing, where ropes and experience are a must, to well-defined, arduous, but novice-quality trails. If you yearn for wide vistas, invigorating outdoor days and quiet moments of relaxation in nature, head for the Central Highlands. Even deep in the mountains, when you feel revitalized and wish to come back to earth, towns like Takayama, Nagano, Matsumoto and Karuizawa yield a regional charm of living history, exotic temples and warm-weather retreats and hideaways.

GIFU

Gifu, (pop. 400,000), lies in the SW corner of Gifu Prefecture, only 30 km N of Nagoya, and is an ideal spot to begin your journey NE into the mountains. It is an industrial city and is internationally known for its greatest attraction, cormorant fishing (*ukai*). *getting there:* By bus from Nagoya Eki in one hour. Gifu is also a stop on the *shinkansen:* 3 hrs from Tokyo, 26 min from Nagoya, and 2 hrs from Osaka. The city is serviced by numerous runs on the Tokaido Main Line and is the junction of the Takayama Main Line heading N to Toyama on the Japan Sea via Takayama and the Japan Alps.

ukai: Traditional fishing with birds, dating back 1000 years. The fishermen no longer make their livelihood from their hauls of fish, but instead from their hauls of tourists watching them fish. *Ukai* now is simply an attraction, but over and above this it is also a night of unusual fun. Today tourists watch the fishermen from the bows of comfortable excursion boats carrying from 10 to 30 people. Although the actual fishing lasts only 45 min, the excursion boats cruise for about 2 hrs, and it's becoming more and more customary to serve dinner on them. Boat reservations are arranged at all of Gifu's larger hotels and at the Excursion Office near Nagara Bridge. You get the best views from the boats, but it's pricey, about Y2000. You can save this money by walking along the banks where the bird-fishing is occurring. Sometimes the boats pull close to shore and you can get a better look. Cormorant fishing takes place nightly from mid-May to mid-October. The cormorants used are captured off the coast of Ibaraki Pref. by use of bird lime and decoys. Once caught, their wings are clipped and they're trained for about a month until they get the idea. The cormorants are about the same size as a full-grown goose, but their elastic necks can stretch far enough to hold a half dozen 15 cm *ayu,* a small tasty fish similar to trout. The wooden boats are manned by 4 men. In the bow is the headman, *eboshi,* who wears an ancient ceremonial headdress and a dried straw skirt. His assistant and 2 oarsmen, one stationed midship and one at the stern complete the crew. Traditionally, only 21 men at a time were allowed to be *eboshi* and to pass on this honor to their sons. The midshipman not only poles the boat, but also keeps a fire of pine knots blazing in a metal cage swung from the bow. Cormorant fishing can only be done on a moonless night, the fire being used as well as a gentle tapping of a stick on the boat's side to attract the *ayu.* A flotilla of about 12 boats slowly drifts downstream, herding the fish into a

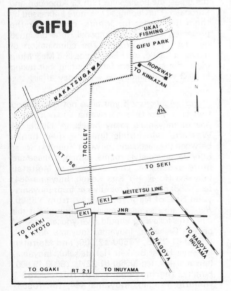

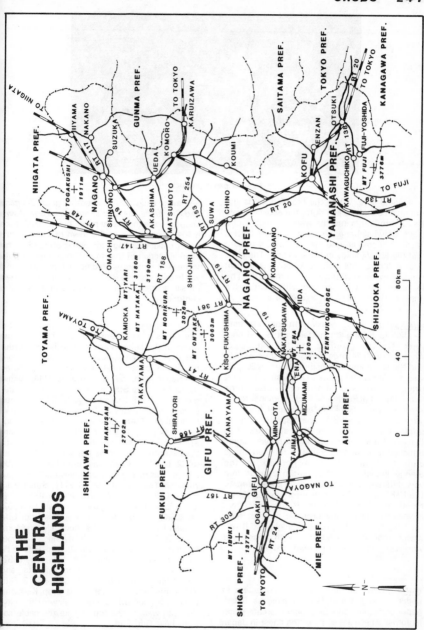

THE CENTRAL HIGHLANDS

fanciful paper products

designated area. When the fire, fish, birds and excursion boats are just right, the *eboshi* lowers his 12 cormorants into the water by means of a piece of whalebone attached to their backs. Each is tethered around the neck by a 4 m cord that the *eboshi* holds in his left hand. The birds duck and dive until their necks bulge with fish, then they're retrieved and emptied. The fishermen are given the honor of presenting the Imperial Household with *ayu* once a year.

other sights: For a relaxing afternoon waiting for the *ukai* fishing at nightfall, visit Gifu (Koen) Park. On the grounds are the Municipal Aquarium with 24 large tanks of freshwater fish, and Nawa Entomology Institute housing 300,000 insects, some dating back to the 18th C. Nawa is privately owned and the proprietor, time permitting, graciously conducts personal tours. Also in town is Shohoji Temple that houses a very different Daibutsu, perhaps the largest papier-mache creation in the world. It is fashioned from over 1000 kg of prayer papers attached to a bamboo frame to form an image almost 14 m tall. It is housed in the orange-and-white building on the grounds. In a very different vein are Gifu's well known *toruku* (Turkish baths). These play-for-pay establishments are dotted throughout the downtown area and attract many clientele through their special services. The prices are high, and if you wish to indulge it is best to go with a Japanese who can help make arrangements.

crafts: Gifu specializes in the production of paper, turning it into fanciful *bangasa* (oiled-paper umbrellas) and *Gifu jochin* (ornate paper lanterns). These are some of the finest in Japan and make excellent, inexpensive gifts. *Bangasa* and *Gifu jochin* are sold in numerous downtown shops. To see the actual paper being made, take a 40 min excursion to the town of Mino where paper making cottage industries abound in the Warabi section of that town. The mulberry pulp to make the paper is traditionally pounded and washed in the Kiso River for a week, then dried on silk screens; a method unchanged over the centuries.

accommodations: This industrial semi-resort city offers a wide range of accommodations. Many of the large Western-style hotels border the river but are pricey. Examples of more reasonably priced ones are: Gifu Grand Hotel, 648 Nagara, Gifu 502, tel: (0582) 33-1111, 15 min by car from Gifu Sta., from Y5000; and Nagara-gawa Hotel, 51 Ukaiya-Nagara, Gifu 502, tel: (0582) 32-4111, 15 min by car from Gifu Sta., from Y6000. There are many *ryokan* in Gifu but expect to pay Y10,000 up. Business hotels are more moderately priced and include Gifu Washington Hotel, 8-20 Kanamachi, Gifu, tel. (0582) 65-4111, 3 min walk from Gifu Sta., 195 rooms, Y3800; and Gifu Daiichi Hotel, 2-5 Fuku-zumicho, Gifu, tel: (0582) 51-2111, 5 min walk from Gifu Sta., 70 rooms, Y4000. YH Kodama-so, Kenei, Nagara-fukumitsu, Gifu 502, tel: (0582) 32-1922, is 30 min by bus from Gifu Sta. and 3 min on foot, 150 beds, closed Mon., every 3rd Sun., the day following a national holiday and Dec. 28-Jan. 3; and Gifu YH, 4716-17 Kami-kanoyama, Gifu 500, tel: (0582) 63-6631, 15 min by streetcar from Gifu Sta., and 20 min on foot, 60 beds, closed Dec.-Jan. 3. Gifu YH is interesting in that it sits atop Kinkazan (Silver Mt.) and offers a great view of the city. You can walk to the top or take the cable car from near Gifu Park.

TAKAYAMA

Takayama (pop. 60,000) is a picture-perfect well-preserved town rarely visited by foreigners. It is saturated with museums, traditional architecture, an artists' commune and excellent specialty shops. If time permits, it's a must.
getting there: Train on the Takayama Main Line 137 km N from Gifu, 2½ hrs, Y2200. From Tokyo, take Chuo Line to Tajami. Transfer to Mini-Ota, then take the Takayama Main Line.
getting around: Excellent bus service to all of the local sights from the train station. A 2 hr walk can cover the entire town. Bikes can be rented near Takayama Eki, the best way of seeing Takayama. An excellent side trip to take while in this area is to Mt. Norikura (3026 m), one of the tallest peaks in the Japan Alps. The views along the sheer-cliffed, serpentine road are magnificent. Return buses are available from Takayama Eki for Y2000, or you can continue directly through Awa Pass to Matsumoto on the other side of the mountains.

ingenious use of water power

sights: The Hida Minzoku Mura (Hida Folklore Village) is situated on a hill overlooking Takayama. Take the bus for a 10 min ride from Stop #4 at Takayama Eki. Return bus fare plus entrance fee is Y520. Preserved or reconstructed are the homes, shops and mills of Japan's simpler days. Each of the 20 buildings is a testament to the use of purely natural materials. Some structures are merely rude farm huts fashioned from vines, ferns and branches lashed with fiber rope. Others are sturdier post and beam constructions using rough-hewn wood, thatching straw and paper, all harmoniously blended. The overall interior effects are subdued and restful. The predominant colors are weathered grays and multi-hued interior browns, ranging from the light tan *tatami* mats to the black-brown ceilings stained by cooking fires. Each building specializes in a different collection of implements and utensils. One is a charcoal kiln; others house looms, tools made from forked branches, kitchenware and sleds. In some, artists fashion hats (*ichi-gasa*) made from yew trees; in others, wood sculptors work and traditional dyeing is done. The most fascinating feature is the ingenious use of water power. Almost like music is the water's gentle tapping rhythm as it powers large rice-pounding mallets, wheels and garden ornaments. Its force is incessantly piped through hollow logs and utilized throughout the village. The nostalgic effect of Hida for the few hours that a tour lasts is pleasant and universal.

museums: The Hida Minzoku Koku-kan (Archaeological Museum) is more than its name implies. Its exhibits include not only archaeological finds, but also wall hangings, weaving machines and all manner of daily utensils. Its displays are not in glass cases and many can be closely inspected. The building itself is of unique structural design with hanging ceilings and hidden passageways. On the stairway to the 2nd floor is a jagged hole broken into the attic. Look in. You will see the unique roof construction and also hundreds of coins littering the floor. Presumably, the universal rule of tourism is that if there is any kind of an opening, pitch in a coin and make a wish. This museum has the only wishing attic in the world. Hours are 0700 to 1900, Y200. Hida Kyodo Kan (General Museum) costs Y200 to enter. Another excellent museum with touchable exhibits, this features masterpieces of weaving and cold-weather clothing. The 2nd floor features geisha wigs and adornments. The wig hairdos look like the frosty toppings for human cupcakes. Other noteworthy museums include Kyodo Gangu-Kan (tradi-

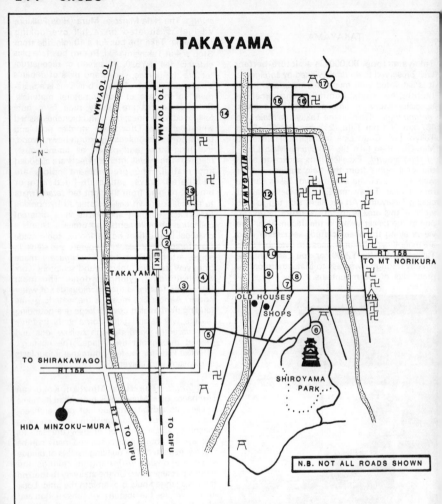

TAKAYAMA

TAKAYAMA

1. bus station
2. tourist info
3. bike rental
4. P.O.
5. Takayama Jinya
6. Kusakabe Mingei-ken (Folklore Museum)
7. Kyodo Gangu-kan (Folk Toys)
8. Kyodo-Kan (General Museum)
9. Minzoku Koko-kan (Archaeology)
10. Hirata Kinen kan
11. Fujii Bijutsu Mingei-kan (Folkcraft)
12. Hachiga Minzoku Bijitsu-kan (Folk Art Gallery)
13. Hida Kokubunji (6th C. temple)
14. Shunkeikan (lacquerware)
15. Hida Kosho-kan (artists at work)
16. Shishi Kaikan (Dragon Dance exhibit)
17. Yatai-Kaikan (festival exhibits)

tional toys), the Shunkei Kan (lacquerware) and Fujii Bijutsu-Mingei-Kan (folkcraft museum). All cost approximately Y200 and are worth a visit. Last but not least, Takayama itself is a museum. Numerous old homes remain completely intact and well-preserved, and a stroll through the town's streets with its numerous temples and shrines is like going back hundreds of years.

crafts: The Hida Kosho Kan is a group of artists under one roof working in glass cubicles making traditional wares. This is a close-up experience of observing the artistry of lacquerware, dollmaking, basket weaving, inlay and other crafts. All articles on display are for sale. One group of items on the 2nd floor is hand-rubbed driftwood. They are used to decorate homes and gardens; many pieces resemble human beings or animals, others are natural abstracts. _Kami Sanomachi:_ An entire street 300 m E of the _eki_ is dedicated to old private houses and fabulous shops which sell every conceivable folk art and traditional craft item made throughout the area. Thankfully they limit the sale of commercial junk. The items are limitless, and for souvenirs that are easy to carry or mail, look for wood block prints or handmade paper (both about Y500).

the Hida Kosho Kan (handicrafts village) in Kayama, master craftsmen ply their trades employing methods handed down over the centuries that would otherwise be lost. This elderly basket maker using handmade tools and all natural materials gathered from surrounding mountains forms containers that could have been carried by merchants and farmers during feudal times

events: The major event in Takayama is the _Sanno Matsuri_ of Hie Shrine on April 14-15. It's one of the grandest events in Japan and attracts droves of tourists. The main feature is the 23 _yatai_ (wagon floats), intricately and superbly embellished with gold and carvings. Many _yatai_ date back 100's of years. The entire populace participates in this event. The floats are exhibited at Yatai Kaikan Museum, 0830 to 1700.

the intricate carved wheels of a _Yatai_ float

accommodations: Western-style accommodations include the Takayama Green Hotel, tel: (0577) 33-5500, 7 min walk from Takayama Sta., from Y6500; and Hida Hotel, tel: (0577) 33-4600, 3 min walk from Takayama Sta., from Y7500. There are numerous _ryokan_ in Takayama starting at Y6000 with 2 meals. Two examples are Ryokan Hishuya, 2581 Kamiokamoto-cho, Takayama 506, tel: (0577) 33-4001, Y6000-15,000; and Ryokan Seiryu, 6 Hanakawa-cho, Takayama 506, tel: (0577) 32-0448, Y6000-7000. _Minshuku_, just as numerous, start at Y3700 (2 meals). An example is Funsuke, 77 Shimoichino-cho, Takayama, tel: (0577) 33-0315, 10 min on foot from Takayama Station. There is only one YH in town at a temple, Tenshoji YH, 83 Tenshoji-machi, Takayama 506, tel: (0577)

32-6345, 15 min on foot from Takayama Sta., 150 beds. Kokumin Shukusha is a people's lodge offering accommodation but reservations are a must. Kokumin Shukusha Hida, tel: (0577) 32-2400, is a 20 min walk from Takayama Sta., Y3400 up with 2 meals. _food:_ Asa-ichi is a morning bazaar (0620-1200 except Jan.) where local farmers gather to sell their reasonably priced fresh and delicious fruits, vegetables and nuts. A profusion of colorful flowers is also for sale. The bazaar is set up at Takayama Jinya (Otokugawa Manor House) along the banks of the Miya River, about 50 m from Kami Sanomachi shopping street.

services: Information and excellent area maps are handed out at Takayama Eki. JNTO also offers a good brochure of the area. For further information contact: Takayama Municipal Office, 2-115 Babacho, Takayama 506, tel: (0577) 32-3333.

MOUNTAINEERING IN THE JAPAN ALPS

Matsumoto: A small town of 170,000 deep in the mountains, Matsumoto is the main staging area for mountaineerng in the Alps. This entire area is a wonderland of snow-capped peaks, glittering lakes and gaily colored mountain flowers. The Alps are wild-and-raw Japan at its best. Before they lure you to their wild vistas and invigorating heights visit Matsumoto-jo (castle).

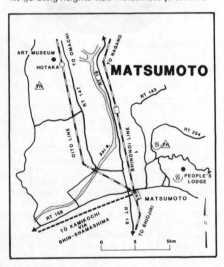

Its 6-storied black _donjon_ is unique in Japan and is colloquially called "Crow Castle" in marked contrast to the "White Egret Castle" of Himeji, considered the most beautiful in the land. While on the castle grounds visit the museum, a collection of over 60,000 folklore items. _getting there:_ From Nagano, Matsumoto is 40 km SE on the Shinonoi spur line of the Shinetsu Main Line about one hour. From Tokyo (4 hrs) or Nagoya (3 hrs) on the Chuo Main Line to Shiojiri, then take the Shinonoi Line 20 km into Matsumoto.

Kamikochi: From Matsumoto to Kamikochi, take the Matsumoto Electric Railway for 30 min (Y380) to Shin-Shimashima, then by bus one hr 25 min, to Kamaikochi (Y1250). Buses are available from mid-April to early November. A bus is also available from Takayama to Hirayu Spa, one hr 20 min, Y1000; then to Kamikochi, one hr 5 min, Y960. At one time accessible only on foot, Kamikochi is now opened by bus routes to a flood of trekkers. Each season more than 100,000 hikers come to this beautiful alpine plateau. Most plan their trips for July and Aug., the period of finest weather, and the mountain huts are crowded at this time. June is rainy, and late Sept. has the fewest climbers as the weather is extremely changeable. The first stop is usually at Weston Memorial, dedicated to the English mountaineer who pioneered mountain climbing in Japan at the turn of the century. Since then, the Japanese have become insatiable climbers embarking to all continents looking for ever-new challenges. Kamikochi is a small area of level land on the upper reaches of the Azusa River. The Azusa's cascading waters have been harnessed at 3 sites, producing 900,000 kilowatts of power, the largest hydroelectric output in Asia. Pick up your supplies in Kamikochi and then head for the mountains.

mountaineering tips: The Japan Alps are visited by hundreds of thousands of mountaineers every season, from May to Nov. Every season a few lives are claimed by the mountains. Careful preparation, a discerning eye on the weather, and staying within your physical limits will insure a safe and exciting experience. These mountains are moody and fickle: a brilliant day of dazzling, clear skies can quickly turn into a dismal day of rain, fog, howling winds and even snow at the higher elevations. Besides your normal camping gear, be sure to take with you the following essential items: sturdy boots, 3 changes of socks, a woolen sweater, windbreaker/raincoat, hat, sunglasses, canteen, matches in a watertight container, flashlight, candle, first-aid kit

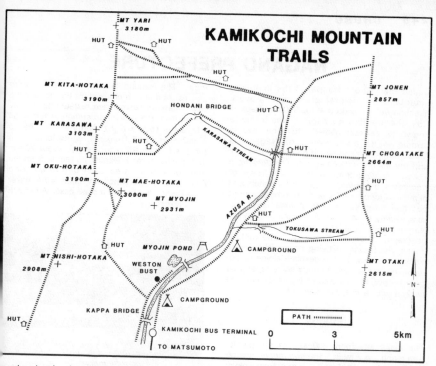

KAMIKOCHI MOUNTAIN TRAILS

MT YARI 3180m
HUT
HUT
MT KITA-HOTAKA 3190m
HUT
HONDANI BRIDGE
HUT
MT JONEN 2857m
MT KARASAWA 3103m
KARASAWA STREAM
HUT
HUT
HUT
MT CHOGATAKE 2664m
MT OKU-HOTAKA 3190m
MT MAE-HOTAKA 3090m
HUT
MT MYOJIN 2931m
AZUSA R.
HUT
TOKUSAWA STREAM
HUT
MYOJIN POND
CAMPGROUND
MT NISHI-HOTAKA 2908m
WESTON BUST
MT OTAKI 2615m
N
CAMPGROUND
KAPPA BRIDGE
HUT
KAMIKOCHI BUS TERMINAL
TO MATSUMOTO
PATH ....
0   3   5km

and a sleeping bag. Light, easily prepared provisions are also recommended since the food provided in the mountain huts is expensive and unpalatable. Also, remember that your sleeping bag, fondly regarded as a downy soft cocoon, turns into a mass of smelly, lumpy feathers when wet. If possible, hike with a partner and stay on the trails. If the weather gets bad, don't foolishly push on. Head back to the nearest known shelter. A bandana around your neck not only soaks up perspiration, but also doubles as an ankle bandage or sling in an emergency. A compass is always a good idea, but unnecessary if you stay on the trails. Take short steps walking uphill, frequent rest breaks, and be aware that the long awaited downhill section is tough on knees and weary ankles twist easily.

accommodations: Matsumoto/Kamikochi has a wide range of accommodations from ultra-modern hotels to camping areas. The mountain huts can be dismal with cramped quarters at high prices (Y4000) including marginal food. They are, however, warm and dry after a long day of hiking. You can stay in Matsumoto at Matsumoto Town Hotel, 2-1-38 Chuo Matsumoto, tel: (0263) 32-3339, 2 min walk from Matsumoto Sta., 108 rooms, Y4200; Hotel New Station, 1-1-11 Chuo Matsumoto, tel: (0263) 35-3850, one min walk from Matsumoto Sta., 64 rooms, Y4000; and Hotel Iidaya, 1-2-3 Chuo Matsumoto, tel: (0263) 32-0027, one min walk from JNR Matsumoto Sta., 57 rooms, Y4200. In Kamikochi the following are all grouped near the bus terminal: Kamikochi Imperial Hotel, tel: (0263) 95-2001, from Y20,000; Gosenjaku Ryokan, tel: (0263) 95-2111, from Y18,000, and Gosenjaku Dormitory, same number, from Y3800; also So Nei Hotel, tel: (0263) 95-2231, Japanese-style from Y6000, dormitory from Y3700. There are 4 YHs throughout the Matsumoto/Kamikochi area. The 2 most convenient are: Asama-Onsen YH, 302-1, Asama-onsen, Matsumoto 390-03, tel: (0263) 46-1335, 20 min by bus from Matsumoto Sta., and 5 min on foot, 150 beds, closed Dec. 28-Jan. 3; and Azumino YH, 4509, Kashiwabara, Hotaka-cho 399-83, tel: (0263) 82-4265, 20 min by bus from Hotaka Sta. and 2 min on foot, 20 beds, closed Jan. 17-Feb. 7. Other accommodations include: People's Lodge Misuzu-so, tel: (0263(46-1727, Y3400 with 2 meals; and Norikurura Kogen Vacation Village, tel: (0263) 93-2304, from Y3400 with 2 meals. Accommodations at Kamikochi are generally closed from mid-Nov. to late April.

NAGANO PREFECTURE

Called the "Roof of Japan," the imposing mountains of this prefecture soar in every direction with 11 peaks that top 3000 m. Nagano City, the prefecture's capital, was formerly known as Zenkoji, named after the revered temple in its area. South of Nagano is Matsumoto, the jumping-off point to Kamikochi and the mighty peaks beyond. Travelers from Tokyo will pass through the resort town of Karuizawa, a summer retreat for foreigners and dignitaries for over 100 years. From here, a short bus ride takes you to Mt. Asama (2542 m), second only to Mt. Aso in volcanic activity. In Nagano you feel the truly mountainous geography of Japan. Climbing to the roof of Japan, the feeling of being on an island slips away in this moody and desolate alpine world. But even in this mountainous solitude, as you peer below, the twinkling lights of villages beckon with a cozy, huddled charm.

NAGANO

The major city [pop. 300,000] of the prefecture and a main transportation center heading S from the Japan Sea or N from Tokyo. It is 5 hrs from Tokyo on the Shin Etsu Main Line, or 1½ hrs from Naoetsu on the Japan Sea (same line). The city is flooded by pilgrims heading for Zenkoji Temple where ancient Buddhist rites predominate.

food: The Nagano area is famous for *ringo* (apples) sold at numerous stalls throughout the city. There are inexpensive restaurants directly across from the main train station in the small alleyways to the right. Nagano also has a MacDonald's and Dunkin' Donuts located on the bus route leading to Zenkoji, about 200 m after the bus turns R leading up the hill from the main downtown area. Just before entering Zenkoji, on the L watch an adept *soba* maker produce noodles behind a glass case. Very fresh and inexpensive.

soba maker

accommodations: The usual range of budget accommodation is lacking in Nagano. There are no convenient *minshuku* or *ryokan* in the downtown area. There are numerous Western hotels close to the *eki* but all are pricey, starting at Y6500. Business hotels provide the budget alternative. Try: Nagano City Hotel Kikuya, 2377 Gondomachi, tel: (0262) 32-4166, 5 min drive from Nagano Sta., 87 rooms, Y3000; Hotel Aoki 1356 Suehirocho, tel: (0262) 26-1271, one min walk from Nagano Sta., 76 rooms, Y4000; and Nagano Palace Hotel, 1325 Minaminagano Ishidc-minami, tel: (0262) 25-2221, one min walk from JNR Nagano Sta., 30 rooms, Y3500. Nagano is also lacking in YHs. The only one in town is Kyoju-in YH, c/o Zenkoji, 479 Motoyoshi-cho, Nagano 380, tel: (0262) 32-2768, 10 min on foot from Nagano Sta., 30 beds, closed Dec. 28-Jan. 6. Unfortunately, the woman running this YH is particularly unfriendly to foreigners and will try to turn you away. Only a confirmed reservation will open the door. *services:* JTB is located at the *eki*. A few attendants speak English. The Temporary Parcel Storage is next door to the JTB, Y200 for the day.

ZENKOJI TEMPLE

Ten min by bus, 1.5 km from the *eki*, or 3 stops on the Nagano Electric Railway. The main street leading to Zenkoji has smaller and lesser temples on both sides. Most pilgrims come to Zenkoji to walk through the 40 m long tunnel beneath the main alter. They hope to touch the Key of Paradise, a stone in the wall of the tunnel, as they move along in total darkness. This they believe will ease their way into paradise. Every day there is some sort of ritual happening. The faint rhythm of drums, clapping sticks and sonorous chanting is always in the background. The feeling is theatrical for the non-Buddhist. San-mon, the main wooden gate into Zenkoji, is strikingly ornate. Usually there are a number of women sitting cross-legged under it selling small religious articles such as beads, and just through the gate is a small bazaar where you can buy fruits, knick-knacks, Japanese kites and other items. To the R of the main walkway are 6 Buddhas with halos of bronze, representing different aspects of life. The grounds are crowded with pilgrims, many of whom approach the main temple to deposit a stick of incense into a giant brass burner and waft the smoke into their faces as part of a purification ritual. The main building is a massive, weather-beaten structure. Inside are 3 giant drums and near them is a temple scribe writing Japanese characters into the small books which the pilgrims carry. The interior roof is completely covered by a fish net used to dissuade the numerous pigeons from perching (and then dropping *their* offerings). Food is available in inexpensive stalls to the right rear of the main structure. Behind Zenkoji is a pink and white 3-storied pagoda, and nearby is a gigantic bird house. A number of attendant buildings are in the compound. One, located to the L of the main structure on the stone pathway leading over the bridge, has 2 stone pillars with wheels that actually spin carved into them. The waters below the bridge are home to 100's of turtles. There is also an impressive statue of Kannon, the Buddhist goddess of benevolent, motherly love and purity. This figure was often adopted by Japanese Christians during the Edo Period as a clandestine symbol of the blessed virgin.

KARUIZAWA

The old resort town of Karuizawa (pop. 14,000) is the most interesting and accessible stopover heading NW from Tokyo into the mountains. Its name is derived from the Ainu words for "Great Pumice-Stone Moor." Foreigners began heading for this cool summer mountainous retreat in 1888 in the wake of the Rev. Shaw, who built a villa here. Since then, its popularity has been assured, attracting 100,000 summer visitors yearly. Old-time Westernization is apparent in the homes with many driveways leading to elegant, colonnaded porches of country manor houses. Some are rustic cabins, and most are distinctly un-Japanese. People came and still come to escape the dripping heat of a Tokyo summer, and many Westerners arrive looking for space and yearning for elbow room. The trails to Mt. Asama, the main hiking area in the vicinity, are heavily trekked and well-defined. There are numerous bike rental shops in town, horses for hire, tennis courts and field archery centers. The emphasis is on the outdoors, although there are over 200 Tokyo-affiliated shops lining the downtown streets. The main boulevard has a Western air, being wide and divided and lined with shops bearing names like "Matsua's Garage," "Jerry's Place" and "Coffee Here."

getting there: From Ueno Station in Tokyo on the Shin-Etsu Line, it takes about 2 hrs by limited express (Y3100) or 2 hrs 30 min by ordinary express (Y2200). From Nagano, same line in 2 hrs 20 min; express Y860, add Y500 for limited express, but save only 20 minutes. From Tokyo by road, take Rt. 17 to Takasaki, then Rt. 18 to Karuizawa. Good hitchhiking with plenty of traffic. *getting around:* Buses are available to all of the local sights. The terminal is just across the street from the *eki*. To get around in

nearby rinks (from Nov. to March). Western-sized skates are available. You can also try field archery at Onoishidashi Lava Rocks, 20 min beyond Minenochaya, open 0900-1700, Y300 for a course of targets. Golfing is available (fees: Y5000-20,000) as well as horseback riding at Kyu-Karuizawa and other local stables (Y3000 per hour). You can rent a bicycle in town, or at the Karuizawa Prince Hotel, where you can cycle through the elegant grounds complete with mountain cabin-type accommodations, and even park for a dip in the outdoor pool.

a 19th C. engraving from, *Asia: Carpenters Geographical Reader.*

own, rent a bicycle. There are at least 5 shops in he immediate vicinity of the bus terminal. Rickshaws in season are also available, but this novelty is costly.

ights: Mt. Asama (2542 m) dominates the Karuizawa area. A ½ hr bus ride costs Y530 through backwood dirt roads to Minenochaya nd the beginning of the walking trails to Asama. The bus ride gives you a close view of many villa hide-a-ways, and stops at Shiraito Waterfalls. At Minenochaya is a small store where you can buy a few provisions and across he street is a billboard-sized map of the mountain trails. Let your energy be your guide s far as climbing goes. The trails are well-marked and easy, although the climb is steady. or the summit, allow 4-5 hours. For a shorter ip, take the same bus for only 5-10 min to yu-Karuizawa where most of the old time villas e located. From here, walk 30 min to Usui Pass d the nearby Kumano Shrine. From a platform op the pass, you get a wide panoramic view of t. Asama and the jagged peaks beyond.

creation: For outdoor fun throughout the area y ice skating at Karuizawa Skate Center and

accommodations: Besides the normal range of accommodations in Karuizawa, there are also camping grounds nearby and even some of the fashionable villas in the mountain recesses can be rented. Western-style places, with some Japanese-style rooms, include Mampei Hotel, 925 Sakuranosawa, Karuizawa, tel: (02674) 2-2771, 4 min by car from Karuisawa Sta., from Y10,000; Green Hotel, 2147, Nagakura, Karuizawa 389-01, tel: (02674) 5-5155, 7 min by car from Naka-Karuizawa Sta., from Y10,000; and Karuizawa Prince Hotel seizan Honkan, 1016 Karuizawa, Karuizawa-machi 389-01, tel: (02674) 2-5211, 3 min by car from Karuizawa Sta., from Y5000. *Ryokan* are plentiful throughout the area and at nearby Hoshino Spa. Some examples are Shiotsubo Onsen Hotel, Karuizawa-machi, Kita-Sakugun 389-01, tel: (02674) 5-5441, Y6000-20,000; Hoshino Onsen Hotel, Karuizawa-machi, Kita-Sakugun 389-01, tel: (02674) 5-5121, Y7500-15,000; and Hotel New Hoshino, Karuizawa-machi, 389-01, tel: (02674) 5-6081, Y9000-15,000. Karuizawa also offers two YHs. A very friendly and accommodating YH is Karuizawa Yuai-Sanso YH, 1608 Karuizawa-machi 289-01, tel: (02674) 2-2477, 10 min on foot from Karuizawa Sta., 60 beds. The other is Karuizawa YH, 1362 Kyu-Karuizawa, Karuizawa-machi 389-01, tel: (02674) 2-2325, 4 min by bus from Karuizawa Sta. and 18 min on foot, 50 beds. For a People's Lodge, try Karuizawa Kogenso, tel: (02674) 8-2111, Y3700 with 2 meals. *services:* JNTO and TIC offer a brochure on the Karuizawa area. If you are interested in renting a villa there, you can also check with JNTO or TIC.

NORTHERN HOKURIKU REGION

In the far N of the Hokuriku region is Niigata (pop. 400,000), the prefectural capital, and Sado Island (pop. 93,000), Japan's 5th largest island, 40 km offshore. Although industrialization has been slow to creep into Hokuriku, Niigata, located on the Shinano River, Japan's longest, is slowly going that way. Modern transportation to Sado is eroding its ancient secluded charm, except when visitors are rare during the winter, when rough waters close its harbors and soupy weather shuts down its airport. *getting there:* Take the Joetsu Main Line from Tokyo (Ueno) in 4 hrs via Takasaki or the Hokuriku Line along the coast via Fukui, Kanazawa, Toyama and Joetsu. TOA also flies from Tokyo in 50 minutes. By ferry from Maizuru (Hyogo Prefecture) it's 13 hrs via Niigata to Otaru in Hokkaido (18 hrs).

NIIGATA

The center of the most fertile plain in the district its agricultural lands irrigated by the now-tamed Shinano River. It was opened to foreign trade in 1869, and the numerous canals cutting through the city's center at one time saw heavy marine traffic. *Hakusan Park:* Only 15 min by bus from Niigata Eki, offers a zoo and Hakusan Shrine Large sand dunes in the NW protect the city from winter storms; Hiyoriyama, nondescript, is one of the tallest, offering a view of the city from its sandy summit. Now the city produces chemi cals from the by-products of its numerous o refineries. Niigata is still an important transpor

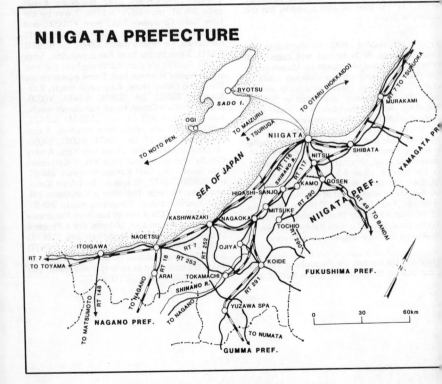

NIIGATA PREFECTURE

the farm fields of Niigata have long been meticulously terraced into mud and water natural sculptures. The Shinano River passing nearby provides the irrigation necessary to sustain these wet ricefields and to make the general area one of the most productive in all of Japan.

tation center to and from Tohoku and Hokkaido, but is rather uninteresting.

ccommodations: For Western-style hotels, try the Niigata Silver Hotel, 1-1-25 Benten, Niigata 50, tel: (0252) 45-7111, one min walk from Niigata Sta., from Y5000; Handai Silver Hotel, -3-30 Bandai, Niigata 950, tel: (0252) 43-3711, 7 min walk from Niigata Sta., from Y5000; and he Italia-Ken, 7-1574 Nishibori, Niigata 951, tel: (0252) 24-5111, 10 min by car from Niigata Sta., rom Y6000. Business hotels include Hotel Kawai, 1-37-5 Bentencho, Niigata, tel: (0252) 1-3391, 3 min walk from Niigata Sta., 52 rooms, 3300; Niigata Station Hotel, 1-21 Bentencho, Niigata, tel: (0252) 47-3225, one min walk from Niigata Sta., 40 rooms, Y3540; and Green Hotel, -4-9 Hanazono, Niigata, tel: (0252) 46-0341, one min walk from Niigata Sta., 33 rooms, Y3000. There is only one YH in Niigata, but there are almost in a row just a few km S of the city long the coast. Some to choose from are Niigata Hiyoriyama YH, 5932-591 Nishi-funami-ho, Niigata 951, tel: (0252) 29-0935, 20 min by us from Niigata Sta. and 5 min on foot, 15

beds; Knosenji YH, Takeno-machi, Maki-machi 953, tel: (02567) 2-3339, 10 min by bus from Maki Sta. and 5 min on foot; and Myokoji YH, Kakuda-hama, Maki-machi 953, tel: (025677) 2025, 30 min by bus from Maki Sta. and 6 min on foot, 40 beds.

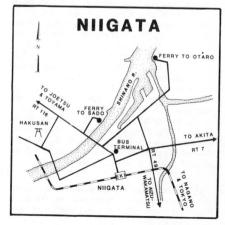

Okesa ballad dancers

SADO ISLAND

At one time an island of exile for prisoners and for powerful men fallen from grace with the authorities. The island is divided by 2 imposing mountain chains in the NW and SE, Mt. Kimpoku (1173 m) in the NW being the tallest. Between the mountains, fertile volcanic soils yield abundant rice harvests. The NW and NE coasts are wild and virtually uninhabited. The Japan Sea pounds their rock face beaches and the winds howl out of Siberia. Separated from the mainland by rough waters and horrifying winter storms, the people of Sado have developed a unique culture preserved today in soulful *okesa* ballads and dances performed for the tourists by the island's women. The bamboo of Sado is also prized as the best for making *takohochi*, the plaintive Japanese flutes that accompany the ballads. Here, too, making a last stand against extinction are 12 *toki* (Japanese crested ibis), the last of their breed in all the world. *getting there:* Take the ferry from Niigata to Ryotsu, the main port, in 2 hrs 10 min or to Akadomari in 3 hrs 20 minutes. From Joetsu to Ogi Port in 3 hrs; or from Suzu (Noto Peninsula) to Ogi Port in 4 hours. By air from Niigata, Nippon Kinkyori Airlines flies to Ryotsu Airport (Sado) in just 20 minutes.

sights: Located at Myoshoji Temple is a small hut, a memorial to Nichiren, the famous Buddhist priest who lived and meditated here while in exile. Another famous exile was Emperor Juntoku, who in the 13th C. was sent to Sado because of an attempt to overthrow the Kamakura Shogunate. His Kuroki Goshi (Unhewn Timber Palace) is located at Izumi, about 10 km SW of Ryotsu, the island's main city located on the SE coast along the shores of Lake Kamo. *Akiwa:* population 15,000, located on the SW coast, is the home of Gold Mountain. The mine here produced voluminous quantities of gold during the Edo Period when prisoners were sentenced here to labor and to die. Now the old mine is a museum complete with wax

a 19th C. prisoner in irons

figures of the toiling prisoners. The mine, though supposedly worked out, still produces 2000 tons of gold and silver each year. It also produces a distinctive red clay used to fashion *mumyoi-yaki*, the island's famous and much sought-after pottery, sold at numerous outlets throughout the island. Bus service is adequate and routes intersect at all of the main cities and completely circle the island. Listening to the women perform their sad and liquid *Okesa* ballads, now only for tourists, you can feel the lingering specters of long ago exiles and prisoners, longing for their lost homes across the sea.

<u>accommodations:</u> There are some hotels and *minshuku* from which to choose in the larger towns of Sado Island. There are, however, 5 YHs dotted around the island. They are: Kazashima-Kan YH, 397 Katano, Ryotsu 952-35, tel: (025945) 3, 45 min by bus from Ryotsu Port, 29 beds; Hosen-Kan YH, 1111 Katagami, Niibomura 952-01, tel: (025942) 3125, 10 min by bus from Ryotsu Port and 5 min on foot, 60 beds; Sotokaifu YH, 131 Iwayaguchi, Aikawa-machi, 952-23, tel: (025979)3815, 2 hrs 40 min by bus from Ryotsu Port, 70 beds; Senkaku-So YH, 369-4 Himezu, Aikawa-machi, 952-21, tel: (02597) 5-2011, 80 min by bus from Ryotsu Port and 5 min on foot, 20 beds; and Sado Hakuzan YH, Yamada, Sawada-machi, 952-13, tel: (02595) 2-4422, 40 min by bus from Ryotsu Port and 25 min on foot, 15 beds.

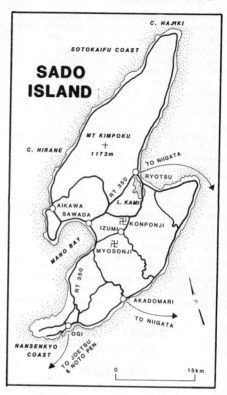

SOUTHWEST HOKURIKU REGION

Toyama, Ishikawa and Fukui are the least industrialized prefectures of the Chubu District. Lying far from the traditional power in Kyoto and Tokyo, their main cities were allowed to develop without undue interference and produced some remarkable results. *Fukui City:* Pop. 220,000, is the prefectural capital. It historically paid taxes and tribute to its ruling *daimyo,* not in the usual bales of rice but in bundles of silk fabrics. Today, Fukui produces 40% of the national output of silks in its distinctive style called *habitae.* Ishikawa's prefectural capital, Kanazawa, is a study in survival, and a thriving art center. In its confines is Kenrokuen Park, one of the most distinguished landscaped gardens in all Japan. Projecting into the Japan Sea is the Noto Peninsula whose shoreline facing Toyama Bay is tranquil with quiet villages nestled in coves and inlets, while on its Japan Sea side, heavy waves

pound the cliffs. Toyama, its prefectural capital, is a traditional center of patent medicines. This entire coastal area is filled with provincial towns where the people live in the rhythm of bygone days.

KANAZAWA

The main city of the Hokuriku district (pop. 407,000). During the Edo Period the ruling Maeda Clan avoided military pursuits and turned Kanazawa into a thriving art colony, thereby mollifying the shogunate and preserving their power in the region. During WW 11 the karma of Kanazawa prevailed once again and no bombs fell here. Entire sections of winding streets and alleyways are lined with original homes and shops. The atmosphere is perfect for a thriving "art city." Kanazawa boasts an impressive *noh* theatre with 100's of citizen actors, superb lacquerware, *kaga yuzen*, an age old dyeing technique and famous *kutani* pottery. <u>getting there:</u> By train, Kanazawa is a main station on the Hokuriku Line. From Tokyo, take the Shinkansen to Maibara, then travel N on the Kokuriku Line, 5 hrs, Y10,000. On the limited express from Tokyo, the trip takes 9 hrs and costs Y5000. There's also a direct one hr 10 min flight from Tokyo, or from Nagoya fly 55 min to Komatsu, 25 km S of Kanazawa. Frequent buses go to the city from there in 50 minutes. Inter-city buses from Kanazawa Eki go to all points of interest.

sights: Kanazawa Castle, located on Hyakkenbori-Dori (street), was almost completely destroyed by fire in 1881; Ishikawamon Gate and a samurai residence are all that remain. This is an excellent place to start a walking tour of the city. Behind the castle is Kanazawa University, and across the street is the entrance to Kenrokuen Park. The park was originally built by Lord Maeda in 1673 and then expanded to its present 10 ha in 1819. There are several cultural attractions within the park; it would take a whole day to really enjoy the setting. The seasons provide colorful makeup for the face of Kenrokuen, but underneath it is always naturally beautiful. The grounds are placid with running streams, and with its artistic arrangements of trees, shrubs and well-placed buildings, the park's atmosphere is respectfully solemn. It is art on a grand scale and it is said that even the stones in the streams are scrubbed and realigned. On the grounds is Seison Kaku, a mansion built in 1863 for the mother of the ruling Lord Maeda. The architecture is distinctly feminine with graceful beams, delicate timbering and gold-flecked walls. The mansion is now also a museum, and the chief exhibits are exquisite kimono, painted *shoji* screens and a wide variety of woodblock prints. The Western-style chandeliers show the influence of the Meiji Restoration. Next door is Ishikawa Prefectural Museum. Again, there is a large display of kimono, prints and folding screens, but the best exhibits here are lacquerware and ceramics dating back to the 17th century. The most distinguished piece is a phoenix-shaped enameled incense burner created by the master ceramicist, Ninsei, in the 17th

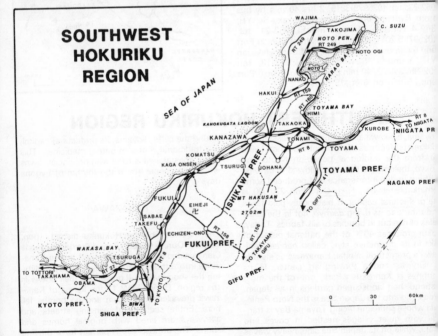

SOUTHWEST HOKURIKU REGION

century. The park is open daily from 0630-1800, admission Y100. Seison-Kaku is open daily and admission is Y300. The Art Museum is open from 0900-1600 daily, Y200.

a walking tour: Leave Kenrokuen Park by the main street across from the Ishikawa Art Museum. Pass the Ishikawa Gokuku Shrine, built in 1939 and used as a memorial to WW 11 soldiers. Continue on to Kanazawa's famous Noh Theatre. This theatre is very active, with new performances scheduled every month. During the Maeda rule, artists were required to do extra curricular activities and many chose the performing arts. This legacy has been handed down, and many ordinary townsfolk take an active role in the performances or related theatrical fields. One outstanding example is a local miller who is so adept at traditional comic monologue that he is considered a human cultural asset. Close by is the Hanro Honda Zohin-kan, a museum containing the feudal belongings of the prestigious Honda family from the Maeda Era. Open 0900-1700 except Thurs., Y400. Notice the twisting alleyways (no roads were built straight so that invading armies were unable to follow a direct route to the castle) and high walls surrounding samurai residences. Many date back 100 years and are still occupied and privately owned. The Higashi (East) Quarter, at one time a red light district, now features numerous *ryokan* and restaurants. Edo Village is a cluster of 25 buildings offering representative reconstructions of the typical homes of the Edo Period. Take a bus to Yuwaku (30 min), a nearby spa town where Edo Village is located; open 0800-1800 daily, Y650.

crafts: Distinctive *kutani* pottery, dating from the mid-17th C., is still being produced in kilns around Kanazawa. Of all Japanese pottery this may be the best known overseas. Unfortunately, many kilns have geared themselves to comercial production and the quality of *kutani-yaki* has suffered, but some pieces done by traditional potters are superb. Many pots are glazed with classical pastoral scenes and natural motifs while others are gaudy bright colors, a Japanese interpretation of foreigner's tastes. To become acquainted with *kutani* ware before purchasing, see excellent examples at the Art Museum at Kenrokuen Park. Kanazawa also produced lacquerware and *kaga yuzen*, an age-old traditionally dyed cloth. Most craft items are available in numerous downtown shops.

Eiheji Temple, Fukui

accommodations: This artistic city offers accommodations to everyone's tastes. Holiday Inn, 1-10 Horikawa Cho, Kanazawa, tel: (0762) 23-1111, from Y7000; Kanazawa Miyako Hotel, 6-10 Konohana-cho, Kanazawa 920, tel: (0762) 31-2202, 3 min walk from Kanazawa Sta., from Y5000; and Hotel New Kanazawa, 2-14-10 Honmachi, Kanazawa 920, tel: (0762) 23-2255, 2 min walk from Kanazawa Sta., from Y4500. There are numerous YHs throughout the area. The most convenient to Kanazawa are: Kanazawa YH, 37 Suehiro-cho, Kanazawa 920, tel: (0762) 52-3413, 25 min by bus from Kanazawa Sta., 120 beds; Matsuiya YH, 1-9-3 Kata-machi, Kanazawa 920, tel: (0762) 21-0275, 14 min by bus from Kanazawa Sta. and 4 min on foot, 15 beds; and Izuminodai YH, 1-1-31 Izumigaoka, Kanazawa 921, tel: (0762) 41-2802, 20 min by bus from Kanazawa Sta. and 2 min on foot, 15 beds, closed Dec. 27-Jan. 5.

The Noto Peninsula: Buffeted by the sea and crossed by rugged mountains, this wild area offers untamed scenery and typical fishing villages. A tour of the peninsula takes at least one full day. From Kanazawa, go by train on the

the rugged coast of the
Noto Peninsula

Nanao Line via Nanao, Wakura and Anamizu. At Anamizu, proceed due N to Wajima on the W coast, or E to Suzu. A ferry is available from Suzu to Sado Island. The peninsula's inland area is terraced with numerous rice fields with the turbulent ocean as a backdrop. In Wajima there is an open air market where farmers, fishermen and artists specializing in lacquerware sell their wares. _accommodations:_ There are no less than 12 YHs lining the E and W coasts of the Noto Peninsula. Except in mid-summer, there is no problem finding a room.

Toyama: Pop. 280,000. Sixty km E of Kanazawa on the Hokuriku Main Line, Toyama is surrounded by fantastic scenery. Due E is the Tateyama Mt. Range and in the W is the Kurehayama Range. Numerous peaks reach 3000 m and steep, v-sided valleys are formed by the raging Jinzu River in the south. Toyama is faced by the Japan Sea in the N; at its back rise the Alps. The city gained prominence in the 17th C. as a center for patent medicines. Numerous pharmacies throughout the city still brew the home remedies, and traveling salesmen do a thriving door-to-door business throughout Japan selling these time-proven concoctions. _accommodations:_ Unfortunately there are no _minshuku_ or youth hostels in Toyama City, although there are plenty nearby on the Noto Peninsula. The best bet for budget accommodations would be any of the business hotels in the downtown area around the _eki_. Hotels that have sauna baths will allow you to stay there over night, but charge Y2500—a bit more than usual for these usually cheaper sauna accommodations.

THE KINKI DISTRICT

INTRODUCTION

300 km W of Tokyo is the largest lake in Japan, Lake Biwa. On its western shores is Kyoto Prefecture, backed by Hyogo Prefecture reaching to the Japan Sea. Dipping S into the Pacific are the surrounding prefectures of Osaka, Shiga, Nara, Wakayama and Mie. These 7 prefectures make up the Kinki District. Neatly packed into this district's boundaries are the colossal tourist trio of Kyoto, Nara and Ise, and the dynamo of Osaka. This area enjoys worldwide acclaim for its art, architecture, performing arts and religious centers. Kyoto and Nara alone are visited by 30,000,000 tourists per year. A visit to Japan without at least a short immersion into this area would be like dining on an exquisite gourmet meal and forgetting to open the vintage wine. Kyoto is Big Ben, the Louvre, the New York Museum of Fine Arts and the Vatican all rolled into one. For 1000 years Kyoto served as the capital, the jewel case of Japan, and the Japanese adorned its precincts with the finest that their minds, hands and souls could conjure. Kyoto was a grand city when Tokyo was merely a mudfield with rude huts, populated with backwoods country folk. Nara, one hour S of Kyoto, is where the seeds of Japanese culture, art, literature and history found fertile ground. It was the first permanent Imperial Court and the surrounding countryside is rich with mythical legends. Ise, yet further S in Mie Prefecture, provides the serene quiet of the Grand Imperial Shrines, the most venerated in Japan. For many centuries the enthroned living deities, the emperors, came here to bow to the gods of Japan. The shrines and their grounds are impeccable. SW of Kyoto is Osaka and its neighboring city, Kobe. Osaka, because of its central location, is the main port of Japan. It is the vibrant, smoke-belching, mechanically gurgling behemoth of the modern industrial nation. Osakans have long enjoyed the reputation of being progressive and indeed stand at the vanguard of 21st C. Japan. Amidst the flash and staccato rhythm of this undisputed commercial center of Japan, Osaka manages to provide the finer pleasures, still locatable through the smog. Next door is Kobe. Delicately marbled, savory, tender beef is produced here. The cattle, exalted members of the farm family, never leave their dimly lit stalls where they are fed the best grains, while their rumps are soaked with beer and massaged into soft-muscled kabobs. They meet their ultimate end as steaks in the finest, intoxicatingly priced restaurants throughout cosmopolitan Japan. The Kinki District is rounded out by heading N from Kyoto to the Japan Sea, deep into the heart of Hyogo Prefecture. Here is *Amanohashidate*, (The Heavenly Bridge), one of the 3 especially favorite spots of elderly Japanese (the other 2 being Miyajima and Matsushima). The Kinki District is no doubt a heavily touristed area, but to miss it on a trip to Japan would simply mean that your trip is culturally incomplete.

the land: The Kinki District lies in a triangle of 3 bodies of water; along the N coast is the Sea of Japan, on the SW is the Inland Sea and the SE is bordered by the Pacific. The N coast is on the fringe of the Hakusan Volcanic Zone which continues inland until it reaches the tall and rugged Chugoku Mts. approaching in a N-eastward direction. The Chugoku Mts. tail off and there is a small basin between them and the Tanba Mts. further to the NE. The Tanbas are much less rugged and form many high plateaus. At the E foot of this range is Lake Biwa (674 sq km), the largest lake in Japan. The main body of the Kinki District lies between these 2 mt. ranges and the Kii Mts. extending from Shikoku beneath the Naruto Straits and across the Kii Peninsula. This area is generally low and dotted with numerous plains and basins, the main ones being those of Kyoto and Osaka. Flowing through the Kyoto and Osaka basins out to the Inland Sea is the Yodo-gawa. Now used for hydroelectricity and irrigation, it was at one time a major communication and transportation link for the region.

climate: The central part of Kinki around Osaka has a climate dominated by the Inland Sea. It is mild for most of the year, and as you move further inland there is a greater range in temperature between summer and winter. Kyoto can experience snow in winter but it is generally short lived, while Osaka normally remains snow free. Kyoto's average summer temperature is 28 C. The S half of the Kii Peninsula below Ise is temperate but has much more rain than the remainder of Kinki, especially during the summer. In N Kinki across the Chugoku Mts., the climate is characteristic of the coast along the Sea of Japan. The winters are bitter and snowy. The best time, comfort-wise, to see Kinki is in the spring and autumn.

economy: The coastal area centered around Osaka is Japan's second-largest industrial zone. Japan's modern industrial furnace roars here. The results are all manners of heavy industry including steel mills, ship building, automobile production and chemical manufacturing. Kobe, Japan's most important port in tonnage, ships what the area produces. The economy is the factory, and the factory is the core of existence. The land and the people are secondary, viewed only as raw materials to make the factories grow. All of the farm villages in a great arc stretching from Kyoto to Okayama are being steadily sucked into the great factory complexes. These farms traditionally produced fruits, vegetables and flowers but the truck farmers are becoming city commuters and their agricultural life is terminating. The Kii Peninsula, especially in the S, is still holding on. The abundant summer rains and fertile soil combine to form the perfect conditions for large forests. Cryptomeria and cypress are the main trees harvested and lumbering is still an important source of income. The growing of mandarin oranges, deep sea fishing and pearl oysters are still quite healthy family-run businesses. The mountainous interior and the coast along the Japan Sea are not industrialized. Cattle raising, rice farming and cottage industries provide most economic activities, although the young men and women so desperately needed to keep them alive are siphoned off more and more by the industrial cities along the Inland Sea.

getting there: Rail service is particularly well developed through the Osaka/Okayama region of the Kinki District. The *shinkansen* stops at all the main cities while the Tokaido and San Yo main lines meet at Osaka to offer innumerable expresses E and W respectively. The Kii Peninsula is entirely looped by the Kisei Line. Kyoto is also serviced by the *shinkansen* as well as the Hokuriku Line converging upon it from the NE and the San-In Line from the west.   *by air:* Osaka has an international airport with flights from all over the world. ANA, JAL and TOA have connecting flights to all of Japan's domestic airports. The Kii Peninsula has 2 domestic airports; one in the N just a few km SE of Osaka and one at Shirohama on the SW coast. The airports at Tottori and Fukui on the Japan Sea border the Kinki District on the NW and NE and provide domestic air service to the cities of this region.   *by bus:* The Tokyo-Nagoya and Nagoya-Kobe Expressways are the main highway arteries of S Kinki. JNR highway express buses make this journey around the clock. Route 24 leads to Kyoto from Nagoya via Gifu and skirts the eastern shore of Lake Biwa. Route 27 heads N from Kyoto, deep into Hyogo Prefecture and connects at Maizuru, a main terminal for rail, land and ferry connections N and S along the Sea of Japan.   *by ferry:* Osaka/Kobe are the main ferry ports in S Kinki. From here, there are numerous coastal ferries heading E to Tokyo and then to points N all the way to Hokkaido. Others plough W to Shikoku, including port cities along the Inland Sea and some head S to Kyushu and then to Okinawa. Maizuru, in Hyogo Prefecture in the western extremity of Wakasa Bay, has a ferry route running NE to Niigata and then continuing to Otaru in Hokkaido.

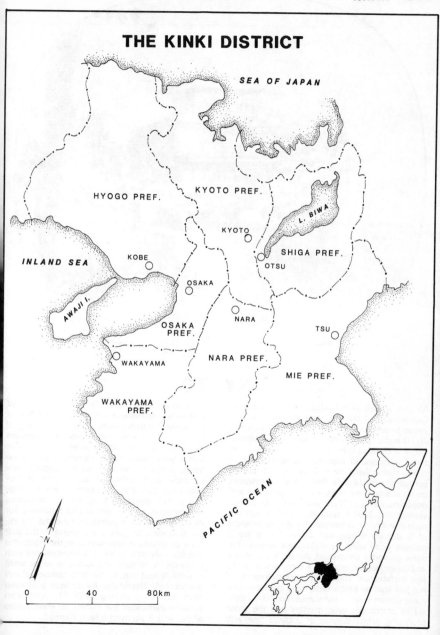

THE KINKI DISTRICT

SEA OF JAPAN

HYOGO PREF.

KYOTO PREF.

L. BIWA

KYOTO

SHIGA PREF.

OTSU

INLAND SEA

KOBE

OSAKA

AWAJI I.

OSAKA
PREF.

NARA

TSU

WAKAYAMA

NARA PREF.

MIE PREF.

WAKAYAMA
PREF.

PACIFIC OCEAN

N

0   40   80km

KYOTO

All the guidebooks lead to Kyoto (Western Capital) pop. 1,500,000, and so they should. Japan's semi-governmental tourist agencies, JNTO and JTB, provide volumes of pamphlets, maps and brochures relating to Kyoto, and travel agencies all over the world attempt to direct their clients here. It is an overflowing cornucopia of Japan's finest, and superlatives go on and on. The number of things to see and do is staggering. There are over 200 Shinto shrines and 1600 + temples, 30 of which are main administrative temples for the major sects of Buddhism throughout Japan. There are 3 palaces once used by Tokugawa Ieyasu, the most powerful shogun of Japan, 9 museums and countless gardens. Yet, Kyoto, with all of its fine architecture and visual accouterments, is not just another pretty face; there is deeper and more vibrant creative substance. For 1000 years, skilled craftsmen, wise masters and the most promising prima donnas of Japan's fine arts

have been lured here. The deep impress of culture and refinement is indelible. A long line of Japanese emperors were enthroned here, and the city retains a myriad of festivals, customs and industries from feudal times. In diminutive home workshops, down narrow, cobblestone alleys, some no wider than a footpath, one happens upon artistic products such as lacquerware, cloisonne, damascene, kimono fabrics, pottery, porcelain, fans, dolls, embroideries and bamboo ware. Kyoto is also renowned for its *noh* and *kabuki* theaters, and the last 2 traditional schools for geisha are found in the soft glow of lantern-lit side streets in the Pontocho and Gion sections. Kyoto is a smorgasbord with every dish a delicacy; the idea is to savor small mouthfuls and not to become uncomfortably overstuffed. Thankfully, Kyoto was preserved from bombing during WW 11. American scholars persuaded the military to leave Kyoto alone, and it survived intact. Karma?

getting there: Kyoto is a swirling hub of railway traffic. Ninety super expresses (longest wait between trains 16 min) streak from Tokyo to Kyoto. The Hikari and Kodama *shinkansen* make the trip in less than 4 hours. Express trains running E from Kyushu (Nagasaki) are fast, frequent and plentiful. Kyoto is the starting point of the San-In Main Line to Shimonoseki and the Nara Line, reaching that city in just one hour. *by air:* Osaka Airport services Kyoto. The flight from Tokyo is one hr and then a bus ride into Kyoto is 75 minutes. There is really no time or money saved in flying rather than training, especially when you consider connection times from the airports. To reach Kyoto from the far reaches of the archipelago such as from Tohoku or Okinawa, a flight might be advisable. But for any travel up to 500 km, take the train. *by road:* There is an expressway linking Kobe and Tokyo/Nagoya/Kyoto/Osaka. Hitchhikers: post yourselves at main entranceways and get off at rest stops to talk your way onward. It is advisable to carry a sign with your destination written in Japanese since you cannot hitch on the expressway itself. To avoid getting lost, take a train or bus to the outskirts of the city where the maze of streets and intersecting highways is less confusing. *by bus:* JNR operates buses connecting Tokyo/Nagoya/Kyoto/Osaka. These buses operate at various times during the day, with one making the Tokyo-Kyoto run at night. The night bus leaves Tokyo at 2300 arriving in Kyoto the next morning at 0745. It departs from Kyoto at 2200 and arrives in Tokyo at 0645. Reservations are a must with a reserved seat adding Y1500 to the basic bus fare. The TICs in Kyoto and Tokyo offer a mimeographed sheet explaining these services. Reservations can be made through any travel agency or JTB. The terminals are located at the S side of the Yaesu exit of Tokyo Eki, and at the W side of the Karasuma exit, Kyoto Eki.

Kyoto information: Kyoto has a TIC (Tourist Info. Center) and it is the wisest first stop for any traveler or tourist. (Open 0900-1700, closed Sat. afternoons, Sundays and holidays). The multilingual staff offers excellent maps and brochures covering the many facets of a stay in Kyoto. Fortunately, unlike the Tokyo TIC they will also make reservations for both travel and accommodations, offering a list of reasonably priced lodgings throughout the area. Sometimes all of the information available is not on display, so if you have any particular query, don't be afraid to ask. They have file cabinets full of mimeographed material just for this purpose. The TIC is

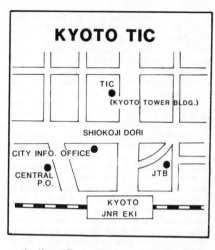

at the Kyoto Tower Bldg., Higashi-Shiokojichu, Shimogyu-ku, tel: (075) 371-5649. It is within 5 minutes walk of Kyoto Eki (see map). While at TIC (also at Tokyo TIC) be sure to pick up a copy of *Kyoto Monthly Guide*. It gives a detailed description of the happenings slated in Kyoto for the coming month, along with other useful phone numbers and addresses. Another useful publication is *Monthly Guide Kyoto*, stuffed with excellent general information. It also lists the outstanding features of the better-known shrines and temples. If you have a Japanese address where it can be mailed, send Y600 to *Monthly Guide Kyoto*, 30-5 Chashiri-cho, Arashiyama, Nishikyo-ku, Kyoto-shi. Before you even arrive in Japan you can get many useful brochures about Kyoto from any JNTO and most JAL offices abroad, free of charge. Another useful stop is the YMCA Thrift Shop, Muro-machi Dori, Demizu-agaru, Kamikyo-ku, Kyoto-shi 602. Many foreigners congregate here on the 3rd Sat. of each month both to socialize and to pick up some bargains at the flea market. They also publish *The Resident's Guide to Kyoto* which is an invaluable tool for anyone contemplating a long-term stay in Kyoto. It can be purchased for Y500 at the YWCA Thrift Shop, or upon request for Y1000 (domestic mail) or Y1500 (foreign airmail). For more travel information see ''services'' at the end of the Kyoto chapter.

getting around: Intra-urban bus lines travel every quarter of the city. Many start from and eventually return to Kyoto Eki. A wide-ranging central area has a fixed fare of Y90; the outskirts can be reached for about Y150. The city bus routes are shown on the back side of *Tourist Map Kyoto/Nara*, available from TIC, JNTO etc. The 2 most useful bus routes are 206 and 214, that run circular routes along the major thoroughfares, stopping at many of the most interesting sights. There are also tour buses that hit the high spots in both Kyoto and Nara. Information is available at TIC and reservations can be made at the English-speaking JTB office at Kyoto Eki, tel: 361-7241, the cheapest for the most limited tour is Y2500. Taxis are numerous but are an unnecessary expense unless time is essential. *on foot:* A combination of bus and a willingness to walk is the best and only real way of savoring the sights of Kyoto. You get so many freebies along the way to major attractions that you might normally miss—the side streets, small stalls and innumerable art shops of old Japan. These side trips down nameless streets often become the most memorable and enthralling part of your visit. Don't worry about getting lost, it's one of the best things that can happen to you. Drop into a coffee shop, relax, recoup your energies and then walk to the nearest bus stop. When a bus arrives, simply say "Kyoto Eki;" the answer will most likely be "hai." Make your way home from there. If that fails, hail a taxi (as common as ants at a picnic), show the driver a matchbook cover of your lodgings or merely point to it on your map and you'll be deposited home safe and sound. TIC offers a pamphlet called *Walking Tour Courses in Kyoto*. They can also give you information on bicycle rentals, but Kyoto is, after all, a large city with heavy downtown traffic. Bicycles save money but the congestion makes them unenjoyable.

SIGHTS

There is no Japanese city documented for tourist attractions as completely as Kyoto, even including Tokyo. Foreign and domestic JNTOs, JTBs and JAL offices, as well as larger travel agencies, have shelves and display cases veritably groaning with literature on Kyoto. The survey presented here is by no means exhaustive; it simply couldn't be. The main attractions are thus listed with particular emphasis placed on cultural importance, historic significance or special situations, and the lesser-known sights are suggested for their sometimes overlooked outstanding features. Kyoto can only be subjectively interpreted.

three palaces and a castle: Gosho (Kyoto Imperial Palace), the lovely Katsura Imperial Villa and Shugakuin Imperial Villa can only be visited after obtaining a pass from the Kyoto office of the Imperial Household Agency. Apply at the Imperial Park Office (at the entrance to Gosho Palace), Kyoto Gyoen-mai, Kamigyo-ku, Kyoto, tel: (075) 211-1211. Open 0900-1600, Mon. to Fri., 0900-1200 on Saturday. No visitors allowed Sat. afternoons, Sun., public holidays or from Dec. 25-Jan. 5. The Gosho is open to the general public for one week in early Apr. and in Nov.; the crowds are horrendous, so try to avoid these times. The Gosho allows large numbers of visitors, so just apply (passport a must) 20 min before the 1000 and 1400 tour times. Katsura and Shugakuin are slightly more difficult to see because the number of tourists allowed in is kept to a minimum. You must apply 2-5 days before your intended visit. This can be done by phone or mail; ask at any JTB or JNTO office. Pick up your pass 24 hrs in advance. Don't complain. Japanese tourists can wait 3 mos before being issued a pass. Remember that these tours are a privilege. You will be escorted by English-speaking guides. Stay with the group, feel free to ask questions, but maintain decorum.

Gosho (Kyoto Imperial Palace): Take Bus 206, 36, 214 or 215 one km N of Kyoto Eki to the Imperial Park. Here you will find the Gosho cushioned by acres of carefully raked white gravel. The original Gosho was built by Emperor Kammu further to the NW, but it was razed by fire in 1788. The present site was chosen and a new palace modeled after the old was built but it, too, met a fiery end. The present structure dates from 1854. Gosho is modestly furnished, delicately decorated, with simplicity its main charm. The gardens are graceful. The Shisenden is the main palace hall where the emperors were enthroned and contains the actual thrones from which they ruled. The throne area is draped in silk with the smaller area to the rear designed for the empress. The buildings are a triumph of the Heian Period, offering open, restful spaces rich in dignity. Shisenden is flanked on the L rear by Seiryoden and on the R by Kogosho. Seiryoden Hall is where the emperor worshipped his ancestors. The 16-petalled chrysanthemum is everywhere in evidence. If you have the inclination you can also visit Sento Imperial Palace. It is also located in the Imperial Park in the SE section. You must obtain a separate pass. The buildings which have been razed and rebuilt over

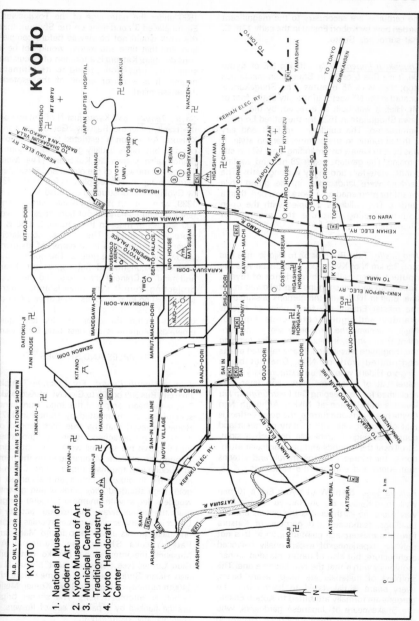

KYOTO

N.B. ONLY MAJOR ROADS AND MAIN TRAIN STATIONS SHOWN

1. National Museum of Modern Art
2. Kyoto Museum of Art
3. Municipal Center of Traditional Industry
4. Kyoto Handcraft Center

the centuries are secondary to the magnificent garden built by Kobori Enshu in the early 17th C. that surrounds Sento.

Shugakuin Imperial Villa: 10 km NE of Kyoto Eki. Take Bus 5 or 36 to Shugakuin-machi bus stop, then walk 15 minutes. The Shugakuin is located in the NE sector of the city at the foot of Mt. Hiei. It was built as a retreat by the Tokugawa Shogunate in 1629 for the retired Emperor Gomizuno-o. The buildings are light and airy with tea-rooms in the summer garden style. It was built to have a commanding view which still remains. The gardens cover 28 ha. and contain ponds, waterfalls and many walking paths. The gardens were landscaped in the grand style meant for promenading—more like a park than a garden. The buildings, coupled with the open country feeling, capture the essence of Shugakuin.

Nijo Castle: Take Bus 9 or 52 to Nijo-jo-mae bus stop 3.5 km N of Kyoto Eki. Nijo Castle was the opulent, artistically rich residence of Ieyasu Tokugawa and the shoguns that followed in his line. Built in 1603, with the gardens designed by the master Enshu, the focal point of Nijo is grandeur and dignity. Later, under Emperor Meiji, it became the temporary seat of government from where, ironically, the edict banning the shogunate was issued. Many talented artists contributed work on Nijo. One notable is Jingoro Hidari, who did an extraordinary wood panel cut of phoenixes here, and later was acclaimed for his Sleeping Cat (*nemuri-neko*) at Ieyasu's burial place at Nikko. Although Nijo Castle has moats and turrets, the overall effect is that of a quiet villa with military conquest and court espionage unthinkable on such a sight. Stroll over the grounds and pay particular attention to the filigree, carvings, murals and screens that adorn and enhance the structures.

Katsura Villa: 5 km W of Kyoto Eki, a 10 min walk from Katsura Eki on Hankyu Electric Railway. Here the earth itself is the canvas and the buildings, teahouses and gardens of Katsura form the masterpiece painted upon it. It is not only an experience of exceptionally balanced architecture, but also of nature blended so harmoniously with it that the two become one. The simplest of materials are used; every beam, every board is calculated to harmonize. The gardens are formally attributed to Kobori Enshu, the Shakespeare of Japanese gardeners, who designed and built them for Prince Toshito in

1590 under the patronage of the Tokugawas. Enshu placed 3 conditions on the Shogun: that the work would not be viewed before completion, and that time and money would not be a consideration. Katsura is a triumph of calculated simplicity, precision carried to its ultimate degree. It is a mirror image of the esoteric Japanese mind.

Saihoji Temple: SW Kyoto just N of Katsura on the Hankyu Electric Railway. Get off at Kami Katsura. Admission is restricted to 1000 people per day, but this is usually given a loose count. Saihoji, also known as Kokedera (The Moss Temple), is the sight of the oldest and rarest Zen garden in Japan. The temple was founded in 731 by Gyoki and reconstructed by Muso-Kokushi in 1339, who laid out its remarkable garden. The fancy brochures handed out here attest to over 100 species of moss in the garden, but 30 is a more likely number. The mosses completely cover the ground in a deep carpet of luxuriant yellow and varicolored greens. The pond in the center is so constructed that it spells out "heart and mind" in Chinese characters, and the rocks projecting from it symbolize islands where sailors rest on long voyages. Just after a rain or morning mist, the garden is dazzling. The droplets capture the color and drip like liquid emeralds. Morning is the best time for a visit.

TEMPLES AND SHRINES

East and north Kyoto: For Chion-in Temple take city Bus 300 or 205 to Gion NE of Kyoto Eki. This is the head temple of the Jodo (Pure Land) sect of Buddhism initiated by Honen in 1175. Honen believed that the true path hinged on simplicity. He preached "return to ignorance" meaning that the spiritual world was not found through the intellect. Meditating upon the name of Buddha was the main requirement. Chion-in is painted in dazzling colors and accented in gold. High standard *shoji* screens and gigantic wooden doors with mammoth metal hinges mark the entranceway. The religious activity at Chion-in is very active with ceremonies occurring daily. In this area is also found Maruyama Park, Yasaka Shrine, the Municipal Art Museum, the international Miyako Hotel and Gion Corner (see "entertainment"). Due N also Heian Shrine built to commemorate the 1100th birthday of Kyoto in 1895. Komei, Meiji' father, is entombed here. The shrine, bright orange flanked by a painted sea of flowers, is spectacularly picturesque.

a stone mason's back-yard shop near the Shisendo

Ginkakuji (Silver Pavilion): Continue 3 km further N from Choin-in on Bus 300 to Ginkakuji-mae. The Silver Pavilion (though there is no silver in evidence) was built by Yoshimasa Ashikaga as a shogun's retreat in 1482, and upon his death became a temple. The garden, designed for moon viewing, was built by Soami. High officials came here to practice esotericism in the form of incense buring and the tea ceremony. The tiny tea room in Togudo Hall, believed to be the oldest in Japan, serves as the classical example. In the general vicinity is Kyoto University and Yoshida Shrine.

Shisendo: From the Silver Pavilion continue further N to the slopes of Mt. Uryu and you'll reach Shisendo, the Hermitage or Poet's Retreat (Bus 5 or 36 from Kyoto Eki). The Shisendo was founded in 1631 by Jozan Ishikawa, a one-time commander of the shogun who turned his attentions to poetry and artistic pursuits. The Shisendo is quiet, unobtrusive and although well known, not heavily tourisited. The garden is simply raked sand. A _sozu,_ a type of water-propelled bamboo mallet, beats rhythmic, poetic, endless time upon the rocks. This area has a countrified feeling. Numerous craftsmen make their shops on the steep hillsides around Shisendo. Curiosity opens many doors. Listen for the sound of hammers and follow your ears to stone masons or woodworkers, as temple building is a specialty of the area. Notice back-yard lots of trees girdled with wire pressing hard plastic strips into the bark of trees. As the trees grow, the logs are indelibly marked (an example of Japanese artisans giving nature a hand and also helping their bank accounts). They are considered aesthetically beautiful and are used in the best construction, especially for _toko-noma_ and family alters. _Basho-an:_ On the grounds of Kompukuji Temple on the nearby slopes of Mt. Hiei high on a hill overlooking the city, is a small thatch-roofed cottage once used by the haiku poet Basho in 1670. It became derelict and fell into disrepair until Buson, another haiku poet, reconstructed it in 1776 in memory of Basho. It is a lovely small hideaway, perfect for artistic contemplation. It is still used by the disciples of the poet Gekko for recitals and meditative _sake_ drinking. On the grounds are stones inscribed with Basho's poetry. The most touristed facility in this section of Kyoto is Shugakuin Villa. If this is your primary destination, check out these other sights for beauty in a setting of peace and quiet.

extreme NE Kyoto: For a bucolic flavor and less crowded temples, take Bus 18 from Kyoto Eki to Ohara. The main temple here is Jakko-in. Since 1185 it has served as a hermitage for royal princesses seeking the religious life. The head nun has always been from the royal family. The temple displays paper screen panels depicting episodes from the classic _Tale of Heike._ The garden of Jakko-in is deep, dark and rich. A poem in appreciation of it was written by Isamu Yoshii:

"The deepest of all solitudes
in this transitory world
We find here
in the moss-covered world of Jakko-in."

West Kyoto: Kinkakuji Temple is located in NW Kyoto; take Bus 204 or 214 to Kinkakuji Michi. Or take Bus 26 from Kyoto Eki to Tamagoe, and _norikae_ (change) to Bus 59. Yet another alternative is to take Bus 12 or 59 from Sanjo Keihan directly to Kinkakuji-mae. Kinkakuji (Gold Pavilion) is one of the most visited temples in Kyoto and for good reason. Whether you perceive it to be outlandish or intoxicatingly beautiful, it is by all measures astounding. This 3-storied pavilion is entirely covered with gold foil. On its roof perches a golden phoenix which is especially symbolic. Kinkakuji was deliberately burned to the ground by one of its priests. A book about this tragic episode was written soon after by Yukio Mishima. It is an insightful psychological study of the reasons behind the priest's rash act. An exact replica was erected in 1955. The original temple dating from 1397 was built by the shogun Yoshimutsu as a retirement villa where he pursued a life of luxury and aesthetics. Though the gardens offer delights of their own, the eye is attracted to the pavilion itself. It overpowers rather than blends with its surroundings and titillates rather than soothes the mind.

Ryoan-ji: Temple of the Peaceful Dragon. Bus 59, just one km S of Kinkakuji. The ultra-famous garden at this temple is the epitome of the adage that beauty is in the eye of the beholder. Proponents of its garden of 15 stones in white sand arranged in the groupings of $5-2-3-2-3$ consider it the ultimate conceptualization of Zen. Its detractors see it as 15 ragged rocks in dirty grey gravel. The temple was founded in 1473 by Katsumoto Hosokawa and the garden is the masterpiece of Soami, completed in 1499. It is so contrived that viewed from any vantage point there is always one rock hidden from view. Interpretations of the garden have been offered for 500 years, but as in the Zen philosophy, the answer lies within. The garden is fondly called Kutei, "Garden of Emptiness" or derisively, "The Nothing Garden." Pamphlets handed out on the premises gush with romantic interpretations. Read them; make your own decisions. Then, while contemplating, use them to sit on. Don't make the mistake of rushing through the grounds to see just the Zen garden. The remainder is lovely and can be appreciated often more so than the Zen garden itself.

Ninna-ji Temple: 1.5 km S of Ryoan-ji. Begun in 886, this is one of the headquarters of the Shingon sect. Until the Meiji Restoration, Ninna-ji always had an imperial prince as the head abbot. The cherry trees growing on its grounds are indigenous to this area only. They are short and thick, bearing many petals during cherry blossom season. In mid-April, this is one of the most frequented cherry blossom viewing areas in Kyoto.   _Tenmangu Shrine:_   One km E of Ninna-ji. This shrine is famous for its festival, _Tenjin Matsuri,_ held on July 24-25. It is one of the greatest festivals in Japan. The main feature is a boat procession on the Yodo River. Dances, musical entertainment and puppet shows are all part of the festival. Arrive early to get a choice spot on the river bank.

the zen garden of Ryoanji

Central Kyoto around Kyoto Station: Nishi-Hongan-ji Temple, 500 m NW of Kyoto Eki, is the headquarters and founding temple of the Jodo Shinshu sect established by Shinran (Kenshi-Daishi) in 1224. This sect disregards celibacy in the priesthood, abstinence from meat and asceticism. Buddhism for the common man, it has one of the largest followings in Japan. Nishi-Hongan-ji is a classic example of Buddhist architecture. It is open for visiting 4 times a day at 1000, 1100, 1330 and 1430. Make application for entry at the temple office. The temple buildings, many named for their predominant artistic motif, contain some of the finest paintings in Japan, with literally dozens being considered National Treasures. An example is Daishon Hall, originally part of Hideyoshi's Fushimi Castle, brought to the temple grounds in 1632. The carvings on the main gate, *Shikya-kumon,* are excellent examples of the artistry of Jimgoro Hidari. Hiunkaku Pavilion in the SE corner of the grounds is 3-storied, each floor housing superb works of art. See the painting of Mt. Fuji on the 3rd floor done by Kano Motonobu; kneel down to get the best perspective. There are 2 excellent *noh* stages on the grounds.

Higashi-Hongan-ji temple: Located 500 m N of Kyoto Eki, is the Otani headquarters of the Jodo-Shinshu sect. In 1602, Ieyasu granted permission for its founding in order to weaken the growing strength of the original sect. Most buildings, except for the Main Hall and Founders Hall, are closed to the general public. Apply one day in advance to get permission to view all of the buildings. The Daishido (Founder's Hall) is the double-roofed structure opposite the main gate. Inside are portraits of all of the head abbots of the sect, including a self-portrait of Shinran himself. The 2 temples combine to exhibit some of the most precious Kano-school art in Japan. The gigantic main structure at Nishi-Hogan-ji with its towering supports and curving roof is the largest wooden structure in Kyoto and second largest in all of Japan (the largest is Taidoji, housing the Daibutsu in Nara).

Sanjusan Gendo: Ten min walk E of Kyoto Eki. Sanjusan (33) Gendo was so named because of the 33 spaces between the pillars supporting the elaborate main building. These pillars were at one time ornately decorated, but age has faded most of the work. The main structure is approximately 120 m long. The original was commissioned in 1164, but the present building dates from 1266. Sanjusan Gendo is the repository for the famous 1000-handed Kannon (Buddhist deity of mercy). It sits 3.3 m high and was carved

the 1000 kannon's of Sanjusan Gendo

by Tankei in 1254 when he was over 80 years old. Surrounding this main Kannon are 1000 smaller gilded Kannons, all in various poses. If this is not enough to overwhelm you, go to the back and you'll see statues of the "28 Faithful Followers." A mixture of fantasy and spiritual ecstasy, these statues are humanoids with animal features and their expressions, captured in wood, are unforgettable. In Jan. of every year, there is a *toshiya* (archery contest) held along the back veranda.

WALKING TOURS

The best plan for Kyoto is to have no plan at all. Of course you'll want to see the major temples and shrines, but 2 days of guided tours and jostling crowds and you'll reach the saturation point. So much the better, because it will free you to be your own guide. All sections of the city are safe, both day and night. Choose small side streets instead of larger ones. Each has its own treasure or curiosity. You'll come across private gardens, unobtrusive mansions, curio shops, mini-temples and bleating, garish discos. A good locale for meandering is around the Daikoku-ji Temple just E of Kinkakuji in an area called Nishijin. Here you'll find tiny shops where fine silks, embroideries and textiles are produced for the finest kimonos in Japan. To the NE around Ginkakuji, stroll around the old canal on a path called "The Philosopher's Pathway." Here old Kyoto unfolds with sedate, tiled houses and quiet secluded gardens.

a *maiko* (apprentice *geisha*)

<u>*Gion Corner:*</u> At Yasaka Kaikan Hall (Bus 206 to Gion) is a potpourri of Japanese art and entertainment designed for the tourist. But don't let this dissuade you, as Gion is unique in Japan. At this one stop, you can see the tea ceremony, flower arranging, geisha performances, court music, *kyogen* farces and *bunraku* puppet performances. There is English commentary and all of the performers and artists are top professionals offering authentic renditions in their fields. Gion lacks the charm of intimately viewing these aesthetics, but it is convenient— like a one-a-day vitamin capsule. Shows take place twice daily at 2000 and 2110, Mar.-Nov. 29; admission Y1500.

<u>*Toei Uzumusa Movie Village:*</u> Only 5 min walk from Uzumusa Eki on the Keifuku RR Arashiyama Line. Hollywood sets, Japanese style. Most sets depict feudal Japanese life with castles, villages, farmhouses, samurai residences, etc. Good for families. Open 0930-1700, Apr. to Nov.; 1000-1600, Dec. to March. Closed Dec. 21 to Jan. 3. Admission Y500 weekdays, Y600 Sun. and holidays.

<u>*arts, crafts and shopping:*</u> Matching Kyoto's extraordinary wealth of temples and shrines is its wealth of accomplished craftsmen and artists. On almost any street you can find shops selling the best in traditional arts with many of the artisans on the premises. Again there are so many that an exhaustive list would be impossible. It is better just to wander around and to enter when a display catches your fancy. Before embarking on a shopping spree it is best to acquaint yourself with quality work and to have an approximation of the cost. Most large *depato* have a floor for traditional works, and visiting 2 or 3 will give you an idea of what's offered in a nutshell. It is also wise to visit a few handicraft centers and museums before you start reaching for your wallet. Keep in mind that, as always, you will not be cheated, but the fact that the article is made in Kyoto will always add to the price. For very expensive yet exquisitely fashioned articles, visit the shopping arcades of the Miyako, Kyoto and International Hotels. For a walking course and window shopping try: 1) Both sides of Shijo St. from the Yasaka Shrine W to Daimaru Dept. Store; 2) Shinkyogoku Arcade parallel to Kawaramachi St.; 3) Teramachi St. from Marutamachi down to Shijo St.; 4) Nawate St., Shinmozen and Furumonzen Sts. for curios and antiques; 5) the N side of Gojo St. between Higashiyama St. and Kawaramachi Street. For a jam-packed day where you can see

the famous balcony of
Kiyomizu Temple

Kyoto's best works on display, take Bus 206 to Heian Shrine. Here in a cluster are some of the best art works and exhibits that Kyoto has to offer. Just S of Heian adjoining the grounds themselves are the Municipal Center of Traditional Industry, The Kyoto Museum of Art, The National Museum of Modern Art and (one min) N across Kumano Jinja-mae is Kyoto Handicraft Center.

Kyoto Handicraft Center: A heavily touristed, must-see art establishment. A retail cooperative of Kyoto's foremost shops and artists make up its several floors. Here you can see the artists making pottery, silks, damascene, lacquerware, woodblock prints, dolls, etc. Most stalls sell authentic works, but there is always a sprinkle of a few selling junk. Even if you don't wish to buy it is a very worthwhile experience watching the artists at work. *Kyoto Dento Sanyo Kaikan:* (Kyoto Center of Traditional Industry). Although you can watch many traditional arts being made here as at the Handicraft Center, this establishment is more of a museum. Just across from the Museum of Modern Art, you can spot it by its distinctive curved wall sweeping upward to the 2nd floor. Some of its most fascinating exhibits are the long, thin corridors used as shops in traditional Kyoto homes and colloquially known as *unagi-no-nedoko* (eel's bedrooms). Open daily except Wed., 0900-1700, Y200. After visiting these 2 establishments you should have a good overview of what Kyoto has to offer.
Kyoto Museum and National Museum: If you still have energy left to be overwhelmed by masterpieces, either or both of these are certainly worth a visit. The Kyoto Museum exhibits contemporary works of Japanese artists skilled in the Kyoto school of painting. The National Museum also features contemporary artists, both Japanese and foreign (100 yrs old is considered contemporary). The Japanese ceramics collection is outstanding.

pottery: Visit Teapot Lane, a small roadway leading to Kiyomizu Temple. Take Bus 206 to Kiyomizu-machi and follow Higashiyama Dori (street) towards Kiyomizu Temple. It is jampacked with pottery shops of all kinds with goods ranging from bargain souvenirs to cherished works of art. While in the area, visit Kiyomizu Temple itself, famous for its wooden veranda suspended over a deep gorge, and its panorama as the city blends into the western horizon. The Japanese saying, "To jump from the balcony of Kiyomizu" is used when one must make a difficult or daring decision. Also try Kawai Kanjiro's House (board Bus 214 to Umamachi Bus Stop, then 50 m on foot). The workshop and house of this world-famous potter are preserved. The house itself is typical Japanese, and the pottery exudes with the spirit of the master. Centrally located and often overlooked, open Tues. to Sun., 1000-1630, Y500. *markets:* There are 3 monthly flea markets worth visiting. Go early for the best selections and don't be suckered into thinking that the old dusty tea cup for Y100 is really a priceless antique. The merchants know the price of things. At: YWCA Thrift Shop, 3rd Sat. of the month; Toji Temple, 21st of the month; Kitano Shrine, 25th of the month.

KYOTO FESTIVALS AND EVENTS

Kyoto is so rich in culture and color that there is an event, festival or happening almost every day of the year. For a month-to-month list, be sure to pick up copies of *Kyoto Monthly Guide* and *Monthly Guide Kyoto* (previously mentioned under "Kyoto Information"). The following list deals primarily with the larger events, though smaller lesser known ones are perhaps even more interesting.

Jan. 8-12: Toka Ebisu (10th day festival honoring Ebisu). Ebisu is one of the 7 gods of fortune and his image is seen in the *takara-bune* (treasure ship). The patron of prosperity, he is especially important to businessmen. Thousands of merchants turn out at Imamiya Ebisu Shrine to pay homage.

Jan 15: Toshiya (archery contest) at Sanjusangendo Hall. This archery contest dating back to the 16th C attracts archers from all over Japan. The winner is the one who can shoot the most arrows over the length of the corridor of the back hall (120 m). The reigning champion is one Daihachiro Wasa who, in 1696, shot 13,053 arrows, hitting the mark with over 8000.

Feb. 25: Baikasai (plum blossom festival) at Kitano Shrine. The plum blossoms are in full bloom and an open air tea ceremony is held in honor of Sugawara Michizane, the patron of scholars and literature. The shrine precincts are lined with flea market stalls.

Mar. 15: Nehan-e at Tofukuji and Seiryosi Temples. Scrolls depicting the life of Gautama Buddah are displayed at Tofukuji on the anniversary of the sage's death at age 79. At Seiryoji, 3, 7 m long pine torches, are burned to ward off evil spirits and to predict the fertility of the coming year.

Apr. - May: Miyako Odori. This is a cherry blossom dance held at the Kabureno Theater in Gion where the colorful dancers are accompanied by traditional music played on *samisen* and drums. 1st- and 2nd-class ticket holders also take part in a huge tea ceremony.

Apr. 2nd Sun.: Yasurai Matsuri at Imamiya EbisuShrine. Ancient beliefs held that plaques summoned by demons swept the land after cherry blossom time. Crowds gather together ot watch "dancer demons" in the hope that the festivities will placate them. There are numerous other dance festivals in and around the city. Most are worth a visit, so check to see where and when they are offered. TIC is the best source of information.

Apr. 21-29: Mibu Kyogen. At Mibu Shrine daily from 1300. Pantomime farces dating back to the 13th C are portrayed at the rate of about 20 per day. These short earthy counterparts to *noh* are universal and easily understood although English translations are available. The most famous *kyogen* skit is the plate-breaking farce called *horoku-wari*.

May, 3rd Sun.: Mifune Matsuri (Boat Festival) at Kurumazaki Shrine. Along the banks of the Oi River at Arashiyama, this is a re-enactment of the Heian Period when the emperor and nobles floated down the river in magnificent barges, soaking up the balmy weather. Today the boats carry dancers·and musicians who perform on the 2 lead boats which are fashioned into the shapes of a dragon and phoenix.

May 5: Fujinomori Matsuri at Fujinomori Shrine. This ancient horse race dates back to the 10th C. The gaily costumed riders gallop around the precinct grounds. The same festivities also take place at Kamikamo Shrine.

May 15: Aoi Matsuri (Hollyhock Festival) at Kamikamo and Shimokamo Shrines. This is one of the major Kyoto festivals, dating from the 6th century. For a time it went unobserved, but then was revived in 1885. The angry gods of these shrines raked the land with horrible storms. To appease them, a royal messenger made a pilgrimage to show homage and this is re-enacted to this day. Starting at 1000, a royal messenger and 300 courtiers leave the Imperial Palace in procession. They proceed to Shimokamo Jinja and commence ceremonies at 1140. At 1400 they head for Kamikamo Jinja and perform the rites again at 1530. The procession is spectacularly ornate and includes pages, standard bearers and guards all in authentic costumes. The route is lined with droves of visitors, so come early to get a choice spot. Seats are also available at the Palace for Y500 (reservations a must).

June 1-3: Takigi-noh. A torchlit performance of *noh* is held at Heian Shrine beginning at 1800. The outdoor atmosphere is turned magical by the flickering light of the torches used to illuminate the stage. The effect is so intense that even the non-aesthete will be drawn into the spectacle. Admission Y200-Y300; book well in advance.

Jul. 1 - Aug. 31: Ukai (cormorant fishing). Displayed every moonless night on the bank of the Oi River in Arashiyama.

Jul. 16-24: Gion Matsuri. Centered around Yasaka Shrine, this is Kyoto's biggest blowout of the year, so accommodations are very tight.

The festival began in the 9th C when the priests of Yasaka Shrine organized the populace to accompany huge shrine wagons to appease the gods and lift a plague that was paralizing the city. The parade of floats today is just magnificent. There are 2 types: *yama*, which are carried on the shoulders of men and depict ancient legendary characters, and *hoko*, which are massive ornamental floats mounted on 4 large wheels and pulled by ropes. Often-times the *hoko* carry orchestras and dancers. The main parade occurs on Jul. 17 from 0900 to 1100. When the entire city joins in, many people display their ancient family heirlooms and treasures. There is no better time to glimpse the treasure chest which is Kyoto. The crowds are literally and figuratively staggering.

Aug.: This month is marked by the *O-Bon* (departed souls) festival, (see "General Introduction") held throughout Japan, but especially observed in Kyoto. The month is punctuated with numerous rites and ceremonies, many employing fire as a remembrance of departed souls and as ritual purification. TIC can provide invaluable information on the locations and times of the most spectacular events. The following lists the main ones only:

Aug. 7-10: *Toki Matsuri* (ceramics festival). All day along Gojo St. Ceramics from throughout Japan are overflowing on numerous stalls. The bargains and the bargaining for excellent works are astounding; it's one of the best times to purchase a sought-after ceramic artwork.

Aug. 15: *Daimonji Okribi*, on the slopes of Mt. Nyogatake. An enormous bonfire visible for kms is lighted in the form of the Chinese character *dai* (large). Other fire characters are also lit on the surrounding hills. The people of Kyoto watch from many vantage points throughout the city as the fires lick heavenward to light the paths of the souls of the dead as they return to the netherworld.

Aug. 23-24: *Jizo-ban.* Jizo Boasatsu is the guardian deity of children. Many temples throughout Kyoto offer lantern-lit festivities in his honor for the protection of their children. This is one of the most touching festivals in Japan. Almost every shrine and temple has a candle-lighting ceremony during August. Some of these are lit at Rokukaramitsu Temple and Higashi Otani. Floating paper lanterns are also sent down the river near Arashiyama and if time permits you should go one evening and participate in this magical time-honored tradition.

Oct. 10 - Nov. 6: *Kamogawa Odori.* Held at Kaburenjo Theater in Pontocho Ward. This is a fall rendition of the springtime Gion Festival, featuring once again dancing and classical music.

Oct. 22: *Jidai Matsuri* (festival (Festival of Historic Time). A huge procession almost 2 km long starts at the Imperial Palace and winds its way through the streets to Heian Shrine. The 2000 traditionally costumed participants celebrate the founding of Kyoto in 794, their costumes representative of the changing historical eras over the intervening centuries. The main procession begins its journey at 1000 and reaches Heian Shrine by 1530.

Oct. 22: *Kurama-no-Himmatsuri* (Great Fire Festival). At Kurama Village about 30 min by train from Kyoto Eki. The entire length of one of Kurama's narrow streets (leading to Yuki Shrine) is lined with blazing torches. The people of the village open their magnificently preserved homes to display family heirlooms that have been lovingly handed down over the centuries. When the last torch burns out, a priest cuts a rope strung across the entranceway to the shrine and the participants stampede to see the sacred rites and ceremonies. Arrive by 1800 and try to pick a spot where you won't be trampled during the frenzy.

Nov. 3-6: *Gion Odori* at Gion. This is a chance to see Kyoto's best *geisha* performing their entertaining arts. You can watch the entire repertoire of these facinating, lovely artists for only Y1000-Y1500.

Nov., 2nd Sun.: *Momiji Matsuri* (Maple Festival). At Arashiyama Park. The music and costumes of this festival date back to the 10th century. a boat parade down the Oi River is similar to that of the *Mifune Matsuri* held in May.

Dec. 1-26: *Kaomise* (Superstars). The most reknowned and celebrated *kabuki* actors make spotlight appearances at the Minamiza Theater. This event is reminiscent of bygone days when actors and authors renewed their contracts with theater managers at this time of year.

Dec. 21: *Shimai Kobo* at Toji Temple. This is the last memorial rite of the year dedicated to Kobo-Daishi, the great spiritualist and Buddhist saint, who founded Toji Temple. Large crowds visit the temple and enjoy shopping in the numerous stalls set-up in and around the precincts.

Dec. 31 - Jan. 1: *Okera Mairi* (at Yasaka Shrine): All day long women promenade down Shijo St. dressed in their finest kimono. The *geisha* of Kyoto attempt to visit all the tea houses in Gion and the Ponto-cho District. At night a huge fire is kindled at Yasaka Shrine. Worshippers try to carry a few embers home in earthen or metal pots with which to cook the first New Year's meal. The belief is that this sacred fire will ward off sickness during the coming year.

ACCOMMODATIONS

To handle the tremendous tourist flow into Kyoto, the city has an exceptionally wide range of accommodations, from ultra-luxury international hotels down to holes-in-the-wall. If you intend to visit Kyoto at any time during the major festivals, especially during April, it is best to book ahead. The Kyoto TIC will make reservations for you once you are in the city and will try to match your pocketbook with a suitable place to stay. Both the TICs in Tokyo and Kyoto readily hand out mimeographed sheets of budget accommodations. The following should at least give you a general idea of what's available and the price range.

Western-style: All of the following hotels offer services to assist the foreign guest, including guided tour reservations, international telephone and post office service and many brochures in foreign languages: Miyako Hotel, (ultra-luxury), Sanjo Keage, Higashiyama-ku, Kyoto 605, tel: (075) 771-7111, 20 min by car from Kyoto Sta., from Y6500; New Miyako Hotel, 17 Nishi Kujoin-cho, Minami-ku, Kyoto 601, tel: (075) 551-7111, one min walk from Kyoto Sta., from Y6000; Kyoto Grand Hotel, Horikawa Shiokoji, Simogyo-ku, Kyoto 600, tel: (075) 341-2311, 5 min walk from Kyoto Sta., from Y7500; Holiday Inn Kyoto, 35 Nishihiraki-cho, Takano, Sakyo-ku, Kyoto 606, tel: (075) 721-3131, 20 min by car from Kyoto Sta., from Y6500; Hotel Gimmond, Takakura Oike-dori, Nakagyo-ku, Kyoto 604, tel: (075) 221-4111, 10 min by car from Kyoto Sta., from Y6500; Kyoto Park Hotel, 6442 Sanjusan-gendo, Mawari-machi, Kyoto 605, tel: (075) 541-6301, 5 min by car from Kyoto Sta., from Y4500.

ryokan: Although offering an authentic Japanese experience, most of the *ryokan* in Kyoto are more expensive than the Western-style hotels, even with the price of 2 meals included, but there are a few exceptions: Hotel Sanoya, Higashi-no-Toin-dori, Shiokoji-agaru, Shimogyo-ku, Kyoto 600, tel: (075) 371-2185, Y8000-12,000; and Hiiragiya Ryokan, Fuyacho-Anegakoji-agaru, Nakagyo-ku, Kyoto 604, tel: (075) 221-1136, Y16,000-25,000.

reasonable ryokan: Rozankaku, Myohoin-Maekawa-cho, Higashiyama-ku, Kyoto 605, tel: (075) 561-4981, Y9000-11,000; Ichiume Ryokan, Higashi-Kiyamachi Gojo-sagaru, Shimogyo-ku, Kyoto, tel: (075) 351-9385, take Bus 215, 200 or 214 to Gojo (5th) Bus Stop, then one min walk, Y2000 per person; Sanyu, Kamogawasuji Shomen-agaru, Shimogyo-ku, Kyoto, tel: (075) 371-1968, take Bus 200 or 215 to Kawaramachi-Shomen Bus Stop, then a few min walk, Y1500 per person, and Yuhara, Kiyamachi-dori, Shomen-agaru, Shimogyo-ku, Kyoto, tel: (075) 371-9583, Bus 200 or 214 to Kawaramachi-Shomen, 3rd bus stop, then a 3 min walk, Y2500.

old standbys: The following 3 lodgings are unique; they have been used for years by budget travelers in Kyoto, so are well accustomed to dealing with foreigners. It is difficult to give them an actual category because they are a mixture of *ryokan*, private home and transient hotel, with some rooms available for long-term stay. What makes them most interesting is the other travelers that you will meet there. Many have been through Asia or in Kyoto for awhile and can give you the best first-hand travel information. It is well worth the time to go to any of these 3 places to talk to the guests and check out the bulletin boards, even if you don't intend on staying there. The directions given start from Kyoto Eki. The 1st is: Tani House, 8 Daitokuji-cho, Murasakino, Kita-ku, Kyoto, tel: (075) 492-5489, Bus 204, 214 or 222 to Funaoka Koen-mae Bus Stop (35 min), then a 2 min walk, Y900 for one person, Y1800 for 2. The one drawback with Tani House is that it is not centrally located and you must bus to and from there to tour Kyoto. The rooms are kept separate for men and women, but there are a few offered for couples, though you can't always count on them being vacant. The 2nd is: Uno House, 108 Maruta-machi-sagaru, Shin-Karasuma-dori, Nakagyo-ku, Kyoto, tel: (075) 231-7763, Bus 4, 14, 54, 200 or 215 to Kawaramachi-Maruta-machi near the SE corner of Kyoto Gosho. Y900 w/o meals or cooking facilities. Uno House is conveniently located within the city and Mrs. Uno is simpatico to foreigners. The 3rd choice is: Mr. Akira Tani's Home, 13 Inokuchi-cho, Kisshoin, Minami-ku, Kyoto, tel: (075) 681-7437, Bus 78 from Hachijo-guchi or Minami-guchi exit of JNR Kyoto Sta., 5 min walk from Nishi-Oji Kujo Bus Stop, Y800 per bed, dormitory style.

business hotels/reasonable Western-style: The following are a combination of business and reasonably priced Western-style hotels. For the most part the accommodations offered at each

shukubo (temple lodgings): A handful of Kyoto's temples (Zen only) open their doors to foreigners and Japanese alike. Along with the accommodations, vegetarian meals (_shojin ryori_) are also provided. The prices range from Y1500 w/o meals to Y5000 w/meals. This is an excellent opportunity to see the workings of Japanese Buddhism at close hand. TIC and JNTO provide a list of _shukubo_ and will help to make reservations.

YHs: There are 7 YHs located in and around Kyoto. The 2 closest to city center, which also means they are often booked solid, are: Higashiyama YH, 112 Shirakawabashi-goken-cho, Sanjo-dori, Higashiyama-ku, Kyoto 605, tel: (075) 761-8135, Bus 5 from Kyoto Sta., (20 min) then 5 min walk, 112 beds; and Matsusan YH, 331 Ebiya-cho, Sanjo-sagaru, Goku-machi, Nakagyo-ku, Kyoto 604, tel: (075) 221-5160, 15 min by streetcar from Kyoto Sta., 4 min on foot, 40 beds. The 5 others which are up to one hr away are Otsu YH, tel: (0775) 22-8009; Kitayama YH, tel: (075) 492-5345; Utano YH, tel: (075) 462-2288; Ohara YH, tel: (075) 744-2721; and Oharago YH, tel: (075) 744-2721.

PRACTICALITIES

food: Once again TIC is a good place to start. They offer a booklet entitled "Kyoto Gourmet Guide" that lists the full gamut of Kyoto's restaurants. To avoid high prices use common sense. Tips are given in the "food" chapter of the "General Introduction." Most importantly, to save money, avoid the restaurants in the large luxury-class Western hotels. The streets around all of the train stations have clean and inexpensive eateries with the dishes and prices displayed in the windows. Kyoto is also beset with Western fast-food chains. There is a McDonald's on Shiso-dori, a Kentucky Fried Chicken on Sanso-dori and there are numerous pizza parlors, ice cream and donut chains throughout the city. Many of the chain pizza parlors offer all you can eat from 1000-1400, Y500.

entertainment: Kyoto offers the full range of entertainment common to all Japanese cities. There are bar hostess clubs, strip joints, stand-up bars and _kissaten_ (coffee shops) that have all been described in the "General Introduction." You can try any of the bars at the larger hotels but they lack Japanese atmosphere and although they will not pad the bill, they will be expensive. Never enter a bar that employs a

would not be qualitatively different. Hokke Club in Kyoto, Nishi-deguchi Shomen, Kyoto, tel: (075) 351-1251, in front of Kyoto Sta., W exit; Kyoto Business Hotel, Oike-agaru, Kiyamachi, Nakagyo-ku, Kyoto, tel: (075) 222-1220, Bus 4 or 14 to Kawaramachi Nijo Bus Stop (20 min) then a 3 min walk, from Y4000; Traveler's Inn (Honkan), 91 Enshojicho, Okazaki, Sakyo-ku, Kyoto, in front of Heian Shrine Otori Higashi and Kyoto Municipal Museum of Art, tel: (075) 771-0225, Bus 5 to Heianjingu Bijutsukan-mae Bus Stop (25 min), then 3 min walk, Y3800; Kyoto Central Inn, Nishi-iru, Shijo Kawaramachi, Shimogyo-ku, Kyoto, tel: (075) 211-1666, Bus 4, 5, 14, 45 or 54 to Shijo Kawaramachi Bus Stop (10 min) then one min walk, from Y5100; Pension Utano, 110-5 Narutaki-honmachi, Ukyo-ku, Kyoto, tel: (075) 463-1118, Bus 25 to Narutaki-honmachi Bus Stop (35 min) then one min walk, single Y3900, breakfast Y500, dinner Y1200; and Kyoto YWCA (women only), Demizu-agaru, Muromachi-dori, Kamigyo-ku, Kyoto, Bus 2, 36 or 203 to Karasumano Shimochoja-machi Bus Stop (20 min), then 2 min walk, Y3500.

sidewalk barker. They will price gouge mercilessly and can be downright nasty. What makes
Kyoto unique is that there is a shrinking, yet
active and authentic, geisha community. Firstly
and simply a budget traveler cannot afford a
geisha. Geisha parties are designed for about 5
patrons with a bill easily reaching Y100,000. The
best tea houses are in effect private clubs and
you will be denied admittance unless you have
an introduction from a well-known patron. The
only reasonable chance of seeing a geisha or
maiko (apprentice geisha) is to be in the Gion
and Pontocho areas at 1500-1700 and after 1900
when many of these ladies are setting off for
their evening's work. The budget traveler can
see them perform during spring and autumn
festivals (see "Festivals") but there will be large
crowds and a lack of the cultured intimacy for
which they are famous. Some tours offer a
geisha party but at best they are a watered-
down facsimile.

services: The Kyoto Central P.O. (in front of W
exit Kyoto Eki) offers 24 hr, 7 days-a-week
service including *post restante*. It is possible to
receive and send overseas mail from other P.O.s,
but the central P.O. is more efficient and geared
toward the foreigner, even offering rates posted
in English. *medical services:* The Japan Baptist
Hospital, tel: (075) 781-5194 and the First Red
Cross Hospital have English-speaking doctors.
Many larger hotels also have doctors that will
make house calls. *guided tours:* Any of the
following can arrange foreign-speaking guided
tours: JTB tel: 361-7241, Fujita tel: 222-0121, and
Kinki Nippon Tourist tel: 222-1224. *foreign
exchange banks:* No problem. Get a full list from
TIC. *interpreters:* Both JTB and TIC can
arrange interpreters. Often-times these will be
students from the local universities who wish to
practice English. There may be an hourly charge,
but picking up the tab for the day's activities is
the usual payment. They will try very hard to
please you and show you sights that you might
miss. Giving them a small memento at the end of
the day is also a polite gesture. Often-times
these same students will babysit in the evening
(Y500 per hr) if you want to do the town without
the kids. Another language service is offered by
Tescort (free of charge). To arrange an interpreter for Kyoto, call (06) 445-6116 (an Osaka
number). *home visit program:* To visit a
Japanese home, contact Tourist Section, Dept.
of Cultural Affairs and Tourism, Kyoto City
Govt., Kyoto Kaikan, Okazaki, Sakyo-ku, Kyoto
tel: (075) 761-0016. TIC and JTB will also make
arrangements and although many of the host

families speak foreign languages it might be
wise to check first and, if they don't, take a
student interpreter. Always bring a small gift of
thanks for the host family. *general information:*
Besides TIC, try Kyoto City Information Office,
in front of Kyoto Eki, tel: 371-2108, hrs
0830-1700; JTB, in front of Kyoto Eki, tel:
361-7241; or the Kyoto Tourist Section,
mentioned under "home visit program."

museums: JNTO and TIC offer a brochure
listing the museums in Kyoto. Some are just
interesting while others, especially those that
give demonstrations, are fascinating. Pick and
choose for yourself, but some worthwhile ones
in Kyoto are: Kyoto Yuzen Dyeing Hall, Inaba
Cloisonne Factory and the Tatsumura Silk
Works. All offer demonstrations of the age-old
techniques employed in producing these fine
articles.

VICINITY OF KYOTO

Lake Biwa: The largest lake in Japan with a
circumference of 235 km, only 10 min by train
from Kyoto. Take the Keishan Line of the Keihan
Electric RR from Keihan Sanjo (Kyoto) to
Hama-Otsu, or JNR Kosei Line to Omi-Shiotsu
on the W shore of the lake. Lake Biwa's outline
roughly resembles the *biwa*, a Japanese instrument from which the name was taken. A combination of fact and tradition attests to the fact
that Lake Biwa, along with Mt. Fuji, was formed
in one cataclysmic eruption on a single night in
286 B.C. The lake has sweeping views and is
studded with islets. The most beautiful view
were selected in the 15th C. and named Omi
Hakkei, "The 8 Views of Omi." The selections
are now debatable. The lakeshore is also dotted
with temples, vilages, campgrounds and plenty
of *minshuku* and *ryokan*. Sightseeing boats are
plentiful in Otsu City.

Uji: A small town 15 km S of Kyoto; take the
JNR or Keihan Electric RR. This area is known
for producing the finest teas in Japan, which
can be purchased at the numerous teashops in
the downtown area. Visit Biodo-in Temple (10
min from Uji Eki), famous for its Phoenix Hall
(Ho-odo), and architectural representation of
the mythical bird descending to earth. A model
of the Ho-odo was presented at the World's Fair
of 1893, and is also the building depicted on the
Y10 coin. The airy temple is intriguing as it is

VICINITY OF KYOTO

SEA OF JAPAN

KUMIHAMA
TO TOTTORI
MINEYAMA
OKU-TANGO PEN.
AMANOHASHIDATE
TO OTARU (HOKKAIDO)
WAKASA BAY
MIYAZU
RT.27
TO TOTTORI
MAIZURU
RT.9
RT.27
TAKAHAMA
TO FUKUI
OBAMA
FUKUI PREF.
RT.303
OMI-SHIOTSU
GIFU PREF.
AYABE
IMAZU
HYOGO PREF.
KYOTO PREF.
TAKASHIMA
TO NAGOYA
SONOBE
RT.312
L. BIWA
KAMEOKA
MT. HIEI
HIKONE
KYOTO
YOKAICHI
TO OSAKA
OTSU
EXPWY.
SHIGA PREF.
OSAKA PREF.
ISHIYAMA
KIBUKAWA
UJI
RT.24
TSUGE
NARA PREF.
MIE PREF.
N

0   30   60km

April: Cherry Blossom time. Dates vary according to the weather, but the month of April marks exceptional festivities centered around cheery blossoms. The dates and sites of particular events are listed in Kyoto's visitor's magazines. If you intend to view the blossoms in and around Kyoto, try to schedule your trip for a weekday. Weekends bring out more people and picnickers than the blossoms themselves

Feb. 3-4: Setsubun, the end-of-winter celebration held throughout Japan, is particularly festive in the Kyoto area. The main objective is to visit a temple where *fuku mame* (beans) are cast about. The participants shout, *"Oni wa soto, fuku wa uchi."* ("In with good fortune, out with the devils.") Of particular interest is the demon-exorcising pantomine held at Rozan-ji Temple in Kyoto

reflected by the deep green pool at its entrance but the inside murals, ravaged by time, are losing their beauty. Vegetarian fare can be enjoyed at Manpuku-ji near Biodo-in on the temple grounds, or at a small restaurant near the gate.

Hozu Rapids: The Hozu Rapids boat trip is a 2 hr, 15 km trip down white water. Train on the JNR San-In Main Line, 22 km from Kyoto Eki to Kameoka. Direct bus is also available from Kyoto bus terminal. The boats are flat-bottomed craft, holding a dozen people and manned by 2 polemen and a helmsman. The descent from Kameoka to Arashiyama is spirited, exciting, but perfectly safe. Sunburn is the only danger. Take a plastic bag to protect cameras against spray. JTB offers a rapids-shooting tour from 1400-1700 on Tues., Thurs. and Sat., from April to October. Arashiyama is on the Oi River, close to where you disembark from the boats. Cormorant fishing is held every moonless night July-Aug., from 1900-2200.

Amanohashidate (the Bridge to Heaven): A fashionable resort in Hyogo Prefecture, known for its scenery. Located 80 km NW of Kyoto on the Sea of Japan. Train from Kyoto in 2 hrs 20 min, or from Osaka in 3 hrs 40 minutes. Amano-hashidate is one of 3 classical sightseeing spots in Japan, inevitably evoking nostalgia in older Japanese. It is no doubt beautiful, but a trip to Amanohashidate for its own sake is simply not worth it. If you intend to travel further along San-In, then by all means stop at Amanohashi-date. What you will see is a sandbar from 35-100 m wide going out to sea for 3.6 km. Big deal. But mythology says that this is the very spot where Izanagi and Izanami-no-mikoto, the Japanese gods of creation, stood while fashioning the islands of Japan. Japanese tourists bend over and stick their heads between their legs (not easy in a kimono) to get the proper perspective for seeing the bridge float to heaven. The dizzier you get, the more the bridge seems to float. No one assuming this undignified posture would ever admit that they didn't see it.

riding the Hozu Rapids

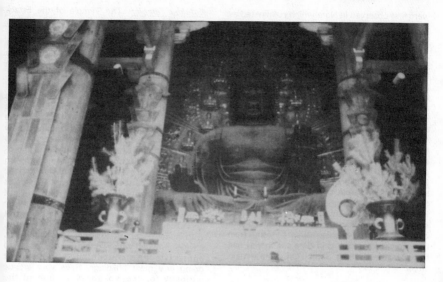

NARA

Means "Level Land." Pop. 250,000, Nara is situated in a basin of the former Yamato Province, "Land of Great Peace," now known as Nara Prefecture. Imperial Japan was born here 124 succeeding emperors ago on Feb. 11, 660 B.C. (legendary date). Jimmu Tenno, the grandson of Ninigi-no-Mikoto, who in turn was the grandson of the sun goddess Amaterasu, was enthroned here as Japan's first emperor. The crest of every mountain, the slope of every hill, the mute testimony of every rock, waterfall, rivulet and valley of Nara is indelibly connected to the dawn of Japanese civilization. To the Japanese, the Yamato Meguri (Yamato Pilgrimage) answers the questions of who we are, and where we began. Even the casual traveler, unversed in the mythical and ancient history of Japan, cannot help but be impressed by the wealth of architectural remains and relics of Japan's earliest civilization still preserved at Nara. Each year, 1,250,000 people come to Nara, mostly on commercialized, package tours. The surrounding area has been swallowed by massive industrialization, with smokestacks, ferro-concrete houses, and green fields turned to asphalt. But the essence of times past lingers; like meditation focus your eyes. The beauty comes when you look "into" not "at" what is offered.

history: Nara predates even Kyoto as the first permanent imperial court. For centuries the capital moved with each successive emperor, finally establishing itself just W of Nara at Heijokyo under the Empress Gemmyo in 710. There it remained until 784. The capital was finally established in Kyoto in 794, where it prospered for over 11 centuries. The dynasty's 84 yrs in Nara thus began what could really be termed "Japanese civilization." Here in the 8th C. were compiled the first history, book of poetry, chronicle of mythology and geographical treatise. The court was heavily influenced by China which also was the gateway for Mesopotamian and Greek culture. The arts, architecture, industry, food, dress, religion and almost every facet of life were Japanified here and flourished. The "Kingdom of the Land of Great Peace" reached its zenith. The spiritual, creative, political and artistic psyche of the Japanese people blended and solidified, the essence lasting to become the Japan we know today. The greatest and longest-lasting influence came from Buddhism. At first rejected by many nobles, it grew into prominence until it became the national religion, establishing itself in Nara. It was felt that Buddhism would keep the country safe and the rituals and festivals such as Bon were first observed in Nara which culminated as the paramount religious center with the casting of the great Daibutsu.

getting there: From Kyoto, take the Kinki Nippon RR to Nara in 33 min, Y600. One train departs every hour. The JNR offers trains from Kyoto, but they take one hr 10 min and aren't any cheaper. From Osaka take the Kinki Nippon RR in 31 min, Y650. One train per hour or by JNR from Osaka's Minatomachi Sta. to Nara in 40 minutes. *getting around:* City and tour buses run to all main sights from the railway stations, but a slow, leisurely walk is best. There are 2 ways to enjoy Nara. One is as a day-tripper from Kyoto, travel time a mere 40 minutes. This saves the rigamarole of moving accommodations, checking in, baggage, etc. The alternative is to lodge in Nara. This is better if you plan to spend 2 or more days taking in the sights, including the outskirts, and also saves the return train fare. To visit most sights in Nara one merely has to go eastward along Sanjo-Dori, Nara's main street.

TEMPLES OF NARA

Nara Park: The largest municipal park in Japan, covering 525 ha, with most of the important sights of Nara within its confines. The park ranges from very busy (Nara's main street, Sanjo-Dori, runs right through its center) to quiet and secluded (around the Manyo Botanical Gardens in the SE). Much is made of the deer running around the park, but like all the royal deer found in various spots throughout Japan, they are too tame to be interesting and their begging for food and their penchant for overturning junk-food-laden garbage cans is actually an annoyance. One by-product are curios made from the antlers found in many side-street shops. Carnival-type vendors throughout the park sell plastic, blow-up deer dolls, deer pins, hats, pennants, and so on. Do your best to ignore them. One thing worthy of note about these "divine messengers" is that they respond to a trumpeter in the evening, heading obediently to their pens.

Kofukuji Temple: The Temple of the Establishing of Happiness. Your 1st stop 200 m SE of Kintetsu Nara Eki, or 500 m E of Nara Eki. Kofukuji was built as the main temple for worship by the Fujiwara Clan in 710. Many of its monks were warriors fighting for the Fujiwara in the civil wars of the 11th and 12th centuries. When the Fujiwara lost, Kofukuji was burned down. Fires have periodically destroyed all the buildings dating from the Nara Period. Even the famous 5-storied pagoda met a fiery end; the present one dates from 1426. Kofukuji is now the headquarters of the Hosso sect. On the grounds are the Kondo (main hall) and the 5- and 3-storied pagodas; the Nan-Endo, an 8-sided hall with a famous image of Kannon; the To-Kondo (N of the 5-storied pagoda) with its famous statues of Nikko and Gekko (sunlight and moonlight); and finally the Kokuho-Kan (museum), a ferrous concrete building that periodically displays all of Kofukuji's treasures, with concise English explanations. Kofukuji is always crowded with pilgrims, so it is better to appreciate the architectural design without going into most buildings. Save your artistic curiosity for the Kokuho-Kan. Behind the 5-storied pagoda are a series of ponds, the most famous being Sarusawa. For a light snack, find one of the many black wagons that sell sweet potatoes roasted over a wood fire. Delicious and nutritious for Y100.

Kasuga Shrine: The Fujiwara Clan's Shinto counterpart to Kofukuji Temple. Follow Sanjo-Dori E until you pass the 2nd *torii* of Kasuga. Kasuga was built in 768 and, as was the fashion, was reconstructed every 20 years. The Fujiwaras, like most Japanese, fulfilled their spiritual needs through Buddhism, but their hearts belonged to Shinto. Kasuga is famous for its 3000 lanterns, ⅔ of which are stone, the remaining being bronze. They are lit twice yearly on the eve of the *Mandoro* Festival (Feb. 3 or 5 and Aug. 15). The shrine is actually made up of 4 structures which, collectively, are the best examples of Kasuga-zukuri architecture. The grounds are simple, impeccably clean, moss covered and quiet. The Heiden (Offering Hall) has a packed dirt floor upon which offerings are made. Behind the main structure, connected by a walkway, is Utsushidondo, the transfer hall where the relics are kept during the rebuilding process. *Kasuga Matsuri*, the main shrine festival, is held on March 13.

Kasuga Wakamiya Shrine: Located 200 m SE of Kasuga Shrine. This shrine was built in the Kasuga style, one elongated building divided

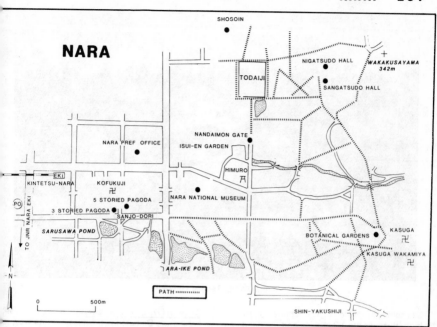

NARA

SHOSOIN

NIGATSUDO HALL

WAKAKUSAYAMA
342m

TODAIJI

SANGATSUDO HALL

NARA PREF OFFICE

NANDAIMON GATE

ISUI-EN GARDEN

HIMURO

EKI
KINTETSU-NARA

KOFUKUJI

5 STORIED PAGODA

3 STORIED PAGODA

NARA NATIONAL MUSEUM

SANJO-DORI

SARUSAWA POND

BOTANICAL GARDENS

KASUGA

KASUGA WAKAMIYA

ARA-IKE POND

TO JNR NARA EKI

PO

N

0   500m

PATH ....

SHIN-YAKUSHIJI

into 3 sections. The S section is known as Kaga-unden (Sacred Dancing Hall). Here *miko* (temple maidens wearing white garments with red-pleated skirts) perform the ancient, sacred *kagura* dance. They each carry a fan, a branch of the sacred *sakaki* tree and bells. The dancers are accompanied by a *kagura* band made up of flutes, clappers, pipes, harps and drums. At this shrine, *On Matsuri* (Dec. 16-17), the greatest festival of Nara, takes place. There is a procession of many participants dressed in feudal armor or ancient costumes. Anyone in Japan that can possibly attend *On Matsuri* does so. The crowds are staggering, but the festival is resplendent.

Daibutsu and Todaiji: The Todaiji (Great Eastern Temple) and the Daibutsu (Great Buddha) are the biggest attractions of Nara, open daily, Y200. Just follow the crowds one km E of Kintetsu-Nara Eki. The Daibutsuden, the main hall of Todaiji which houses the Daibutsu, is reported by the Japanese to be the "largest wooden structure on earth," while the mammoth Daibutsu inside, seated on an enormous pedestal, is the largest bronze casting in the world. The Daibutsuden is truly huge, measuring m long, 50.5 m deep and 48.7 m high. The

pillars and beams are hewn from giant trees. The Daibutsuden has undergone a series of fiery calamities. It was burned down, along with the Kofukuji Temple, by the Taira Clan in 1180. The present structure, ⅓ smaller than the original, was completed in 1709. The latest restoration to the structure was in 1914. There is continual maintenance with scaffolding obvious at most times. The Daibutsuden is a monumental architectural feat by any standards, and although heavy beams have been used, it maintains an elegance of line. The Daibutsu, the giant sculpture inside, was commissioned by Emperor Shomu in 743. The designer was a Korean artist, Kuninaka-no-Kimimaro, from the Kingdom of Paikche. After several failures at casting, the Daibutsu was finally completed and dedicated in 752. The ceremony was lavish, attended by 10,000 priests and nuns, the Imperial Household, and a host of nobles. Huge amounts of metals and materials were used to cast the Buddha, but the most staggering weights included 437 tons of bronze and 130 kg of pure gold. The vegetable wax alone used in the process weighed 7 tons. The pedestal, composed of 56 lotus petals upon which the Buddha is enthroned, is 21 m in circumference. A long list of the Daibutsu's size and measurements would be boring, but a few will give you an idea of its

the Todaiji Temple complex

awesome dimensions. The statue is 15.2 m high, the eyes are 1.2 m wide and the hands are 2 m from palm to fingertip. The Daibutsu personifies Buddha Vairocana, the root, the source of all Buddhas. The pedestal upon which he sits is Rengezokai, "The Lotus Flower of the World," or paradise. The Buddha is guarded by 2 statues. The Komukuten on the left is a figure trampling a demon. This protects the Buddha, and destroys any obstacles in the lives of devotees. To the right is Tamonten with a face snarled in anger, again trampling a demon. He protects the Buddha from the N, an ominous region to Japanese Buddhists. To the right rear is a pillar with a square hole cut in the bottom. Superstition says that anyone who can fit through it will have a place in heaven. Most large-boned Westerners can forget it! The last Western dignitary of note to squirm through was the Prince of Wales in 1922. The Buddha sits in a meditative pose and the posturing of his hands symbolizes peace of mind and the granting of graces. Two sublime gilt wooden statues are placed in front. To the right is Nyoirin-Kannon, engaged in granting good fortune. To the left is Kokuzo-Bosatsu who dispenses wisdom and happiness. You do not have to be a Buddhist to feel the power, dignity and harmony permeating this place of reverence.

Shosoin (Treasure Depository): A one min walk behind the Daibutsuden. Shosoin, in its way, is the most intriguing building of the whole Todaiji complex. This sturdy log cabin, complete with notched corners, looks like the rustic home of a Japanese Davy Crockett, while in actual fact it preserves some of the ancient, intricate, fragile works of art. Shosoin stands 3 m off the ground on *hinoki* (cypress) tree trunks which allow free circulation of air. Though fire periodically rages all around it and tumultuous earthquakes even snapped off the head of the Daibutsu in the 9th C., the Shosoin has stood intact for 1200 years. It is now flanked by 2 concrete buildings that help to preserve some of the art works, but inside remains a large potpourri of Nara-Period masterpieces. Here lie swords; embroideries; mirrors; musical instruments inlaid with mother of pearl, gold and silver; human, bird and animal figurines; incense wood; medicines, fabrics and ceramics showing Chinese, Korean and Persian influences. The list is as varied as the fertile imaginations of the artisans. The bulk of the treasure was donated by Empress Komyo upon the death of her husband, Emperor Shomu, in the middle of the 7th century. The Shosoin airs its treasures only during the crisp, brilliant days of Oct. and November. If you are in Japan at that time, make all efforts to attend. Do not despair; in times past, the doors were opened only once evey 200 years. The objects that you will see, including those made of cloth, are so well preserved that it will be hard to appreciate that they are more than 12 centuries old.

Nigatsudo and Sangatsudo Halls: To the R of the Daibutsuden, follow the stone steps to the top of the hill. Nigatsudo (2nd month) is home to 2 mysterious statues, the large and small 11-headed Kannons. The public is not allowed to look upon them, but the latter is reported to be always warm to the touch. The main festival is _Omizutori_ (Water-drawing Festival) held from March 1-14, with a torchlight procession held on the evening of March 12. The lower hall, Sangatsudo (3rd month) is the oldest surviving temple at Todaiji. Inside are excellent sculptures from the Nara Period. The main work is the Fukukenjaku Kannon. He is a male deity of mercy, clutching a fishhook to symbolize his saving people from suffering. Surrounding him is a priceless crown bedecked with 20,000 pearls, crystal, jewels and rare gems. The remainder of the hall is adorned with numerous exquisite statuary of Nikko, Gekko and the 4 Heavenly Guardians, done in dry lacquer work. The view from the hilltop is expansive, presenting the roof of the Daibutsuden, the tree-lined walkways of Todaiji, and a broad vista of the Yamato Plain. Small teahouses dot this section of Todaiji, where for a small fee you can enjoy the tea ceremony. An even better view to the NE is Wakakusayama Hill (343 m), behind the 2 halls. Yearly, on the night of Jan. 15, this entire grassy knoll is set afire in a ritual purification ceremony called _yamayaki_.

FESTIVALS

Jan. 15: Yama Yaki (Grass Burning Festival on Wakakusayama Hill). Festivities begin with a hill-climbing race in the early afternoon. At sundown, a long procession of monks carrying torches, heads for the hill. At approximately 1800, a massive fireworks display heralds the actual setting afire of the 30 ha of hillside which burns for about one hr and ritually purifies the temples of Nara. Crowded and spectacular.

Feb. 3-4: Mandoro (Lantern Festival at Kasuga Shrine). All 3000 lanterns in and around the shrine precincts are lighted at once. In the evening, the temple _miko_ perform ancient _bugaku_ dances originating from central Asia. At nearby Kofuku-ji Temple, _Tsuina-e_ (a demon

exorcising ritual) is performed to celebrate _setsubun,_ the end of the coldest part of winter.

March 1-14: Omizutori (Water-Drawing Festival of Todaiji Temple). This 2-week festival is the culmination of aescetic Shinto and Buddhist practices. On the midnight of March 12, glaring torches are carried by novitiates who visit a sacred well to draw water. The people try to capture a few fallen torch embers as talismans of good luck. Ritual dances are performed inside the temple all night long. No women are allowed in the inner precincts.

March 13: Kasuga Matsuri. A giant procession of people dressed in Heinan Period armor and costumes (794-1185) parades through the streets until they arrive at the Kasuga Shrine where sacred dances are performed.

May 11-12: Takigi Noh at Kofukuji Temple. Beginning at sundown, _noh_ performances are enacted on an outdoor stage in the temple grounds.

May 19: Fan-Throwing Festival at Tosho Daiji Temple. The temple priests hurl fans into the jostling crowds as people try to retrieve them as talismans against evil.

June 17: Saegusha Festival at Isakawa Shrine. This festival is designed to ward off sickness as priests and parishioners offer holy _sake_ and wild lilies to the shrine gods.

Aug. 15: Mandoro. A repetition of the Feb. festivities at Kasuga Shrine when the lanterns are lit once again as part of O-Bon.

September (variable date): Unema, at Unema Shrine near Sarusawa Pond. The highlight is a giant Japanese fan carried in procession and then set afloat upon the pond as the full moon rises. Musicians in accompanying boats provide classical music.

Mid Oct.-Nov.: In the crisp dry days of autumn the Shosoin Treasure Hall is opened and the year's selection of treasures to be displayed later at Nara Museum is chosen.

Dec. 16-18: On-Matsuri, at Kasuga Wakamiya Shrine. This 3-day festival is an elaborate potpourri of processions, dances, *noh*, classical dramas, wrestling and period costumes. Nara's gaiest yearly event. Large crowds and a great time.

PRACTICALITIES

accommodations: If you have not day-tripped from Osaka or Kyoto, Nara offers a range of accommodations. Western-style places (with Japanese-style rooms) include the Nara Hotel, 1096 Takabatake-cho, Nara 630, tel: (0742) 26-3300, 10 min by car from Nara Sta., from Y6500; and Hotel Yamatosanso, 27 Kawakami-cho, Nara 630, tel: (0742) 26-1011, 5 min by car from Kintetsu Nara Sta., from Y7000. Most 1st-class *ryokan* in Nara start at Y8500 (w/2 meals). The Tourist Info Office at Kintetsu-Nara Eki can help with lists and reservations. For reasonably priced *ryokan* try: Osakaya, Nishi-Kitsujicho, Nara, tel: (0742) 22-7107, 10 min walk from Kintetsu-Nara Sta. on the Kintetsu Line, Y3000 w/o meals; Sakae Ryokan, 46 Higashi-Kitsu-jicho, Nara, tel: (0742) 22-2444, 15 min walk from Kintetsu-Nara Sta. on the Kintetsu Line, Y3500 w/o meals; Rakuyo, Higashi-Jurincho, Nara, tel: (0742) 22-5538, 15 min by bus from JNR Nara Sta., Y4000 up w/o meals. For business hotels, try the People's Inn Hanakomichi, 23 Konishi-machi, Nara, tel: (0742) 26-2646, 2 min walk from Kintetsu-Nara Sta., on the Kintetsu Line, from Y4500, English is spoken; Business Hotel Shoroku, 1288 Kita 2-chome, Horencho, Nara, tel: (0742) 23-1351, 2 min walk from Kintetsu-Nara Sta. on the Kintetsu Line, from Y4200; and Business Hotel Takatsuji, 315 Shibatsujicho 4-chome, Nara, tel: (0742) 34-5371, 2 min walk from Shin-Omiya Sta. (one stop before Nara Sta.) on the Kintetsu Line, English is spoken, Y4200. Nara has 2 YHs, the most centrally located being Nara YH, Sogo-undo-koen, 64 Handa-Hiraki-cho, Nara 630, tel: (0742) 22-1334, 5 min by bus from Nara Sta. and 7 min on foot, 120 beds. The more friendly is Nara-Ken Seishonen-Kaikan YH, 72-7 Ikenokami, Handa-hiraki-cho, Nara, tel: (0742) 22-5540, 9 min by bus from Nara Sta. and 5 min on foot, 54 beds, closed Dec. 29-Jan. 4.

services: Before you arrive in Nara, JNTO (available at TIC also) provides pamphlets and brochures on Nara with the *Kyoto-Nara Tourist Map* especially helpful. In Nara, try the City Tourist Info. Center, located on the 1st floor of Kintetsu Nara Sta., tel: (0742) 24-3611, open daily 0900-1700. They also hand out excellent maps and brochures of Nara.

VICINITY OF NARA

Dreamland: Just N of Nara is the nightmare of Dreamland (bus 20 min from the train sta.). It was fashioned after the attraction that most Japanese hold such a childlike fascination for— Disneyland. There is nothing basically wrong with the giant amusement park, but to travel to Nara to visit Dreamland is anti-thema. Families with children who are restlessly bored with the subtleties of Nara, could work off a great deal o' pent-up energy, and preserve their sanity by spending an afternoon there with the kids, bu' most people should pass it by.

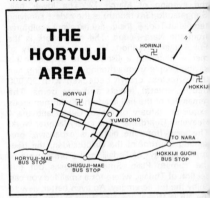

Horyuji Temple: Twelve km SW of Nara. Fron Nara, bus from Kintentsu-Nara Eki to Horyuj mae (30 min). From Osaka, train from Minate machi to Horyuji. The bus from Nara also stop at Toshodaiji and Yakushuji, 2 temples wort seeing. Allow 5-6 hrs to visit all 3. Horyuji is th oldest temple in Japan, built in 607 by Princ Shotoku. Accordingly, it holds some of th rarest art treasures in the country. This famou temple is one of the "7 Great Temples of Nara It is divided into 2 sections, the Toin (E Templ and Saiin (W Temple). These headquarters the Shitoku sect consist of 45 buildings, man being among the oldest wooden structures the world. The classical way to view Horyuji from the S, first passing through Nandaimo (Great S Gate) and then through Chumo (Middle-Gate) into the confines of the We Temple (Saiin). In Saiin is the Kondo (Main Ha and the 5-storied Pagoda. The Kondo is one the oldest buildings, quite small, but impre sively built with 28 massive pillars. The Kond holds numerous Buddhist images; the mo noteworthy is the Sakya Trinity, dating fro

623. The Four Heavenly Guardians are here too, and concealed deep underground in the NE corner is Fukuzo, a hidden repository of treasures known only to its keepers. The 5-storied Pagoda is so devised that as the stories taper from ground to roof, each succeeding one becomes exactly half in size. The murals on the 1st floor depict holy scenes of Buddhism. The pagoda was disassembled during WW 11, but the original timbers were used in the reconstruction. Under the central pillar is believed to be a bone fragment of Buddha. Behind the Kondo is Dai Kodo (Great Lecture Hall) flanked by Kyozo (Sutra Library and Shoro (Belfry). To the extreme rear is the less-visited Kami-no-Mido and further to the R is the octagonal Saiendo, built as a meditation hall for Lady Tachibana, Empress Komyo's mother. E of the Kondo, leading to Toin E Temple is the Daihozoden (Great Treasure Hall), 2 ferro-concrete buildings holding the greatest treasures of Horyuji. Don't let appearances fool you; this block-house modern repository is dripping with priceless art works.

the Toin (E temple): Reached by following the pathway under the Todaimon (8-Pillared Gate). The main edifice is Yumendono (Hall of Dreams), the most beautiful octagonal building in Japan. Here the monk-prince Shitoku would retire to meditate on the holy sutras. It was said that if he could not discern the answer, a wise old sage with a golden aura would appear from the E and enlighten him. The main object of worship here is the Guze-Kannon, covered in gold foil and measuring 1.8 m (the supposed height of Prince Shotoku). This statue was rediscovered by an American scholar, E. Fenelossa, in the late 1800s and is now open to public view. The Denpodo (Sermon Hall) to the L of Yumendono once belonged to Lady Tachibana, (the most looked-after mother-in-law in history) and in the rear of the compound is Chuguji, a temple nunnery, containing the oldest existing Japanese embroidery, the Tenjukoku Mandala. It has not survived intact, but enough remains to give an idea of the craftsmanship of the Asuka Period (552-645).

OSAKA

Means "Big Slope." Pop. 3,000,000. The industrial center of the world's 3rd richest industrialized nation. Ten million people work within the megalopolis running from Kyoto to Kobe, and their efforts produce the lion's share of Japan's domestic and foreign industrial commerce. To a traveler without a keen eye for discovery, this adds up to one big bore. Osaka is not a people's city. It is choked by traffic, and the soot, smog and clatter of unceasing industry blights the environment. Efforts have recently been made to improve this condition with green belts, a few scattered parks and a new emphasis of worth being placed on the city's intriguing history. When Japan is ridiculed for industrial spoilage, loss of a sense of beauty, and money-before-people attitude, Osaka is a prime target. *Shikata ga nai* (it can't be helped) should become the city's motto. Yet, there are a few sights worth ferreting out. Osaka is the premier city for *bunraku* (puppet theater), performed at the Asahi-za theater. These performances preserve the finest and oldest traditions of the art. Osakans have also built a resplendent Kabuki Theater, the Shin-Kabuki-za, where the best performers in Japan are featured. These 2 stunning artistic endeavors are seemingly out of place and are almost an apologia for the city's urban blight. Osaka's Kabuki Theater is grander than Tokyo's and should not be missed.

history: Naniwa (Rapid Waves), the original name of Osaka, was ruled by Emperor Nintoku in the 4th century. Its location on the eastern extremity of the Inland Sea and in the middle of the then-known empire, made it a natural as the trading center of Japan. Nintoku realized that trade was the way to prosperity, and in a unique move suspended taxes on his people for 3 years. This was the financial boost that Osakans needed and the city's awesome mercantile history dates from this period. In remembrance, Nintoku's keyhole-type mausoleum was built here on a grander scale than even the Egyptian Pyramids. Located in Sakai suburb, 1.5 million cubic meters of sand were conveyed by over one million workers. Much later Toyotomi Hideyoshi, the dominant warlord of the 16th C. who unified Japan and laid the groundwork for the Tokugawa Shogunate, built his enormous castle fortress here in 1583. Again, Osaka was infused with prosperity and the merchant class grew like never before. The *samurai* class, firmly entrenched by 250 yrs of Tokugawa peace, paid little attention to trifles like money. The merchants of Osaka were looked down upon and for the most part were ignored and thereby freed to amass fortunes. The arts were pursued, but they were by-products, not the foundation upon which Osaka developed. World War 11 leveled the city, but the scars are paved over.

Osaka missed a tragic, but nonetheless golden opportunity to rebuild with people in mind. Old habits die slowly. Business as usual won out in the end.

getting there: Osaka's International Airport is located at Itami, 15 km from city center. Frequent shuttle buses make the trip in 20 minutes. International air flights connect Osaka with Europe, N and S America, and Asia. Most flights land in Tokyo and go on to Osaka at no extra charge. ANA and JAL have frequent 55 min flights to Osaka from Tokyo and Fukuoka. JAL, ANA and TOA provide regular flights to Osaka from throughout major cities in Japan, including Sapporo in one hr 45 min, and Naha in 2 hrs 5 min. *by rail:* Osaka is serviced by the Tokaido *shinkansen.* To Hakata, the furthest point W (624 km), the journey takes 3 hrs 49 minutes. To Tokyo, the furthest point E (515 km), the time required is 3 hrs 10 minutes. About 100 trains per day of the Hikari and Kodama *shinkansen* travel to and from Tokyo. The *shinkansen* is the most expensive public transport in Japan. Except when time is of the essence, it is not worth it, but anyone visiting Japan should experience one joy ride. Whisk from Osaka to Kyoto (39 km) in 17 min, or Kobe (37 km) in 17 minutes. The Tokaido and Sanyo (JNR) Main Lines connect Osaka with all points throughout Japan. Private rail connects Nara-Nagoya by Kintetsu Line, Kobe-Nagoya by Hankyu Line, and Kyoto-Nagoya by Keihan Line and Hankyu Line. JNR also offers Inter-urban Rapids (*kaisoku*) from Kyoto and Kobe. *by ocean liner:* The few shipping compaines still offering service to Japan usually dock at Kobe, about 30 min by JNR from Osaka. *by bus:* Most buses serving Osaka use the Meishin Expressway (Nagoya, Kyoto, Osaka, Kobe). Many JTB Package Tours from Tokyo terminate in Osaka. *hitchhiking:* Use on-ramps and service areas of the Meishin Expressway and highways for best results. Highway No. 1, Osaka-Kyoto-Nagoya-Tokyo. Number 2, Osaka-Kobe-Hiroshima-Shimoneseki. Highways 25, 26, 43, 176 and the Chugoku and Kinki Expressways also converge on the city from various points. *by ferry:* Main ferry routes are Kobe/Osaka to Kawasaki-Tokyo, 19 hours. Routes are also available to Hiroshima, Tokushima, Beppu and other points. The Kato, Kansai and Muroto Steamship Companies service the majority of these routes. Schedules, fares and reservations are available at JNTO and JTB offices.

getting around: Subways go to most quarters of the city. Schedules and subway maps are available from JTB at Osaka Station and at Osaka Municipal Tourist Office just outside the E entrance of Osaka Station. The subway lines are numerous and confusing. The 2 most practical and best for travelers are No. 1 and No. 2. Number 1 runs from Shin-Osaka-Eki (terminus for the *shinkansen*) to Osaka Eki, S across the Shin-Yodo River. It has stations at Umeda (Osaka Eki), Shin-Saibashi, Nanba and Tennoji and a change at Tenmabashi, heading to Osaka Castle on No. 2. JNR runs a loop line completely around the city. It does not pass through the downtown area, but is good for getting to the port. *buses:* Go everywhere, but there are no signs in English. Your route must be mapped and you must be primed for bus stops for them to be of any use. *taxis:* Always the best alternative in a pinch, but in Osaka there is a catch. Drivers (they take correspondence classes from New York cabbies on bad manners) might refuse you for short hops. At rush hour, or in rainy weather they price gouge mercilessly. When you flag them down, the number of fingers that you hold up indicates the number of times that the fare will be multiplied. Thank you Emperor Nintoku. *car rentals:* Available, but there is no place to park. You can become an expert on at least one block of Osaka after you've gone around it 200 times. *sightseeing buses:* In many cities, bus tours are unnecessary for touring, but in Osaka they are a viable alternative. Three main tours are offered. Osaka Afternoon Tour leaves major hotels at 1300 and returns at 1500. It hits the highlights: Osaka Castle, Expo '70, etc. Mid-Mar. to Mid-Nov., the Osaka Golden Night Tour leaves major hotels at 1900 and returns at 2300; a watered-down version of "acceptable" night spots. Apr.-May, mid-Sept. to Mid-Nov., JTB Tour leaves from Umeda Office at 1300 and offers Osaka-Kyoto. The tour lasts a ridiculous 3 hours. Canned commentary. The best part is the return to Osaka on the *shinkansen.*

SIGHTS

Osaka station: In the Umeda area. Popularly called Kita (North), this is the busiest area in Osaka, loaded with *depato*, theaters, restaurants and cabarets. The Umeda Underground Center is a frantic, buy-anything marketplace. Over 300,000 people pass through this area everyday. The Japanese phenomenon of graceful scurrying is at its best here as is the unabashed face of modern Japan.

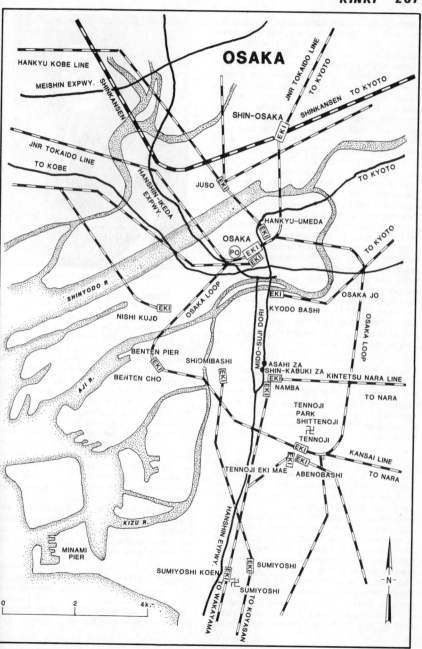

OSAKA

HANKYU KOBE LINE

MEISHIN EXPWY.

SHINKANSEN

JNR TOKAIDO LINE

SHIN-OSAKA EKI

SHINKANSEN TO KYOTO

JNR TOKAIDO LINE TO KOBE

HANSHIN-IKEDA EXPWY.

JUSO EKI

TO KYOTO

HANKYU-UMEDA EKI

OSAKA PO EKI EKI

TO KYOTO

SHINYODO R

EKI

OSAKA LOOP

EKI KYODO BASHI

OSAKA JO

NISHI KUJO

OSAKA LOOP

BENTEN PIER

SHIOMIBASHI

MIDO-SUJI DORI

ASAHI ZA SHIN-KABUKI ZA EKI

KINTETSU NARA LINE

AJI R.

BENTEN CHO

EKI

EKI NAMBA

TO NARA

TENNOJI PARK SHITTENOJI 卍 TENNOJI

KANSAI LINE

EKI EKI

TO NARA

TENNOJI EKI MAE

ABENOBASHI

KIZU R.

HANSHIN EXPWY.

MINAMI PIER

SUMIYOSHI KOEN

EKI EKI SUMIYOSHI

卍 SUMIYOSHI

TO WAKAYAMA

TO KOYASAN

-N-

0 2 4km.

Osaka Castle: Take the subway to Tenmabashi, then walk SE 300 m. Or bus to Ote-Mae, then walk E 500 m. Japan was a system of loosely-knit feudal states ruled by _daimyo_ (warlords). The Imperial Family had presided over their empire for 20 centuries, but often-times they were only figureheads with political power resting in the hands of the strongest _daimyo_. Hideyoshi Toyotomi finally unified Japan in the 1580s, centralizing the government, and fittingly built the largest castle in Japan at his main city of Osaka. The complex was completed in 1586 after 3 years of construction employing 600,000 workers. Their creation was staggering. The original massive stone walls were almost 3 km long by 2 km wide. The Tokugawa Clan, in their bid for power, completely destroyed the castle in 1615 when they defeated Hideyoshi's heir. They rebuilt the castle and used it as a symbol of their authority until 1867 when the last remnants of the Tokugawa Shogunate burned it in withdrawal before submitting to the Meiji Restoration forces. The castle was last renovated in 1931. The grounds today are a park, sorely appreciated as an escape from the clamor of the city. Inside the main 5-storied _donjon_ (actually 8 floors within) is a museum (Y200) displaying artifacts of the 250 years of Tokugawa reign. The top floor presents a dazzling panorama of the city and a bird's-eye view of modern Japan.

Midosuji Boulevard: Runs N-S from Osaka Eki to Namba Eki. It is wide, tree-lined and along it are found the Central P.O., exchange banks, department stores, restaurants and all travel amenities. It is the central street of the grid pattern upon which Osaka was laid, dividing the city in half.

Namba Station: Five km S of Osaka Eki on Subway No. 1. The most interesting section around Namba is Dotonbori Street. Everywhere neon flashes, advertising the profuse array of wares for sale. This street also a hive of restaurants, bars and nightclubs, is, according to Japanese brochures, for the "mental relaxation of the people." The 2 best attractions are the _Shin-Kabuki-za_ (_kabuki_) and the _Asahi-za_ (_bunraku_) theaters within walking distance of Namba on Dotonbori. _the Shin-Kabuki-za:_ This theater is a modern extravaganza and, despite its name, rarely presents _kabuki_ performances. Instead, it features primarily _manzai_ comedies, modern plays, _kyogen_ farces and a host of "variety shows." Japan's _kabuki_ stars

the _bunraku_ puppet, Kumagai

perform here for only 3 weeks, from May 1-25. The theater is large and lavish, seating 2000 people. To sample the performances and save money, tickets can be purchased on a "by the act" basis. If you like what you see, purchase another ticket until you are satiated. With these tickets you must stand. _Asahi-za:_ This theater presents the finest _bunraku_ performances, elevated to an art in Osaka about 300 yrs ago. These performances take place about 5 times a year; check with JTB upon your arrival for more information. The puppeteers are masters; their black-cloaked appearance on the stage quickly blends into the background as they deftly manipulate their magical puppets through the drama. The puppets themselves are realistic, colorful, exemplary works of art. Often-times the drama depicts a scene from the tragedy of the civil war tale of the Heike Clan. _Bunraku_ was raised to an art form by Chikamatsu Monzaemon (1653-1724), Japan's Shakespeare, who provided the finest dialogue and staging for this classical Japanese theater. Performances can also be enjoyed in the area at the lesser visited theaters of Kado-za and Naka-za.

Tennoji: Two km SE of Nanba by subway. Just N of the _eki_ is Tennoji Park, offering some quietude with its flowers, ponds and a walking path. In the park is the Municipal Art Museum, Zoological Park and Botanical Garden. The

provide a good afternoon escape. Nearby is Tsutenkaku (Heavenly Tower), heralded in tourist brochures for its view. What a promotional blunder! The city fathers should have left well-enough alone when the original tower was dismantled in 1943 and melted down for the war effort. Bring an oxygen mask and a machete to cut through the smog. The quiet aquarium on the 1st floor, ignored by the hordes of student visitors, offers an interesting array of tropical fish in dimly-lit surroundings. Shin-Sekai (New World), and you must be brave to enter it, is located W of Tennoji Park. This entire section is a bawdy pinball parlor, teeming with cheap restaurants, cheap thrills, strip shows, and great for a belly laugh. The workers of Osaka, disinclined or unable to afford the slightly more refined attractions around Dotonbori, come here to play.

temples and shrines: Shitennoji Temple, near Tennoji Park, is reported to be even older than Horyuji in Nara. Prince Shotoku dedicated it in 593. *Bugaku* (sacred dances) are performed here on Apr. 22. They originally came from India via China and their dignity and drama are preserved best here in Osaka. *Sumiyoshi Shrine:* Near Sumiyoshi-koen (Park) Eki on the Nankai Line. Known for its style of architecture using natural timbers and bark-thatched roofs. This ancient style was well established long before Buddhist temple architecture was introduced. An arched bridge, pond and 600 lanterns are the main features. The shrine was dedicated to the gods of the sea because at one time Sumiyoshi was the main port of Osaka. *Konda Hachmangu:* (Furuichi Eki on the Kintetsu Minami-Osaka Line). This shrine believed to be over 1400 yrs old, enshrines the Emperors *Ojin, Chuai* and *Jingu.* Recent examination of the Ojin Mausoleum in the area has uncovered artifacts and treasures which are exhibited in a museum on the grounds.

museums: The Osaka Castle Museum is on the 2nd and 7th floors of the castle *donjon.* Its exhibits include folding screens, armor and histories of Japanese castles of the Momoyama Era along with many personal artifacts of Toyotomi; open 0900-1700, Y200 entrance. *Osaka Municipal Art Museum:* At Tennoji Sta., offers ancient and modern works of art and features Jomon-type pottery and artifacts found at local digs; open 0900-1700, admission Y200. *Japan Local House Museum:* Hattori Park, Tyokuchi-koen Eki. A dozen or so representative farmhouses were reconstructed here to give an authentic view of Japanese rural life and display many articles of daily use from by-gone days. Simple and fascinating; open Tues.-Sun., 0930-1630; also most holidays, Y300.

others: Notable local museums include Fujita Art Museum near Katamichi Eki, Japan Industrial Art Museum near Namba Eki, and the Traffic Science Museum, Benten-cho Eki, JNR Loop Line, which exhibits fine old locomotives and automobiles. Osaka also offers 2 dozen industrial tours of major companies in the area. Inquire at JTB.

EVENTS

Jan. 9-11: *Toka Ebisu* at Imamiya Ebisu Shrine (Imamiya Eki, Nankai Line). Ebisu is the patron of business and good fortune. The Osakan merchants do not neglect their sacred duties on this day when enormous offerings are made to Ebisu. A palanquin procession (*hoekago*) of women in fine kimono caps off the festivities.

Mar. 18-24: *Higan-E* (Holy Service of Nirvana) at Shitennoji Temple, pilgrims remember the dead while small stalls sell trinkets and souvenirs to the bereaved.

Apr. 1-10: *Ashibe Odori* (at the Asahi-za). Osakan geisha perform dances to musical accompaniment. Twice daily and weekends.

Apr. 22: *Shoryo-E* or *Oshorai* at Shitennoji Temple, this commemorates Prince Shotoku. Highlighted by *bugaku* dances. Impressive and dramatic at night.

Apr.-May: Osaka International Festival at Osaka Festival Hall, Nakanoshima. Internationally-known artists participate. Classical Japanese theater is also offered.

June: Osaka International Trade Fair takes place on even-numbered years at various sites throughout the city. Many countries display their wares.

June 14: *Otaue Matsuri* at Sumiyoshi Shrine begins about 1200. Young temple maidens ceremoniously plant rice in the shrine paddies. Traditional costumes, folk dancing and music. Rustic influence deep in the heart of the city.

June 30-July 1: Aizen Matsuri takes place at Shoman-In Temple near Shitennoji Eki. Gay and lighthearted, this is the 1st of the summer festivals and is presided over by the mystical *yamabushi* (magical mountain priests), who build a fire to Aizen, the fire god. The light drives away evil spirits.

the Tenjin Matsuri (festival)

July 24-25: Tenjin Matsuri, at Tenmangu Shrine (Minami-Morimachi Subway Eki). Certainly Osaka's, and one of Japan's, biggest festivals. The night sky is lit by fireworks as fantastically decorated boats carry portable shrines up the Yodo River to Osaka Castle. Excellent, but crowded. Foreigners are given special consideration. A stand for viewing is set aside and special tickets for the boats are available from JTB.

July 31-Aug. 1: Sumiyoshi Matsuri, at Sumiyoshi Shrine, is the last of the summer festivals. Young men, well-fortified with *sake*, parade, carrying an enormous palanquin across the Yamato River. Dancing and festivities take place all night at the local fish market.

Aug. 11-12: Noh Drama, is staged at the Ikutama Shrine near Tennoji. Torchlights romantically light the outdoor stage for this purely aesthetic art form. The *noh* dramas offer abstract design coupled with deep human emotions carved into the traditional masks. The emphasis is placed on the fleeting and tragic aspects of the human condition. Crowded, but impressive.

Nov. 22-23: Shinno Festival held at Sukuna-Hikona Shrine (near Kitahama Subway Sta.), originated 160 years ago during a cholera epidemic. The local pharmacists prayed to Shinno, the legendary Chinese god of medicine. They handed out pills, talismans of bamboo grass, and papier-mache tigers. The tigers are still handed out.

PRACTICALITIES

accommodations: Western-style/first class hotels include: Hotel Hanshin, 3-30-2 Umeda, Kita-ku, Osaka 530, tel: (06) 344-1661, one min walk from Osaka Sta., from Y6000; Royal Hotel, 5-3 Nakanoshima, Kita-ku, Osaka 530, tel: (06) 448-1121, 5 min by car from Osaka Sta., from Y7000; and Osaka Airport Hotel, 3-555 Nishimachi, Hotarugaike, Toyonaka, Osaka 560, tel: (06) 855-4621, in the Osaka International Airport Bldg., from Y6500. For information and reservations for *minshuku* and *ryokan*-type accommodations throughout the Osaka area contact Osaka Minshuku Center, Osaka-eki-mae, Dai-ichi Bldg. B300, 1-3-1 Umeda, Kita-ku, Osaka, tel: (06) 344-2501. For business and reasonable Western-style hotels, try Shin-Osaka Seni City Hotel, Nishi Miyahara 2-chome, Yodogawa-ku, Osaka, tel: (06) 394-3331, 10 min walk from Shin-Osaka Sta., from Y4000; New Oriental Hotel, Nishi Honmachi 2-chome, Nishi-ku, Osaka, tel: (06) 538-7141, 3 min walk from subway Awaza Sta., from Y4000; Osaka YMCA Hotel, Tosabori 1-chome, Nishi-ku, Osaka, tel: (06) 441-0892, 5 min by taxi from Osaka Sta., from Y4000; and Osaka Tokyu Inn, Doyama-cho 2-chome, Kita-ku, Osaka, tel: (06) 312-0109, 5 min walk from Osaka Sta., from Y5000. There are also a number of YHs in and around Osaka, including those in nearby Kyoto and Nara. The most convenient and exceptionally inexpensive YH (Y600, no card necessary) is Osaka-Shiritsu Nagai YH, 450 Higashi-Nagai-cho, Higashi-Sumiyoshi-ku, Osaka 546, tel: (06) 699-5631, 20 min by subway from Osaka Sta., and 16 min on foot (in the Municipal Sports Grounds), 108 beds, closed Dec. 28-Jan. 4; Sayama Yuen YH, 40 Aobagaoka, Tondabayashi 584, tel: (0723) 65-3091, 8 min on foot from Sayama-Yuen-mae Sta., 24 beds; and Hattori Ryokuchi YH, 1-3 Hattori-tyokuchi, Toyonaka 560, tel: (06) 862-0600, 5 min by bus from Sone Sta., 25 min on foot, 108 beds, closed Dec. 28-Jan. 3.

food: One of the fringe benefits of being a gigantic commercial center is that Osaka is a huge food distribution center as well. An enormous array and volume of food flows to Osaka Port, both from agriculture and from the sea. Osakans have long been looked upon as Japan's connoisseurs, _kuidaore_ (extravagant gourmets). The restaurants along Dotonbori, as well as the underground arcades throughout the city, offer the full array of Japanese cuisine at its _kansai_ best, with a heavy sprinkling of Western fare. For vegetarian and macrobiotic foods, try Fukuen, 3-Umeda, Kita-Ku, Osaka, tel: (06) 341-7798. They also have a _kampo-yaku_ (Chinese homeopathic medicine) clinic on the premises. For another choice along the same line, try Sekai Seishoku Kyokai, 9-2 Tani-machi, Tennoji-ku, Osaka, tel: (06) 779-0172.

services: Excellent tourist information is offered at the main thoroughfare at Osaka Eki. The counter is marked by a sign in English, and the staff help not only with travel information but with arranging accommodations as well. They have no brochures on Osaka, but do provide (in English) an excellent city map including the subway system. Open 0530-2400. The Osaka Municipal Tourist Office is at the E exit of Osaka Eki, open 0900-1700, tel: 345-2189. The staff speak little English, but they do complement the other information booth by offering tourist literature. Pick up your _Guide to Osaka_ here for general information and a good city map. JTB has offices located in larger hotels dotted around the city. The most convenient is at Osaka Eki, open 0900-1800, tel: 361-5471. For information regarding festivals in Osaka contact Osaka International Festival Society, 2-22 Nakanoshima, Kita-ku, Osaka, tel: 231-6985. The tourist map of Japan, available from any TIC or JNTO, has an Osaka city map on the back side. The Osaka Immigration Office is located at 2-31 Tani-machi, Higashi-ku, Osaka, tel: 941-0771. For medical emergencies, most larger Western hotels have doctors on call, or contact Osaka National Hospital, tel: 942-1331. For the businessman: All inquiries concerning business arrangements including contacts, industrial tours, interpreters and secretaries can be made to the Commerce and Industry Dept., Osaka Prefecture Govt., Otemaeno-cho, Higashi-ku, Osaka, tel: (06) 941-2880, or at the Osaka International Trade Center, located next door to the Royal Hotel in Nakanoshima. Interpreters, free of charge, are provided by Tescort. To make arrangements, phone Mr. Kira at 445-6116. To arrange a home visit, contact the previously mentioned Osaka Tourist Info. Office at Osaka Eki.

KOBE

Kobe (Sacred Households), pop. 1,400,000, lies squeezed between the sea and the Mt. Rokko range. Some sections of the city are only 3 km wide, while the metropolis complex stretches for 30 km lengthwise. Kobe is the major port of western Japan, accommodating over 10,000 vessels per year. It was one of the 1st ports open for trade with the W, the 1st contact made on Jan 1, 1868. Since that time, its link with the outside world has given Kobe a cosmopolitan air, and it is now home to 60,000 foreign residents. Many Western-style homes from the 1800s still dot the hills behind the city. Western busi-

nesses, banks and hotels are very much in evidence around Sannomiya, the main train station. Most ferries from the Inland Sea arrive at Naka Pier about halfway between Kobe Eki and Sannomiya Eki, so head NE to this area where most of the action is. Kobe has lost a great deal of its charm, having been gobbled up by the industrial complexes surrounding it, but it is still a vital crossroads and a main jumping-off point for ferries through the Inland Sea. A large number of passengers arriving in Japan by oceanliner (a quickly declining proposition) land at Kobe.

KOBE AND VICINITY

getting there by air: Kobe is served by Osaka's International Airport at Itami, reachable by frequent buses from Sannomiya Eki in one hr 10 minutes. _by rail:_ Kobe is on the _shinkansen_, which links it with Tokyo in 3 hrs 30 minutes. Numerous JNR expresses and super expresses connect Kobe with Osaka and Kyoto. The Hanshin and Hankyu Electric Railway Lines (private) provide excellent and frequent service to Osaka, Kyoto and Nara. The San-Yo Main Line (JNR) and the Tokaido Main Line provide connections to all parts of the archipelago. _by bus:_ JNR Highway buses connect Tokyo, Nagoya, Kyoto, Osaka and then on to Kobe. A direct bus departs from Tokyo Sta. at 2140, arriving in Kobe at 0720; Y7500, reservations a must. _by ferry:_ A large network of ferries connects Kobe to most ports along the Inland Sea and the points south. Service is provided by the Kansai Steamship Co., Tokyo, tel: (03) 274-4271; Osaka, tel: (06) 572-5181. Most ferries depart from Naka-Tottei Port located 10 min on foot from Kobe Station. The Port Terminal Bldg. has foreign exchange banks, a Tourist Info. Office (good maps), JTB office, lockers and restaurants. Bus 92 runs between the port and Sannomiya Eki. _getting around Kobe:_ JNR provides intra-city trains running basically E-West. Buses and trams criss-cross all quarters of the city. Minimum bus fare is Y50. Subways are still under-developed, but one now links Suma New Town with Shinnagata.

sights: Sannomiya Eki is the main station in Kobe with lines of the JNR and Hankyu and Hanshin Railways. There are numerous restaurants, cabarets and shops frequented by many of the foreign residents. Tor Road is a favorite strolling promenade. Many of the smaller lanes along this way offer inexpensive restaurants with a small cosmopolitan menu. Suwayama Park rising up a hill overlooking the bay, provides extensive views of Awaji Island and the Inland Sea. The night view from here of Kobe's lights is also impressive. Near the park entrance is the Budokuden, a martial arts hall famous for displays of _kendo, aikido_ and karate. Nunobiki-taki waterfalls are located one km behind Shin-Kobe Eki. A popular hiking trail leading from here to Odaki (Male Fall, 45 m) and Medaki (Female Fall, 19 m) takes you out of the bustle of the city and provides an excellent vantage point to view the port below. _shrines and temples:_ Ikuta Shrine is 400 m W of Sannomiya Eki. This shrine was founded in the 3rd C. by Empress Jingu. Nagata Shrine, 200 m N of Nagata Eki, is dedicated to a Shinto deity of good fortune and prosperity. Minatogawa Shrine, 300 m N of Kobe Eki, is actually a ferro concrete reconstruction, but Minatogawa Park nearby is good for a breather. Fukushoji (Suma) Temple, 200 m N of Sumadera Eki, San-Yo RR, is the headquarters of the Sumadera-Shingon sect founded in 886. Renowned for its famous 11-headed Kannon, it is quiet most times, except in April when crowds converge to view the cherry blossoms.

EVENTS AND FESTIVALS

Jan. 2: _Irizomeshiki_ at Arima Spa is the wintertime opening ceremony of the baths, dedicated to the Buddhist saints that discovered them. Their statues get the 1st plunge. Nice time of year for a hot bath, but crowded. Arima also offers a Hot Springs Festival on Nov. 2 and 3.

Feb. 3-4: _Tsuinashiki_ Festival, when evil spirits are driven out at Nagata Shrine in preparation for the coming spring. These spirits take the form of 7 dancers circling the shrine with flaming torches.

May 24-25: _Nanko_ Festival takes place at the Minatogawa Shrine. Sixteen warriors on horseback commemorate Masashige's heroic death in 1336.

3rd week of May: The Kobe Festival is a hodge podge of processions, music, marching bands and even a beauty contest. A modern festival to celebrate prosperity.

Mid-October: The *Matsubara Matsuri* takes place in nearby Himeji. Popularly known as the Fighting Festival, 3 groups of men carrying *mikoshi* (portable shrines) clash at full speed. Colorful and crazy.

shopping: Kobe has come a long way from 1868, when it was known only for its textiles and matches. Now, products from all over the district pour into the port. The best city area catering to foreigners is between Sannomiya and Motomachi Eki. Tor Road and Kobe International Center also offer good shopping. Kobe Commerce/Industry/Trade (C.I.T.) Bldg. organizes trade fairs and provides excellent information on shopping and what's available.

accommodations: Western-style places include the Kobe International Hotel, 1-6-8 Goko-dori, Fukiai-ku, Kobe 651, tel: (078) 221-8051, 3 min walk from Sannomiya Sta., from Y6000; New Port Hotel, 6-3-13 Hamabe-dori, Fukiai-ku, Kobe 651, tel: (078) 231-4171, 5 min by car from Shin-Kobe Sta., from Y5500; Oriental Hotel, 25 Kyomachi, Ikuta-ku, Kobe 650, tel: (078) 331-8111, 5 min by car from Sannomiya Sta., from Y5500. For *minshuku* available in the area, contact Kobe Minshuku Center, Sun Kobe Chikagai, Aioi-cho 1-chome, Ikuta-ku, Kobe, tel: (078) 341-7056. For business and reasonable Western-style hotels there is Hotel Minakami, 1-1-15 Mizuki-dori, Kobe, tel: (078) 575-5871, 2 min walk from Hankyu Shinkaichi Sta., 64 rooms, from Y4500; Green Hill Hotel, 2-18-63 Kanocho, Ikuta-ku, Kobe, tel: (078) 222-1221, 8 min walk from JNR Sannomiya Sta., 100 rooms, from Y4800; and Kobe YMCA, 2-15 Kano-cho, Ikuta-ku, Kobe, tel: (078) 241-7201, 3 min by taxi from Sannomiya Sta., from Y3800. In nearby Himeji, try Himeji Business Hotel Tokai, 151 Gokenyashiki, Himeji, tel: (0792) 24-9233, 5 min drive from JNR Himeji Sta., 50 rooms, from Y3500. The best bet for a YH in the Kobe area is to take the ferry to nearby Awaji Island. The closest port to Kobe on Awaji is Iwaya on the NE tip of the island. The YHs here include: Senpukuji YH, 4-3-51 Sakae-machi, Sumoto 656, tel: (07992) 2-3309, 40 min by bus from Iwaya Port, 5 min on foot, 65 beds; Asahi Ryokan YH, 239 Gunge, Ichinomiya-cho 656-15, tel: (07998) 5-0018, 55 min by bus from Iwaya Port and 3 min on foot, 150 beds; and on

the S tip of the island is Awaji YH, Ama Nandan-cho 656-07, tel: (07995) 2-0460, 10 min by boat from Fukura Port, 116 beds.

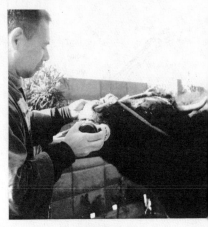

beer fed Kobe beef

food: Everyone has heard about sumptuous Kobe beef and the horror stories about the prices charged. Well, they're true. Just walk along Tor Road and stop at any fancy restaurant to get an idea of costs and the platters served. The prices start at ridiculous and go up quickly from there. If you are still interested, go to Arakawa at 2-9 Nakaya Mate-dori. Another excellent restaurant is the Texas Tavern, which serves a variety of American food as well.

services: General information can be had from the Tourist Info. Office on the 2nd floor of the Kobe Kotsu Bldg., on the W side of Sannomiya Eki. JTB has an office at Sannomiya Eki, tel 231-4111. For business info and industrial tour go to Kobe C.I.T. Center Bldg., 6F 1-14-Hamabe-dori, Fukai-ku, Kobe, or call (078) 251-2911. Kobe Immigration Office is at Kaigan-dori, Ikuta-ku, Kobe, tel: 391-6377. For a home visit, contact Tourist Section, Kobe City Office, 6-7 Kano-cho, Ikuta-ku, Kobe, tel: (078) 331-0252.

VICINITY OF KOBE

Mt. Rokko (932 m) is actually part of the Inland Sea National Park. It is Kobe's and Osaka's playground. Board your train from Rokko Eki or the Hankyu RR or Rokkomichi Eki on the

Tokaido Main Line, then bus 10 min to Do Baishi. A ropeway takes you to the summit in 10 minutes. The summit provides an extensive view of Kobe and the Inland Sea. The area has been developed and provides a man-made "natural" pasture, complete with horses, cows, a passable golf course, plus skiing on artificial snow in winter. Not really exciting, but a reasonably good getaway from the city.

Arima Spa, located 22.5 km N of Kobe, is a favorite resort of Kobe and Osaka. The area provides 30 *ryokan,* each offering its own mineral baths. The surroundings are pleasant, although developed, and the fall foliage is brilliant. The trip from Kobe takes about 1 ½ hrs, but the mountain scenery of the Rokko range is inspiring.

<u>beaches:</u> Along the coast S of Kobe are some good swimming beaches (Suma, Shioya and others) but they are generally crowded in season. A good taste of the Inland Sea can be had by taking a short excursion to Awaji Island, where beaches are less crowded and even border on secluded.

Himeji: Pop. 423,000. Lies W of Kobe (55 m) along the Inland Sea. Get there by JNR local train. For anyone heading to Okayama or Hiroshima, a brief stopover in Himeji to view Himeji Castle is recommended. The castle, only a 10 min walk from Himeji Eki, is known as Egret Castle because of its white plastered walls, and is considered one of the most beautiful in Japan. As usual with castles, it sits high on a hill and offers an excellent view from the top of the *donjon.* Restored in 1964, it is an exact reproduction of the original built in 1581 by Toyotomi Hideyoshi and renovated in 1608 by Ikeda Terumasa. The craftsmanship and design are exemplary.

Himeji, the White Egret Castle

THE KII PENINSULA

Wakayama, Southern Nara and Southern Mie Prefectures comprise the Kii Peninsula. This peninsula is completely surrounded by the Pacific and is separated from Shikoku in the W by the relatively narrow Kii Channel. Cape Shionomisaki on the very tip of the peninsula marks the southernmost point of the main island of Honshu. Only a few hrs from Osaka or Nara, the entire peninsula is untouristed. Yoshino Kumano National Park (bordering all 3 prefectures) is bisected by the Kumano River, famous for its spectacular gorges and misty cataracts. At Kumano, on the southern coast, is Onigajo, a series of grotesque rocks and caves chiseled by the sea. Only 14 km SW along the coast is Shingu, where Nachi-no-taki, the tallest waterfall in Japan, plummets 120 m. The mere mention of Yoshino in the center of the peninsula brings cherry blossoms to the lips of the Japanese. (Very difficult in a land where almost every town boasts the best). The trees were planted by En-No-Ozuno, a 7th C. Buddhist priest, who put a curse on anyone who tampered with them. The W coast below Wakayama City, known for an impressive castle built by Hideyoshi Toyotomi, is made up of spectacular coastal scenery and quiet, unassuming villages. In one such village, Gobo, is Dojoji Temple, the scene of an ancient Japanese romantic tale of unrequited love. The entire peninsula bristles with rugged, climbable mountains that oftentimes overlook ancient temples and shrines, one of which is the final resting place of the great Buddhist saint, Kobo Daishi.

getting there: The Kii Peninsula has only a few roads and no railroads running through the S central regions. The main roads are from Yoshino and Gojo in the N central region to Kumano and Shingu respectively on the SE coast. Another main artery runs from Hashimoto (10 km W of Gojo) to Minabe on the SW coast. Air routes are maintained from Kushimoto to Osaka and Nagoya and from Shirahama to Nagoya and Tokyo. Ferries are available from Shingu to Tokyo, Kochi or Shimoneseki.

YOSHINO

The Yoshino area, extending 8 km from Yoshino-guchi in the W, to Yoshino Yama in the E, is the heart of the Yoshino Mountains. Yoshino is a unique town, so built into the surrounding mountains that many shop fronts along the road are actually the 3rd floor of the structure, the 2 below the road used for living quarters and storehouses. A host of temples and shrines surrounding this unique town dot the hillsides. The only way to get to them is by walking, and thanks to En-No-Ozunu, the walk through the cherry woods is simply beautiful. In season, this entire slope is pink. Yoshinom, Yoshimizu, Yoshino-Mikamari and Kinpu are the main shrines of the area with Kinpusenji and Nyoirinji being the main temples. They are all clustered within a 5 km radius around Yoshino-yama. In the middle of a cherry grove is Kinpusenji with its main hall, Zaodo. Along with being the 2nd largest wooden structure in Japan, Zaodo possesses 2 Deva Kings at the main gate, superb sculptures that complement the exemplary architecture of the temple itself. Up a pathway, S of Kinpusenji, is Nyoirinji Temple, where the last remaining 143 warriors prayed before going into battle for the Imperial cause in the 14th century. Behind it is the mauseoleum of Emperor Godaigo.

VICINITY OF YOSHINO

For heavy trekking and remote temples accentuated by superb mountain vistas, head for the series of mountains to the SE between Yoshino and the coast. The 2 most famous peaks are Sanjo-san (1720 m) and Odaigahara-san (1695 m). Sanjo-san is considered the holiest mountain in the area with 2 temples at the summit dedicated to Zao-gongen and En-no-Ozunu. Temple lodgings are offered to pilgrims from May 8-Sept. 27 (check at other times). If the weather is crystal clear you can see Mt. Fuji.

Odaigahara-San: 64 km SE of Yoshino. The Osugidani mountain valley along the Miya River is one of the grandest in all Japan. Its crystal-clear waters, numerous cascades, and gnarled cataracts are superb. The summit of Odaigahara is topped by a temple that offers lodgings. There is a bus through Obamine Pass from Yamato-Kamiichi Eki (2 km N of Yoshinoyama) winding 17 km to the summit (3 hrs). For the fit and hardy, 32 km of trail lead from Odaigahara to Owase on the E coast, or to Toro Gorge on the Kitayama River. *getting there:* From Shimo-ichiguchi (between Yoshinoguchi and Yoshino-yama), bus from the *eki* S to Dokawa (2 hrs); from there the ascent takes 3-4 hours. If you do not wish to backtrack, you can descend to Yoshino, but this takes 8 hrs of heavy hiking. Overnight camping is advised to break up the trip.

Koya-san: The general name given to the mountains of Koya-Ryujin National Park, another mountainous and intriguing area W of

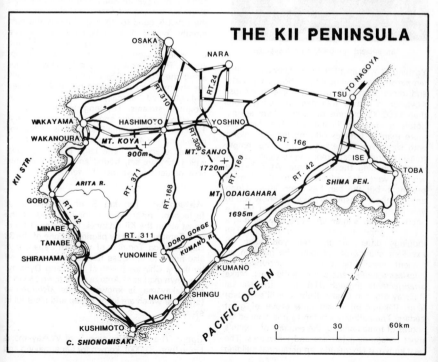

an ancient tombstone on Koya-san

Yoshino. Koya-san (900 m) is famous for the temple on its summit built by Kobo-Daishi in 816 and more than 120 other temple buildings. Koya-san is heavily touristed, attracting more than 1,000,000 pilgrims per year. There are no hotels or *minshuku* in the area, but there are more than 50 temples offering lodgings along with *shojinryori* (vegetarian food). The temple treasures and the early morning services make it worth spending the night here. At one time women were not admitted into the temple precincts, but the ban has been lifted. Upon entering the monastery, a guide will show you to your lodgings. Put the money required for the accommodations in an envelope or wrap it in a piece of paper to show proper respect. The lodgings differ slightly, but you have an excellent chance of spending the night in an ancient, heavily timbered hall surrounded by priceless artworks and sacred antiquities. Make arrangements through JTB or at the Nankai Railway office in Osaka. Kobo Daishi's Mausoleum (Oku-no-In) is set in a grove of giant cedars. The pathway leading to it is flanked by scores of tombs holding the remains of Japan's most outstanding families and luminaries. The best known is Nokotsudo, an octagonal building

where rest the ashes of countless devotees. The experience of Koya-san is unforgettable, unique and timeless. *getting there:* Train to Hashimoto on the Wakayama Main Line and change to the Koya Line of the Nankai Electric Railway, which is a direct line from Namba Eki in Osaka. A bus from Koya-san Cable Car Sta. takes you to Nyonindo (Women's Hall) in 20 minutes.

THE KISEI MAIN LINE SOUTH

Wakayama (pop. 385,000), on the W coast is the main city of the prefecture; the most convenient stopover to replenish film, and other needed travel services before heading south. Wakayama Castle, a facsimile of the original built in 1585 by Hideyoshi, was rebuilt in 1958 following its destruction in WW 11. It's pleasant enough for an hr's visit before training south. The entertainment to be found in visiting this whole region S of Osaka and centering on Wakayama, comes from meandering mountain trails, magical nights in ancient temples, broad vistas and soothing seaside spas. There is no nightlife worth mentioning. Almost any likely spot along the coast is good for fishing; June is the best month. *crafts:* Wakayama, basically rural, is a prime supplier of Japanese handmade paper and the indispensable *waribashi* (wooden chopsticks). The paper is produced at many villages along the Yoshino River. You can frequently see the mulberry pulp being pounded, washed and bleached naturally in the many clear mountain streams. The long, white strips are placed on flat boards and set in the sun to dry. The cedar in Wakayama Prefecture is perfect for producing the 400 million easily split *waribashi* shipped every year. The large platforms upon which they are set, bound and dried resemble neat gardens of wooden flowers.

Wakanoura: Ten km S of Wakayama. A fashionable resort known for its views of the coast along the Kii Channel. Here also is Kimidera Temple, visited by pilgrims as one of the 33 Holy Kannon Temples of western Japan. It is also home to the Guse Kannon sect originated by Iko, a Chinese priest of the Tang Dynasty. The town market of Arita, a small town 25 km S of Wakayama, is known for its *kishu-mikan* (oranges) which are juicy, cheap and plentiful in season.

Gobo: The 1st major stop S of Wakayama is Gobo (pop. 31,000), known for papermaking and

washi (hand made paper) drying

the Dojoji Temple. Dojoji holds a special place in Japanese romantic legends. A young priest of the temple, Anchin, often passed a farmhouse where he was asked by the farmer to spend the night. The farmer's daughter, Kiyohime, eventually fell in love with him and told the young priest about her feelings. He promised to return her love that evening, but had 2nd thoughts and instead ran back to the temple. Kiyohime, who became enraged, transformed into a dragon and pursued him. The young stalwart did the only gentlemanly thing and hid, unfortunately, under the temple bell. The dragon wrapped herself around the bell until it became red hot. The next morning only a few charred bones and ashes remained. (Could this have been the 1st of the "last of the red hot lovers"?).

beaches and spas: For swimming beaches and secluded spas, head for Minabe and Tanabe, 85-95 km S of Wakayama. From Minabe, head inland by bus 3 hrs to the Ryujin Spa, high in the hills on the Hidaka River. The best swimming beach is Ogigahama at Tanabe, from where you can head inland to Yunomine Spa (bus 3½ hrs) at Hongu. This road, which continues to Shingu on the E coast, is known as Nakaheji (Middle Pilgrimage) and has been used for centuries.

Shirahama: 95 km S of Wakayama, offers excellent spas piped into many *ryokan* situated on the coast. A 17 min bus ride from the *eki* takes you into the heart of them. The area has many trails and picturesque scenery along the coastline, a good midway point to stop before continuing around the tip of the peninsula.

Cape Shionomisaki: 165 km S of Wakayama. This cape on the very tip of Kii, is the most southern point of Honshu. Kushimoto, a nearby small resort town offers direct air flights to Osaka and Nagoya.

Nachi: On the SE coast, boasts the tallest waterfall in Japan, Nachi-no-Taki (120 m), along with 40 smaller ones. Take the bus from the *eki* 25 min to the falls. It is a cool, delightful area, and although less striking than imagined, is pleasant. Seigantoji, a nearby temple, is the traditional starting point for pilgrimages to the 33 Holy Kannon Temples.

Shingu: (Pop. 39,000). The jumping-off point for a fantastic river trip up the Kumano River to Toro (Doro), one of the most scenic and pristine gorges in Japan. The flat-bottomed motor boats are comfortable, but the older, air-propelled boats are more exciting. The trip takes about 4 hrs and is spiced with one spectacular scene after another as you manipulate the wild bends of the river. Accommodations are available in Toro. A good alternative is to bus from Shingu to Hashimoto (connections for Nara). The bus skirts the gorge, providing an excellent tour of the mountainous area.

Kumano: On the E coast, is not as spectacular as the surrounding area, but it is well situated as a starting point for visiting the temples, gorges, hot springs and mountain walks surrounding it. Kumano is linked by road to Yoshino, which passes through the heart of Yoshino-Kimano National Park, and by rail to Ise and Nagoya. Even Emperor Jimmu Tennu used it when he was lost in the area and led by a crow from Kumano to Yamato, the ancient capital. Fronting on the Kumano Nado Sea, Kumano features 5 sandy beaches and *onigajo*, sea-eroded caves, connected by a series of walking trails chiseled into the sea cliffs. Accommodations are not as tight here as they are in the more scenic areas.

festivals: Since Wakayama and indeed all of the Kii Peninsula abounds in historical sites, temples and relics, there is no shortage of festivals or events. There are more than 200 scheduled per year, so whenever you visit there will be some festivities. The following is merely a non-inclusive list of some of the major festivals and where they are held: *Feb. 6:* Oto Matsuri (Fire Festival), Kamikura Shrine, Shingu. *Mar. 3:* Hina-Nagashi (Doll Floating), Awashima Shrine, Wakayama. *Apr. 15:* Shishimai (Lion Dance), Fujishiro Shrine, Kainan. *Apr. 28:* Kane-kuyo (Memorial Bell Service), Dojoji Temple, Kawabe.

May 5: Sanada Festival (a procession of feudal soldiers), Sanada-en, Kudoyama. *May 7:* Waka Festival (a procession of feudal lords), Waka-yama. *May 13-14:* Raigoeshiki (Buddha Procession), Tokushoji Temple, Arita. *May 20:* Ebi Matsuri (Fish Festival), Kada Kasuga Shrine, Wakayama. *June 11-19:* Aoba Matsuri (Fresh Verdure Festival), Mt. Koya. *July 14:* Nachi Himatsuri (Fire Festival), Nachi Shrine, Nachi-katsura. *July 14-15:* Kochi Matsuri (Boat Festival), Kochi Shrine, Koza. *July 24-25:* Tanabe Festival, Tokei Shrine, Tanabe. *July 28:* Kokawa Festival, Kokawa Temple, Kokawa. *July 15:* Toroyaki (Lantern Burning Festival), Kokokuji Temple, Yura (Lunar Calendar). *Aug. 14-15:* Hagi Mochitsuki Odori (Rice-cake Pounding Dance), Hongu. *Aug. 16:* Shiide Onimai (Demon Dance), Itsukushima Shrine, Kudoyama. *Oct. 4:* Kehon Dance, Shino-Hachimangu Shrine, Gobo. *Oct. 10:* Warai Matsuri (Laughter Festival), Niyu Shrine, Kawabe. *Oct. 14:* Shishimai (Lion Dance), Kinomoto-Hachimangu Shrine, Wakayama. *Oct. 15:* Nakizumo (Wrestling Festival), Yamajioji Shrine, Shimotsu.

Shiide Onimai (demon dance)

Myoto Iwa (married rocks) of Futami

ISE

At the Grand Shrines of Ise, the Imperial Household of Japan has come to pay homage for countless centuries. The Nai-ku (Inner Shrine) and Ge-ku (Outer Shrine) have a joint history of 1986 years and tower above any other Shinto Shrines in Japan, unparalleled in the sanctity and reverence accorded them. In every instance that may be connected with the Imperial Dynasty, a member of the family or a special envoy is sent to pray at Ise for divine counsel. War, peace, famine, good fortune—all conditions are brought to Ise before a decision is made. Amaterasu-O-Mi-Kami, the Sun Goddess enshrined at Nai-ku, and Toyoke-No-O-Mi-kami, the god of the earth enshrined at Ge-ku, are the 2 basic, fundamental deities of Shinto stands. By extension, the sun and the earth, the givers of all life, are the bedrock upon which Shinto stands. The shrine buildings are simple, unpainted *hinoki* (Japanese cypress), especially timbered from the Imperial Forests in the Kiso Mountains. The architecture is pure, ancient Japanese, a style that prevailed long before the introduction of Chinese-style temple construction. The lines are simple, the crossbeams and roof frames being patterned after prehistoric structures. The shrine buildings are dismantled and new ones are built on adjoining plots every 20 years in a ceremony called *Sengu-Shiki* (the last occurred in Oct., 1973). The wood is cut into bits and distributed as talismans to the hundreds of thousands of pilgrims that attend. For a pure, untainted Japanese experience, Ge-ku and Nai-ku should not be missed.

getting there: Ise is an incorporation of the 2 towns of Uji (E) and Yamada (W). From Nagoya, take the Kinki Nippon Railway (Kintetsu Line) to Uji-Yamada for one hr 20 minutes. Avoid the JNR! From Kyoto, JNR to Ise-shi by express (*kyuko*) in 2 hrs, Y2020. By local this run takes 4 ½ hrs and costs Y1120. From Osaka, take JNR, or the speedier Kinki Nippon RR to Ise in under 2 hours. From Nara, go by JNR in one hr 40 minutes. Ise has 2 *eki* about 5 min apart, Ise-shi and Uji-Yamada. Uji-Yamada is the main *eki* for travel to Ise. *tourist office:* Upon leaving Ise-shi Eki, turn left. Look for a large sign that says NATIONAL. The JTB is on the bottom floor of the building. They have no brochures in English, but their maps are useful, although only in Japanese.

getting around: Ise is small enough to walk almost anywhere in town. There is frequent shuttle-bus service between Ge-ku/Nai-ku Shrine 6 km away. Two bus stops provide this service: one at the road island at the main entrance to Ge-ku, and the other a Uji-Yamada Eki, Bus Stop No. 4. *bike rental:* Good ones with baskets are available at Ise-shi Eki for Y200 per hr, or Y1000 from 0800 to 1700; an excellent way to tour Ise.

THE SHRINES

Ge-ku (Outer Shrine): A 10 min walk from either *eki*. Ge-ku is surrounded by a small forest of Japanese cedars. Tradition says that in the 12th C., an Imperial messenger from the Taira Clan caught his hat on one of the lower branches of a tree at the main entrance and had the offending limb chopped off. Now the lowest branch is about 10 m from the ground. The shrine was permanently established here in 478. Previously, it was in Kyoto. Upon entering, there is a small building to the R, the Kakuraten, where sacred dances are performed. Next door are usually a group of *miko* (temple maiden dancers) clad in white tops and red-pleated skirts. They are friendly and approachable, but it's polite to ask first if you may take their picture. Unfortunately, they will pose. In this area is the Anzaisho (Imperial House of Sojourn). On its doors is the symbol of Imperial Japan, a purple, 16-petalled chrysanthemum on a white background. Pecking around the grounds here are a small flock of chickens donated by various devotees. Religious legends relate that Amaterasu, the sun goddess, was lured from her cave where she hid from her brother Susa-No-O and restored light to the world by the help of a crowing rooster who signalled the dawn. Follow the white gravel road to the main shrine. The grounds are kept meticulously manicured by working priests clad in floppy blue or green ballooning pants. When you approach the main shrine, you'll pass through 2 unpainted fences. Go no further, as only the Imperial Family of Japan may proceed. Photographs are not allowed. Ge-ku itself has a thatched-roof and simple lines. There are no carvings and only a few unobtrusive metal ornaments. This is one of the 2 most sanctified spots of Japanese Shinto. Offerings of food are made at the shrine every morning. These offerings are ceremoniously and symbolically accompanied by the Emperor's white stallion, who awaits his task in a nearby corral. During the week the grounds are not heavily touristed, but one million pilgrims come to share in the New Year's festival. The other festivals take place in June, Oct. (*Kanname-sai*) and in Dec. (*Tsukinami-sai*). They are always dignified. The serenity and general air of these sacred precincts impress anyone who enters. *note:* There is no fee for entering. At one time the shrine was open 24 hrs, but in the early 1970s, the Japanese Red Brigage attacked the airport at Tel-Aviv and made vague threats towards the Imperial Household. The shrine now closes sharply at 1700. Backpacks and other gear may be safely left at the guard station on entering Ge-ku. The shrine office sells a well-done color booklet in English for Y2000.

Nai-ku (Inner Shrine): Dates from 5 B.C. and holds the melted remains of the 8-Pointed Mirror (Yata-no-Kagami), one of the 3 symbols of Imperial Authority. The mirror is believed to have come directly from Amaterasu and the emblem embodies her spirit. The Nai-ku is the more revered of the 2 shrines of Ise. The 6

the simplicity and pure Japanese architecture of the grand shrines of Ise. Here only the Emperor and the highest ranking members of the royal family may come to worship their ancestors

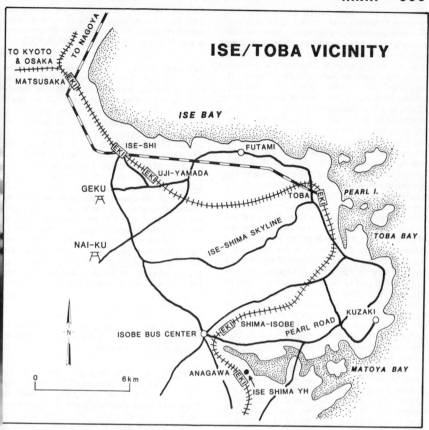

ISE/TOBA VICINITY

TO KYOTO & OSAKA
MATSUSAKA
TO NAGOYA

ISE BAY

ISE-SHI
FUTAMI
UJI-YAMADA
GEKU
TOBA
PEARL I.

NAI-KU
ISE-SHIMA SKYLINE
TOBA BAY

KUZAKI
ISOBE BUS CENTER
SHIMA-ISOBE
PEARL ROAD

-N-
0   6 km
ANAGAWA
ISE SHIMA YH
MATOYA BAY

km-long avenue leading from Ge-ku to Nai-ku is lined with stone lanterns, each curiously displaying an emblem resembling the Star of David carved into it. No buildings in the immediate vicinity of the shrines may be taller than 4 stories; this would be an insult to the gods. On the way you will pass a large building called Jingu Kaikon (Shrine Conference Hall). One of Japan's largest *sumo* tournaments is held here annually, usually during the early spring. When you arrive, cross the bridge over the Isuzu-gawa. Most Japanese walk down to the banks and use the water to wash their mouths in ritual purification. Hats and overcoats are also removed in reverence to the gods and NO SMOKING is in effect. During the Ise

Omatsuri (Festival) in Oct., teams of men hauling on ropes drag a huge beam up this river where virtually tamed overstuffed carp hug the banks, waiting for offered morsels. Gnarled, twisted pines and giant cedars interspersed with pathways give a park-like feeling to the grounds. The shrine buildings, with their thatched roofs and beamwork, are simple and dignified. At the eaves, the thatch rolls under like the curl of a gentle wave. Pictures can only be taken from the bottom of the steps and no further. Here, like at Ge-ku, offerings are made each morning accompanied by another pure white royal horse, and on special occasions, the *miko* will perform their sacred *kagura* dances.

nearby: When facing the 1st *torii* at the main entrance to Nai-ku, look to the L (SW) and you will see a street lined with shops. The shops sell a variety of locally produced souvenirs, featuring woodwork carvings made on the premises. The *sake* stores along this street sell a special, traditional *sake* known as *haku taka*. It resembles Greek Retsina with the resins still present in the bottle. It is quite unique, but costs Y2500, and the flavor takes getting used to. The premier shop along this street is Akafuku, rarely visited by the foreigner. Continue walking down the shopping street for about 5 min, look for smoke rising from a wood fire under 3 enormous bronze pots encased in red porcelain, the symbol of Akafuku. They boil spring water for the green tea which is served along with the *mochi* (glutenous pounded rice) and sweetened red beans, Y100. Akafuku's specialty is known all over Japan. Connoisseurs try to visit Akafuku for the "1st day of *mochi*," made on the 1st day of every month. Each month the *mochi* is of a different variety. Aug. *mochi* is the most traditional, using no sugar and made from millet, a type eaten over 150 yrs ago. Usually sold out by 0900. Although Akafuku *mochi* is a delight to the Japanese palate, most foreigners find it toe-curling sweet. You may not enjoy this special delicacy, but sip the atmosphere along with the tea. Akafuku's history and the purely Japanese building that it occupies predate the American Revolution. There was even a local T.V. program about its Meiji Era history. Fortunately the building survived the fire bombings of WW 11, even thought there was a gun emplacement just outside its doors facing the river. Sit on the raised *tatami* mats, which are a unique form almost like straw, and sip your tea while watching swallows fly around the brown-beamed rooms. There are excellent scroll paintings and fine examples of calligraphy hanging on the walls.

events: The New Year's Celebration takes place on Jan. 1-3 when 100s of 1000s of tourists gush from the train stations. The city streets are jammed. Pilgrims visit the shrines, then attend a huge bonfire where they roast *mochi* as insurance for a year of good health. *July 7:* Goma Festival, part of *Tanabata* held at Futami, a favorite spot to remember the "star-crossed lovers." Burning sticks are taken from the fire and placed at the doorways of many homes to ward off evil spirits. Only a few places in Japan observe this ritual. *July 13-15:* Konkodori during *Obon*. There's a unique dance and costuming during this festival. The participants wear grass skirts, white-and-black striped jerseys and horse-hair headdresses. Pre-

Chinese, very ancient. Almost seems African. *October:* Sengu Shiki is the shrine rebuilding ceremony at Ge-ku and Nai-ku. Occurs once every 20 years. The last occurred in 1973.

shopping: During *Tanabata*, (early July), there is a huge craft fair held at Ise. The streets are lined with street merchants from all over Japan. The trading is hectic, but there are excellent bargains. A few stores in Ise also specialize in magnificent religious carvings of Ge-ku and Nai-ku shrines, the larger ones costing Y150,000 and up. One such store is across from *Oinari* (the Fox Shrine), about 100 m to the L of the Ge-ku entrance. The store exudes a rich camphor smell from the wood used in the carvings. Another is Minge-Ise-Ji, a small shop, specializing in folk art from all over Japan. Exit Ujiyamada Eki. Stay on the lefthand side of the street and walk past the 1st traffic light. In the middle of the 2nd block is Minge-Ise-Ji. Look for the pottery displayed on the sidewalk. Excellent bargains. The shopkeeper also owns the tea store next door. *Meiruin Market:* Across from Ujiyamada Eki is a labyrinth of twisting alleyways housing the semi-open-air market of Meiruin. Shops sell everything from rubber sandals to fine porcelain. There are also a number of snack bars and *akachochin* (small drinking and eating places). Look for the red paper lanterns, the literal translation of *akachochin*; the food is traditional, delicious and inexpensive.

entertainment: The most rewarding entertainment in Ise is its shrines. The entire area, however, is preserved as a National Park, so there are excellent walking trails. The mountains abound in wildlife. On the trails you can encounter wild boar, monkeys and a variety of small forest animals such as squirrel, rabbits and *tanuki* (badgers). Ise's nightlife is subdued in reverence to the shrines, but there are hostess bars. Many offer taped music and a microphone to any patron inclined to sing. Itinerant musicians wander through the nightspots playing guitars and singing old favorites. This is giving way to taped music, but can still be heard in Ise. An old custom still practiced is for the towns people to take turns walking the streets at night clapping 2 wooden blocks together. The noise is a gentle reminder to check the safety of all cooking fires and to retire. Follow the natural rhythm of Ise to enjoy it fully, and allow this natural hypnotic sound to lull you to sleep.

services: There are a number of foreign exchange banks in the central business district. Two efficient ones are the Daichi Bank and the

105th Bank. The main P.O. is across the street from the main entrance of Ge-ku Shrine. There are only 2 copies of the Mainichi Daily News (in English) available at the newsstand at Ujiyamada Eki. Gone by 0800. At the local JTB no English is spoken, but maps, brochures and on-going reservations are available. Turn L outside Ise-shi Eki and look for a yellow-and-blue sign on a building that says NATIONAL, the JTB is on the 1st floor of this building. Martial arts are practiced and can be seen next door to the main police station.

accommodations: The most important thing to remember about lodgings in and around Ise is that they are impossible to get during festival time. Reservations for the New Year's celebration are made even a year in advance. At other times, Ise is not difficult to find a place to stay. For western-style, Town Ise Hotel (turn R at main entrance of Ujiyamada Eki, 150 m on R), is single Y3400, double Y6000. Yamata Business Hotel and Tea Room (sign in English); walk under large _torii_ straddling the road outside of Ise-shi Eki, and it's 2 blocks down on the left. They charge Y3800 for single, Y7000 for double. New Green Hotel (near N entrance of Ge-ku, just past Yamata Business Hotel) charges Y3000 for single, Y5000 for double; best hotel buy in town, tel: 22-4560. For something different, Mitsukoshi Sauna Bath, Y1500 per night, includes free orange juice and cigarettes. Y3000 for a massage. Full of local color and night people. Lockers are available for personal possessions. Located at 8th floor of Josoko Bldg., the large, honeycombed gold building with an orange band around it across from Ise-shi Eki. Sorry, men only! The closest YH to Ise is Iseshima YH, 1219-80 Anagawa, Isobe-cho 517-02, tel: (05995) 5-0226, 7 min on foot from Anagawa Sta., 120 beds. Others are found in the surrounding areas (see "Tobe and Vicinity").

food: The best traditional foods, along with homey, local atmosphere, are available at Meiruin Shopping Arcade across from Ujiyamada Eki. The Keta Snack is directly across from Ujiyamada Eki in the brown building near the entrance to Meiruin. Relax at the counter, no pressure, beer is Y600 per liter; popular with the locals at night. Kame Hachi (8 Turtles) is located at the main entrance of Meiruin. Go down the 1st alleyway to the R and look for the big _akachochin_ (red paper lantern). This is a Japanese neighborhood restaurant with a very friendly atmosphere. Sit on the raised _tatami_. Rice and vegetables Y150, beer Y350, _akadashi_ (strong _miso_ soup) Y150. _Sake_ Y250-300 per bottle. Misogi (past Kame Hachi, on the corner as the alleyway bends) is very tiny, look again for the red lantern. Great food, great value and traditional delicacies. _Tonkatsu teishoku_ (batter-fried meat on rice) goes for Y500; chicken _yakitori_ is Y60 per skewer. With your beer (Y330) you're given free munchies: tiny shrimp and spiced and dried eel backbone, full of vitamins and minerals. Another specialty here is grilled shark meat. There is a health food store on the L about 150 m past the _torii_ at Ise-shi Eki; look for the yellow and green awning. Since health food stores are few and far between, this is a good place to stock up on _genmai_ (brown rice), good bread (a rarity), barley, oatmeal and much more.

TOBA AND VICINITY

On the coast, 10 km E of Ise is Toba, where the cultured pearl industry began in Japan in 1893. You can train from Uji-Yamada Eki in 20 min (Y200) but it is much more visually and culturally attractive to bus over Asamayama (553 m) on the Ise-Shima Skyline. If you have decided to bus along the skyline you will not only get an excellent view of the coastal area once you crest the mountains, but you can also get off and reboard along the way as the bus pulls into various scenic or cultural sights. _getting there:_ Buses depart twice hourly from Uji-Yamada Eki, making the express trip in 30 min (Y800), or from the bus terminal at Nai-ku Shrine (Y660). Another alternative is to hike the back mountain trails passing over Asamayama from Ise to Toba (3 hrs). You can begin in Ise or train to Samayama (10 min) and begin from there. Upon leaving Ise you pass through Furuichi, a now defunct red-light district where pilgrims once mixed earthly pleasures with spiritual aspirations as they converged on Ise from throughout the old empire. Walking along further, you will notice that _jizo_ (small stone Buddhist dieties) line the pathways. At one time all executions that took place in this mountainous region were performed by the _Eta,_ the little talked about untouchable caste of Japan. The "head chopping" _jizo_ still attracts some mourning pilgrims. The one drawback about this otherwise fascinating trek is that the rock outcroppings along the way harbor the deadly poisonous _mamushi_. These snakes are most prevalent during the summer months, so Japanese hikers beat the brush with long sticks as they walk along.

KONGOSHOJI

The bus stops at this inspiring heart-rending temple. Most Japanese tourists visit Kongoshoji superficially and miss a unique experience. Many businessmen look upon the site as a Zen retreat to spiritually apologize for their earthly ways. They act like lowly monks for a few hours and then drink holy _sake_ for the rest of the night. In the morning, their monumental hangovers are a reminder of their now-cleansed souls. Kongoshoji has 2 ferocious and superbly done _emma_ (male devil guardians to the afterworld) at the entrance. The temple was built as an offering to the gods in humility before the building of Todaiji Temple at Nara. The 2 _emma_ serve as a type of "devil filter" against evil spirits descending from the ominous north. Many pilgrims paste little bits of paper on the belfry here at the entrance, each bit containing a name. What most visitors come to see is the exquisite, vermillion Moon Bridge, a perfect semi-circle over a green sparkling pool. Another favorite attraction is the huge Buddha footprint. Toss a coin. If it lands inside the print, you will have good luck for a year. The best attraction is the stony and moss-covered footpath behind the temple. The area is moving, eerie and a unique experience , the whole way lined with tall (4 m) poles used as remembrances of the dead from throughout Japan. This practice is ancient. The top character on the pole is not Japanese, but Sanskrit. The poles are festooned with

the Moon Bridge of Kongoshoji

mementos from the departed's life. Some are hung with *sake* cups, calligraphy brushes, eye glasses and tiny ones with baby rattles, toy fire trucks and the 1000 cranes (mothers will fashion paper into a long string of 1000 cranes to beseech the gods to cure the diseases of their babies). Many strings are unfinished. Superstitious, religious or purely logical, this area will make your spirit vibrate. Inexplicably, you feel as though there are many people about, even though you are there alone. When you walk to the end of the trail (150 m), you will come to a very rustic Rest House operated by a Japanese couple. The husband is usually in the hills hunting. They sell a wide variety of cellophane-bagged munchies, but they specialize in an *oden*-type gelatin called *konyaku* (devil's tongue). It is made from pureed yam and the specialty here is to dip it into a sweet miso sauce. Earthy, traditional, but a bit sweet. After a spiritual immersion into Kongoshoji, reboard the bus. Before arriving in Toba, the bus stops at an official rest center, souvenir shop and restaurant. It is a monument to poor taste—rip-off prices, poor food and commercialized souvenirs. There are, however, excellent vistas as you round the mountain bends.

ama san (pearl divers) at Toba

TOBA

This small port city has been famous ever since 1893 when Kokichi Mikimoto annoyed his 1st oyster by injecting a grain of sand under its shell to produce the world's 1st cultured pearl. Toba, now a known tourist trap, abounds in pearl and jewelry shops where there are reasonable prices, but few bargains. Maps and brochures are available from Mikimoto Pearl in Tokyo. The town exists for the tourist. Next to the bus terminal is the Toba Visitor's Center, a small white building that hands out the usual brochures.

sights: For Pearl I., take the glass-encased bridge over the main road near the terminal, Y500 at the entrance. Here at Toba Aquarium, *ama-san* (woman divers) at one time heavily employed in pearl farming, now play with tanked dolphins. They can still hold their breath for a lung-busting amount of time. Some still actually do work the outlying islands, diving for seaweed and abalone. There are also films in English of ecstatic little oysters, so happy to have helped Mikimoto-san in producing adornments for grateful human beings. The Pearl I. Museum, however, is a complete and fascinating learning experience on cultured pearls. Another attraction is the *Brazil Maru*, a converted ocean liner that at one time took Japanese rice farmers to Brazil. It's now a floating restaurant, boutique, souvenir shop and more. *excursion boats:* Available (near the bridge to Pearl I.) to take you around the bay, but 45 min for Y1400 is not worth it. From the ferry terminal, however, there are regular ferries to the outlying islands that are worth it. The islands are rarely visited and provide good camping on any likely beach, snorkeling, friendly fishermen and spear fishing. (Buy a long bamboo spear propelled by a thick rubber band in numerous shops for Y1000). One of these islands, made famous by Yukio Mishima, the renowned author who committed suicide in the early 1970s, is Kamishima, the setting for his novel *The Sound of Waves*.

Futami: Along the coastal road, halfway between Ise and Toba (bus from either), is a curious natural shrine at Futami Beach called Myoto-Iwa (Married Rocks). The 2 rocks just offshore are 9 and 4 m high. In folklore, they represent Izanagi and Izanami, the male and female creators of Japan. The larger male rock has a *torii* on top, and their marriage is symbolized by a thick straw rope hung between them. Many Japanese lovers come to view the moonlight from here. The rope is replaced every year on Jan. 5th. The beaches in this area are good for swimming, spear fishing and camping, though they're a little too popular in mid-summer. To get to the rocks, you must pass a

Kaeru (Frog) Shrine especially meaningful to fishermen. A play on the word *kaeru* means "to return," therefore, a safe return from the sea.

accommodations: Toba, like Ise, is heavily touristed and has even more accommodations although the prices, because of its popularity, are quite high. Western-style places include the Toba Hotel International, tel: (05992) 5-3121, 15 min walk from Toba Eki, from Y7000; and Shima Kanko Hotel, tel: (05994) 3-1211, 10 min walk from Kashikojima Eki (Toba), from Y6500. Many *ryokan* and *minshuku* are found throughout the area. Including 2 meals, they start at Y15,000 and Y10,000 respectively. European-type lodgings are prevalent in the Toba area. They usually start at Y6000 (w/2 meals). Examples are: Uemura Pension, tel: (069932) 5555, and Pension Fukura, tel: (05992) 5-6234. In Toba and Futami try the Kontaiji YH, 3-24-1 Toba 517, tel: (05992) 5-3035, 15 min on foot from Toba Sta., 7 beds; and Taikoji YH, 1659 Ei, Futami-cho 519-06, tel (059643) 2283, 4 min by bus from Futamiura Sta. and 5 min on foot, 28 beds.

food: Toba is also known for its excellent seafood, especially lobster, sold in local restaurants and *sushi* bars. The many *sushi* bars range in price, but a favorite with the locals (always the best sign) is Edo Kin (Tokyo Gold) on a not-too-difficult-to-find street about a 10 min walk from Pearl Island. For Y2000 you can have a mouth watering, zesty array of excellent *sushi*.

CHUGOKU

INTRODUCTION

Referred to as "Western Japan," this district is the long, thin tail of Honshu stretching toward Kyushu and ending at the port of Shimonoseki. The prefectures of Tottori, Okayama, Shimane, Hiroshima and Yamaguchi make up the district. Although Chugoku is grouped as one geographical region, it is actually divided down the center from E to W by the tall and rugged Chugoku Mountains. To the N of the mountains are the prefectures of Tottori, Shimane and a small portion of northern Yamaguchi, collectively known as the San-In Region (literally Shade of the Mountains). Here, the inhospitable and rocky coast is battered by the Sea of Japan. To the S, on the leeward side of the mountains, is the San-Yo Region with its balmy prefectures of Okayama, Hiroshima and southern Yamaguchi, lying along the soft, tame Inland Sea. The 2 regions are not only distinctive geographically, but culturally and historically as well. The cities of Yamaguchi, Hiroshima and Okayama were, from ancient times, ports of call and major way stations along the trade routes linking the empire with its southern territories and the all-important trade with Korea and China. It follows, naturally, that today they are serviced by the *shinkansen* and are vital organs in the industrial underbelly of Japan. The San-In Region, alternatively, was always far removed from the seat of power of the old empires. News and culture traveled slowly and, even today, Tottori and Shimane are left underdeveloped and (thankfully) lagging behind mainstream Japan.

San-Yo Region: Today, a traveler in the San-Yo Region of Chugoku can quietly scream along by *shinkansen* stopping at Okayama. Only 20 km distant is Kurashiki and its old quarter, a living museum of ebony and white plaster walks. Rickshaws can still be hired here to slowly soak up the sights in the intricate alleyways. You are never far from the Inland Sea, laced with ferry service for a quick step to Shikoku. Next express stop is Hiroshima, with the A-bomb site, man's testament to the way the future must not be. Within 15 min is Miyajima, the Sacred Island, framed in its floating *torii*. From olden times, it was considered a place too sacred on which to die or be born. Here, Kamikaze pilots mustered and prayed before taking on their last assignments. On the western tip of Chugoku is Shimonoseki, a useful city where travelers can catch the inexpensive Kampu ferry to Korea to re-up on a Japanese visa, or to move on into mainland Asia. *San-In Region:* In the western regions of San-In are Shimane Prefecture and the cultural city of Matsue, where can be found the home of Lafcadio Hearn, a turn of the century writer on "things Japanese." There is also an impressive castle built by the cousins of the Tokugawas. Close-by in Izumo is the Taisho Jinja, the oldest Shinto Shrine in Japan. The Shinto gods gather at Taisho in Nov., leaving vacant their resting places throughout Japan (even gods need a vacation). Seventy km out into the Sea of Japan are the Oki Islands, still uninvaded by tourists, but gaining in prominence as a rustic, uncluttered vacation spot. The largest tree in Japan is on the Okis where it is lovingly wrapped with burlaps to protect it from the cold, and braced by stout beams like crutches for an old man. Finally, there are the sand dunes of Tottori, where you can ride camels and where Techigawara, the well-known Japanese director, filmed *Woman of the Dunes.* Crowning the San-In is Mt. Daisen (1713 m) with excellent skiing and walking trails, along with Daisenji, its own mountain people.

GETTING THERE

by rail: San-Yo is serviced by the *shinkansen* from Tokyo (4 hrs 10 min), Nagoya (2 hrs 9 min), and Kobe (one hr) to Okayama. Add one hr to continue on to Hiroshima. The San-Yo Main Line, offering both limited express and ordinary express, operates numerous runs along all points of San-Yo. Branch lines, such as the Yamaguchi Fukuen, Hakabi and Tsuyama, cross Chugoku from S to N, running inland to all major towns. *to San-In:* The San-In Main Line runs along the coast of the Japan Sea with stations at all major towns and cities. Points along the lines are usually so close together that you can save money without sacrificing much time by taking the *futsu* instead of paying the express charge on the *kyuko*. *by bus:* The 2 major roads in Chugoku parallel the 2 major rail lines along both coasts. The Trans-Chugoku Expressway, designed to run through the center of the

district, is a long-term project still in progress. Buses give a clearer window on Japanese life because the routes pass through the main streets of villages that are only a blur from a train window. A good sightseeing route is from Hiroshima to Matsue for Y2300 (express train Y3300), approx. 5 hours. Buses also depart from Hiroshima, Okayama and Yamaguchi for all points within Chugoku, and for major cities on Kyushu and Honshu. The drawbacks are that buses are not nearly as numerous as trains, and you must wait for sometimes infrequent comfort stops. *by air:* There are 2 major airports in Chugoku, at Okayama and at Hiroshima with Hiroshima carrying the most traffic. From Tokyo to Hiroshima, 2 hrs 30 min by ANA. Osaka to Hiroshima, one hr 5 min by TOA. In the far W, Ube services Yamaguchi and along the Sea of Japan, Izumo and Miho (Matsue) are linked directly to Hiroshima and in turn, both are linked with Dogo Island, the largest of the 2 Okis. Tottori Airport farther to the E completes the chain.

by ferry: The ferry routes connecting San-Yo with Kyushu, Shikoku and the main ports of central Honshu (Kobe, Osaka, Tokyo) look like a spilled bowl of spaghetti on the map. A main and frequently used route is between Kobe and (Shimonoseki) Kokura, 15 hours. Shimonoseki is also the embarkation point for the 15 hr 30 min Kampu Ferry to Pusan, Korea (see "General Introduction—Visa" and "Shimonoseki" this chapter for more information). San-In has no ferry routes connecting it to greater Japan. The Oki Islands, however, are serviced by ferry from Shichirui (30 km NE of Matsue) by a 3 hr ferry ride. *note:* The best way to experience Chugoku is by rail and bus. The Inland Sea route undoubtedly has its own serene beauty, but this is limited to scenic panoramas. The distances covered by the ferries are too large, and you move from port to port, leaving all in between undiscovered. A good alternative is to make short hops by ferry; but a person choosing this way must have the time. A full list of ferry schedules throughout the region is offered by TIC and reservations can be made at any JTB. The main ferry companies are: Seto Naikai (STS Line) Steamship Co., which runs numerous boats throughout the Inland Sea. Tokyo, tel: (03) 567-8740; Hiroshima, tel: (0833) 51-5291. Hiroshima Green Ferry Co. operates boats from Osaka and Hiroshima and then on to Kyushu; Osaka, tel: (06) 532-3121, and Hiroshima, tel: (0822) 28-1665. Ocean Tokyu Ferry Co. plies from Tokyo, docks at Tokushima and terminates

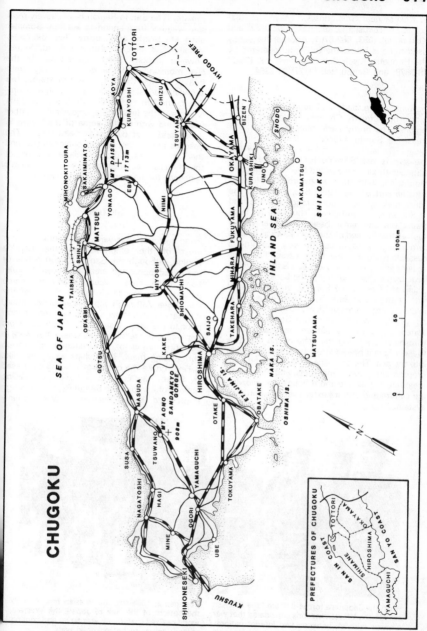

CHUGOKU

PREFECTURES OF CHUGOKU

at Kokura near Shimonoseki. Tokyo, tel: (03) 567-0971; Tokushima, tel: (0886) 62-0489; and Kokura, tel: (093) 582-6761. Another frequently used route is Hiroshima to Beppu operated by the Hirobetsu Kisen Co., Hiroshima, tel: (0822) 48-2678; and Beppu, tel: (0977) 21-2364.

the land: Like a toad sunbathing on a log in the middle of a stream, Chugoku is divided into 2 regions. The horny back with its bumps and creases is San-In, braced against the Sea of Japan. The soft, smooth belly turned towards the sun is the San-Yo Region, stretching somnolently along the Inland Sea. The Chugoku Mountains, with their windward face leaning into the surf of the Japan Sea, extend to the coast, making the harbors craggy and the land of San-In rocky and steep. There are no large plains, but only small basins and river valleys such as that formed by the Gonokawa as it flows tumultuously towards the sea, forming a passable route that has been a trade link since ancient times. The one exception is the relatively large Izumo Plain that forms the banks for Lake Shinji at Matsue. The San-Yo, on the leeward side of the mountains, is far less rugged. The relatively large plains of Okayama and Hiroshima dip gently towards the Inland Sea where the waters are calm, the harbors deep and wide. Hiroshima is actually the delta of the Otagawa River, where it breaks into 6 branches emptying into the sea. The shoreline is embroidered with promontories, bays and islets and the inland areas are flatter and more hospitable allowing agriculture and a more extensive transportation system.

climate: The San-In Region has relatively pleasant weather from spring to autumn. Summer days are bright and sunny. The beaches, although few, are clean and uncrowded. Winter, however, is nasty. The region is struck by the NW monsoon and the days are foggy with heavy clouds. Close to the mountains, the snowfall is considerable and the skiing is magnificent. The San-Yo Region, which is actually the N shore of the Inland Sea, enjoys mild weather year round with rainfall some of the lowest in Japan and most days sunny and bright. The beaches are numerous, but overcrowded, and the San-Yo coast is grossly polluted because of the immense factories spurred on by Japan's penchant for unchecked industrialization.

HISTORY

In an historical overview of Chugoku places, most of the emphasis on the San-Yo Region, although the San-In Region is one of the oldest populated areas of Japan. Populations, trade, communications and commerce moved more readily along the shores of the Inland Sea. Although Japan is an island nation, it never developed as a great seafaring nation prior to the Meiji Restoration. Japanese sailors felt secure on the Inland Sea where they were in constant view of the islands of Japan surrounding them. Their ships were more like galleys, unlike the deep water sailing craft used by Elizabethan England and the great sailing nations of Europe. The San-In Region, although it provided limited anchorage, was primarily

when the Japanese forces defeated the Chinese in 1894, the Western nations considered that war a minor skirmish between two inferior nations. But when the Czar's forces were soundly trounced in 1905 and the Russian fleet sent to the bottom of the Sea of Japan, the Western world realized that Japan was an up and coming military power to be reckoned with

Moritsuma Sasaki, commander of the victorious Minamoto (Genji) Clan

below rather than surrender. Her actions were considered tragic, but extremely noble. Shimonoseki paradoxically came into prominence again in 1863, but this battle marked the end of shogunate rule close to the same spot where it had begun centuries before. The Choshu clan rallied under the battle cry of "Expel the Barbarians," and attempted to seal off the straits to foreign ships. In a grossly lopsided battle, American, English, French and Dutch ships bombarded the port, bringing about its defeat in 3 days. The shogunate dissolved and the Meiji Era began, hurling Japan headlong into the 20th Century. Japan, realizing its power as an emerging nation, came into conflict with China in 1894 and later with Russia in 1905. In both conflicts the Japanese fleet was based at Hiroshima, the best and safest western port for war. Chugoku served as an excellent staging area for Japanese troops sent to fight the Chinese, and later as a naval headquarters for Admiral Togo, the hero of the Russo-Japanese war, who annihilated the Russian Baltic Fleet in the Sea of Japan. Japan's rapid and heady ascendancy came to a shattering end in Hiroshima on August 6, 1945, when the first atomic bomb fell and reduced the once mighty city into a blackened, smoking cauldron.

reached by arduous overland routes. It nonetheless was totally integrated, but played a much lesser role in the country's development. Its history is steeped in folklore, but it served mostly as a spring to water the spread of Japanese culture that flowered further downstream. There was a brief period during the 8th C. in San-In when the Izumo culture blossomed under the Yamato Kings. This period was marked by the construction of large tombs along the Japan Sea. The Oki islands, by today's standards a short ferry ride from Matsue, were considered so remote that they were used as islands of exile for recalcitrant emperors such as Godaigo in the 14th Century. Shimonoseki, overlooking the Kanmon Straits in the far W, was the scene for 2 important battles that changed the history of Japan. The first was the battle of Dannoura in the 12th C. when the 2 powerful clans of the Minamoto's and Taira's (Heike) clashed in their bid for power to unify Japan. The Minamoto were victorious, and thus began almost 7 centuries of militaristic rule known as the shogunate. The downfall of the Taira clan is immortalized in a work called the *Tale of Heike*. This narrative epic relates that when the battle was nearing a conclusion, the loyal Lady Nii of the House of Heike took the young emperor into her arms and plunged from the castle battlements into the sea

economy: The San-Yo Region today is primarily industrial with waning secondary industries of agriculture and fishing. The region's harbors and bays are quickly being turned into kombinats, which are huge industrial complexes producing new materials to feed lesser factories attached to them by rail and sea connections. The shorelines fume with petrochemical refineries and steel mills. The harbors are dredged to accommodate larger vessels and the dredgings are dumped into low water areas to create more land for the factories which go to make up more kombinats. Beautiful natural areas are being destroyed and the waters are thick with pollution. Along the San-Yo coast of the Inland Sea is where the Japanese must bear the taunt that they have lost their sense of beauty. Yet, the corporate heads say that the wheels of industry must turn, and the catch-all apologetic phrase of *shikata ga nai* (it can't be helped) is their only sad retort. The San-In Region is temporarily being saved from rapid industrial development by its inhospitable coastline, but plans are in the works. The land itself is not agriculturally productive for rice cultivation, but drainage projects since WW 11 have opened more land. On mountain slopes as well as on the sand dunes of Tottori, pears, grapes and tobacco are raised with limited success. The real financial backbone of the area is in fishing. The once timid Japanese seafarer today puts out from numerous fishing villages along San-In to the deep ocean shelves. Like all lesser industrialized area of Japan, the San-In District is preserved only by dwindling time and temporarily inadequate technology.

ARTS AND CRAFTS

pottery: Chugoku has 2 of the most famous types of pottery in Japan: *bizen-yaki* in Okayama Prefecture, and *hagi-yaki* in Yamaguchi. Bizen (Imbe) is a small town 35 km E of Okayama on the JNR Ako Line. Its pottery history dates back to the 9th C., making *bizen-yaki* one of the oldest potting centers in Japan. Bizenware is distinguished by a deep brown hue, a result of the firing of the iron-rich clay found in the area. A second, less favored type, is a light, off-white. A distinctive feature of *bizen-yaki* is that it is encircled by salt-soaked straw during the firing which produces the burnished irregularities so prized by collectors. Unfortunately, in Bizen there is no annual pottery fair typical of most pottery centers, so to acquaint yourself with the pottery, visit: Bizen Ceramics Hall, Imbe, Bizen, Okayama (near Imbe Eki), tel: (0869) 64-1001, open 0930-1700, closed Mon., Y200; and Bizen Old Ceramics Art Museum, 998 Imbe, Bizen, Okayama (10 min walk from Imbe Eki). tel: (869) 64-3775, open 1000-1700, Y200.

Hagi-yaki: Hagi City is located on the Japan Sea coast of Yamaguchi Prefecture, 20 km E of Nagato. Take the *shinkansen* from Osaka to Ogori (3¼ hrs) and then bus (1½ hrs) to Hagi, or train from Nagato to Hagi on the San-In Line (approx. 35 min). *Hagi-yaki* began as the spoils of the ill-fated war waged by Toyotomi Hideyoshi against Korea at the turn of the 16th Century. Indentured Korean potters were taken to Japan where they began recreating their masterly works in Japanese clay. *Hagi-yaki is* known for its translucent glazes. Early works are distinguished by transparent yellow-green and hazy, milk-white glazes, whereas modern works have turned to the use of soft beige and muted pink. One quality of *hagi-yaki* that is particularly delightful is the gentle transformation of the beige glaze into pink as the cups are used over the years for tea drinking. Unfortunately, there are large numbers of johnny-come-latelies plying their unaccomplished trade in Hagi. A resurgence in the popularity of *hagi-yaki* caused a boom, and the number of potters has increased 500% in the last 10 years. The result is that there is a high density of inferior pottery competing with truly excellent work. Let the buyer beware. For well-done displays visit: Hagi City Tourist Association, 15 min walk from Higashi-Hagi Eki, tel: (0838) 25-1750; the Kumaya Art Museum, 47 Imauotanacho, Hagi (near Higashi-Hagi Eki), tel: (0838) 22-7547, hours: 0900-1700, Y300 entrance; and Ishii Tea Bowl Museum, 35 Higashidamachi (2 min from Hagi Bus Station), hours: 0900-1600. Closed the 9th and 19th of each month. Y300 admission.

folk toys: Kijigangu (wooden tops, dolls and animals) are made at Iwami, Tottori Prefecture. The 12 gaily painted animals correspond to the months of the year, an adaptation of the 12 year cyclical Chinese calendar. *Tsuchi ningyo* (clay dolls), called *koga-ningyo* in Hiroshima, are fashioned after foreigners, namely Dutch and Chinese, who traded at the tiny island of Dejima during the Edo period. During their heyday, they were considered very exotic. A unique *tora-no-gangu* (paper tiger) is made at Izumo, Shimane Prefecture. Compared to most, it is extremely well done, with big ears, whiskers and large, golden eyes. It was depicted on the New Year

stamp of 1962. A master of *tora-no-gangu* is Tatsunosuke Tanaka of Tottori, who specializes in giving his tigers a full range of facial expressions from mirth to disappointment. A famous type of *fune-no-gangu* (decorated wooden boat) is made at Onomichi, Hiroshima Prefecture. It is called *tanomobune,* and is customarily given to baby boys on their first birthday. It is made of thick, wooden slats and mounted on wheels. It is a good luck omen depicting rice-laden junks that at one time sailed into the port of Onomichi. *Omen* (papier mache masks) are made throughout Tottori, but a particularly famous one is the *tengu* (long-nosed goblin) mask of Kurayoshi. Others found in Tottori City include a blazing red orangutan with flax-fiber hair, considered a minor work of art. This mask wears an expression similar to that of the Classic Greek Comedy Mask and similar ones may be used in Kabuki plays.

CHUGOKU FESTIVALS AND EVENTS

Feb., 3rd Saturday: Hadaka Matsuri (Naked Festival). Eyo, the Naked Festival of Saidaji Temple, Okayama, is one of the largest Hadaka Matsuri held in Japan. The festivities begin on the temple grounds at midnight and the participants are all men. The men wear only a fundoshi (loincloth) to show the kami that they have been purified and as a sign of equality and comraderie in the boisterous, jostling event. Two batons made of camphor wood are thrown into the darkened courtyard. The object is to retrieve them and take them to the waiting priests to receive blessings and a large prize. Fun, but crowded.

Mar. 3: Hina Matsuri (Doll Festival). An interesting variation of the Doll Festival held throughout Japan on the same day, is held at Tottori. Little straw baskets carry paper dolls of a man and a woman down the river and into the sea. The paper dolls, surrounded by peach blossoms, represent evil spirits that vex little children. This ritual symbolizes good-bye and good riddance to youthful woes.

Apr. 15: On this date, Gumonji-do (Fire Walking Ceremonies) and ancient bugaku dances are held atop Mt. Misen at Miyajima. This festival centers around a temple founded by Kobo-Daishi 12 C ago. The fire walking is both a purification ceremony and a testament to the religious zeal of the devotees. The bugaku dances, which originated in Central Asia, have been preserved only in Japan. Firewalking ceremonies are repeated on Nov. 15, but no dancing. Fascinating, and an excellent time of year to see Miyajima.

Apr. 23-25: Senteisai Festival of the Akama Shrine, Shimonoseki. This festival commemorates the noble tragedy of Lady Nii who threw herself and young Emperor Antoku into the sea when the Heike clan was defeated. Particularly touching for women, who dress in their best traditional attire and pay homage at the shrine.

mid-Jul.: Kangensai Music Festival of Itsukushima shrine, Miyajima, is the gayest festivity held on this holy island. The god of the shrine is ferried across to the mainland, while gagaku (classical court music) and bugaku are performed on the barge which is returned the next morning after staying one night on the mainland. A performance of classical music and dance like those of the music festival can be arranged at the large, open-air stage at the shrine at anytime for an appropriate fee. The cost, however, is too high for a personal performance and is usually split by an interested group.

Aug. 6: Peace Memorial Park, Hiroshima. This memorial service begins at 0815, the time of the blast. The family of man looks, remembers and prays.

mid-Aug.: Tamadori Matsuri at Itshukushima Shrine, Miyajima. Thousands of loinclothed young men gather at high tide under the torii. A ball is thrown into the water, and there is a scramble to recover it. It is brought to the awaiting priests for prizes and blessings. Biggest water polo event in the world. Amazingly, no one drowns.

Nov.: At Izumo-Taisho Shrine, Matsue. It is believed that all the Shinto deities of Japan gather at this shrine in Nov. in a sort of heavenly vacation. This time is called kamiarizuku (the time when the gods gather) at Izumo, and kannazuki (the month without gods) in the remainder of Japan. The celebrants of the festival carry lighted torches from the beaches to the shrine to welcome back the gods. Young lovers usually gather, because the shrine is renowned as a place of marriage. The feeling in the air is electric.

THE SAN-YO REGION

OKAYAMA CITY

Okayama (pop. 500,000) is the transportation gateway to San-Yo and the main commercial city of the whole prefecture. Already, plans are inching ahead to fully include Okayama in the great industrial megalopolis building steadily along the Inland Sea. The slowly yielding Chugoku Mountains are being transversed by a superhighway and minds are plotting the building of a bridge to Shikoku across the whirlpools of Naruto. Okayama stands poised, ready to dive into the industrial pool, but before the backwash covers its beauty, there are still some lovely sights to see. *getting there:* By *shinkansen* from Tokyo (4 hrs 10 min), Y10,000, and by numerous express and limited expresses from all points of Honshu. Also the junction of the Tsuyama Line to the interior and ferry from Uno (Okayama's port, 30 min by bus from the *eki*) to Shodo Island and Takamatsu on Shikoku.

sights: The most fascinating sights are not found in Okayama City itself but in the surrounding areas. The pottery town of Bizen and the cultural center of Kurashiki provide full days of touring and cultural exploration. Both are easily reached by train or bus from Okayama Eki in less than one hour. While in the city make sure to visit Korakuen Park, 1.6 km E of Okayama Eki by frequent bus, one of the 3 most celebrated gardens of Japan. It was built in 1700 by Tsunamasa Ikeda on the banks of the Asahi River and offers wide expanses of tended lawns interspersed with perfectly manicured gardens. Here is Japanese landscape gardening at its best on an unusually grand scale. Look across the park to see Ujo (Crow Castle) purposely painted black to balance the pure white Egret Castle in the nearby town of Himeji. Japan abounds in parks, but Korakuen is unique and superb. Korakuen and Ujo are connected by a walking bridge with Okayama Art Museum nearby.

accommodations: Okayama offers a full range of accommodations and is an excellent base from which the surrounding cultural and scenic areas may be explored. Western-style hotels include Hotel New Okayama, 25-1-1 Ekimae-cho, Okayama 700, tel: (0862) 23-8211, in front of Okayama Station, from Y3500; and Okayama Royal Hotel, 2-4 Ezu-cho, Okayama 700, tel: (0862) 54-1155, 2 min by car from Okayama Station, from Y4500. Most Western-style hotels offer Japanese-style rooms, but for a totally Japanese experience, try Shinmatsunoe Ryokan, Ifukucho, Okayama 700, tel: (0862) 52-5131, Y8000-15,000. The budget-minded should try the following business hotels: Okayama New Station Hotel, Ekimae, Okayama, tel: (0862) 53-6655, 44 rms., Y3300, one min walk from JNR Okayama Station; and Okayama Business Hotel, 1-1-42 Minamikata, Okayama, tel: (0862) 22-2224, 82 rms., Y3400, 5 min walk from JNR Okayama Station. One YH is available in Okayama. It is Okayama-ken YH Seinen Kaikan, 1-7-6 Tsukura-cho, Okayama 700, tel: (0862) 52-0651, 20 min on foot from Okayama Station, 65 beds. Closed Jan. 18-24.

services: In Okayama, for maps and general information concerning Okayama Prefecture contact Okayama Tourist Section, Uchisange Okayama, tel: (0862) 24-2111. *excursion buses* Two regular excursion bus tours are operated daily, including Sunday, departing from Okayama Eki. The earlier tour departs at 1050 and its 6 hr itinerary includes Kurashiki and its museums, Washuzan Skyline and hill, and the Mizushima Industrial Zone (see following descriptions). The later bus departing Okayama Eki at 1230 offers a 4 hr 30 min tour and includes stops at Ikeda Zoo, Bizen and Shizutani Korakuen Garden, Okayama Castle and various sights in the immediate Okayama area. There are other lesser tours offered, but these are the best Only Japanese is spoken.

VICINITY OF OKAYAMA

Bizen: If heading for the nearby pottery town of Bizen (see "arts and crafts"), it is easier to find accommodations in Okayama. Besides the pottery works, Bizen sights also include Shizutani, the first school in Japan designed for the education of the common people. The distinctive roof of the main hall and attendant buildings of Shizutani are tiled with *bizen-yaki*. Shizutani is 10 min by bus from Yoshinaga Eki. Open daily 0900-1600. An interesting stopover on the way to Bizen is Saidaiji Temple famous for its Naked Festival (see "events").

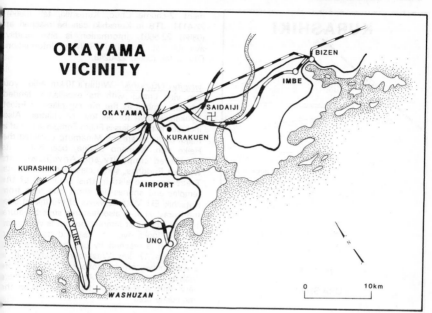

OKAYAMA VICINITY

BIZEN

IMBE

SAIDAIJI

OKAYAMA

KURAKUEN

KURASHIKI

AIRPORT

SKYLINE

UNO

WASHUZAN

N

0   10km

Kasaoka: An interesting stopover is at Kasaoka (15 km W of Kurashiki). Kasaoka preserves a special *bon* dance at Shiraishi performed on the beach on Sat. nights during the summer. The dance especially remembers the spirits of the warriors fallen during the clash of the Heike and Minamoto clans. Amidst all the beauty of this area is the Mizushima Industrial Area, a telling glimpse of the future. Rows and rows of petrochemical tanks, textile factories and steel works stand shoulder to shoulder. Here the beautiful shoreline is no more, and the specter of Japan to come treads on heavy feet through thick mists of smog.

KURASHIKI

This town, 20 km W of Okayama on the JNR Main Line, was an important grainery and shipping port during the Tokugawa Era. The waterways of the city, lined with willow trees, once saw barges laden with grain heading for ships on the Inland Sea. The black-tiled graneries (*kura*) have been preserved and the city abounds in galleries, museums, folk arts and temples. Though surrounded by industrialization, Kurashiki is a jewelcase of culture. Along the canal, with willows gently swaying in the

breeze, old Japan is captured. For precious moments, the specter of simpler times floats on still wings. Rickshaws can be hired for Y100 per half hour.

sights: The Ohara museum of Art is just one km S of the *eki*, and is just what its name implies. The main building is a ferro-concrete Greek-style structure built in 1930. Classical Japanese buildings were added in 1961. The museum houses works of art from the world over, including El Greco, Cezann, Van Gogh, Renoir and comtemporary artists. The newest collections include works from Japan and antiquities from China. _Kurashiki Archaeological museum:_ This museum is dedicated to relics found in the neighboring Kibi District, as well as shards of Yayoi and Jamon pottery. Many of its exhibits come from the Tsukuriyama burial mound of the 5th C., the 4th largest of its kind found in Japan. _Kurashiki Museum of Folkcraft:_ This exhibit begins with buildings which are folk art in themselves. The adventure unfolds as you walk the inlaid cobblestone and marble pathway. Inside are thousands of exhibits of Japan's finest woodwork, ceramics, textiles, glassware and all manner of handmade objects.

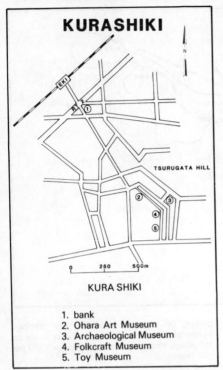

KURASHIKI

TSURUGATA HILL

0   250   500m

KURA SHIKI

1. bank
2. Ohara Art Museum
3. Archaeological Museum
4. Folkcraft Museum
5. Toy Museum

accommodations: Business hotels in the Kurashiki-Washuzan area include Kurashiki Station Hotel, 2-8-1 Achi, Kurashiki City, Okayama Prefecture, tel: (0864) 25-2525, 134 rms., Y3500, 3 min walk from JNR Kurashiki Station; Mizushima Grand Hotel, 1-8 Minamisaiwaicho, Mizushima, Kurashiki City, Okayama Prefecture, tel: (0864) 46-4040, 30 rms., Y3300, 15 min drive from JNR Kurashiki Station. Reasonably priced *minshuku* accommodations are available at Kurashiki Tokusan Kan, 8-33 Hon-machi, Kurashiki City, tel: (0864) 25-3056, Sanyo Main Line, Kurashiki Station, 12 min on foot. Youth Hostelers in the area have a choice of two. They are Kurashiki YH, 1537-1, Mukaiyama, Kurashiki City 710, tel: (0864) 22-7355, 10 min by bus from Kurashiki Station and 10 min on foot, 80 beds; and Washu-zan YH, 1666-1, Obatake, Kurashiki City 711, tel: (0864) 79-9280, one hr 20 min by bus from Okayama Station and 3 min on foot, 60 beds. *services:* For maps and information on the museums and sights of Kurashiki, contact Kurashiki City Tourist Department, 2-chome Chuo, Kurashiki, tel: (0864) 22-4111. JTB in Kurashiki can be reached at (0864) 22-5601. Information is also readily available at Kurashiki Railway Information Office, tel: (0864) 22-0249.

vicinity of Kurashiki: Within a 10 km radius, you can visit Entsuji with its excellently tended garden, famous as the training place of Priest Ryokan, known for his love of children. Also included in the radius is Fujito Temple, a site of a major battle where the Minamoto defeated the Heike clan. Kumano Shrine, beautiful in its weathered simplicity and Anyoji, with its wooden Buddhas, some classified as National Treasures, are also in this area. All of the temples and shrines are short bus trips from Kurashiki Eki. With its views of the Inland Sea, the Kurashiki area also features superb natural beauty. The most famous lookout is Washuzan Hill that looks over the sea and its pine-clad islands. It is reached by bus from Mizushima along the 17 km Washuzan Skyline. It is a well-known, official lookout and draws more than its share of tourists. Accommodations here vary, with a resthouse, hotel and YH in the immediate area.

the cobble stone street and distinctive tiled buildings of Kurashiki are best exemplified at the Kurashiki Museum of Folkart

HIROSHIMA PREFECTURE

HIROSHIMA

Like a Phoenix from its own ashes, Hiroshima rose. Less than 4 decades since its obliteration, it is once again the most vital city of the San-Yo Region, with a growing population of 750,000. It is referred to as the "River City" because in its confines, the Otagawa branches into 6 delta tributaries that flow into the bay. In the years just following the A-bomb blast, scientists doubted if Hiroshima could ever live again. Today the streets hum with activity, trees and flowers grow, and birds perch to sing. Nature does not forget, but it does forgive. *getting there:* Hiroshima is a main station on both the *shinkansen* and the San-Yo Main Line. The *shinkansen* from Tokyo makes the trip in 5 hrs, from Kyoto in 2 hrs, 15 min, and from Shin-Osaka in one hr 56 minutes. A sleeping train from Tokyo is also available, making the overnight journey in about 12 hours. By air, ANA operates daily flights from Haneda (Tokyo) to Hiroshima Air-

port. Bookings can be make at Tokyo Reservation Center (03) 747-5111. Frequent buses shuttle between the airport and Hiroshima Eki, making the trip in 35 minutes. Besides the ferry service mentioned in the chapter introduction, the Hiroshima Green Ferry offers daily sailings between Osaka Minami-ko Ferry Terminal and Hiroshima Dejima Port. The daily ferry departs from Osaka at 2020 and arrives in Hiroshima the next morning at 0710. Return sailings depart from Dejima Port at 2020, arriving in Osaka the next morning. *getting around:* Hiroshima offers streetcars servicing the downtown area, Y90. Kokutetsu (JNR blue buses) and Hiroshima Kotsu (orange buses) service all the suburbs of the city. Most stop at Hiroshima Eki or at the bus center near the A-bomb site. Take the elevator from street level to the 3rd floor of Sogo Depato where you will find the bus center. For inter-city and long-distance buses, the 3rd floor is the place. English speaking personnel offer maps and information at the Tourist Information Center at Hiroshima eki. JTB office is at Kamiyo-cho, tel: (0822) 47-5131.

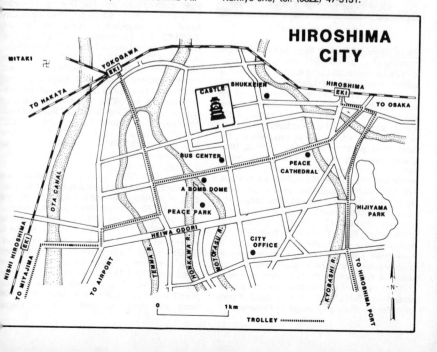

the A-Bomb Dome

Peace Memorial Park: It happened here. On the morning of August 6, 1945, the people of war-torn Japan hurried to begin the day. Overhead, a solitary airplane flew, a parachute drifted downwards, and a small man-made sun touched the earth. Buildings melted, people evaporated, and the family of man lost the first battle of the atomic age. Seventy thousand buildings in 13 sq km were flattened, 200,000 people perished, the lucky ones quickly; the unlucky lingered. Hiroshima, fringed by mountains forming a natural amphitheatre, seethed and fumed. Now we remember; the Peace Memorial Park is there. The Cenotaph, shaped like an ancient tomb, holds the names of the dead. The prayer, the hope in Japanese reads, "Repose ye in peace, for the error shall not be repeated." The skeleton of the Atomic Bomb Dome turns green with age against a blue sky. Pretty young girls stop to have their pictures taken. Families row in brightly colored boats on a light-hearted Sunday picnic. A lost balloon floats at treetop level; a child cries. An international law should be passed—the first official act of any head of state must be a solitary pilgrimage to Hiroshima.

Hiroshima Peace Memorial Museum: More life-like and chilling than Madame Troussaud's House of Wax, here are the charts, graphs, photos and modern sculptures of the living dead crawling through a ghastly city. It's all here, chronicled behind squeaky clean glass cases. Rent tapes and earphones in German, French, Italian, etc. No one should be uninformed. One exhibit, a shadow of a one-time person sitting on steps when it happened. That's all—just a shadow. Across the way at the auditorium, motion picture reels portray the same. Open 0900 to 1630 every day except New Year week; admission, Y50.

other sights: For an hour's relaxation, head only 700 m W of Hiroshima Eki to Shukkein Park. The park, familiarly known as Sentei, features a tea house, pools and gardens. It's prolific with azaleas as well as cherry blossoms in season. *Hijayama Park:* Located 10 min by bus E of the city, built on the slopes of Mt. Gako. The panorama lying at your feet is an extensive logistical view of this mountain-bound city.

accommodations: Hiroshima is an internationally visited city providing first-class Western style accommodations. For fine accommodations with prices to match, try: Hiroshima City Hotel, 1-4 Kyobashi-cho, Hiroshima 730, tel (0822) 63-5111, 3 min walk from Hiroshima Station; Hiroshima Kokusai Hotel, 3-13 Tate-machi Hiroshima 730, tel: (0822) 48-2323, 5 min by car from Hiroshima Station, single from Y4000; and Hotel Hiroshima Grand, 4-4 Kami-hachobori Hiroshima 730, 5 min by car from Hiroshima Station, single from Y4000. There are a cluster of *ryokan* within walking distance of Peace Memorial Park. They include Amagi Ryokan (0822) 47-1113, Kakusui-en Ryokan (0822) 48-1221 and Sera Bekkan (0822) 48-2251. Business hotels of Hiroshima include: Hokke Club Hiroshima-ten 3-7 Nakamichi, Hiroshima, tel: (0822) 48-3371 single w/bath Y3500 (tax and service charge are included); Hiroshima Central Hotel, 8-1 Ginzan cho, Hiroshima, tel: (0822) 43-2222, single w/bath Y3350; and Hotel Silk Plaza, 14-1 Hachobori, Hiroshima, tel: (0822) 27-8111, single w/bath Y3500. The Hiroshima YWCA Hostel is located at 3-10-4 Otemachi, Hiroshima, tel (0822) 41-5313, single w/o bath Y2000, women only. There are 2 YHs in Hiroshima. They are Hiroshima YH, 1-13-6 Ushita-shin-machi, Hiroshima 730, tel: (0822) 21-5343, 10 min by bus from Hiroshima Station and 8 min on foot, 100 beds; and Hiroshima Saka-machi YH, Ueda

Saka-machi, Hiroshima 731-43, tel: (0828) 85-0700, 20 min on foot from Saka Station, 25 beds. Hiroshima YH is the more convenient of the two. The staff speaks passable English and they have prepared maps of Hiroshima to help with sightseeing.

MIYAJIMA

This diminutive, sacred island is also known as Itsukushima or Shrine Island. Its 16 m high floating vermillion *torii* is a well-known symbol of Japan. Miyajima is an over-touristed "must see" area that millions of Japanese and foreigners visit yearly. Nonetheless, it is exquisite. *getting there:* There are numerous ways of getting to Miyajima from Hiroshima, including rail, ferry and bus. Information is available at Hiroshima Eki. The easiest and most economical route is to buy a return ticket from Hiroshima Eki to Miyajima-guchi Eki. This Y740 JNR ticket also includes the 10 min ferry to Miyajima. When you arrive at Miyajima-guchi (the ferry port), expect almost opressively large crowds. Resist the gamut of souvenir shops as there are better ones on Miyajima itself. A 10 min ferry ride, (Y120 if you haven't purchased the JNR RT ticket) and you're there.

MIYAJIMA ISLAND (ITSUKUSHIMA)

MT MISEN
+
530m

ROPE WAY

TSUBAKI DANI COURSE

MOMIJIDANI PARK

HIRAMATSU PARK

DAISHOIN COURSE

OMOTO COURSE

DAISHO IN

PIER

ITSUKUSHIMA

N.B. NOT ALL PATHS, SHRINES & TEMPLES SHOWN.

MIYAJIMA ISLAND (ITSUKUSHIMA)

1. Five Storied Pagoda
2. Sen jo kaku
3. Treasure House
4. Daiganji Temple
5. Treasure Museum
6. Tahoto Pagoda
7. Historical and Folk Museum
8. Aquarium
9. people's lodge
10. Ohmoto Shrine
11. Sesshu-en
12. Oku-no in
13. Misen Hondo
14. Misen Observation Platform

students interpreting the famed
floating *torii* of Itsukushima

sights: The main shrine draws you like a magnet
and *you* draw the tame, sacred deer which are
everywhere. They have long since lost their wary
instincts, and now obnoxiously overturn garbage cans looking for morsels. The braver ones
try to beg sandwiches from your hands, while
the scoundrels of the group steal them outright.
The main shrine at Miyajima, Itshukushima, was
founded in 592 on a spot calculated to be most
affected by the tides. The illusion of the main
shrine and *torii* floating on the high tide is most
realistic. The shrine is dedicated to 3 goddesses
of the sea who dwell there. Only the priests may
enter the inner shrine. An ancient religious rule
forbade birth or death on the island. There is
nothing recorded on this rule ever having been
broken. Pregnant women were ferried to the
mainland, as well as the gravely infirm and their
soon-to-be mourners, who underwent a 50-day
purification at Ono on the opposite shore before
returning. The shrine cherishes various treasures, the most outstanding of which are
decorated sutras, masks, armor and swords of
noted warriors, along with paper and bamboo
fans over 1000 years old. The easements and
shrine precincts have a wealth of bronze and
stone lanterns which are lighted on auspicious
occasions. In the waning days of WW11, kamikaze pilots gathered on a tiny island near Miyajima to muster their loyalty before doing their
final duty. If the spirit of bravery eluded them, a
small concrete bunker was provided for self dis-
embowelment. What an alternative!

Senjokaku (The Hall of 1000 Mats): There are
actually 450 *tatami* mats of normal size, but
who's counting? Senjokaku is a time-weathered
building just to the L of Itsukushima. Senjokaku
was built by Toyotomi Hideyoshi at the end of
the 16th C. from the wood of one giant camphor
tree. Inside are thousands of rice scoops
attached to the walls and engraved with the
names of the donors. This practice began in
1894 with soldiers quartered there awaiting
transport to the Sino-Japanese War. They
played on the words *meshi-toru* which mean
"taking up rice," and also "conquer China."
They whittled the rice scoops and offered them
as a prayer to the gods. The practice continues,
and rice scoops can be bought at any souvenir
shop on Miyajima. Today's practice is to attach
the proper postage and send them through
the mails. A few 100 m behind the main shrine
are Hiramatsu and Momijidani Parks. Buy your
lunch at one of the numerous stalls and eat in
one of these parks by a bubbling stream. A
break from the crowds is refreshing. The next
attraction is the Ropeway to Mt. Misen (Y600,
50 min), from Momijidani Station just next to the
park. There is also a lovely unused trail by the
station leading to the summit. Most Japanese
take the ropeway. To see the same sights and
save money, take the trail. There is a good
chance of encountering semi-wild monkeys on
this route and if you do, don't stare them in the
eye as this may trigger an aggressive reaction.
At the top, the view to both the N and S is
breathtaking. Continue E along the trail for a 4 hr
circular tour of the entire island. Miyajima has
been given special attention and devotion for
over 1500 years. It is brimming with exemplary
shrines, temples, pagodas, museums and parks.
They are found at almost every turn of the pathway as it skirts the shoreline and climbs into
hidden recesses on the hillsides. English-
language pamphlets on Miyajima describing the
sights and providing a map are available near the
pier area. Miyajima holds frequent and impressive festivals that have been described in the
"events" section of this chapter. The most
mysterious is the Fire-Walking Festival held atop
Mt. Misen. To thoroughly enjoy Miyajima, and
to experience all of the highlights, you should
expect to spend an entire day of touring. Also, if
you are souvenir hunting, Miyajima has many
small shops that offer quality wood carvings of
turtles and gods, as well as a host of regular
run-of-the-mill mementos.

accommodations: Accommodations on Miyajima are very tight during the summer months;
reservations are a must. There are no budget

accommodations. The Miyajima Grand Hotel, tel: (0829) 44-2411 starts at Y10,000, but 2 meals are included. A handful of superb *ryokan* are available, but they start at Y15,000. There is, however, Miyajima People's Lodge (Miyajima Kokumin Shukusha), tel: (0829) 44-0430, offering rooms and 2 meals from Y3500. Remember that the Japanese plan their trips to Miyajima well in advance, and getting a room may be very difficult. There is also a YH on

Miyajima: Makoto Kaikan YH, 756 Sairen-cho, Miyajima 739-05, tel: (0829) 44-0329, 10 min by boat from Miyajima-guchi and 5 min on foot, 75 beds.

services: For accommodations listings and prices on Miyajima, call the Municipal Hotel Information Office, tel: (08295) 60-600. A telephone tourist service answering general questions can be reached at (08294) 42-011.

YAMAGUCHI PREFECTURE

Yamaguchi City (pop. 105,000), the prefectural capital, is also known as "Western Kyoto" because of a slight resemblance in topography to the renowned city and the abundance of temples found there. The most noted is the Joeji Temple, an attempt to mimic Kinkakuji Temple (the Golden Pavilion) of Kyoto. Joeji is superb, featuring an impressive garden laid out by Sesshu (1420-1506), who was a master of *sumi-e* (black-ink drawings). *getting there:* Ogori (13 km, 20 min S of Yamaguchi, connected by the Bocho Bus Line), is the actual transportation terminal of the area. It is a station for the *shinkansen* (one hr from Hiroshima), serviced by numerous limited expresses, and the junction of the Yamaguchi Main Line which connects with the San-In Main Line at Masuda and is also connected with the San-Yo Line by the Ube and Onoda Line. Besides the Bocho Bus Line, numerous local trains (*futsu*) connect Yamaguchi and Ogori.

VICINITY OF YAMAGUCHI

Ogori to Tsuwano: If the San-In coast is your destination, an alternative routing from Ogori to Tsuwano by a vintage steam locomotive may prove to be fun and a welcomed respite from the usually slick Japanese rail system. Tsuwano, 60 km NE of Yamaguchi, is also efficiently serviced by the Yamaguchi Main Line as it heads further N to Masuda on the Japan Sea coast. In 1979 JNR saw their chance to cash in on the raging nostalgia that Japanese have for steam locomotives and so in that year a vintage *kisha* "puffing billy" began making the 60 km run between Ogori and Tsuwano. Very difficult to get a ticket during the tourist season (June to Aug.). Tsuwano itself is a small town of only 10,000, but it attempts to preserve the age-old richness of yesteryear Japan. Its former rulers were lovers of art and learning, and strove to bring the burgeoning culture of Kyoto to their provincial out-

post. They succeeded in a limited way; and the finest architectural specimens are along Tonomaachi Street where a number of well-preserved samurai houses are located. Tsuwano also has unique man-made ditches running in front of many residential areas that are filled to capacity with carp. Pop: Tsuwano, 10,000; carp, 100,000. *local festivals: Yabusame* (horseback archery) is held at Washihari Hachimangu yearly on April 13. The largest city festival is the Gion Festival, July 20-27, when all accommodations are fully booked. *accommodations:* Provided by a dozen well-preserved *ryokan* and a people's lodge. Tsuwano YH is located at 819-ko, Washihara, Tsuwano 699-56, tel: (08567) 20-373, 8 min by bus from Tsuwano Station and 3 min on foot, 44 beds. Check bookings through JTB during the tourist season.

Akiyoshi Cave: 30 km NW of Yamaguchi by JNR Express Bus. This limestone cave complex is one of the largest in the Orient, stretching for at least 10 km underground with only one km open to the public. The features of this hobbit-like world are universal: stalactites, stalagmites, wierdly shaped stone pillars and deep crystalline pools. The largest chamber is 150 m wide by 80 m tall. The authorities suggest a guide, but this is unnecessary. The trails are well-lit and the map, even in Japanese, is easy to follow. Exit the caves by the 80 m elevator and make bus connections to Ogori or Hofu on the San-Yo Main Line.

SHIMONOSEKI

This important port city is the westernmost extremity of Honshu where the San-In and the San-Yo Lines meet. It is basically an industrial city, and one of Japan's major fishing centers. Due to its position, it is a heavily trafficked sea and land transport center. The Kanmon

in 1863 the Choshu Clan of Shimonoseki rebelled against the new order initiated by the Meiji Restoration. The shogunate as a ruling power in Japan was rapidly coming to an end and along with its decay came increasing trade with the West and an influx of new unsettling social ideas. The Choshu, true samurai as they were, threw caution to the wind and fired upon a combined fleet of French, English, Dutch and American ships. The clan was hopelessly outgunned and after a 3-day naval pounding Shimonoseki Port surrendered. This defeat, in effect, marked the downfall of the shogunate, and Japan was ushered into the modern age

Undersea Tunnels connect it to Moji on Kyushu, and the Kampu Ferry to Pusan, Korea. It is also a port of call on the Inland Sea ferry route from Tokyo.

getting there by train: A well-oiled network of land, air and sea connections make Shimonoseki readily accessible. Shimonoseki is one hr 22 min from Hiroshima by *shinkansen.* Many limited expresses make the same journey in about 3 hours. From Shimonoseki, you can easily proceed to Kita-Kyushu and Fukuoka and from there to all points on Kyushu. Trains also depart from Shimonoseki to various points along the San-In coast including the major cities of Hagi, Matsue and Tottori. *by air:* Two airports are located nearby. One is at Ube, a small town 30 km SE of Shimonoseki, and the other is at Kita-Kyushu just across the Kanmon Straits. They're both on the main air routes and are connected to Tokyo by domestic flight. *by ferry:* Shimonoseki is the western gateway to the Inland Sea. The Ocean Tokyu Ferry Company operates a ferry between Tokyo and nearby Kokura on Kyushu on a daily basis. Details are given in the "getting there by ferry" section in the introduction of this chapter. Ferries are also available to Kobe, and one local car ferry makes the short hop to Kokura at various times throughout the day.

sights: The Akama Jingu Shrine is 10 min by bus from Shimonoseki Eki. This shrine is dedi-cated to the memory of Lady Nii and Emperor Antoku, a fateful liason dating from the clash of the Minamoto and Heiki (Fujiwara) clans in the 12th century. The Sentei-sai Festival is held here April 23-25. At Dannoura Beach (one km E of the shrine) the actual battle occurred. Here are found curious crabs called *heike-gani,* whose

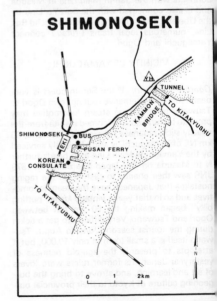

SHIMONOSEKI

creased shells resemble grimacing human faces, and *koheiki,* golden-colored sea bream. Legend says that the fallen warriors of the Heike became the crabs, and the women became the golden bream. *Shimonoseki Aquarium:* 15 min by bus from Shimonoseki Eki. This well-stocked aquarium contains at least 300 varieties of fish. Connected to the aquarium is Marine Land. Here is an entire day of family recreation and fun. A good place to spend some time while waiting for onward-going travel. *Hinoyama Hill:* Offers an extensive view of the Kanmon Straits. A cablecar goes to the top. Take any bus to Ropeway Mae, and then walk or cable to the top.

accommodations: Shimonoseki offers a selection of inexpensive business hotels clustered in the downtown area around the *eki* and the nearby port. For Western-style hotels that also offer a few Japanese-style rooms, try Sanyo Hotel, 2-9 Minosusogawa-machi, Shimonoseki 751, tel: (0832) 32-8666; Western-style rooms for Y4000, Japanese style from Y9000. Shimonoseki Grand Hotel, 31-2 Nabecho, Shimonoseki, tel: (0832) 31-5000, from Y3800 Western to Y6000 Japanese. Shimonoseki also offers a YH where the house parents are very friendly, speak halting English and can offer good information on the Kampu Ferry. The hostel is excellently situated with a grand view of the straits, harbor area and with a bus stop conveniently located nearby that takes you to Shimonoseki Eki. The adrress is Shimonoseki-Hinoyama YH, 3-47 Monosusogawa-machi, Shimonoseki 751, tel: (0832) 22-3753, 15 min by bus from Shimonoseki Station, and 2 min on foot, 52 beds. Hinoyama can oftentimes be booked up, so reservations are advisable. If there is no room, try going to nearby Ube and staying at Ube Tokiwa Kohan YH, Tokiwa-kohan 654, Takahata, Kami-ube, Ube 755, tel: (0836) 21-3613, 25 min by bus from Ube-shinkawa Station and 10 min on foot, 80 beds.

THE KAMPU FERRY TO PUSAN S. KOREA

The ferry between Shimonoseki and Pusan, S. Korea, is a well-used route by travelers wishing to move on through Asia, and for travelers desiring to lengthen their stay in Japan by acquiring a new visa. There are other ways of carrying out his visa procedure (see "visas" under general "Introduction") but the Kampu Ferry route is the tried and usually true standby. The procedure, although hampered by bureaucracy, is relatively simple. You will need a Korean visa, a return ticket on the ferry, and then when you arrive in Korea you must visit a Japanese consulate to get your new visa. The Kampu Ferry Co. operates 3 sailings a week on Mon., Wed. and Fri., leaving Shimonoseki Port at 1700 and arriving in Pusan the following morning at 0800. The dock is only a 10 min walk from Shimonoseki Eki. The ferry leaves Pusan on Tues. and Thurs. at 1700, arriving in Shimonoseki the next morning at 0830. On Sat. a ferry leaves Pusan at 1000 and arrives in Shimonoseki at 1900 the same evening. You should arrive at Shimonoseki Port 3 hrs in advance to insure your reservations and a spot to sleep at night if you are going *tatami* class. The fares range from Y8000 *tatami* (minus a 20% student discount), to Y10,000 for a cabin. You can book in advance from any JTB or large travel agency, or directly from the Kampu Ferry Co., 4th fl., Ginza Asaki Bldg., 3-8-10 Ginza, Chuo-ku, Tokyo, tel: (03) 567-0971; or at the Shimonoseki Office, 1-10-38 Higashi-Yamato-cho, Shimonoseki, Yamaguchi-ken, tel: (0832) 66-8211. First acquire a Korean visa. This can be done in one day but it is best to allow more time if possible. For Korean visas (Y300 plus passport photo), go to the Consulate of the Republic of Korea, 7-32-1 Minami-Azabu, Minato-ku, Tokyo, tel: (03) 455-2601. There are various ways of reaching the consulate, but the least confusing is to take the Yamanote Line 5 stops W of Tokyo Eki to Shinagawa Eki. From there, take Bus 91 and get off at Ninohashi. Walk for 100 m in the direction that you arrived, and look for a large white building. The Korean Embassy is also in Tokyo, tel: (03) 452-7611, but they do not issue visas. They do, however, provide useful general information. Korean consulates are also found in major cities throughout Japan from Sapporo to Naha. There is also one in Shimonoseki near the ferry dock, tel: (0832) 66-5341, but they are less efficient than the Tokyo branch. Call either the Korean Embassy or Consulate in Tokyo for a complete listing of where to acquire a visa. When you arrive in Korea, apply for your Japanese visa at the consulate in Pusan, or further N in Seoul, if you intend to spend a little more time in Korea. The addresses are: Japan Consulate General, No. 1147-11, Choryang-Dong, Dong-Ku, Pusan, tel: 43-9221; and Japan Embassy, 18-11, Chunghak-Dong, Chongro-Ku, Seoul, tel: 73-5626. The procedure should not take more than 24 hrs, so you could conceivably return to Japan on the next ferry, but don't count on it. If time is of the essence and money is not a factor, you

(cont.)

can also fly to Korea by a number of carriers. Flights to Korea are offered by JAL, KAL, NWA and CP. The most expensive flight is Tokyo-Seoul (Y35,400, 2 hr 20 min); the cheapest is Fukuoka-Pusan (Y11,400, 40 min). See "getting there" under general "Introduction" for phone numbers and addresses.

re-entry: After going through all of this rigamarole, there is no guarantee that you will be readmitted to Japan. The officers in Shimonoseki, especially, know what's going on and are known to be unduly difficult. Try flying back to another Japanese port of entry (Tokyo-Osaka) if you are unsure. If this is your first attempt at getting a new tourist visa, you are generally OK. The second time is pushing it, and the third time you are at the mercy of the gods. Remember that the Immigration Officer decides admittance to Japan on a "case by case" basis. All of your papers, money, visa and tickets may be in perfect order, but you can nonetheless be turned away. Usually an official protest will not help. If you are entering Japan for the first time via the Kampu Ferry, you are scrutinized even more closely because the officials know that it is the cheapest route, and your intentions for visiting Japan as well as your financial status will be thoroughly queried. Without an onward-going ticket and provable sufficient funds for your visit, you haven't got a prayer of entering. Those who have gone to Korea to change their tourist status to a more respectable study or work visa find it almost no problem to re-enter Japan, providing all papers are in order.

IMPORTANT TIPS FOR KOREA

money: There are money changers at the ferry terminals at both ends of the line that offer the official exchange rates, so cashing TCs is no problem. Korean currency (*won*), however, is worthless outside Korea, so make sure to change it while in Korea. Yen and U.S. dollars are available at Korean banks. There is a thriving black market in Korea dealing in U.S. currency, and some hard-pressed travelers use it to help offset the cost of their trips. The black market pays between 5% and 10% higher than the official rate. The procedure is to take large denominations ($50 or $100 bills) to Korea. In the downtown market area there are little old ladies with handbags literally overflowing with *won.* The surplus is used to live on while in Korea. There is also a ready and open market for whiskey and coffee. It is legally allowed to take in 6 jars of coffee and 2 liters of whiskey. The coffee must be Nescafe Red Label, and the whiskey Johnny Walker Black Label. It is easily sold for a profit at almost any shop. The Koreans are also clamoring for Japanese

cameras. Bringing in only one camera can turn a neat profit (50%), but more than one camera will raise suspicion at customs, and you'll run the risk of having the serial numbers officially listed. Nikon and Canon cameras are the most sought after. Tape recorders, radios and almost any electrical device can easily be sold in Korea. Japanese goods of all types are highly prized. For those with ethical problems, it should be remembered that the Korean economy is in relatively good shape. Most Koreans do have the money to spend on these items; they lack only the availability.

theft: Even the most hardened travelers soften up on watchfulness in Japan, since there is virtually no theft. Most Koreans are honest, but there are thieves, especially in big cities. You must be very careful with cameras, money, etc., or they will grow legs.

accommodations: Large Korean cities have everything from ultra-modern luxury hotels down to inexpensive *yogwon,* found around most bus and train stations, and primarily used by Koreans. They may or may not have private toilet facilities, but most are clean.

food: Unlike Japan, the water is not always safe to drink, and vegetables should be cooked because of the use of raw "night soil" as fertilizer. Drinking hot tea and bottled drinks is the safest course. Western-style restaurants are expensive. Chinese restaurants are cheaper, but the best prices are found at *makkoli* houses, which sell rice wine and some meals. Only Korean is spoken, but the prices are cheap and the experience is totally genuine.

information: The Korean Tourist Bureau has offices in most provincial capitals. In Seoul, they can be reached at 72-119115, and there is also an office in Pusan (inquire at the ferry terminal). Many Koreans, especially officials and those dealing with tourists, speak English. Main ports of entry offer Information Offices to get you started.

CAPSULE VOCABULARY

where?	*audie?*
restaurant	*schick dahng*
cheap local restaurant	*makkoli*
hotel	*hotel*
toilet	*pyuhn so*
how much?	*uhl mom nee kah?*
yes	*ne*
no	*aniyo*
thank you	*kam sa hamnida*
telephone greeting (hello)	*yaba seo*

HAGI

40 km N of Yamaguchi on the Japan Sea is the artistic town of Hagi (pop. 52,000). Although it has recently become prominent because of *hagi-yaki* (see "folk art" in "Introduction"), it is still only moderately touristed. Hagi sits surrounded by mountains on 3 sides and to its front is the sea. There are excellent swimming beaches, numerous shops in which to purchase folk art, preserved temples, and a slow-paced, back-country air. The town has changed very little over the centuries, and samurai houses surrounded by gardens and stone walls are still prominent. Hagi provided a disproportionate number of leaders prominent in the Meiji Restoration from the local Choshu clan. The homes of these men have been preserved and are open to the public as museums. *getting there:* From Shimonoseki, the San-Yo Main Line heads N and skirts along the coast stopping at Hagi. From Yamaguchi Eki, take a JNR bus for the one hr 30 min trip (Y850) available every hour. From Ogori, JNR or Bocho bus to Hagi in one hr 40 min (Y1200), available every hour. From Tsuwano, take the Bocho bus to Hagi in one hr 45 min (Y1000). Ordinary express train from Matsue, 220 km to the NE, makes the trip in 4 hrs for Y3500.

sights: Hagi Castle is 25 min on foot to the W of Higashi-Hagi Eki. This castle was built in 1604, but razed in 1871 during the Meiji Restoration. The grounds now serve as a park. In the immediate area surrounding the old castle site are numerous *hagi-yaki* kilns. Many are open for inspection, and you can watch the potting process at close hand. No fee. The houses of Hagi are well preserved with many over 100 years old. Excellent examples are the houses of Shinsaku Takasugi and Koin Kido (25 min on foot SW of Higashi-Hagi Eki). These 2 men were instrumental in bringing about the Meiji Restoration. The homes, now open to the public, offer numerous relics of feudal times.

accommodations: The following hotels offer Western-style as well as Japanese-style rooms. Hagi-Kanko Hotel, 15 min by bus from Higashi-Hagi Eki, tel: (0838) 25-0211, from Y8000; and Hagi Kokusai Kanko Hotel, tel: (0838) 25-0121, from Y7000. Hagi also offers a unique *minshuku* experience at Tsuchi-no-Yado (Inn of Soil). This *minshuku* is especially designed for the handicapped. The philosophy at Tsuchi-no-Yado is simply for all men to live a full life and to reach their potential regardless of the handicaps they may carry. The *minshuku* also has Gallery Kohagi attached to the main building where folk arts and hand-crafted items are sold. Everyone is

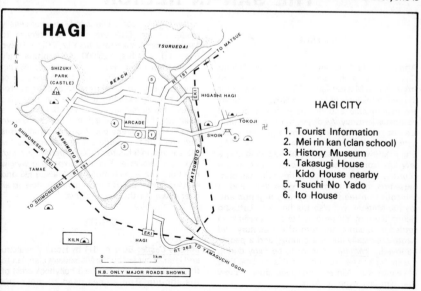

HAGI CITY

1. Tourist Information
2. Mei rin kan (clan school)
3. History Museum
4. Takasugi House
   Kido House nearby
5. Tsuchi No Yado
6. Ito House

N.B. ONLY MAJOR ROADS SHOWN.

welcome to stay. The address is Tsuchi-noYado, 2-1 Hamasaki Shin-machi, Hagi, tel: (0838) 25-4505. The price is a very low Y2000, and includes a self-service breakfast. A few minutes walk from the *minshuku* will take you to Kikugahama Beach. YH accommodations are available at Hagi Shizuji YH, 109-22 Jonai, Horinouchi, Hagi 758, tel: (0838) 22-0733, 20 min on foot

from Tamae Station, 74 beds. Closed Jan. 10 through Feb. 10. This YH is well situated on a small peninsula of land that is designated as a park. Numerous kilns are in the immediate area. *services:* For general information and maps of Hagi, contact Hagi City Tourist, tel: (0838) 25-3131, or Hagi Tourist Association (0838) 25-1750.

THE SAN-IN REGION

MATSUE

Although billed as an "International Culture City," don't let the fancy title discourage you from visiting Matsue (pop. 130,000). Except for the shrine festivals of Izumo in Nov., the crowds are manageable and the pace in this cultural outpost is leisurely. As of yet, Matsue and Izumo are not on the itinerary of any organized international tours. Lying on the shores of Lake Shinji (known for its striking sunsets) and only a few km from Izumo, the oldest shrine in the country, the area at large is ripe with temples, museums, ancient archaeological digs, and is the fountainhead of numerous legends and myths. Matsue was also the home of Lafcadio Hearn (Koizumi Yakumo), a literary traveler who settled in Japan at the turn of the century and wrote prolifically about a country and a people he loved. *climate:* Known to be rainy during the spring and early summer, fall is the best time of year to visit. Winter brings deep, downy snow that can last even to April.

getting there: Connections to Matsue are easily made. By air, TOA offers a daily service to Matsue from Osaka (one hr, Y12,500) or Tokyo (Haneda), 1½ hrs, Y25,000. ANA offers daily flights from Tokyo (Haneda) to Yonago, 45 min E of Matsue. By train, take the *shinkansen* or any express to Okayama and change for Matsue. From Okayama to Matsue on the Kyuko takes 3 hrs 20 min and costs Y5000. Matsue is a main stop from all points E or W on the San-In Main Line. A direct bus from Hiroshima Bus Terminal (3rd fl. of Sogo Depato) also makes the Matsue run in 5 hrs for Y2300. *getting around:* Taxis are available. The least expensive way is city bus. The 2 main stops are Matsue Eki and Matsue Onsen Eki. Buses from either stop go all over town, to the major sights.

SIGHTS

Matsue Castle: Built in 1611 by Horio Yoshiharu and later occupied by the Matsudaira clan, kin to the Tokugawa. Look for the 3-hollyhock crest of the shogun. The stones used to make the foundation for the fortress were donated by serfs from distant regions because the local stone is too soft. Lafcadio Hearn captured the military mood of the castle when he began a description with "From under the black scowl of the loftiest eaves..." Matsue-jo was built as a fortress, not as a residence. Look for the fishtails on the roof, a symbol of water and a prayer against fire. When you enter (Y200), leave your shoes in the little lock boxes provided. The wooden floors are constantly polished by the

visitors' stockinged feet, and their soft rub as you walk around is like a massage. See the extraordinary lacquered screens on the 2nd floor uniquely depicting the lives of the peasantry. *Matsue Cultural Museum:* Down the steps from Matsue Castle through the carnival-atmosphere area; Y200. Artifacts here are mostly from the Edo period.   *Lafcadio Hearn Residence and Memorial Museum:* Y100, open daily, 0900 to 1700. Side by side, they contain mementos of Hearn's artistic life as well as everyday personal

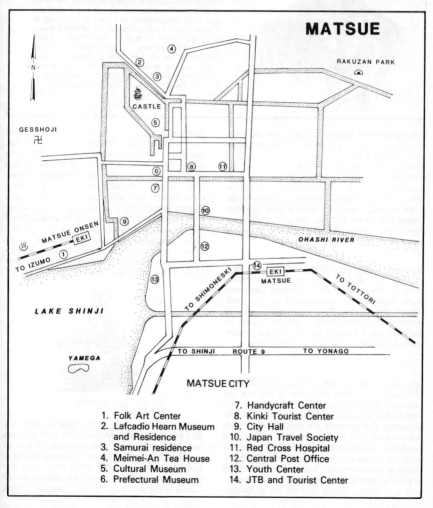

MATSUE

MATSUE CITY

1. Folk Art Center
2. Lafcadio Hearn Museum and Residence
3. Samurai residence
4. Meimei-An Tea House
5. Cultural Museum
6. Prefectural Museum
7. Handycraft Center
8. Kinki Tourist Center
9. City Hall
10. Japan Travel Society
11. Red Cross Hospital
12. Central Post Office
13. Youth Center
14. JTB and Tourist Center

LAFCAIDO HEARN (1860-1904)

Lafcadio Hearn: Hearn is perhaps the best-known western writer on Meiji-era Japan. He was of Greek-Irish lineage, and as a young man migrated to the U.S. where he worked as a newspaper correspondent in New Orleans, and in 1890, was sent to Japan by *Harper's* of New York. He became enamored with Japan, married Koizumo Setsuko, a 23-year-old woman from an old Matsue samurai family, and became a naturalized Japanese citizen, adopting the name of Koizumo Yakumo. The couple had 4 children, and their descendants are said to be living in Tokyo. Hearn lived in Matsue for almost 2 years, and then moved on to Kumamoto then to Kobe, and finally became a professor at Tokyo University. He died in 1904, disillusioned with Japan as he watched it adopt the western materialism that he had tried so desperately to escape. He is buried at Zoshigaya Cemetery in Tokyo. His best-known works include *Japan: An Interpretation*, and *In Chostly Japan*

belongings such as pipes, slippers and clothing. Hearn wrote *Glimpses of an Unfamiliar Japan* here, and the love he had for the people of Matsue is returned by their honor of his memory. A portrait of Hearn shows him with bulging eyes. Some felt that it was a generalization of Western features by the Japanese artist, while in fact, Hearn did have a false eye that bulged out. Hearn felt that this was a disfigurement so he insisted that photographs of him be taken in profile.

Bukeyashiki Samurai House: Y120, open 0900 to 1700 daily. A fully preserved samurai house open to the public. Soft, classical Japanese music plays in the background as you walk around the garden. Peer in at the traditional *tatami* rooms where clothing and utensils are on display. Contrast this to the wonderfully smoke-stained kitchen in the rear of the house.

Meimei-an: An authentic replica of a 200-year-old tea house used exclusively for the tea ceremony (*cha-no-yu*). The best feature is the thatched roof and split bamboo used for rain guttering. The grounds are quiet, distant from the crowds, and create just the right mood needed for the ceremony. There are 2 other tea lodges in the area where you can watch or participate in the ceremony: Kanden-an is N of the city limits towards Mt. Makuragi, and Kangetsu-an is E of Matsue Castle, just off the waterway.

Matsue Onsen area: As well as being loaded with cultural spots, Matsue has excellent hot spas. They are found clustered around Matsue Onsen Eki. Tenriji, 200 m W of the *eki,* is the most famous. Here also, just across the street from the *eki,* is the Matsue Folk Art and Souvenir Center. Fair prices and authentic goods. Watch for plastic replicas of lacquerware, although they too can be quite beautiful. Good buys include handmade paper (*washi*), paper dolls (*anesama ningyo,* which means "older sister"), paper tigers, local pottery, agate jewelry (*menou*). Local foodstuffs include *ita-wakame* (dried kelp) and *yaki-wakame* (roasted kelp).

Izumo Shrine

shrines: The Kamosu and Yaegaki shrines are a 25 min bus ride from Matsue. The area includes ancient burial mounds surrounding the site of an ancient village and amuseum. Kamosu Shrine is believed to be even 400 years older than the shrine at nearby Izumo, and the oldest form of Taisha architecture in Japan. Yaegaki Shrine

Yaegaki shrine mural

houses the oldest existent Japanese mural painted on wood. Age has deteriorated the treasure, but a few figures can still be seen. Behind the shrine is Mirror Pond where young girls wash their hands and faces in prayer to the deity to provide a good husband. *Izumo shrine:* This illustrious shrine is famous as a vacation spot for the Shinto gods. The belief is that during the month of Oct.-Nov. (depending on the lunar calendar), all the gods leave their shrines and travel to Izumo. In Izumo itself, the month is called *kamiarizuki* (the month of the present gods), while in the remainder of Japan this period is called *kannazuki* (the month without gods). The resident deity is Okuninushi, whose heavenly parents live at Yaegaki. A tale relates that Okuninushi's princely father courted and married his mother at Izumo. From that time, the shrine has been a special place for marriage, and Japanese arrive from distant areas to be married here. Approaching the shrine are small compartments. These are the "hotel rooms" that the visiting gods occupy when they come to Izumo. Majestic trees line the pathways leading to the shrine. See "Introduction — events" for a description of the festivities.

accommodations: Western-style hotels include the Hotel Ichibata, which offers both Western and Japanese-style rooms. The price is from Y500 Western and Y15,000 Japanese-style for two. Hotel Ichibata is located at 30 Chidoricho, Matsue, tel: (0852) 22-0188. For a *ryokan* experience in this traditional city, try Horaiso, 101 Tonomachi, Matsue 690, tel: (0852) 21-4337, Y8500-12,000; Meirinkaku, Kuniyacho, Matsue 690, tel: (0852) 22-3225, Y7000-12,000; and Suimeiso, 26 Nishichamachi, Matsue 690, tel: (0852) 21-6235, Y6000-20,000. Matsue, unfortunately, only has one YH, Matsue YH, 1546 Kososhi-machi, Matsue 690-01, tel: (0852) 36-8620, 30 min by bus from Matsue Station and 15 min on foot, 82 beds. You can also take the train from Matsue Onsen Eki for one stop to Furue, and then walk for 15 minutes. The house parent here goes by the book and is a stickler for reservations. Even if the YH is not full, he may turn you away. Getting back to town in the evening can prove troublesome. Setting up camp in the tree-covered back yard of the YH is a good way to get your point across and may even soften *parento-san's* heart. Yakumo Honjin Ryokan is a traditional inn, considered an important cultural asset. It is used by visiting dignitaries and even Emperor Taisho once lodged here. It is located at Shinji, about halfway between Matsue and Izumo. Also, Matsue provides a civic rest-and-recreation village on the road to Inbe. Reservations are required.

food: Some specialties of the area include: *shijimi,* a tiny, purplish-black shellfish served in *miso shiru,* and reputed to be an excellent elixir for problems of the liver. *Kabayaki* are eels that have been charcoaled; delicious with *tare* (sweet soy sauce). *Hoshoyaki* is sea bass wrapped in Japanese paper and slowly cooked over glowing embers. The delicate flavor is captured and enhanced by soy sauce. *Kaiyaki* is wild duck stewed in a tangy sauce in a large sea shell, usually served in winter.

services: Limited English spoken at the Matsue City Hall Tourist Information, tel: (0852) 24-1111, and the Matsue Tourist Information Center (0852) 21-4034. Pick up good maps and brochures at the Travel Service Center at Matsue Eki.

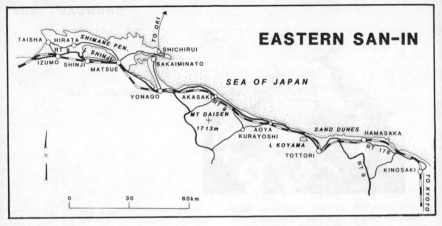

EASTERN SAN-IN

Yonago: Pop. 114,000, is considered to be the fastest growing industrial city along the San-In. Yonago has little to recommend it, but it is a main gateway to Mt. Daisen and the Oki Islands. Here is the terminus of the 144 km Hakubi Line from Kurashiki. If you leave Saigo (Dogo) by the 1540 ferry, you'll miss the last bus to Mt. Daisen and will arrive in Yonago at 1920 (the bus from Yonago for Daisen leaves at 1840). If you are stuck, stay at the _ryokan_ only 50 m down the small street behind the bus terminal (Y3000, no meals). There are no YH or inexpensive hotels in Yonago. Get excellent "morning serbisu" at Port Young Coffee Shop before 1000, located in the building just near your bus stop. After breakfast, head for Daisen.

Mt. Daisen (Great Mountain): At 1711 m, this mountain turns its Fuji-like face to the sea and looms over the San-In coast. A one hr, Y450 bus ride from Yonago deposits you at Daisenguchi. Grouped along the main cobblestone streets are restaurants, hotels, souvenir shops, and ski rentals. Maps in Japanese are also available from the larger stores. Follow Daisenguchi's cobblestone street up a series of steps, perhaps 100 or so, and you'll arrive at Daisenji, a Tendai sect temple founded in 718. Because of the altitude, spring comes later here and cherry blossoms are still framed in the _torii_ as late as mid-May. The mountaintop remains snow-covered and the deeper ravines, shielded from the sun, contain pockets of icy snow. On the grounds of Daisenji is a magnificent, life-sized bronze bull. Walk to the back of the main edifice and continue following the trail up the mountain. As you go further, the terrain becomes more rugged and the slopes are oftentimes covered in a deep, downy mist. In a few minutes the trail forms a Y, the L fork takes you to Golden Gate, the R to Ogamiama Jinja, where you'll find another animal creation in bronze. This time it's a bronze horse with pilgrim-sandled hooves of straw. Ogamiama Jinja celebrates its festival on the first Sat. and Sun. of June. The buildings are weather-beaten split wood crouching beneath the towering slopes of Daisen. Again, follow the path behind the temple. The rock strewn path becomes less defined. Few tourists venture this far. Now, all is the mountain. The face is tortured, barren rock. The trees give out as the altitude increases. The summit is about 3 ½ hrs straight up. Don't be surprised to see Japanese ski enthusiasts lugging their skis up the trail to get in some final runs, even as late as June. Finally, after a huff-puff climb, the summit. You are on the roof of Chugoku. On clear days the vista southward reaches all the way to the shores of Shikoku across the Inland Sea. To the N, the Oki Islands dot the horizon.

accommodations: Daisen YH, Daisen, Daisen-cho, Saihaku-gun 689-33, tel: (0859) 52-2501, 50 min by bus from Yonago Station and 3 min on foot, 102 beds. Daisen YH is very modern. The front is all glass, and there is even a glass case with plastic food like a restaurant. The YH offers separate rooms as well as dormitories. Daisen-guchi has a handful of _ryokan_ and moderately priced hotels. It is much better to stay in this resort area than to return to Yonago. Official campsites are found on the eastern and western slopes of the mountain close to the ski grounds.

THE OKI ISLANDS

In a setting of blue-green sea are the tranquil gems of the Oki Islands. Remote to most Japanese, only 80 km separate these sparsely visited, enthralling islands from Honshu. The tourist season is July and Aug., when accommodations are heavily booked. The island cluster is made up of 4 islands with a scant combined population of only 30,000. The main and largest island is Dogo, and the 3 others to the W are grouped under the name Dozen. There is excellent fishing, wilderness camping, bullfights, and unsurpassed seascapes at such locales as Matengai and Tsutenkyo (Dozen), and at Shirashima on Dogo. At Kasuga Shrine near Fuse-mura on the E coast of Dogo are found the tallest trees in Japan. The island's interior offers rustic temples where *sumo* matches are still held outdoors in the traditional clay ring. Here is unhurried, traditional Japan that most foreigners come to see, but usually cannot find.

getting there: The main port for the Oki Is. is Saigo, on Dogo. Ferry service is available daily from Sakaiminato (Shichirui Port) 10 km N of Yonago, and 15 km NE of Matsue. The morning ferry departs from Shichirui at 0930 and arrives at 1220 (Y1480 economy class). From Matsue,

take the 0810 bus from Station No. 5 at the bus terminal. Arrive at Shichirui at 0913. Look for the ship's flag of 3 red balls forming a triangle. The ship is very modern, and the crossing is pleasant. Direct service is also available from Shichirui to Beppu (Dozen I.) in 3 hrs 10 minutes. Regular inter-island ferries throughout the day connect the Oki Islands. By air, TOA flies from Osaka to Saigo in one hr 50 min; from Yonago to Saigo in 25 minutes. *getting around:* Bus service is available to all points on the main islands. Taxis for short hops are available, and bicycles — the best means — can be rented at Saigo and Beppu. Hitchhiking is easy and fun.

DOGO ISLAND

Saigo, this island's main port, offers a P.O., exchange banks, airport, *minshuku,* and hotels on the main street. OK for a base, but move on as soon as you can to the remainder of the island (which is much more fascinating). Travel first along the E coast till you reach Fuse-mura (15 km). *Fuse-mura:* A quiet, one-street fishing town 15 km NE of Saigo. The main attraction

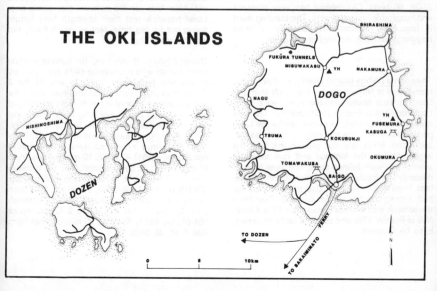

THE OKI ISLANDS

SHIRASHIMA
FUKURA TUNNELS
MISUWAKABU
YH
NAKAMURA
NAGU
DOGO
YH
FUSEMURA
KASUGA
TSUMA
KOKUBUNJI
OKUMURA
TOMAWAKUSA
SAIGO
DOZEN
NISHINOSHIMA

TO DOZEN
FERRY
TO SAKAIMINATO

0   5   10km

here, as in all of the Oki Is., is the coastline. The delights are visual. Walk 5 min N of town to the little community park, and follow any trail down to the sea where the spectacle begins. The coves and inlets are canyon-like along razorback mountains, tumbling to the sea. White duck-prowed fishing boats bob about 300 m from shore. The water is absolutely transparent to a depth of 30 m. Golden seaweed, like giant fans, sway on the bottom amidst pink and purple coral. As the depth increases, the green tint becomes more pronounced until it becomes a rich turquoise. The stone backdrop is blackish. A few m and the coves tunnel under the mountains. Here, the waves roar and foam bubbles through. The intricacies are endless. Walk on. The mountains to your back are spiny and rugged with green, verdant pines covering them completely. The sunrise and sunsets are tearfully beautiful. *Kasuga Shrine and the trees:* Just to the L as you cross the bridge into Fuse-mura. There is no way to ensure scientific accuracy, but Fuse-mura claims the tallest trees in Japan. To be sure, these giant pines are whoppers. The oddity is that these stately conifers lean over a working lumber mill, the jaws of which they have somehow miraculously escaped. Kasuga Shrine is nestled in the trees—small, unimpressive, but deliciously quiet. The local people have seen it before, so you usually have the grounds all to yourself. *accommodaations:* Okinoshima YH, 101 Fuse, Fuse-mura 685-04, tel: (0851) 27-28, 60 beds. Okinoshima has very pleasant and hospitable house parents. The building itself is large and modern, the scenery is mind boggling, and the atmosphere is quiet.

Shirashima (White Island) *Overlook:* Take a bus from Saigo to Nakamura and then to Nishimura. One km from Nishimura, the road bears right. Look for signs in English to Shirashima. The area is obviously touristed, as evidenced by the large parking lot where the trail begins. Don't be disappointed. Most tour bus passengers take the largest trail to the lookout and few take the smaller, but well-defined trails. The view is magnificent. The locals claim excellent fishing for *tai* (sea bream) in this area. Use *ebi* (shrimp) for bait. Ten kg catches are not unusual. Peer from the summit into endless ocean. Due W is Korea, NW is Russia. This emptiness, a rarity in Japan, is to be savored.

Fukura Tunnel: NW Dogo. These are a combination of man-made and natural tunnels dead-ending at the sea. Here is an excellent swimming beach and camping area. Along the coast in this small area it's not uncommon to see small leopard-spotted fish caught in pools in the rocks left from high tide. DO NOT EAT THEM. They are poisonous.

Misuwakasu: A village in the N central area. Incongruously, there is a stately old Dutch-style mansion in the center of town. Almost next door is Oki Jinja, a rustic temple/youth hostel. The most interesting feature is the ½ m thick thatched roofs. The grounds are uncluttered, simple, countrified Shinto, taken care of by elderly local women. Misuwakasu is peaceful, but not as stunning as the coastline. Observe the local women in the rice paddies. They supply the hand labor while the men work the machinery. *accommodations:* Misuwakasu YH (Oki Jinja), 723 Kori, Goka-mura, 685-03, tel: (0851) 25-2123, 45 min by bus from Saigo Port and 2 min on foot, 30 beds. Closed Dec. 21 through Jan. 10.

Tamawakasu Jinja: Southcentral Dogo on the N outskirts of Saigo. This shrine boasts another famous tree. This old fella, wrapped in burlap and propped by tree canes, is all of 10 m in circumference. The belief is that he is 2000 years old. Also, look for the outdoor clay sumo ring. Local hopefuls test their strength here before trying out for big time. Not as much flash, but it's the real thing.

Dozen Islands: If you long for remote uncluttered islands where towering cliffs are pounded by the sea, ferry from Saigo to any of the 3 Dozen Islands. These islands are also famed for wild ponies who travel in herds over the rugged interior plains. They have long furry coats and are a Japanese version of Shetland ponies. *accommodations:* Each island offers a YH. They are: Oki Jinja YH, 1783 Ama, Ama-machi 684-04, tel: (0851) 42-0212, 10 min by bus from Hishiura Port, 37 beds, closed Dec. 26 through Jan. 10; Takuhi YH, Hashi, Nishino-shima-cho 684-03, tel: (0851) 46-0860, 2 min on foot from Hashi Port, 100 beds, closed Dec 31 through Jan. 3; and Chibu YH, 1020-2 Chibu-mura 684-01, tel: (0851) 48-2355, 20 min on foot from Raii Port, 36 beds.

THE INLAND SEA (SETO–NAIKAI)

INTRODUCTION

Many discerning and experienced travelers consider the Inland Sea (*Seto-Naikai*) as the most beautiful body of water in the world. It is visually the most romantic area in Japan. It is a perfect archipelago, a harmonious blending of land and sea that fulfills the most basic aspect of traveling—that of looking and relaxing. Numerous ferry services are available through these waters from hour-long hops between tiny islands, to luxury cruises through the length of *Seto-Naikai* taking up to 2 weeks and costing up to Y300,000. At every turn there is beauty. At times *Seto-Naikai* is like a narrow lake with land on every side only a few hundred meters away. You can look from the boat into tiny fishing villages huddled under their black-tiled roofs with fields in the background terraced up the sides of mountains. Suddenly a channel will open up between 2 islands and you'll be ploughing through open waters. Then more islands, some uninhabited used as farm fields with the farmers coming by boat from a larger island to tend them. Always, on even the tiniest island, there are steps leading to a temple or shrine, the *torii* gate sihouetted against the sky. Here is the best place in Japan to let fancy be your guide. If you want a city, disembark at Hiroshima, visit the A-Bomb site, or head for the spas of Beppu. From Beppu catch a short hop to the western shore of Shikoku, spending time at one of the 88 temples on the famous pilgrimage route, or just cruise leisurely from Kobe to Beppu, taking in the sights and getting your 2nd wind. Everywhere are onward going ferry connections. All small cities have inexpensive *minshuku,* or business hotels; all larger cities offer luxury hotels, and there are YHs dotted all along the shoreline. Every area of Japan has its specialty: in the N, Tohoku and Hokkaido represent the Japan of old and budding individualism; Kyushu is the font, the beginning, Okinawa the southern cousin, and Tokyo, the heartbeat of the modern sprawling industrial giant. The Inland Sea is the "Romantic Face" of Japan, tempting, shy and quietly lovely.

getting there: The *Seto-Naikai* Steamship Co. offers the most extensive range of tours through the Inland Sea. They operate from Mar. to Nov., and they offer everything from a 2-day mini tour for Y55,000 to an extended 13-day excursion at Y300,000. For information, contact: Setonaiki Kisen Co., Ltd. Hiroshima Head Office, 12-23 Ujina Kaigan 1, Hiroshima 734, tel: (0822) 55-3344; or Tokyo Office, 19-10 Kyobashi

1-chome, Chuo-ku, Tokyo 104, tel: (03) 567-8740. Reservations may be made through travel agents, major airlines, hotels, or through JTBs Sunrise Centers in Tokyo, New York, Los Angeles, San Francisco, Honolulu, Paris, Sydney and Hong Kong. Also check out Fujita's De Lux Imperial Coachman Tours at any Fujita Tour office throughout Japan. A scheduled tour for the budget traveler is actually unnecessary. To save money, you can ride dozens of ferries regularly operating throughout *Seto-Naikai* that offer student discounts with the proper identification. For information contact the Kansai Steamship Co., Tokyo, tel: (03) 274-4271; Osaka, tel: (06) 572-5181. All JNTOs and TICs hand out useful literature including ferry schedules and the names and locations of steamship companies operating in this area.

The Sea: Since ancient times, the Inland Sea has been a major link between Kyushu and western Japan and the cultural centers of Kyoto and Tokyo to the north. It was really a large Japanese lake whose shores linked the whole country. Seafarers felt safe here, surrounded by Japan on all sides and protected from the unknown. Today, as in the past, art, culture and learning flow freely on this waterway, binding Japanese thought and cultural advancement from one region to another. The Inland Sea is really a series of 5 small seas (Harima, Bingo, Aki, Suo and Iyo), and the Bay of Osaka connected by channels and stretching from Osaka in the E to Shimoneseki in the W for a distance of 500 km. From N to S, the distances vary considerably; the widest point is 65 km, and the narrowest a mere 7 km. Some channels passing between islands are only a few hundred meters wide. The Naruto Straits in the E connecting the Inland Sea to the Pacific, are just over one km in width and are famous for their roaring whirlpools formed by the ebb and flow of the tide rushing through the channel. The new and full moons whip the pools to their greatest fury, and boats can be hired to view this phenomenon at close quarters. Depending upon your definition of an island, there are between 700 and 3000 separate land masses emerging from the water. The largest is Awaji, lying a few km out to sea SW of Kobe and measuring 600 sq km. Others are mere boulders separated from the coast by a few meters of water. The sea's coast touches 11 prefectures on 3 of the 4 main islands of Japan; Honshu, Kyushu and Shikoku. Along the coast is every conceivable geographic feature found in Japan: beaches, bays, volcanic mountains, basins, plains, peninsulas and capes.

Because it is surrounded by land, *Seto-Naikai* is usually as smooth as a temple pond. It is relatively shallow, measuring an average depth of only 40 meters.

the climate: The Inland Sea region is sunny and clear year round. It is even relatively protected during the typhoon season. Whenever you choose to go is the right time. If you wish to escape the cold winter, disembark at Takamatsu and head for Kochi in the S of Shikoku. If you are sweltering in the summer heat, pick an island and sunbathe on one of the numerous balmy beaches.

places of interest: With over 750 inhabited islands to choose from, it is difficult to single out particular ones. Most are unvisited fishing villages, quaint, traditional and quiet. There are a few that deserve special mention. *Awaji,* just off the coast from Kobe, is the largest island. The best way to get there is to take a one-hr speedboat from Kobe to the port of Sumoto, or from Naruto on Shikoku to Fukura (the best place from which to see the whirlpools) in 50 minutes. Fukura Cove is also one of the best places from which to view the whirlpools. The bus takes 40 min from Sumoto to Fukura. Awaji is known as the birthplace of *bunraku,* the slightly smaller-than-life-size puppet theater of Japan. This earthy puppet theater was the forerunner of classical Japanese theater.

Shodo Island: 28 km off the coast of Shikoku from the port of Takamatsu. Ferries are available from Takamatsu with Kansai Steamship Co., from Uno on Honshu (on the coast due S of Okayama) by the Shodoshima Transport Co. and from Okayama by the Ryobi Marine Co. The main port on the 155 sq km island is Tonosho. The island features a mediterranean climate complete with olive groves. It is believed that the stone quarried to build Osaka Castle came from Shodo. There are fine fishing and bathing beaches, and even a monkey garden (*Choshikei*), easily reached by tour bus service. Shodo also features 88 sacred spots, a miniature of the 88 temples of Shikoku. Many pilgrims come here because the tour on foot takes only 4 days compared with the 2 months necessary to walk the temples of Shikoku.

Omishima: Is a small island between Mihara on Honshu and Imabari on Shikoku. It is the setting for the Oyamazumi Shrine dedicated to

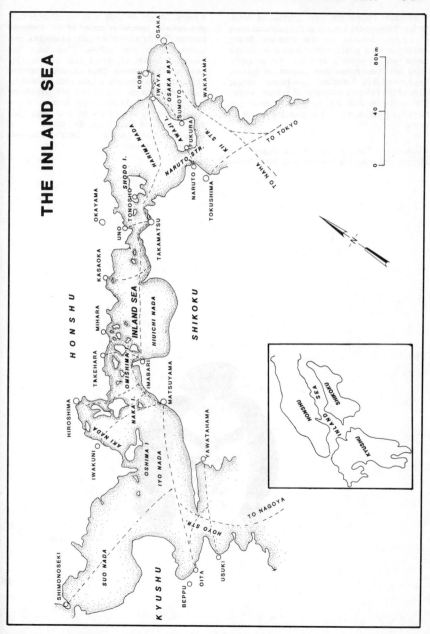

THE INLAND SEA

Oyamazumi-Okami the elder brother of Ama-terasu, traditionally known as the guardian deity of pirates. Because of the inherent daring needed to be a pirate, many Japanese *daimyo* came here to worship and pray for strength. They left their armor and swords as tribute. Because of this, the island now houses almost 80% of the nation's treasures of ancient armor. The shrine is also surrounded by enormous camphor trees, some dating back thousands of years.

Ikuchijima: Twelve km off the coast from Mihara. This island is the home of Nishi Nikko Kosanji Temple. In 1946, a common sailor built this colorful temple in honor of his deceased mother. The buildings are painted in gold, red, green, purple and yellow. They copy the Toshugo Shrine of Nikko built in the 17th century. The grounds have numerous statues of Buddha, and there is a cave with representational paintings of heaven and hell. Whenever you decide to alight from your ferry, or if you decided merely to lie back on your deck chair and breath the balmy air, the magic that is Seto-Nakai will linger like the blood-red sunsets for which it is famous.

KYUSHU

INTRODUCTION

Kyushu is the source, the mountain spring from which the long river of Japanese civilization began its flow. Archaeological evidence points to Kyushu as the earliest inhabited area of Japan. From Kyushu, traceable Japanese history emerged from the dark mire of antiquity. There is strong evidence that Jimmu Tenno began his northward push from here, planting the seeds of what would be the world's longest living line of nobility, lasting to include the present emperor. Less definable, but vastly more important, the cohesive concept of "we Japanese" began to take form and the psyche of what would become Japan was structured. In Kyushu, the climate is mild, almost Mediterranean, and this is reflected in the temperament of the people. The climate, coupled with a long history and assuredness of who they are, tend to make the people of Kyushu more fiery. Here the stoic, public Japanese mask cracks a bit to reveal the emotional side of the Japanese personality. The leadership of Kyushu seemed to be more receptive to accepting Western ways. When the Tokugawa slammed the door shut for 150 years, a tiny island at Nagasaki, Dejima, provided the only peephole to the West. The first Japanese muskets and cannons were cast in primitive factories in Kagoshima. This long legacy of contact with the West is still in evidence. In Kyushu, more so than in any other area of Japan, the *gaijin* is viewed as an individual and not merely as an unknowable, amorphous alien. In the S is Kagoshima, ancestral

home of the Shimazu clan, the conquerors of Okinawa. Remaining today, a legacy to their gentler side, is their idyllic Iso Garden, one of the most exquisitely manicured formal gardens in Japan. Kagoshima Bay is dominated by Sakurajima, an active and fuming conical volcano crisscrossed with numerous walking trails leading to the summit. Just N is Kirishima, a series of volcanos on a high plateau. Underrated and under-visited, Kirishima provides camping and hiking, numerous relaxing mineral baths, and Kirishima Jinja, an ancient mountain shrine which is a Mecca to Shinto pilgrims. In the center of Kyushu is Mt. Aso, the world's largest volcano. Oftentimes, because of its unstable activity, the summit is closed to hiking. It is an ugly giant, but its awesome strength is fascinating; its constant rumbling and fuming fissures inform the visitor that the giant is not asleep. Nagasaki, etched on the sides of rolling mountains, lies on a peninsula on the W coast. The 2nd atom bomb fell here during WW 11, but the natural mountain formations absorbed much of the blast, and the city suffered much less destruction than Hiroshima. Today the city is rebuilt and thriving. Overlooking hastily constructed "pragmatic architecture," Nagasaki remains one of the most beautiful Japanese cities. In the N is Fukuoka and its sister city, Kita-Kyushu, one enormous industrial complex, the gateway to Kyushu by overland routes from Honshu. On the E coast is the ultra-famous spa town of Beppu. It has long been known for its

Hells—bubbling multi-colored waters forming ponds as it oozes from the active volcanic soil below. White steam and dampness fill the air, while Beppu lives up to its name and looks like hell. A few km S of Oita, Beppu's closest neighboring city, are the Seki Butsu. The Seki Butsu are fascinating Buddhist rock carvings set in a deep mountain ravine. No one is quite sure why such art, fashioned with obviously painstaking dedication, is found in such a secluded sector of the country. Kyushu, with its wealth of scenic beauty, historical sights, balmy climate and enduring culture, is a Japanese treasure chest just waiting to be opened.

getting there: Kyushu has 7 airports which are located in the main cities throughout the island. They include Omura (Nagasaki), Kumamoto, Kagoshima, Oita, Miyazaki, Kita-Kyushu and Fukuoka, all accessible by direct flight from major cities throughout Japan. Fukuoka, the largest city in Kyushu, is the principal airport for international flights to the island. Fukuoka Airport is a modern facility with all the amenities. A good place to pick up travel brochures and maps, it is located at Itazuke, in the SE end of the city, and is connected by frequently departing buses heading for Hakata Eki in 20 minutes. Hakata and Fukuoka are now considered one metropolis. JAL and ANA connect Fukuoka Airport to Osaka (one hr) and Tokyo (one hr 40 min). From Fukuoka, get connecting flights to other airports on Kyushu. TOA connects Fukuoka to Miyazaki (one hr) and Kagoshima (40 min). Again, the obvious is true: except for emergencies or when time is of the essence, air travel in Japan is unnecessary, unrewarding and costly.

train service: Kyushu is readily accessible by train from any area of Japan. The *shinkansen* operates between Tokyo and Fukuoka (Hakata) and this is an excellent chance to ride the bullet. It covers the distance in just under 7 hrs and costs Y15,500. This is one of those times where it is worth spending the extra money for the *shinkansen*, especially if you are going to travel the entire distance from Fukuoka to Tokyo. The limited express (*kyuko*) costs Y11,500, but it takes almost 17 hrs from Tokyo, a long time to bounce along in a train. If you want a berth for this marathon, it costs an extra Y4000, and there goes your savings. It is possible to cover this distance by ordinary express (*futsu*) for Y9000, but you might have to renew your 90-day tourist visa by the time you arrived. For short hops, ride the *kyuko and futsu,* but if you're going to take

the big step, ride the bullet. *getting around:* Because Kyushu's location has its NE tip at Kita-Kyushu almost touching the SW tip of Honshu, you will most likely wind up there or in nearby Fukuoka. From either, you can catch trains (excellent service) all over Kyushu. The 3 main rail arteries leading from Kita-Kyushu are: the Nagasaki Line terminating in Nagasaki and including a branch line to Sasebo on the extreme western shore of Saga Prefecture. The Kagoshima Main Line services the western shoreline of Kyushu stopping at all main towns until it arrives at Kagoshima in the extreme south. The eastern seaboard of Kyushu is tracked by the small but adequate Nippo Line that runs from Kita-Kyushu to Oita and then southward to Miyazaki where it branches westward, tying in with the Kagoshima Main Line. Basically, this rail network circles the entire island of Kyushu with branch lines such as the Kyudai from Oita to Saga and the Hohi Line from Oita to Kumamaoto dissecting it horizontally.

ferry service: The outlying islands to the N and W are connected to Kyushu either by bridges or local ferry service. The famous Inland Sea Ferry Route connects Kyushu to Shikoku and Honshu, and is perhaps the best way to travel to Kyushu. It gives a seaside, romantic window on Japan as it slowly cruises along the coast. There is also ferry service from Hakata and Kagoshima to Okinawa. These ships island-hop down and back, (see "Okinawa") and give you an opportunity to visit the beautiful sub-tropical islands in the extreme SW of Kagoshima Prefecture.

schedule to Okinawa: The RKK plies the Hakata to Naha, Okinawa route every 4-5 days, Y11,800 to Y29,500, 26 hours; the Kagoshima to Naha, Okinawa run every 4-5 days, leaving Kagoshima at 1700, arriving in Naha at 1300 the next day. Oshima Unyu, every other day; leave Kagoshima at 1800, arrive in Naha at 1830 the next day, Y10,500-Y25,400. The RKK also sails from Naha to Kagoshima, Kyushu every 4 days, leaving Naha at 1100, arriving Kagoshima at 0800 the next day. Oshima Unyu, every other day, leaving Naha at 0900, arriving Kagoshima 0830 the next day.

the land: Kyushu is the 3rd largest island of Japan (44,300 sq km) and the most southern of the 4 main islands. It is comprised of the prefectures of Fukuoka, Saga, Nagasaki, Oita, Kumamoto, Miyazaki, and Kagoshima, which

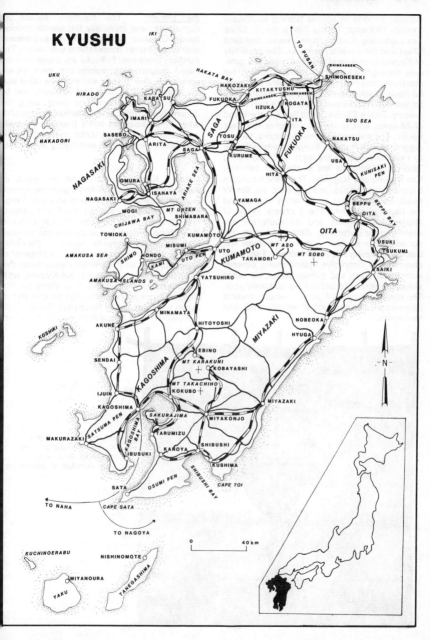

KYUSHU

IKI

UKU

HIRADO

NAKADORI

NAGASAKI

KOSHIKI

KUCHINOERABU

NISHINOMOTE

MIYANOURA

YAKU

TANEGASHIMA

HAKATA BAY

TO PUSAN

SHINKANSEN

SHIMONESEKI

KARATSU

HAKOZAKI

FUKUOKA

KITAKYUSHU

SHINKANSEN

SHINKANSEN

NOGATA

IIZUKA

ITA

IMARI

SASEBO

ARITA

SAGA

TOSU

KURUME

FUKUOKA

SUO SEA

NAKATSU

USA

HITA

KUNISAKI PEN

OMURA

ISAHAYA

ARIAKE SEA

YAMAGA

BEPPU

BEPPU BAY

OITA

NAGASAKI

MOGI

MT UNZEN

SHIMABARA

CHIJAWA BAY

KUMAMOTO

MT ASO

MT SOBO

OITA

USUKI

TSUKUMI

TOMIOKA

MISUMI

UTO PEN

UTO

KUMAMOTO

TAKAMORI

SHIMO

HONDO

KAMI

YATSUHIRO

SAIKI

AMAKUSA SEA

AMAKUSA ISLANDS

MINAMATA

HITOYOSHI

NOBEOKA

MIYAZAKI

HYUGA

AKUNE

EBINO

MT KARAKUNI

KOBAYASHI

SENDAI

KAGOSHIMA

MT TAKACHIHO

KOKUBO

IJUIN

KAGOSHIMA

SAKURAJIMA

MIYAKONJO

MIYAZAKI

SATSUMA PEN

KAGOSHIMA BAY

TARUMIZU

MAKURAZAKI

KANOYA

SHIBUSHI

IBUSUKI

KUSHIMA

SATA

OSUMI PEN

CAPE TOI

SHIBUSHI BAY

TO NAHA

CAPE SATA

TO NAGOYA

0   40 km

-N-

includes a string of islands fanning southward towards Okinawa. To the SW is the E. China Sea separating Kyushu from Taiwan, mainland China and the Korean peninsula. The proximity of Kyushu to mainland Asia has made it a gateway through which culture has flowed for countless centuries, mostly by means of peaceful trade. It also served as a prime staging area for war with Russia and China at the turn of the century. To the E is the Inland Sea and the island of Shikoku, and to the SE stretches the wide Pacific. The volcanic Kyushu Mountains, tall and rugged, stretch from the Bungo Straits in the NE to Yatsushiro Bay on the west. The low, rolling Tsukushi Mountains are in the NW between Kita-Kyushu and Nagasaki. There are numerous bays and peninsulas, more prolific on the W coast. The peninsulas are generally rugged, and the bays are shallow. The 3 coastal plains of Miyazaki, Kumamoto and Tsukushi are the island's most extensive. Active volcanos are dotted all over Kyushu, with Aso, Kirishima and Sakurajima being the most famous. They have given rise to distinctive upland plains covered with volcanic ash and pumice which are called *shirazu*, generally considered agriculturally poor. The islands running S from Kumamoto towards Okinawa are an aggregate of volcanic and coral formations.

the climate: The southern section of Kumamoto, and especially the islands running toward Okinawa, can be considered sub-tropical with warm, humid temperatures year round. The northern areas near Fukuoka are cooler and the inland mountainous regions can even experience snow due to their altitude. The rainy season (*baiu*) is early June, and typhoons can be expected in September. The coast along the Japan Sea is drier and experiences droughts while other areas are being flooded. Generally the summer is hot and sticky, the winters mild and balmy, and autumn and spring are superb.

history: Kyushu is considered the cradle of Japanese civilization, holding a prominent place in Japanese mythology. Legend says that Ninigi, a descendant of Amaterasu (the Sun Goddess) first came to earth here on Mt. Takachiho in Kagoshima Prefecture and that he was invested with the regalia of royalty: the sword, the mirror and the jewels which symbolize the Emperor of Japan to this day. Opinion concerning the original migrations is divided, but Kyushu, with its proximity to mainland Asia aided by the stepping stone islands, was the easiest island of Japan to be reached in times past. The mild climate would have also aided the earliest settlers.

the battle flag of the Kyushu Christians when they rose in a disasrous rebellion at Shimabara

a monoment on Tanegashima I. commemorating the introduction of firearms to Japan

from Asia and later for the temporarily aborted contact with the West. For the most part this was accomplished through peaceful trading, but war was also a factor. Kublai Khan sent an expeditionary force of 100,000 warriors to Hakata (Fukuoka) in 1281 to subjugate Japan after an earlier small force had failed. The Japanese defenders fought valiantly, and providentially were aided by a typhoon that arrived just in the nick of time to sink the Khan's great fleet. The people believed that this *Kami Kaze* (Divine Wind) was sent by the gods in answer to their prayers—a name that would symbolize terror and desperation 7 centuries later. Kyushu was also the home port of Japanese pirates who roamed the Yellow Sea and the Pacific seeking plunder and bringing back news from abroad. The first recorded contact with the West also occurred in Kyushu in 1543. Three Portuguese merchants traveling in a Chinese junk were blown off course and landed at Tanegashima Island, just off the tip of Kagoshima. They paved the way for 2 opposite Western commodities that would alter Japanese history: firearms and Christianity. The Lords of Satsuma, the Shimazu clan of Kagoshima, immediately recognized the value of cannon in warfare and instructed their swordsmiths to begin casting them a few years later. St. Francis Xavier came to Japan through Kyushu in 1549. Catholicism spread rapidly, and was eventually considered a threat to national security by the Tokugawa Shogunate. This resulted in civil war between the converts and the shogunate. A battle was fought at Shimabara in 1637 in which 40,000 Catholics were killed. The new religion went underground and did not emerge until the reopening of Japan in the mid-1800s. Kyushu is also known for its mili-

To the N where the climate is harsher, and nature at odds with the people, a far more advanced technology, including a structured division of labor, would have been necessary. In Kyushu it was simply easier to live. The pertinent history of Kyushu begins with the half-real, mythically embellished founder of the Japanese nobility, Jimmu Tenno. Jimmu allied his roving privateers with the queen of Kyushu and drove back the barbarians in the mountainous hinterlands. Once accomplished and firmly fortified with an alliance with the Queen, he moved on to Honshu and established his reign around the present Nara. His kingdom, Yamato, became the strongest and in time the largest, and thus began the Imperial Japanese State. Those early alliances proved a solid bond between Yamato and Kyushu for centuries to come. Increasingly, as the centuries rolled on, Kyushu became a wide-open gateway for culture, art, manufacturing and religion which flowed into Japan

Takamori Saigo

Heihachiro Togo

tary leaders. The Shimazu clan subjugated Okinawa in the 17th C. and expanded Japanese rule into the Pacific. Takamori Saigo was instrumental in establishing the Meiji Restoration in the 1860s. Later he rebelled against the new order and led the Satsuma Rebellion, only to be defeated. He lived according to the old rules of *bushido,* and committed *seppuku.* Another more modern leader was Heihachiro Togo. He was Admiral of the Japanese Imperial Fleet and annihilated the Imperial Russian Baltic Fleet in the Russo-Japanese War of 1905. The most modern historical city of note on Kyushu is Nagasaki. When Japan closed its doors, it was the one and only link to the outside world. Here, Chinese, Korean and Dutch merchants came to trade. The traders were sequestered on one tiny island, Dejima, linked to the mainland by a small bridge. Only Japanese merchants and prostitutes could cross that bridge. It can also be considered that WW11 effectively ended in Nagasaki on the morning of Aug. 9, 1945, with the flash of the second atomic bomb blast.

economy: At one time, Kyushu, especially the northern sector, was a thriving center of industry and manufacturing. This was largely due to its coal deposits and its traditional role as gateway to Asia. In the early part of the century the coal supplied almost half of the nation's yearly consumption. In recent years, these sectors have seen a decline in production which has resulted in both a loss of revenue and population. Kita-Kyushu still produces steel and heavy machinery, but the large industrial areas of northern Japan, as well as those of Tokyo, Osaka and Nagoya, have long since eclipsed it. In today's market, N. Kyushu is at a disadvantage

because of its distance from the main ports of Tokyo and Yokohama. Nagasaki and Sasebo on the W coast are still important shipbuilding areas (the A-bomb was meant for the huge Mitsubishi Shipyards in Nagasaki, but missed) and these yards still employ a large number of workers. There is a small but growing oil refining industry on the W coast centered around Oita; this area has been designated as a new industrial city, and should, unfortunately, see rapid growth in the next decade. Southern Kyushu's economy is based on agriculture and forestry. The upland plateaus of southern Kyushu are comprised of *shirasu,* the pumice and ash outpourings from the numerous volcanos. This soil will produce crops, but is very susceptible to erosion from frequent typhoons. It is also very porous and unable to hold water. This combination makes farming risky and leads to many crop failures. In the mountain villages, the traditional way of earning money is forestry, but with modern communications and the lure of big wages in the cities, there has been a constant population drain.

the people: There is a long tradition of contact with the West in Kyushu, especially in Nagasaki and the larger towns, so the people are more apt to be curious and inquisitive towards a Western traveler without being as awed or intimidated as they might be in other regions of Japan. *Gaijin* will find this a refreshing change from always being kept at a very polite arm's length. Most of the social interactions are up to you: if you are friendly and open, you will be treated likewise. It is also said that the people of Kyushu will show their emotions; they are a bit more expansive with their gestures and their faces are more animated. Though another Japanese can easily perceive these differences, a Westerner will find them less obvious.

ARTS AND CRAFTS

Although this section deals primarily with the potter's art, the most famous of Kyushu's crafts, there are also a multitude of other arts and crafts found throughout Kyushu. For information on these handicrafts, please refer to specific regions. The manufacture of fine ceramics and porcelain is a thriving art throughout Kyushu. This art dates back to the early 17th C. when Korean potters were brought into Kyushu after the abortive invasion of their homeland by Ieyasu Hideyoshi. The finest kilns were founded by the Koreans and even today the influence of the Yi Dynasty can be seen in the exquisite wares of Kyushu. There are numerous and varied kilns throughout Kyushu, but there are 4 main groupings by which most of the pottery produced is designated.

Satsuma *yaki* (pottery)

Satsuma ceramic ware: Satsuma ceramics are produced in southern Kyushu in and around Kagoshima. There are 2 main types: *shiro* (white) and *kuro* (black). *Shiro Satsuma* has unique designs of elegant birds and flowers, but has become very popular, especially as an export item, so its high standard has suffered. The once-elegant hand designs are merely stamped on. You can find excellent pieces, but the novice buyer can only be guided by instinct and price. *Kuro Satsuma* are the dark-glazed ceramics of Kagoshima. Their history dates back to the Shimazu clan when these ceramics were used in tea ceremony. The glazes vary from black to dark green. Many of the pieces today are utilitarian and along with *shiro* are found in numerous shops in Kagoshima. The 2 most famous kilns producing these wares are Ryumonji and Naeshirogawa, where excellent pieces can still be purchased. The addresses are Ryumonji-Gama, Koyamada 5945, Kajiki-cho, Aira-gun, Kagoshima-ken, tel: (09956); and Naeshirogawa, whose master potter Samejima Sataro, is located at Miyama 456, Higashiichiki-cho, Hioki-gun, Kagoshima-ken, tel: (09927) 4-2450.

Arita (Imari-yaki): This pottery is manufactured in Western Kyushu, S of Fukuoka and W of Saga. *Arita-yaki* is beautiful enameled porcelain whose main patterns are flowers and animals. Its history dates back to the 15th C. when it was patterned after Ming porcelain from China. This ware can be seen at the Arita Ceramics Museum, 1356 Aritacho, Nishimatsura-gun, Saga Prefecture, tel: (09554) 2-3372, from 0900 to 1630, closed Mondays. Admission is Y100.

This museum displays old *Arita-yaki* and gives a history of its origins. There are numerous kilns in and around Arita. Close by is Imari, the port from which Arita ware was once shipped, and the mountain village of Okawachi—dedicated exclusively to pottery. At one time the inhabitants of Okawachi were prevented from leaving in order to safeguard the secrets employed in the production of the distinctive porcelain. Today the village is becoming more and more touristed, but fine examples of family-owned and operated shop/kilns are everywhere. A visit to any of the following kilns in the Arita area will give you a good cross-section of the pottery available: Kakiemon Kiln, Minamigawara, Arita-cho, Nishimatsura-gun, Saga Prefecture, tel: (09554) 3-2267; Imaemon Sankokan Gallery (across from Imaemon Kiln), Akae, Arita-cho, Nishimatsura-gun, Saga Prefecture, tel: (09554) 2-3101; and Fukagawa Seiji Kiln, 1361 Arita-cho, Nishimatsura-gun, Saga Prefecture, tel: (09554) 2-5215. There's also a ceramic market held

Imari *yaki* (pottery)

yearly May 1-5 in Arita at which time the streets are lined with open-air stalls selling the yearly stockpile of ceramics. This is the largest fair of its kind in all Japan. Some works are treasures, while other items are of the dimestore variety. Another important center for pottery is Karatsu, located on a bay of the Japan Sea, approx. 20 km due W of Fukuoka in Saga Prefecture. Pottery works in Karatsu are everywhere, and it seems as though every shop sells *Karatsu-yaki* Karatsu, being so close to Korea, has been an important trading port for centuries. A number of families in town have handed down their ceramic traditions for over 4 centuries, and these wares have been a favorite in tea ceremonies for as long. Most pieces are of simple buff tones with dark brown underglazes. Other prominent glazes are deep, rich blacks and striking oranges.

See fine examples of *Karatsu-yaki* at: Nakazato Taroemon Kiln, Choda, Karatsu, Saga Prefecture, tel: (09557) 2-8171; and Ochanomizu Kiln, Katanamachi, Karatsu, Saga Prefecture, tel: (09557) 2-2685. Also visit Karatsu Castle, a 10 min walk from Higashi-Karatsu Eki, to see old Karatsu ware chronologically catalogued along with local archaeological finds. The castle is open from 0900-1700; admission Y150.

Onita-yaki: In the N-central section of Kyushu, in and around the village of Hita, you'll find *Onita-yaki.* This pottery is perhaps the best example of true folk art in Kyushu. It is a no-frills utilitarian pottery designed for everyday use. It has been manufactured in this area for 3 centuries and its simple design and unpretentious colors and shapes give it an earthy beauty. Again, Korean potters, taken from their homeland, populated the nearby villages. Train to Hita and bus (40 min) to the village of Sarayama, where you'll find almost every family employed in one form or another with the manufacture of *Onita-yaki.* There is a pottery fair held every year on the second weekend of October. There are numerous excellent kilns in the village, but 2 fine examples are: Sakamoto Haruzo Kiln, Sarayama, Motoe-cho, Hita, Oita Prefecture, tel: (09732) 9-2405, and Sakamoto Shigeki Kiln, Sarayama, Motoe-cho, Hita, Oita Prefecture, tel: (09732) 9-2404.

Hakata Ningyo: These famous clay dolls are made in and around Fukuoka. These figures come in a wide range of shapes and sizes, and are usually dressed in classical Japanese kimono and molded into poses of grace and beauty. The finer ones have delicately painted, life-like features. They can be found in shops all over the city and in fact all over Japan, with prices ranging from Y200 for small, hastily made models, to Y20,000 plus for those of superior workmanship.

KYUSHU FESTIVALS AND EVENTS

Kyushu is where the gods were believed to have made their descent to earth. Rituals and traditions carried out at Kyushu's numerous festivals, and prayers offered before out-of-the-way shrines, date back to antiquity. The Shinto shrine at Kirishima, one of the oldest and most venerated in Japan, is the final resting place of many emperors. Kyushu stages quite modern festivals as well as festivals heavily laced with foreign influence. In Nagasaki, the victims of the atomic bomb blast are remembered each year, and processions glorifying the Holy Virgin and the Christian martyrs from the 1600s are held, usually in May by the city's Catholic population. Festivals, obviously of chinese origin, are held testifying to the fact of Kyushu's proximity to mainland China and its past role as a gateway of foreign influence. Dragon masks, the dragon dance and Chinese-style temples are all part of this heritage. The following are merely the main festivals held. You will find numerous others in the small villages throughout the island with their own unique rituals and distinguishing characteristics.

Jan. 1: Horai En Ya, at Oita. Fishermen in white loincloths, head wrapped in bright scarves, and children in ritual attire ride in boats down the Katsura River. As they row they chant, "Horai," beseeching the river gods for a good catch, and safe voyages. The boatmen praise their own benificent *kami*, Funadama, at this festival. The ever-present sea provides the sparkling background.

Jan. 7: Hi Matsuri, at Fukuoka. This is basically a fire festival. Giant 5 m pine torches are burned to purify the participants and to drive off lurking evil spirits.

late Apr.: Kite (*tako*) Flying, at Nagasaki. This festival turns eyes toward midair as participants launch their huge kites and attempt to gain favorable positions in combative but fun-filled aerial maneuvers. In Nagasaki, the kites are called *hata*. Sometimes as many as 20 participants man the strings of the huge kites, some measuring 12 by 8 m. One kite motif often seen is that of a giant demon sitting atop a warrior. this particular demon harassed the people with his wrongdoings until he was punished by the hero Yuriwaka. This kite is an honorable reminder of the event.

Lord Soga's Umbrella Burning Festival

May 3-5: Hakata Dontaku, Fukuoka. This is the grandest festival of the area. Farmers arrive to join in from all over the island. Huge stre nered decorations are hung in doorways and participants on horseback ride through the streets representing ancient gods. The music is traditional, being performed on *samisen* and huge drums. This festival provides a good time in a usually dull city.

May 28: Lord Soga's Umbrella Burning Festival, Kagoshima. At this festival, a bonfire is made from umbrellas. The fire is tended by men in ornate ritual costumes as well as those clad only in loincloths. The burning umbrellas symbolize Lord Soga's defeat of an enemy in the 12th century.

Jul. 13-15: Tobata-no-Chochin, Fukuoka. this festival is the culmination of the Hakata Yamagasa that begins on Jul. 1, when large floats representing castles bedecked with dolls are pulled through the streets. The *Tobata-no-Chochin*, a giant pyramid constructed of lanterns, is pulled through the streets. The glowing fire, colored by the paper lanterns, purifies the participants and drives off evil spirits.

Jul. 28: O Taue, at Mt. Aso. Large drums herald the approach of *mikoshi* (portable shrines) bearing the representatives of the local *kami*. They are paraded around so that the *kami* can "see" the area that they protect. This festival is simple and without flash, but captures the roots of Shinto belief.

Aug. 9: Peace Festival, at Nagasaki. A gathering of mankind at the Peace Memorial commemorates the 70,000 killed by the A-bomb on this day in 1945. Dedicated by all men to all gods, one unified prayer for peace.

Oct. 7-9: Suwa (Okunchi) Festival, at Nagasaki. This festival is largely Chinese in origin. The mythical Chinese dragon floats through the streets surrounded by people dancing and singing. The center for the festival is the Suwa Shrine where huge floats and palanquins begin their route through the city. If you intend to participate, be sure to come early for a seat because this festival lures tremendous crowds. The highlight is the rapid descend down the precarious steps of Suwa Shrine by the sure-footed *mikoshi* (portable shrine) bearers.

Nov. 3-5: Karatsu Kunchi, at Karatsu. Fourteen floats from different districts of the city depicting helmets, lions, ships, etc. are drawn through the streets. Historians say that this festival is a local spin-off of the Gion festival held in Kyoto. Others believe that the obverse is true; Kyoto borrowed the festival from Kyushu. The festival is colorful, folksy and provides a good opportunity to visit this famous pottery center.

Karatsu Kunchi Floats

FUKUOKA PREFECTURE

Kita-Kyushu is an industrial giant in the NE sector of Fukuoka Prefecture and the transportation hub of Kyushu. It is a conglomerate of the 5 cities of Moji, Tabata, Yahata, Wakamatsu and Kokura. All overland traffic from Honshu to Kyushu passes through or near Kita-Kyushu. It is an excellent staging area for making connections to all points in Kyushu, but its size and industrial profile make it of little interest to the traveler. The constant whir of machinery, belching smoke stacks and kilometers of sprawling factories are better off quickly left behind. *getting there:* Kita-Kyushu is linked to Honshu by the Kanmon Bridge, stretching from Shimonoseki to Moji, a section of Kita-Kyushu. It is the longest bridge in the Orient and its 6 lanes can handle 60,000 vehicles per day. The *shinkansen* from Tokyo (6 hrs 30 min) and Osaka (3 hrs 15 min) pass under the Kanmon Straits through the Shin-Kanmon Tunnel, the longest undersea tunnel on earth. Two other undersea tunnels are for rail traffic and automobiles with the lower sections for pedestrians passing for a distance of 3.5 km under the straits. Rail and bus service flow through Kita-Kyushu from all points. Ferry service is available by way of the Inland Sea from Nagoya in 20 hrs 40 min, from Kobe in 13 hrs (3 boats per day), and Tokyo, 36 hours. Take a break, make onward-going connections and head out as soon as possible.

sights: As previously noted, Kita-Kyushu serves admirably as a way station, but is singularly uninteresting as a tourist attraction. The best itinerary if caught between trains is to bus (10 min) to Cape Mekari 2.5 km NE of Mojiko Eki. Cape Mekari has been turned into a park and offers some quietude amidst the hustle and bustle of the city. Here is Mt. Kojo and from its heights you get an excellent view of the Kanmon Bridge and the port. Here is also a Peace Pagoda of mild interest dedicated to the SE Asians who died in WW 11. Mekari Shrine is at the tip of the cape and it was supposedly founded by Empress Jingu in the 3rd C. after her return from an early war in Korea. If time permits, visit Kokura castle (5 min walk from Kokura Eki). Next door is Kita-Kyushu Municipal Hall where the 15th floor has been turned into an observation platform. The final and probably most reasonable suggestion is to embrace rather than wince from the clutches of this industrial giant of a city. Find a pleasant *kissaten* (coffee shop) and watch modern industrial Japan hurry by.

accommodations: If you must spend the night in Kita-Kyushu, here are some suggestions. For Western style, Kokura Castle Hotel, 1-2-16 Muromachi, Kokurakita-ku 803, Kita-Kyushu, tel: (093) 571-2345, 5 min by car from Kokura Station, from Y4500; Kokura Station Hotel, 1-1-1 Asano, Kokurakita-ku 802, Kita-Kyushu, tel: (093) 521-5031, 2 min walk from Kokura Station, from Y5000; and Hotel New Tagawa, 3-46 Furusenba-cho, Kokurakita-ku 802, Kita-Kyushu, tel: (093) 521-3831, 3 min by car from Kokura Station, from Y5000. Business hotels are: Kitakyushu Daiichi Hotel, 11-20 Konyamachi, Kokurakita-ku, Kita-Kyushu, tel: (093) 551-7331, 105 rooms, from Y3400, 10 min walk from Kokura station; and Yukata Business Hotel, 2 Asanomachi, Kokura-ku, Kita-Kyushu, tel: (093) 511-0101, 96 rooms, from Y3700, 2 min walk from Kokura Station. The youth hostels are: Kita-Kyushu YH, 7 Hobashira, Yahatahigashi-ku, Kita-Kyushu 085, tel: (093) 681-8142, 12 min by bus from Yahata Station and 3 min on foot, 96 beds. For *minshuku* accommodations, contact: Kita-Kyushu Minshuku Ctr., Kokurazabo 4th fl., 1-4-1 Uo-machi, Kokura, Fukuoka Prefecture.

FUKUOKA

This neighboring metropolis is connected to Kita-Kyushu by the Kagoshima Main Line. Fukuoka is the commercial, industrial and governmental center of Kyushu. It is divided into 2 sections by the Naka River—Hakata on the E bank, and Fukuoka on the west. Its size, industry and crowded streets make Fukuoka, like Kita-Kyushu, more of a way station than a place to sightsee. Do your traveling business and head out to the much more charming sections of Kyushu to the W and south. Fukuoka is an ancient trading port. It was here that Kubla Khan sent his fleets in the 12th C. and the word *kami-kaze* was born. In the closing months of WW 11, young fanatically brave Japanese pilots attempted to emulate this timely typhoon by flying their planes into American warships. As history shows, they wreaked havoc, but were unsuccessful in stopping the American juggernaut.

sights: Again if caught between trains, a few of the following sights could fill an afternoon. Within 10 min walking distance from Hakata Eki is Shofuku-ji Temple. This temple is the cradle

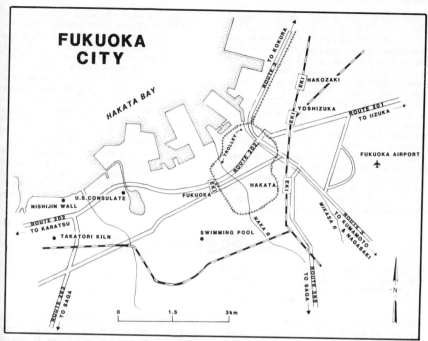

FUKUOKA CITY

HAKATA BAY

TO KOKURA

EKI HAKOZAKI

EKI YOSHIZUKA

ROUTE 3

ROUTE 201
TO IIZUKA

FUKUOKA AIRPORT

ROUTE 202

TROLLEY

HAKATA

EKI

FUKUOKA

NISHIJIN WALL

U.S. CONSULATE

MIKASA R

TO KUMAMOTO & NAGASAKI

ROUTE 3

ROUTE 202
TO KARATSU

TAKATORI KILN

SWIMMING POOL

NAKA R

ROUTE 3B
TO SAGA

ROUTE EKI
TO SAGA

TO SAGA

-N-

0   1.5   3km

Zen Buddhism in Japan. Founded by Eisai in 1195, it established the concepts of Zen that became so ingrained into the Japanese psyche. The grounds are serene and quiet and the temple is designated as an Important Cultural Property. Nearby is Sumiyoshi Shrine sitting atop a hill overlooking the Naka River. The restored buildings date to the early 1600s and *sumo* matches are held yearly in early October. For an afternoon out of the city, head for the remains of the Anti-Mongol Wall, locally called Boheki, and marked on handout maps from tourist information at Hakata Eki as Genko Fort. The walls were constructed to repel Kublai Khan's soldiers in 1281. About 100 m have been excavated to show their girth and size. Hakata Bay surrounding the walls is relatively clean, providing good swimming in season. Take the Nishi-no-Ura (Yuki bus) from Haakata Eki (2 hrs).

accommodations: Western-style places include: Hakata Zenikku Hotel, 3-3-3 Hakata-ekimae, Hakata-ku, Fukuoka 812, tel: (092) 471-7111, 3 min walk from Hakata Station, from Y6500; Hotel Takakura, 2-7-21 Watanabe-dori, Chuo-ku, Fukuoka 810, tel: (092) 731-1661, 5 min by car from Hakata Station, from Y4000; and Hakata Miyako Hotel, 2-1-1 Hakata-eki Higashi, Hakata-ku, Fukuoka 812, tel: (092) 441-3111, in front of Hakata Station, from Y6500. Business hotels include: Hakata Green Hotel, 4-4 Hakata-eki-chuo-gai, Hakata-ku, Fukuoka, tel: (092) 451-4111, 225 rooms, from Y3300, 2 min walk from Hakata Station; Hokke Club Fukuoka-Ten, 3-1-90 Sumiyoshi, Hakata-ku, Fukuoka, tel: (092) 271-3171, 298 rooms from Y3500, 7 min walk from Hakata Station; and Heiwadai Hotel, 1-3-26 Otemon, Chuo-ku, Fukuoka, tel: (092) 781-6066, 62 rooms from Y2400, 10 min walk from Nishitetsu Fukuoka Station. Among the *ryokan* are: Fukuoka Hotel, 2-9-3 Takasago, Chuo-ku, Fukuoka 810, tel: (092) 531-5931, 40 rooms from Y3000; Fukuoka Kanko Hotel Marumeikan, 5-6-1 Nakasu, Hakata-ku, Fukuoka 810, tel: (092) 291-0715, 32 rooms, Y8000-10,000; and Ryokan Gekkoen, 2-3-15 Kiyokawa, Chuo-ku, Fukuoka 810, tel: (092) 531-5531, 24 rooms,

Y8000-18,000. There is also a youth hostel, the Jodoji YH, 1-8-53 Tojin-machi, Chuo-ku, Fukuoka 810, tel: (092) 751-3377, 30 min by bus from Hakata Station and 3 min on foot, 16 beds, closed Aug. 8-23 and Dec. 25-Jan. 7. *special accommodations:* For a very inexpensive and relaxing night you can also stay at the Sauna Bath in the Sunhact Building just across from Hakata Eki. For Y1200 you not only get a place to stay (on the floor of the sleeping room, blanket provided) but also the complete sauna facilities. Once checked in, however, you can not leave and come back. You must be out by 0900 the next morning. Cigarettes and over-stuffed lounge chairs are provided free of charge. There is also an inexpensive snack bar in the lounge area. In the morning the coffee shop on the first floor has a good *morningu sabisu.* One drawback—the sauna admits men only!

services: Excellent city maps marked both in English and Japanese are available from the Tourist Information Office at Hakata Eki. If you are arriving from or going to Korea, pick up a visa or general information at the Korean Consulate, 1-10-20 Akasaka, Chuo-ku, Fukuoka, tel: (092) 771-0461 (for more info on Korea, see "Shimonoseki"). *from Fukuoka:* The Fukuoka International Airport is the main air gateway to Kyushu. Its facilities accommodate flights from the South Pacific and mainland Asia. JAL and ANA connect Fukuoka to Osaka (1 hr) and Tokyo (one hr 40 min). TOA has flights to Miyazaki (one hr) and Kagoshima (40 min). The airport is located at Itazuke in the SE corner of the city. There is an information center at the airport where maps and brochures are available in English. The bus to the city center (Hakata Station) covers the 4.5 km in 18 minutes.

SAGA PREFECTURE

The gnarled, jagged promontory extending into the Japan Sea W of Fukuoka and N of Nagasaki is Saga Prefecture. Its S shores run along the Ariake Sea, while Nagasaki Prefecture extends N along its western borders. Most travelers drawn by Nagasaki's magnetism overlook this portion of Kyushu. Iki and Tsushima Is., although technically a part of Nagasaki Prefecture but geographically closer to Saga, lie in the Japan Sea off its N shores. The latter is only 100 km or so from the S tip of Korea. Saga's interior villages such as Imari and Arita are renowned for pottery, the art being the spoils of many wars with Korea. Tranquil spas add a romantic touch to many secluded areas throughout the prefecture. The chief city is Saga, which serves as a main transportation terminal S to Nagasaki or W to Sasebo, the home of Japan's Maritime Self-Defence Force, and a U.S. Naval Base. Just off the coast is Hirado I., where Will Adams, the indomitable English pilot of the 16th C. is believed to have died. Natural beauty is preserved in numerous parks along the coast, and a strong, vibrant religious heritage offers many colorful and unusual festivals. *getting there:* The 2 main rail arteries through Saga originate in Fukuoka. The more southerly route (Nagasaki Main Line) passes through Saga (54 km from Fukuoka) and then branches S to Nagasaki and W to Sasebo. The northern Chikuhi Line runs from Fukuoka along the northern seaboard to Karatsu. It then heads S with one branch passing through Imari and Arita and one going directly to Saga.

KARATSU

Saga's north coast: The main city and chief port along the northern coast is Karatsu, a long established trading port with Korea. Numerous kilns throughout the area turn out high-quality porcelains, and archaeological digs in the surrounding hillside often unearth Ko-Karatsu (old Karatsu ware) dating back to the 16th century. *sights:* The town is ideally situated around a beautiful harbor. One stretch of 6 km is known as Niji-no-Matsubara (Rainbow Pine Cove) where the sea and land meet to form an almost perfect rainbow arc. The seacoast around Karatsu is wealthy with natural beauty and phenomena. Nanatsu-gama Caves (14 km NW of Karatsu Eki) have been formed by the swirling waters of the Genkai Sea. Seven deep caves have been formed in the basalt out-cropping. Sightseeing boats can be hired at Yobuko, a nearby town, and smaller craft can enter on calm days. Karatsu itself boasts a fine example of a castle that affords an impressive view of the Rainbow Pine Grove and the lonely Matsura Bay. To mix history with sightseeing, visit Nagoya Castle at the tiny port of Nagoya, 45 min by bus from Karatsu. The castle was built by Hideyoshi Toyotomi in 1592 when he embarked on his war against Korea. As you look from its *donjon* seaward, on the horizon will be Iki I. and further out Tsushima.

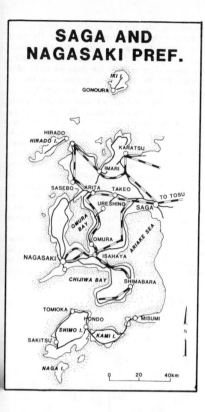

SAGA AND NAGASAKI PREF.

IKI AND TSUSHIMA ISLANDS

Take a ferry from Yobuko (near Karatsu) or Hakata (4 times a day). Flights are also available from Fukuoka. Iki I. is a favorite recreation area for Japanese students during the summer. The islanders are isolated most of the year and almost never see foreigners. Their dialect is even incomprehensible to most Japanese. This remote spot gained international notoriety when Dexter Cate, a Hawaiian school teacher, journeyed there to protest the slaughter of dolphins. This episode has been well-documented, showing dolphins being fed live into giant grinders, their grizzly remains forming a large pool of blood that would be used as fertizer. The islanders are now somewhat suspicious of foreigners, but their good-natured ways soon overcome any initial mistrust. Besides the swimming beaches, the high point of Iki I. is

literally the high point. Bus to the top of the central mountain and enjoy a 360 degree vista. On top is a Monkey Shrine with the famous motif of See-Hear-Speak No Evil. The women in attendance fight a constant battle to dissuade the many real monkeys in the area from dining on the fruit offerings made to the shrine. Mostly the women win, but a few marauders make off with their ill-gotten gains.

Tsushima Islands: Tsushima is made up of 2 islands: Kami (247 sq km) and Shimo (435 sq km). Kami I. was ruled for 700 yrs by the So clan, and their castle compound can still be seen on the outskirts of Izuhara, the principal city. Tsushima is even more rugged and isolated than Iki. It is a base of drug smuggling from Korea, so foreigners may be given a scrutinizing lookover by the local police. Besides this mild intrusion, there are usually no hassles. The mixture of Japanese and Korean culture is evident and adds an exotic color to many of the festivals.

accommodations: For an extended stay in this area, it is best to put up in Karatsu, where there is a small range of accommodations to choose from. There is one youth hostel: Niji-no-Matsubara YH, 4108 Kagami, Karatsu 847, tel: (09557) 2-4526, 5 min on foot from Niji-no-Matsubara Station, 56 beds. Unfortunately there are no YHs on Iki I., but there are _ryokan_. Tsushima, however, offers 2 YHs: Tsushima Seizanji 1453 Kokubu, Izuhara-machi 817, tel: (09205) 2-0444, 10 min on foot from Izuhara Port, 16 beds; and Kita-Tsushima YH, 983 Otsu, Sasuna, Kamiagatai-machi, tel: (09208) 4-2009, 15 min by taxi from Hidakatsu Port, 20 beds.

SAGA AND ENVIRONS

Heading SW from Fukuoka on the Nagasaki Main Line will take you through Saga, the prefectural capital. The city itself offers a pleasant afternoon of sightseeing with many interesting sights lying in the small towns just beyond. Visit Kodenji Temple, also known as Enichi-Zan, a Zen temple with the graveyard attached to it holding the tombs of the successive lords of the Nabeshima family. Those particularly interested in the samurai and their code of _bushido_ may wish to visit the Yamamoto Jocho Hermitage, where this sage taught young disciples in the code of the samurai. The house and grounds are well-preserved and give a feel for these old aesthetic traditions. An autumn scene from times past occurs throughout Saga in early

a *hangii* washtub boat

October. On any appropriately sized stream, women can be seen floating in washtub-sized boats (*hangii*), gathering water nuts called *hishi-no-mi*. This practice endures only in the Saga area.

vicinity of Saga: Heading W from Saga will take you through a series of picture-perfect spa towns, religious centers of ancient ascetic practices, and famed pottery centers. Ogi-machi (20 km W of Saga and 10 km N on the line from Karatsu) is the sight of one of the oldest purification rituals in Japan. Here in early spring, plum blossoms turn the rolling countryside resplendent with their soft-white petals. This is a perfect backdrop for Tamasudare (Bead Curtain), a 75 m high waterfall that sends its spidery webs over a sheer rock wall forming a knee-high pool at the base. Devotees come here to bathe themselves in the water offering special prayers through this ancient rite. The hope is to purify the spirit, thereby facilitating the good graces of the gods before setting out on pilgrimages. Further W (20 km) the rail line branches S to Nagasaki, passing through Hizen Kashima, renowned for its vermillion lacquered shrine, Yutoku Inari. Before taking this route, however, head another 40 km W passing through Takeo and Arita. The backtracking here is worth it. Takeo offers a spa whose history dates back to Japan's earliest times. Empress Jingo of the 1st C. is believed to have bathed in its waters. The approach is marked by a superb gate with the familiar *onsen* sign being the central character of the writing. The spa is an authentic delight; one of Japan's pleasures offered at its best. The next stop along the way is Arita, where porcelain tradition is still a thriving business dominating the town. The pottery fair here in early May attracts 500,000 visitors to its row upon row of street stalls. Accommodations are tight, but this is an excellent time to pick over the commercial offerings to some real treasure hidden under the piles. After visiting some of the local potteries for an up-close look, an alternative to backtracking on the rail line is to bus to the spa town of Ureshino. Hot springs line both sides of the Ureshino River, with many *onsen* tucked away in the surrounding hills. The atmosphere is quiet and the spas extra soothing in their traditional settings. Many hotels have been built to accommodate visitors. Finally, back on the track to Nagasaki, pass through Kashima City, where majestically on a hillside sits Yutoku Inari Shrine. It is considered one of the 3 greatest Inari shrines (fox shrines) in all of Japan, and its architectural splendor is second only to the shrines of Nikko. As a superb specimen of shrine architecture, it shouldn't be missed.

Tamasudare waterfall

accommodations: A Western-style place is the New Otani Saga, 1-2 Yokamachi, Saga, tel: (0952) 23-1111, from Y7000. The youth hostels are Takeo YH, Nagashima, Takeo-machi, Takeo 843, tel: (0954) 22-2490, 6 min by bus from Takeo-onsen Station, and 10 min on foot, 100 beds; and Saga-ken Seinen Kaikan YH, 1-21-50 Hinode, Saga 840-01, tel: (0952) 31- 2328, 10 min by bus from Saga Station and 2 min on foot, 56 beds. Also, all the towns mentioned, especially the spa towns, offer numerous *ryokan, min-shuku,* and a smattering of business hotels. *services:* For information concerning Saga and the nearby towns, contact Tourist Section, 1-1-59 Jonai, Saga City, tel: (0952) 25-2148.

NAGASAKI PREFECTURE

NAGASAKI CITY

Nagasaki is a romantic city. Physically, it looks like a child's drawing of dome-topped hills, touching each other at the base and rolling on and on. The mountains come down to the sea, and Nagasaki, like an enormous terraced garden, is etched on their sides. Its deep harbor is one of the best and safest in Japan, and the port, surrounded by the hills, is at the end of a land-locked inlet about 5 km long. Nagasaki is the western end of Japan and lies only 800 km from Shanghai. This accessibilty to the mainland has made Nagasaki one of the oldest Japanese ports and an entry point of foreign influence into Japan. The Chinese and Japanese traded for centuries through Nagasaki and finally in the late 1500s came the Europeans. Nagasaki maintains its cosmopolitan flavor to this day. Its history is a potpourri of the incredible, the adventurous, the swashbuckling, and the tragic. Nagasaki began as a small fishing vīllage lying at the foot of a minor castle. It did not come into prominence until the 16th C. when it became Japan's premier trading port with the outside world.

Merchants from Asia as well as the Portuguese, the Spanish and Dutch came to trade. Along with the Spanish and Portuguese came Jesuit and Franciscan missionaries. For a time, the rulers of Japan permitted the new religion and thousands of converts were made, including high-ranking *daimyo.* The Catholic priests, unfortunately, began to meddle in affairs of state, and many intrigues were carried on, especially concerning the court of Kyoto. The Toku-gawa clan observed the priests with watchful eyes and learned that in Europe, the Catholic church was directly involved with the state and that it held vast political powers. They viewed the Pope as a secular leader similar to the *shogun.* The Shogunate assessed this situation as intolerable, and it was for political reasons, fueled by a fear of a Catholic rebellion against the Japanese state, that the Spanish and Portu-guese priests were expelled and the new religion banned. The Protestant Dutch, who had shown that their aim in Japan was trade, were permit-ted to stay. The doors of Japan clanged shut to all foreigners, including Asians, in 1612. Only one miniscule island in Nagasaki Bay, Dejima, remained opened. Dutch ships were permitted to anchor here, but the traders could not cross the small bridge connecting Dejima with the mainland. Only prostitutes and Japanese mer-chants, under constant surveillance, could visit Dejima. And thus it remained until the 1850s. Everything foreign was outlawed and even hap-less Japanese sailors that had blown off course and touched down in a foreign land were put to death on their return to Japan because they were considered tainted. A trickle of Western technology entered through Dejima, but it was confined to medicine and warfare. Secret Chris-tian societies, in and around Nagasaki, went underground and disguised their beliefs as Bud-dhism. It is believed that the Buddhist female deity, Kannon, whose statue took the form of a benevolent mother with babe in arms, came secretly to represent the Blessed Virgin Mary. Only after the doors of Japan were opened over 250 years later in the 1850s, did the faithful emerge. It is considered a miracle that the Japanese Christians endured so long without benefit of clergy or church. Nagasaki remains a stronghold of Christianity to this day. It was a strange quirk that the atomic bomb dropped on Nagasaki in August 1945 fell almost on top of Urakami Catholic Church, built in 1914 and at that time the largest Catholic church in the Far East. After the bomb fell and the war ended, Nagasaki began to rebuild into a once again flourishing international city.

getting there: The train from Fukuoka by limited express takes 2 hr 40 min (Y2200). From Osaka, 12 hrs 30 minutes. Nagasaki Airport is located at Omura about 25 km NE of the city; bus into Nagasaki takes one hour. There are also direct ferry routes to and from Nagasaki to Sasebo, the

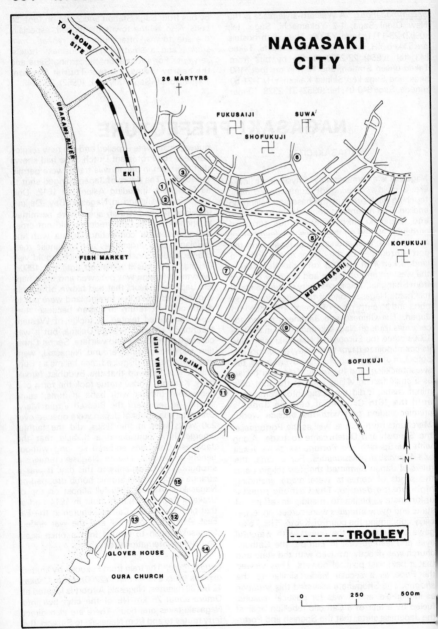

NAGASAKI CITY

26 MARTYRS

FUKUSAIJI

SUWA

SHOFUKUJI

KOFUKUJI

MEGANEBASHI

SOFUKUJI

TO A-BOMB SITE

URAKAMI RIVER

EKI

FISH MARKET

DEJIMA PIER

DEJIMA

GLOVER HOUSE

OURA CHURCH

-N-

- - - - - - - - TROLLEY

0   250   500m

Amakusa Is. and the Goto Islands. _by bus:_ Direct bus service is available from the Kumamoto Kutsu Center. Purchase your ticket at window 5 and board Bus 5 for the 4 hr trip which costs Y1990 including the 1 hr ferry ride from Misumi to Shimabara. Get back on the bus when the ferry begins to dock because it rolls off and leaves very promptly. _getting around:_ Nagasaki has excellent bus service throughout the city and charming vintage streetcars (_densha_), only Y70 per ride. Be sure to take your pink transfer slip when changing cars. combining a ride on these slow-moving dinosaurs with a few min of walking will take you to all the sights in Nagasaki. City buses as usual are also available to all points but their routes are much more complicated than the streetcars.

THE SIGHTS

Emerging from Nagasaki Eki, get good maps and tourist information at Nagasaki Tourist Center just outside the main entrance to the L next to the police box. A good first stop is Dejima. Take Streetcar No. 1 for 3 stops to Dejima. There is an excellent museum and a few old Western-style houses left standing on this one-time island that is now reclaimed land. The museum is free and offers exhibits related to the Dutch trading years. Just outside the museum is a large model of old Dejima that is worth looking at.

the Western influenced architecture of Hollander Heights testifies to its long history as a European enclave

Tsukimachi: The commercial heart of Nagasaki. It is a main streetcar junction, and at Tsukimachi are the Nagasaki Bus Terminal, exchange banks, large _depatos_ and numerous shops. For a cheap cup of coffee, stop at Mr. Donut under the large Toshiba sign, or at Keyaki, a small jazz-oriented coffee shop nearby in Hamanomachi. Keyaki also specializes in pottery from all over Japan. The walls are lined with hand-chosen works and the owner himself is a potter. If you like your coffee cup and saucer, you can buy it. Take care of business in Tsukimachi before continuing your tour. For an inexpensive lunch, try _champon_ in the numerous small restaurants in the area. _Champon_ is nourishing Chinese noodles, a specialty of Nagasaki, similar to ramen, but served in a much richer broth at Y300 anywhere. _Hollander Heights:_ From Tsukimachi, the main intersection on the line, take Streetcar No. 5 to the end of the line at Ishibashi. From Ishibashi you are a 5 min walk to the Nagasaki Oranda-Zaka Youth Hostel. This area is called Hollander Heights. Just on the corner where you get off the streetcar is a good French pastry shop. The area has a number of Western-style houses still standing. Climb the cobblestone street and get a good wide-angle view of Nagasaki. The temple below with the

NAGASAKI CITY

1. Nagasaki Information Center
2. JTB
3. Lucky Taxi and Bus
4. Post Office
5. American Japanese Info Center
6. Nagasaki Art Museum
7. Telephone and Telegraph Office
8. shopping arcade
9. Keyaki coffee shop
10. exchange bank
11. Nagasaki Bus Terminal
12. Tojin Kan Chinese Museum
13. Minzoku Shirokan Museum
14. Youth Hostel
15. Cezanne Bar

Meganebashi, the oldest style stone bridge in Japan built by the Chinese citizens of Nagasaki in 1634

golden roof is Tojin-kan and it houses Nagasaki's Chinese Museum. Stay on the cobblestone street and follow it past the YH and back down the hill. You will come to a small area just at the foot of the hill that sells souvenirs and artifacts at reasonable prices. Look for Cezanne Bar, a great spot to relax before moving on. It is marked by an artist's palette hanging outside that says BAR AND COFFEE. The owner is an artist himself and speaks English.

Glover House: About 400 m W from Hollander Heights (take the streetcar back towards Dejima) is this British merchant's house built in the 1860s. From the uppermost steps leading there you get an excellent vantage point to view the city and the bay. It is said that Glover House was the original setting for Pucchini's heartwarming, but fictitious tale *Madame Butterfly.* Avoid paying the Y200 to go on the grounds proper which you can see quite well from the steps. From Glover House it is an easy walk to Tsukimachi. Oura Church can also be seen to the R from Glover House. It is the oldest Gothic structure in Japan, built in 1865 by a French missionary.

Meganebashi and Kofukuji temple: From Tsukimachi, take Densha No. 2 or 5 for 5 min to Okeyamachi, Y70. Meganebashi was built in 1634 by the Chinese priest Niyojo, the abbot of Kofukuji Temple. It is the oldest foreign-style stone bridge in Japan. When you look over the side, you will see carp trying to swim upstream. Unfortunately you will also see garbage in the water. Actually, there are 7 bridges in the immediate area, Meganebashi being the largest. The

entire area is good for sightseeing. Cross the bridge and immediately on your L is a fine little pottery shop. Continue walking until you come to the stone wall surrounding Choshu Temple. Turn L and follow along the ivy-covered wall. The beautiful yellow flowers growing from the wall are *yamabuki.* About 100 m along, you'll come to a stonecutter's yard. He specializes in stone lanterns. Just listen for the rap of his hammer. The first gate you will come to is the entrance of Choshu Temple, made of weather-beaten wood. About 50 m further is the vermillion gate of Kofukuji (Y100). Kofukuji is the main Chinese temple in Nagasaki; its structural style and architecture derive from southern China. This and other Buddhist temples throughout Nagasaki got a popular boost when Christianity was outlawed. The populace flocked to the temples to show their dedication to Buddha, and to save their skins. The grounds are manicured and serene, perfect for sitting and contemplating. Tea is offered for a small charge. Look for the Bell Tower and Masodo Hall, housing the God of Voyages. The temple and grounds are well worth the Y100. *Suwa Shrine:* Recross Meganebashi and walk 10 min to this fantastic shrine. Climb the 73 steps to the shrine and look down on an outstanding view of the city. Suwa Shrine is home to the *Okunchi* Festival, Oct. 7-9, when its steps are jam-packed with participants. Check out the 2 fearsome gods guarding the gates against evil demons. Suwa Shrine is very popular and not a day goes by without some service or festivity occuring.

other sights: Take the streetcar one stop past Nagasaki Eki to the Site of Martyrdom of the 26 Saints. The actual shrine is a mural done, probably, in the throes of religious fervor, and commemorates the slaughter of Christians and foreign priests when the new religion was outlawed in the 17th century. There are a hodge podge of colors, whirligigs, stars, stairways to the stars—the meaning cloaked in religious symbolism. Just across the street is the church of San Phillipo, another architectural curiosity. Made from slabs of grey, ferrous concrete, its twin spires loom into the air like twisted phallic symbols fashioned from broken bits of old pottery. The idea is good, but the effect is quite grotesque. The entire scene is topped off when you stand back and look through the main arches leading into the church. They perfectly frame an enormous silver Buddhist goddess, Yakoshine Urai, standing on a distant mountain. It's as if the 2 religions were attempting to outdo each other in bizarreness. A 5 min walk almost directly behind the Nagasaki Eki is the Nagasaki Fish Market, renowned for its array of fresh fish and seafood. The best fish is available before 0800, an inexpensive way to eat if you do your own cooking at the youth hostel.

the Okunchi Festival beginning on the steps of Suwa Shrine features a Chinese dragon. This is a remnant pointing to the long historical and cultural contact between Nagasaki and China

The Peace Park: Located in Matsuyama-cho, the western sector of the city, this monument is 7 streetcar stops from Nagasaki Eki. Here is ground zero of the atomic explosion of Aug. 9, 1945. In the center of the park is the Peace Statue, a unique, but controversial bronze sculpture (9.7 m high) of a male figure sitting on a pedestal with one arm stretched to the horizon and the other pointing skyward. The art may not be to everyone's liking, but the message is clear: Let this never happen again. In the park is also the Cultural Hall, housing a museum of the bomb blast, and close by is the Urakami Catholic Church. The exhibits displayed are of the same heart rending variety as those at Hiroshima.

PRACTICALITIES

accommodations: Since Nagasaki is a main point of interest on the tourist trail, both domestically and internationally, a large array of varying accommodations are available to handle the year-round flow of visitors. *western-style:* New Nagasaki Hotel, 14-5 Daikoku-machi, Nagasaki 850, tel: (0958) 26-6161, 2 min walk from Nagasaki Station, from Y5500; Nagasaki Heights Hotel, 3-19 Kozen-machi, Nagasaki 850, tel: (0958) 22-3156, 2 min by car from Nagasaki Station, from Y5000; and Nagasaki Grand Hotel, 5-3 Manzai-machi, Nagasaki 850, tel: (0958) 23-1234, 5 min by car from Nagasaki Station, from Y6000. *ryokan:* Nagasaki Kanko Hotel Shumeikan, Chikugomachi, Nagasaki 850, tel: (0958) 22-5121, 65 rooms, Y10,500-16,500; Nagasaki Kokusai Hotel Nisshokan, Nishizaka-machi, Nagasaki 850, tel: (0958) 24-2151, 111 rooms, Y9500-15,500; and New Hotel Chuoso, Manzaimachi, Nagasaki 850, tel: (0958) 22-2218, from Y7500-12,500. *business hotels:* Business Hotel Dejima, 2-13 Dejimacho, Nagasaki, tel: (0958) 24-7141, 45 rooms from Y3500, 5 min drive from Nagasaki Station; Nagasaki Business Hotel Futaba-so, 2-11 Aburayamachi, Nagasaki, tel: (0958) 27-3922, 35 rooms, from Y3400, 7 min drive from Nagasaki Station; and Nagasaki Plaza Hotel, 13-10 Motofunacho, Nagasaki, tel: (0958) 24-5151, 57 rooms, from Y3700, 7 min walk from Nagasaki Station. *youth hostels:* Nagasaki Oranda-zaka YH, 6-14 Higashi-yamate-cho, Nagasaki 850, tel: (0958) 22-2730, 20 min by bus from Nagasaki Station or take Streetcar No. 5 from Tsukimachi to Ishibashi and walk to the top (5 min to Hollander Heights), 55 beds; Nagasaki Kenritsu YH, 2 Tateyama-cho, Nagasaki 850, tel: (0958) 23-5032, 15 min on foot from Nagasaki Station, 90 beds, closed Dec. 28-Jan.3; and Nagasaki Nanpoen YH, 320 Hamahira-cho, Nagasaki 850, tel: (0958) 23-5526, 20 min by bus from Nagasaki Station and 6 min on foot, 20 beds.

services: The tourist information office at Nagasaki Eki offers good maps and tourist literature. More information can be had at the Nagasaki Tourist Center across the street from the *eki* (2nd floor). JTB may prove helpful for reservations, etc., and can be contacted at 24-3200. For guided tours, call Lucky Taxi and Bus Co. at 22-4123. The Japan-American Cultural Center is located at 3-163 Sakurababa-machi. For information on Nagasaki Aquarium which features almost 400 species of marine life (12 km from Dejima Pier), call 38-3131. Nagasaki Municipal museum at Dejima, hours 0900-1700, closed Mondays, tel: 25-5027.

UNZEN-AMAKUSA NATIONAL PARK

This extensive park of 250 sq km includes the central and southern parts of the Shimabara Peninsula and the Amakusa Islands. It is bordered on the E by the Ariake Sea and on the W by Chijiwa Bay.

Amakusa Islands: A diminutive archipelago of more than 120 islands make up the Amakusas. The 5 major ones are linked by the Five Amakusa Bridges. The 2 largest islands are Amakusa Kami and Amakusa Shimo. The seas around the Amakusa Is. are bathed in the warm Tshushima current, which gives rise to abundant coral growths and provides a haven to tropical fish with its numerous underwater grottoes. The islands have historically been known as a haven for Christianity. When Christianity was banned by the Tokugawas, the Christians of Amakusa rebelled and seized the 2 castles of Tomioka and Shimabara. They were annihilated and the shogunate, to enforce its will, took over direct control of Amakusa. The Christians here went underground and preserved their faith for 300 years. The islands abound with historic Christian relics, old battlefields, tombs of martyrs and Catholic churches. Besides the historical attractions, the western beaches of Amakusa Shima are quiet and lovely. Small rustic hot springs are found in the villages.

getting there from Misumi: To head W from Kumamoto to the Amakusa Is., Shimabara and on to Nagasaki, you must pass through Misumi, the main junction for land-sea transportation to these areas. From Misumi, you can board a steamer to Shimabara (one hr), to Amakusa-

Shimo I. (one hr 30 min) or you can bus to the Amakusa Is. over the Five Amakusa Bridges to Matsushima I. or Amakusa Kami I. in one hr 30 min or to Hondo or Amakusa Shimo in 30 minutes. Besides busing from Misumi, you can ferry from Mogi (5 km S of Nagasaki) in one hr 20 min, to Tomioka from Minamata (NW coast of Kagoshima Prefecture) to Hondo on Amakusa Shimo in 2 hrs and from Shimabara to Hondo (2 hrs) or to Atsushima (1 hr 30 min).

UNZEN

The Unzen area on the Shimabara Peninsula has been a summer oasis for foreigners in Asia since the 1800s. Missionaries and their families, businessmen, diplomats and members of various foreign services stationed throughout Asia made for Unzen to escape the sweltering Asian summer heat. The peninsula is washed by balmy breezes and the air is cool atop the highest peak of the central attraction, Mt. Unzen (1360 m). Although the area is pleasant and offers climbs, trails and spas, it is over-touristed. A one-day stopover en route to or from Nagasaki should be sufficient. The waters of Unzen Spa, situated at 727 m above sea level, provide relief from rheumatism and general aches and pains. Relax, soak the bumps of the road away, and move on. *getting there:* Take a bus directly from Nagasaki to Unzen (2 hrs 10 min) or train from Nagasaki to Obama and thence by bus. Or, bus from Kumamoto to Shimabara and on to Unzen in 50 minutes.

accommodations: Throughout the Unzen-Amakusa-Shimabara area there are a large number of accommodations to choose from. They include Western-style/*ryokan:* Unzen Hotel, Unzen Onsen, 854-06, tel: (095773) 3201, from Y5000; and Unzen Kanko Hotel, Unzen Onsen 854-06, tel: (95773) 3265, from Y6000. There is also the Western-style Unzen New Grand Hotel, Obamamachi 854-06, tel: (95773) 3291, Y8000-11,000; and Hotel Honda, Obamamachi, 854-06, tel: (095773) 3391, Y8000-13,000. As for youth hostels, there is the Seiun-so YH, 500-1 Unzen, Obamamachi 854-06, tel: (095773) 3273, 90 min by bus from Isahaya Station, and 10 min on foot, 300 beds; and Shimabara YH, 7938 Shimo-kawashiri-machi, Shimabara 855, tel: (09576) 2-4451, one min on foot from Shimabara-gaiko Station, 60 beds. Near Honda on Shimo I. is also found Amakusa YH, 180 Hodo, Hondo-cho, Hondo 863, tel: (09692) 2-3085, 90 min by bus from Misumi Station and 10 min on foot, 60 beds.

OITA PREFECTURE

Oita Prefecture is primarily agricultural dotted with football field-sized farms, and also the site of one of Japan's oldest and most popular tourist attractions, Beppu. Even at the turn of the century, over 2,000,000 visitors per year strolled through this remarkable spa town with international passenger liners making it a regular port of call. With Beppu being so popular, most travelers visit it, leaving the countryside around it, especially to the S, unseen. Oita Prefecture lies S of Fukuoka, bordered on the W by Kumamoto with its eastern seaboard lying entirely along the western shores of the Inland Sea. Second perhaps only to Kita-Kyushu, it is the main gateway to the island of Kyushu. Its interior encompasses part of Aso National Park. Near Usuki, a small village just S of Oita, is found the Seki Butsu, a religious mystery which to this date remains unsolved.

getting there by rail: Overland, the Oita/Beppu area is services by numerous express trains of the Nippo Line, originating in Kita-Kyushu and terminating in the extreme S at Kagoshima with most trains stopping at Oita/Beppu. The Kyudai Line connects Oita to Kurume in the W, a terminal of the Nagasaki Line. Kumamoto via Mt. Aso National Park is easily reached by the Hohi Main Line cutting diagonally across the island. *by ferry:* Even more so than trains, ferries provide the most direct routes to Oita/Beppu, with most cutting a wake through the beautiful Inland Sea. Beppu is linked to Osaka by 3 ferries per day in each direction. They all depart from early to late evening. Beppu departures 1700, 1730, 1930; Osaka departures 1630, 1700, 1740; The trips take approx. 17 hrs with *tatami*-class costing Y5000 (student discount available). The last ferry from Osaka presents the largest and best daylight view of the Inland Sea. Oita only 10 km S also has 2 ferries per day to and from Kobe (Osaka). The schedules vary, but many ferries stop at Shikoku en route where you can disembark and then carry on at your leisure. The main ferry company is Kansai Steamship Co., tel: (03) 274-4271, Osaka (06) 572-5181. For a ferry via Hiroshima/Beppu, contact Hirobetsu Kisen Co., tel: Hiroshima (0822) 48-2768, Beppu (0977) 21-2364. *by bus:* Regular express buses travel between Beppu and Kumamoto on the Cross-Kyushu Expressway making the trip in 4 hrs 30 minutes. The route parallels the Hohi Main Line and runs past Mt. Aso. *by air:* Oita airport is located at Kunisaki 40 km N of Oita (many shuttle buses). The airport is linked to all main cities of Kyushu and TOA connects it to Tokyo in one hr 35 min, while ANA connects with Osaka in less than one hour.

BEPPU

The epitome of a traveler's cliche. It attracts over 12,000,000 visitors per year, mainly Japanese with a heavy smattering of foreign tourists from throughout the world. The drawing cards are its medicinal baths, its Jigoku (mud pools) known as Hells, along with hot sands that together steam, boil or poach vitality into aching

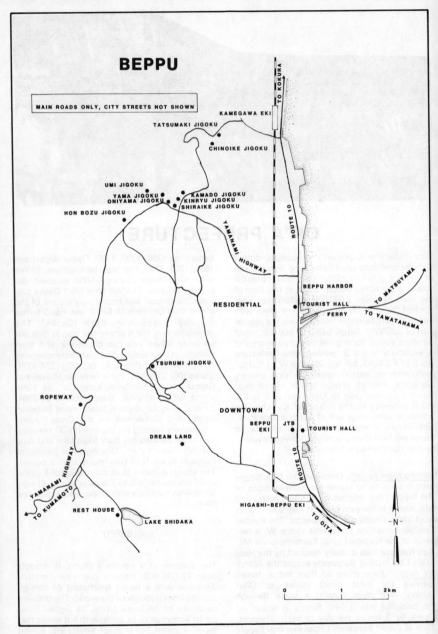

BEPPU

MAIN ROADS ONLY, CITY STREETS NOT SHOWN

TO KOKURA

KAMEGAWA EKI

TATSUMAKI JIGOKU

CHINOIKE JIGOKU

UMI JIGOKU

YAMA JIGOKU
ONIYAMA JIGOKU
KAMADO JIGOKU
KINRYU JIGOKU
SHIRAIKE JIGOKU

HON BOZU JIGOKU

YAMANAMI HIGHWAY

ROUTE 10

BEPPU HARBOR

RESIDENTIAL

TOURIST HALL
FERRY

TO MATSUYAMA

TO YAWATAHAMA

TSURUMI JIGOKU

ROPEWAY

DOWNTOWN

DREAM LAND

BEPPU EKI
JTB
TOURIST HALL

YAMANAMI HIGHWAY

TO KUMAMOTO

REST HOUSE

LAKE SHIDAKA

ROUTE 10

HIGASHI-BEPPU EKI

TO OITA

—N—

0   1   2 km

muscles and tired bodies. Beppu is totally geared toward tourists. There are hundreds of accommodations from multi-storied Western hotels to small, secluded family operated *minshuku*. <u>*getting around:*</u> Information is readily available from the JTB and the Beppu Sightseeing Association, only 5 min walk from Beppu Station. There is regular sightseeing bus service, originating from Beppu Station (Mar. to Nov.) whose route passes most spas and Hells. It has an English-speaking guide and takes about 2½ hours. Many colorful brochures with maps in both Japanese and English are available from most large hotels in the area and at all tourist facilities at the *eki* and the ferry terminal.

<u>*sights:*</u> There are no in-betweens with Beppu. You either love it or despise its obvious gaudy tourism. The geography that forms Beppu (actually 8 different spa areas) is laden with truly remarkable thermal activity that is mismatched with the most gimmicky advertising to lure the overwhelmed tourists. There are so many spas to choose from that a pay-your-money-and-take-your-choice attitude is as good as any. Most large hotels open their baths to the public. Even if you don't stay there, you can enjoy their best attraction. Soaking can be done in the most entertaining ways. Along with conventional spas there are: falling water hot springs, thatched huts such as those at Myoban Spa which make delightful saunas and open-air mixed bathing at Hoyurando Spa. It's as if nature itself contrives to make the experience monumental. If the spas aren't enough, go stick everything but your head in the hot-sand saunas (*sunaya*). For this you have a choice of indoor or outdoor facilities. For indoors, go to Takegawara, a monstrous old building offering steaming black sands just for the purpose. The attendants are quite familiar with foreigners and will give you all the directions needed to proceed. Basically, strip and follow the women attendants to a cozy hole they have dug for you. There is an outdoor facility near Kamegawa Eki that offers the same experience. Ask for the *sunayu*. Novices should remember that more tender body parts cook a lot quicker than hands and feet. The results for over-indulgence can be not only painful but embarassing. The remainder of your time in Beppu can be spent with a tour of the Hells (*jigoku*). Some offer picturesque gardens while others are pure tourist traps. Many are like circus sideshows featuring a 3-legged chicken—no one really wants to see it, but you just can't pass it by. Some examples of the most remarkable ones dotting the hillsides of Beppu are: Mountain Hell (Yama Jigoku), a health resort for animals; Oniyama Jigoku breeds crocodiles; huge Umi-jigoku (Sea Hell) features exotic tropical plants and can accommodate 1000 visitors. Chinoike Jigoku (Blood Pond Hell) has vermillion waters and is especially renowned for its ability to cure skin diseases. Frequently the steam from the *jigoku* is piped into greenhouses as well as being used for cooking in brick ovens, and in heating many homes. Tourists are shown eggs in wicker baskets dunked into the hot water and hard boiled. If you can manage to overlook many of the man-made "wonders," you'll see a most amazing display of thermal activity. The pucking mud, forming concentric circles as it oozes through the ground, and the colors of the ponds in this hell-on-earth surrounding are more than enough to fascinate and entertain.

the Hells of Beppu

the Seki Butsu of Usuki

accommodations: Hundreds to choose from; let your pocketbook be your guide. *western hotels:* Suginoi Hotel, Kankaiji, Beppu 874, tel: (0977) 24-1141, 7 min by car from Beppu Station or Beppu Pier, from Y7500; Kamenoi Hotel, 5-17 Chuo-machi, Beppu 874, tel: (0977) 22-3301, 3 min by car from Beppu Station, from Y5000; Beppu New Grand Hotel, Kijima-kogen, Beppu 874, 20 min by car from Beppu Station or Beppu Pier, from Y6500; and Hinago Hotel, 7-24 Akiba-cho, Beppu, tel: (0977) 22-1111, 2 min by car from Beppu Station, from Y7500. *ryokan:* Hotel Hakuunsanso, Minami-tateishi, Beppu 874, tel: (0977) 23-1151, 131 rooms, Y9000-15,000; Hotel New Showaen, Minimi-tateishi, Beppu, tel: (0977) 22-3211, 32 rooms, Y14,000-44,000; and Nogami Hotel, Kitahama, Beppu 874, tel: (0977) 23-2141, 34 rooms, Y6000-8000. *minshuku:* Many small *minshuku* are available in Beppu. Many are tiny homey affairs with just a few guest rooms. Considering that they include 2 meals and lodging for about Y4000, they would be an excellent budget choice. Check with the Tourist Center at the *eki* for a complete list. *youth hostel:* Beppu YH, Kankaiji-onsen, Beppu 874, tel: (0977) 23-4116, 20 min by bus from Beppu Station, and 4 min on foot, 150 beds. This YH is always booked solid and reservations are a must. An alternative to staying in Beppu is to train a mere 10 km further S to Oita. Although so close, it does not enjoy the fame of Beppu which helps to cut down on accommoda-

tion costs. Besides the Western-style hotels, you might try the following business hotels: Oita Daini Oriental Hotel, 1-15 Suehirocho, Oita, tel: (0975) 32-0131, 98 rooms from Y3400, one min walk from Oita Station; Hokke Club Oita-Ten, 2-1-1 Miyakomachi, Oita, tel: (0975) 32-1121, 207 rooms from Y3100, 7 min walk from Oita Station; and Oita Daiichi Oriental Hotel, 3-9-28 Funaicho, Oita, tel: (0975) 32-8238, 102 rooms from Y3200, 10 min walk from Oita Station. *special accommodations:* The Japan Rural Mission was founded and is operated by Rev. Philip Visser and his wife Wilma who arrived in Japan 25 yrs ago with little more than their hand luggage and a deep faith in God. They have graciously decided to open a few rooms in their home to travelers. For a moderate fee they provide a Western oasis of food, conversation and travel information to remote areas that they have explored throughout their years in Japan. The real beauty of staying at the Mission is the Visser family themselves. They live their religion and teach more through lifestyle and example than by Biblical harangue. If you are so inclined Rev. Visser will be more than happy to discuss religion with you, but the choice will be yours. Contacting Rev. Visser in advance of your planned visit is a must. To make arrangements write: Japan Rural Mission, c/o Rev. Philip Visser, P.O. Box 142, Oita City 870-91, Oita, Japan, tel: 41-4739. The mission is located 5 km S of Oita. Rev. Visser will provide directions.

Oita City and vicinity: Oita is basically an agricultural area consisting of tiny farms and neat houses clustered together. To Westerners, the farms look more like suburban homes with large back yards, which belies the fact that this area manages to produce a considerable amount of produce. The main attraction in the area is the Seki Butsu of Usuki, located 31 km SE of Oita. The area consists of 60 elaborate rock carvings of Buddha (entrance fee Y200). No one is quite sure why a center of this magnitude and obvious dedication was built in such an out-of-the-way area. The Seki Butsu is designated as a Special Place of Historical Importance. The grounds are quiet, moderately touristed, and pleasantly mysterious. The quietude and introspection is delicious after Beppu and its tourist hype. Once satiated with the Beppu/Oita area, you basically have a choice of a southerly or westerly direction. Heading W from Beppu on the Cross-Kyushu Expressway will take you through some of Kyushu's most resplendent countryside including Mt. Aso (see "Kumamoto" chapter for details). Four buses per day leave Beppu along this route. Three terminate at Kumamoto and one goes on to Nagasaki. What lies S along

coastal Rt. 10 and the remainder of the Nippo Line is Miyazaki Prefecture, probably the most unvisited area of Kyushu.

MIYAZAKI PREFECTURE

Miyazaki is a long, thin prefecture fronting the Pacific Ocean S of Oita. Passing through its length along the coast heading to Kagoshima is a reasonable alternative to cutting across Kyushu through its center. From Kagoshima you can go N to Kumamoto and Nagasaki, thereby completely touring the entire island of Kyushu. Miyazaki has been populated since Japan's earliest history and offers natural phenomena, ancient temples and shrines and unhurried traditional village life. _getting there:_ Route 10 and the Nippo Main Line parallel each other down the coast of Miyazaki. Trains can be boarded in Oita or at Kagoshima, the southern terminus to make this run. Highway buses are also available and the hitchhiking along the one primary route is both uncomplicated and easy.

HEADING SOUTH

The first major cities after visiting the Seki Butsu are Nobeoka, and 10 km further, Hyuga. Nobeoka supposedly has excellent fishing inland along the banks of the Gokase River that flows into its bay. More importantly it is a major acess point (Rt. 218) to Takachiho and its famous gorge located about 40 km W towards Mt. Aso. Takachiho Gorge should not be confused with Mt. Takachiho 100 km to the S in the Kirishima area although both lay claim to being part of

Japan's earliest civilization, even being among the first earthly stepping stones of the gods. Takachiho Gorge is included in the Sobo-Katamuki National Park known for its vast forests and water-eroded rock formations. Takachiho Gorge is heavy with ancient myths and traditional dances (Iwato-kaguro) celebrating these myths, which can be seen from Nov. to Feb. at the local Iwato Shrine. Over 300 ancient burial mounds also testify to the area's antiquity. Most are found around Saitogaru. Hyuga is a main ferry port for Miyazaki. A coastal streamer runs from Beppu and another from Hiroshima. A long-distance ferry goes S of Shikoku from Hyuga to Osaka-Kobe in 14 hours.

MIYAZAKI CITY AND VICINITY

Miyazaki City (pop. 216,000) is in the southern end of the prefecture. It is the prefectural capital and also boasts Miyazaki Shrine, and the tomb of Jimmu Tenno, the first emperor of Japan. _getting there:_ Besides the train and bus routes previously mentioned, ANA links Miyazaki to Tokyo and Osaka while TOA flies to Fukuoka.

sights: Haniwa Park is located within the city. It features replicas of ancient burial mounds found

clay figurines symbolically replaced court retainers who were at one time buried alive upon the death of their leige lord, so that they could carry on their service in the nether world

throughout the area, especially at Saitogaru. Clay figurines, replaced symbolic offerings to deceased lords, are exhibited in the park. At one time very early in Japan's history, human retainers were buried instead of the figurines. In the far southern reaches of the prefecture below Miyazaki is Nichinan Coast National Park. Here the blue skies and balmy seas conspire to form an idyllic coastline. One famous area is Aoshima, a one-time island now connected by a causeway. A small train line runs along this coast to Aoshima and local buses also connect it to Miyazaki in 45 minutes. Aoshima is covered in *biro* (beetle nut palms) as well as 200 varieties of imported and native sub-tropical plants. At low tide the sea reveals an eroded coastline here in a series of rugged bumps. This is of great interest to geologists and is popularly called The Devil's Washboard. Further S from Aoshima are the natural and rustic Udo Shrines (about 45 min by bus from Aoshima). The main shrine is housed unusually in a cave, while smaller shrines sit like sentinels on lonely rock out croppings. Finally, at the tip of Miyazaki is Cape Toi. It is home to the largest lighthouse in Asia and on its 300 m high plateau overlooking the sea a herd of wild horses runs free.

accommodations: Most of the cities mentioned offer moderately priced hotels. Miyazaki also has a handful of business hotels. Two examples are: Miyazaki Daiichi Hotel, 5-4-14 Tachibana-dori, Higashi Miyazaki, tel: (0985) 24-8501, 152 rooms, from Y3400; and Miyazaki River Side Hotel, 1-18 Kawaramachi, Miyazaki, tel: (0985) 24-1655, 30 rooms, from Y3020, 5 min drive from Miyazaki Station. Further S in Nichinan is Central Hotel, 1-16 Iwasakicho, Nichinan, tel: (09872) 3-3118, 24 rooms, from Y3200, 5 min walk from Aburatsu Station. Youth hostelers can put up at Hama-so YH, 151 Azuma-cho, Miyazaki 880, tel: (0985) 24-3019, 18 min on foot from Miyazaki Station, 100 beds; Seiryu-so Bekkan YH, 164 Azuma-cho, Miyazaki 880, tel: (0985) 22-6191, 18 min on foot from Miyazaki Station, 50 beds; Miyazaki-ken Fujin-Kaikan YH, 1-3-10 Asahi, Miyazaki 880, tel: (0985) 24-5738, 15 min on foot from Miyazaki Station, 50 beds, closed Dec. 30 through Jan 3; Miyazaki-ken Seinen Kaikan YH, 130 Umizoi, Oriuzako, Miyazaki 889-22, tel: (09856) 5-1103, 5 min on foot from Kodomonokuni Station, 100 beds, closed Dec. 28-Jan. 3; and Nichinan City YH, 889-311, tel: (09872) 7-0113, 20 min on foot from Odotsu Station, 68 beds.

KUMAMOTO PREFECTURE

Kumamoto City (pop. 500,000), located on the central W coast, is the prefectural capital and the 3rd largest city of Kyushu. This bustling commercial center contains Kumamoto-jo, one of the 3 grandest castles in all of Japan (the other 2 being in Osaka and Nagoya). Also here is Suizenji Park, one of the finest examples of Japanese landscape gardening, going back almost 300 years. With Kumamoto lying at the western terminus of the Cross-Kyushu Tourist Highway, its main function, however, is that of gateway to more scenic areas such as Mt. Aso, Unzen National Park, the Amakusa Islands and Nagasaki.

getting there: From Fukuoka (120 km) it takes one hr 30 min by limited express. From Beppu via Oita (160 km), 3 hrs 20 min on the Hohi Main Line. There are also direct flights from Tokyo (one hr 40 min), Nagoya (one hr 15 min) and Osaka (one hr 5 min). Misumi, a port town 20 km W of Kumamoto on the tip of the Uto Peninsula, is an important travel link to the Kumamoto, Aso, Nagasaki area. Ferries ply from Misumi to Shimabara and Hondo, the main island ports

in the Urizen Amakusa National Park. Buses also cross the 5 Amakusa bridges into this area originating in Misumi. *getting around:* At Kumamoto Eki there's an information booth with good maps and brochures of Kumamoto. The real heart of Kumamoto is Kutsu (Transportation) Center. All city buses originate from here. Take City Bus No. 8, Y90, from the *eki* to the Kutsu Center, and make connections from there all over the city. There is an excellent bus service throughout the city and if you get lost, you will eventually wind up back at the Kutsu Center. There are coin lockers. The attendants at nearby Jal Pak speak English, so inquire there for specific information.

SIGHTS OF KUMAMOTO

Suizenji Park: A paradox. It is man-made natural beauty. Every stone, tree and grassy knoll has been crafted. This exquisite landscaped garden is over 300 years old. It was constructed by the Hosokawas, who were the rulers of the district, and is a miniature of the 53 Stages of the Old

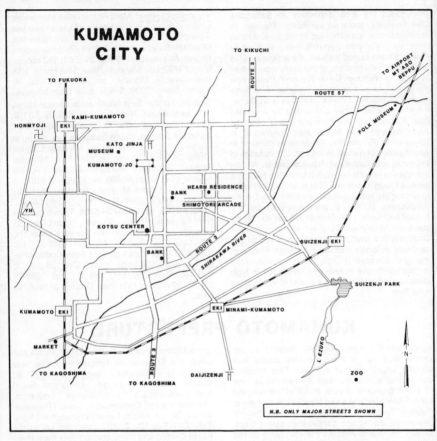

KUMAMOTO CITY

TO FUKUOKA

TO KIKUCHI

ROUTE 3

ROUTE 57

TO AIRPORT
MT ASO
BEPPU

FOLK MUSEUM

KAMI-KUMAMOTO

EKI

HONMYOJI

EKI

KATO JINJA
MUSEUM

KUMAMOTO JO

HEARN RESIDENCE

BANK

SHIMOTORI ARCADE

YH

KOTSU CENTER

BANK

ROUTE 3

SHIRAKAWA RIVER

SUIZENJI EKI

SUIZENJI PARK

KUMAMOTO EKI

EKI MINAMI-KUMAMOTO

L EZUKO

MARKET

TO KAGOSHIMA

ROUTE 3

DAIJIZENJI

TO KAGOSHIMA

ZOO

N

N.B. ONLY MAJOR STREETS SHOWN

Tokaido Highway. _getting there:_ Take Bus No. 10 from the Kutsu Center, 20 min. Y100. Alighting from the bus, walk back about 25 m to the T intersection, and turn R down the side street. On the corner is a French pastry shop that sells authentic, mouth-watering goodies. This entire area has inexpensive Japanese restaurants, many with tiny gardens. It is also a good place to pick up souvenirs and film.

exploring the park: As you enter Suizenji, take note of the beautifully painted eagle screen that spans the entrance to the small shrine to your left. Continue over the little bridge to see hundreds of fat carp; the little stalls sell bread crumbs for Y30, but these fat boys don't need

them. Check out the construction of the bridge. Follow the path over a number of bridges leading to more shrines. The main spring-fed pond is crystal clear and exceptionally cold. Walk slowly to savor the atmosphere of a piece of living history that hasn't changed in over 300 years. The whole image is one of simplicity, and the tea house further on is a lingering trace of old Japan. The _shoji_ screens, the raked garden, thatched roof, _tatami_ mats and brown, natural wood combine to make a true visual treasure, a perfect, living, breathing painting. Just 200 m away is Kumamoto, the city. Only the Japanese could maintain such stark juxtaposition. Allow 2 hrs for this park. Take plenty of film and a picnic lunch for under the cherry trees. There is also food available at numerous stalls inside Suizenji.

Kumamoto-Jo (castle)

on a Harley Davidson. Imagine riding a horse at full gallop wearing *geta*! There is a fantastically surreal painting depicting a fierce-looking two-sworded *daimyo* riding a large tiger, the eyes of the man and the beast are the same. There are numerous exhibits of fierce-looking armor, particularly the face plates with gaping mouths and wide, flaring nostrils. The 3rd floor has a collection of sea shells. Some are merely polished, but others have been opened up and they hold miniature, intriguing paintings of pastoral scenes and the tea ceremony. Finally, on the top floor, you get a 360 degree panorama of Kumamoto and the surrounding hills. As you leave the castle, don't miss the Higo Flower Gardens. The flowers here have been handed down from generation to generation and cultivated as symbols of spiritual education since the time of Shigetaka Hosokawa, feudal lord of Kumamoto over 200 years ago.

Lafcadio Hearn's residence: Hearn (Yakumo Koizumi) spent part of his life in Japan in a small home in Kumamoto which still stands and is presently occupied. Look for this old-fashioned structure on a side street in the city center across from Tsuruya Depato near the Shimotori Shopping Arcade. (See "Matsue" for more details on Lafcadio Hearn.)

PRACTICALITIES

Kumamoto-jo: This castle, built in 1607 by Koyomasa Kato, was one of the grandest in all Japan. This becomes immediately evident when you see the massive stone walls extending for over 9 km that surround it. With warriors atop them slinging arrows and being generally nasty, it was believed that no invader could scale them. How strange that this one-time symbol of mighty authority is now a playground for children and on its formidable grounds are now gentle scenes of families viewing cherry blossoms. The original *donjon* was destroyed in 1877 by Saigo and his forces from Kagoshima, but a ferrous concrete facsimile was built in 1960. Although it is new, it still gives a feeling of its former grandeur. The entrance fee to the grounds is Y100 and to enter the castle's museum is another Y200. The museum gives a history of Kumamoto's rulers for the last 500 years. As you go from floor to floor, you will notice that each room gets smaller. The 2nd floor is dedicated to a Rogue's Gallery of former *daimyo*. It holds such exhibits as hats, armor, a Japanese drum (*taiko*), palanquins, and a Japanese saddle with stirrups like the foot pads

accommodations: Western-style places to stay include the New Sky Hotel, 2 Higashi Amidaji-machi, Kumamoto 860, tel: (0963) 54-2111, 3 min by car from Kumamoto Station, from Y4000; Togiya Hotel, 1-8 Shima, Senba-cho, Kumamoto 860, tel: (0963) 54-3131, 5 min by car from Kumamoto Station, from Y4000; and Kumamoto Hotel Castel, 4-2 Joto-machi, Kumamoto 860, tel: (0963) 53-6111, 8 min by car from Kumamoto Station, from Y5000. For business hotels, try the Shin-Kumamoto Hotel, 1-11-17 Kuhonji, Kumamoto, tel: (0963) 64-6151, 60 rooms, from Y3000, 5 min drive from Kumamoto Station; Business Hotel Konan, 1-16-12 Kasuga, Kumamoto, tel: (0963) 53-0101, 21 rooms from Y3400, one min walk from Kumamoto Station; and Hokke Club Kumamoto-Ten, 20-1 Toricho, Kumamoto, tel: (0963) 52-5001, 153 rooms from Y3700, 10 min drive from Kumamoto Station. The Suizenji YH is on 1-2-20 Hakusan, Kumamoto 860, tel: (0963) 71-9193, 25 min by streetcar from Kumamoto Station and 2 min on foot, 40 beds, closed Dec. 31-Jan. 1; Ryokan Shokaku YH, 1-2-41 Nihongi, Kumamoto 860, tel: (0963)

52-1468, 8 min on foot from Kumamoto Station, 50 beds; and Kumamoto-Shiritsu YH, 5-15-55 Shimazaki-machi, Kumamoto 860, tel: (0963) 52-2441, 20 min by Bus No. 6 from City Bus Center, 64 beds, closed Dec. 28-Jan. 3.

food: Local dishes include *tofu-dengaku*, a simple, delicate tasting dish of skewered tofu, browned over charcoal and then spread with a sweet bean paste; *uma-sashi* is sliced horse meat, distinguished by its pink color. It can be found in small bars; wash it down with lots of sake. *Karashi-renkon* is an exotic dish of bean paste and mustard inserted into the holes of the lotus root. The mixture is dipped in flour, seasoned, and deep fried. Very tasty. _services:_ Tourist information, brochures and maps are available just outside Kumamoto Eki. Detailed information is offered at Kumamoto Tourist Section, Suizenji, Kumamoto, tel: (0963) 66-1111.

crafts: Shimotori Shopping Arcade is in city center; its every nook and cranny filled with shops selling everything from traditional folk products to motorcycles. Here, pick up all of your traveling necessities as well as Kumamoto's special products. _higo zogan:_ A traditional metal work (a variety of damascene) that gained popularity with the samurai almost 400 years ago. The basic product is hand-forged black steel that has been inlaid with silver and beaten gold. *Higo zogan* is still handmade by artisans in small shops throughout the city, but most is marketed in large *depatos* and the boutiques of Shimotori in the form of tiepins, necklaces, brooches, compacts, etc. The prices vary with the amount of gold and intricate inlay, but expect to pay Y5000 and up for a decent

piece. *Yamaga doro* is the traditional Japanese paper lantern crafted only from glue and gold foiled paper. It is usually 6 sided with a pointed knob on top, and the motif is that of leaves and chrysanthemum. The *Yamaga Doro* Lantern Festival (the night of Aug. 16 yearly) features young women parading through the streets while performing traditional folk dances wearing these lantern headdresses.

VICINITY OF KUMAMOTO

Mt. Aso: The collective name of 5 peaks in the center of the world's largest crater basin. All are extinct, puffing only small wisps of white smoke, except virulent Nakadake (1323 m). This volcano's activity often closes the crater rim to hikers. The original crater, whose boundaries are readily visible, is 17 km wide and 24 km long. Inside the original basin are towns (pop. 70,000), railroads, and highways. The Aso area is not beautiful and is perhaps best described as mighty. Nature reveals its stark forces here and the entire area is awe inspiring. To make the ascent of the crater, start from Aso Station by way of the Aso Kanko Toll Road (50 min bus ride), or from Miyaji Station by way of the Sensuikyo Gorge Toll Road (15 min bus ride). Both routes lead to a ropeway that takes you up to the rim of the crater. _getting there:_ Take the Hohi Main Line from Kumamoto to Aso Station in one hr 30 minutes. You can also make the ascent of Mt. Aso from Tateno, Akamizu or Uchinomaki, all on the Hohi Main Line. There is also a direct bus service to Mt. Aso from the Kutsu Center in Kumamoto. It takes approx. 1 ½ hrs along Rt. 57. From Beppu, board the Hohi Main Line or take a bus on the Cross-Kyushu Highway (approx. 3 hrs) to Aso Station. The

Mt. Aso, the ugly giant

MT. ASO VICINITY

best way to enter the Aso area is from Aso Station, located near the village of Ichinomiya. Ichinomiya is known for the Hiburi-Shinji (Sacred Fire Ritual) dedicated to the Aso Shrine held on March 3. Walk to the main crossroads in town and head towards the mountains. In about 100 m, you will come to an old Buddhist temple, Saigon-Denji, which is worth a look.

accommodations: Just outside Aso Eki is a built-up area offering a few inexpensive hotels at approx. Y4000. A well-known Western-style hotel in the area is Aso Kanko Hotel, Yunotani, Choyo-mura 869-2, 15 min by car from Akamizu Station, Y7000 up. For a mixture of Western-style and *ryokan,* try: Ryokan Sanrakuso, Aso-machi 869-23, tel: (09673) 2-0511, 37 rooms from Y8000-12,000; Hotel Soyokaku, Asomachi 869-23, tel: (09673) 2-0621, 88 rooms from Y6000-12,000; or Aso Hotel, Asomachi 869-23, tel: (09673) 2-0525, 56 rooms from Y6000-12,000. The most easily reached youth hostel is Aso YH, 922-2 Bochu, Aso-machi 869-22, tel: (09673) 4-0804, 16 min on foot from Aso Station, 60 beds, closed Dec. 31-Jan. 4. Others in the area are: Kumamoto YMCA Aso Camp YH, Kuruma-gaeri, Aso-machi 869-21, tel: (09673) 5-0124, 30 min on foot from Akamizu Station, 35 beds; and Murataya-Ryokan YH, 1660 Takamori, Taka-mori-machi 869-16, tel: (09676) 2-0066, 8 min on foot from Takamori Station, 36 beds.

KAGOSHIMA PREFECTURE

Kagoshima Prefecture lies at the extreme southern tip of Kyushu and includes the long strip of islands leading towards Okinawa. The principal ones are the Amami Is., and the most southern is Yoron Jima, visible from Hedo Point on the N tip of Okinawa. In all, there are over 140 islands in this prefecture, most boasting a sub-tropical climate and surrounded by coral reefs and dark blue seas. Yaku I., lying 100 km off the tip of Satsuma Peninsula, has the tallest mountain in the prefecture, Mt. Miyanoura at 1935 m. The total area of the prefecture is just over 9000 sq km and is comprised of small mountain ranges, swift unnavigable rivers and tiny plains. Rich volcanic soil is present in almost every area of the prefecture, forming extensive *shirasu* plateaus. The climate of the prefecture is mild, due to its geographical location, and aided by the balmy waters of the sub-tropcial *kuro* (black) current that laps its shores. The main climatic

drawbacks are the numerous and violent typhoons that squall ashore, usually in September. On its NE border is Mt. Takachiho where the sun goddess Amaterasu descended to earth and Japanese mythology began. Kagoshima also served as home port for Japanese pirates and later as a port of call for the Portuguese. This link with the West brought Francis Xavier and Christianity to Japan. The most dominant and inspiring family in the area were the lords of Satsuma, the Shimazu clan, who began their reign with Tadahisa in 1185. They spread the Japanese culture to the S by subjugating Okinawa, and maintained a longstanding relationship with China and the countries of the South Seas. The Shimazus were not merely warriors, but men of culture, art and foresight. Nariakira introduced manufacturing to Japan and was a guiding force in the opening of the country to the West. Under his rule, ironworks, photography, telegraphy and mechanization were introduced. The Iso Gardens, beautiful in their simplicity and harmony with nature, were home to Mitsuhisa Shimazu. Next door is one of the first factories in Japan. The Meiji Restoration, which roused Japan from its long slumber and catapulted it into the 20th C., was largely brought about by the support of Takamori Saigo, Toshimichi Okubo and Koin Kido, native sons of Kagoshima. Lying on the S tip of Satsuma Peninsula is Ibusuki, an international resort where the rage is to be buried neck deep in steaming sands. In Kagoshima City is the fabulous volcano Sakurijima, majestic and fuming, providing one of the most amazing backdrops to any city in the world. Northeast, high in the *shirasu* plains, is Ebino, starting point for the climb of Mt. Karakuni and home to rustic, relaxing mineral baths. Here also is Kirishima Jinja, one of the oldest and most revered Shinto shrines in Japan. The feeling in Kagoshima is one of adventure and exotic beauty tempered heavily with a strong feeling of antiquity.

KAGOSHIMA PREF.

FROM KAGOSHIMA CITY TO:

Airport - 60 min. - bus
Sakurajima - 15 min. - ferry
Ibusuki - 80 min. - bus,
        70 min. - train
Kirishima - 2 hrs - bus
Izumi - 90 min. - train

KAGOSHIMA CITY

The city of Kagoshima is the prefectural capital and lies on the W coast of the peanut-shaped Kagoshima Bay. Though it is a large thriving international port town, its back streets beat with a slow-paced charm. Museums, parks and the Shimazu Castle provide hours of sightseeing

Lady Jimesa

and the numerous shops offer traditional pottery and folk crafts. *getting there:* Kagoshima International Airport lies 30 km NE of the city center. Excellent and readily available bus service connects it directly with the city in 50 minutes. There are coin lockers available (Y300, 24 hrs), but take your baggage with you as there is no reason to return unless you plan to depart from the airport. The airport is an international gateway from the Asian continent. There are direct flights from Hong Kong (2 hrs 15 min), and via Hong Kong the airport services Manila, Bangkok, Singapore and Jakarta. Direct flights are also available from Nauru and Port Moresby. Internal flights connect Kagoshima to Tokyo (one hr 45 min), Osaka (one hr 5 min) and Sapporo (2 hrs 30 min). Connecting flights can be made to Kagoshima from anywhere in Japan. By train, Kagoshima is linked to Fukuoka in 4 hrs 40 min by the Kagoshima Main Line and to Kokura in 7 hrs 40 min by the Nippo Main Line.

getting around: There are 2 City Tourist Centers located in front of Nishi-Kagoshima and Kagoshima Train Stations. The former is the most central of the 2 while both offer English-speaking staffs and excellent city tourist maps and brochures. Most sights worth seeing are grouped in the downtown area between the 2 *eki* and can be reached on foot by a leisurely walk of only 3-4 km. Kagoshima has an extensive network of city buses with their routes and schedules available from the Tourist Centers. Convenient but slow streetcars also service the city. The most useful route passes through the downtown area between the 2 *eki*. There is also a City Sightseeing Bus Service. It departs from Kagoshima Eki at 0910, 1310 and

from Nishi-Kagoshima Eki at 0900, 1010, 1300 and 1410. These tour buses do hit the high spots, but it's a whirlwind tour mostly from behind the bus windows and at Y2000 is much more expensive than the adequate public transportation.

sights: The following sights can easily be seen on foot in about 2-3 hours. Combined they make an interesting mini tour of the downtown area. *Tsurumaru Castle:* A good central starting point. The former castle was called Tsurumaru because of a nearby mountain that resembled a crane (*tsuru*). The walls are surrounded by a muddy moat and local children wade around in it, trying to capture goldfish with long bamboo poles with small nets attached. The walls, made from enormous, rough-hewn stone, are about 4 m high and form an impressive 300 m square. *Museum of Fine Arts:* Near the castle. As you enter the museum grounds, immediately the quiet sets in. To your L as you face the museum, you will see a curious sculpture of a face hewn out of a large rock. This is the face of the medieval princess Lady Jimesa who, legend says, was graced with noble virtues but not beauty. When her husband Iahesu lost a battle to Hideyoshi Toyotomi, she was carted off to Kyoto as a hostage. There she composed a poem that touched the heart of Hideyoshi and he in compassion released her. She returned home to her husband, but was unable to bear children. She obligingly raised a son of her husband's mistress as her own, and became renowned for her gentleness and kindness. Every year on Oct. 5th, young girls come to put powder and lipstick on her statue, praying that they will become gentle and kind like Lady

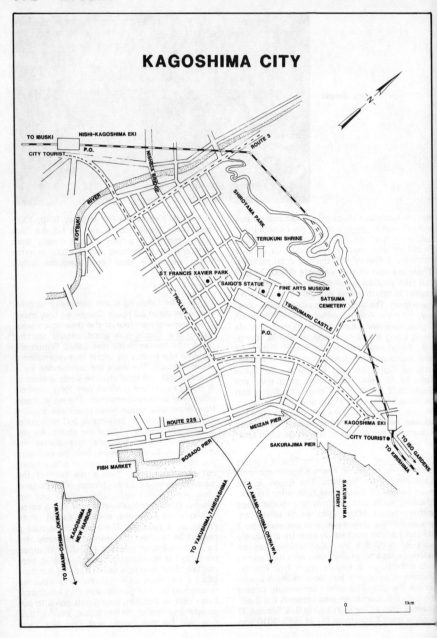

KAGOSHIMA CITY

TO IBUSKI

NISHI-KAGOSHIMA EKI

CITY TOURIST

P.O.

ROUTE 3

NISHIO BRIDGE

KOTSUKI RIVER

SHIROYAMA PARK

TERUKUNI SHRINE

ST FRANCIS XAVIER PARK

SAIGO'S STATUE

FINE ARTS MUSEUM

SATSUMA CEMETERY

TSURUMARU CASTLE

TROLLEY

P.O.

ROUTE 225

MEIZAN PIER

KAGOSHIMA EKI

CITY TOURIST

TO ISO GARDENS

TO KIRISHIMA

SAKURAJIMA PIER

BOSADO PIER

SAKURAJIMA FERRY

FISH MARKET

TO YAKUSHIMA/TANEGASHIMA

TO AMAMI-OSHIMA/OKINAWA

KAGOSHIMA NEW HARBOR

TO AMAMI-OSHIMA,OKINAWA

0   1km

Jimesa. The museum itself is dedicated to art, and that's what you get—a remarkably wide scope of exhibits in a relatively small area. The L wing of the first floor is devoted to exquisite examples of Satsuma pottery. Anyone interested in buying ceramics should come here first to see quality work. The next room is filled with contemporary paintings, mainly cubist, impressionistic and abstract. Indeed, many of these artists perfected their art while sipping cognac on the West Bank in Paris. They learned well, and their work shows it. In yet another room is an outstanding, lifelike representation of a typical Kagoshima farm at about the time of the Meiji Restoration, the best display in the museum. Marvel at the number of items fashioned from straw such as a horse collar, sandals and raincoats. There are fine examples of farming implements and an old wooden machine used to separate rice from the stalk. Everything in the exhibit seems to be made out of wood, straw and thatch and this fine exhibit gives a true feeling of the times. The second floor of the museum is dedicated to artists from Kagoshima, most notably Kinosake Abihara and Seiozi Togo. Before leaving the grounds, compose yourself in the serene courtyard before heading out into Kagoshima's noisy, frenetic city streets.

a Shinto priest from Terukuni Shrine preparing to bless a Toyota truck

St. Francis Xavier Park: Amid the clatter, the neon signs and the billboards written in _kanji,_ you suddenly come across an archway inscribed in Latin. This is St. Francis Xavier Park. There is a bust of St. Francis under an archway that is a facade of a church entrance—almost like a Hollywood set. Behind it is a grassless park where children ride swings and teeter totters. Across the street is the church rebuilt in 1949 to replace an older one bombed out in WW 11. If you go in, remove your shoes and wear the plastic slippers that are provided.

Terukuni Shrine: After looking at the origins of Christianity in Japan at St. Francis Xavier Park, head for Terukuni Shrine. There is a gigantic stone _torii_ over 10 m high and 15 m across. As you look through it, it frames the city. This is a symbol of modern Japan. As you stand there, the modern city throbs at your feet and at your back, ancient Shinto rites are performed.

Saigo's Cemetery: The last stop on this mini tour is the Memorial to the Satsuma Loyal Retainers, or more colloquially, Saigo's Cemetery. A small museum takes you through all of the periods in the life of this very formidable

man. It's worth a look, offering a window to the political turbulence and lifestyle just at the time of Japan's emergence as a 20th C. nation.

Iso Gardens: Don't miss them! They are the best thing to see in Kagoshima. They are located on Rt. 10 on the eastern outskirts of the city along the bay. Take City Bus No. 1 from Nishi Kagoshima Eki (about Y100). Taxis are available, but cost Y1200. Entrance Y400. These gardens, filled with mossy nooks and crannies, were built by the Shimazu clan as a sanctuary of peace and beauty where courtesans and lords once composed poems to the glory of nature. Smoking Sakurajima volcano provides the backdrop across the bay. The gardens are meticulously manicured and flowers are everywhere; also, under almost every overhanging rock or mossy recess there is a tiny shrine. There is even a clock set in the ground made from flowers. As you walk in, pick up the map of the gardens in English. There is natural art everywhere. On the side of the mountain, behind the gardens, are huge rocks inscribed with Chinese characters called Senjin Gan. The translation, appropriately enough, is "a huge rock." This was ordered by Narioki, the 27th lord of Shimazu. Fortunately,

Iso Gardens

most of the other Shimazus had more imagination. The last Shimazu lord, Tidayoshi, commissioned a famous artist, Ohshige Isanji, to build Seimon, the main gate. It is constructed from camphor trees found in the area. Look for the emblem of the lords on it: a circle surrounding a cross. Nearby is a smaller gate, the curious Suzu-mon, made from tin and painted red. History relates that only the *daimyo* and his successor were permitted to walk through it. There is one spot, Kyokusai-no-Niwa, where garden parties were held by Yoshitaka, the 21st lord. Each guest seated on a stone by a small stream was requested to compose a poem before a cup filled with sake came floating by. The same Lord Yoshitaka introduced 2 shoots of bamboo (*moso-dake*) from Okinawa, which he transplanted in the present bamboo grove and from there they spread all over Japan. Pecking around the floor of the grove are chickens, effectively keeping down the undergrowth. It will take an entire afternoon to thoroughly enjoy the gardens, but you can't help walking away from them refreshed and revitalized. The ancient beauty to which they were dedicated permeates the air. <u>*Shoko Shuseikan:*</u> Next door to the gardens. Shoko Shuseikan was one of the first factories in Japan which began operations in 1851, its 1200 workers making everything from land mines to glass. It is now a museum and worth a quick look. This factory is where Japan took its first shaky step into the age of technology.

<u>*special products:*</u> As well as the previously mentioned pottery and ceramics introduced into Kagoshima by indentured Koreans, the prefecture is known also for other unique folk arts.

tinware: Its highly polished, lustrous surface makes excellent goblets and wine sets. It was first manufactured under the Shimazus from a successful tin mine founded in 1655 at Tani-yama. <u>*bamboo products:*</u> These make inexpensive souvenirs and some baskets are even suitable as incidental travel bags. Bamboo products are found at numerous sidewalk shops and include such practical items as handbags, curtains, fruit baskets and fans. Bamboo dolls, toys and wind instruments have a long history as traditional folk art. <u>*Oshima silk pongee:*</u> This pure silk handwoven cloth goes back 2 centuries. Try the large *depatos* and ladies' kimono shops. An entire kimono made from Oshima pongee is outrageously expensive (Y40,000 up), but you can get decent prices on handbags, ties and smaller items. To save money, buy a length of it and do your own sewing. Its quality is further enhanced by a unique dyeing method which consists of repeatedly washing the raw silk in iron-laden mud, and then dipping the sections into a solution of boiled sap of the *sharinbai* which grows in the Amami Islands. The dye is permanent and lasts for as long as the material itself lasts. <u>*Yaku cedar products:*</u> Perhaps next to pottery these fine, hand-tooled wooden products are the best souvenirs from Kagoshima. The best pieces—furniture, chests, woodcarvings and curios—are made from *yakusugi* trees over 100 years old. Less distinguished pieces are made from *kosugi*, a younger cedar. <u>*where to buy:*</u> Any of the above-mentioned products can be found in numerous shops and large department stores. The prices are usually fair. To get an idea of quality and pricing before you look around town, the prefectural government operates a souvenir display shop located at the Sangyo Kaikan (Industrial Building), tel: 23-9171.

services: Kagoshima offers the cultural delight of the Home Visit Program. If you wish to visit a Japanese family at home, contact the following to make arrangements: Tourist Section, Kagoshima City Office, 11-1 Yamashita-cho, Kagoshima, tel: (0992) 24-1111; or City Tourist Information Center Service, 1 Chuo-cho, Kagoshima, tel: (0992) 53-2500, in front of Nishi-Kagoshima Eki. Some useful numbers include: City Tourist Services located in front of Kagoshima Eki, tel: (0992) 22-2500. The City Hospital can be reached at tel: 22-2101; the Central P.O. at 54-5390; and JAL at 58-2314.

accommodations: For Western-style accommodation offering more expensive Japanese-style rooms, try Kagoshima Sun Royal Hotel, 8-10-1 Yojiro, Kagoshima 890, tel: (0992) 53-2020, 10 min by car from Nishi-Kagoshima Station, from Y5000; and Shiroyama Kanko Hotel, 41-1 Shinshoin-cho, Kagoshima 890, tel: (0992) 24-2211, 10 min by car from Nishi-Kagoshima Station, from Y7000. *Ryokan* include Hotel Tsurumaru, Shiroyamacho, Kagoshima 892, tel: (0992) 22-4131, Y7000-12,000; and Daiichiso, 1-38-8 Shimoarata, Kagoshima 890, tel: (0992) 57-2121, Y7000-12,000. Among the business hotels, Kagoshima Gasthof, 7-3 Chuomachi, Kagoshima, tel: (0992) 55-0256, 40 rooms, Y3360, is a 4 min walk from Nishi-Kagoshima Station; Kagoshima Daiichi Hotel, 1-4-1 Takashi-cho, Kagoshima, tel: (0992) 55-0526, 40 rooms, Y3360, 5 min walk from Nishi-Kagoshima Station; and Hokke Club Kagoshima-Ten, 3-22 Yamanokuchicho, Kagoshima, tel: (0992) 26-0011, 127 rooms, Y3400, 3 min drive from Nishi-Kagoshima Station. Kagoshima City has only one youth hostel, Kagoshima-ken Fujin Kaikan YH, 2-27-12 Shimo-arata, Kagoshima 890, tel: (0992) 51-1087, 12 min by bus from Nishi-Kagoshima Station and 2 min on foot, 45 beds. An alternative is to stay at Sakurajima YH, Hakamagoshi, Sakurajima-cho 891-14, tel: (099293) 2150, 6 min on foot from Sakurajima Port, 95 beds. (See "Sakurajima" on the following pages for a description of this enthralling, volcano-dominated peninsula.)

local food: The complete range of Japanese cooking is found in Kagoshima, but some dishes, collectively called *Satsuma-ryori,* are a specialty found only in this district. Due to Kagoshima's long history of involvement in wars and conflicts, it is believed that these dishes originated from battlefield campfires and that the original recipes came from China through Okinawa. They have come a long, tasty way since then. Typical examples are *tonkotsu,* pork spare ribs cooked in miso. A *tonkotsu teishoku* (full meal including rice, soup, etc.) costs between Y600 and Y900. *Satsumajiru* is miso soup laced with vegetables and strips of pork (Y300-500). *Shunkan sake sushi* is specially prepared *sushi* with a unique, zesty sauce served on vinegared rice. *Tsukeage* is deep fried and battered minced fish. To get a full sampling of all of these dishes, order the works: a 10-course meal called *Toku Satsuma Teishoku.* It costs Y3000 and up. It obviously can't be your daily fare, but it makes an excellent once-a-week blow out! Enjoy. The alcoholic complement to these foods is the locally produced *shochu* distilled from sweet potatoes. Don't be fooled. This mild-tasting brew packs a wallop. If you want *shochu* as a souvenir or gift, it comes in a pottery bottle. The larger bottles (like whiskey bottles) have the best quality and higher potency *shochu.* There are also local sweets called *karukan, harukoma* and *korai.* These very sweet cakes go back hundreds of years. Most Westerners find them *too* sweet. *Karukan* is made from yams and rice. They were first commissioned by Nariakira Shimazu during the Edo Period when they were first produced commercially in Rokubei Yajima's cake shop named Akashiya. Two curiosities that grow in Kagoshima: one the *Sakurajima daikon* (radish) grows only on Sakurajima, to a diameter of 1.5 m and weight 30 kg; the other, the diminutive Sakurajima orange, measures only 3 cm in diameter, abut is very juicy and sweet.

Sakurajima

SAKURAJIMA VOLCANO

No matter which way you enter Kagoshima, this towering volcano will become immediately obvious. Like most travelers, you will be uncontrollably attracted to it. Don't fight, because it is not only an excellent place to visit, but also makes a perfect base from which to tour the city. *getting there:* Take the Sakurajima Ferry which runs every 15 min and costs a meager Y60. Sakurajima Pier is only 100 m from Kagoshima Eki (don't become confused with Nishi-Kagoshima Eki). From Nishi-Kagoshima Eki, take the streetcar to Kagoshima Eki or take City Bus No. 1 from in front of the station (Y90) directly to the pier. When you arrive at the pier, you will see a spiral staircase. Go up. Tickets are dispensed through machines. The ferry ride itself is short, but you have a good chance of orienting yourself and seeing the lay of the bay. Before you will be a hustling, bustling port city of heavy maritime traffic. Ahead you will see Sakurajima seared by the amazing lava flow from an eruption in 1914 that spewed millions of cubic meters of lava, turning the one-time island into a peninsula now connected to the mainland from the E by a highway. When you dock at Sakurajima, follow the flow and hand in your ticket. In the ferry terminal is a model of Sakurajima along with maps of the area. Unfortunately, they are in Japanese, but there is a small portion written in Japanese-style English. Not perfect, but it gives a good capsulized history of the mountain's activity. When you leave the terminal, the first thing you notice is the lush vegetation, especially the giant ferns. The air has a sulphurous smell and there is fine dust floating everywhere.

touring Sakurajima: To begin your tour o' Sakurajima, from the ferry terminal follow the road N out of the town (with the terminal at you back, go L). In a few 100 m, the town will give way to tiny cottages nestled away in orange groves. They are of traditional weatherbeaten timber with tile roofs, but the ever-present dus makes them look greyer. After 2 km the road wi branch off to the R heading up the mountains Signs direct you to the Yunoshira Observatio Platform. If you continue along the coast road in another 2 km you will come to a rathe unappealing bathing beach. The premier spot t head for is the Observation Platform. The road i steep, so expect to push your bike. Miniatur

SAKURAJIMA

SWIMMING

SAKURAJIMA

YUNOHIRA
VIEW NORTH PEAK
  + 1118m

FERRY LAVA FIELD

SOUTH PEAK
  + 1060m

FURUSATO

0   2.5   5km

farms cling to the sides of the mountain. Their major crops are oranges, scallions and giant *daikon* (radishes). The smell of onions for once is welcome as it helps to blot out the sulphurous fumes as you climb nearer the volcano. The view from the top is worth every drop of sweat that it took getting there. It is magnificent. The bay and Kagoshima lie at your feet. In the far distance are tall mountains promising further adventure, and to the S lies the broad Pacific with silhouettes of islands on the horizon. The one eyesore (there always seems to be one) is that some modern engineer built Sakurajima's garbage incinerator smack dab in the middle of the view! *Shikata ga nai*—It can't be helped!). The tour up and back takes about 3 hours.

accommodations and food: The best place to stay is at the Sakurajima YH, only 5 min on foot up the hillside from the ferry terminal. When you get off the ferry, turn R and walk about 100 m until you see the first road going up the mountain on your left. Follow this to the YH. Once you get to the top of the hill, you will have your first close-up view of Sakurajima. They also offer maps of Sakurajima. There are at least 3 hotels on the Mt., but their cheapest rooms will be about Y3500 without meals. South, out of town (with the ferry terminal at your back, go R) is a public Camping Area in about 1 km along the fairly secluded shore. There is no charge for camping. If you decide to camp, what you will need, even more than usual, is a good Japanese bath (*ofuro*) because of the dust that seems to seep into every pore. From the camping area, head along the coast road away from town and in a few km you will come to Furusato Onsen. A good soak never felt so good. To really save

money, try your hand at fishing for supper. The fishing is good wherever you dunk a line. There is a built-up area just outside of the terminal where you can buy fruit and groceries. There are a few small restaurants but prices are perhaps Y100 per dish more than usual.

SOUTH FROM KAGOSHIMA

Ibusuki and Mt. Kaimon: The main attraction S of Kagoshima on the E coast of the Satsuma Peninsula is Ibusuki. Unfortunately, Ibusuki is a victim of its own fame. Its main attraction is its steaming sands which you lie in buried up to your neck, letting their heat soothe your body. Sounds great, but there are just too many people. Ibusuki is heralded as the "Hawaii of Japan" and is a famous honeymoon resort, something akin to Niagara Falls in the U.S. You can take a hot bath and be buried in the sands at any of the large hotels. Prices vary, but expect to pay Y1200, which usually includes use of the swimming pool too. Bathing suit rental, if you can find one to fit, is an additional Y300. If you do wish to visit this area, don't plan on staying overnight-the prices are too high. Instead, take a day trip from Kagoshima. _getting there:_ By train from Nishi-Kagoshima Eki (one hr, Y500) or by Kagoshima Kotsu Bus from Yamakataya Bus Center (at Yamakataya Depato, 10 min walk from Kagoshima Eki along the streetcar route). The bus trip to Ibusuki takes 1 hr 20 min and costs Y700. _sights:_ Mt. Kaimon is about 10 km further S along the coast. Known as Satsuma Fuji because of its perfect conical shape rising 100 m, the view from the top encompasses the entire Ibusuki Peninsula. Visiting Ibusuki and Mt. Kaimon will take an entire day. The first hourly train leaves Kagoshima at 0515. Trains back to Kagoshima from Kaimon Station leave at 1425, 1759 and 1957.The fare is Y520 one-way for the one hr 15 min trip.

accommodations: Due to its resort status, Ibusuki's accommodations are high priced. Here are a few examples of the dozens of ultra-modern hotels/*ryokan* to choose from: Ibusuki Coral Beach Hotel, Junicho, Ibusuki 891-04, tel: (09932) 2-2241, Y10,000-20,000; and Ibusuki Kanko Hotel, Junicho, Ibusuki 891-04, tel: (09932) 2-2131. If the hot sands are not enough, the massive Ibusuki Kanko offers a jungle bath. Expensive, but worth a once-in-a-lifetime visit. Ibusuki Oriental Hotel is located at Junicho, Ibusuki 891-04, tel: (09932) 2-3141, 28 rooms, Y6000-9000. Ibusuki YH, 1850 Junicho, Ibusuki

KAGOSHIMA PREF. SOUTHERN ISLANDS

KYUSHU

KAGOSHIMA

IBUSUKI

TANEGASHIMA

YAKUSHIMA

NAKANOSHIMA

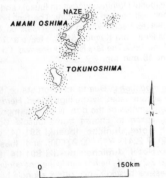

NAZE

AMAMI OSHIMA

TOKUNOSHIMA

-N-

0   150km

891-01, tel: (09932) 2-2758, 6 min walk from Ibusuki Station, 96 beds. *services:* the Tourist Information Office at the *eki* offers maps and general tourist information of the area. The staff speaks halting English.

Osumi Peninsula: Across Kagoshima Bay from Ibusuki, the Osumi Peninsula is a virgin tourist area. Train as far as Kanoya, then bus along Rt. 269 from Kanoya to the tip of the peninsula at Cape Sate. This area is gaining prominence with archaeologists who have found ancient burial mounds dating to the very beginnings of civilization in Japan. The Rocket Space Center from Tokyo University also uses the peninsula as a launching site. Cape Sate is the most southern point of the Japanese main islands. The area is covered in sub-tropical jungle. A day trip from Kagoshima is the best way to see Osumi, but with so few people in the area, camping spots are numerous and easy to find. There are a number of villages close by to pick up provisions and the fishing from the rocky promontories is especially good. You can also ferry from Sate to Ibusuki (1 ½ hrs).

Southern Islands: Lying directly S of Kagoshima are the islands of Tanegashima and Yakushima. Further out to sea, stretching S towards Okinawa are the Amami Islands. The main attractions on any of these islands are bright blue skies, friendly fishing villages, warm sands, clean waters, coral reefs and tropical fish. Kick back and relax. Yaku I. also boasts the prefecture's tallest mountain, Mt. Miyanoura (1935 m). Here also grow 1000-yr-old cedars that have been designated as Natural Monuments. *accommodations:* No problem. All the island villages have at least one moderately priced *minshuku*. Camp on the sparkling beaches wherever your heart desires and buy fresh fruit and fish in the town market. *getting there:* Ask for details of stopovers at the ferry offices. As well as the main ferries, there are local ferries to the islands leaving Kagoshima from Basado Pier, Meizan Pier and Kagoshima New Port. For reservations and information, call JTB at 0990-22-8135, (5 min walk from St. Francis Xavier Park) or stop in at Kagoshima's 2 City Tourist Services in front of the train stations. There is a boat daily to Yakushima (4 hr 30 min) from Kagoshima and Naze, the main town of Amami-Oshima is a regular port of call. From there, you can get local boats to any of the smaller islands. By air, TOA Domestic Airlines flies from Kagoshima International Airport to Amami-Oshima (one hr 15 min).

KIRISHIMA-YAKU NATIONAL PARK

In south central Kyushu, on the border of Kago-shima and Miyazaki Prefectures, is Kirishima, the mountainous section of Kirishima-Yaku National Park. Its name means Fog Is. as the peaks sticking through the mists resemble islands surrounded by fog. It is one of the premier cultural, religious and scenic spots in the entire nation. It is the first National Park, designated as such in 1934, and it is the first place in which the descendants of the Sun Goddess Amatarasu set foot upon Japan at Mt. Takachiho. Unbelievably, at most times of the year, it is not crowded. The tourist flood occurs in mid-summer when people come to the mountains to escape the sweltering heat of the lowlands. The area is studded with 23 magnificent volcanic peaks. There are gorges, waterfalls, pristine lakes, high mountain trails. Kirishima is known for its beautiful pink azaleas (*miyama kirishima*) that bloom from late March to mid-April. The main trees are red pines and maples. The maples turn scarlet in early November. The winter months (Jan.-Feb.) are known for frost-covered plants. The sulphurous mists from the mountains cover the plants and are turned frosty white, presenting a remarkable panorama. Deer, fox and badgers (*tanuki*) are found throughout the area. Manmade wonders are found as well. There is Kirishima Jinja, one of the most revered shrines in all of Japan, the original structure being built 1400 yrs ago, today a living taste of Japanese history. Kirishima has it all, from high-rise hotels at Kirishima Hot Springs Resorts, to primitive camping spots at Ebino Heights. Kiri-shima is one of the best mini-tours that any traveler (long or short-time) can take in Japan. You get to feel the park's natural, volcanic, mountainous beauty while at the same time experiencing its cultural and religious soul.

getting there: From the bus terminal in front of Nishi-Kagoshima Eki, the ride takes 2 hrs (Y1100). The bus takes the high road and you get excellent seascapes as well as broad mountain vistas as you near Kirishima. Sit on the right-hand side. From points N, board the train to Yoshimatsu, or the largest and main station, Kobayashi (Kumamoto to Kobayashi, Y2200). From any of these, bus to Kirishima. There is also direct bus service from Kagoshima International Airport to beautiful Kirishima. *to Kobayashi Train Station:* Bus from Ebino Bus Terminal along the Kirishima Toll Road to Kobayashi in 20 min; check at terminal for schedules. Kobayashi is a "big" little town with most of the amenities. Unfortunately, there's no public place to change money in town. From Kobayashi, make connections to Kumamoto and points north. If you have a choice, depending upon your departure time, avoid the *futsu* and take the *kyuko;* the *futsu* takes 3 long hrs for the 80 km trip to Kumamoto. *getting around:* Buses run throughout the Kirishima area and link up with all main train stations surrounding it. Regular sightseeing buses depart from Kirishima Jingu Eki at 0925 and from Hayashida Onsen Hotel at 1440. The fares vary according to the distances traveled.

EBINO

The best place to head for in Kirishima is Ebino. It is at the base of Mt. Karakuni in the middle of the park. It is a crossroads for mountain trails, has excellent bus service to other scenic spots in the area, and has a wide range of accommodations. To throroughly enjoy this area, spend at least 3 days making Ebino your base. For excellent maps and information, visit the park ranger, Takawa Misuno, at the National Park Office. He will be happy to assist you and he speaks English very well.

sights: The first walk to take from Ebino is to the extinct volcano, Mt. Karakuni (1700 m). It takes about 1 ½ hrs to ascend the moderately rugged, well-defined trail. It was named Karakuni (Korea Mountain) because it was believed that you could see Korea from its summit. This is a fanciful exaggeration, but the view you get is vast and awe-inspiring. You can look S and see the coast and Mt. Sakurajima, to the E Mt. Takachiho (1574 m), and to the N Mt. Shinmoe (1421 m), which last erupted in 1959 and is still active and smoking. Mt. Shinmoe provided the spectacular smoking cauldron for the James Bond movie *You Only Die Twice.* From Karakuni, you look down into Lake Onami, the largest crater lake (4 km circumference, 12 m depth) atop a mountain in Japan. Legend says that this was the site of the first suicide in Japan when a heartbroken young maiden threw herself into the water and was transformed into a mermaid-type dragon. It is said that if men throw themselves in, their bodies are never recovered as the dragon maiden drags them to her lair at the bottom, while women are rejected and are found on the top. The crater of Karakuni itself is enormous and makes you feel insignificant when you ponder the force that created it. Trails lead from one mountain to the next and the very adven-

Mt. Karakuni

turous and very fit can walk from Ebino all the way to Mt. Takachiho. This would take an entire day of hard walking, but you could see it all. You can pick up a bus from Kawara, near Takachiho to Kirishima Jinja and then back to Kirishima Onsen.

EBINO

EBINO

MT KARAKUNI
1700m

1. out door hot springs
2. Karakuni So (lodge)
3. National Park Office
4. parking
5. parking
6. Visitor Center and
   Free Museum
7. Bus Terminal and
   Lindo So (People's Lodge)
8. rest center and
   gift shop
9. Ebino Kogen Hotel
10. gas station
11. Police
12. Ebino Kogen So
    (People's Lodge)
13. Tokyo University Volcanic Lab
14. scenic overlook
15. Ebino Kogen Hotel
16. Ebino camping site
17. parking lot

accommodations: Ebino Kogen Campu Mura (Campground) is operated by Ezo Matsuyama, tel: (0984) 330-800, about one km SW of Ebino's bus terminal. Here you can either pitch a tent (Y200) or stay in a primitive cabin (Y700). For colder months, blankets and a heater are provided for an extra charge. An open-air pavilion is provided with running water, but there are no bathing facilities. This is no problem since any of the people's lodges or hotels in town will

let you use the spas for Y200-300. This is a very economical place to stay, though the summer months are very crowded. There are 3 people's lodges in Ebino that provide _ryokan_-type accommodations for Y3500, including 2 meals. They are Lindo-So, Ebino Kogen-So, and Kara-kuni-So. They are all comfortable, well maintained and provide mineral spring baths. The best is Karakuni-So, about ½ km from the town center. Though the proprietors, Mr. and Mrs. Taniyama, do not speak English, they have excellent knowledge of the area, including a complete slide show of Ebino in all 4 seasons which they will be happy to show you after the evening meal. These kind people provide sumptuous full-course meals and their bath is superb, fashioned from traditional wooden tubs. Slide the screens open if the weather permits and the bathroom becomes an open-air gazebo looking out onto Mt. Karakuni. Lie on the hot stones surrounding the tub for deep soothing heat. Towels, a _yukata_ and a _haori_ for colder weather will all be provided. There are washing machines available, a rare find in Japan. Karakuni-So is the perfect spot for relaxing and revitalizing before moving on. Japanese-style Ebino Kogen Hotel offers a number of western-type rooms at rates of Y5000 up. They will cash travelers checks.

food: The most important information about food in Ebino is that all of the restaurants close at 1700, so if you plan a long day of hiking, this can be a nuisance. Stock up for the evening meal before you go. Across from the bus terminal, the Rest Center restaurant serves decent-sized meals at slightly elevated prices. Add Y100-200 to the normal price for most dishes. The cheapest is curry rice for Y450. The giftshop sells a wide variety of touristy junk, but towards the rear they have excellent posters of the area for Y400. The paper is thick and of good quality. There is a ramen shop at the bus terminal. The bowls (Y400) are large and tasty. The eggs hanging in the wicker baskets are hard boiled (Y50). Pick up a few if you plan a trek. Finally, to the rear of the Visitor's Center and Free Museum there is a small restaurant area with the cheapest food in town, but their menu is limited. They also sell beer.

MAJOR STOPOVERS WITHIN THE PARK

Kirishima Onsen: This is Kirishima's most touristed area with 20 modern, fashionable hotels and scores of _ryokan_. The main attraction is its hot mineral baths. Prices range from Y5000

an elaborate walkway of
Kirishima Jinja

and up, and most rooms are Western-style. The larger hotels cash TCs and this is where the P.O. is located. The mountains are covered with virgin forests and there are numerous gorges and streams. Famous Maruo Waterfall gathers the waters from the hot spring resorts and cascades 60 m into a rocky pool. Senri and Tearai Falls are also well known.

Kirishima Jinja: The shrine is located in the S area of the park, not only a major bus stop on the route from Kagoshima but also on the regular sightseeing bus service throughout the park. The shrine is magnificent. It was dedicated to Ninigi-no-Mikoto, the legendary descendant of the Sun Goddess and was originally built by Priest Keiin about 1400 years ago. The present shrine was rebuilt by Yoshitaka Shimazu in 1715. The shrine is an embodiment of oriental beauty. Black tiled, gabled Chinese roofs sit atop orange and vermillion pillars. The eaves are intricately carved, often featuring animals and painted gold, green, brown, red and pink, an amazing blend of colors. Giant Japanese cedars surround the shrine and you get a sense that the main shrine and lesser buildings are one giant sculpture, fused into the side of the mountain. Priests in flowing robes stroll through the manicured gardens. There are small fountains and a feeling of peace and tranquility hangs lightly on a cool breeze.

Mt. Takachiho: 1574 m. Ten min by bus (15 km) from Kirishima Jinja or a 25 min bus ride from Ebino. You will first see Takachiho as a dome-shaped mountain, looming on the horizon. The main road leads to a *torii* gate announcing the

religious significance of Takachiho. Look for a sign reading TAKACHIHO RIVER FIELD and begin your ascent from here. Just inside is a parking area and a gift shop selling a few light provisions. The climb is well marked and takes about 90 minutes. It's possible to begin from Takachiho and walk the mountain trails back to Ebino in about 8 hours. The climbs are not difficult, but the up-and-down topography is quite tiring. The full walk is recommended for only those in top physical condition.

accommodations: The following is a partial list of the many resort accommodations found in the Kirishima area. Most center around the Kirishima Onsen and nearby Shinkawa Gorge area. Western hotels, with some Japanese-style rooms, include the Kirishima Kanko Hotel, tel: (09957) 8-2531, from Y4000-30,000; Kirishima Hotel, tel: 8-2121, Y3000-10,000; Hotel Otani, tel: 82321, from Y3000. There are 2 *ryokan:* Orihashi, tel: 7-2104, from Y3000; Makizono (town-operated *onsen* center), tel: 6-0007, from Y2000; and Shinkawa Ryokan, tel: 7-2218, from Y3000. For business hotels, try Kirishima Business Hotel, tel: 8-2611, from Y3000. Ebino YH, 8596 Tamakino, Minimi-nishi-kata, Kobayashi 886, tel: (09842) 3-8181, is 25 min by bus from Kobayashi Station and 7 min on foot, 48 beds, closed June 16-25 and Dec. 1-10; and Kirishima-Kogen YH, Kirishima-jingu-mae, Kirishima-cho, 899-42, tel: (09955) 7-0116, 12 min by bus from Kirishima-jingu Station and 10 min on foot, 120 beds. *services:* For tourist information in the Kirishima area, contact Kirishima Hot Spring Information Office at (09957) 8-2256 or Daikarishima Tourist Association at (09957) 8-2256.

SHIKOKU
INTRODUCTION

Shikoku (Four Provinces) is the smallest of the 4 main islands of Japan. Even including the pilgrims who visit the 88 Sacred Temples, and who have a special purpose for being there, it is the least visited. Considering the fact that it has excellent weather, outstanding physical beauty and intriguing cultural and religious centers, this statistic is unbelievable. The swirling Naruto Straits prohibit the building of a bridge from Honshu which helps to preserve Shikoku, in the Japanese mind at least, as not readily accessible. Except for the major port cities of Matsuyama, Takamatsu and Tokushima, lying along the Inland Sea, the rest of the island is comprised of provincial towns and slow-paced villages. Anyone heading inland, away from the coastal towns, will leave modern, industrialized Japan behind. In Ehime Prefecture in the W are unvisited fishing villages whose secondary industry is raising cultured pearls; beautiful specimens can be purchased from wholesalers at greatly reduced prices here. The 2 capes of Ashizuri and Muroto, jutting out to sea in the S provide excellent secluded camping surrounded by fantastically beautiful seascapes. Mt. Tsurugi

(1955 m), in the central E, provides remote camping, hiking and fishing. At Matsuyama, visit the famous Dogo Spa, a favorite of nobility and artists for centuries. And always there are the 88 Sacred Temples of the Buddhist saint, Kobo-Daishi, many providing accommodations (check with TIC for full listings), macrobiotic Zen meals and an atmosphere of tranquility. At the temples, where rituals and lifestyles have not changed for centuries, the emphasis is on communicating with the inner self. Shikoku developed as a major trade link of the old empire. Its native sons provided some of the best seafarers, some even turning to piracy, using the remote coves and harbors of Shikoku as their home base. Shikoku, serving also as a communication link, allowed its people to keep a finger on the pulse of modernity and innovation, though in many ways they chose to remain traditional. Unlike Tohoku and Hokkaido which developed later in Japanese history, Shikoku has always been a vital and vibrant part of Japan, but it was not in the mainstream like Kyoto, Osaka, and Tokyo. It was more like the banks along which the cultural river flowed.

getting there by ferry: The benign Inland Sea separates Shikoku from Honshu in the N and Kyushu in the west. Crossing it is pleasant, visually attractive and easily done from many ports. Shikoku is linked with Honshu and Kyushu by ferries of the JNR and by various private steamship companies. A frequently used route is the JNR Uno-Takamatsu Line. Uno is located 20 km S of Okayama. The Kansai Steamship Company, tel: Tokyo (03) 274-4271; Osaka (06) 572-5181, operates daily ferries from Naka-Tottei Port (Kobe) to Beppu. En route, the ferry docks at both Takamatsu and Matsuyama on Shikoku. The STS Line (Setonaikai Kisen Steamship Company) operates numerous ferries through the Inland Sea. In Tokyo, tel: (03) 567-8740; Hiroshima (0833) 51-5291. The Nihon Kosoku Ferry Co. sails between Tokyo and Kochi in southern Shikoku. The ferry departs from the Tokyo Ferry Terminal on odd numbered days. Telephone Tokyo (03) 274-1801; Kochi (0888)310520. The Ocean Tokyu Ferry Co. sails between Tokyo and Kokura (near Kita-Kyushu on Kyushu) on even numbered days of the month. En route, the ferry docks at Tokushima; tel: Tokyo (03) 567-0971; Kokura (093) 582-6761; Tokushima (0886) 62-0489. Sailings are from Tokyo Ferry Terminal at 1820, arriving in Tokushima the following day at 1130. The ferry arrives at Kokura on the 3rd day at 0630. *by air:* There are 4 airports on Shikoku at Tokushima, Takamatsu, Matsuyama and Kochi. Tokushima is connected with Osaka by direct flight, and the remaining 3 are connected with both Osaka and Tokyo by direct flight. ANA and TOA Domestic provide the air services. The longest flight is Tokyo-Kochi (2 hr 10 min); the shortest is Osaka-Tokushima (30 min).

internal travel: The rail service on Shikoku is provided by 4 lines of the JNR. The Yosan along the N and E coasts; the Tokushima Main Line from the E coast to the center at Ikeda; the Dosan Line from Tadotsu in the N to Kochi in the S; and the Kotoku Main Line along the NE coast. Although it's no problem along the coastal areas, the train service to the interior of the island, especially in western and central eastern sectors, is non-existent. *by bus:* For any out of the way areas, bus service is the only means of transportation. Again, you must use the basic rule of thumb for traveling in Japan—if there is a road passing through a village, there is always a local bus. It only takes a bit of patience and 2 small phrases. Pull out your map, point to the desired village and say, *"koko"* (here), then *"Basu noriba wa doko desu ka?"* (Where is the bus stop?) That should do it.

the land: Shikoku, comprised of the 4 prefectures of Ehime, Kagawa, Tokushima and Kochi, is approx. 19,000 sq km and is bordered by the Inland Sea to the N, and the Pacific on the south. These 2 bodies of water are connected by the Bungo Channel on the W and the Kii Channel on the east. Running E-W through the center of the island are the rugged and tall Shikoku Mountains, the highest peaks of which are Mt. Ishizuchi (1981 m) in Ehime, and Mt. Tsurugi (1955 m) in Tokushima. There are numerous unnavigable rivers running from the interior to the sea. The longest river (*kawa*) is the Yoshino (194 km), which empties into the Kii Channel. A particularly beautiful river, well suited for camping and hiking, is the Iya-kawa near the town of Ikeda in Kagawa Prefecture. There are a few small plains on which farming occurs. The 2 most important are the Tokushima along the lower reaches of the Hoshinogawa River, and Kochi Plain, bordering the Pacific in the southwest. The coastline along the Inland Sea is punctuated with numerous harbors, capes and promontories. The remainder of the coastline is generally mountainous with the exception of the relatively flat coasts of the Maruto and Ashizuri peninsulas.

the climate: Shikoku can be divided into 2 climactic regions, separated by the Shikoku Mountains running the length of the island. The Inland Sea region to the N is sunny and bright most days of the year. Except for the typhoon season, oftentimes there's a shortage of rain. The Pacific coast area to the S is one of the warmest regions of Japan. Its southern location combined with the Kuroshio (Black Current) keeps southern Shikoku warm year round with especially mild winters. The Pacific Coast area has much more rain than northern Shikoku, especially during the spring rainy season. (*baiu*). A traveler in Japan has an excellent chance of finding fine, balmy weather in Shikoku, regardless of the season. Let altitude be your weatherman. When it gets too hot, go to a temple or spa in the mountains. When the weather is blustery, head down to the sea (no more than a 2 hr bus or train ride).

history: In a small mound just E of Sukumo, a tiny city in southern Ehime, fragments of Yayoi pottery were discovered. Scholars have determined that this primitive pottery dates back to just before Christ and have concluded that Shikoku was one of the earliest inhabited areas of Japan. The island's main function throughout history was that of a cultural pathway. From

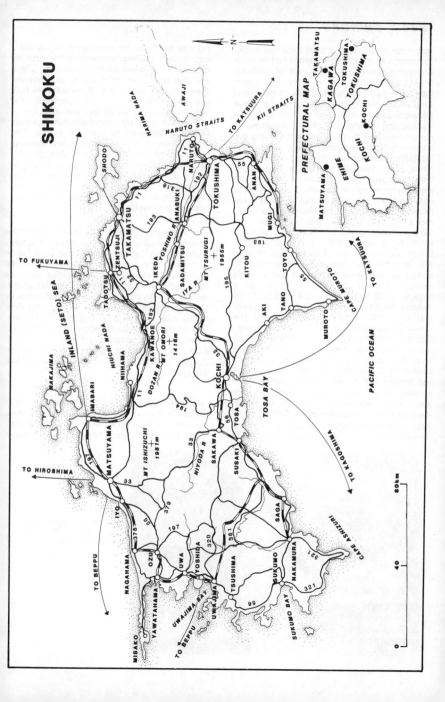

very early times when Japanese culture began its northeastward spread under the half-mystical emperor Jimmu Tennu, the bays of northern Shikoku provided natural stopovers. Later, during the Edo Period, Shikoku and the Inland Sea where the main watercourse for trade between Japan and Asian mainland. Unlike Kyushu and Honshu, Shikoku's development is not underscored by great battles changing the course of Japanese history. There were many local skirmishes between the ruling warlords and many cities (especially along the Inland Sea) began as castle towns, but military encounters played a lesser role in Shikoku's history. Many early seafarers hailed from Shikoku, and some became the scourge of the mainland, operating their pirate activities from this island base. The most outstanding figure in Shikoku's history is the Buddhist saint, Kukai, known also as Kobo-Daishi. He was born in Kagawa Prefecture in 774, and his teachings were instrumental in spreading Buddhism throughout Japan. This energetic founder of the Shingon sect left a legacy of 88 sacred temples dedicated to Buddha found throughout Shikoku. Approximately 100,000 pilgrims per year visit the temples. Some make the journey on foot, spending almost 2 months getting around to all the temples, while others have modernized the procedure and bus the temple circuit in about 2 weeks. As suppliants to Buddha, the pilgrims eat simple Zen meals (*shojin ryori*) while staying at the temples and dress in white kimono, leggings and mittens. Spring is the most popular season for pilgramages. Saint Kobo visited many parts of Japan and numerous miracles have been attributed to him. One popular motif has the saint appearing before a farm house as a poor wanderer. After receiving hospitality, he rewarded the inhabitants with a well that when bathed in had curative powers. Many versions of these myth-miracles are built around this simple plot. The hospitable and humble recipients are always rewarded with a tree, stream or other natural gift that dispenses cures or otherwise benefits the people. The good works of this gentle man have become immortalized over the centuries through such folk tales, and his memory is especially revered in the temples of Shikoku. Much like Christ, Kobo-Daishi focused his attention on the common man. Good works and love are the basis of his teachings.

The 88 Sacred Temples: The temples are distributed all over Shikoku. Prefecture by prefecture, there are 22 in Kagawa, 26 in Ehime, 24 in Tokushima and 16 in Kochi. Some are close to cities and towns, while others are nestled away in deep mountain gorges. A map pinpointing the temples can be obtained from any JTB office in the larger cities, but it will be in Japanese. One of the most famous is Zentsuji, the 75th of the 88, and the birthplace of Kobo-Daishi. It features a treasure house, pagoda and original works of Kobo-Daishi. Zentsuji is located one km W of Zentsuji Station, and is the headquarters of the Shingon sect.

economy: Before WW11, Shikoku was supported by the primary labor-intensive industries of forestry, livestock breeding, salt making, agriculture and fishing. The people lived a simple

a white clad pilgrim visiting one of the "88 Sacred Temples"

Kono san the dollmaker exemplifies the tradition of the solitary craftsman. He produces *ushi oni* (devil monsters) in his one man shop in the city of Uwajima

life, centered around the village. Since Japan began its rapid industrialization after WW11, the villages have been drained of their population by the demands of the large coastal industrial zones on the northern coast, and the primary industries have become economically insignificant. At one time, fields along the Inland Sea produced indigo, *igusa* (reeds used for matting), and cotton. Now they are parking lots for giant steel and petrochemical plants. In the S the people from the Kochi Plain still earn their money from the land, raising supplemental crops of vegetables, tobacco and rice, which can be harvested twice a year because of the mild climate. In the foothills of the Shikoku Mountains, paper mulberry is cultivated. It is used for the special paper in *shoji* screens, and for the printing stock for Japanese money. The Pacific S of Shikoku provides excellent fishing grounds and is fertile in bonito and tuna. Many towns and villages in this area serve as bases for fishing fleets, and have thus far escaped the mammoth industrialization of the northern coastal areas.

arts and crafts: One of the premier potters of Japan, Omori Terushige, resides in the village of Masahiwara near Zentsuji (the birthplace of Kobo-Daishi) in Kagawa Prefecture. The pottery itself is known as *nanzan*. Omori-san has gained worldwide recognition for his fine artistry, especially in his use of glazes. A visit to his studio will provide a display of glazes unmatched for their diversity of color and

beauty. His studio in Zentsuji is well known and easily found. Another famous pottery coming from Naruto is *otani-yaki*. What distinguishes it from other pottery is its sheer massive size. These giants are used for raising water lillies and as garden pots. Some large bowls are over one meter in diameter, while the larger garden pots can hold 1000 l. of water. They are thrown on a unique wheel, a *nerokuro*, operated by one potter who works the clay while another lies on the floor and spins the wheel with his feet.

paper products: Kochi has long been known for paper products. Numerous small shops feature every facet of Japanese paper craft from *chochin* (lanterns), to *kami saifu* (paper wallets). The raw material is pulp from Japanese mulberry cultivated in the nearby mountains. A specialty of the region is a *daruma* known as *okiagari,* whose original design was borrowed from Tokyo in the early 1800s. This colorful ''princess *daruma*'' is sold as a charm for good health at numerous shrines in the area. Part of this paper-making tradition led to the manufacture of *omen* (paper masks). The most famous are *tosa* (the feudal name for Kochi). These masks are colorful and humorous and can be purchased almost anywhere. *dollmaking:* An excellent, but little-known folk artist is Kono-san, the dollmaker, who lives in the city of Uwajima. He specializes in wooden toys, particularly *ushi-oni,* which have the head of a devil and the body of a cow. Giant papier-mache *ushi-oni* are carried by local men during a special festival in

October. Another of Kono-san's specialties is a red fighting bull, *yokuzuna*. His *yokuzuna* was chosen by the Ministry of Industry as an official souvenir in Japan's Southeast Asian Floating Fair. He uses *sakura* (cherry wood) aged for 15 yrs to carve his folk toys. Many cheap facsimiles of these folk toys are available in the area, but Kono-san's are by far the best. These authentic folk art items make excellent gifts; they are packed in a special wooden box, and sell from Y10,000 to Y30,000 for the larger ones (about 50 cm high). (See the Uwajima map for the location of Kono-san's studio).

the people: The people of Shikoku are earthy, hospitable and traditional. Few have ever had close contact with *gaijin* and will view you with open curiosity always tempered with respect. Being contantly center stage can be a bit tiring, but a good-natured approach is always the best one. You will be rewarded with helpfulness and unpretentiousness. In the smaller fishing villages or mountain hamlets, it is not uncommon to be invited to dinner or to be guided to the most rustic temples or tucked-away spas that you could easily otherwise miss. Be open, and doors will open in return.

SHIKOKU FESTIVALS

Jul. 23-24: Summer Festival. Held at the Warei Shrine in Uwajima, this event features a parade of decorated fishing boats whose fishermen pray for a large catch. A *togyo* (bullfight), one of 6 held throughout the year, is also scheduled for this festival. The bulls are pitted against each other in a show of strength, and the winner is the one who drives its opponent from the ring. Tradition says that the first bulls came in the early 1800s as a gift of thanks from a Dutch ship that was saved from a typhoon by local fishermen. The bulls were so fierce that the tradition of fighting them began.

Aug. 9-11: Yosakoi Festival. Held in Kochi City, this midsummer festival is full of dancing and frivolity. The emphasis is placed on the simple joys of living.

Aug. 15-18: Aw Odori Dance Festival. Held in Tokushima, this is the largest and most spirited summer festival in Shikoku. Thousands of people in fancy attire dance away their cares through the streets, accompanied by flutes, drums and *samisen*. Onlookers are encouraged to join in the revelry. TV cameras beam the festival to the homes of those who wish to participate but can't actually attend. The festival is also known for *bunraku* puppet shows that are performed by amateur, but highly skilled farmers. *Bunraku* theater also occurs during the farmer's slack season, but there are no fixed dates.

Oct. 10-11: The Grand Festival of Kotohiragu Shrine. At Kotohira. This shrine is dedicated to *Omononushi-no-Mikoto,* the Shinto protector of travelers. The adoration accorded this shrine is 2nd only to the Sacred Shrine of Ise. Fantastic floats are paraded through the compound and the participants are dressed in attire from the Heian Period.

Oct. 14: Funa Odori. Held at Gogoshima, a small island a few km off the coast from Matsuyama. Features pantamime dancing on floating barges.

Oct. 28-29: Ushi-Oni (Ox Devil). Giant ox devils are paraded at Uwatsuhiko Shrine, midway between Uwajima and Yoshida. This is a basic, down-to-earth rural festival full of tradition and local color.

KAGAWA PREFECTURE

TAKAMATSU

Kagawa is the smallest prefecture on Shikoku, situated in the NE corner of the island. It encompasses, however, Takamatsu (pop. 310,000), the busiest and most important city in Shikoku. Although Takamatsu is sprawling and hyperactive, it offers superb scenic areas, unparalleled formal gardens, and serves as a gateway to the second most revered shrine in Japan, Kotohiragu. Unlike most Japanese cities that were bombed out during the Pacific War, Takamatsu escaped the hurried, haphazard rebuilding spree that followed. Some inexplicable oversight was made, and Takamatsu was actually rebuilt with human habitation in mind. The city was planned to include wide avenues, tree-lined parks and arcades for leisurely strolls, the latter being an unadmitted, but joyous pastime of the business minded Japanese. The ferry port, main *eki,* and downtown area are all within walking distance. The immediate coastline is dotted with islands, many with histories steeped in legend and folklore. From the hills and rock outcroppings around Takamatsu you see them stretch westward on the smooth surface of the Inland Sea. The sunlight and the time of day create the backdrop. In early morning they are soft blue and mysterious, peeking through the mist. In broad daylight they are painted islands on a painted sea. And at night they are hazy, twinkling silhouettes in the blackness. At all times, they are ethereal and contemplative.

getting there: Takamatsu is the island's main air and seaport, serving as the transportation hub to all parts of Shikoku. Numerous flights link the city with the major islands of Japan. Ferries ply many routes from Kyushu and Honshu (see "Introduction"). The most frequently used route is by train from Tokyo. The rail cars are loaded on a ferry at Uno (Okayama) and cross the Inland Sea in one hour. The Yosan Kotoku Main Line running into the city connects with all the rail lines throughout the island. *getting around:* The city provides taxi, bus and electric railway to all points in the metro area. JTB operates a 3 hr bus tour of the city in English. Tickets are available at any JTB office.

sights: Whether in Takamatsu by design or merely en route some sights are a must. *Ritsurin Koen:* This 78 ha park is 2 km S of Takamatsu Eki. Take the Kotohira Electric Railway to Ritsurin Koen. Then walk W for 300 meters. Ritsurin Park was, at one time, the private quarters of the Matsudaira Clan. It is of classical design, containing the requisite 6 ponds and 13 mounds. The feudal lords engaged their serfs for over 100 yrs to complete the formal gardens. Besides the excellent arrangements of flowers, shrubs and trees, the park contains a zoo, folk-craft exhibit, museum and art gallery. A thorough tour takes an entire afternoon. Ritsurin is considered one of the finest classical gardens in Japan. *Tamamo Park:* A lesser park than Ritsurin, but a quiet place for a stroll or picnic lunch. It is only 100 m from the *eki* just behind the Sightseeing Bus Terminal. It is the former site of Takamatsu Castle and gives a good view of the Inland Sea, but you must overlook the congestion of the modern ferry port.

vicinity of Takamatsu: Megashima Island (Demon's Island) is the folklore setting for the adventure of Momotaro, a tiny boy born from the center of a peach who, with his band of monkey, pheasant and dog, defeated the horrible 3-toed, 3-eyed man-eating demons of the island. A 20 min ferry ride connects this quiet island with Takamatsu. The Yashima Plain is ½ hr E of Takamatsu by direct bus. It rises 300 m above the sea on precipitous sea walls and is the site of Yashima Temple, the 84th of the 88 Sacred Temples.

Momotaro, the Peach Boy

accommodations: Inexpensive western-style accommodations include: Takamatsu City Hotel, 8-13 Kameicho, Takamatsu, tel: (0878) 34-3345, 35 single rms at Y3300, and 10 twin rms at Y6000; and Okura Hotel, 1-9-5 Jyotocho, Takamatsu, tel: (0878) 21-2222, 272 single rms at Y3500 and 78 twins at Y6000. Ryokan in Takamatsu are Hotel Kawaroku, Hyakkensho, Takamatsu 760, tel: (0878) 21-5666, Y8500-20,000; and Tokiwa Honkan Ryokan, Tokiwacho, Takamatsu 760, tel: (0878) 61-5577, Y7000-12,000. For business hotels, try Hotel Tokuju, 3-5-5 Hanazonocho, Takamatsu, tel: (0878) 31-0201, 121 rms at Y2800, 5 min drive from JNR Takamatsu Station; Takamatsu Station Hotel, 10-17 Nishinomarucho, Takamatsu, tel: (0878) 21-6989, 26 rms at Y3500, one min walk from JNR Takamatsu Station; or just W of Takamatsu in Sakaide at Hotel Sun Route Sakaide, 1-1-2 Komadomecho, Sakaide, tel: (0878) 46-6111, 90 rms at Y3000, one min walk from JNR Sakaide Station. There are a number of YHs throughout the area. The most centrally located is Takamatsu Yuai-sanso, 2-4-17 Nishiki-cho, Takamatsu 760, tel: (0878) 22-3656, 10 min on foot from Takamatsu Station, 32 beds. If you plan to visit Ritsurin Park, you can stay close by at Takamatsu Yashimasanso YH, 774 Yashima-naka-machi, Takamatsu 761-01, tel: (0878) 41-2318, 8 min on foot from Yashima Station, 50 beds. In Takamatsu, a less centrally located YH is Takamatsu-shi YH, 531-3 Okamoto-cho, Takamatsu 761, tel: (0878) 85-2024, 15 min on foot from Okamoto Station, 52 beds.

TADOTSU, ZENTSUJI AND KOTOHIRA

If you are bound for Kotohiragu Shrine (Kompira) at Kotohira or Kobo-Daishi's birthplace at Zentsuji the best route is the train on the Yosan Line to the old port city of Tadotsu. Tadotsu is also the junction of the Dosan Line to Kochi, via Ikeda. *getting there:* Regular ferry service between Tadotsu and Honshu is available. Ferries to Fukuoka, 15 crossings per day, Y1130. At Tadotsu *eki* there is a small bus (free) with a ship's wheel painted on it that will take you to the ferry terminal. *accommodations:* Tadotsu has a full range of accommodations, but an excellent place to spend the night is at Kaiganji YH, 997 Nishi-shirakata, Tadotsu-cho 764, tel: (0877) 32-3433, 5 min on foot from Kaiganji Station, 150 beds, which is a Buddhist temple open for accommodation. It is one stop (Y140, 5 min) from Tadotsu Eki. The food is delicious and the temple provides purely Japanese-style lodging. At the entrance to the temple are 2 slightly larger-than-life bronze sumo wrestlers. They stand in silence, exuding strength and patience as they guard the temple. Purchase your return ticket to Tadotsu at the small grocery store 50 m on the L leading to the train stop.

the great Buddhist saint, Kobo Daishi

Zentsuji: From Tadotsu, head 6 km S on the Dosan Line to Zentsuji, the headquarters of the Shingon Sect of Buddhism, founded by Kobo-Daishi. The temple is one km W of the station, where St. Kobo was born. The grounds upon which the temple is built were believed to be owned by the great priest's father. The temple is the 75th station of the 88 temples. *Kotohira:* Five km S of Zentsuji is the Kotohira (Kompira) Shrine, one of the most revered Shinto shrines in all of Japan. When you get off the train, the *torii* gate is just in front of you. No entrance fee. This shrine is dedicated to Omononushi-no-Mikoto, the protector of seafarers and voyagers. The entire shrine area is densely forested with cedar, pine and camphor. The air and buildings seem to get more refined as you steadily climb Mt. Zozu. The main shrine is 251 m up the mountain, accessible by 785 steps. The panoramic view of the surrounding Sanuki Plain is breathtaking. The carvings, sacred halls and works of art blend with the shrine, and the whole presents a picture of ordered, yet natural beauty. *accommodations:* In the area, stay at Kotohira Seinen-no-Ie YH, 1241 Kawanishi-otsu, Kotohira 766, tel: (0877) 73-3836, 15 min on foot from Kotohira Station, 68 beds. Two *ryokan* found at Kotohira are: Kotohira Kadan, Kotohira 766, tel: (0877) 75-3232, Y8000-20,000; and Toraya Ryokan, Kotohira 766, tel: (0877) 75-3131, Y7000-12,000.

EHIME PREFECTURE

This prefecture encompasses the entire western and northcentral coast of Shikoku. It runs W from Kawanoe, a small city bordering Kagawa Prefecture on the Inland Sea, to the tiny town of Johen, on the SE coast at the mouth of the Bungo Straits. The main city is Matsuyama, which is also the most populous city (pop. 390,000) of Shikoku. Rural Ehime is rarely visited and the coastal towns of the SW are some of the most untouched areas of the island. Ehime offers serene Zen temples, cultural oases such as Dogo Spa in Matsuyama, fishing villages virtually unruffled by modern times and provincial towns offering quiet accommodations and generally rustic festivals.

getting there: The most popular route to Ehime is from Hiroshima (via Kure) by hydrofoil to Matsuyama (one hr 10 min). Ordinary ferry from Hiroshima takes 3 hrs and disembarks at Mitsuhama a few km W of Matsuyama. Ferries are also available from Iwakuni, Kobe or Osaka. From Kyushu, ferry from Beppu or Usuki to Yawatahama on the W coast in 3 hours. _by air:_ ANA from Tokyo to Matsuyama (one hr 40 min), Osaka to Matsuyama (50 min). _by rail:_ The Yosan Main Line runs all along the western and northern coasts and connects the major cities of Ehime with Takamatsu. The JNR also operates direct bus service from Matsuyama to Kochi. The route runs through the interior of the island and takes 3 ½ hours.

MATSUYAMA

Although the most populous city of Shikoku, Matsuyama is saved from the hustle, bustle and congestion that you would normally expect to find because it is not the main industrial port of Shikoku. That dubious honor belongs to Takamatsu. Matsuyama gives the impression of being a large town instead of a city, although it has a full range of travel amenities. Historically, it was known as a mecca of art and literature; this tradition adds to its slow paced ease and charm. Anyone heading S or inland would be well advised to take care of banking, travel necessities and film in Matsuyama as opportunities to buy these necessities become less frequent as you move away from the northern cities. One day in Matsuyama is sufficient to see the sights and to round off your visit with a trip to Dogo Spa, the premier spot. _getting around:_ The orientation point in Matsuyama is the train station (_eki_). For some unknown reason, there is not the usual temporary baggage storage in this station. Here it is a private enterprise run by the car park attendant. Stand in the main doorway and look to your right. There is a large Coca-Cola sign and a small building under it where you can leave your luggage at a slightly inflated rate of Y300. Matsuyama has a streetcar system that will bring you to the most important spots in town: Matsuyama Castle, Dogo Onsen, and Kinokunia Book Store, where you can stock up on books in English and other languages. The JTB in Matsuyama can help you with travel bookings but the staff does not speak English. This is frustrating, but you can work things out if you are only interested in ongoing travel.

Dogo onsen (spa)

Dogo Onsen: This remarkable public bath is one of the oldest known hot springs in Japan. A part of it was set aside for the royal family at the turn of the century. It is steeped in tradition, art, and

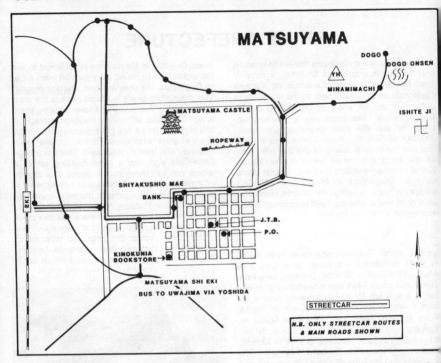

MATSUYAMA

DOGO

DOGO ONSEN

MINAMIMACHI

ISHITE JI

MATSUYAMA CASTLE

ROPEWAY

SHIYAKUSHIO MAE

BANK

EKI

J.T.B.

P.O.

KINOKUNIA BOOKSTORE→

MATSUYAMA SHI EKI

BUS TO UWAJIMA VIA YOSHIDA

STREETCAR

N.B. ONLY STREETCAR ROUTES & MAIN ROADS SHOWN

legend, and should not be missed. Getting there is simple. Board the streetcar and ride it to the end. If in doubt, just say "Dogo Onsen" to anyone and you will be directed. The current building housing the public baths was built during the Meiji Era and has been in service for 100 years. It is a triumph of traditional Japanese architecture. Many folk stories revolve around the founding of the baths, but it is commonly held that Okuni Nushi Nomikoto founded them almost 3 millenia ago. Legend says that a local bird called a *sagi* had injured its legs. It flew to the *onsen,* splashed around, and its legs were healed. Many famous people from all walks of life visited the *onsen* through the ages. Some of the early Tenno emperors sought out these baths. Shotoko Taishi, a famous Buddhist priest, came to soak and meditate. Haiku poets such as Shiki and novelists such as Soseki came to clear their minds and find inspiration. The baths literally drip with past glories and culture. The entrance fee for the baths ranges from Y150 for a basic bath to Y1000 for bath, green tea and sweet cakes. Upon entering, undress and place your clothes and valuables in the basket

provided for safekeeping. Take the attached number. You are then given a *yukata* and a towel. Follow the steps to the lower level where the baths are located. Here the modern world slips away and you're in the middle of a Japanese birthright — the hot mineral bath. There are buckets for dousing, and wooden stools to sit on while washing. The atmosphere is ancient, and the waters are bubbling hot. Part of the ritual at Dogo is to lie flat out upon the worn stone floor. The heat is soft and soothing. Stay as long as you like. After the bath, round off the experience by going upstairs to the *tatami* room where you will be served cakes and *ocha.* You'll abe given a comb and a mirror for grooming, and for Y10 you can rent a hair dryer. There is a little anteroom with some paintings and relics from the past that are mildly interesting. Out on the balcony is a view over a garden and courtyard that hasn't changed for centuries. In the background the rhythmic *kurang-kurang* of *geta* on the cobblestoned streets can always be heard as the people of Matsuyama arrive for their nightly ritual bath.

Matsuyama Castle: Built in 1602, this is one of the best preserved castles in Japan. Like visiting cathedrals in Europe, it is easy to get bored with castles after awhile, but this one is a great specimen and very representative of castle architecture. You get an excellent view of the surrounding countryside from its heights and the grounds around it have been turned into a spacious, nerve-soothing park. Most of the castle is now a museum, and a few hours inspecting it and the grounds is well worth the Y200 admission fee. Either walk the pathway to the top of Shiroyama Hill, or take the cable car from the E side.

shopping: After leaving the Dogo baths, there is a modern looking arcade just across the street with varied and moderately priced restaurants. There are a number of shops selling junk, but the ceramic and wood carving shops have some fine pieces at bargain prices. The wooden pieces are made from pine specially chosen for the beauty of its grain. Most carvings come from trees that are hundreds of years old. A number of shops sell *geta*, and they have such a large selection that you have a good chance of finding a pair that will fit "massive" western feet. *Kinokunia Bookstore:* Located at Shiyakusho Mae, this bookstore has a good selection of foreign books (mostly English) and maps on the 4th floor, and the attendants speak English. This is a good place to stock up on reading material because the pickin's get mighty slim as you travel through Shikoku. This is also a good place to go if you need some particular information or have an important question that the staff may be able to help you with.

accommodations: In Matsuyama around the area of Dogo Ōnsen are a number of first-rate *ryokan.* Many of these establishments look like western-style hotels from the outside, but the rooms are pure Japanese with only a few western-style rooms offered. Some of the best are: Funaya Ryokan, Dogo-Yunamachi, Matsuyama 790, tel: (0899) 47-9278, Y12,000-32,000; Juen Ryokan, Dogo-Sagidanimachi, Matsuyama 790, tel: (0899) 41-0161, Y7000-10,000; and Hotel Okudogo, Suemachi, Matsuyama 791-01, tel: (0899) 77-1111, Y8000-20,000. Okudogo has more than 100 western-style rooms. All of these *ryokan* offer excellent baths and beautiful, contemplative gardens. The YHs in the area include: Shinsen-en YH, 1-28 Dogo-imaichi, Matsuyama 790, tel: (0899) 24-7760, 15 min by streetcar and 5 min on foot (35 beds); and

Okudogo YH, Sugitate-cho, Matsuyama 791-01, tel: (0899) 77-0303, 30 min by bus from Matsuyama Eki, 7 min by ropeway and 5 min on foot (48 beds). For a reasonably priced business hotel, try Hotel Taihei, 3-1-15 Heiwa-dori, Matsuyama, tel: (0899) 43-3560, (Y3500), near Matsuyama Eki. There is one Kokumin Shukusha in Ehime Prefecture located at Ozu about halfway between Matsuyama and Uwajima at Garyuen, 670 Yunoki, Ozu-shi. Rooms plus 2 meals run Y3500. Reservations are necessary. Forty km N of Matsuyama at Imabari is a Kokumin Kyukamura, Tohyo, Sakura Kaigan, Imabari City. Again, reservations are a must for this reasonably priced vacation village.

FUKUOKA'S EXPERIMENTAL FARM

Mr. Fukuoka is a born teacher (*sensei*). He is patient, naturally descriptive and full of energy. He has an unassuming bearing about him. He is a simple man, a farmer, but it is his lot in life to

the *sensei* (teacher), Masunobu Fukuoka

students from around the world come to learn back to nature techniques at Fukuoka-san's experimental commune

spread a philosophy, and this seems to weigh heavily upon him. Fortunately the earth to which he is so attuned bears him up, and his inward strength and sense of peace is contagious. The bounce in his step and his general vigor belie his 68 years. His farm is run on a totally natural basis, and the food is macrobiotic. His philosophy is that man does not grow food—nature grows food, and the less man and his "science" interfere, the better it will be. He attempts to pass this on to the world by training young people in his philosophies. Fukuoka-san calls his farming method the "no work method." This is not totally true, but it is about as close as you can get. He does not plow, cultivate, or use any chemical fertilizers. He rolls his seeds in mud, creating a pellet, and broadcasts them onto the ground. His crops are dry field rice, alternated with wheat. After he spreads his seeds, he lets nature work for him. As one crop comes up, he harvests it, and cuts the stalks to serve as mulch and to cover his broadcast seeds. In turn, they come up and he repeats the processes. He says he works a little at the beginning and then reaps his yield at the end. That is all. He has employed this simple, but effective method for over 3 decades, and has become the most successful farmer in the region. The *sensei* has also turned his attentions to Japan's beloved, dying pine trees. Most scientists feel that the blight infesting them comes from the outside, but Fukuoka-san thinks that the trees have been changed internally and have lost their innate strength to fight off disease. He works daily with fungi in his rustic laboratory attempting to find a natural cure.

getting there: Fifteen km S of Matsuyama is the small town of Iyo. Iyo is not important in itself, but it is a perfect halfway point between Matsuyama and the back-to-nature experimental farm. Take the bus S from Iyo for 5 km to a stop called Ohira. Walk to the built-up village area and just say "Fukuoka-san" to anyone you meet. You'll be directed. *accommodations:* People are welcome to stay at Masanobu Fukuoka's semicommunal farm on a daily basis, or on an extended stay as a student of his unique form of farming. The price is a day's work for accommodations and food, but for those intending to observe only, it is best to stay at Iyo. There is a *ryokan* in Iyo called Kuro Mori (tel: 202 19) that offers comfortable accommodations and excellent food for Y3500.

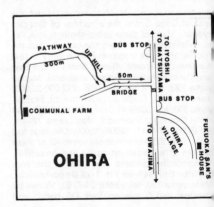

OHIRA

PATHWAY   UP HILL   BUS STOP   TO IYOSHI &
TO MATSUYAMA
300m
50m
BRIDGE   BUS STOP

■ COMMUNAL FARM

TO UWAJIMA   OHIRA VILLAGE   FUKUOKA SAN'S ■ HOUSE

information: To gain a personal view of Mr. Fukuoka, there is a fine article that appeared in *East West Journal* entitled, "The Natural Farmer (Replanting the Garden of Eden)," Nov., 1979. He also has authored a book that covers his life, philosophy and farming methods entitled *The One Straw Revolution*, published by Rodale Press ("Organic Gardening"), Emmaus, PA 18049, USA. It must be stated that anyone intending to go visit the commune must be in serious pursuit of knowledge. The accommodations are extremely basic: thatched huts, no electricity, outdoor toilets, and plenty of hard work. If you plan to visit, please write a letter of your intentions to: Masanobu Fukuoka, Iyo Shi, Ohira, Ehime Ken, 201-2-799-31, Shikoku, Japan.

UWAJIMA BAY

Seventy km S of Matsuyama on the coast at Uwajima Bay is the small town of Yoshida, and 7 km further S is the city of Uwajima. These 2 out-of-the-way places hold some of the most engaging and fascinating sights in Shikoku including a newly opened Zen training center that welcomes foreigners, a Buddhist temple whose priest is nothing short of a modern-day wizard, a museum dedicated to sex and phallic symbols, bullfights, folk artists, and inexpensive cultured pearls. *getting there:* The Yosan Main Line runs S from Matsuyama to Uwajima. The basic fare is Y1080. Slightly more costly express bus service is available from Matsuyama to all points south. Make reservations at Matsuyama Eki, or at JTB. The train is quicker and more comfortable, but you get a better view of numerous villages riding the bus.

sights: Uwajima offers a secluded formal garden, Tenshaen, and an excellent castle preserved from the mid 1600s. But the most exotic feature of Uwajima is Taga Jinja, a shrine dedicated to erotica collected from all parts of Japan. It is a giggling, slight embarrassment to the local people, but everyone visits it just the same. The courtyard is filled with huge penises carved from trees, and gigantic wooden vaginas complete with well placed moss. Even the statue of a hooded Buddha becomes a phallus viewed from the right direction. The museum takes up 3 floors of a modern building. Admission Y600. Every exhibit is slanted towards sex. There are statures of women giving birth, tiny geisha riding penis sleds down hills, little Buddhas gaily masturbating, even a clothespin becomes 2 lovers copulating. A strange oddity is that whenever female pubic hair is drawn in a picture or placed strategically on a carving, it is demurely taped over with white cotton. Animals are not exempted from the exhibits. Lions, tigers, giraffes in tree-top bliss, and even hippopotamuses are caught in the act. The most

a giant phallus points the way to the entrance of Taga Jinja

bizarre exhibit of all is one collected by a Dr. Kato at the turn of the century. Here, catalogued by name, age, region and occupation are thousands of snippets of pubic hair; an example: Miss Nokano, Age: 19, Birthplace: Osaka, Occupation: shop assistant, Remarks: virgin. The why and wherefore of this painstaking collection is now only a matter of speculation. The shrine is usually visited by young married couples learning what there is to know, and older couples praying for fertility and perhaps the birth of a child before time closes the door, and troupes of ribald, older women, no longer hampered by decorum, laughing and pointing at the collection of malehood and remembering when. *events:* Uwajima is primarily known for its bullfights held 6 times a year (no set dates). The bullfight arena is the large, white-domed structure sitting high on a hill overlooking the bay. It is also the setting for the 2 rustic festivals of Ushi-Oni (Ox Monster) and Yatsu Shika Odori (8 Deer Dance) held on Oct. 28-29.

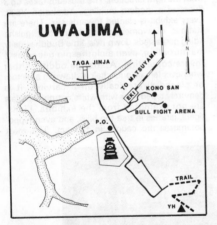

Kono-san: Tucked away on a hillside is the home of Kono-san, the woodcarver (see "arts and crafts"). Here this quiet man taps away with his hammer and chisels creating his unique folk toys. His house is a tiny bastion of culture. The walls are covered with carved artifacts from around the world, while piano, saxophone and various exotic instruments take up the corners in his small, artistic home. Kono-san does not speak English, but is willing to admit guests to his workshop for a short visit. Have a Japanese speaking acquaintance call to arrange a visit (tel: 08952-3256). He is well known in the area, and any taxi driver should know the way.

shopping: Miyatamo Pearl is located in downtown Uwajima, close to the main shopping arcade. Miyatamo is a warehouse and retail outlet for cultured pearls produced in the Uwajima area. This is where the local pearlers bring their products for distribution, as well as being a low-keyed shop where you can find a bargain. Discounts are offered, especially to *gaijin*. Merely repeat the amount you wish to spend, and the shopkeeper will produce multiple strings of pearls to fit your budget. Hand pick the ones that you like, and they will be promptly strung for you. You will be given the proper value for your money, no rip-offs. The shopkeeper's daughter, Riyoko, speaks English and is a good contact for information about the area.

accommodations: The Uwajima area has the full gamut of accommodations including numerous inexpensive business hotels, *ryokan* and *minshuku*. Many hotels are located just S of town on the main road leading to Sukomo. Bus service is available from the city center. A typical *ryokan* is Jonanso, Hirokoji, Uwajima 798, tel: (0895) 22-4888, Y7000-10,000. Uwajima YH is beautifully situated on top of a mountain S of the city center. The 30 min uphill hike along the winding cobblestoned pathway offers an excellent view, with friendly accommodations at its end. The address for the YH is Atago-koen, Uwajima 698, tel: (0895) 22-7177, 80 beds. In Yoshida, the San Mai So Hotel, located next door to the P.O., offers reasonable accommodations. During the last 2 weeks of July, the Uwajima area offers an English-speaking Summer Camp for local students. The camp is located at beautiful Nometako Waterfalls, where one can find cool mountain air, refreshing dips in bubbling streams, and country living. Anyone willing to teach English at the camp is offered free room and board. This is a great way to save money and an excellent opportunity to have an up-close, personal view of the people.

local interpreter: Mr. Tadashi Kikuchi, an English teacher at Yoshida High School, can provide information on Nometako English Camp. He has kindly offered his services to any foreigner in the area needing a guide or interpreter. He speaks English very well, and has a wealth of information to offer on the temples and scenic spots of the area. Please remember that Mr. Kikuchi has a full-time job and that his time is limited. If you plan to be in the area, please write to: Tadashi Kikuchi, 1373-5 Kakihara, Uwajima, Ehime 798, Japan. Tel: (0895) 25-1078.

THE AMAZING TEMPLES OF YOSHIDA

In the nearby small town of Yoshida are 2 Buddhist temples that are opposite sides of the coin. Both are proponents of the same religion, but the paths that they follow are totally different. One, Dai Raku Ji, is baroque, almost rococco. The priest, Gyogon Asano, is the 15th generation of his family to head this temple. He is worldly, drives a sports car, and has attempted to transform the grounds of his temple into Paradise on Earth. The other temple, Dai Jo Ji, is an ascetic Zen training temple. The priest, known only as *roshi*, is the epitome of what you would think a Zen Buddhist priest should be. He is a small, thin, shaven-headed, bespectacled, macrobiotic, orange-and-brown robed, serene man. Both temples in their own right are truly full of wonder and offer the widest possible view of practicing Buddhism.

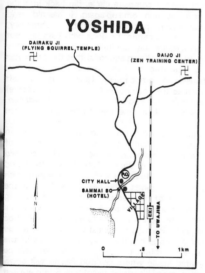

YOSHIDA

DAIRAKU JI
(FLYING SQUIRREL TEMPLE)

DAIJO JI
(ZEN TRAINING CENTER)

CITY HALL

SAMMAI BO
(HOTEL)

EKI

TO UWAJIMA

N

0   .5   1km

Dai Jo Ji: Two km NE of Yoshida Eki. It opened its doors as a Zen training temple in mid-1980. The priest, given the honorific title of *roshi*, follows the Buddhist tradition of seeking enlightenment through meditation. The students, known as *deshi*, follow a rigorous schedule of study, meditation and public works. The *deshi* must live the Buddhist tradition of roaming the countryside, singing prayers and begging for their food, a rite known as *taku hotsu*. Finally,

Roshi of Dai Jo Ji

under close scrutiny of their master, they are instructed in the meditative training of Za Zen. It is impossible to capsulize the intricate philosophy of Zen into a few words, but the main idea is to fuse the self with the oneness of the universe. There is no past, or future, only the all-encompassing now. Materialism is stripped away. The *deshi* live a humble life in the training temple, sleeping on one *tatami* mat (1 m by 2 m). They have a small shelf for their personal possessions, and they spend a great deal of their time sitting *seiza* (lotus position). Through self-denial and sometimes torturous ritual, they attempt to empty themselves and seek fulfillment. Their diet is purely *shojin ryori* (vegetarian). Obviously, this is a vocation to which few are called. The *roshi* opens his temple to everyone. You are welcome to visit for one day, or a week just to clear your mind, or you can join the temple as a way of life. Anyone visiting Dai Jo Ji will come away richer. All it takes is one glimpse of this enlightened Zen master meditating in his orange-and-brown robes on a *tatami* mat to see why.

Gyogan Asano of Dai Raku Ji

Dai Raku Ji: This truly amazing place is locally known as Musasabi (Flying Squirrel) Temple because the grounds are home to a number of these small, nocturnal animals. Gyogon Asano, the current priest of the temple, is the 15th generation of his family to live at Dai Raku Ji. The family have been collectors for centuries. There is a museum that is overflowing with artifacts, mementos and bric-a-brac so that it resembles a flea market more than a museum. There is no apparent cataloguing or order to the displays. They are just there in heaps. Visitors are permitted to enter the museum free of charge, and you can wander around handling any exhibit that catches your eye. The list is endless, but a few examples are clocks, bows and arrows, swords, bamboo products of all sorts, fans, stuffed animals, palanquins, erotic sculptures, and old passports. These "treasures" have been collected from all parts of Asia and the western world. You can spend an entire afternoon in the museum alone, but force yourself to leave because there are many wonders awaiting you on the grounds of Dai Raku Ji. Gyogon Asano is happy to serve as your guide. He is proud, worldly, and full of life, a man who

delights in delighting his guests. He has a large family, smokes cigarettes, eats meat, and uses every manner of modern contraption and convenience; still he glows with inner peace and joy. His path is different than that of the *roshi* at Dai Jo Ji, but he gets there just the same. The temple grounds are on a steep hillside; at the top of one of the hills he has created a miniature (replica) of the sea. This sea pond has rising and falling tides, saltwater fish, oysters, and marine plant life. When asked how he does it, his eyes twinkle, and he chuckles. You can see that the water is piped by a small motor and heated by solar energy, but how he maintains the proper chemical balance of the sea water is his secret. High on one of the hills is a flower-viewing platform that he and his son have built. He says that oftentimes his family takes tea here while his wife plays the *koto.* Gyogon Asano has also turned his attention to creative gardening. One of his favorite mediums is bamboo. He twists it, turns it, and ties it in knots. He has some plants that make a complete circle, dip back into the earth, and then come up again. He has old, dead trunks that sprout new shoots. Technically, most of this cannot be done with bamboo, but here it is, anyway. Dai Raku Ji also has a number of *musasabi* (flying squirrels) that the priest has documented over the years. He has a few families in semi-captivity (their cages are left open so they can come and go as they please) and they have had offspring. To his knowledge, this is the first time that flying squirrels have been born in captivity. The best feature of the temple is the formal gardens. It has been planned and laid out for centuries. It is one of the most manicured and superbly tended gardens in all of Japan. Every flower, bush and tree is meticulously groomed to harmonize with the surroundings. The best view is from the veranda of the temple, sitting and looking through one of the opened screens. This forms a frame through which the living art work can be enjoyed. Perhaps the priest will even show you old drawings documenting the progress of the garden through the years. Finally, you will be invited inside where Gyogon Asano will show you some of his varied inventions. Some are just gimmicks, while others are truly ingenious. He has made a water-powered stereo, a flush toilet from plastic garbage cans, a portable motorcycle, a double-necked acoustic guitar, and simply hundreds of household gadgets. What pours out of Gyogon Asano is unbridled vitality and love of life. There is wonder and amazement in everything, if you only look, and as you walk down the steps of Dai Raku Ji, you cannot help feeling that you have just stepped from wonderland.

THE SOUTH COAST

Take the bus S along the coast from Uwajima to Sukomo, as this is the only form of transport to the area. The service is regular, comfortable, but expensive (Y1600). About one hr S of Uwajima, you'll pass through the town of Iwamatsu. To experience a totally unvisited area, change buses at Iwamatsu and head W out onto the peninsula to the fishing village of Shiragai (Y300 RT). This detour takes only 2 hrs (tour included), and here you'll find a basic coastal fishing village cupped in a tiny rocky bay. Shiragai is never visited by foreigners and so the no-frills experience is delightful to the villagers and traveler alike.

SUKOMO

Located on the extreme SW corner of Kochi Prefecture, it has one main attraction. Ten km from Sukomo, a mound was discovered holding shards of *yayoi* pottery. It was one of the oldest inhabited areas of Japan. A few specimens are on display at Sukomo Chuo Kominkon located one block from the bus terminal. They are on the second floor, and they will be shown to you simply by saying "*yayoi*." The entrance fee is Y3000, and this quasi-museum is open everyday except Sunday. The main floor houses local, modern works, mainly pottery, and is worth a fast tour.

accommodations: The bus from Uwajima terminates at the Sukomo Bus Station where another short ride (Y300) will take you to the Sukomo YH, 196 Kamiari, Hashigami-machi, Sukomo 788-01, tel: (08806) 4-0233, one hr 10 min by bus from Nakamura Station, or 30 min from Sukomo, and 6 min on foot, 19 beds. There are a few reasonably priced *minshuku* in Sukomo, but the YH is the best deal. The food is good and the hostel sits surrounded by mountains with walking trails to the summit. The hostel is privately owned and the *parento-san* has built a traditional thatched Japanese house on the grounds where you can spend the night if you wish. Nakamura offers 2 temple hostels: Ishimiji, 4288 Yasunami, Nakamura 787, tel: (08803) 5-3033, 8 min by bus from Nakamura Station and 15 min on foot, 30 beds; and Taiheiji YH, 1-4-27 Motomachi, Uyama, Nakamura 787, tel: (08803) 4-5155, 5 min on foot from Nakamura Station, 50 beds (closed Dec. 29-Jan. 4). Taiheiji is the more rustic of the two. If you decide to proceed to Cape Ashizuri, there are 2 hostels. One is a temple: Kongofukuji YH, 214-1 Ashizuri-misaki, Tosa-shimizu 787-03, tel: (08808) 8-0038, one hr 30 min by bus from Nakamura Station and 2 min on foot, 80 beds (closed Feb. 14-16, July 9-10); and the other close-by is a shrine: Shirao Jinja YH, 1351-3 Ashizuri-misaki, Tosa-shimizu 787-03, tel: (08808) 8-0324, 90 min by bus from Nakamura Station and 3 min on foot, 20 beds. While heading S from Sukomo to the Cape, you'll pass through Tosa-Shimizu. Here you will find Fujiidera YH, 3940 Misaki, Tosa-shimizu 787-04, tel: (08808) 5-0120, 2 hrs by bus from Nakamura Station and 5 min on foot, 21 beds. If you desire more sophisticated accommocations, try Ashizuri Pacific Hotel Ryokan, Ashizuri-misaki, Tosa-shimizu 787-08, tel: (08808) 8-0341, Y6000-8,500.

vicinity of Sukomo: South of Sukomo is Cape Ashizuri. The main gateway is by express bus from Nakamura, but service is available from Sukomo. Many Japanese students head for the cape, considering it a romantic refuge. There is a white lighthouse, and Kongofukuji Temple, the 38th of the 88 temples of Shikoku. The Cape ends in a sea cliff and the vegetation is sub-tropical. The area is well suited for camping, offering secluded precipices, numerous trails and outstanding scenery. Tosa-Shimazu is the main town in the area where camping supplies can be obtained and onward travel arranged. Twelve km W are found Tatsukushi and Mino-koshi, 2 semi-developed tourist spots housing a museum and underwater observatory respectively. *Nakamura:* Ten km E of Sukomo is the terminus of the Nakamura Line. Use it as a way station for bus service W or train service E to Kochi. For Kochi, change trains at Kubokawa.

KOCHI

Kochi City, the prefecture capital (pop. 264,000) is located on the central southern coast of Shikoku. The city has particularly mild weather, but is buffeted by typhoons during the fall season. Kochi is a farming as well as important fisheries center. The farming, however, is a precarious business. Many local agriculturists attempt to get their produce to the large city markets before the regular season. This takes expensive greenhouses, heating systems and fertilizers. If they are within the first wave at the markets, they can price gouge. If there is mild weather and produce flows through the normal channels, they take a financial beating. Kochi also serves as a fishing port. It produces huge amounts of *katsuobushi* (dried bonito), a flavoring used in soup bases and many Japanese dishes. Kochi has taxis for finding a particular address, buses to all corners of the city, and a N-S, E-W streetcar which is the main way to get around in town. *getting there:* Linked directly to Tokushima on the NE coast by the Tokushima and Dosan lines, running through the center of

the island. If you wish to travel to the SE coast, by bus is the only way. Bus from Kochi to Mugi via Muroto (Y3200). Train from Mugi to Tokushima (Y750). For ferry service, see "getting there" in the "Introduction."

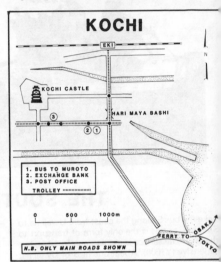

KOCHI

EKI

KOCHI CASTLE

HARI MAYA BASHI

3

2 1

1. BUS TO MUROTO
2. EXCHANGE BANK
3. POST OFFICE
TROLLEY ·······

0   500   1000m

FERRY TO OSAKA TOKYO

N.B. ONLY MAIN ROADS SHOWN

sights: In the central western section of town is Kochi Park with the castle sitting in the center. As usual, it provides a panorama of the city. The 5-storied *donjon* is an "Important Cultural Property" and dates from the mid-1700s. Entrance Y300. The park surrounding the castle is quiet and is a good spot for an afternoon siesta (*hirune*). *onagadori:* A remarkable feature of Kochi is the raising of roosters with 10 m long tails. These *onagadori* have been raised for centuries and are used to grace the grounds of local shrines. Their caretakers take special pains to preserve the tail feathers, often walking behind and supporting them.

shopping: When in Kochi be sure to shop for the noted traditional paper products famous in this area. These products can be purchased in many shops in the central arcade. They range from inexpensive but gaily decorated pocket notebooks, to classically rendered woodblock prints. They are affordable, distinctive, easily carried and mailed, and make excellent gifts.

accommodations: For *ryokan* accommodations in Kochi, try Joseikan, Kamimachi, Kochi 780 tel: (0888) 75-0111, Y7000-12,000; or Sansuien Hotel, Takajomachi, Kochi 780, tel: (0888) 22-0131, Y9000-16,000. For a more reasonably priced stay, try Business Hotel Itcho, 3-11-12 Harimayacho, Kochi, tel: (0888) 83-2166, 55 rooms, Y3000, 5 min walk from JNR Kochi Station. Kochi also offers 2 Youth Hostels: Kochi Ekimae YH, 3-10-10, Kita-hon-cho, Kochi, 780, tel: (0888) 83-5086, 7 min on foot from Kochi Station, 104 beds. This is centrally located. Leave the *eki* through the main entrance. Turn L and walk 3 blocks: Turn L again for one block. The other less conveniently located YH is Hitsuzan YH, 30-4 Koishiki-cho, Kochi 780, tel: (0888) 33-2789, 10 min by bus from Kochi Station and 20 min on foot, 50 beds. The Kochi area also offers 8 temple lodgings (*shukubo*) that are often crowded with pilgrims, so make reservations. A list is available from TIC.

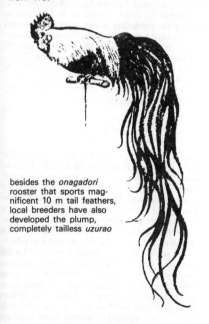

besides the *onagadori* rooster that sports magnificent 10 m tail feathers, local breeders have also developed the plump, completely tailless *uzurao*

VICINITY OF KOCHI

__Katsurahama:__ A white-sand swimming beach 35 min by bus from Kochi Station. The beach is interspersed with ruggedly weathered rocks and small pines. The local people head there in the autumn for moon viewing. __Ryugado Cave:__ A stalactite cave 25 min by bus from Tosa Station (10 km W of Kochi). The cave meanders for 4 km underground. Prehistoric pottery was unearthed in the caves, indicating occupation from very early times.

__Muroto Peninsula:__ Located in the extreme SE corner of Shikoku on a point of land jutting deep into Tosa-wan (bay). From Kochi, bus for 2 hrs (Y1650); sit on the right-hand side to get the best view of the coastline. Muroto Town provides practicalities, but is uninspiring. The surrounding area, however, has many points of interest. _vicinity of Muroto:_ Nearby, 15 min by bus, is Muroto-zaki Todai, another lonely lighthouse looking over an expanse of the Pacific. Camping, walking trails and breathing fresh sea air is the attraction. Perched pensively on a mountaintop overlooking Tosa-wan is Hotsumi-saki Temple, popularly called Higashidera. Take the bus from Muroto to the first stop; stress Higashidera or the bus will not stop and you must backtrack for 5 km. Follow the paved trail up the mountain. Higashidera is 24th of the 88 Sacred Temples, founded by Kobo-Daishi in 807. It is open to the public as a hostel (Y2250 with meals) and is a pilgrimage retreat. The communal *tatami* rooms can sleep as many as 20 people on *futon*. The food is delicious vegetarian fare. The buildings of the temples are of warm, brown, hand-hewn beams and the gray pebbled grounds are stately and quiet. The pilgrims and their families are not. The pilgrims are a microscopic cross-section of Japan. Some are old, with weathered faces, wearing the all-white regalia and prayer beads around their necks. They go from altar to altar uttering prayers and attaching small papers (*omikuji*) to propitious spots. Others are young families with bright-faced, skipping children who shortcut the rituals and wear only white vests over street clothes. Age seems to be proportional to devotion. If you do not wish to lodge at Higashedera, head for the Muroto Hotel at the bus stop at the bottom of the hill where you had previously asked to be let off. Prices are moderate and the rooms are adequate. On the main highway between Muroto and Mugi, you will pass boulder-ridden coastline with black sand beaches. This is uncommon. Approximately 10 km N of Muroto in a cluster of black, sandy beaches is an area called Little Hawaii. These 50 m stretches of beach are broken by natural seawalls. Here, young Japanese sit with surfboards on the roofs of their Toyotas, waiting for the sea to challenge. There is a bus stop and this is a good spot for a refreshing dip.

TOKUSHIMA PREFECTURE

TOKUSHIMA

Tokushima City is the capital as well as the cultural center of Tokushima Prefecture. It is a hub of industry, commerce and transportation, second only to Takamatsu, and has a population of 245,000. Located on the E central coast of Shikoku, it is linked by steamer and air service to all parts of Japan, and is a major crossroads to all points of Shikoku. The Tokushima Plain surrounds the city, which is situated on the lower stretches of the Yoshinogawa, the longest river in Shikoku. Rice is the main product, but vegetables and flowers are grown for the markets of Osaka and Kobe. Commercial crop cultivation is still important, but rapidly giving way to industry. The city craftsmen produce woodwork products and a cotton crepe called *awa chijimi*. Much of the traditional architecture of the city was destroyed during WW11, but the city has long since been rebuilt. A Portugese naval officer by the name of Wenceslao de Moraes made his home in Tokushima at the turn of the century. He was a prolific writer on "things Japanese" and in the same league as Lafcadio Hearn. He is entombed at Cho-Onji Temple, one km SW of Tokushima Eki. Tokushima is the doorway to Mt. Tsurugi, a magnificent mountain deep in the eastern interior. It is also the home of Tokushima University, a number of superb city parks, and culturally important temples. *getting there:* By air it's 30 min from Osaka, 2 hrs from Tokyo. Tokushima Airport is located between Tokushima and Naruto, connected in 40 min to the city center by frequent bus service. By ferry, it's 3½ hrs from Osaka S Pier, 2½ hrs from Fuke, 3½ hrs from Higashi Kobe, and one hr 45 min from Kobe by hydrofoil. See "Introduction" for details. By train, it takes 1½ hrs by express from Takamatsu on the Kotoku Main Line. The Tokushima Main Line runs W to Ikeda where it connects with the Dosan Line running S to Kochi.

sights: Tokushima Park, ½ km E of the station, contains an intricately landscaped formal garden as well as an amusement area complete with zoo. Bizan Park, located ½ km SW of the *eki*, centers around Otaki Hill (279 m). A bus is available to the summit. An extensive view of the city, surrounding plain and the Inland Sea has long been famous. During cherry blossom time, the hill is blazing pink and white. There is a Peace Memorial at the foot of the hill, as well as a museum containing artifacts from SE Asia. The fee is nominal and the exhibits are well prepared.

accommodations: Tokushima offers a number of hotels in city center. A good one, well-accustomed to foreigners is the Awakano. *Ryokan* in Tokushima include Sumiya Ryokan, Makadorimachi, Tokushima 770, tel: (0886) 52-9161, Y8000-12,000; and Kanko Hotel Bizan Honkan, Higashi-Yamatecho, Tokushima 770, tel: (0886) 22-7781, Y9000-12,000. If you're looking for moderate prices, stay at Business Hotel Tokushima, 1-15 Shinkuracho, Tokushima, tel: (0866) 52-6131, 40 rooms, Y3200, 10 min walk from JNR Tokushima Station. Tokushima has one YH: Tokushima YH, 7-1 Hama, Ohara-machi, Tokushima 770, tel: (0886) 63-1505, 30 min by bus from Tokushima Station, and 3 min on foot, 80 beds.

NARUTO

Naruto is a small town on the E coast of Shikoku 10 km N of Tokushima and 73 km SE of Takamatsu. The town overlooks one of the most impressive natural phenomena to be found in Japan. Here, just off the coast in the narrow channel (1.3 km wide) separating Shikoku from Awaji Island, are whirling, roaring tides known as the Naruto Whirlpools (Awa-no-Naruto). The phenomenon is caused by the almost 2 m difference in sea levels on the N and S sides of the Kii Channel. The best time to observe this spectacle is one hr before, and one hr after the changing of the tides. The ebb tide whips the water to a frothy, deafening series of maelstroms which reach their greatest fury at the new and full moons. The onslaught of rushing water reaches speeds of 20 km per hour and more. Rocks jutting from the sea throughout the area help to create a giant egg beater effect. Excursion boats from the pier area offer views of the whirlpools from close quarters. For a bird's eye view of the entire area, go to the observatory at Naruto Park on Oge Island about 8 km NE of Naruto City.

Easily accessible by bus. You can also walk to the top of Naruto Hill within the confines of the park for another view. *getting there:* Train from Takamatsu (change at Ikenotani) in one hr 35 minutes. Train from Tokushima in 40 minutes. Buses are also available from both cities. A direct hydrofoil makes the trip from Kobe to Naruto in one hr 30 minutes. Many ferries are available to and from Awaji Island.

accommodations: Tokushima has the wider range of accommodations but Naruto also offers some limited places to stay. For a moderately priced *ryokan,* stay at Mizuno, MuyachiOkazaki, Naruto 772, tel: (08868) 5-4131, Y6500-15,000. Naruto YH is found at 149-12, Kitatono-cho, Hayasaki, Muya-cho, Naruto 772, tel: (08868) 5-4561, 5 min by bus from Naruto Station and 7 min on foot, 50 beds. Awaji Island also offers accommodations, but they are exceptionally crowded in the summer season and reservations are a must.

ANABUKI

Forty km or 40 min due W of Tokushima by express is the town of Anabuki. It primarily serves as a starting point for the ascent of Mt. Tsurugi and the surrounding gorges along the Anabuki River. This is one of the most beautiful areas in all of Shikoku, complete with alpine walking trails for a 2-day romping and camping excursion. *getting around:* Anabuki provides a bus and taxi service to all sections of town. Two busses per day, one at 0700 and one at 1200, leave for the 2 hr 20 min 40 km trip to Mt. Tsurugi. The bus terminal is across the street from the *eki.*

sights: Anabuki has 2 minor, but entertaining sights. Earth Pillars (NE of town, 15 min by bus) are natural phenomena of eroded earth 18 m tall, topped by a scruffy covering of weeds and bracken. Other phenomena of this type are said to be found only in the Tyrol of Switzerland and the Rocky Mountains of the U.S. The sight is partially fenced. No admission charged. At the foot of the hilly area leading to the Earth Pillars is O-Me (Man-Woman) Jinja. This shrine is a smaller and homier rendition of Taga Jinja, the phallic shrine of Uwajima. The proprietor delights in showing his curiosities to his guests, giving a whirlwind talk complete with visual aids on the positions for making love. Tittering like school children and statements of "Will you look

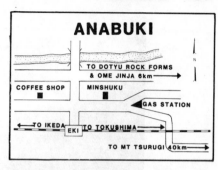

at that" are both expected behavior from all comers. *accommodations:* There is no YH in the area, though numerous hotels, mainly *minshuku* and *ryokan* are scattered throughout town. The best deal is Iguchiya Ryokan only 60 m from the *eki* (Y3000 with supper). The *ryokan* has sleeping rooms over a small Japanese restaurant. The proprietors are congenial and the lady of the house will do a small load of laundry free of charge.

MT. TSURUGI

A 40 km stretch of unpaved, but well-graded road links Anabuki with Tsurugi-san (1955 m). Bus (twice a day), prohibitively expensive taxi, thumb and walking are the only means of getting there. For the robust wishing to walk this invigorating trail, it is best to plan on 2 days. Camping spots are numerous, and fresh water is available at frequent mountain springs. The road parallels the Anabuki River and 30 km of Tsurugikyo Gorge, formed by its forceful cascading waters. The river, the gain in altitude and the umbrella of vegetation keep the trail cool and damp. Part of the trail was newly constructed following a violent typhoon in 1975 that changed the natural course of the river and destroyed parts of Anabuki itself.

walking the trail: The first of many pristine views is at Kanjono Taki (waterfall) about 6 km from Anabuki on the trail. The waterfall is marked by a sign on your right. The waters gush through a gap in the rock and plummet to the river below. Everywhere there are deep pools for swimming and the area boasts of excellent fishing. *Aiyu, ida* and *unagi* (eel) are some of the pan fish there for the catching. There are also 2 edible plants that grow prolifically along the trail.

from atop Mt. Tsurugi, Shikoku lies at your feet

One is *itadori*, a broad-leaved, hollow-stemmed plant that resembles rhubarb. Eat this semi-tart plant with a bit of salt. The other plant is *uro* which is sweeter and grows among thorn bushes. Any villager along the road can point them out. The mountains become razor sharp as you climb into the clouds, and the terraced fields hanging precariously over the ravines give way to scraggly pines. The rocks have a peculiar green tint, and mist cloaks the valleys below. Six km from the summit is Misogibashi, the official entrance to the mountain. Two km above it, on a steep trail, are Ryokoji and Tsurugi shrines. Here also is Fujinoike (Fuji Lake) and several spacious prayer halls where accommodations can be found for Y3000. July 17th is the annual shrine festival when thousands visit the area. The festival is enchanting, but accommodations are tight. Between Misogibashi and the summit is Minokoshi (go through the tunnel to your R)

where a 900 m chairlift will take you to within one hr of the summit. Minokoshi has a small souvenir shop and basic restaurant (ramen Y300). At the summit you'll cross a wide, floral plain known as Ohana-batake. Just above it is the summit of Tsurugi from where Shikoku tumbles away at your feet. Autumn is the best time for trekking, the flora bathing the mountainsides with spectacular colors. Check with the locals for road conditions in winter. To make a complete walking tour of this area, descend on the W side to Kubo and spend the night there. Next day, hike to Deai where en route you'll pass Iyadani Gorge with its 50 m high rock walls. From Deai, bus to Ikeda. An alternative route is to bus back to Anabuki or to Sadamitsu, where you link up with the rail line to Ikeda. This entire area is excellent for hiking and camping, and the best suggestion is to combine bus and foot to see all the sights.

HOKKAIDO

INTRODUCTION

Hokkaido is the child of modern Japan. It is scarcely 100 years since the Meiji Restoration that the Japanese have seriously considered it a viable place to live. Before that it was home only to the vanquished, homeless, and the aborigines of Japan, the Ainu. It is the only area of Japan that merits the word wilderness. Hokkaido possesses Japan's most precious resource-land. The pioneer spirit prevails, and enterprising young Japanese still come here to homestead and carve out their futures. Get your second wind here when you are "templed out" and need a break from the crowds. The ancient trappings of tradition that are borne by age are left far behind on Honshu and the southern areas. Here you will find wide open spaces, brazen frontier towns, vibrant villages clinging for life on spectacular shores. Its people are concerned more with survival than decorum. The beauty is not in the towns, but rather in the mountains behind the towns and in the shores surrounding

them. The towns look temporary, as though they are just waiting for someone to knock them down and put up something permanent. In Hokkaido, bears still roam, and in outlying villages you can get *soba* with *shika*, venison. Japan's newest volcano is here, Showa Shinzan, created in July of 1945. Natural wonders and impressive vistas are everywhere; Noboribetsu Spa in Shikotsu-Toya National Park is known for its medicinal waters and the last vestige of communal bathing. The Valley of Hell (Jigokudani) in this area has seen many suicides as even entire families have jumped into its bubbling cauldrons. Lake Mashu reflects Mt. Mashu towering over it, and the air is full of deep, mysterious vibrations. Kushiro is a wild and woolly town full of horse traders, loggers and fishermen. The women either break their backs in the local canneries, or lie on them in numerous brothels. Hokkaido is the land of the backpacker, wilderness explorer, skier and trout fisherman. It is rustic, rural Japan. Remember that Sapporo is here also with a population of one million plus, with fine restaurants, cushy hotels and a university. In Hokkaido, you won't need your black tie and tails, but you will need good hiking boots and woolen shirts. You won't see ancient temples steeped in tradition, but you will walk miles of trails to snow-capped mountains. Hokkaido is the other face of Japan; new, bright, untamed.

GETTING THERE

The most time-saving but expensive way of arriving in Hokkaido is by air. The fares are constantly changing, but you can expect to spend around Y40,000 from Tokyo to Sapporo. JAL, ANA and TOA all fly regularly to Hokkaido. There are 8 main airports scattered throughout the island. Chitose and Okadama (Sapporo), Asahikawa, Hakodate, Obihiro, Kushiro, Memambetsu and Wakkanai. All but the last two are connected to Honshu by direct flight.

by ferry: There are 2 main ferry routes to Hokkaido, both originating at the Tokyo Ferry Terminal, but terminating at opposite ends of the island. The Kinaki Yusen Ferry Co. goes to Kushiro in the SE of Hokkaido, while Nippon Enkai Ferry Co. arrives at Tomakomai in the SW, 70 km below Sapporo. The latter route is the most popular. Both take about 35 hrs.; a 20% discount on 2nd class tickets is allowed upon presentation of a valid International Student Card. First-class ticket holders get their own cabins. If you travel the more economical 2nd class, you will be human cargo allotted you own 1 m-by-2 m space on the carpeted floor of the large communal cabin. Meals are expensive; expect to spend Y1000 for a basic dinner, so take canned food and fresh fruit. Hot water is always available, so carry instant drinks: tea, coffee, etc. Dates of departures are variable. To get to the ferry terminal in Tokyo, there is a bus available from Tokyo Station (Marunouchi Minami-guchi Exit) departing at 2000. The only other way is by taxi (expensive).

alternative ferry routes: There are a number of less-traveled alternative ferry routes to Hokkaido. Along the Japan Sea side, you can board a ferry at Maizuru or Tsuruga, located at Wakasa Bay about 70 km N of Kyoto. Its destination is Otaru (33 hrs) about 30 km NW of Sapporo. This ferry stops at Niigata in SW Tohoku where you can board and continue your journey

to Hokkaido (18 hrs, 30 mins). There are 2 ferries available from the E coast of Tohoku that make port at Tomakomai in Hokkaido. The one from Sendai makes the voyage in 16 hr and the other from Hachinoche, further N along the coast, takes about 9 hours.

combination rail and ferry: This is the most common method of getting to Hokkaido. If you tour Tohoku, you will inevitably arrive in Aomori. In Aomori you will find the two most traveled and crowded ferries to Hokkaido. The main one plies the Tsugaru Strait between Aomori and Hakodate (4 hrs, Y1300, 2nd class), while the other makes for Muroran (4 hrs, 20 mins) about 130 km S of Sapporo. When you arrive at Aomori Eki, turn left after getting off the train. You will see an overpass. This is the way to the ferry terminal. Don't leave the *eki*. Buy your ticket and fill out your boarding pass to save time and hassle. When boarding is called, get in line as quickly as possible as these ferries are often overcrowded and seats are at a preimium. There are 2 other less-traveled ferries in this area that go to Hakodate. One leaves from Noheji, about 30 km E of Aomori (4hrs) and the other embarks at Oma at the northern tip of Shimokita Peninsula, and makes the crossing in one hour. The longest tunnel in the world (55km) is nearing completion under the Tsugaru Straits. This will link Tokyo and Sapporo in only 5 hrs. by Shinkansan and its opening, scheduled for 1983, will mark the end of Hokkaido's isolation.

TRANSPORT WITHIN HOKKAIDO

Hokkaido's main cities and towns are all linked by rail, which is the most convenient means of transportation on the island. One drawback is that due to the distances between places of interest, it can be very expensive. There are fewer convenient *futsu* available in Hokkaido, so in order to travel with even moderately good connections and speed, you are always being charged extra for the *kyuko*. *shuyuken:* The one simple and economical way around these prices is to use the special rail pass called the *shuyuken*, which allows unlimited train travel for a specified number of days from the point of purchase and back again. The best *shuyuke* available for Hokkaido is purchased in Senda and enables you to travel for 21 days including all JNR ferries (Aomori-Hokadate) and all JNR operated buses. It costs Y20,000 and a student discount of 20% is available. In other parts of Japan the pass isn't really necessary, but it

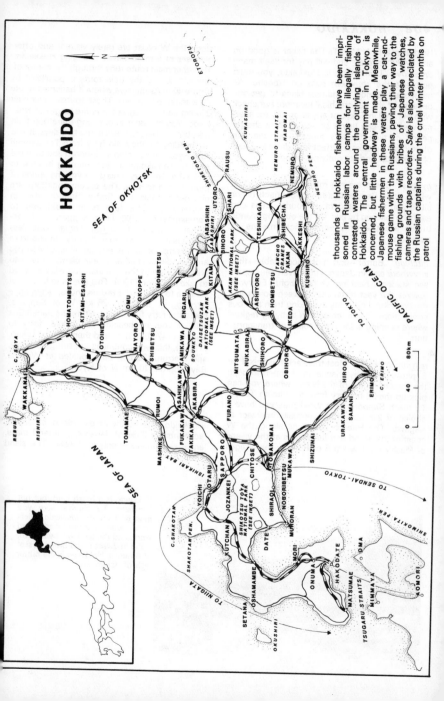

HOKKAIDO

SEA OF OKHOTSK

SEA OF JAPAN

PACIFIC OCEAN

ETOROFU

KUNASHIRI

NEMURO STRAITS

HABOMAI

NEMURO PEN.

C. SOYA

WAKKANAI

REBUN

RISHIRI

HOMATOMBETSU

KITAMI-ESASHI

OMU

OKOPPE

MOMBETSU

OTOINEPPU

NAYORO

SHIBETSU

ENGARU

KAMIKAWA

ASAHIKAWA

KITAMI

ABASHIRI

ASAHIKAWA-UTORO

SHIBETORO PEN.

RAUSU

SHARI

TESHIKAGA

SHIBECHA

AKKESHI

TANCHO CRANES AKAN

HOMBETSU

ASHIYORO

KUSHIRO

DAISETSUZAN NATIONAL PARK (SEE INSET)

SOUNKYO

AKAN NATIONAL PARK (SEE INSET)

FUKAGAWA

TAKIKAWA

AKABIRA

RUMOI

MASHIKE

TOMAMAE

ISHIKARI BAY

FURANO

MITSUMATA

NUKABIRA

SHIHORO

OBIHORO

IKEDA

HIROO

SAMANI

URAKAWA

SHIZUNAI

MUKAWA

TOMAKOMAI

CHITOSE

SAPPORO

OTARU

JOZANKEI

KUTCHAN

YOICHI

C. SHAKOTAN

SHAKOTAN PEN.

SHIKOTSU-TOYA NATIONAL PARK (SEE INSET)

SHIRAOI

NOBORIBETSU

DATE

MURORAN

MORI

ONUMA

HAKODATE

MATSUMAE

MIMMAYA

OMA

AOMORI

TSUGARU STRAITS

SHIMOKITA PEN.

OKUSHIRI

OSHAMAMBE

SETANA

C. ERIMO

ERIMO

TO TOKYO

TO SENDAI - TOKYO

TO NIIGATA

0   40   80km

N

thousands of Hokkaido fishermen have been imprisoned in Russian labor camps for illegally fishing
contested waters around the outlying islands of
Hokkaido. The central government in Tokyo is
concerned, but little headway is made. Meanwhile,
Japanese fishermen in these waters play a cat-and-
mouse game with the Russians, paving their way to the
fishing grounds with bribes of Japanese watches,
cameras and tape recorders. *Sake* is also appreciated by
the Russian captains during the cruel winter months on
patrol

Hokkaido it is A MUST. The ticket is good on any *kyuko* or *futsu*, and will pay for itself many times over. Unavailable in Hokkaido, you must purchase the *shuyuken* pass on Honshu. As mentioned, Sendai is the best place to get one because of the geographical location, but check with the JNR in Tokyo or any large city for alternatives. You can buy a *shuyuken* for a shorter period of time for less money, but the one offered for 3 weeks is perfect for a complete tour of Hokkaido and its outlying islands.

by bus: Buses are the major means of travel within cities. Regular bus service connects major cities and towns, and major tourist areas can easily be reached by bus. On the outlying islands buses are the only economical means of transport.

hitching: Better—and more acceptable—than anywhere else in Japan, you'll even see Japanese students hitching—a rare sight. Everyone realizes the vast distances between points and the occasional difficulty in making train and bus connections. There are certain outlying regions where hitching is *the only* means of transportation.

leaving Hokkaido: Most travelers must head for Sapporo unless by chance you happen to be in the eastern region of the island where you can pick up the 32 hr ferry from Kushiro to Tokyo. To reach Sapporo from Wakkanai, you have a choice of 2 routes that eventually intersect at Kagawa. The Haboro Line runs along the W coast of the island and terminates at the village of Mashike, a few km S of Rumoi. The villages along the W coast are rarely visited, and offer glimpses of a more slowly changing Hokkaido. The other main route runs through the center of the island, and the train route is paralleled by Route 40 to Asahigawa where it becomes Route 12 leading to Sapporo. These routes cover over 350 km and cut across the entire length of Hokkaido. You can do it in one long marathon train ride, but it is best to break it into two days. If you are heading for the main ferry from Tomakomai to Tokyo, you can stop in Sapporo and take the train to Tomakomai in the morning in time to make the 1145 ferry. This gives you the option of more places to stay. The accommodations are cheaper and easier to find in Sapporo than in Tomakomai. The fare from Wakkanai to Tomakomai is Y5700. From Sapporo to Tomakomai it is Y1380. *from Tomakomai;* Unbelievably, it is very difficult to find a bus running from Tomakomai *eki* to the ferry terminal. Unless you are very determined and have plenty of time to walk the 6 km to the terminal, you will be forced to take a taxi for Y1000. This seems to be a local scheme to bolster the taxi revenues. *alternative ferry route;* In Otaru, 25 km W of Sapporo, board the ferry for Honshu along the Japan Sea side. If you are heading for Tokyo, ferry to Niigata (Y4700, 19 hrs), and then train to Tokyo, (Y3000), this ferry continues to Tsuruga (31 hrs), and Maizuru (33 hrs) both located at Wakasa Bay, approx. 70 km N of Kyoto.

THE LAND

Hokkaido, the northernmost island of Japan, accounts for 23% of Japan's total land mass, and is second in size only to Honshu. The island

Hokkaido is a harsh land, but not merciless. To survive here you must back up your idealistic beliefs with good old-fashioned hard work, and the land will bear forth. If the midwest is the bread basket of America, Hokkaido is the butter dish of Japan

encompasses 83,500 sq km, including outlying islands. At one point, Hokkaido is separated from Honshu by only 18 km across the Tsugaru Straits. Hokkaido lies at about the same latitude as Pittsburgh, Pennsylvania and Genoa, Italy. The seas around Hokkaido are dotted with numerous islands. The Habomai islands lie off the E coast, with Shitokan further out to sea. Kunashiri and Etorofu are due E of Cape Shiretoko, and the outstanding islands of Rebun and Rishiri lie W of Wakkanai. Sakhalin, a large island N of Wakkanai, covered in dense forest and surrounded by excellent fishing grounds, was captured along with 3 other, smaller islands in the Kurilies by the Russians when they entered WW11 during its final week. This remains a bitter injustice in the minds of the Japanese, who unsuccessfully try from time to time to reclaim these islands in the UN. Sixty percent of Hokkaido's interior is covered in forest; 36% of the trees are conifers, and the remaining various leaf varieties. The coastlines are dramatic, the rivers are clear and deep, and the blue skies and crisp, brisk air remain unpolluted. Hokkaido's shape resembles a tall mountain reflected in a tranquil lake. It stretches 400 km from N to S from Cape Soya to Cape Erimo, and 440 km E to W from Nemuro to Setana. In this area lie the last stretches of wilderness in Japan: wild bubbling hot springs; majestic lava-seared mountains; trout-filled lakes and lush, untrampled meadows, home to deer, rabbit and wild bear. Though aesthetics are manifested in flower arranging, garderning and the tea ceremony, the Japanese spirit of adventure and freedom thrive in Hokkaido. Inevitably, the completion of the tunnel under the Tsugaru Straits, scheduled now for 1983, will finally link Hokkaido with mainland Japan. It has been a dream that has taken a long time to materialize, but when it does, it will be a marvel—at 55 km, the longest tunnel in the world.

climate: Hokkaido experiences 4 distinct seasons like the rest of Japan, but lying so far north, it is generally cooler in summer (22 C in July) and cold, snowy and blustery in winter (-5 C average in Jan.). Because of the cool summers, various groups including students, affluent Japanese, and foreigners head for Hokkaido to escape the hot, stuffy climate of southern Honshu. The main tourist flood occurs from June through September, spilling its banks in August. The cherry blossoms burst forth in late May and a variety of colorful wild flowers cover the floors of the deep northern forests all summer long. The fall—Oct. to Nov.—is clear, crisp and brilliant. The nights are coal black and the stars seem only an arms-length apart. Autumn is the least touristed time of the year in Hokkaido, and also the most underrated. The days are sunny, and nature has one last magnificent fling, turning the leaves into dazzling reds, oranges and yellows. In winter, Hokkaido is either the hostile, frozen north or a white diamond-studded wonderland, depending on your point of view. The snows lasts 4-5 months, from Nov. to March, on the Japan Sea side, reaching depths of 3 m, while on the E coast they average only ½ meter. Sapporo was the home of the 1972 Olympics and the skiing was magnificent. Anyone arriving in Japan during the winter should not discount a trip to Hokkaido. It is feasible that you could be shushing the slopes of Teine Olympia near Sapporo and a few days later, by a combination of train and ferry, or just a matter of hours by plane, can be luxuriating on the sandy sun-drenched beaches of Okinawa. This is a desirable combination, and even a visit of 10 days, with the use of internal flights, would be sufficient.

FLORA AND FAUNA

The woodlands of central Hokkaido still team with wildlife, although these timberlands have continuously decreased to make room for man's expansion. Bear (*kuma*) still roam the thickets and natural pastures deep in the mountains of central Hokkaido. There is an open hunting season on these animals. Though they have been known to very infrequently attack domestic animals and even man, their main diet consists of berries, rabbits and fish that they manage to snag in the upland streams. The villagers believe that the bears hibernate (Dec.-Apr.) with their paws laden with honey and ants to eat on awakening. Their fur brings good money from the dealers, and their intesttines and glands are sought by drug manufacturers. This helps lead to their demise. Hikers should be aware of *kuma*, and take basic precautionary measures. Remember that a bear is more frightened of you than you are of it, and will make every effort to run away. If you are attacked, lie down and play dead. Don't run—this only triggers its killing instinct and this lumbering beast can do the 100m dash in 6 seconds. At night, keep a fire burning and, most importantly of all, hang your food in a bag high in a tree away from your campground. Your chances of encountering a bear, however, are extremely remote.

the bear, an Ainu totem, is the symbol of untamed Hokkaido

shika (_deer_): Deer roam freely in Hokkaido, and are hunted for food. Shika soba, which is an exceptionally tasty dish, is available in the small villages of the interior. Deer feed at dawn and dusk, so your chances are best at these times to observe them.

oshorokoma (_Ainu_), _iwana_ (_Japanese_): A type of trout indigenous to Japan and a delight for the fisherman. Your casting arm will uncontrollably itch when you pass the clear mountain streams and deep blue lakes of Hokkaido. Lakes Shikaribetsu and Nukabira are famous for their rainbow trout while the small, fighting, snake-eating _iwana_ have the firm light taste of the wild mountain streams. An ultra-light collapsible pole, a mini reel and a film cannister which can easily hold all of the tackle necessary for trout fishing (swivels, split shot and hooks) will add less than a pound to your pack and provide hours of relaxation and entertainment. Dig

mushi (worms) for bait or turn over rocks for insects. Heat up the old skillet. Trout wrapped in foil and baked over hot coals is delicious, or poke a slender stick through your catch and turn slowly over your fire.

tsuru (_cranes_): The crane is the symbol of a long life filled with happiness, because the Japanese say that they live for 1000 years. In truth, some specimens have been known to live for 80 years. The most outstandingly beautiful crane in Japan is the _tancho_ (red-crested crane). It is a long-legged, pointed-billed, white-bodied bird trimmed in black. It has scarlet plumage on its head. It inhabits the Kushiro plain and the base of Mt. Akan. The birds mate for life and after an elaborate and surprisingly graceful courtship dance, the female lays 2 eggs in late March. The parents choose only one to nurture, which the male helps incubate. The chick is born into a gigantic reed nest, and the cycle repeats itself. The crane is a national monument, but this distinction, instead of helping the bird, may lead to its extinction. Although only 200 cranes remain, this number is a big improvement over the meager 25 that neared extinction only 40 years ago. The _tancho_ does not migrate like other birds of its species but stays in Hokkaido and moves to established feeding grounds in the winter. The local villagers jealously regard the cranes as their own, and when a pair come to visit an area, they consider it a good omen. The people of Hokkaido resent any outside study of the birds, and this attitude is mirrored by the government which refuses to issue study permits to scientists who are forbidden to study the birds or even go within 30 m of their nests. This is a case in which misguided love is killing the

birds. Encroachment upon the habitat by agricultural and building demands is the largest factor leading to the birds' demise. Land has been set aside for *tancho,* but experts say more is needed. The crane is a long-established artistic motif and its graceful outline appears in art forms from delicate paintings to patterns for kimonos and to New Year's cards. Let us hope that these majestic birds lifting into the twilight of a Hokkaido sunset and trumpeting their deep, resonant song will fulfill the legacy of their symbol and live for 1000 years.

trees: This is a land of trees. In the southern areas of Hokkaido, where the climate is a bit milder, there are forests of broad-leaved trees such as the native beech, and a few imported varieties such as maples lining the avenues and streets of towns. As one heads N, the broadleaved varieties give way to the heartier conifer specimens such as larch, spruce and fir. *Yesso* spruce and *Sakhilan* fir also cover the outlying islands. They can tolerate the harsh winter blasts and they provide excellent windbreaks when you pitch your tent among them. *flowers:* People usually associate mild climates and balmy breezes with flowers, but this assumption also applies to chillier northern climes. Hokkaido becomes a rhapsody of wild flowers as soon as the snows disappear. There are cherry blossms and lilacs; and their viewing provides hours of meditation for the Japanese and traveler alike. The islands of Rebun and Rishiri are particularly known for their flowers. Mid-June on Rebun features a flower festival. Hikers head for Mowiwa, a famous spot on Rebun, just to soak up the natural beauty and view the flowers. *Usuyuiso,* a white pointed flower with a yellow center, is found only on Rebun. There is also the *uki torano,* a long purple flower on a thin stem resembling a bush caterpillar. As you climb above 1000 m on Fuji-shaped Rishiri, the alpine plants take over and the ground is covered like a giant, intricate colorful embroidery. Delicate, yellow *botan kinbai* are among the most common.

marine products: The sea also pitches in with edible seaweed called *kombu.* This yellowish green seaweed is harvested off the northern coasts and islands. Fishermen and women in rubboots gather it and place it along the shore to dry. *Marimo* is another curious specialty found only at Lake Yamanaka near Mt. Fuji, and at Lake Akan in Hokkaido. This curious green spherical duckweed serves as a barometer and forecasts the weather. When the weather is fine,

it floats. When the weather turns nasty, it sinks. At one time people gathered *marimo* to place in their aquariums. Biologists feared that this would cause it to diminish. A plea was sent out to return it to the lake. Over 2,000 people complied, yet another testament to the national pride of the Japanese. When you visit Lake Akan, look, but don't touch. You will still be able to buy this curiosity in some of the many gift shops in the area.

HISTORY

When Tokyo was a metropolitan giant in the 18th C., Hokkaido was still the domain of the Ainu who hunted wild bear. Formerly known as Ezo (alien people who live in the north), Hokkaido was the last area of Japan to be developed, and indeed for centuries was not considered a part of Japan. It was a hostile, northern wasteland, inhabited by barbarians and steeped in mystery. The Japanese certainly knew of its existence, but made no attempt to colonize it. Hokkaido appeared in Japanese literature as early as the 6th C. when Abe-no-Hirafu vanquished the Ainu and drove them out of Tohoku and into Hokkaido. The people of Tohoku, sometimes straggled to its shores in times of war and famine, but no political or social ties were made until the Ainu Chieftain, Koshamain, rebelled in the 15th C. and was defeated by Nobuhiro Takeda, opening Hokkaido to expansion. At the turn of the 16th C., Yoshihiro Takada, the 3rd-generation progeny of Nobuhiro, joined forces with Ieyasu Tokugawa and brought Hokkaido under the influence of the shogun's cen-

statue of Hokkaido's 19th C. American agricultural advisor, Dr. W. S. Clark

tral authority. This marked the official subjugation and consequent settlement of Hokkaido. Ieyasu closed Japan for 2½ centuries, and this included Hokkaido. Finally, in 1854, after the arrival of Commodore Perry, Hakodate was opened as one of the free ports of Japan. Western culture flowed freely in Hokkaido, especially American farming methods. One of the earliest advisers, Dr. W.S. Clark of Amherst College, established the Sapporo Agricultural College in 1876. Along with the Americans came the barns, silos and dairy herds sitting on large farms of 64 hectares and more. (The average Japanese farm is only .8 hectares). A statue erected to Clark bears his departing words, "Boys be ambitious." Obviously there must have been no girls educated in Hokkaido at the time, and modern Japanese students remember this prophetic phrase as "Boys be undershirts," thereby allotting it the place in history that it deserves. In 1869, the name of the island was changed from Ezo to Hokkaido. In 1870, Sapporo became the capital city. It was planned by the American, Horace Caprin, and laid out in 1872 in checkerboard fashion with wide avenues and parks. Today, it remains the easiest Japanese city to get around in and even has numbered streets and addresses. After WW11, the development of Hokkaido was dramatic. It now produces quantities of dairy products, wood and fish. Still, only 5% of the Japanese population lives here. There is still elbow room and scattered farmhouses where you can't see your nearest neighbor.

THE ECONOMY

The basis for Hokkaido's economy are the primary industries of agriculture, dairy farming, forestry and wood products, fishing, steel production and coal. The tourist trade is important but small. A 10-year Hokkaido Development Program, directed at elevating the productivity of the island, was launched in 1971. One goal was to create a pollution-free industrial area south of Sapporo geared toward heavy industry. _farming:_ Hokkaido has the space for large, mechanized farms. Unlike the rest of Japan, it engages primarily in dry-field farming, which produces potatoes, sugar beets, beans, animal fodders, and peppermint — as well as rice. Here you will see New England-style farms complete with red barns and Harvestore silos. Hokkaido is slightly smaller than Maine and shares its climate. Bumper stickers read "Drink more milk" — at one time milk was an anaethema to the Japanese; now it is slowly but steadily becoming a part of the diet. Hokkaido butter is renowned for its

purity and flavor. White-fenced farms are homes to thoroughbred horses on the W coast as well as for draft horses, at one time used for farming, and now only used for bamba — an old-fashioned horse pull. _forestry:_ Hokkaido accounts for 30% of Japan's wood resources. The forests in the N are made up of Yesso spruce and Sakhalin fir, which make fine pulp and lumber. The southern forests consist of Japanese beech, a hardwood. With proper management, the forests of Hokkaido can provide years of this useful, renewable resource. The reserves are well

when Hokkaido was pioneered, its rich coal deposits were mined by hand. The fledgling industries of the S depended upon the backbreaking work of Hokkaido's tireless turn-of-the-century settlers

tended and conservation is ingrained. Wherever the trees are felled, they are replanted or become productive fields. Japan learns its lessons well.

other industries: The other major industries are steel production and mining. Along with the production of steel comes the manufacture of heavy equipment and farm machinery. Murora is the center of the smelting processes. Coal the primary reason for mining. Over 50% of the nation's total lies in thick veins in western Hokkaido. Gold, platinum and even oil, although extremely limited, are also found here. Sapporo produces beer, and a number of distilleries produce wine, sake and the potent _shochu._ Hokkado is alive with factories and manufacturing, but the areas are concentrated, and the space available is vast. Pollution is essentially under control.

fishing: In Hokkaido, as in all of Japan, the sea is the most fertile natural resource; its indominable presence is felt not only in fishing villages, but far inland. The smell of drying fish and seaweed flavors the air. Nets, glass buoys and a menagerie of boats are seen in every coastal town and village. Most farmhouses keep racks for drying fish and seaweed; as a large percentage of the daily diet is seafood. The Japanese fishermen set out to sea in everything from motorized canoes to enormous sea-going canning factories. Offshore, the women gather oysters and don hip boots and rakes to gather

the edible kelp from the coastal waters to lay on the rocky shores to sun dry. King crab, salmon, mackerel, squid and cod are caught further out to sea. These hauls account for 20% of Japan's yearly total. Women in bonnets and *monpe* wait at the canneries for men to come home. The preparation of the fish is a communal, cooperative effort. Japan and Russia have been feuding for years over the islands N of Hokkaido seized during WW11. Russia extended its coastal boundaries, severing most of the prime fishing spots from the Japanese. The fishermen, driven by necessity, quietly fish these waters. Over 10,000 have been arrested, fined or imprisoned. A quiet battle rages. The Russo-Japanese treaty remains unsigned, and the yearly tonnage gets smaller and smaller. Only world opinion and pressure can change the situation.

the Ainu heritage and ways are dying. A few sad tourist areas feature them in their *kotan* (traditional Ainu villages) where they are as captive as the bears they worship

THE PEOPLE

The "average" Japanese person does not live in Hokkaido. In Hokkaido there is room to breathe, the spaces are bigger. Those born here find it ludicrous to live in cramped cities, in miniscule apartments fighting rush-hour traffic jams. Those that move here have the pioneer spirit or are escaping the cities. Some look for a better life, some seek themselves. Surely there are young people who pine for the flash and

excitement of Tokyo, but once the spirit of the north country takes hold, it is hard to shake it off. Most Hokkaidoans are a bit less refined than city dwellers, but much more expansive. Survival against the elements produces a simplicity that puts life into a basic perspective. Hokkaidoans laugh more heartily, speak more loudly; they don't worry about social graces, they have fun. They smoke less and drive faster. These are the Asian counterparts to rural Americans, outback Australians and North-Country Canadians: kind, curious and open. Enjoy what they have to offer.

the Ainu: Scholars differ on the origin of this light-skinned, round-eyed, full-bearded race. Some say that they are a caucasoid strain whose origins are from the steppes of Siberia. Others believe that they are of Mongolian descent. One fact is uncontested: they are the original settlers of Hokkaido and northern Tohoku, and like many indigenous peoples, the Indians of North and South America, the Aborigines of Australia and the mountain peoples of Viet Nam, they have been driven off their ancestral lands, their culture has been destroyed, and they are now 2nd class citizens. It is difficult to say how many pure-blooded Ainu remain. Some say none, others put the figure at 100 or so. There are probably 15,000-20,000 people with some Ainu blood. They were long defeated before the Meiji Restoration, but this period forced them to abandon their language, customs and dress. Their heritage has lingered on the brink of extinction ever since. A few cling to their roots in an attempt to preserve the rituals and the language. Unfortunately for them and for the Japanese, no support is forthcoming from the government. Today, these small, charming people ply the tourist trade for their livelihood. Two model villages (*kotan*) are located at Shiraoi on the shores of Lake Shikotsu, and Chika Bumi on the outskirts of Asahigawa. Here for a small fee the elders (*emeshi*) will give you a tour of their thatch-and-reed homes, and relate stories of the olden times. The women and young people will dance, and all will pose for pictures. Tips are expected. In Akan National Park, a few small groups of Ainu live in the more traditional manner, although none actually live without the touch of modern civilization. These groups are made up of old men, still sporting their long, flowing beards, and their wives, a few of whom have the traditional blue tatooing around their mouths. This practice is now prohibited by law.

ARTS AND CRAFTS

Perhaps it is a fact of life that where survival in a harsh land is a preoccupation of daily life, arts and crafts become secondary pursuits. This is not to say that in Hokkaido there are not fine sculptors, potters, caligraphers and artists, but there are no real specialized centers for these activities. In the cities, towns and villages, numerous shops sell locally produced artifacts, but these are the whims of the artists and follow no set patterns or traditions. A few notable exceptions are Ainu-inspired carvings, including long, pointed, intricately worked sticks used as moustache lifters. High-flying kites are made throughout Hokkaido; especially famous are those from Rebun Island, where kite flying from Mt. Rebun is outstanding. Unfortunately, these kites do not readily dismantle, so would be difficult to send home, but the painted paper used in making them can be easily stripped off and make excellent framed pictures. The few remaining Ainu, and other Hokkaidoan craftsmen, make skillful carvings of bears, birds and totems. The better could be elevated to objects of art; unfortunately, these carvings are not really traditional. They are the good idea of an Austrian who visited the Ainu at the turn of the century and suggested their manufacture as a way of making money.

Ainu art: If you are interested in authentic Ainu art, visit the Bachelor Museum, a western-style house built in 1891, at the Hokkaido University Botanical Gardens in Sapporo. John Bachelor was a British missionary at the turn of the century who dedicated his life to the Ainu and the preservation of their ways. There are 20,000 artifacts in this museum, featuring simple designs on cloth, weavings, and implements of daily life. Here is captured the essence of the Ainu way of life. Here you will see fine examples of *attushes*, long coats worn by men and women woven from Japanese witch elm. For Ainu woodcarving, go to Tonako, Noboribetsu, Shiraoi, Onneyu, Akan; for *atsushi* (cloth), try Asahikawa City.

an *Ainu* woodcarving

FESTIVALS OF HOKKAIDO

Feb., 1st weekend: Yuki Matsuri (Sapporo Snow Festival). Here the Japanese celebrate the most obvious wonder of Hokkaido—the snow. The entire city turns out and the main avenues feature a contest of gigantic, but intricately carved ice sculptures. The atmosphere is festive, and the emphasis is on the great outdoors. This is one of the most renowned winter festivals in Japan. The skiing at this time is great, but accommodations are tight, and the slopes are jammed. This festival is also held at Mombetsu, Abashiri and Asahikawa, Obihiro.

May, last weekend: Lilac Festival, Sapporo. These beautiful purple flowers are abundant in Hokkaido and signal the coming of summer. Lake Onuma, a few km N of Hakodate, is also famous for its heady-scented lilacs.

mid-June: Shrine Festival, Sapporo. This is a parade of _mikoshi_ (portable shrines) carried from their temples through the streets and back, to give thanks to the _kami_. If you like parades, attend. If not, give it a miss.

Late-June: Orochon (Fire Festival). Held at Abashiri on the Sea of Okhotsk. Both fire and hearth are an integral part of Ainu belief. Fire is the domain of Fuchi, the fire goddess, benevolent grandmother who provides Ainu households with light and warmth. Celebrated with dancing and gaiety, this festival is a perfect time to see the Ainu in costume, when shaman and _miko_ exhibit their dances to the spirits.

early Aug.:   Mid-summer Festival. Held in Sapporo, this festival resembles a German Beer Festival with drinking stands and beer gardens. The wise will come prepared with their best hangover remedy.

Oct. 8-10:   Marimo Matsuri. On and in the depths of Lake Akan roll around fuzzy, moss-like weeds called _marimo_. These bright green balls are the focus of a new festival featuring Ainu dancing in traditional dress, and culminating, on the 10th, in a ceremonious scattering of _marimo_ over the waters—in thanksgiving for it having lured tourists, and thus a measure of prosperity, to the lake's surrounding inhabitants.

Winter, date flexible: Bear Festival. At many Ainu villages and at L. Akan. This festival is a vestige of the times when the Ainu governed Hokkaido and their shamanist religion was universally practiced. The bear has special significance to the Ainu. They believe that bears live deep in the mountains at the "source of water" and, while living there, they dress and act like men. When a bear wanders close to a village, it is believed that the _kami_ (spirit) of a man trapped inside is asking to be released so that it can return to the spirit world. In olden times, the killing of the bear followed strict rituals. Special arrows were made to shoot the bear from four directions. One was aimed at the heart. The carcass was dragged to a special altar adorned with carved poles and _sake_ and _mochi_ were offered. The body was dismembered and the head became a talisman, displayed at the home of the tribal chief. The bear meat was served to all the participants, to celebrate the liberation of the spirit. At first, observance of this practice may appear cruel, but take into consideration that the Ainu, living so close to the land, depended upon the creatures of the forest for nourishment. In killing the bear, they believed that they were performing an honorable service to the spirits of the Ainu. Today, Ainu hunters trap a bear cub and bring it to the village, placing it into a log cage. It becomes an attraction, like its keepers. It is not so much mistreated as not treated at all. It sits dazed, captured and helpless. The tragedy is in its loss of freedom. Today the captive bear is a symbol of the Ainu more so than ever. The modern Japanese in this more enlightened age should realize that the Ainu are neither a disgrace nor a detriment, but a unique race and cultural asset and that their heritage must be preserved.

SOUTH OF SAPPORO

HAKODATE

If you have wound your way overland through Honshu towards Hokkaido, you will most likely arrive in Hakodate by ferry from Aomori. Hakodate is merely a port town and a stop along the way. It holds little interest and you should head N towards Onuma as quickly as possible. If you have a few hours between trains in Hakodate, there is one place worth visiting. Goryokaku Fort, completed in 1864, is a massive earth-and-stone European-style fort built in the shape of a 5-pointed star. (Bus from Hakodate Eki, or street car to Goryokaku). It was a stronghold of the Tokugawa Shogunate defended by Takeaki Enomoto, which fell in 1868 after a bitter siege. The grounds are now a park, and a museum holds relics and mementos from the battle.

accommodations: Western-style hotels include: Hakodate Kokusai Hotel, 5-10 Ote-machi, Hakodate, 040, tel: (0138) 23-8751, a 5-min walk from Hakodate Eki; and Hotel Hakodate Royal, 16-19 Omori-cho, Hakodate, tel: (0138) 26-8181, 5 min by car from Hakodate Eki. Both offer single rooms from Y5000 up. However, the best accomodations are at the nearby spa town of Yunokawa Onsen. From Hakodate Eki, take streetcar number 5 or 8 to Yunokawa. Also many buses. There are numerous _ryokan_ starting from Y7000 with 2 meals. Three of these are: the Hanabishi Hotel, Yunokawa Onsen, Hakodate City 042, tel: (0138) 57-0131; Ryokan Yunokawa Kanko Hotel, Yunokawa Onsen, Hakodate City, 042, tel: (0138) 57-1188; and New Kokusai Hotel Asahikan, Yunokawa Onsen, Hakodate City 042, tel: (0138) 57-1161. Yunokawa Onsen also offers a youth hostel: Hokusei-so YH, 1-16-23 Yunokawa-machi, Hakodate City 042, tel: (0138) 57-3212, 25 mins by bus from Hakodate Eki, and 2 mins on foot.

ONUMA

Onuma is an agreeable little town to spend your first overnight stop in Hokkaido. It is flanked by 2 alluring lakes, Onuma and Konuma, topped by a very oddly shaped mountain, Mt. Koma (1133 m) that looks like it's wearing a beenie. The shores of Lake Onuma feature numerous camping areas, but beware of the mosquitos (_ka_). Onuma becomes crowded from late June to August. The town has a park and the grounds are manicured. There is a pathway leading over bridges which connect little islets along the shore. The scene—small rowboats (Y800/hr), frolicking families, and lily pads—is very civilized. Purple wisteria add a subtle touch in early summer. Although it is a park, people still earn their living as fishermen on this lake. Among the tourists glides a fisherman with his long-prowed boat... life goes on. Bicycles are available in town, but they cost Y300 per hour. Look around, relax, and head N in the morning.

ONUMA

getting there: If you have not purchased a _shuyuken_ (point-to-point ticket [see transport by rail, Introduction],) you will experience your first squeeze of falling into the grasp of JNR (kokutetsu). Heading toward Onuma, a mere 28 km N of Hakodate, you will be charged Y320 for your ticket, and a shocking Y400 for the _kyuko_—a charge that eliminates only 10 min of this 40-min run. This is a well-designed plot. The _futsu_ runs so infrequently that unless you pay the _kyuko_ charge, you can wind up twiddling your thumbs for hours at Hakodate Eki, a truly malignant thought for any serious traveler.

accommodations: There are a smattering of hotels and pensions in the area. The pensions average Y5000 per day including meals. Three youth hostels offer bunk and bath: Onuma Keiun-so YH, 326 Onuma-koen, Nanae-machi, Kameda-gun 041-13, tel: (013867) 2100, 5 min on foot from Onuma-koen Eki; and Ikusanda

Onuma YH, 498-6-7, Omuma-cho, Nanaemachi, Kameda-gun 041-03, tel: (013867) 3419, 8 min on foot from Onuma or Onuma-koen Eki.

from Onuma: Two main arteries head N toward Sapporo from Onuma: Hwy 5 (*Kokudo Go*), or by rail on the Hakodate Main Line. Both pass through the town of Oshamanbe where a decision has to be made. You can either continue NE to Sapporo or head E on to Muroran on Hwy 37 (*Kokudo San Ju Nana*) toward Date and Lake Toya, and further E toward Noboribetsu and the Ainu *kotan* (village) at Shiraoi. If you choose the eastern fork, you can swing back N toward Sapporo from Tomakomai on the Chitose Line or from Date on the Iburi Line, but you would miss Shiraoi. This detour will take an entire day. If you leave Onuma early on the *kyuko,* you can conceivably make Sapporo by nightfall, but it will be a long all-day haul. A more leisurely alternative is to stay at Lake Toya or move on to Shiraoi, spending the night there and heading for Sapporo in the morning.

SHIKOTSU-TOYA NATIONAL PARK AREA

Lake Toya: Located in the Shikotsu-Toya National Park, the closest to Hakodate and Sapporo. The heaviest tourist flow is late June through August. On the S shore is Showa-Shinzan, Japan's newest volcano. Created in July of 1945, a potato farmer saw its birth while tending his fields. He quickly gave up farming and became a civil servant. The volcano grew 20 cm per day for 7 months until it again erupted and formed a peak 400 m high. In 1978, Mt. Usu, close to Showa Shinzan, once again displayed the unsettled geology of this area. Fortunatley, preceding earthquakes warned the nearby villagers of the impending disaster and no lives were lost. Small quakes shook the surrounding countryside at the rate of 200 per hour. When the lid finally came off, steam and ash blew straight up but strong winds blew them back again and the nearby empty village (Toyako Onsen) was buried. Even in Sapporo the sun was darkened as soot and ash fell to earth for days. Follow Route 230 around the perimeter of Lake Toya for excellent scenic views. At the foot of Showa Shinzan is a museum with exhibits chronicling the volcanic activity of the area and nearby is the Ainu Memorial Hall with displays of artifacts of the Ainu people. Mt. Usu also boasts a fantastic museum (Abuta Kazan Kagaku-Kan) that realistically simulates the eruption of 1978. The entire natural drama is displayed on actual film footage complete with lightning, thunder and smoke. It is very close to the bus station. Just look for the fishing boat near the entrance way. The area abounds with hiking and trout fishing. Excursion boats are available, but expensive. Hakajima Island is in the center of Toya-Ko. It is the peak of an extinct volcano. The shoreline is rugged with many bays and inlets. This will be your first tame taste of Hokkaido's great outdoors. Toyako Spa is located here, famous for its curative waters.

accommodations: For the yen conscious, there are 2 youth hostels: Toya Kanko-kan YH, 83, Sobetsu-onsen, Sobetsu-cho, Usu-gun 052-01, tel: (01427) 5-2649, 22 min by bus from Toya Eki (200 beds): and Showa-Shinzan YH, 79, Sobetsu-onsen, Sobetsu-cho, Usu-gun, 052-1, tel: (01472) 5-2776, 30 min by bus from Toya Eki, and 2 min on foot. Numerous *ryokan* include: Manseikaku, Toyako Onsen, Abutacho 049-57, tel: (01427) 5-2171, 90 (w/b 75); Toya Kanko Hotel, Toyako Onsen, Abutacho 049-57, tel: (01427 5-2111, 103 (w/b 26); and Toya Park Hotel, Toyako Onsen, Abutacho 049-57, tel: (01427) 5-2445.

IN THE VICINITY

Noboribetsu: Ten km E of Toya-Ko is the largest resort in Hokkaido, and famous throughout Japan. The spa at the Dai-Ichi Takimoto Hotel is enormous with a gigantic bath over 100 m long where mixed bathing (_konyoku_) still occurs. Many bathers are either old women or children, so the experience is not as eye-opening as you might think. For the modest, there is a "women only" section. The Japanese keep their eyes down and mind their own business besides being masters at preserving modesty with a well-placed arm and strategically held towel. Western women and sometimes even men can experience some unwanted, mostly curious, leering. The best defense is to stare unsmilingly back. Few Japanese, especially when they are acting rudely, can sustain direct eye contact. Even the crudest will get the message. The little squirrels, poised around the perimeter, spout drinking water. If you feel woozy from the heat, take a dip in the shallow pool at the far end that holds refreshing cool water. The baths close to non-hotel guests at 1700. If you haven't had enough by then or if you intend to arrive later you can make arrangements at the front desk.

Jigokudani (The Valley of Hell): A few hundred m away. This is a vast ravine filled with bubbling streams and springs gushing boiling hot mineral waters and covered in swirling steam. The nearby slopes present a stark contrast of placid green. Above the crater is a seething mud lake, the devilish fountainhead of the sulphur springs (_oyunumo_). Many suicides have occurred here including entire families who have cast themselves into the Dante-like inferno. Clouds of smoke and steam fill the air. Walk only on designated paths. Some areas (roped off) have only a thin crust of ooze over boiling hot water. Take the road to the right on the way to Oyunumo Lookout. This leads (2.5 km) to Lake Kuttara and provides an excellent panorama of the area.

accommodations: Noboribetsu offers 5 YHs in the area surrounding Noboribetsu spa, as well as one in Noboribetsu itself. (Noboribetsu-Ekimae YH, 2-2-1-, Noboribetsu-higashi-cho, Noboribetsu City 059-04, tel: (01438) 3-1039, one min on foot from Noboribetsu Eki, 50 beds. Closed Dec. 28 through Feb.). Noboribetsu is an extremely well-known spa area with numerous _minshuku_ and _ryokan_. Most _ryokan_ start at Y10,000; the least expensive is Noboribetsu Grand Hotel, Noboribetsu Onsen, Noboribetsu City 059-05, tel: (01438) 4-2101, from Y7000.

konyoku (mixed bathing)

turn of the century *kotan*

Shiraoi: A model Ainu village (*kotan*) 20 km E of Noboribetsu on Rt 36 leading to Tomakomai. Modern-day Ainu recapture the past sitting in representative Ainu houses which display old family heirlooms. If there were a real vibrant culture still in existence and this were only a display, it would be fun. But realizing that this is all there is dampens your spirits and makes you feel plain bad. Perhaps instead of avoiding Shiraoi, it is best to go and see and observe another lesson of what happens when man doesn't LET IT BE. When you've had enough of the obviously staged and lifeless tourist displays and you can't stand to look at another sad little bear in a miniscule cage, head down the paved trail beside the pond near the *kotan*. This will take you with a little imagination back to primeval times. Lush vegetation and dense overhanging foliage create an eeriness evocative of the old Ainu culture and the spirits that they cherished. It's a reflective, refreshing hour's walk; a change from the contrived smartness of the tourist-enticing souvenir stands. Another notable exception to the dreariness of Shiraoi is the Ainu Museum. The well-appointed displays dramatize the simple and earthy Ainu culture that once was. Pick up the booklet "Shiraoi and Ainu" for an account of the Ainu's point of view on history and their absorption into modern day Japanese society. *accommodations:* The Shiraoi YH, 24-1, Shiraoi, Shiraoi-machi, Shiraoi-gun 059-09, tel: (01448) 2-2302, is 15 mins on foot from Shiraoi Eki

Lake Shikotsu: Also located within the confines of Shikotsu Toya National park. The best way to get here is to get to Chitose and then bus in. The lake has excellent trout fishing and succulent *zarigani* (crawfish). Lake Shikotsu at 363 m is the deepest lake in Hokkaido and 2nd only to Lake Tazawa on Honshu in all of Japan. Cruise boats can be hired from the marina near the bus terminal for a leisurely tour of the lake. You can disembark at Poropinai from where you can begin a climb of Mt. Eniwa. Mt. Trumae (1024 m) and Mt. Eniwa (1320 m) are 2 climbable, active volcanos, on the southern and northern shores of the lake, respectively. Mt. Eniwa is the tougher climb. Mt. Tarumae has bus service ¾ to the top with only a 40 min walk remaining to reach the summit. Either one presents a fantastic view of the park and Sapporo to the north. Neither is worth an entire day, but a long afternoon on the way to Sapporo should do it. *accommodations:* Two YHs serve the area: Shikotsu-ko YH, Shikotsu-kohan, Chitose City 066-22, tel: (012325) 2311, 40 min by bus from Tomakoamai Eki, and 3 min on foot, and Utonai-ko YH, Uenae, Tomakomai City 059-13, tel: (0144) 58-2853, 30 min by bus from Tomakomai Eki, and 7 min on foot.

SAPPORO

Sapporo (pop. 1,000,000 +) is the first prefectural capital and premier city of Hokkaido. In winter it is snowy, but relatively mild, with temperatures warmer than Boston and crack snow removal services. Sapporo was a planned city from its conception about 100 years ago. The downtown area, sprawling along the banks of the Toyohira River, has broad streets and avenues laid out in a 100-m grid system. This is very untypical of the maze of twisting, turning alleyways common to most Japanese cities. The streets have names and addresses which follow in numerical order. From all this order, don't get the impression that Sapporo is bland. It is not. Before Sapporo became a Japanese city, it was an Ainu village. Its name derived from a combination of Ainu words meaning "long, dry river." In 1870 the Governor of Hokkaido visited the United States and persuaded President Grant to send advisers. He complied, and Sapporo was built on the American plan. Most travelers to Hokkaido will eventually arrive in Sapporo. When you arrive, take advantage of what it has to offer before moving on into the interior. One or two days should be sufficient.

services: The Sapporo Eki is the hub of the city. All trains, subways and buses go to this station. Here you will find information booths with good maps, English-speaking tellers to make onward

going reservations, and a temporary parcel storage (Y200). As usual, there is _soba,_ available for a quick cheap lunch, and the restaurant at the top of the steps overlooking the main floor has good _teishoku_ for about Y600. A stroll through downtown Sapporo is definitely worth the time and effort. In a one km radius from Sapporo Eki you can hit all the high spots. The central P.O. is close-by. Exit S and turn R (W); it is 100 m down on the lefthand side. For those traveling for awhile, this is a good Poste Restante address. There are a number of foreign exchange banks in the vicinity. The Fuji Bank one block S from the _eki_ on your left is a convenient one. Sapporo is the place to cash your travelers checks. Except in a handful of main cities in Hokkaido, this can be tough to do. You are quite safe carrying cash, but for those still fretful, buy travelers checks in yen. These can be cashed anywhere in any bank. The few dollars you lose in the transaction will save hours of unproductive hassle. Also stock up on film in Sapporo. Slide film is hard to come by in the smaller towns.

sights: The Botanical Gardens (open April to Nov.) is 500 m SW of the _eki,_ go past the central P.O. 2 blocks and turn left. There are still a few stands of natural trees, but the most interesting aspect of the Gardens is the collection of over

4500 specimens of flora from every corner of Hokkaido. This will enable you to become familiar with the flora that you will encounter as you range over other parts of the island. The University Museum is in the Gardens, and here are examples of stuffed birds (many from the collection of Blakiston), and animals such as bear and wolf, as well as minerals found throughout Hokkaido. Here also is the Ainu (Batchelor) Museum (see *Ainu art*, Introduction). Preserved here and on display is the colorful past of these men of the north. Utensils, artifacts and costumes make up most of the exhibits—probably the closest that the casual traveler can come to witnessing the culture of a vanishing race. The simple yet classical designs and motifs of the displays testify to the richness of the Ainu tradition. If you wish to become more involved with what you have seen at the Gardens, there are 2 libraries (*toshokan*) at your disposal. The public library is only one block further W from the Botanical Gardens and there is another at the university only a few blocks away.

a walking tour: To continue your mini tour from the Gardens, head E on Kite-ichido Dori for about 8 blocks and on a side street to your L (see map) you will see the Clock Tower. It is not really impressive, but it is free, so look. It was built in the Russian style, and has been trying to keep time since 1881. Head for O-dori Promenade 2 blocks south. This is a great spot

SAPPORO CITY

1. Sapporo International Hotel
2. Central Post Office
3. Sapporo Youth Hostel
4. Seikatei
5. Ainu Museum
6. City Library
7. City Hospital
8. Museum
9. Clock Tower
10. T.V. Tower

to relax, people-watch, and eat your brunch. There are various food vendors, but the best is the sweet corn for Y150, available in the multi-colored tent-covered stalls. After it is boiled, the corn is roasted over charcoal and a dash of soy sauce is added. It's not as sweet and buttery as what Americans are used to but try ordering a bowl of miso *shiru* in Iowa. Look up and you will see the TV tower famous for its view of Sapporo. The bottom floor has some refreshment stands and junk shops (underground, toilets are available). Here you will find the tower elevator which will take you to the 3rd floor; there you will be deposited and asked for Y500 to continue to the top. Don't do it unless you have a burning desire to see downtown Sapporo (you can actually see it better from most of the top floors of the high-rise hotels in the area). As you walk around, combine business with pleasure. Buy film, etc., and stop at an exchange bank. There is one more stop that you should make. Head S from the tower toward Tanukikoji Shopping Arcade, a covered arcade featuring thousands of shops selling everything. Here also is Susukino (ask any cab driver), the entertainment quarter of Sapporo. There are over 25,000 people employed here in cabarets, snacks and discos and bars of every description, a typical Japanese phenomenon. If you want to go out in Sapporo at night, this is where to go. The final stop in Sapporo proper is the Sapporo Beer Hall located at the Sapporo Beer Factory. Return to the *eki*, turn E on the main street, and the brewery is about 600 m E on the left. The Beer Garden is a good place to kickup and have a raucous beer. Brewing in Hokkaido is traced back to a German who, in the 1880's, found wild hops growing and taught the Japanese how to make beer.

accommodations: Western style hotels include: Century Royal Hotel, 5, Nishi, Kita-Gojo, Chuo-ku, Sapporo 060, tel: (011) 221-2121, 2 min walk from Sapporo Eki; Hotel New Miyakoshi, 3, Nishi, Kita-Nijo, Chuo-ku, Sapporo 060, tel: (011) 221-2141, 3 min walk from Sapporo Station; and Sapporo International Hotel, 4-1, Nishi, Kita-Yojo, Chuo-ku, Sapporo 060, tel: (011) 261-1381, 2 min walk from Sapporo Station. *business hotels:* (from Y3500) Hotel Washington Sapporo, Nishi 4-chome, Kita 4-i, Chuo-ku, Sapporo City, tel: (011) 251-3211, one min walk from Susukino Subway Station; Sapporo Plaza Hotel, Nishi 1-chome, Minami 7-jo, Chuo-ku, Sapporo, tel: (011) 511-7211, 5 min walk from Susukino Subway Station. The least expensive is Hotel Highland, tel: (011) 511-0726, 7 min walk

from Susukino Station on Namboku Subway Line, from Y3000. *ryokan:* (from Y8500) Hotel Maruso, 3-3, Kitai-ichijo-Nishi, Chuo-ku, Sapporo 060, tel: (011) 221-0111; and Sapporo Daiichi Hotel, 10, Odori-Nishi, Chuo-ku, Sapporo 060, tel: (011) 221-1101. *minshuku:* For information and reservations contact the Hokkaido Minshuku Center, Sapporo Station Meitengai, Nishi 4-chome, Kita 5-jo, Chuo-ku, Sapporo City, Hokkaido, Japan. *Y.H.:* There are over 80 YHs scattered throughout Hokkaido and the main islands surrounding it. Most cities, spa towns and national parks have at least one. There are 4 large YHs in Sapporo with accommodations for more than 400 people. Mid-summer and winter skiing seasons are the most popular. The best and most convenient is: Sapporo House YH, 3-1, Nishi 6-chome, Kita 6-jo, Kita-ku, Sapporo City 001, tel: (011) 721-4235, 7 min on foot from Sapporo Station. From the *eki* pass the P.O., turn R at the next block. Cross the tracks, and the YH is on the right.

food: Seafood is a specialty of Sapporo as it is throughout Hokkaido. Many inexpensive restaurants are found around the *eki* and the Susukino shopping arcade has shoulder-to-shoulder eateries offering light snacks to full-course meals. The hot buttered corn from vendors around Sapporo Tower is an inexpensive treat. Try Genghis Khan, charcoaled mutton dipped in savory sauce. Many restaurants feature this, but for a special treat try to attend a cookout at Tsukisappu Sheep Farm. Ask at the JTB for particulars. There is also a Shakey's Pizza with all the pizza you can eat until 1400. For beer snacks and Genghis Khan, try the Sapporo Beer Hall. An internationally approved restaurant is the Kaiyotel, Inishi, Minami-Juichijo, Chuo-ku, tel: 511-3361.

Sapporo services: Sapporo Immigration Office (for ARC) 4 Nishi, O-dori, Chuo-ku, tel: (011) 261-9211. *diplomatic delegations:* American Consulate, 221-5121/3; French Consular Agency, 261-1311; Korean Consulate, 621-0288. *private travel agencies:* Hokkaido Kanko Travel, 241-1131; Sapporo Express, 251-411 ; JTB, Nihon Seimei Bldg., 4-1-3, Nishi, Kita, Chuo-ku, Sapporo.

vicinity of Sapporo: On the western outskirts of the city is the legacy from the 1972 Olympics. Here is the Mt. Moiwa Sightseeing Toll Road leading to a skiing area (take a bus from the *eki*). The summit of Mt. Moiwa (530 m) is commercialized, but it still presents a commanding view of Sapporo and the surrounding mountains. Maruyana Park and Zoo are 4 km N of Moiwa, and this area also features virgin forests. These western mountains abound in ski grounds (see skiing guide) and winter sports facilities. Mt. Arai is only 20 min from the Sapporo Eki by bus. It is the closest, and consequently is jammed. Beginners congregate here and very politely fall all over the slopes. If you are a serious skier, go farther W to Mt. Teine (1024m) to find excellent and challenging skiing. If you arrive in Hokkaido in the winter especially for the skiing, stay in Sapporo in one of the numerous youth hostels, *ryokan* or hotels and commute each morning, easily and conveniently, to the slopes. After having a breather in Sapporo and taking care of business, head out. Don't worry if you haven't seen everything; you'll be here again as you swing back S after visiting the northern and eastern regions of this invigorating, hardy northern island.

skiing: Teine Olympia, 55 min by bus from Sapporo Eki, mid-Nov. to mid-April. Night skiing. Twelve lifts, one ropeway and 2 ropetows. *Jozankei:* Only 26 km S of Sapporo (and one hr by bus). Besides being a famous spa, it has excellent skiing. The spa is at 300 m and the waters from the hotsprings are piped into the local homes and hotels. Jozankei is set in beautiful surroundings and well worth an afternoon visit. From here you can continue S on a tortuous mountain road to Shikotsu Toya National Park covered earlier in chapter. *accommodations:* Stay at Jozankei Hotel, Jozankei Onsen, Minami-ku, Sapporo City, 061-23, tel: (011) 365-2111 and Hotel Shikanoyu, Jozankei Onsen, Minami-ku, Sapporo City 061-23, tel: (011) 365-2311, both *ryokan* start at Y8000, or stay at Jozankei YH, 4-310, Higashi, Jozankei-onsen, Minami-ku, Sapporo City 061-23, tel: (011) 365-2858, one hr. by bus from Sapporo Station and 5 min on foot, closed Nov. through April.

DAISETSUZAN NATIONAL PARK

Daisetsuzan National Park constitutes not only the geographical center, but the essence of Hokkaido. Here are vast plains, cascading mountain streams, lofty, lonely mountain peaks, and unending km of hiking trails. *getting there:* Head N from Sapporo to Takikawa (80 km) either by thumb or bus on Rt. 12 (Kokudo Ju-Ni) or by train on the Satsu Sho Line. At Takikawa you must make a decision for continuing on to Daisetsuzan. The common and most heavily trafficked route is to proceed N to Asahikawa. From here bus to Sounkyo, the N entrance to the park, 2 hours. Take Rt. 39 from Asahikawa or continue by train to Kamikawa and from there bus to Sounkyo, 35 minutes. The alternative, slightly more difficult, but more rewarding route is to head E from Takikawa and follow Rt. 38 or train for 130 km to Obihoro (Y500). From here enter Daisetsuzan from the S where few tourists venture and where the park is at its wild and woolliest best. The entire trip from Sapporo takes 12 hrs and if you're not up for a train marathon a good halfway point at which to stop is Furano. There is nothing exceptional about Furano but it does have 3 convenient business hotels just across the street from the *eki* (Y3000). You can rest and continue on to Obihoro the next morning.

travel tip: Because of the lack of public transportation in this area, you must break one of the cardinal rules of economy traveling and do some backtracking. For instance, there is no public transportation running from Nukabira in the S to Sounkyo Gorge in the N of Daisetsuzan. Don't let this stop you. There is a way, but you must hitchhike. These interior areas of Daisetsuzan should not be missed because they contain some of the most premier wilderness areas in all of Hokkaido. If you wish to see the length and breadth of both Daisetsuzan and Akan National Parks, as well as the SE coast of Hokkaido, you should follow a circular routing. Allow 7-10 days for a thorough inspection of these truly magnificent areas.

the circular routing: From Obihoro, train or bus on Rt. 241 to Kami-Shihoro, then train or bus (Tokachi Bus Co.) from Kami-Shihoro to Nukabira; bus from Nukabira to Mitsumata. From Mitsumata, thumb (only) to Sounkyo, then bus from Sounkyo to Rubeshibe. Then train to Ikeda, perhaps, with a stopover at Hombetsu. From Ikeda, train to Kushiro. Bus from Kushiro to Tsurimura (Akan Kibbutz). Stop over, and then go onward to Akan National Park.

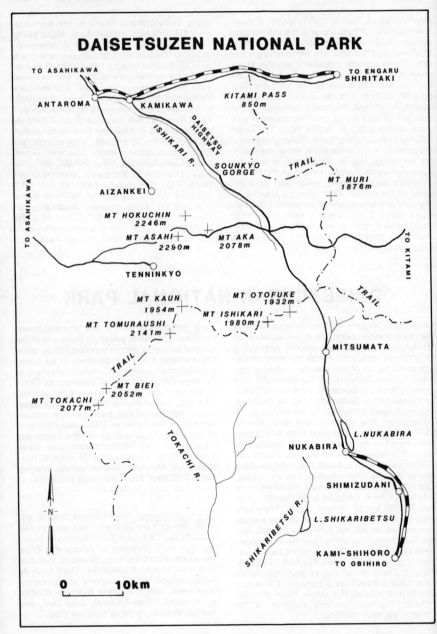

DAISETSUZEN NATIONAL PARK

TO ASAHIKAWA

TO ENGARU
SHIRITAKI

ANTAROMA

KAMIKAWA

KITAMI PASS
850m

DAISETSU HIGHWAY

ISHIKARI R.

SOUNKYO GORGE

TRAIL

MT MURI
1876m

AIZANKEI

TO ASAHIKAWA

MT HOKUCHIN
2246m

MT ASAHI
2290m

MT AKA
2078m

TO KITAMI

TENNINKYO

MT KAUN
1954m

MT OTOFUKE
1932m

MT ISHIKARI
1980m

MT TOMURAUSHI
2141m

TRAIL

MITSUMATA

MT BIEI
2052m

TOKACHI R.

MT TOKACHI
2077m

L. NUKABIRA

NUKABIRA

SHIMIZUDANI

SHIKARIBETSU R.

L. SHIKARIBETSU

KAMI-SHIHORO
TO OBIHIRO

-N-

0   10km

NUKABIRA

The main village in the southern region of Daisetsuzan is Nukabira. It is the last train and bus stop heading N through the park. It consists mainly of one central street, but it is an excellent place to head for. *getting there:* There is a small white bus (Kokutetsu Daiko Bus Co.) that travels out to Mitsumata. It leaves Nukabira at 0757 and 1442 from the *eki*. The other alternative is to hitchike. There is no problem getting a ride, but there is very little traffic. Count on only one car every 15-20 min.

accommodations: There is a Youth Hostel, Nukabira Ko. The Minshuku Minaru at Y2500 and Y3600 with meals, and the modern Fujimi-kanko Hotel at Y6000 per night. Ken Nakamura manages this hotel and speaks English very well. He is a good person to contact for information and directions in this area. *food:* There is an excellent *soba* shop in town and 20 m up the street is a restaurant, Fujiya, that specializes in Genghis Khan (marinated charcoal lamb) at a reasonable rate: Y600. A few shops line the main street where you can purchase groceries and excellent Ainu carvings done on the premises. They start at Y1200 and go upward quickly.

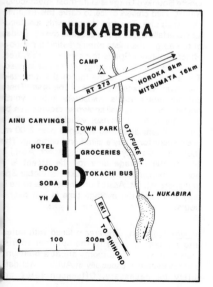

sights: This area consists of wide, broad valleys and rolling mountains. The Otofuke River and Lake Nukabira have excellent fishing (*tsuri*), and there is even a small slope for skiing in town. Camping spots are plentiful. A one km hike out of town is all that is necessary. An excellent spot is to head out of town on the road to Mitsumata. Turn R at the Y, Rt. 273 (*ni-hyaku nan-ju san*) and when the bridge crosses the river (300m), head down to it and camp along its banks. The thick northern forest here is thickly carpeted with soft moss and flowers resembling white lillies of the valley and purple pansies. *Mitsumata:* Continue N on 273 to Mitsumata. Eight km out along this well-banked, gravel road, you will come to Horoka Onsen, one km from the road, featuring mineral baths costing Y250.

MITSUMATA

A frontier, semi-ghost town 16 km N of Nukabira on the road to Sounkyo with only 7 families living in town, and numerous empty cabins and buildings in the vicinity. There is only one restaurant, the Mitsumata Sanso. It is operated by Tamie Tanaka, a lovely young woman who serves *shika* (deer) *soba,* which is absolutely delicious. The deer is hunted by her husband, Oyaso, who runs the small bus company. He also made all of the rustic wooden furniture in the restaurant. On the walls are a few deer head trophies. The table vases are full of wildflowers that Tamie has picked in the neighboring mountains. The roof of the *soba* shop has a daisy painted on it, and there is a Fuji Film flag hanging over the entrance. Tamie also has a few essential groceries: crackers (*senbei*), cans of fish, candy bars, etc. This is absolutely the last place to pick up a few supplies. You can camp anywhere in Mitsumata, and Mr. Tanaka graciously offers a night's lodging to any hitchhiker unable to go farther. Please avail yourself of his hospitality only if you are really stuck. This area is the epitome of outback Hokkaido; no factories, towns, farms, just untamed, untrampled wide-open spaces.

sights: To the E are 2 anatomical mountains known locally as Opai Yama (Tits Mountains). A small road leading in their direction will take you to a very rustic *jinja.* From this summit, you get an excellent view of the surrounding countryside. You must hitchhike N from Mitsumata along the gravel road for another 30 km until you intersect Rt. 39 (Kokudo San-Ju Kyu); the hale

the outback of Daisetsuzan National Park

and hearty might even consider walking it. You will begin to pass through fantastic gorges cut through the mountains. Eventually the road will crest the mountains at Mikun Tobe 5 km N of Mitsumata and here at your feet lies all of Diesetsuzan, a fitting reward for those bold enough to get off the beaten track. As you head N along Rt. 273, the scene gets more and more spectacular. The wide valleys begin to give way to mountains that are pointed and jagged. The mountains are covered with an amazingly lush growth of trees. There are no bare spots. Another 10 km N and you will arrive at Kaisetsu Lake. Here, the Japanese have dammed the Ishikari River. The dam is a wonder, made from earth and rubble with no concrete used. The lakeshore is perfect for camping, and the lake itself is dotted with islands. In a few more km you will intersect Rt. 39. Turn L (W) and in a few km you will reach Sounkyo. The road is well traveled and you are back in civilization. There will be a road sign that reads Obako and there is a tunnel that goes through the mountain.

SOUNKYO AND ENVIRONS

This entire area is well touristed and in stark contrast to the interior of Daisetsuzan. Here at Obako are fantastic gorges that have been cut through the mountains. An old bridge no longer used except by pedestrians crosses the river and gives excellent vantage points for photography and just soaking up the sights. Further down the road towards Sounkyo (2 km) is Chu Jo Setsuri, a natural, abstract still life. It is long spires of rock, geometrically cut and resembling squared pipes of an old-fashioned church organ running vertically up the side of the mountain. This is where Sounkyo Gorge is at its most spectacular. Nature used chisels of ice to carve this magnificent sculpture. The area is laced with spectacular waterfalls (*taki*) which cascade over the sides of the gorge, the mists often creating a rainbow effect. Sounkyo Spa is the center of this area. The spa and its surroundings are well developed. There is a ropeway to the top of the mountain that gives an excellent view of the area. There are numerous hotels, *minshuku* and a youth hostel. This area is well known so crowds can be a problem. Mt. Daisetsu, which is actually a group of conical shaped volcanos over 2000 m, is excellent for a day's climb and camping. The route from Sounkyo culminating at Mt. Asahi is 14 km; the average time for the ascent is 7 hours. You can also bus to Yukomambetsu Spa and approach Mt. Asahi from there. This route is only 7 km and the average time is just over 4 hours.

accommodations: The area is laced with hotels and *ryokan* catering to the summer tourist crowd, at which time rooms are at a premium, and reservations, especially in August, will definitely be necessary. Offseason rates are cheaper. Try the Minshuku Association and JTB for reservations. The most centrally located YH is Sounkyo YH, Sounkyo, Kamikawa-machi, Kamikawa-gun 078-17, tel: (016585) 3418, 35 min by bus from Kamikawa Station and 7 min on foot, 90 beds. Others in the area are: Daisetsuzan YH, Shirakaba-so 1418, Higashikawa-machi, Kamikawa-gun 071-03, tel: (01669) 6-2055, one hr 40 min by bus from Asahikawa

Station, 38 beds, and Ginsenkaku YH, Sounkyo, Kamikawa-machi, Kamikawa-gun, 078-17, tel: (016585) 3003, 35 min by bus from Kamikawa Eki and 5 min on foot, 84 beds, closed Sept. 16 through June 14; as well as the previously mentioned Nukabira-ko YH, Nukabira, Kamishihoro-cho, Kato-gun 080-15, tel: (01564) 4-2221, 8 min on foot from Nukabira Sta., 52 beds in the S of Daisetsuzan.

HEADING EAST:AKAN NATIONAL PARK

From Sounkyo, there are some fancy zigs and zags to get E to Akan; unfortunately, there are no direct train lines. You can bus or hitchhike E on route 39 to Rubeshibe, from where you can make a train connection further E to Kitami. In Kitami, transfer and head S to Ikeda and onward to Akan. In Rubeshibe, you can hitchhike S on Hwy. 242 and intersect the train (10 km) at Oketo or with luck, just keep going to Ikeda. Both the train and Rt. 242 pass through the town of Hombetsu, about 80 km S of Kitami and 30 km N of Ikeda.

Hombetsu: Although lacking tourist attractions, and rarely, if ever visited by foreigners, a stop here is a delight. Hombetsu is a backwater, average Hokkaido community similar to any midwest town in the United States. It lies in a low, flat plain and is surrounded by rolling hills. The serious traveler should make an effort to stay in a place like this at least once in every trip. In Hombetsu you will meet a remarkable man by the name of Mr. Hayashi. He and his wife operate Seikatsu Gakko (New Life School), and Seikatsu Gakko Restaurant. Mr. Hayashi speaks English well and is a fount of information. In his life, he has been a politician, editor of a travel magazine, and now a restaurant chef. No directions are necessary—just ask anyone in town. In the afternoon, school children stop by his restaurant and are amazed to see a gaijin. They will try a few words of English and watch your every move. Sitting in the middle of the restaurant is a life-sized, papier mache and chicken-wire cow, covered in fur. This oddity is a creation of one of Mr. Hayashi's friends. Mr. Hayashi has a back room at his restaurant where you can stay overnight free of charge. Repay his kindness by buying one of the many excellent western-style meals at his restaurant. Beef stew, deep-fried chicken and homemade bread are just a few of his specialties. He also makes an excellent dessert from homemade mint gelatin

floating in creamy Hokkaido milk. There is an English conversation class in town; it would be an excellent gesture, time allowing, to offer your services as a guest speaker. In town there is a fine, inexpensive _sushi_ bar. Walk from Mr. Hayashi's towards the station, and it will be on the right, about halfway there. The _sushi_ is fresh and excellent. A little night out including a bottle or two of beer here will cost less than Y1000. Local people stop in, and the atmosphere is cozy and friendly. _local sights:_ Hombetsu Onsen is a fine spa featuring an excellent bath only 2 km N of town on Rt. 242. It is located in a large hotel and costs Y250 for a bath. The baths are spacious with many showers. Towels are provided.

KUSHIRO

After spending a day or so in Hombetsu, head for Ikeda. The train leaves Hombetsu at 1046 and arrives at Ikeda at 1347. There is a small shopping area at Ikeda near the train station. There is also the largest champagne glass in all of Japan. It is the plastic fountain just in front of the _eki_. Very kitsch. _getting there:_ Change trains at Ikeda and head directly for Kushiro. The charge from Hombetsu to Kushiro is Y2200, Y700 is the _kyuko_ charge. Kushiro is a frontier town full of swaggering fishermen, loggers and back-country boys. It is sprawling and ragged around the edges. A perpetual mist lies over it, caused by the cold water currents. Trawlers with their holds full of salmon make port and fly gaily colored flags signalling their catch. The town teems with cheap hotels and women cruising the night spots attempting to net the fishermen. Kushiro is the largest town in this district, and here you will find all the amenities. If you have any banking to do, Kushiro is the place. _sights:_ The most interesting attraction of the immediate area is the Natural Park for Japanese

a swarm of fishing
trawlers in Kushiro
Harbor

Red-Crested Cranes (see *tancho* under "fauna"
in "Introduction"). It is easily reached by bus
from Kushiro Station in about 30 minutes. From
Kushiro, head due N on the Senmo Line directly
to Teshikaga, the southern entrance to Akan
National Park.

AKAN KIBBUTZ

There is an extremely worthwhile alternative to
heading directly to Teshikaga, and that is to
make for Tsuruimura where you will find Akan
Kibbutz, which is a back-to-nature commune
where visitors are welcome. At Kushiro Station,
30 m to the L as you walk out of the main
entrance, you will find Akan Bus Terminal. Here
you can pick up a bus to Tsuruimura. The one hr
ride costs Y550. When you get off the bus, continue walking in the direction in which you
arrived in town for about 40 m until you come to
the main crossroads. Here, make a R, and follow
the road for about 700 m until you cross an
orange metal bridge. After this bridge, take the
first dirt road on you right and look for the
commune about 200 m on your left. The main
building is a large, rectangular structure and
looks somewhat like a hotel. The farming done
here is totally organic; no chemical fertilizers are
used. The main agricultural thrust of the
commune actually takes place at a dairy farm:
Yiyasa No Koan, 18 km away. There is much
coming and going between the two, so getting
over there is no problem. However, there are

more accommodations at Akan Kibbutz. You
will be charged a very reasonable Y1500 for a
private room including meals. Don't expect to be
entertained. The people are very busy and are
very serious about their work. Lend a hand and
observe. If you are willing to stay and work for
one month, there is no charge. You will even
gain Y2500 in pocket money at the end of the
month. You will be expected to work 8 hrs a day,
6 days a week. The work is very flexible. If you
arrange it in advance,. you can work for a couple
of weeks, go off and tour for a week or so, and
then come back and finish your month. The
food at the Kibbutz is natural and nutritious. A
typical meal might include rich brown bread,
homemade marmalade, pitchers of goat's milk,
golden fried potatoes and fresh eggs. The
commune is not vegetarian, but all of the food is
wholesome. A prominent member of the
commune is an expatriot Englishman, Moshe
Matsube, who lived in Israeli Kibbutzim for 30
years. Long talks with him in the evening are
both interesting and informative. Other, Japanese members of the commune speak English, so
communicating is no problem

information: There is an excellent book published by the Japanese Commune Movement
available from Akan Kibbutz. It lists all of the
communes throughout Japan and includes their
philosophies, addresses and accommodations
for visitors. This is an excellent sourcebook to
have if you plan to visit and observe the com-

munes of Japan. It can also save you a great deal of money in accommodation costs as you travel around Japan. For your copy, send $7.00 U.S. (including postage: sea mail, allow 6 weeks) to: The Japanese Commune Movement, Kibbutz Akan, Shin Skizen Juku, Nakasetsuri, Tsuruimura, Akan Gun, Hokkaidao 085-12, Japan.

LAKE MASHU

There is a bus running directly to Teshikaga from Tsurui. It takes only one hr and costs Y600. At the bus station in Teshikaga, make a connection for Lake Mashu. The trip takes only 20 min and costs Y380. On your way to Lake Mashu, you will pass the Matsuko YH on your L where there's a bus stop. A good idea is to stop and drop off your gear at the hostel before heading the 3 km to the lake. Walk and enjoy the countryside instead of taking the bus. The mountains in this area are rolling and round-topped and the fields are broad and covered with flowers.

Lake Mashu and beyond: It is obvious when you arrive at the lake because of the built up touristy area with hundreds of tourists. There are some people selling broiled corn at a usurious Y300 apiece. About 100 m up the road is a gate that closes it off to traffic. Go under this gate and walk on for about one minute. The crowds disappear and you have the view to yourself. Lake Mashu lies far below, completely surrounded by mountain peaks. The most impressive of these is Mt. Mashu (858 m) on the E side of the lake. There is no apparent inlet or outlet, and to reach the shores of the lake is very difficult because of the steep slope. The waters are the clearest in the world, and on sunny days you can see to a depth of over 40 meters. Following the road to the summit for another km, you arrive at a view of Lake Kucharo to the W, and the spa town of Kawayu, 3 km further along the road. Here you can pick up the train to Abashiri if you don't wish to return to Teshikaga. *accommodations:* Kawayu is a hot spring resort with numerous rather expensive *ryokan* lining the downtown area. There is a youth hostel in town, Nomura Kawaya YH, Kawayu, Teshikagamachi, Kawakami-gun 088-34, tel: (015483) 2037, 15 min on foot from Kawayu Station, 72 beds; but for a special treat, head for Kushuro-ko YH, Nibushi, Kawayu, Teshikaga-machi, Kawakami-gun 088-34, tel: (015483) 2415, 15 min by bus from Kawayu Station, and 3 min on foot, 65 beds. Kusshuro Ko is situated on the shores of Lake Kucharo, and hostelers can soak in the lovely bath of a nearby resort hotel.

LAKE AKAN

To see Lake Akan you must return to Teshikaga and bus along the Akan Transverse. This takes you through fantastic mountainous country until you arrive at Akan and the 2 famous mountains of Me-kan and O-Akan, or Mr. and Mrs. Akan. Akan is noted for the curious *marimo* duckweed (see "events," "flora," "marine products" in "Introduction") and is surrounded by alpine jungle. The porous volcanic rocks sprout vegetation and the entire area has the feeling of mystery. Excursion boats can be hired from Akan-Kohan to view the *marimo*. On Oct. 10, the Marimo Festival occurs but is not really an Ainu tradition. It is modern hype where the few remaining Ainu thank the *marimo* for luring the tourists.

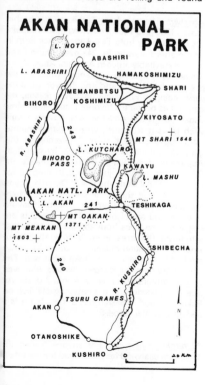

AKAN NATIONAL PARK

L. NOTORO
ABASHIRI
L. ABASHIRI
HAMAKOSHIMIZU
MEMANBETSU
SHARI
BIHORO
KOSHIMIZU
243
KIYOSATO
MT SHARI 1545
L. KUTCHARO
BIHORO PASS
KAWAYU
L. MASHU
AKAN NATL. PARK
AIOI
L. AKAN
241
TESHIKAGA
MT OAKAN 1371
MT MEAKAN 1503
SHIBECHA
240
R. KUSHIRO
TSURU CRANES
N
AKAN
OTANOSHIKE
KUSHIRO
R. ABASHIRI

the Marimo Festival of L. Akan

accommodations: Akan-kohan is a resort featuring Ainu craftsmen whittling away. *Ryokan* and hotel prices are high in season. There are 3 YHs in the immediate area: Akan-Kohan YH, Akan-kohan, Akan-machi, Akan-gun 085-04, tel: (015487) 2309, 70 min by bus from Teshikaga Station and 4 min on foot, 58 beds; Choritsu Akan YH, Akan-kohan-Bangaichi, Akan-machi, Akan-gun 085-04, tel: (015467) 2445, 70 min by bus from Teshikaga Station and 5 min on foot, 60 beds; and Akan Angel YH, 5-1, Shurikomabetsu, Akan-kohan, Akan-machi, Akan-gun 085-04, tel: (015467) 2309, one hr 50 min by bus from Kushiro Station and 12 min on foot, 90 beds.

THE ABASHIRI AREA

getting there: From Akan, continue by bus until you reach Kitami-Aioi, where you can pick up a train to Bihoro and Abashiri, or you can return to Teshikaga and bus or hitch along Rt. 243 past Lake Kucharo and over Bihoro Pass where you get another outstanding view of the vastness of Hokkaido. Japanese film makers have used Bihoro as a backdrop to "period films." This underdeveloped town is a perfect setting for a romantic or traditional theme. Before you arrive at Bihoro you will pass Lake Kucharo where aquatic life was strangled when sulphur poured into the lake after a recent volcanic erruption.

Abashiri: The train from Teshikaga to Abashiri costs Y1080 plus Y500 *kyuko*. Whether you take the train directly from Teshikaga or pick it up in Bihoro after following Rt. 243 over Bihoro Pass, you will inevitably arrive in Abashiri. Abashiri is a fishing town that has a strange attraction, the prefectural prison and the flower gardens surrounding it. For some unknown reason, the garden has become a favorite picnic spot. Most Japanese think it odd that any traveler would wish to visit Abashiri, whose name means "Wearing the Red Kimono," referring to the garment worn in times past only by convicts. Abashiri is a way station. Unless you are caught there in the evening, just use it to prepare for your thrust NW along the Sea of Okhotsk. If you have time, visit the municipal museum where artifacts excavated from the nearby Moyoro Shell Mound are displayed. These artifacts are believed to be relics from aboriginal people that inhabited the area even before the Ainu. Another interesting museum is Oroke Kinenkan run by Mr. Gendaanu, an Oroke tribesman. The Orokes are nomadic reindeer herders who lived on the northernmost islands. About 3 dozen reside in Hokkaido and a smattering still live on Sakhalin Island. Abashiri has a YH, but it is a perfectly dismal place.

Shiretoko Peninsula: For anyone having the time, turn eastward here and head for the totally untraveled Shiretoko Peninsula (Ainu for "World's End"). One problem is that you will be forced to backtrack if you head for Shiretoko. From Abashiri, train to Shari and here you can pick up a ferry (Y4000 RT) that will take you around the peninsula to Rausu and back again. On the boat trip you will pass impressive sea cliffs over 200 m high. They are streaked with black and white deposits that wind and rain have sculpted into fantastic shapes. Rausu is pure Hokkaido fishing village. The fishermen here are the ones involved with the Russians in a cat-and-mouse border game. The area has some distinctive mosses that are featured. A trip here

is only for those who have the time and money and a desire to visit virtually untouched grounds. There are a few hot water pools (*rotemburo*) along the shores where waters collect from nearby hot springs. These natural spas are favorite spots for young Japanese travelers. Au natural. *accommodations:* There are 5 YHs on Shiretoko, 2 of which are at Rausu. There is also one at Shari and one at Shibetsu, the northern and southern bases of the peninsula. A ferry is available from Shibetsu to Nemuro where you can make train connections to Kushiro and then ferry back to Tokyo.

ALONG THE SEA OF OKHOTSK

Heading W along the coast from Abashiri, you will once again be forced to take long steps. Mombetsu is a good halfway town to head for after leaving Abashiri for Wakkanai. The train from Abashiri to Mombetsu costs Y1200 plus Y500 *kyuko*. Mombetsu is a rough little town about halfway between Abashiri and Wakkanai on the Sea of Okhotsk. It is a stop for sailors and fishermen and the nightlife is sleezy, somewhat like a miniature Kushiro. To find the nightlife is simple, the town is small—just head for the lights. All of the towns along the coast are minor variations on the same theme. You really don't have to worry about being hassled, but you will be approached by drunken seafarers and ladies looking for a good time. Don't be surprised if someone asks you if you are Russian. Tell them clearly where you're from—anyplace is good as long as it's not Russia. Sorry Comrade.

sights: Mombetsu does boast a museum, the Mombetsu Hakubutsu-kan, located just behind the train station next to the shrine (*jinja*). Look at the hills behind the train station for the *jinja* roof, then head for it, and the museum is right there on your left. Entrance is free. The main room is dedicated to natural history, containing stuffed animals including deer, bear, seals, fish, birds, and even a monkey. It is a good example of the flora and fauna of Hokkaido. There are also stone arrowheads and some ancient pottery. Another room is dedicated to seafaring equipment: oars, anchors, harpoons and canoes. There are more modern exhibits from the war with Russia, including rifles, swords and helmets. It is a touchable museum. The displays are not encased in glass, and you can inspect them fully. It's a good place to spend an hour or two between trains.

accommodations and food: Mombetsu has many inexpensive hotels lining the downtown area. You can find a place to stay for around Y3000. There are no luxury hotels in town. There is an excellent YH, however, Mombetsu Ryuhyo-Ho-Yado, tel: (01582) 4-4321, walking distance from the train station. The houseparent is especially cordial and the YH overlooks the sea. Inside is a small *tatami* room set up as a museum where you can also sit and drink coffee. The room contains artifacts from all over Japan. Notice the traditional rice-straw boots, capes and mittens used to brave the winters of Hokkaido. They don't appear comfortable, but it is amazing to realize that you can survive the raw, biting cold bolstered only by straw clothing.

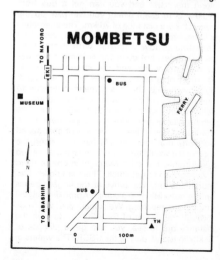

pack-ice along the Sea of Okhotsk

NORTH TO WAKKANAI

The train trip between Mombetsu and Wakkanai (Y3100) is simple, but disappointing. Unfortunately, the spur along the coast is unfinished, so you must head inland to Nayoro and then through the center of the peninsula up to Wakkanai. This means that you miss some fantastic coastline. Route 238 runs along the coast and you can get a bus from Wakkanai to Esahi where you can pick up the train. This is a distance of 70 km. The alternative is to hitchhike which is fun and usually easy. The coastline is low and flat with many rock promontories, not good for swimming because of the cold water and the strong undertow. There are no official campsites along this stretch but anywhere is OK. It is somewhat difficult to find a spot out of sight of the road, but there are some rolling sand dunes that will serve. The fishing villages are more like supply stations for the fishing fleet. There are scores of abandoned buildings that look like old barracks along the road and it would be possible to spend a not too comfortable, but sheltered night in one of them if you happen to get stuck. There are no accommodations until you arrive at the larger villages on the outskirts of Wakkanai. Approximately 50 km before reaching Wakkanai, you will pass through the village of Saru Futsu. Here, in the distance out to sea, you can get a glimpse of Sakhalin Island, part of the USSR. The waters in this area are very rough and choked with pack ice in the winter. The mountains begin to reach down to the sea on this unique coastline, and the seascapes are quite romantic, with picturesque villages scattered here and there in the coves. Bald-topped rolling hills tumble towards the sea, and small scrub brush manicured by nature becomes prominent. The impression is of neatly trimmed lawns. Eventually Rt. 238 winds its way up to Cape Soya, the northernmost limits of Japan. As you enter Omisaki Mura, there is a little monument on a diminutive island 200 m out to sea. This is the borderline of Japan. Also, if you look out to sea off to the W, you will have your first glimpse of Rishiri Island floating majestically with its conical-shaped volcano.

Wakkanai: Wakkanai is a working town, a functional town, dingy and beaten up. Although the buildings are unattractive, the natural setting is beautiful. To get to Rebun and Rishiri by ferry, you must stop in Wakkanai. Do your banking here and there are a few spots to visit while waiting for the ferry. From anywhere in town, you will see two dome-shaped mountains A bus runs to the summit, and at the top is a park. Just at sunset is the best time to go for an absolutely commanding view of Wakkanai huddled along the coast. Out to sea are numerous islands including Kraft Island, another seized by the USSR. The lights of the town are quite romantic from this distance, and you can even tolerate the petrochemical tanks in the harbor. Take note of the ferry terminal down in the harbor where you

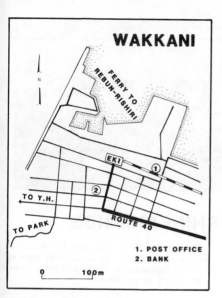

might be leaving for Rebun in the morning.
accommodations: Wakkanai has numerous hotels and a few *minshuku*. There are 2 youth hostels in town, but the best is the Wakkanai YH, about 10 min W of the train station by bus. The houseparents have seen countless thousands heading for Rebun and they will wake you early enough in the morning to catch you ferry. (Heaven forbid if you wish to sleep in and catch the late ferry, you'll be awakened anyway.) Any bus heading down the main road in front of the

youth hostel will take you to the *eki*. The ferry terminal is only a short walk away. Wakkanai YH, 5-3-18, Horai, Wakkanai City 097, tel: (01622) 3-7162, 12 min on foot from Minami Wakkanai Station, 100 beds, closed Nov. through April.

from Wakkanai: If you follow the main road from town W, in 2-3 km you will come to the sea. Here in summer the sunset is superb as it sets over Rishiri Island. Even in July, the wind can be nippy, although the Japanese current keeps the port open all winter. This is a good spot for picturetaking and some light introspection. The ferry schedule to Rebun (Y1260, 2 hr 30 min) and Rishiri (Y1110, 2 hr and 5 min) varies according to the month, but there are basically 3 per day to each island. Flights are available to Oshidomari on Rishiri in the summer. It really makes no difference which island you visit first. Convenient ferry service connects them in only 40 minutes. One suggestion is to take the 1130 ferry to Rebun. This will give you time to stroll around the pier area of Wakkanai and take care of banking and the post office. The P.O. in Wakkanai is another good place to have mail sent Poste Restante. There is no temporary parcel storage at the ferry terminal, but for once, the Y200 lockers are large enough to hold a backpack. Store your gear here and meander about town. (Warning: Once you lock the locker, you can't close it again unless you pay another Y200. Take your camera, etc., the first time. Bad weather sometimes cancels the ferry so there is a chance that you will have to take the later ferry or you might even have to stay another day in Wakkanai.

REBUN AND RISHIRI ISLANDS

Rebun and Rishiri are 2 of Japan's premier spots. They are so close and yet their attractions are so varied. Rebun is a low, rolling island offering wide mountain meadows lush with flowers and extraordinary rock formations jutting out to sea. You should allow 3 days for a thorough tour of Rebun. It is a relaxing, slow-paced island where you can regroup your thoughts and energies before moving on. The entire island is transversed by the Hachi-Ji Kan (8 hr) HIking Trail, and a 2 hr trail leading to Mt. Rebun in the center offers a 360 degree panoramic view of the surrounding seas and Rishiri Island.

accommodations: No problem on Rebun. The crowds don't arrive until July, and camping is quite easy and acceptable. The main towns of Funadomari and Kafuka have plenty of _ryokan_ and _minshuku_, but the youth hostel at Funadomari, Rebun Choritsu YH, tel: (01638) 72717, should not be missed. What a delight!! When the ferry puts in at Kafuka, the YH sends a free bus to pick up travelers for the 19 km trip from Kafuka to Funadomari. The houseparent operating the YH is not the usual demagogue. He is a friendly, open man who enjoys letting people enjoy themselves. Set your own limitations and they will even vary their schedule (sleeping and eating) to accommodate your individual needs. The atmosphere is free and friendly, which blends perfectly with the vibes of Rebun Island. The houseparent is even an unofficial matchmaker, and the walls of the YH are covered with the names of couples who met here and were later married. In Funadomari you can find all the camping supplies that you need and the going rate for a _minshuku_ with meals is Y3500. Rebun would be an excellent place for an entire family to go camping.

accommodations: Rebun Choritsu Funadomari YH, Ohsonae, Funadomari, Rebun-cho, Rebun-gun 097-11, tel: (01638) 7-2717, 20 min on foot from Funadomari Port, 56 beds; Rebun YH, Tsugaru-cho, Kabuka, Rebun-cho, Rebun-gun 097-12, tel: (01638) 6-1608, 13 min on foot from Kabuka Port, 80 beds; and Momoiwa-so YH, Motochi, Kabuka, Rebun-cho, Rebun-gun 097-12, tel: (01638) 6-1390, 15 min by bus from Kabuka Port and 7 min on foot, 74 beds, closed Oct. through May 20.

walking trails: There are 2 walks on Rebun that are almost obligatory. The shorter of the 2 is the 3 hr RT hike to the summit of Mt. Rebun (490 m). Bus from either Funadomari in the N, or from Kafuka in the S, approx. halfway along the E coast to the village of Nairo. In Nairo, locate the P.O. and a small red and green building next door. Walk along the pathway next to this building (through someone's yard, but don't worry, it's OK). As you pass the vegetable garden, you will locate some new wooden steps leading up the side of the hill. You are now on the path to Mt. Rebun. There is no water available along this walk, so bring some, and food for a picnic. For the first 25 min of the walk you pass through low-lying vegetation that resembles mountain laurel. This eventually gives way to a forested area with tall pines and birch. Finally,

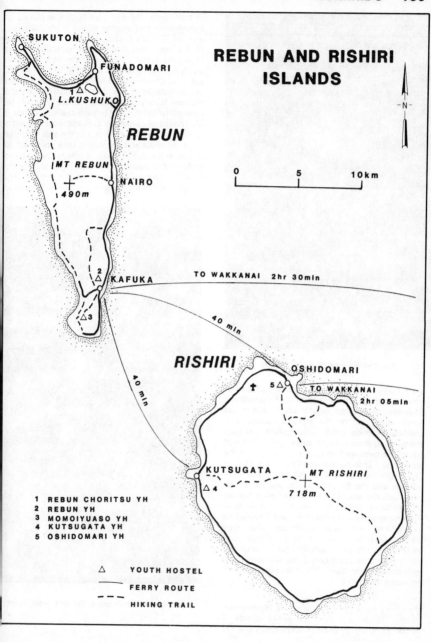

REBUN AND RISHIRI ISLANDS

SUKUTON

FUNADOMARI

L. KUSHUKO

1

REBUN

MT REBUN

490m

NAIRO

2

KAFUKA

TO WAKKANAI 2hr 30min

40 min

3

40 min

RISHIRI

OSHIDOMARI

5

TO WAKKANAI 2hr 05min

40 min

KUTSUGATA

MT RISHIRI

718m

4

0   5   10km

-N-

1 REBUN CHORITSU YH
2 REBUN YH
3 MOMOIYUASO YH
4 KUTSUGATA YH
5 OSHIDOMARI YH

△   YOUTH HOSTEL

———   FERRY ROUTE

- - -   HIKING TRAIL

spectacular rock spires of Rebun

your course will take you over a number of small, humpbacked mountains until the summit of Rebun comes into view. If you intend to eat lunch, don't eat on the summit, where it is always extremely windy. Just before you gain the summit, there is a little valley with a grove of trees, the best spot to take a breather. On the summit is a little marker and Rebun lies at your feet. Your view is total of the tiny ports, little villages and the flowered landscape as it rolls away into the sea. (There is a wildflower festival the 3rd Sunday of each June). The craftsmen of Rebun make very colorful kites, and it would be excellent to take one along. Unfortunately they do not fold, so even the most delicate mail handling would be insufficient for getting one home. The walk takes only 3 hrs, but when you include busing to Nairo, this little sojourn will fill an entire day.

the Hachi-ji-kan Hiking Trail: The Hachi-ji-kan Hiking Trail (8 hrs) runs the entire length of Rebun along the W coast. Luckily there is a YH

at both ends, the one previously mentioned ·at Funadomari and another to the S at Momoiyu-aso, tel: (01638) 6-1390, so you can take your choice and start from either direction. Bring food and water. You will pass little streams along the way, but DON'T DRINK THE WATER, which is contaminated with organic pollutants and can cause severe stomach distress. As the trail winds its way along the coast, you will be treated to absolutely breath-taking scenery. Multitudes of waterfalls cascade over sea cliffs turning to mist before they join the sea. The trail hugs the coast and monolithic rock spires jut 30 m above the sea. Miniscule villages snuggle in protected coves. The efforts at survival here are totally communal. Some of the homes are merely temporary shacks made from orange

a lace like waterfall along Rebun's west coast

a temporary warm weather fishing village of Rebun which lies dormant in winter.

crates and used only during the spring and summer months. Others are more substantial affairs built from hand-hewn rough logs. There are only 2 ways to get to these villages — on foot, or by private fishing boat. One typical village is Meshikuni, containing about 7 shacks anchored to the rocky shore. The fishermen bring in their catches, usually *nukaboke*, a small 15 cm fish, to these working camps where the fish are dried. The drying process is usually an old metal drum with the top and bottom removed. A slow, smoldering fire is made from sawdust and the fish hang above the drum on string covered by wet burlap. The women spend their time clad in hip boots raking edible seaweed from the shore and laying it on the rocky coastling to sun dry.

They also climb into the foothills and gather *fuki*, a wild vegetable that resembles rhubarb. They cut the leaves from the stems and then boil the stems in large, black cauldrons left lying here and there along the beach. Although few western visitors enter these villages, they are welcome and treated to an unpretentious hospitality. The fishermen are known to indulge in heavy drinking and you will most likely be offered a beer or a cup of *sake*. Food will most likely be offered, perhaps a cup of *ocha* and some dried fish, or a long octopus tentacle (*tako*), highly seasoned and very chewy. Cut off bite-sized bits of *tako* with a knife. Don't try to sever it with your teeth, it's like leather. Relax and enjoy yourself before moving down the trail.

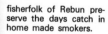

fisherfolk of Rebun preserve the days catch in home made smokers.

Rishiri Island: There are 2 ferries from Kafuka on Rebun to Rishiri. They both take about 40 min and cost Y500. One goes to the main port of Oshidomari on the northern section of the island and the other arrives at Kutsugata on the W coast. Again, accommodations are plentiful in the main towns, featuring moderately priced _minshuku._ Camping spots are available on the southern slopes of Mt. Rishiri (718 m) and there are 2 YHs in Oshidomari and Kutsugata, the one at Kutsugata being the more liberal of the two. A highway has recently been built completely encircling the island, and bus service is available.

The main attraction on Rishiri is obviously the climb. There are 3 main trails from the NE and NW which are well marked and mildly rugged, taking approx. 8 hrs to complete. Rishiri, like its neighbor Rebun, is superbly suited for outdoor fun. Soothing, refreshing sea breezes and wide sea-dominated panoramas are what it's all about. As you climb the mountain, trees give way to alpine flora, and the view improves with every step. Take one good long-lasting look at this northern wonderland before heading back to mainland Japan.

OKINAWA

INTRODUCTION

Okinawa Prefecture stretches southward for 685 km off the SW coast of Kyushu through the Pacific and East China Sea, and is Japan's most southerly prefecture. It consists of 65 sub-tropical islands in 4 main groups: Okinawa, Miyako, Yaeyama and Daito. The population is just over 1,000,000. Approximately 45 islands are inhabited, with many boasting their own unique cultures and distinctive histories. These islands, bathed in the tropical sun, are often bordered by coral reefs, changing the waters to fantastic colors, and providing a haven for numerous species of tropical fish, luring the scuba and skin diving enthusiast. Sandy sunny beaches and secluded fishing spots abound. Taiwan lies less than 10 hrs by ferry from Iriomote, one of the Yaeyama Is., which served as a gateway through which ancient Chinese culture entered Okinawa for centuries. Naha, the main city of Okinawa Is., is a mixture of the sublime and the gaudy. Visit an exquisite, diminutive temple and then party next door at a blasting, flashing discotheque. Frequently and unexpectedly come across delicate and intricate works of art and a thriving traditional culture, and yet go 4 times a day (8 times on Sundays and holidays) to watch an imported mongoose and cobra fight to the death amongst the cheers of vacationers and islanders alike. For those interested, snake burger and snake kabob are a specialty. Contrast this to the time-honored tradition of the bull fight, bull against bull, like 4-footed *sumo* trying to jockey each other out of the ring. Interisland ferries link scantily touristed islands dotted with traditional fishing villages, the fishermen and women engaged in community cooperative ventures to wrest their livelihood from the sea. Compare this to inner city buses and a fleet of LPG-powered taxis linking the throbbing, pulsating semi-seedy night spots of Naha. Major airport facilities on Okinawa and smaller strips on the major islands connect Okinawa to Tokyo and SE Asia, and regular and frequent steamships and interisland ferries ply between Okinawa Prefecture, the main islands of Japan, and Taipei, Taiwan. Age-old folk dances, classical arts, and serene customs and manners are a way of life on the islands. With ferocious ceramic lions (*shisa*) sitting atop red-tiled roofs, the culture of old, though quickly disappearing on the mainland industrial islands, lingers and thrives on the remote islands and in the provincial towns and villages of Okinawa.

GETTING THERE

getting there by air: An efficient network of air and sea travel both internationally and domestically is available for traveling to Okinawa. Naha

OKINAWA ISLANDS

FERRY OFFICES IN OKINAWA

Ryukyu Kaiun	In front of Naha Futou Terminal	TEL (0988) 68-1126
Arimura Sangyo	3-25-21, Maejima Naha City	TEL (0988) 68-2191
Kansai Kisen	2-12-5, Minato-machi, Naha City	TEL (0988) 68-7591
Ohshima Unyu	2-12-5, Minato-machi, Naha City	TEL (0988) 68-7783
Terukuni Yusen	2-12-5, Minato-machi, Naha City	TEL (0988) 68-9098

FERRIES TO OKINAWA FROM MAIN JAPANESE PORTS

Course	Name of Ship	No. of People	Time Required
Tokyo ↕ Naha	Daiyamondo Okinawa	1,033	45 : 00
	Shin Sakuramaru	815	41 : 00
Hanshin ↕ Naha	Goalden Okinawa	995	32 : 00
	Ferry Kuroshio	641	36 : 00
	Hiryu	1,007	27 : 00
Hakata ↕ Naha	Emerald Okinawa	603	26 : 00
Kagoshima ↕ Naha	Nahamaru	902	19 : 00
	Princess Okinawa	500	20 : 00
Kagoshima ↕ Amami	Akebonomaru	1,020	23 : 30
	Emerald Amami	804	20 : 00
Amami ↕ Naha	Queen Coral I	904	23 : 30
	Queen Coral II	1,080	23 : 30

International Airport is a converted U.S. military base located at the extreme western end of Naha, the main city of Okinawa Island. Use Bus 8 which departs from the terminal every 30 min (1300 to 1900) and arrives at the bus terminal at the S end of Kokusai Dori, the main avenue in downtown Naha. The airport is relatively small with the most important signs written in English. Pan Am flights from San Francisco and NWA flights from New York land at Naha in route to Taipei, and again on return. TWA and JAL flights originating in Hong Kong or Taipei also land at Naha. Other international carriers land in Tokyo, Osaka, Fukuoka, Nagoya, Kumamoto and Miyazaki to Naha. The longest flight time is Tokyo-Naha (2 hrs 30 min). Reservations can be made at any JTB, or by calling the airlines: JAL Okinawa Branch, 3-21-1 Kumozi, Naha, tel: (0988) 62-3311, and ANA Okinawa, 1-9 Kumozi, Naha, tel: (0988) 66-5111. NWA also operates 2 flights weekly from Naha to Manila. In Naha tel. NWA at (0988) 54-0581. The Philippine Consulate in Naha can be reached at tel: (0988) 97-3626. Continental Airlines operates 3 flights weekly between Okinawa and L.A. stopping at Honolulu and Guam. For information in Naha, tel: (0988) 37-0142.

internal flights: South West Airlines operates flights originating from Naha and connecting the surrounding islands including Miyako, Ishigaki, Yonaguni and Kume. For complete information call SWA at the Naha Booking Center, tel: (0988) 57-4961.

by sea: Naha has 2 international ports: Naha Shin Ko, known also as Tomari Port, is the smaller of the two. It is less trafficked and about 3 km NW of city center. Coin lockers are available. A small, free shuttle bus will pick you up at dockside and take you the ½ km to the terminal building. As you leave the terminal area, make a R and head up about 300 m to the bus stop. Go in the direction that says AIRPORT, or taxi to the city center for Y600. It is easy to arrange splitting the fare with young Japanese from the boat. Naha Ko, the main port, is situated at the foot of Kokusai Dori and only a short walk from the bus terminal. Naha Ko is large and bustling, and is the main shipping port with Tomari taking a share of the passenger service.

shipping companies: Ryukyu Kaiun Kisen (RKK), Oshima Unyu (OU), and Kansai Kisen (KK) operates sea-going ferries between mainland Japan and Okinawa. Their schedules and rates vary and many island hop, docking at Amami, Oshima, and various stepping-stone island ports on their way to Okinawa. Regular departures are made from Tokyo, Osaka, Fukuoka, Kagoshima and other ports throughout mainland Japan. The Tokyo-Naha trip takes 46 hrs. and costs approx Y20,000 (2nd class [*tatami* mat]) to Y40,000 (1st class [*cabin*]). As usual, carry fresh fruit, vegetables and easily prepared foods to keep prices down. Hot water for drinks, etc. is always available. Student discounts (20%) are offered with valid identification. In Tokyo: RKK, Mitsuyoshi Bldg., 3-5-13 Nihombashi, Chuo-ku, tel: (03) 281-1831; OU,

INTERISLAND NAVIGATION CHART

Starting Port	Name of Course	Name of Ship	Time Required	Reference Telephone
Naha Port	Miyako	Princess Okinawa	13:00	68-1126
Naha New Port		Gyokuryu	12:00	68-2191
	Ishigaki	Gyokuryu	13:00	68-2191
Naha Futou		Princess Okinawa	14:00	68-1126
Tomari Port	Kume Island	Ferry Kumezima	3:00	68-2686
		Dai Ichi Kumimaru	5:00	68-2686
		Dai San Shirasemaru	4:30	68-7540
	Iheya	Dai Ichi Iheyamaru	3:30	68-4449
	Aguni	Dai Ichi Yokyumaru	3:00	68-4449
	Tonaki	Dai Ichi Kumimaru	3:00	68-2686
	Zamami	Zamamimaru	1:30	68-4567
	Tokashiki	Dai Ichi Keramamaru	1:10	68-7541
	Nanbokudaito	Kyoeimaru	15:00	68-3549
Tokuchi	Ie Island	Ferry Ie Island	0:35	(098049)-2255
		Ferry Shiroyama	0:35	(098049)-2255
	Iheya	Dai San Iheyamaru	2:30	(098046)-2001
	Izena	Dai San Izenamaru	1:30	(098045)-2002
	Minna	Minna	0:40	(09804) 7-2140
Hamazaki	Sesoko	Dai Go Sesokomaru	0:10	(09804) 7-3741
Unten	Kouri	Dai Go Kourimaru	0:15	(098056)-3129
Yakena	Hama	Kasugamaru	0:30	(09897) 8-2335
		Asahimaru	0:30	"
		Ebisumaru	0:30	"
	Higa	Kasumimaru	0:30	(09897)-8251
		Matsukazemaru	0:30	"
	Tsuken	Dai Ichi Daishomaru	0:40	(09897) 8-2453
		Jyodaimaru	0:40	"

Starting Port	Name of Course	Name of Ship	Time Required	Reference Telephone
Miyagi	Ikei	Dai Ichi Okisuimaru	0:15	(09897)-8548
		Dai Hachi Ikemaru	0:20	"
Baten	Kudaka	Dai San Shipoumaru	1:00	(09894) 7-6215
		Dai Go Ryukyumaru	1:00	"
Hirara	Naha	Princess Okinawa	13:00	(09807) 2-2047
		Gyokuryu	12:00	(09807) 2-2128
	Ishigaki	Gyokuryu	4:45	"
	Irabu	Heiwamaru	0:30	(09807) 2-3263
		Kariushi	0:17	"
	Sarahama	Hayate	0:15	(098079)-2665
	Tarama	Dai Ichi Futenmamaru	3:00	(098079)-2665
Karimata	Ikema	Ikemamaru	0:40	(09807) 5-2011
		Ohgonmaru	0:20	"
Yonaha	Kurima	Raikoumaru	0:15	"
Ishigaki	Naha	Princess Okinawa	14:00	(09808) 2-2050
		Gyokuryu	13:00	(09808) 2-3844
	Hirara	Gyokuryu	4:45	"
	Taketomi	Taketomimaru	0:30	(09808) 2-3961
	Kohama	Dai San Tohkohmaru	1:10	"
	Kuroshima	Dai Ichi Tohkohmaru	1:50	"
	Ohhara	Ohharamaru	2:00	"
	Funaura	DaiSanSumiyoshimaru	2:00	(09808) 2-2128
	Shirahama Hatoma	Keityomaru	2:30	(09808) 2-2880
	Haterumu	Dai Hachi Shineimaru	3:15	"
	Yonaguni	Yonakuni	6:10	(098087)-2103

NOTE: NOT ALL PORTS SHOWN ON MAP

Asano Bldg. 9th fl., 1-3-11 Nihombashi, Chuo-ku, tel: (03) 273-8911; and KK, Nakagawa Bldg., 1st fl., 1-14-13 Yaesu, Chuo-ku, tel: 274-4271. In Naha: RKK, Naha Port Terminal, tel: (0988) 68-1126; KK, 2-12-5 Minato Machi, Naha, tel: (0988 68-7591; and OU (same address), tel: (0988) 68-7783. TIC offices offer complete information on ferries to Okinawa as well as the best ways to reach the ferry terminals in the larger cities. Reservations are available from JTB or any travel agency.

interisland ferries: Ferries are available to virtually every inhabited island throughout Okinawa with a few being connected by high-speed hydrofoil. The schedules are regular with the smaller island being serviced with fewer sailings. Specific information can be found in the "getting there" section of each Japanese island. As well as the 3 major shipping companies previously listed, 2 others operate interisland ferries as well as sailings to mainland Japan. For further information, in Tokyo contact: Arimura Sangyo, Echo Kyobashi Bldg., 2nd fl., 3-3-1 Takara-cho, Chuo-ku, tel: (03) 562-2091; in Osaka: Arimura Sangyo, Daiichi Bldg., 4-20 Sonezaki-ue, Kita-ku, tel: (06) 345-7421; in Naha: Arimura Sangyo, 3-25-21 Mae-jima, Naha, tel: (0988) 68-2191, or contact Teru-kuni Yusen Co., 2-12-5 Minato-machi, Naha, tel: (0988) 68-9098.

ferry to Keelung (Taiwan): A ferry to Keelung is operated by Arimura Sangyo once a week, leaving Naha Friday nights at 1800. The ferry docks at Miyako for 1½ hrs and at Ishigaki for 9 hrs. en route to Keelung, arriving there at 0700 Sunday morning. The return sailing trip leaves from Keelung at 1600 on Sunday, and sails directly back to Naha, arriving at 1300 on Monday. Reservations are a must, and can be made from 2 to 90 days in advance. Fares start at Y12,000 (*tatami* mat); 20% student discount available. TIC has full information. For a visa to Taiwan, you must have a passport, 2 photos, tickets in advance, and a Y2000 visa fee. Apply: Association of East Asian Relations, Heiwado Bldg., 2nd fl., 8-Higashi-Azabu 1-chome, Minato-ku, Tokyo, tel: (03) 583-2171. Hours are Mon.-Fri. 0900 to 1100, 1300 to 1600, Sat. 0900-1100. For more travel information see "getting around," Naha chapter. To obtain a Japanese visa in Taiwan, contact Interchange Assoc., 43 Tsinan Road, Section 2, Taipei, Rep. of China

THE LAND

The total area of the islands that make up the Okinawa Prefecture is 2244 square km. The largest, Okinawa Island, encompasses over half of this area. Okinawa Island is long (100km), thin and jagged. It is only 30 km wide   where sprawls into the sea at the Motubu Peninsula. The central area is a mingling of rugged ravine, sheer cliff, and rolling verdant hills. The southernmost region is hilly and capped with limestone plateaus. The coastline is varied, with craggy, rocky shores in the N, coral reef and sandy wasteland in the center, and elevated beaches ending in sea cliffs in the south. The whole island is gouged with caves, which made a natural and formidable barrier for the Japanese defenders against invading American G.I.s in WW11. The outlying islands making up the rest of the prefecture vary considerably in size and terrain. Miyako (176 sq km) escaped the ravages of bombardment during WW11 and remains a preserve for traditional Okinawan architecture. Flat and low, fringed by coral reef, Miyako is ideal for the cultivation of pineapples and sugar cane. Wild and secluded Iriomote (322 sq. km) lies in the extreme south. This mountainous island is covered in verdant sub-tropical jungle, and is home to a recently discovered wildcat, quite primitive from an evolutionary standpoint. Ie Jima, one hr off the coast of Motobu Pen. in the N of Okinawa Island, is peanut-shaped, flat on the periphery and dominated by one towering mountain in the center. Some of the smaller uninhabited islands are the peaks of sunken volcanos jutting out of the sea, covered in deep tropical green. On all, beaches and coral reefs invite the sun worshipers while a network of trails and paths lures the trekkers inland. Climbing to the top of any mountain provides a breathtaking sea panorama in all directions. Interisland ferries connect them all and an adventurous traveler would be rewarded with a quiet, uncluttered, traditional island setting. *Minshuku* are available, and camping on your own secluded beach is no more difficult than finding a good palm-sheltered spot to pitch your tent to enjoy a vista of sand and surf.

CLIMATE

Any season in Okinawa will be generally warm with luxuriant tropical plants and profuse blazing blossoms. Fruits such as bananas (the little reddish ones are called island [*shima*] bananas, a bit sweeter than the usual), and papayas grow year round and are available at most food stalls. October to April is considered a fine time to visit Okinawa. Cherry blossoms can be seen in January; lillies adorn the sea cliffs in April. May and June are rainy; average rainfall in Naha is 2118 mm per year. July-Sept. are the best swimming months. Violent but usually brief typhoons rake the islands in Sept. and October. When it's rainy, visit temples, shrines and historical sights; when fine, hike trails and go to the beach.

village homes in Okinawa are built low to the ground, surrounded by thick coral walls and have heavy tiled roofs. These features ensure protection against the typhoons that suddenly sweep inland wreaking havoc

FLORA AND FAUNA

fauna: The wealth of Okinawan wildlife lies in the sea. Exquisite varieties of tropical fish inhabit the coral reefs. Lobsters, *tai*, prawns, and abundant game fish provide the traveler equipped with snorkeling gear or pole with entertainment and a fine meal. The sea around Kabira Bay is used to farm black cultured pearls. Sharks and eels lurk in the deep waters. Turtles waddle ashore to lay their eggs on many islands. Dolphins steal the show at Ocean Expo Memorial Park. *reptiles*: The *habu* is a deadly poisonous snake with a slim neck, broad head, and erratic diamond pattern. It is found throughout Okinawa and the adjacent islands. Like all snakes, it will definitely try to avoid man. If camping out, take your boots inside the tent, crush tin cans, don't poke your hand around when foraging for firewood; when trekking step on fallen trees in the path, never over them. An antidote is available. If bitten, stay calm, wash and bind the wound, seek help immediately. You will sometimes see signs, "BEWARE OF SNAKES." Take caution, but don't panic.

a photo of a stray Irimote kitten rescued in June 1981, the only one ever captured alive. Now living at the animal Protection Center in Okinawa City.

Iriomote wildcat: This primitive wildcat was discovered only in the past decade. There are believed to be only 50-60 in existence. They are found only on Iriomote I., one of the last unexplored regions of Japan. A primitive form of wildcat, these last examples are considered living fossils. Slightly larger than a house cat, this curiosity has white spots, a mangy reddish gray coat, and doesn't dilate its pupils in bright light as other cats do. The chances of seeing one would be remote. They are found in the deep recesses of the mountainous interior of Iriomote.

bird life: The *noguchigera*, living in the deep forest of northern Okinawa, is red and black and has a long pointed beak. It is designated as a Natural Treasure, and doubles as the prefectura bird. The *noguchigera* dines on the larvae of logicorn which makes it a natural insect controller. The *akahige* is a reddish brown bird with a beautiful song. Found only on Iriomote, Ishigaki and Yonaguni Islands, it lives in dark recesses near rivers and streams, and eats insects and nuts. *insects*: The *yonagunisan* is a moth, said to be the largest in the world. It can be found on Yonaguni I., the most extreme southwestern island in Japan.

flora: Hibiscus (*akabana*) is a species of Chinese rose found in all parts of Okinawa Prefecture. It is used to decorate graves and Buddhist altars. The brilliant red flower of the *deigo* tree is the official flower of the prefecture. The wood is used to make excellent pieces of lacquerware. The blazing red flower symbolizes passion. The *sakura* (cherry blossoms) begin to bloom in late Jan. and mark the beginning of Spring and the earliest cherry blossom festival in Japan. The most frequently found trees are palms, traveler trees, and pandanus. There are also broadleave evergreens such as the camphor tree, evergreen oaks, plus a variety of pines. *Fukugi* trees form a high green hedge and provide a windbreak against the violent typhoons of the area. The *yaeyama* coconut palm faces extinction. It has been cut down for building, the leaves used as thatch, and the young sprouts eaten; it is now found in only a few secluded spots on Iriomote. The largest bottle-shaped palms in Japan are at S. E. Botanical Gardens not far from Naha. *Hinpungajumaru* is a tree 20 m high and the symbol of Nago City in the N of Okinawa Island. It is 300 years old and the name is derived from the Sanbushi monument found under its immense spreading boughs. Orange *okocho,* red poinsettias, deep pink bougainvillaea, yellow *ohambou,* strings of white "moon pearls," camellia "dropping flower" with fluff-like newborn chicks, and long trumpet lilies are only a few the natural flowers that grace village stone walkways and punctuate the paths of deep green tropical forests. Large, white drooping *datsun,* yellow and orange *kaenboku* and *sharinbai,* delicate white flower of the rose family, are also abundant. These flowers play heavily in the motifs of woven cloth and bright costumes local festivities.

THE YAMATO

a last ditch effort to repell the American invasion in
[Ok]inawa the super dreadnought *Yamato* was given a
[su]icide mission called "Heavenly Code." Oil was
[pr]eciously short in war-ravaged Japan and the Yamato
[ha]d only enough fuel for a one-way sortie. The Yamato,
[its] name (meaning "Mountain Road") the same as that
[of] ancient Japan itself, was the pride of the
[ad]mirality as well as being considered a mystical
[sy]mbol of military Japan. It measured 246 m long,
[we]ighed 72,800 tons and its nine 46 cm guns were the
[lar]gest ever mounted on a battleship. These enormous
[can]non could hurl dufflebag sized shells for over 40 km.
[Th]is powerful giant with a full company of 2,500 men
[cou]ld cruise at a steady 16 knots for 11,500 km. In the
[ear]ly afternoon of April 6th 1945, the Yamato and its

small cover fleet of destroyers slipped out of Tokuyama
Naval Base. Its desperate mission was to steam for
Okinawa, destroying the enemy wherever encountered
and to finally scuttle itself in Okinawa Harbor blazing
away with its massive guns until it was swallowed
whole by the sea. It never made it. The supership was
spotted by American submarines and Naval Task Force
58 sent no less than 350 planes to engage it in bloody
battle. After being struck with 5 bombs and 12
torpedoes the Yamato sunk in 375 m of water about
160 km SW of Nagasaki, almost exactly 24 hours after
its mission began. In May of 1982 a Japanese group lead
by a Mr. Ishida, a former naval officer, reported that
they had found the hulk of the Yamato and a salvage of
the wreckage is now underway

HISTORY

[T]he Chinese referred to Okinawa as *Shurei no
Kuni*, or, the "nation that keeps the peace."
[A]ctually, the kings of the Ryukyu Is. (former
[n]ame of Okinawa) who held court at Shuri, now
[a] part of the Ryukyu University in Naha, had no
[c]hoice, as they were caught between the colos-
[s]us of China and the mighty and rapid ascen-
[d]ancy of Japan. Jimmu Tennu, the first (semi-
[l]egendary) emperor of Japan, to whom all
[s]ubsequent emperors trace their lineage, was
[t]hought to be an Okinawan pirate who invaded
[K]yushu about 1800 yrs. ago. Written records
[d]escribing Okinawa begin about 1400 yrs. ago.
[B]etween that time and the mid-14th C.,
[O]kinawa was united under the king of the
[m]iddle kingdom" who vanquished his rivals to
[t]he N and S and set up his permanent court at
[S]huri. Here, the impressive main gate, along
[w]ith 90 % of the traditional architecture
[t]hroughout Okinawa, was destroyed during
[W]W11. It served as the HQ of the Japanese
[d]efending forces, but has since been rebuilt. In
[t]he 14th C. China dominated Okinawa and
[d]emanded nominal tribute and subordination.

The kings at Shuri complied, and Chinese culture flowed into Okinawa, which was repaid by a
period of peace and tranquility. A Tax Stone
(*bubakariisu*), 1.4 m high, erected during this
period, still exists on Miyako Island. It is said that
all inhabitants who grew to its height must pay
taxes. In the 17th C. the Shimazu clan of
southern Kyushu subjugated Okinawa, appealed
to the Shogun for possession, and brought
Okinawa under the dominance of Japan.
Okinawa developed in relative seclusion with
some internal political turmoil until the late 19th
C. when it was officially annexed as a Japanese
prefecture under the Meiji government. Ties to
China were completely severed when 66 Okinawan fishermen drifted off course and landed in
Formosa (now Taiwan) and were promptly executed by the authorities. The Japanese government protested and China, accepting the
protestation, acknowledged Japanese sovereignty over the islands. The ancient tribute paid
to China ceased. The Japanese exploited and
dominated the area until Easter Sunday, 1945.
On that date, total devastating war swept across
the islands. Five American divisions, supported
by an overwhelming naval barrage and aerial
bombardment, invaded Okinawa. In the grisly
battle that ensued, lasting 82 days, numerous

acts of bravery, fanaticism, honor and down-right insanity occurred on both sides. The Japanese had been totally prepared for the invasion. Their battle cry was:

> "One plane—one warship
> One boat—one ship
> One man—ten of the enemy, or one tank."

They had honeycombed the natural caves and rock outcroppings of the entire island with a labyrinth of tunnels. Even the ancient tombs were fortified and used as gun emplacements. The fighting was hand to hand. The gains and losses after a day of fighting resulted in a few bloody meters of shell cratered ground. Civilians and Japanese died horribly by bayonets, flame throwers and hand grenades. Mothers took their babies in their arms and leaped into the sea. *Kamikaze* pilots swooped from the sky and crashed their planes into American warships. There were heavy and severe daily losses to the American Marine divisions. American generals died alongside their men in harrowing *bonsai* attacks. At the end of the fighting, 250,000 Japanese soldiers and civilians lay dead; 13,000 americans would never return home. On June 22, 1945, the American flag was raised. The Japanese commander, General Ushijima, and his chief of staff, General Cho, fulfilled their last obligation according to *bushido* and commiteed *seppuku*. The unbelievable had

Okinawan civilians suffered terribly during the invasion of their island home. Hoodwinked by propaganda from Tokyo they were taught to believe that American G.I.'s were animalistic bloodthirsty murderers, rapists and thieves. Many civilians at first chose suicide instead of falling into the grips of the Americans. They were overjoyed to discover that the feared G.I.'s were mostly kind young men from a far away land caught up in a war that sickened them and which they longed to end

happened. For the first time in Japanese history, the "land of the gods" had been invaded and vanquished by a foreign nation. The U.S. occupied Okinawa until 1972, when it reverted back to Japan.

government: After 27 years of U.S. occupation, Okinawa once again became a sovereign part of Japan in 1972. The last vestige of foreign influence disappeared when driving went from the right-hand side of the road (to cater to Americans) to the left-hand side to match the rest of Japan. The transition period was a nerve jangling but very polite mess. Everyone has the message now so don't worry. It was a long political issue to get the Americans out. When the Americans left, however, the economy took a nose dive. Okinawa has traditionally been looked upon as an area that is to be exploited by the central government. Japanese people have recently altered this view slightly and are trying to bolster the economy, a task which is showing moderate success though Okinawa still lags behind the main islands. Farming (sugar cane, pineapples, tobacco), fishing, and the tourist trade are the main props of the economy. The tourist trade is on the rise, but there will always be uncluttered beaches, remote islands, and infrequently visited villages to be explored and enjoyed.

THE PEOPLE

The people of Okinawa are of the same general stock as the main body of Japanese people with a bit heavier smattering of Chinese and Indonesian blood. They have the same general features as the Japanese except that many seem to be of a swarthier complexion (due to climate) and have naturally wavy hair. Okinawans have been under the dominance of one power or another for centuries (Chinese, American, Japanese) and being powerless to oppose the dominance, have developed the ability to "get along." They have been referred to by the Japanese as *shurei-no-tami*, (people who treat others with respect). Perhaps they've had no choice. They speak their own dialect of Japanese, and would find it difficult communicating with someone from the mainland. Their customs and traditions are unique. Because of their geographical location, these islands have been a touchstone for Chinese culture. A Japanese soldier's diary from WWII reports that the village reminded him of China, not Japan. Okinawa has also been referred to as "the island of the dead

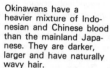

Okinawans have a heavier mixture of Indonesian and Chinese blood than the mainland Japanese. They are darker, larger and have naturally wavy hair.

because of the vast number of tombs, some roughhewn, others elaborate, carved into the sides of mountains and found in the midst of fields everywhere. The Okinawans are second-class citizens of Japan. They are accepted as part of, yet as a people slightly less than "we Japanese." The climate, remoteness and tropical island atmosphere have all combined to develop an easygoing personality that hasn't suffered the ravages of modernization and anxiety to the same degree as is typical in the northern cosmopolitan centers of Japan. Due to American Occupation, Okinawans are not as awe struck by the *gaijin* as in other parts of Japan. The obverse may be true, at least in Naha and the bigger towns. Perhaps this is due to the fact that soldiers from any country usually do not make the best diplomats. Okinawans love life, are interested in meeting foreigners, enjoy sharing cross-cultural experiences, and will treat you with a warm hospitality which is easy to reciprocate.

ARTS AND CRAFTS

The beautiful fabrics of Okinawa personify the strength and brilliance of sub-tropical nature. The designs are simple, powerful, and in harmony with the surroundings. Nature, in a word, has been absorbed by the Okinawans and abstractly manifested in their outstanding handiwork. *bingata:* This unique dyeing of linen and cotton, using vegetable dyes of wild plants mixed with natural pigments, is the most famous traditional fabric of Okinawa. It is said to resemble the *yuzen* dyeing of Kyoto. It is created by a stencil and dye process employing brilliant colors and specializing in such Okinawan themes as flowers, shells, country scenes, fans and birds. The patterns are untamed and elegant. Wildflowers provide the inspiration for color. An experienced craftsman can spend 2 painstaking weeks on a small piece of cloth. They make excellent wall hangings, and when blocked and framed are truly superb. Kimono and neckties are also made out of this material. The process can be observed at Shuri in Naha. They are expensive, but definitely worth the money. Beware of mass-produced facsimiles on synthetic materials in the markets. You get what you pay for. *minsa:* This fabric is only produced on Taketomi Island, but is available in Naha. It was presented by a woman to her lover as a sign of acceptance to a marriage proposal. Its main pattern is the centipede which symbolizes eternal love. The red thread, signifying passion like the red bloom of the *deigo,* can be seen drying on the stone walls of the villages of Taketomi. *miyako jyofu:* This dark blue fabric with a smooth texture was traditionally a tax payment. Today the villagers of Miyako preserve the tradition by working communally, usually in their gardens after the rainy season, to produce this fine cloth. *bashofu (abaca cloth):* This cloth has a 600 year tradition. It is made from the fiber of the banana tree. It produces a faint yellow lightweight cloth, perfect for kimono and *obi* in this hot, humid land. *kasuri cloth:* Another traditional art form, the warp in this particular cloth is raised, resembling fine needlework. Introduced 400-500 years ago as a result of trade with Indonesia and Taiwan, it is produced at Keijan, Motubu and Teruya from plant fibers. Twenty thousand *tan* (218,000 m) are produced per year, mostly silk.

a ceramic *shisa* (lion dog) placed on the roofs of Okinawan houses to ward off evil spirits.

Tsuboya pottery: This exquisitely made pottery, which takes its name from the Tsuboya section of Naha, has been produced for the last 500 years. It was influenced at its inception by that time's fledgling trade with Europe, and so most pieces were used as wine and water jars. To this day *tokkuri* (*sake* bottles) with a thin spout and curved body (designed to be carried by means of a small rope on the hip) are produced. Also the *shisa* (lion dog) is designed to ward off evil spirits and is one of the most common products; this diety is rendered both as male and female and is available everywhere. The prices range from a few 100 yen to Y10,000 for the larger ones. The kiln techniques were introduced from China and are preserved by master potters to this day. Some of the best known are Masaharu Kobashikawa, Toshio Kinsho and the most famous is Kiro Kinjo. Any piece he signs is considered a national treasure. All of these masters work in the Naha area. Just after WWII, pottery suffered because G. I.s bought it up as souvenirs and the quality declined as the demand went up. There are still inferior pieces made that cater to the tourist trade, but fine works are also available. Unless you are skilled at recognizing fine pottery, your best bet is to purchase it at a large department store (*depato*) where the selection has been made for you. If you are just after a nifty souvenir, buy at the markets and set your own standards. Two other motifs that are most common are burial urns and boxes. The boxes have a dragon (usually greeen) sitting on the lid. If you plan to buy household items for daily use, such as cups and plates, be careful when washing them. The glaze is thin and can wear off with constant washing.

lacquerware: This immensely intricate art form has been in existence for about 500 years, the natural humidity and heat of Okinawa providing the perfect climate for its manufacture and development. Okinawan lacquerware is made from the light wood of the *diego* tree and is lacquered and relacquered until a perfectly smooth, shiny black finish is achieved. Onto this, the design is finally drawn. It is usually a flower or a fern, and the main colors are red, gold, brown and green. The pieces can be serving trays, bowls, and jewelry boxes. They are expensive but gain in beauty as they age. Don't let them sit on a windowsill in the bright sunlight. Beware of cheap plastic facsimiles. Bembo Lacquerware Factory (Naha) is reputed for its high quality of workmanship. Tours can be arranged.

the Okinawan *samisen*

musical instruments: The *samisen* (Okinawan *jabisen*) is a three-stringed instrument introduced from China in the 14th Century. It has been referred to as the Japanese banjo and at times, when vigorously played, resembles one. It is a classical instrument of Japan, oftentime played by a geisha. It has a long, slim, fretless neck, a broad head and 3 large friction pegs to hold the strings. The body is round, about 8 cm thick, and covered in snake skin, or cat skin. One of the most famous producers is Matayoshi-san who lives in Kamoji, Naha City. There are no music books for this instrument written in English, so Western players will have to teach themselves. If you purchase one, you'll receive a few basic lessons. The *mitsu dake* is a rhythm instrument made out of 3 pieces of bamboo held by the 3 main fingers of the hand and struck by the other hand, making a castanet-type sound.

This basic type of instrument is produced in one form or another by many cultures throughout the world.

weaving an *Antsuku* basket

folk arts: Antsuku is the true art form of the common man. These rough baskets are woven from the fibers of the pandanus (screw pine). Traditionally used by *adan* (fieldworkers) as lunch buckets, *antsuku* are found in all markets and shops. They make fine souvenirs, inexpensive yet practical gifts, or incidental traveling bags. *Ryukyu ningyo:* These superb dolls are dressed in traditional costumes in colors of red, gold and blue. They are adorned with elaborate headpieces and usually carry fans. The prices vary from Y3000 to Y15,000. The more expensive ones are in glass and wood cases, which are impressive in themselves. The less expensive ones come in plastic cases. The poses of these dolls reflect the grace and serenity of the women of Okinawa. Other minor crafts include stonework, shell and beadwork, tortoise shell, jewelry and weaving; available all over Okinawa.

the performing arts: There are a great variety of dances, with each island having its own special form. The main occasions for dancing are village festivals such as the August dance (*mo-asobi*) and the seed-gathering dance (*Sangatsu-asobi*) performed by the village youth and maidens.

Many dances are held during August to pray for a good harvest and peace. Every member of the village joins in dance after dance. Many festivals include the fan dance, the stick-wielding dance of the men and boys, the dance drama (*shishimai*), and many others. There is also the rain dance (*amagoi-odori*), and the *usudaiko* dance performed by women. The *ryukyu* dance is divided into 3 parts: *iriha* (entrance), *nakaha* (dance proper), and *dewa* (exit). Some dances are performed to songs and others to instruments alone. Some are boisterous mixed affairs and others are refined, danced by couples. The *odori* dances are restricted to definite patterns while the *mai* dances are performed as freely as the emotions dictate. The *jabisen* is the main instrument, supplemented by a particular type of harp, and mouth whistles. Yaeyama I. during Oct. has a seed-gathering festival with dances that last for 2 days. At the *anagama bon* festival, the entire village joins in. Miyakojima I. features the *kuicha-odori*, which is performed by men and women who clap their hands as the only musical accompaniment.

FOOD

The best and most easily obtainable food for the traveler in Okinawa is fresh, tropical fruit which is available in any town or island market. In a very hot climate, a light meal at noon is recommended. Fruit will not only provide energy, but will save on the pocketbook too. Eat your fill of papaya, banana, pineapple, mango and kiwi fruit. Most Japanese do not eat in public, but a traveler eating a banana on a bus stop bench or under a palm tree is acceptable.

special dishes: Most Japanese dishes are available in Okinawa, but Okinawans haved added a few tasty delights of their own. Some of them are: *soki soba*, the Okinawan variety of *soba*. *Soki* means pork, and the soba is prepared in the normal style with 4 small spare-ribs floating on top. This is usually the special dish in most *soba* shops, and is accordingly a bit more expensive (about Y450). Okinawan *soba* (Y300) is prepared in the same way except that 2 small pieces of bacon-like pork are substituted for the ribs. Both dishes contain 2 pieces of *kamaboko* (processed fish cake), and are served with side dishes of *takuan* and a rice ball (*onigiri*) containing a sweet, tangy sauce. With *soki soba* you will be provided with a small bowl; don't pour your tea into it, it's for the bones. Also on the table will be *togarashi*, (red pepper), or *shichimi* (7 tastes), a

OKINAWA FESTIVALS AND EVENTS

Throughout Okinawa, the year is heavily interspersed with festivals and celebrations, most stemming from primitive nature rituals. They are unique in many ways from the festivals found in the mainland prefectures of Japan. These festivals are heavily steeped in tradition, having been handed down almost unchanged for centuries. Most, having maintained their original form, constitute a type of living history. The following is a list and brief description of the major festivals shared by all Okinawans, but bear in mind that each village, town, and shrine have numerous local festivals throughout the year that are distinctive to the area and maintained only by a small group of people.

Jan. 20: *Juri Uma*, at Tsuji, Naha, near and at the "Tea House of the August Moon." Hundreds of dancing girls from various tea houses around Naha parade through the streets riding toy horses, accompanied by gongs, *jamisen*, drums and flutes. Traditionaly, this was a rite of the *geisha* who entertained the visiting noblemen in times past. Now most of the women participating are only a modern facsimile.

May 4: *Haryusen* (Hary). This festival is held on 4 May at Tomari Port in Naha and at Itoman. It is dedicated to the gods of the sea, to whom prayers are offered for a big haul, and for safety for the fishermen. The festival features a boat race in a traditional canoe (*sabani*) manned by 12 oarsmen and one at the tiller. Officially, winning is not as important as participating, but try telling that to the local "bookies." The *sabani* are festively decorated, featuring painted patterns on the gunwales, and the oarsmen are all in traditional costume.

May 4: *Haryusen* (Hary). This festival is held on 4 May at Tomari Port in Naha and at Itoman. It is dedicated to the gods of the sea, to whom prayers are offered for a big haul, and for safety for the fishermen. The festival features a boat race in a traditional canoe (*sabani*) manned by 12 oarsmen and one at the tiller. Officially, winning is not as important as participating, but try telling that to the local "bookies." The *sabani* are festively decorated, featuring painted patterns on the gunwales, and the oarsmen are all in traditional costume. Chinese influence on the craft is apparant.

Jul. 13-16: *Eisa*. During the *Bon* Festival (13-16 Jul.), young men and women dance and sing through the streets shouting, "Eisa! Eisa!" The participants, whose main task is to form a link between the living and the venerable dead, are

accompanied by the *jabisen* (snake-covered *samisen*) as they make their way from house to house. They paint their faces and wear a white cloth around their heads. During this festival fine delicacies are offered to the departed.

Aug. 15: Nakagusuke Castle. A moon-viewing festival is held at this site Nakagusuke is 22 km NE of Naha (take Bus 30, Awase East Line along RL 329). The castle itself is worth seeing, and this is also the setting for traditional Okinawan Court dancing. A beautiful woman/man and a bottle of *sake* are also recommended in case of clouds.

Nov. 10: The purpose of the *Tanetori* Festival is to pray for a good harvest as well as to prepare spiritually for the harvest. This festival (highly regarded by the farmers) is steeped in tradition. The farmer's bodies along with the actual implements for harvesting are purified and offered to the *kami*.

Tsunahiki Matsuri (Giant *Tug-of-War*): This festival is held at 3 different dates throughout Okinawa. First Sun after 27 June at Yonabaru (10 km E of Hana), 15 Aug. at Itoman, and 10 Oct. at Naha. Two teams pull against each other

with 2 giant rice-straw ropes representing male and female. The ropes are 60 cm in diameter, 500 m long, and can weight 1000 kilos. Smaller ropes are attached to them, and the giant tug begins. Traditional songs and dances are performed to accompany the strenuous tug. The exact location chages each year, so find out exactly where it is planned to occur. Ask at TIC or any JTB.

every 12 years: Noro, held at Kudaka I. during the Year of the Horse. One distinguished woman is selected as *noro*. A *noro* must be over 70 years old and well versed in the discipline of the *miko* (temple priestesses). These women, who traditionally communicated with *kami* now work at shrines where they perform the duties of clerks, dance at religious ceremonies, et. The *noro* represents the villages to the *kami*, offers prayers, and receives messages that she relates in the classical oracle tradition. The women of the island who wish to become *miko* (ages 30-42) gather at this date. They carry a huge bow that forms a circle and are tested for their knowledge and worthiness. If successful, a red seal is applied to forehead and cheeks and they then enter the lowest ranks of the *miko* in some areas, the *noro* is hereditary.

Sundays: Bullfights. These tremendous animals, at one time used primarily for farming can be seen in action only a few km N of Naha. Traditionally, the contests were held only during the farmers' slack season. The bulls, head down and shoulder muscles rippling, try to gain dominance in the ring. Like giant *sumo*, they try to force their opponent out of the ring, or cause the opponent to withdraw. The bull and its trainer form a real bond of affection as well as a team. Rarely is a bull killed or injured, the tournament being instead a test of strength and endurance with the trainer plotting strategy. The audience, in full participation with more than a few *yen* wagered, stomp their feet and harangue the bulls to battle.

mixture of red pepper and spice, to be sprinkled on top. Vegetarians can enjoy these dishes also; the meat is just placed on top, not cooked into the soup, so you can pick it off. Wash down these 2 dishes with Japanese tea (always provided) and you have a delicious, inexpensive, substantial meal. Any *soba* shop will serve almost exactly the same dish, and they are always meticulously clean family affairs. A good one is Maruichi on Kokusai Dori, 150 m N of Mitsukoshi Depato on the right-hand side; look for the blue-tinted door just next to the optometrist's. *Yasai chanpuru* is a good, filling, inexpensive staple of stir-fried slivers of pork, green peppers, onions, cabbage and carrots in soy sauce, spices, and oil, served with a side dish of rice, and a pot of tea. On mainland Japan it is called *yasai itami*, and sometimes beef is substituted for the pork. It costs about Y400, and is available everywhere. Don't buy it when visiting Itoman, where it is locally prepared with Spam—a disastrous meeting of east and west. *Nakami* is a stir-fried dish of tripe (beef or pork stomach) served in a savory sauce over rice; inexpensive, and tastes much better than it sounds. *Yakitori* is easily available everywhere in Naha, but especially good at the stalls around the Makishi Public Fair. Only Y50 per skewer; combined with fruit it makes a dandy mid-day repast.

bar food (otsumami): These are the little ripoff dishes that are served to you in bars, whether you want them or not. Unfortunately, this snack-with-drink convention exists in Okinawa also, but sometimes these little delicacies are exotic enough to be worth the money. In the bars around Okinawa you will get little slices of raw turtle, very delicate in flavor; ground pigs ear, gristly and made up almost like cole slaw; or

goya, a gourd-like vegetable called *nangauori* on mainland Japan, extremely bitter, but believed to provide stamina and vigor. If the mind is willing but the stomach weak, have your trusty beer mug ready to quickly wash down any surprisingly unsavory tidbit. It hurts too much to pay for something that you don't eat, and you will be charged regardless if you eat them or not.

drinks: Most bars carry a full shelf of whiskies and scotches as well as beer and sake. Okinawa is known for *awamori.* This special sake is believed to have entered Okinawa about 500 years ago through Thailand, as recorded by Chi Ryu, a Chinese historian. The Japanese say that the colder climates of northern Japan are perfect for making sake, but that *awamori* needs the warm climate of Okinawa. Anyway, the Okinawan brewers have captured a small typhoon in every bottle. They are on sale in every town, and often come in distinctive twine-wrapped pottery jars. In bars, *awamori* is served in little clay pots with a large tumbler of ice. You pour a little in the tumbler at a time. Sometimes the Okinawans will add a raw egg and some sugar. It can also be drunk as a cocktail, accompanied by soda and a sprig of peppermint. *Shochu,* a vodka-like spirit, is not as sweet as sake and can oftentimes be rough and bitter. It is a heavy duty no-nonsense drink. The rule for any of these strong Japanese drinks is "sip it; don't swill it."

Habuzake urume: Real snake juice—this type of *sake* comes in a large, wide-lidded jar. It is also believed to enhance stamina and sexual prowess. The *sake* is ordinary, but in the bottom of the jar is coiled the deadly poisonous *habu* snake. The snake will slowly disintegrate into bones after 10 years. This sake is potent and known to really get you slithering.

NAHA

Naha grew as a city because of the foreign trade that poured in from Luzon, Annam, Malacca, China, and finally the West. It is the heart of Okinawa and the center of government, industry and education. Much was destroyed during WW11 when the city was reduced to a smoldering cinder. The Americans brought in the bulldozers and americanized the city with such thoroughfares as the Naha Bypass and Kokusai Dori (International Blvd.). Kokusai Dori remains the heart of Naha. Much of the charm and quiet living of the city has disappeared due to modernization influenced by mainland Japan, unfortunately the fate of many provincial towns. Naha is the closest example to a modern Japanese city in the prefecture and can be thought of as the 'Tokyo' of Okinawa. Naha holds 3 fascinations for the traveler: art, history, and nightlife. The University of the Ryukyu's is here, built on the ruins of old Shuri Castle. Banks, tourist bureaus, ferry services linking the outer islands, plus an international airport are all found in Naha. Old men and women in bright kimono walk with a dignified air while teenagers in T-shirts and jeans cruise the city streets. Here you will find a potpourri of all that Okinawa has to offer. Established shops selling magnificent art works are next door to fly-by-night ones selling pure junk. *Obasan* with quiet manners and quick smiles sell *soba;* their shops sandwiched between McDonalds and A&W Root Beer. (Meet other foreigners with a goldmine of travel tips at the McDonalds just up the street from Mitsukoshi Depato.) The city has 2 main ports: Tomari, and Naha Ko about 2 km apart. Both have excellent service to the city center.

getting around: Bus service is excellent in Naha and throughout the Okinawan mainland. LPG-powered taxis are on almost every downtown corner in Naha, and they are easily hailed as they circle the streets. Most buses originate at the bus terminal located at the S end of Kokusai Dori (see map). Since there is no rail service on Okinawa, the bus system is sophisticated. The lack of rail service is due to the spongy Okinawan ground, being composed primarily of coral. Bus routes travel the length and breadth of the mainland. For example, Bus Rt. 20 (Nago West line) follows Rt. 58 to Nago along the W coast, while Bus Rt. 21 follows the E coast to Nago. Branch lines go to virtually every town

and village. For information on prices and schedules, check the bus terminal or contact: Okinawa Bus, 1-10-5 Izumizaki, Naha, tel: (0988) 67-3382 (the regular line to all points throughout Okinawa); Ryukyu Bus, 2-365 Makishi, Naha, tel: (0988) 63-3636 (sight-seeing tours); and Naha Transportation, 1-19-11 Nishi, Naha, tel: (0988) 68-2931 (Naha city buses).

travel services: Okinawa Tourist Hall is located at Naha Port close to Meiji Bridge. The building is covered in red tiles and can be easily spotted. Sight-seeing tours and schedules for interisland flights and ferry services are offered. Reservations can be made from here for onward-going travel. More information is available from: Okinawa Federation of Sightseeing, Sightseeing Bldg., 42-1 Asahi-machi, Naha 900, tel: (0988) 67-4716. In Tokyo contact Okinawa Prefecture, International Sightseeing Bldg., 1-8-3 Marunouchi, Chiyoda-ku, Tokyo 100, tel: (03) 215-0546. For travel agents in Naha try JTB, tel: (0988) 68-9781; or Okinawa Tourist Services, tel: (0988) 55-1111. In Okinawa City (Koza) try American Express, tel: (0989) 37-3142. For car rentals, contact K. K. Japaren, 20-2 Higashi-machi, Naha, tel: (0988) 68-5942, or Okinawa Tourist Car Rental, 261-3 Matsuo, Naha, tel: (0988) 68-6013.

SHOPPING

First Makishi Public Fair: Across from Mitsukoshi Depato on Kokusai Dori (open 0700-2100, 7 days a week). This fair is the most crowded, most amazing hodgepodge of food, art, crafts, softgoods, and bric-a-brac in all of Okinawa. It was originally built only from free formed pitch. It's a twisting, turning maze of stalls and booths providing an entire day of entertainment. The shopkeepers are usually women, and pressureless browsing is the norm. You can buy anything: *bingata* cloth, *tsuboya* ware, *ryukyu* dolls and cigarette lighters made from 50-caliber machine gun bullets. The main entrance arcade is covered by a tent, but go further. Don't worry about getting lost; you will. The area is relatively small, but jam packed. If you spot an item that you really like, buy it; you probably have been given a fair price. Finding your way back to the same shop later could prove *muzukashii* (diffi-

open air shopping along the alleyways of Naha's Makishi Fair offers the island's best in folkarts, food and clothing along with a heavy mixture of cheap souveniers.

cult). This is the spot for souvenirs and art hunting. All products from throughout the islands flow into here. They are authentic and, believe it or not, you usually won't find them cheaper at their places of origin. This market is a true oriental delight. Visit it whether you intend to purchase or just look around. _food:_ The eatery section is an over-stuffed cornucopia. Big bags of mushrooms, noodles, squash, carrots and cucumbers spill into the aisles. Cabbages of various sizes, tomatoes, usually big beauties, daikon (the long white radishes), raw peanuts, beans and rice are easily had from bargain stalls. There is also excellent fresh fruit. Small, reddish and sweet *shima* bananas (island bananas), mouth watering mangos, and kiwi fruit are all available. A vegetarian's delight! Next—fish, fish everywhere. The pungent odors and slippery wet floors mark the fishmarket area: you may be greeted by the smiling face of a fish monger as she holds up an octopus for your inspection and rubs her belly (the international sign for delicious). Delight in the displays of big, red, plump prawns; snappers; *maguro* (tuna); bags of dried and fresh seaweed; *awabi*, (abalone); tiny multi-colored clams to throw shell-and-all into the soup; and a psychedelic fish of blazing orange, green and blue (a favorite for sushi). In another section find meat cut by women butchers on tree-stump chopping blocks. Pigs feet, knuckles, knees and ears are a favorite with Okinawans. These are served as *otsumami* in the little red-lantern bars (*akachochin*) all over town.

miscellaneous: There is no theft even though shop owners leave their wares unattended on the sidewalks. Jewelry shops here specialize in *sango*, a pinkish to blood-red coral (Y2000-Y20,000) that looks like a little ornamental bush which is fashioned into pendants, earrings and tie clips. The more blood-red the piece, the more expensive it is. There are shops for household items featuring multi-colored *futon* and *zabuton*, quilts, and *tatami* mats. The thicker the *futon*, the more expensive it is (a decent one can be purchased for Y6000). An expensive but superb kimono shop in the area is Toma Gofu Kuten. Japanese men will not enter because it is a "ladies" store, but *gaijin* men can break the barrier, although they will cause unending giggles. _glassware:_ For a detailed look at traditional Okinawan glassware, visit Okuhara Glass Factory where export-quality hand-blown glassware is produced. In Okinawa, glassware was first produced in 1902 after the art form was learned from the west. The unique process has been preserved here while at the same time becoming a lost art in the west. The glassware has a cracked effect somewhat like a shattered windsheild in an automobile. There are small goblets for Y1200, milk pitchers for Y1700, and ornamental pieces like *fugu* (blowfish) at Y3500.

carving: Stores featuring carvings, usually wood and tortoise shell, are also quite common; elaborately carved 1.5 m Buddha for Y500,000, or a small table model for about Y5000. Tortoise shell ware includes hair clips and other fancy feminine accoutrements. These are mostly delicate yet practical items. Another odd specialty of some stores is matched, mounted and carved (often with a dragon motif) bull horns. Up to one m across, they are designed to be hung on a wall. *lacquerware:* The main and most interesting product of this area is the lacquerware. For lacquerware, visit the Bembo Lacquerware Factory, long renowned for its craftsmanship. For *tsuboya,* walk about 4 short blocks behind the markets to the *Tsuboya* section and visit the Okinawa Pottery Factory and the smaller but more interesting kilns of the independent craftsmen in the area. Finally, the area abounds in cheap but unique curios, trinkets and toys. Paper wallets, bound notepads, stick pins, and *ryukyu* dolls make excellent gifts and momentos. Also a good practical and authentic item is footwear. *Geta* for men and women, indispensable if you plan to stay in *minshuku* and YHs, sell for about Y1000. They slip on and off very easily but be careful of slide slipping on wet walkways. In this category are *odi,* special thongs worn by women in kimono. These are fancy, colorful, and about Y8000. They are too delicate to take any type of heavy use. Here also is a unique type of *geta* for men with a cork bottom, rubber sole, and a little feminine heel. They may look too exotic to be worn by most men back home.

ENTERTAINMENT

bars: These neighborhood red-lantern bars (*akachochin*) are usually small, cozy and smoky. A typical one is Inaka, downstairs from the Ichi-Dollar Minshuku (see map). They are all a variation on the same theme. Inaka is about 3 m by 4 m, and would hold a dozen Westerners comfortably. The Japanese cram in twice that number. The atmosphere is relaxing and friendly. Small oil lamps provide subdued light. A TV blares in the corner with no one watching. A woman behind the counter prepares light snacks. The *otsumami* include 8-legged starfish, Y200; *sashimi,* Y800; and various little tidbits. A liter of Orion Draft is Y400, sake and *awamori* Y250, a shot of whiskey Y150; and a "key bottle" of scotch that will be kept for subsequent visits Y5000. These places are good for relaxing. No one will hurry you to drink. Meet local people and have a good night out for a reasonable price.

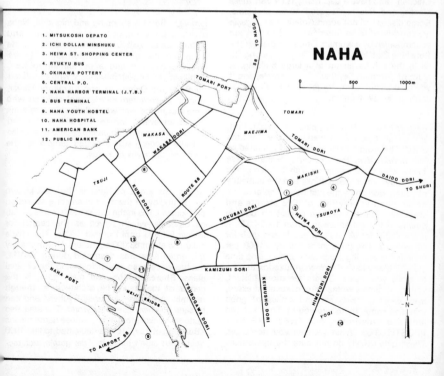

NAHA

1. MITSUKOSHI DEPATO
2. ICHI DOLLAR MINSHUKU
3. HEIWA ST. SHOPPING CENTER
4. RYUKYU BUS
5. OKINAWA POTTERY
6. CENTRAL P.O.
7. NAHA HARBOR TERMINAL (J.T.B.)
8. BUS TERMINAL
9. NAHA YOUTH HOSTEL
10. NAHA HOSPITAL
11. AMERICAN BANK
12. PUBLIC MARKET

0 — 500 — 1000m

TO NAGO
TOMARI PORT
TOMARI
MAEJIMA
TOMARI DORI
DAIDO DORI
TO SHURI
WAKASA
WAKASA DORI
MAKISHI
TSUJI
KUME DORI
ROUTE 58
KOKUSAI DORI
HEIWA DORI
TSUBOYA
NAHA PORT
KAMIZUMI DORI
KEIMUSHO DORI
HIMEYURI DORI
MEIJI BRIDGE
TSUBOGAWA DORI
YOGI
TO AIRPORT 58
-N-

nightlife: Naha teems with nightclubs and discos. It comes alive at night, a carry-over from the Occupation. The better and certainly expensive nightclubs, complete with doormen, are found throughout the city, but especially around Kokusai Dori. They usually provide high-class bar hostesses who are there to salve your ego and to help you spend wads of money. This type of place is universal and no real cultural exchange takes place. If you wish to spend more money in one night than you would ordinarily spend in a month, go there. If not, avoid them completely.

discos: The same in Naha as they are on the mainland. They are frequented by fastidiously fashion-conscious younger people, and are complete with loud music, pulsating light shows and dancing. Discos are really the only places where boy meets girl. For an entrance fee of Y3000 (sometimes this includes only one drink, so ask), you can spend the night drinking, dancing and eating. A *gaijin* is usually a minor celebrity, so brush up on the old "Funky Chicken" and have a ball. Many G.I.s visit these places, and this has caused some problems. Some discos will not admit Americans (all *gaijin* are considered to be Americans) unless they are accompanied by a woman. One such place is the Sunshine Club located in the Tsuji area along Rt. 58 in the sub-basement of a large building. A team of doormen "eyeball" the clientele, and if you're on your own, forget it. This does not apply to single women.

hostess bars: In Maejima, close to Tomari Port, is the main Okinawan variation of the "hostess club." These are mostly owned and operated by the *boruku den,* the Okinawan Mafia. These bars—with such names as Tahiti, Miami, and Pink Lady—offer cheap drinks and the company of young women by the half hour. The area is a noisy, neon-lit labyrinth of side streets and alleyways. The charges are posted on bulletin boards at the entranceway. From 1000-2030, it costs Y2000 for all you can guzzle and grab for 40 minutes. The price increases by Y1000 per hour as the evening progresses until closing time at 2430. Many have doormen in tuxedos that try to smile you inside. Others are more blatant; young, attractive women provocatively dressed, eyes winking, skirts slit and smiles of good things to come, try to lure you in. They act and look like prostitutes, but THEY ARE NOT PROSTITUTES. What you see you don't get. These girls usually do not date the customers.

They are there to smile, to get you drunk (they leave hardened New Orleans hustlers back at the starting gate), and to quickly separate you from your money. The area is humorous, but not rewarding. A stroll through the streets alone is sufficient to soak up the atmosphere that spills onto them. Going inside is really unnecessary.

the heavy stuff: There are 3 main red light sections in Naha. Makishi, W of Kokusai Dori; Naminoue; and Toruku. Any cab driver knows the way. Again, the areas are a maze of alleyways, but the neon lights and gaiety are missing. Side glances, forced smiles and hushed voices come from fading older women nestled in doorways. A pall of sadness hangs in the air. The women charge Y5000, and the time alloted is short. No Hollywood set, however, could match these areas for authenticity and color; they look just like what they are. They are the epitome of the cliche, and straight-forward business transactions are the norm.

IN AND AROUND NAHA

temples: Besides shopping and nightlife, Naha offers a good many temples, shrines, and cultural spots. Visit Gokuku Otera which is the main temple for the Shingon Sect. In its confines you will find a monument to Rev. Bettlhaim, an English missionary who translated the Bible into Okinawan, and Kozakura Tower, erected to commemorate school children who were lost in the war when their ship was sunk during an evacuation to Kagoshima. Namino Uegu and Sogenji Ishimon are 2 famous temples in Naha. Sogenji was a sacred temple for the spirits of the Ryukyu Kings.

Shuri: Six km E of Naha is the best-known temple and by far the most interesting attraction on Okinawa. It is in the oldest town (same name) on Okinawa, which served as the capital for almost 500 yrs until the mid 1800s. The castle occupied about 63,000 sq meters. Unfortunately this entire area was destroyed during WW11, but has since been rebuilt following the original plans. Shurei-no-Mon, the main gate, is the center of the area. The architecture, though resembling Chinese, is purely Ryukyan and can be seen nowhere else in the world. The area also features Kankai Mon, a gate whose name means "Boasting of Joy." It was dedicated to last 1000 years, but didn't make it. This gate's architec-

the second of 6 gates leading to Shurei Castle. The original gate destroyed during WW 11 has since been restored. "Shurei-no-kuni" is the Chinese name for Okinawa which means "The Nation that keeps peace."

tural style is mainly Chinese and Korean, modified to fit the Ryukyan style. Tamaudon, the final resting place of the kings and courtesans, is in the compound. The Prefectural Museum is also here, housing art, textiles, sculptures, and industrial objects. A tour will provide insight into the unique Ryukyan culture. Allow one day for a thorough tour of Shuri. *getting there:* From the bus terminal, take Bus Rt. 16 (Tonokura Line), which operates every 25 min from 0630 until 2200. It passes Tonokura in Naha, proceeds through the university, then onto Shuri, Kinjo (famous for stone pavements by Shoshin in the late 15th C.), Daido, Yogi (don't miss Yogi Park), and back to Kokusai Dori. Other routes are Bus Rt. 25 (Nakagusuku/Shuri Line) from Naha to Enobi via Shuri, Tanahara, Futenma, Okinawa City and Chibana every 20 min from 0600-2200. Bus Rt. 26 (Yakena/Shuri) goes from Naha to Yakena via Shuri, Futenma, Okinawa City, Agena, and Gishikawa every 60-90 min from 0610-2150.

PRACTICALITIES

accommodations: Western style places include: Naha Tokyu Hotel, tel: (0988) 68-2151, or Tokyo office, (03) 264-4436, single Y11,000 up; and Naha Grand Castle, tel: (0988) 54-5454, or Tokyo Office (03) 281-4321, single Y12,000 up. *ryokan:* Kanko Hotel Kyuyokan, Kumoji, Naha City, tel: (0988) 63-4181, Y6000 up; and Okinawa Hotel, Daido, Naha City, tel: (0988) 84-3191, Y8000 up. *budget hotels:* Kanko Tyokan Hisagoen, 2-23-3 Tsuji, Naha, tel: (0988) 68-4167, Y2000 up; Kanko Ryokan Katoriso, 1-13 Wakasa, Naha, tel: (0988) 68-4679, Y2200 up; and Hotel Ginza, 2-105 Makishi, Naha, tel: (0988) 33-3847, Y2500

up. *cheap:* Ichi Dollar Minshuku is a grotty fleabag for Y1000. Around the corner is a newer *minshuku* run by the same man, Hideyo Niwa, called Ishi Gachiya. It is clean and well kept; ask for the rooftop room—good for stargazing at Y2000. Directions: face the Mitsukoshi Depato, walk to R for 50 m to the first intersection. Turn left. Ishi Gachiya is on the R just before you reach the next intersection. Painted pink with a wood slab door; Niwa-san lives on the 2nd floor. Tel: 69-9261; he will also lead you to the Ichi Dollar Minshuku, but remember it is rock bottom. *youth hostels:* Naha has three. All are decent and can offer good information. The closest to city center is Naha YH, 51 Onoyama-cho, Naha City 900, tel: (0988) 57-0073, 15 min on foot from Naha Port, 100 beds; Harumi-so YH, 2-22-10 Tomari, Naha City 900, tel: (0988) 33-3218, 15 min by bus from Naha Port and 3 min on foot, 40 beds; and Tamazano-so YH, 54 Asato, Naha City 902, tel: (0988) 33-5377, 15 min by bus from Naha Port and 5 min of foot, 30 beds.

reading matter: "Okinawa Pastime" and "This Week on Okinawa" are magazines offering up-to-date information on events and what's happening in and around Naha. Available at newsstands and larger hotels. The "Morning Star" is the daily English newspaper. For an excellent selection of Western books, visit the Charles E. Tuttle Bookstore, Urazoe City, tel: 77-2140. Take Buses 20-29. Get off at Minato-gawa and walk 2 minutes. *useful phone numbers and addresses:* American Consulate (0988) 77-8142, Phillipine Consulate (0988) 97-3642, and Chinese Consulate (0988) 55-3381. *emergencies:* Western doctors are available at the 7th Day Adventist Medical Center, Naha.

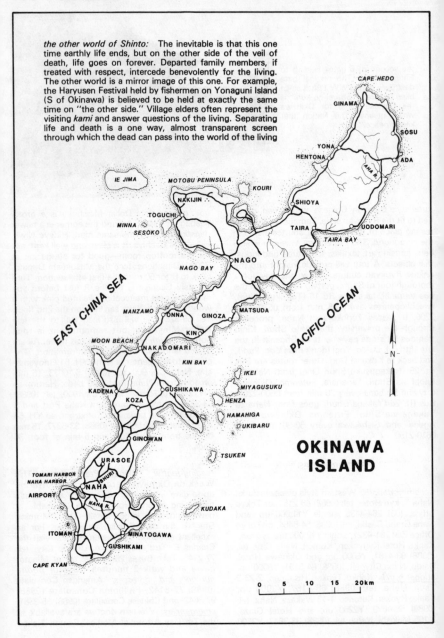

the other world of Shinto: The inevitable is that this one time earthly life ends, but on the other side of the veil of death, life goes on forever. Departed family members, if treated with respect, intercede benevolently for the living. The other world is a mirror image of this one. For example, the Haryusen Festival held by fishermen on Yonaguni Island (S of Okinawa) is believed to be held at exactly the same time on ''the other side.'' Village elders often represent the visiting *kami* and answer questions of the living. Separating life and death is a one way, almost transparent screen through which the dead can pass into the world of the living

OKINAWA
ISLAND

EAST CHINA SEA

PACIFIC OCEAN

CAPE HEDO
GINAMA
SOSU
YONA
HENTONA
ADA
AHA R.
UODOMARI
IE JIMA
MOTOBU PENINSULA
KOURI
NAKIJIN
SHIOYA
TOGUCHI
TAIRA
MINNA
SESOKO
TAIRA BAY
NAGO
NAGO BAY
MANZAMO
ONNA
GINOZA
MATSUDA
MOON BEACH
KIN
NAKADOMARI
KIN BAY
IKEI
MIYAGUSUKU
KADENA
GUSHIKAWA
HENZA
KOZA
HAMAHIGA
UKIBARU
GINOWAN
TSUKEN
URASOE
TOMARI HARBOR
NAHA HARBOR
ISHURI
AIRPORT
NAHA
NAHA R.
KUDAKA
ITOMAN
MINATOGAWA
GUSHIKAMI
CAPE KYAN

-N-

0   5   10   15   20km

NANBU

This is the colloquial name for southern Okinawa, with Itoman as its center. Nanbu was hit particularly hard during WW11, and part of the attraction is Okinawa Old Battlefield Quasi-National Park. The park contains a number of monuments to the war dead. The most tragic are the Himeyuri-no-To; The Lily Tower, commemorating the death of 13 teachers and 190 students of the prefectural girls senior high school who gave their lives to protect their island home. The other is Mabuni Hill, a small knoll only 80km high where tens of thousands died in the famous closing battles. Here, General Ushijima committed *seppuku* when sure defeat became a reality. There is a tower called the Peace Prayer Statue designed by renowned artist Yamada Shinzan at the venerable age of 90. It is 5.5 m high and built in a distinctive lacquerware method called *tsukin*. Now peaceful panoramas of sugar cane fields and sea seem immortal. The hills are dotted with blooming bougainvillea and hibiscus. The death and destruction once vivid here are only a dim, haunting memory. Of historical interest in the immediate vicinity is Nansan Castle, the oldest in Okinawa. Here is where the king of the southland held court from the 14th C. until, after more than a century of civil war, the island kingdom was united under Shuri.

getting there: Direct, Bus 89 leaves from Platform 13 in Naha. Locate Platform 13 across from the bus station, then use the overhead walkway to cross the main street. On the way to Itoman you will pass innumerable tombs; some are elaborately carved, while others are built of modest cinder blocks. You will also see the modern Okinawan housing; unattractive boxy buildings with external stairways. Finally you will pass through scenic countryside with rows of neat fields and immense plant greenhouses. A few other good bus routes are: Bus Rt. 32 (Itoman/Takara) via Naha, Kainan, Oruku and Takara, 0600-2218 every 10 minutes; Bus Rt. 33 (Itoman/Tomigusuku) via Naha, Perry, and Takamine, 0600-2245 every 15 minutes; and Bus Rt. 34 (Itoman/Kochinda) via Naha, Tominoru, 0600-2200 every 20 minutes.

Itoman: The main city of the area, 12.5 km S of Naha, is the center of the fishing and sugarcane industry in Nanbu. It was renowned in times past for its liberated women who held the purse strings and who were reputed to have practiced polygamy. This practice is long dead, but the women do appear to be a bit more forward than usual. Itoman is a large small town. The buildings are mainly ferrous concrete with a liberal smattering of traditional architectural designs squeezed in. The city, built in a horseshoe around the bay, is dominated by the sea. The famous Dragon Boat Race (*Haryusen*) takes place here in May. Hakugingo Hall, dedicated to fertility and safe sea voyages, is here. In Itoman is also the Kochi Family grave, containing the ashes of over 2500 people of this famous Okinawan clan. This is characteristic of the still powerful belief in ancestor worship thriving in Itoman and the vicinity.

the rich foliage of the sub-tropical jungle is captured in the *kasuri* fabrics produced in Nanbu. They bear uncanny resemblance to the Pekalongan style of batik from the N coast of Java

vicinity of Itoman: Not far away are the villages of Kiyan, Motobu and Teruya, known collectively as Kasuri, where the manufacture of the famous cloth of the same name is believed to have begun more than 500 years ago. Here you can find the best *kasuri* fabrics that the islands have to offer. From Itoman, bus across the peninsula and then N along the E coast following Rt. 33l. This routing takes you past Nanzan Castle, Gyakusendo Caves and further N past Chinen Castle on the coast and Oshiro Castle further inland. Oshiro Castle dates back 400 yrs and the high ground here gives an expansive view of the bay. Chinen Castle close-by is famed for its magnificent arched gates on the northern and eastern approaches. Along the E coast are fine examples of Okinawan beaches. Niihara Beach, clean and warm, is a typical example. Take your swim suit for a refreshing dip before returning to Naha.

THE GYAKUSENDO CAVES

The most fascinating attraction of Nanbu. From Itoman, take Bus 82 across from the large green terminal building to the village of Minatogawa for Y300. From here walk down the hill to where the road forks. Go L (not over the bridge), and follow this road 2 km to Gyokusendo. This road is heavily trafficked, so try hitchhiking, though a walk through the countryside after the confines of Naha is pleasant. *stay:* About 200 m along this road on the right-hand side is a small *minshuku*, Minato So, owned by Suzoko Arakake who speaks *sukoshi* (a little) English. Her *minshuku* is conveniently located for this area, and the price is reasonable at Y3000. If you don't stay here refresh yourself with a soft drink from

one of the most dazzling subterranean grottoes of the Gyokusendo Cave complex. Discovered only in 1967 by a spelunking expedition from Ehime University. The fantastic stalagmite and stalactite limestone formations number over 300,000

her machine. She also has a toilet available. Across the street is a small cemetery with excellent examples of the famous and ubiquitous Okinawan tombs, and in the fields along this road are a few more. The caves themselves are open Mon.-Sat. 0900-1800, Sun. 0930-1730. Entrance Y500. No smoking or photography. Discovered in the late 1860s, Gyokusendo is the 3rd largest limestone cavern in Japan, after Shuhodo in Yamaguchi, and Ryusendo in Iwate.

the tour: It contains over 450,000 stalagmites and stalactites that grow at the rate of 1 mm every 3 years. The caves extend for 5000 meters. The walk inside is well lit by a series of colored lights, while loudspeakers like tiny jukeboxes (Japanese only) explain the natural formation process. There are also a few signs in English that make a brave but sometimes unclear attempt at explanation. Tread firmly because the trails inside are treacherously slippery, especially the wooden walkways. The walk is pure fantasia. At the center is Golden Cup, a rimstone pond 20 m high by 20 m long. "The water in this spring of happiness is ever blue and inhabited by prawns," says the sign. Next is the Hall of Love, featuring stalagmite formations like couples embracing, and stalactites like elongated breasts attached to the ceiling. The grand finale, Toyoichi-Do, is an immense cavern where nature has turned sculptor. The stalagmites take on statuesque form. Some look like classical Roman sculpture, others amazingly resemble the silent sentinels of Easter Island. Still others, gargoyle-like, seem to have come from the brush of Hieronymus Bosch. For those inclined, take a sketch book. Emerging, you will walk under a long, orange canopy which will lead directly into a souvenir shop selling commercial junk. One worthwhile buy is the postcards, some with fine photos of the caves.

returning to Naha: One obvious way is to return to Minatogawa and bus back, but a walk in another direction will take you through some totally unvisited countryside. Upon leaving the main entrance, turn L and walk 50 m to a small road on the right. There is an arrow and a sign that says NO TRUCKS OR BUSES. Follow this road for about 2½ km to a small village. Turn L at the main intersection and there on your R is the *basu noriba* (bus stop) in front of a small grocery store run by an ancient old man. Wait there for a bus to Naha (Y300). This detour eliminates backtracking and offers a fleeting glimpse of unpretentious Okinawan life.

HEADING NORTH ON OKINAWA ISLAND

There are a number of bus routes, but the 2 best and easiest are Bus Rt. 20 (Nago West Line) — Naha to Nago via Urasoe, Ginowan, Kadena AFB, Nakadomari (Moon Beach), and Kyoda. It follows Hwy. 58 along the W coast and runs from 0530 to 2200, every 12 minutes. Bus Rt. 21 (Nago East Line) goes from Naha to Nago via Urasoe, Ginowan, Ishikawa and Kin along the E coast from 0505 to 1935, every 30 minutes. As usual, you pay only as far as your ride, so get on and off the bus whenever you see a good spot. The first major stop N of Naha is Urasoe (8 km), where the Charles E. Tuttle Bookstore, located at Minatogawa, tel: (0988) 77-2140, has an excellent selection of books, maps and literature available in English for the traveler. The American Consulate is also located here, open Mon. to Fri. 0900 to 1700, tel: (0988) 77-8142.

Okinawa City (Koza): About 18 km NE of Naha this city is strictly G. I. Most Americans congregate in the Goya section of Koza. The city is one large flashing neon light full of dives offering cheap women and expensive drinks. G.I.s looking for action travel in groups, and bar fights are ordinary. Drugs are available. Rip-offs can and do happen.

Kadena AFB: A stop at Kadena is both useful and mind-boggling. Asia transforms to America instantaneously. The signs are in English; guys are jogging; bra-less blondes are riding bikes; 6-foot tall black ladies are pushing baby carriages; and EVERYONE MEETS YOUR EYES AND SAYS HELLO. Head for the USO Club just inside Gate 2; it offers good maps and traveling information. The food bar has a wide selection of hard-to-get American junk food, and absolutely delicious, homemade, authentic apple pie. Make sure to get off the bus at Gate 2. If you disembark at Gate 1 it means an 8 km hike, but there are taxis available if you make that

mistake. There is usually no trouble getting permission to visit the USO Club, but to be on the safe side, ask a G. I. (plenty around) to escort you onto the base. Even the most jaded traveler will enjoy this quick deposit back into the West. If it's too much, just walk out the gate and—POOF—Asia again.

Nakadomari and Moon Beach: Eight km N of Kadena on Bus Rt. 20 you will begin to see signs for an amusement park where the mongoose and cobra fights take place. You are approaching the village of Nakadomari and nearby Moon Beach, a very famous but nonetheless excellent bathing beach. Ferrous concrete buildings begin giving way to traditional wooden homes with thatched roofs as you approach this area. Get off Bus 20 at Nakadomari, if not for an extended visit, at least for lunch and a refreshing dip. At the beach you will see a mixture of Japanese civilians and U. S. military personnel enjoying the sunshine. The familiar smell of suntan oil as well as frisbees fill the air. Moon Beach is wide and clean. Food stalls with a Polynesian flair complete the scene. Scuba diving on the surrounding coral reef is excellent. Gear is available at the beach area. Many teenagers, dependents of the military personnel, hang out in this area. They give a traveler a good welcome and are hungry for stories from "back home." One of their pastimes is to race hotrods at about 0400. These car crazies are known as "boogie boys."

along the west coast: After refreshing yourself at Moon Beach, reboard Bus 20 and head north. You will pass through Onna Mura, where Monzano, a famous sea cliff, is located. A Ryukyan king said about 250 years ago that this place would seat 10,000 people. Quite true if they were diminutive Japanese. Monzano is a wide expanse of grassy knoll buttressed by the sea.

Maeda Point, on the S side of Onna Mura, has an observatory providing an all-encompassing view of Motobu and Ie Jima. This is an excellent fishing spot, used at night for partying. Remeber the teenagers from Moon Beach? The view is spectacular but marred by the litter of beer cans. Further N about 15 km you arrive at Imbu, another famous beach. As you travel along the coast you will observe mossy rocks protruding from the sea, cliffs honeycombed with caves, and tiny uninhabited islands. Traditional boats (*sabani*), like those used in the Haryusen festival are prominent. They bob around with their high prows protruding like ducks on a pond. These vessels are quite seaworthy and maneuverable in these jagged coastal waters. The Imbu area is excellent for camping; just choose a beach that strikes your fancy, or at low tide walk across the sand to one of the tiny islands and camp there. There are numerous hotels and a variety of reasonable *minshuku* in this area, if camping doesn't suit your taste.

NAGO

More of a large town than a city, Nago has a distinctly countrified atmosphere. It is an excellent place to put up for a day before heading N to Hedo or W to Motobu. Nago has a deep-water bay with a volume of traffic including everything from family fishing boats to dandified yachts. Looking southward you can see Mt. Nabu, remote and peaked, rising 338 m. This area is virtually untrekked, and could provide rugged camping. Looking northward, the land is flatter and stretches to Motobu. Do all your banking at the downtown banks and any important mailing from the Nago P.O. before heading north. This is also a good place to receive Poste Restante mail. A few other sights in the area are Hinpungajumaru, a 300-yr-old tree located in the middle of the road about 200 m S of Nago X Roads. The ruins of Nago

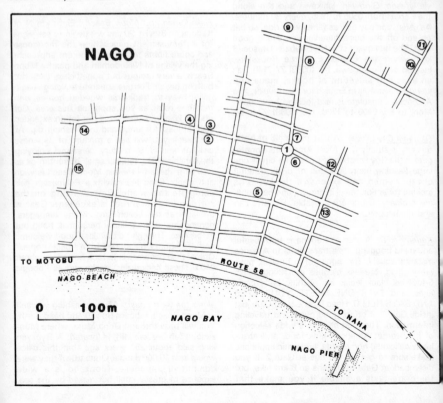

Castle are reported to give the best view of cherry blossoms in all of Okinawa, and from the heights you can get a commanding sweep of Nago harbor and the mountains of Kunigami in the north. The people of Nago are very warm and friendly. They are basically country folk, and the traditional way of life is still deeply engrained in their daily routines. This area can offer a brief glimpse of the fading Okinawa of old. For travel information in Nago contact Nago Association of Commerce, 415 Nago, Nago City 905, tel: (09805) 2-4243.

accommodations and food: The *minshuku* in town are all standardized at Y3000; an excellent one is Nago Minshuku, run typically by a family, with their 2 young daughters serving as maids. A *yukata* is provided, and the *tatami* rooms are spotlessly clean. The meals are full course and superb. A typical dinner includes *sukano furayi* (battered fish), *yasai chanpuru* made with bits of chicken, *sakana no nitsuke* (marinated sweet fish), *sashimi* in sauce with sliced cucumbers, and volumes of *ocha, miso shiru,* and steaming white rice. There are a few business hotels in town such as the Tsukino Ama, tel: 3755 for Y3000 excluding meals. Fancier but too expensive is Hotel Futabaso, 150 m S of Nago X Roads. At Mt. Tanodake, a few km to the E, is the Ikoe no Mura resort which features tennis courts, saunas, roller skating and swimming pools. The rooms are designed to accommodate groups of 4, but a single traveler may also stay there. For what is offered, the rates are reasonable. You can get there by a convoluted bus route, but to save headaches, pay the fare and take a taxi. While in Nago relax at the Shiro

Coffee Shop owned and operated by Morihiko Shiroma, who sports a long, black beard, and has an infectious laugh. Enjoy a liter of Orion beer (Y400) brewed locally in Nago while listening to his extraordinary collection of jazz. He has them all—from Duke Ellington to Dave Brubeck. Morihiko's brother, Yahusuko, is a famous Okinawan jazz guitarist. The overstuffed chairs lining the room are comfortable and you don't have to be a jazz fan to feel right at home. Around the corner from Shiro is the Daruma Sushi Bar, where excellent *nigiri shushi* is served for a reasonable price. The countertop is stainless steel and serves as your plate. If you prefer an individual dish, ask for *ichi numie.* Sharpen your palate with *giri* (pickled ginger) and dip your *gyoku* (egg omelette on rice held with a band of seaweed) into your *wasabi* (hot Japanese horseradish), and enjoy. A poster on the wall gives the English translation for the various fish served. Choose whatever seems appetizing; for about Y1000 you can sample a wide assortment.

HEDO POINT

Hedo Point is the most remote area in Okinawa, in the extreme north. Take bus Rt. 20 (Nago/Hentona Line) via Okuma from 0600 to 1940 every 20 minutes. Change (*norikae*) to Bus Rt. 69 (Hentona/Oku Line) via Ginama and Hedo. From Hentona 0520 to 1720, and from Oku 0645 to 1846. There is no bus service along the E coast for about 30 km from Oku to Taira, but if you can manage a ride to Taira, you can pick up a bus there to Henoko at 0830, 1300 and 1725. This route will take you through the most unvisited expanse of Okinawa. Hedo itself is a wild and woolly area, and from its 100m sea cliff you can see Yoron Jima, a southern island of Kagoshima Prefecture. A curious custom is to throw a bundle of miscanthus from the cliff to hear it hit the rocks below. The word *banta* is used to describe the sound it makes. Along this route you will pass Ogimi Mura, famous for *bashofu,* the pale yellow cloth made from banana fiber and used to make kimono. The Hedo area offers solitude and remote undisturbed beaches. The villages are purely traditional with modern facilities making only slow inroads. This area is as far away as you can get in Okinawa.

MOTOBU PENINSULA

Motobu, Expo '75 (Kaiyo Haku): Head out to this area early so you can explore it and still catch the nearby ferry at 1400 to Ie Jima. To get

---

NAGO

1. Nago roads
2. Bus Stop No. 65
3. small P.O.
4. Okinawa Bank
5. public market
6. shiro coffee shop
7. Daruma Susai Bar
8. police station
9. fire station
10. nago super market
11. Nago Minshuku
12. Ryukyu Bank
13. Central P.O.
14. bus terminal
15. Ryukyu Bus

out onto the Motobu Peninsula, take Bus Rt. 76 (Nago/Toguchi Line) from the bus terminal in Nago, via Izumi and Namisato, from 0630 to 2000. Or take Bus 65 from the bus stop across from the small P. O. near Nago X Roads. Nago to Toguchi is Y3500. Two km before arriving at Toguchi you will see Toguchi Shin Ko (Port) on your right, where you will catch the ferry to Ie Jima. For travel information throughout the Motobu Peninsula contact: Motobu Association of Commerce and Industry, 4-12 Toguchi, Motobu, Okinawa 905-03, tel: (09804) 7-2749.

sights: Toguchi offers 2 attractions, the site of Expo '75 (Kaiyo Haku) and the ruins of Nakijin Castle. They are both in the same direction so you waste no time. You can bus, hitchhike (which is easy) or rent a bike for the 7 km OW trip. You can see Expo from Toguchi, so no directions are necessary. The main building of Expo now has the feeling and look of an abandoned spaceship. Large modernistic hotels for the people who once flocked to this area are now quite empty. From the heights overlooking the futuristic main building, you can see Ie Jima, Sesoko and Minna Jima, a tiny flat island in the bay where it is said that the best sunsets in Okinawa are visible. After having taken a good look, continue straight ahead (about 2 km) until you come to a T intersection. Turn left and proceed 4 km until you see a sign pointing to Nakijin Castle—high on a hill to your right.

traveler's fountain: In a gorge of Mt. Ishidake on the northern side of the Motobu Peninsula is a foundation called Kyoda. It was believed that a water nymph would appear and offer water to a traveler with her hands. The spot is now famous. Anyone reading this book should qualify for her services.

Nakijin Castle: Entrance fee is Y150. Nakijin was built in 950 A. D. It covered 20,000 sq. m, and the wall surrounding it was over 1,100 m long. It was the headquarters for the king of Hokuzan (N Okinawa) until it fell to the Sho Kingdom when the court was united under Shuri. The battle to capture the castle must have been long and bitter. Its defenses are formidable. The mortarless walls are of rough-hewn stone intricately fitted together. Their thickness gives a strong feeling of solidarity. The entrance gate is broad and low, and observation holes flank it on each side. Only the stone stairs and the walls remain, but the view from the heights is as commanding as ever. The sea stretches out at your feet and rugged mountains tower at your back. At the top is an austerely simple shrine where incense is still burned. The battlements from this vantage point look like a miniature Great Wall of China. Now, instead of gazing for approaching enemy columns, people come to enjoy the enchantment of the cherry blossoms.

IE JIMA

Return to Toguchi Shin Ko (port) by 1400 to catch the ferry to Ie Jima. It costs Y460 and takes 40 min, leaving twice daily at 0800 and 1400. If you arrive at the terminal early, there is a raised *tatami* area to nap on while you wait. Ie Jima itself is small and its few roads are easy to

the formidable walls of Nakijin Castle

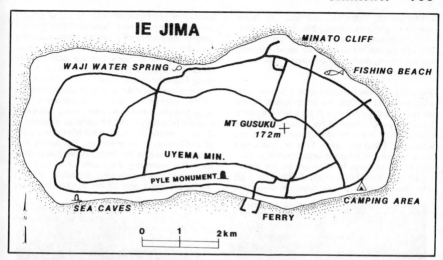

follow. The one-and-only mountain in the center that looks more like a thumb than a finger always provides directions.

transport: Ie Jima is perfect for bicycling. Rent one in town and explore the entire island in about 8 hours. If you don't choose to cycle or walk around the island, there is a bus. It leaves from town and is moderately priced. The local people are aware that you are just visiting and will give you a lift if you hitchhike.

stay and eat: Walk up from the pier area and turn R at the road leading past the sugar refinery. Proceed 4 km and you will come to Ie Campground for Youth. If you are there before mid-April, there is no one around and the camping is free. After April the island is increasingly visited, so you will have a tough time finding a beach to yourself. The *minshuku* on Ie have a fixed price of Y2500 which is a bit cheaper than usual. Y1500 will get you a room without meals. Ie *soba* is nutritious and flavorful, and the going rate is Y300. There are a few coffee shops and *akachochin* for relaxing at night. A good *minshuku* is Uyama, operated by Shizu Uyama. It's only 50 m from the ferry on the top road to the L that runs parallel to the sea.

sights: The U. S. still maintains a gunnery range on the extreme NW corner of the island, and it is restricted. Another grim reminder of the war is the `Ernie Pyle monument, dedicated to the

famous war-time correspondent who was killed here only weeks before the end of the war when his jeep was overturned by mortar fire. The town

the village co-op of Ie Jima

of Ie itself is tasteless modern. For the best view, go for a walk on the breakwater at night. If you are lucky enough to have a full moon, the soft light and the silhouetted palms will give the impression of a tranquil south sea island, while the night cloaks the ferrous concrete boxes. While in town, visit the local cooperative where men and women work together processing seaweed and fish harvested from the local seas. They are pleasant and anxious to show you around. This is a good place to purchase fresh fish to prepare while camping. Most of their products are exported to Tokyo. For a romantic view of the island, head for the interior where the homes remain traditional and the life style is unadulterated. There you will find little farms raising sugarcane, pineapple, and tobacco, which stretches in neat rows down to the sea. The homes are surrounded by salad gardens, and the feeling is of a self-contained mini world.

Yateagama: Famous caves on the S shore only a few km W of Ie. They are worth a visit. Follow the main road out of town W for a few km until it turns to gravel. Proceed for about 300 m and take the first track on the L down to the sea where you'll find the caves. They are just above the shoreline and are quite large, stretching 50 m long by 20 m deep. It is evident by the watermarks that they are partially flooded by high tide. The remnants of fires, however, show that the higher places remain dry. The local people do not frequently visit them and any traveler who is part troglodite would enjoy camping here. No fresh water. Continue W past the caves and you will see many pastoral scenes with people bent over in fields with the sea as backdrop. Beautiful, exotic flowers carpet the fields where numerous older crypts lie partially buried by the vegetation. Some are elaborate with pagoda roofs, while others are merely holes dug into the hills with a slab of stone as a covering. All seem visited and many have wilting bouquets of wild flowers at the entrances. The people that you see working in the fields will one day occupy them. It is interesting, especially for a traveler, to think that these people are born, raised, toil and die on an island only 22 km in circumference.

Ernie Pyle, the famed WW 11 correspondent known as the "G.I.'s Spokesman," was ironically killed during the closing days of the war. He had followed the Allied campaign in Europe for 4 years and had decided to turn his attention to the Pacific War. On april 18th on Ie Jima Island the jeep in which he was traveling was attacked by a Japanese machine gun. It was overturned in a ditc by the fusillade. The correspondent living the life of G.I. and eager to report the horrors of battle throug their eyes lifted his head. The machine gun rattled i mechanical death cry and Ernie Pyle was killed. monument in his honor is maintained on Ie Jima.

THE SOUTHWEST ISLANDS

The islands stretching to the SW from the main island of Okinawa are broken into 2 main groups: the Sakashimas, about 150 km SW, with Miyako as the main island; and the Yaeyamas, including Ishigaki, Iriomote and Yonaguni. From Yonaguni you can see the mountains of Taipei. Known for the world's largest moth (*yonagunisan*), Yonaguni is one of Japan's most remote islands, and produces devastatingly strong sake. For air and ferry service to these islands, see "interisland transportation" in the "Introduction."

MIYAKO

The most heavily touristed island of all the Sakashimas, Miyako offers abundant accommodations, including picture-perfect camping spots lining the jagged, sun-drenched coast. For a good look at the culture of the Ryukyus without the remoteness of Iriomote and Ishigaki, come here. This island was untouched during WW11, so its traditional Okinawan architecture is beautifully preserved. The houses are built low to the ground and fenced by coral to protect them from frequent typhoons that rake this area. Hirara, in the SW, is the main town, the center of culture and industry. It has an airport and harbor. The Emperor Wilhelm 1 of Germany erected the Monument of Philanthropy at Hirara Port in 1873 in recognition of the islanders who provided a ship and safe passage to shipwrecked German traders. Higashi Henna is a cape on the E end of the island. If you walk out onto the promontory, from here you can see the East China Sea on your R, and the Pacific on your left. Located here is the *Bubakarisu,* (the tax stone), a link to times past when the islanders owed tribute to China. There are 7 small islands surrounding Miyako. Frequent ferry service is available. They are virtually unvisited and provide quiet undisturbed subtropical beaches combined with vestiges of traditional Okinawan life. Tarama, one of these, preserves traces of the old dynasty in its many colorful festivals. As you walk the back streets of Miyako, notice Miyako *jofu,* the fine textured blue cloth at one time used as a tax payment, drying on the walls and over the doorways of homes. Traditionally used for kimono, it makes perfect clothing for the hot sub-tropical weather of this area. *services:* For general travel information including maps, ferry schedules, tours and accommodations, try Miyako Sightseeing Association, City Office, 186 Nishisato, Hirara, Miyako, Okinawa 906, tel: (09807) 20-316.

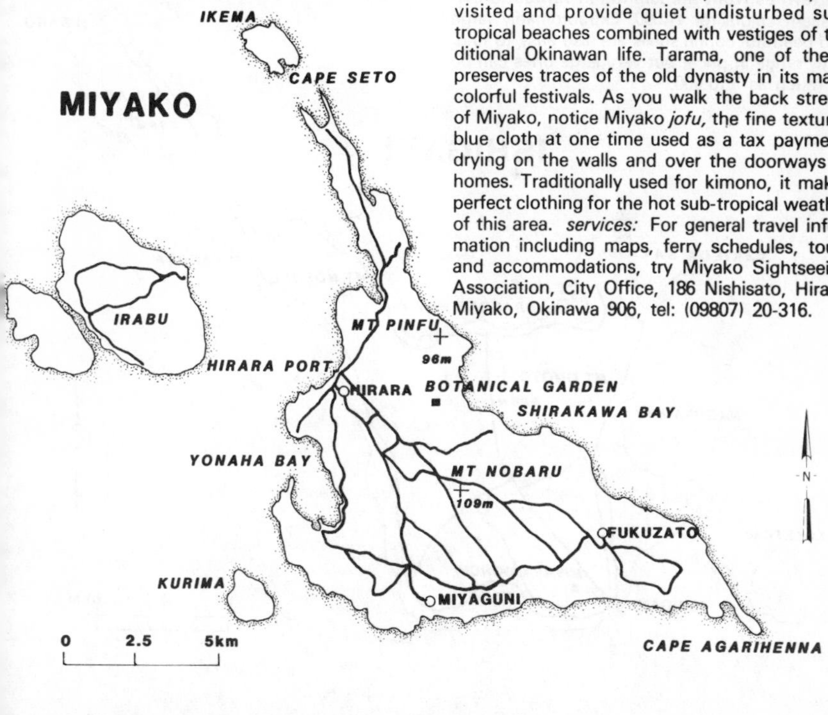

MIYAKO

IKEMA

CAPE SETO

IRABU

MT PINFU
96m

HIRARA PORT

HIRARA   BOTANICAL GARDEN

SHIRAKAWA BAY

YONAHA BAY

MT NOBARU
109m

FUKUZATO

KURIMA

MIYAGUNI

CAPE AGARIHENNA

0   2.5   5km

-N-

ISHIGAKI

Meaning stone fence, is the central island in the Yaeyama group, with a population of 34,000. The ferry ride from Naha (Y4140) is very convenient, leaving at 1900 and arriving at 0800 the next morning (no time is lost for touring, and you save a night's lodging). From Naha take the Ryukyu Kaiun Ferry Line and return on Oshima Unyu. *shopping:* The main street, loaded with more modern shops, is supplemented by colorful smaller shops on any of the side streets. The articles sold range from typical island baubles to minutely carved oyster shells made into flowers. An island specialty is a snake-covered walking stick for Y4000. The shops feature lobsters incased in glass, Y1100; lacquered turtles, Y38,000; and a cobra and mongoose in a hideous death grip for Y11,000. More conventional items are carved bamboo boats (Y8000), pottery, featuring *shisa, sake* flasks, and a Japanese standby, roughly made *wadagi* (rice straw) sandals, once used on the Tokaido pilgrimage. Another unusual item is mounted butterflies from the islands in fantastic irridescent colors for Y4000. Extraordinarily large and beautiful conch shells are also easy to find. They range in price, but very large ones can be as much as Y10,000.

services: The Tourist Information is centrally located near the bus terminal. No English is spoken but you will be able to get detailed Japanese-language maps of the islands. There is also a branch of the Okinawa Tourist in town (see map) where you can purchase tickets for your return to Naha, or to any of the outlying islands. They also service All Nippon Airways and South West Airlines. You can purchase tickets at the pier for Iriomote. For travel information on Ishigaki and the surrounding islands, contact Yaeyama Sightseeing Association, 37 Ishigaki, Ishigaki City, tel: (09808) 2-2809. *note[* Change TCs in Ishigaki at the Ryukyu Ginko. No banking services are available on the outlying islands, including Iriomote. *transportation:* Excellent bus service connects the villages of Ishigaki. The bus terminal is centrally located at the pier area. Bike rentals are also easily available. A good shop is Kamei Cycle, Y250 per hr, Y1200 per day. A bicycle built for two, Y400 per hr, Y2000 per day. Motorcycles are also available at Y500 per hr, Y3000 per day, (8 hrs). Bicycling is really the best way to see the island.

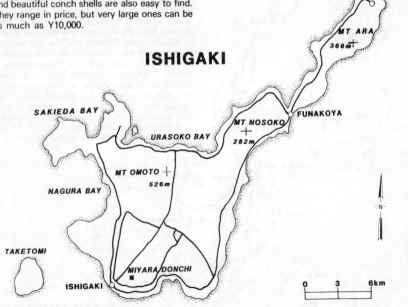

ISHIGAKI

the typhoon resistant roofs and distinctive stone walls of Ishigaki

sights: One of the first things that you will notice on the flower-lined streets are the roofs. They are predominantly of red tile and cemented with thick white plaster to hold them down in typhoons. _Shisa_ sit atop many, and the houses are surrounded with walls of porous stone which were thrown from the throats of volcanos. Neat gardens are everywhere, and flowering _deigo_ (the best tree for lacquerware) brighten the cobbled streets. Miyara Donchi, built in 1819, is a samurai residence open to the public. It is still occupied by the Matsushige family. An old woman sits on the porch collecting the entrance fee of Y100. She is the 10th generation. Her son is the 11th generation living in the home, and the current heir. The structure is simple and constructed of gray weathered wood. There is no admittance to the structure itself, but you can peer inside and see beautiful _shoji_ screens, charcoal drawings, paintings and an ancient Ryukyuan chess set. You can also spot a modern fire alarm and color TV. The construction is superb. The sidewalls are post and beam, and the roof is poles overlaid with young bamboo. The fastenings are pegs. The outside gray coloring contrasts pleasantly with the multi-shaded browns of the interior. The garden surrounding the home is a visual delight. It is built in the Ishigama method particular to the Ryukyus. This is a perfect chance to see living history. _around Ishigaki Island:_ A good trip is to bus N to Hirano. This area is sparsely visited, quiet and beautiful. Stay at the Northern House of the S operated by Shigeru and Madomi Kido. Rent diving equipment (_dokutsu_) in this area at Ishigaki Shima Saihate no Yado, tel: (09808) 9-2343. _fishing:_ There are many tackle shops in Ishigaki. The local poles are long unsplit bamboo. A favorite bait is baby prawns. About Y1500 can put you in business. Dunk a line while tending a campfire at night. Good fun and saves on food costs.

accommodations and food: Ishigaki has various _minshuku_ for about Y3000. The Grand Hotel is just opposite the pier area. They accept VISA. A single room is Y5000, a double Y7500; add Y3000 for meals. More modest business hotels are also in this area. The YHs available on Ishigaki are: Ishigaki-shi-tei YH, 287 Shinkawa, Ishigaki City, tel: (09808) 2-2720, 13 min on foot from Ishigaki Port, 13 beds; and Yashima Ryokan, 117 Tonojo, Ishigaki City, tel: (09808)

2-3157, 5 min on foot from Ishigaki Port, 20 beds. There are a multitude of inexpensive restaurants on the side streets. There is even A&W Root Beer. For excellent *soba* try Jugoya, run untypically by an old man. *Yakisoba* is the specialty (see map). The building is run down, painted blue, and next door to a grocery store with a large 7Up sign. Across the street is a coffee shop with pottery in the window.

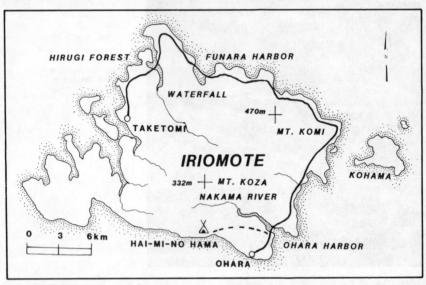

IRIOMOTE

On Iriomote soak up the natural beauty. Swim, snorkel and relax. This is the place. Iriomote is the last unexplored region of Japan. The interior, a primeval forest, is shrouded in mystery and home to the famous Iriomote wild cat. Houses are scattered along the E and W coasts. Many foot trails lead to the interior, and dirt tracks frequented only by sugarcane trucks twist around the coastline. Flag one down, they are happy to give you a lift. Iriomote has 2 main ports: Ohara in the S, and Funara in the north. Many Japanese students visit Iriomote, fascinated by its remoteness. They all follow the same itinerary. Landing at tiny Ohara, they bus N to Funara and on to Shirahama. A small shuttle bus waits at Ohara to take you ½ km to the bus terminal. This service is included in your ferry ticket. At the top of the hill is the town. There is a bus terminal, a post office, and a bike rental shop. In town you will also find a super-market for supplies. The bus service from here runs up the E coast of Iriomote to Shirahama 50 km, the farthest point. Funara is 39 km, and costs Y600. This northern area is beautiful and provides *minshuku* and YH accommodations. There is plenty of camping, crowded to capacity during student holidays.

Haimino Hama: An alternative itinerary, and probably superior because it avoids the crowds, is to stay in the S and hike to Haimino Hama, one of the premier camping spots on all of the islands. Use Haimino Hama as a base to explore the island, while saving on accommodation costs. At the top of the hill from Ohara pier turn L, away from the bus terminal, and follow this road about 3 km. This route will take you through some very rural areas where buffalo are still worked as agricultural animals. You will pass through sugarcane fields. If caught in the rain, look for some broad-leafed plants very common in the area that make very adequate rain hoods. You will eventually come to a little settlement. If you have not bought camping supplies, this is your last chance. There are also snorkels and film available at this little store. Buy rice, canned fish and fruit. The fishing, both pole and spear, is excellent at Haimino Hama, but one never knows. Continue along this road, wide enough for 2 sugarcane trucks to pass, for about one km until it ends in a large hump and turns into a walking track. Go straight and count the mountain peaks on your right. After about one km, turn L onto the beach between the saddle of the 2nd and 3rd mountain peaks. And this is Hamino Hama. There is even a little, metal, over-grown sign with 2 chipmunks pointing the way. There is a freshwater stream for drinking and bathing coming from the mountain; drift-

wood lies along the beach for an evening camp-fire. The local fishermen are curious, but completely trustworthy, so don't worry about leaving your gear to explore the remainder of the island and the beach that stretches for miles. If at night you see small lights upon the water, it is the local fishermen spearing fish and lobster. It is not uncommon to be invited to the feast that follows. They may even offer to lend you their gear so you can try it too. Allow one hr for the walk to and from town. Note: Beware the deadly *habu* (see "fauna" in the "Introduction"). *stay:* Youth Hostels on Iriomote include Iriomote Jima Midori So, 870 Uehara, tel: Iriomote Jima-60, 20 min on foot from Taketomi Port, 15 beds.

Okinawan tombs

Okinawa was called the Land of the Dead because of the numerous tombs that dot the countryside. They are of 3 types: the tortoise-shell type, the lock-and-key type, and the most primitive, the *hafu* (cave type). They were the repositories for the remains of kings

and noblemen. At one time the body was disenterred after 6 years and the bones were scraped, allowing the wind to scatter the gruesome bits. This practice has given way to cremation, but still occationally does occur

NOTES

APPENDIX

THE JAPANESE LANGUAGE

Mastering the Japanese language takes years of intensive study, but you can learn to communicate your basic needs and simple ideas very quickly. Learning a new language makes us realize what simple creatures we are after all. This section will concentrate on the basics; namely, how to move it down the road, how to lay it down at night, how to put food in and how to let it out. These, coupled with a few more niceties and basics like numbers, directions, and days of the week should get you started. The phrases following may not be "proper," but they are simple; have faith, because they will work. English is by far the most common foreign language used in Japan. A few doctors and scientists speak German. This is a carry over from the turn of the century when Germany led these fields. A handful of Japanese artists, who romantically pine for Paris have learned French. Foreigners in Japan from non-English speaking countries make a living teaching English, though their command of the language is at best halting. Foreigners in Japan are assumed to be able to speak English and assumed to be Americans as well.

TIPS

Don't be self-conscious about speaking Japanese. Remember that all Japanese students are taught English from junior high, and after 6 years of study, although they can read and write some, most can't say more than "This is a pen." Even a few words of Japanese will ingratiate you to the people. They are convinced that no *gaijin* can possibly learn Japanese well. Even long-term *gaijin* who speak the language flawlessly cannot be understood at times because the Japanese refuse to believe that their language is coming from a foreign face. Beware of "*Gaijin* Fever" (See "The People" for a thorough explanation). In short, this acute illness strikes the Japanese when confronted by a foreigner, especially a Japanese speaking foreigner. In men the symptoms are open-mouthed, awe-struck faces. In women, look for uncontrollable, hysterical, mouth covered giggles. This can be a nuisance at RR stations when time is of the essence. If hard pressed, choose a young Japanese to communicate your needs to. A student is a good choice. Boys are slightly less shy than girls. Speak simply or *PRINT* your communication. Remember, at times you know what you want to say, but you don't know what you want to hear. Be patient. Almost magically, when you're lost, a Japanese who speaks English seems to alway come along. Though the Japanese are very intuitive, don't ask negative questions like "Can't you show me the way?" The Japanese will answer uncustomarily, but properly with "Yes" (I cannot show you the way.). Don't stress syllables in Japanese words. Speak as evenly as you can, no ups and downs. Japanese rarely address a problem directly. They seem to beat around the bush, but this is really due to their sense of politeness. Don't become unstuck if you don't seem to get a straight answer; "maybe," or "that may be" are proper responses to questions they can't, or don't want to answer directly. *Gaijin* are allowed to speak directly. For example, if you are offered food but are full, though *kekko desu* is correctly polite, you can say, "*iie*" (no). A Japanese, however, would never do this. Speak slowly, distinctly, and as simply as you can. Remember, the Japanese are accommodating you. Some tourists have the mistaken belief that if you can't be understood, speak more loudly. This only aggravates. There is a proper woman's way and man's way of saying things in Japanese. Foreigners, however, regardless of sex, are given wide license. Japanese are hard pressed to distinguish between the English "L" and "R" sounds. Don't be surprised to hear, "Rets Eat Runch" or "Honoruru, Hawaii," as there is no equivalent to an "L." There is also no "th" sound in Japanese and "V" often becomes a "B" as in *balbe* (valve). There are certain Japanese words and phrases used so frequently throughout this book that they are used to replace the English word. At times the English word may be used in the same paragraph in which they occur for clarity or as a reminder. The most frequently used Japanese words are:

eki	train station
gaijin	foreigner
onsen	hot springs or spa
minshuku	guest house serving bed and breakfast
ryokan	Japanese inn
daimyo	Japanese feudal king (warlord)
mura	village
ofuro (sento)	bath (public)

PRONUNCIATION KEY

<u>vowels:</u> Vowels in Japanese are pronounced like those in Romance languages. Italian is the closest. The sounds given are phonetic.

A   Long A, *ah!* That feels good! (*Asakusa, Kamakura*)

E   Short E, pen, dent. (*Kobe, Ebisu*)

I   Short I, when *i* occurs in the middle of words, eg. *inn* or *pin* (*Shinjuku*). Long *i* when *i* occurs at the end of words like *see* or *knee* (*Ryoanji*).

O   Round O, *Oh, no!* (*Osaka, Nikko*)

U   Round U like *do* not disturb! (*deguchi*)

The vowel length in Japanese can change the meaning or a word. Long vowels in this section are indicated by doubling of the vowel. Many *faux pas* occur by not following this rule. For example, if you were in a restaurant and wanted a sweet, you would ask for *okashi* (short i). If you said *okashii* (long i), you would elicit a puzzled expression on your waiter's face—*okashii* means strange. Goodbye in Japanese is *sayoonara*, not *sayonara*.

<u>consonants:</u> Consonants are invariably followed by a vowel, and may be either single or double. A double consonant is pronounced twice as long as a single consonant. Consonants are pronounced as in English. A few exceptions include:

G   hard *g* like *get* in the beginning of words (*Gifu*). Like *ng* in *sing* at the end of words.

W   as *wh* in wheat. (*Wakayama*)

When *i* and *u* follow *h, k, p, s* or *t*, they are voiceless or almost whispered, especially at the end of a word. The famous Japanese food is not *sukiyaki*, but *s'kiyaki*. The often-used phrase, "Where is...?" is pronounced, "Wa doko *des'ka*," not "desu ka."

<u>stress:</u> Generally light stress unless there is a double vowel or a double consonant. Questions have a slightly lower intonation at the end. There are some homonyms (same-sounded words) which are stressed differently, *hashi* (stress on *ha*) means chopsticks, while stress on *shi* means bridge.

<u>basic grammar:</u> Japanese is unrelated to any other language, including other oriental languages. Studies show that there is even a marked difference in the dominant side of a Japanese brain when it comes to storing language. The following rules are enough to get you started.

1. Japanese word order is subject-object-verb. Modifiers go in front of word modified.

2. There are no plurals. More than one is unstood in context, or by special counting words.

3. Adjectives have tenses and moods.

4. Verbs have only present and past tenses. Future is designated by the present and adverbs of time: Next Year I go to Japan.

5. There are many "participles" in Japanese. Some of the most important "connectors" include: Nouns as subjects are followed by the particle *ga* or *we*. Nouns as objects are followed by *o* for action and *e* for direction.

6. *Ka* at the end of a sentence indicates a question.

NUMBERS

Japanese generally use arabic numerals when writing. They also use the decimal system based on units of 10. Verbally the number system works like Roman numerals. For example, to say 15 in Japanese, combine *ju* (10) and *go* (5), therefore, *ju-go*. To complicate matters slightly, the Japanese use 2 number systems. One is designed to stand alone (Japanese origin) and one is to be used with an object (Chinese origin). Numbers designed to stand alone range from 0 to 10, and then the number-object system is employed. These stand-alone numbers (shown below) of Japanese origin are slightly harder to remember. If you were buying oranges and the shopkeeper asks you, *"Ikutsu desu-ka?* (How many?)" you should reply, *"Futatsu* (2)," if you wanted 2 oranges. If you replied, *"Ni* (2 in the number-object system)," you would be incorrect, but perfectly understood. The number-object system changes depending upon the size and shape of the object, but this is far too complicated for the itinerant traveler. Learn the stand-alone Japanese system from 1 to 10, but you will rarely use it past the number 4. In all other cases, use the number-object Chinese system. You will save long, frustrating hours of study. To calm some anxiety, the number-object (Chinese) system is always used when counting money and telling time, 2 of the basic traveling necessities.

Stand Alone System (Japanese origin):

1 *hitotsu*

2 *futatsu*

3 *mitsu*

4 *yotsu*

5 *itsutsu*

6 *muttsu*

7 *nanatsu*

8 *yattsu*

9 *kokonotsu*

10 *to*

(eg.) *"hitotsu kudasai."* (one, please.)

Number Object System (Chinese system):

1 *ichi*

2 *ni*

3 *san*

4 *shi* or *yon* (*shi* sounds like the Japanese word for death and to promote good luck it is often avoided.)

5 *go*

6 *roku*

7 *shichi* or *nana* (*shi* again)

8 *hachi*

9 *ku* or *kyu*, but don't mix it up with *roku* (6)

10 *ju*

To continue counting from 11 to infinity, Japanese numbers are built like Roman numerals.

11	*ju-ichi*
17	*ju-shichi* or *ju-nana*
30	*san-ju*
35	*san-ju-go*
100	*hyaku*
559	*go-hyaku go-ju kyu*
1000	*sen* or *zen*
2267	*ni-sen ni-hyaku roku-ju nana*
10,000	*ichi-man* (or *man* as in *go-man,* 50,000)

56,297   *go-man roku-sen ni-hyaku kyu-ju nana*
(5 x 10,000; 6 x 1000; 2; 100; 9 x 10; 7)

USEFUL PHRASES

yes	*hai*
no	*iie*
no (it isn't so)	*so j'a arimasen*
(I) understand	*Wakarimasu*
(I) don't understand	*Wakarimasen*
Do you understand?	*Wakarimasu ka?*
(Speak) slowly please	*Yukkuri (iite) kudasai*
(Say it) again please	*Mo ichido (iite) kudasai*
(Say it) in Japanese	*Nihongo (de)*
Write it please	*Kaite kudasai*
Is it correct?	*Tadashiidesu-ka?*
Do you speak English?	*(Anata wa) eigo hanashimasu ka?*
I speak Japanese a little	*Watashi wa Nihongo o sukoshi hana-shimasu*
How do you say it in Japanese	*Nihongo dewa nan to iimasu-ka?*
just a moment	*chotto matte kudasai*
not yet	*mata*
Let's go	*ikimasho*
(I) like it	*suki desu*

nice!	*suteki desu!* (women only) *kako ii!* (men only)
It's been awhile	*shibaraku desu*
cute	*kawaii*
sad, unfortunate (thing, person)	*kawaii-so*

GETTING ACQUAINTED

hello	*hello* or *haro*
good morning	*ohayoo gozaimasu*
good day	*konnichi-wa*
good evening	*konban wa*
good night (on retiring)	*oyasuminasai*
goodbye	*sayonara*
go to it!	*ganbatte (kudasai)*
good health	*o genki de* (said on leaving someone for a time)
see you soon	*mata ne*
take care	*ki o tsukete*

POLITENESS

thanks	*domo*
thank you	*domo arigato*
very much (polite form)	*domo arigato gozaimasu*

(The Japanese really appreciate being thanked!)

excuse me	*shitsurei shimasu* (when you need to pass, or when you bump someone lightly)
excuse me	*sumimasen* (usual)
excuse me	*gomen-nasai* (a real knock-down)
that's too bad	*zanen desu*

QUESTION WORDS

what?	*nan desu ka?*
who?	*dare (desu ka)?*
where?	*doko (desu ka)?*
why?	*doshite (desu ka)?*
which?	*dochira (desu ka)?*
when?	*itsu (desu ka)?*
how?	*dare no (desu ka)?*

(These can be used alone as a question, or can be placed at the end of a longer sentence.)

TELLING TIME

For schedules of trains, planes, buses, ferries and boats, the 24-hour time system is used, ie, 1300, 1749, etc. The man in the street will use am (*gozen*) and pm (*gogo*). If you are anxious about this, take a small cardboard clock with movable hands (these are teaching aids for children often sold in novelty stores(. When you buy a ticket, hand the ticket seller your clock. He'll chuckle, but will get the idea. To convert the 24-hr system to am-pm subtract 12 from any time larger than 12 (ie, 1937 - 12 = 7:37pm). Times less than 12 are am and are the same (ie, 0730 = 7:30am) in both systems.

am	*gozen*
pm	*gogo*
...o'clock	*...ji*
one o'clock	*ichi-ji*
...minutes	*...pun, (fun)*

A.M. — P.M.

1:36pm	*ichi ji-san-ju-roppun*
6:45am	*roku-ji yon-ju go fun*
6:45pm	*roku-ji yon-ju go fun*

24 HOUR SYSTEM

(1336)	*ju-san-ji san-ju roppun*
(0645)	*roku-ji yon-ju go fun*
(1845)	*ju-hachi-ji yon-ju go fun*

To express the half hour, *han* is used. For example, 8:30 is *hachi-ji han,* but a half hour is always *san-jippun* (30 min).

morning	*asa*
afternoon	*gogo*
evening	*ban*
night	*yoru*
today	*kyo*
tomorrow	*ashita*
yesterday	*kino*
day after tomorrow	*asate*
day before yesterday	*ototoi*
now	*ima*

MONTHS

January (1st month)	*Ichi-gatsu*
February (2nd month)	*Ni-gatsu*
March (3rd month)	*San-gatsu*
April (4th month)	*Shi-gatsu*
etc...	
one month	*ikkagetsu*
two months	*nikagetsu*
three months	*sankagetsu*
etc...	
this month	*kongetsu*
last month	*sengetsu*
month before last	*sensengetsu*
next month	*raigetsu*

month after next	*saraigetsu*
week	*shu*
month	*getsu*
year	*nen*
every-other (day)	*ichi-nichi oki*
every-other (week)	*i-shukan oki*

WEEKS

one week	*isshukan*
two weeks	*nishukan*
three weeks	*sanshukan*
etc...	
this week	*konshu*
last week	*senshu*
next week	*raishu*

DAYS OF THE WEEK

Sunday	*Nichi yobi*
Monday	*Getsu-yobi*
Tuesday	*Kai-yobi*
Wednesday	*Sui-yobi*
Thursday	*Moku-yobi*
Friday	*Kin-yobi*
Saturday	*Do-yobi*

SEASONS

Spring	*haru*
Summer	*natsu*
Autumn	*aki*
Winter	*fuyu*

DIRECTIONS
(getting around)

north	*kita*
south	*minami*
east	*higashi*
west	*nishi*

straight	*massugu* or *zuto*
right	*migi*
left	*hidari*
up	*ue*
down	*shita*
that way	*achira*
this way	*kochira*
here	*koko*
over there	*asoko*
Draw a map please	*Chizu o kaite kudasai*
Is it near (far)?	*Chikai (toi) desu-ka?*
I'm lost	*(michi ni) mayoimashita*
Please show me	*...e iku michi o*
Please show me the way to the	*...e iku michi o oshiete kudasai*
place	*basho*
street	*michi, dori*
highway	*kokudo*
How long does it take on foot?	*Aruite dono kurai kakarimasu-ka?*
Show me on this map plese	*Kono chizu de oshiete kudasai*
I forgot!	*wasuremashita*
I can't find...	*...ga mitsukarimasen*

TRANSPORTATION

train	*densha* (long distance) or *ressha*
train station	*eki*
electric train or trolley	*romen densha*
bus (stop, station)	*basu (noriba, taminaru)*
ferry	*ferri*
airplane	*hikooki*
subway (station)	*chikatetsu (no eki)*
ticket	*kippu*
one way	*katamichi*
return (round trip)	*ofuku*

special excursion round-trip ticket	*shuyuken*
first	*saisho no*
last	*saigo no*
next	*tsugi no*
How much?	*Ikura (desu ka)?*

HELPFUL TRANSPORT PHRASES

At what time does the train for Kobe leave?
Kobe yuki no densha wa nan-ji demasu ka?

From which platform?
Nanban sen kara demasu ka?

Where is Platform 8?
Hachi-ban sen wa doko desu-ka?

Does the train for Kyoto leave from here?
Kyoto yuki no densha wa koko kara demasu ka?

I want to get off at Ueno Station.
Ueno eki de oritai desu.

Will you tell me when to get off?
Itsu oritara yoi ka oshiete kudasai? (or)
Eki de oroshite kudasai

When buying a ticket after your destination is clear to the ticket seller, just ask, *Doko de norikaemasu-ka* (change where)?

How many stations (before I get off)?
Koko kara nanbanme no eki desu-ka?

TREKKING

How far is the vilage?
Mura made dono kurai desu-ka?

Am I on the correct road to the *temple*?
Kore wa otera ni iku michi desu-ka?

Where does this road lead (go)?
Kono michi wa doko e iku michi desu-ka?

Also see *directions* for maps, etc.

HITCHIKING

Where are you going?
Doko e ikimasu ka?

How far are you going?
Doko made ikimasu ka?

Can you give me a ride to Osaka?
Osaka made nosete kuremasu-ka?

Stop please!
Tomatte kudasai

Straight ahead (on this highway)
Kono kokudo massugu.

Roadside rest area (next)
(Tsugi) no kyu keijo.

Do you know anywhere I can stay tonight?
Doko-ka tomareru tokoro o oshiete kuremansen-ka?

Where is the nearest youth hostel?
Koko kara ichiban chikai yusu hosuteru wa doko desu-ka?

POST OFFICE

aerogram	*koku shokan*
air mail	*kokubin*
package	*kozutsumi*
letter	*tegami*
post office	*yubin kyoku*
post restante	*kyoku dome yubin*
stamps	*kitte*
sea mail	*funabin*
special delivery	*sokutatsu*

ACCOMMODATIONS

How much is it...?	*...ikura desu ka?*
nightly	*ippaku*
weekly	*isshuukan*
for bed and breakfast	*choshokutsuki*
for full board	*sanshokutsuki*
excluding meals	*sudomari desu*
Does that include...?	*...wa suite imasu-ka?*
meals	*shokuji*
service	*saabisu*

Have you anything cheaper?
Nani ka motto yasui (no wa arimasen ka?)

Can you recommend a good and inexpensive hotel?
Yokute takakunai hoteru o oshiete kudasai (or)
Doko-ka yasukute ii yado o oshiete kudasai?

That's too expensive!
Takasugimasu!

RESTAURANTS, FOOD

Breakfast, please	*Choshoku kudasai*
Lunch, please	*Chuushoku kudasai*
Dinner, please	*Yuushoku kudasai*
extra helping	*Omori*
I don't like it	*Ski dewa arimasen*
No thank you	*iie, kekko desu*
Delicious	*Oishii* (or) *Umai desu*
It looks delicious	*Oishii-so*
The bill	*Okanjoo*
restaurant	*resutoran*
Japanese-style	*ryoriya*
bar (Japanese style)	*baa (akachochin)*
coffee shop	*kissaten*
snack bar	*sunaku* (often written "snack")
not enough	*tarinai desu*
I am hungry	*Onaka ga sukimashita*
I am thirsty	*Nodo ga kawakimashita*
How much?	*Ikura desu ka?*
expensive!	*Takai desu!*
Anything cheaper?	*Nani ka motto yasui?*

YOUTH HOSTELS

membership card	*kaiinsho*
with meals please	*shokuji tsuki*
Can I stay?	*Tomaremasa ka?*
Do you have a room?	*Heya wa arimasu-ka?*
full	*ippai desu*

Big	*ookii*
small	*chisai*
(to) order	*chumon (osaru)*

What's the price for the fixed menu?
Teishoku wa ikura desu-ka?

Is service (charge) included?
Sabisu ryo komi desu-ka?

Nothing more, thanks.
E mo kekko desu.

SHOPPING

camera store	*kameraya*
dept. store	*depato*
grocery	*shoku ryoohinten*
laundry	*sentakuya*
liquor store	*sakaya*
(local) market	*ichiba*
supermarket	*supa maaketo*
travel agent	*ryokoo dairiten*
I want...	*...ga hoshii desu*
Have you anything...	*Nanika no wa... arimasen ka*
...smaller	*...motto chisai na...*
...larger	*...motto ookii na...*
...cheaper	*...motto yasui...*
...more expensive	*...motto yoi...*

EMERGENCY

(I'm) ill	*(watashi wa) byooki desu*
Get a doctor	*Oisha-san o yonde kudasai*
Get help	*Sugu ni tasuke o yonde kudasai*
Quickly	*hayaku*
Danger	*kiken*
It's dangerous!	*Abunai!*
Fire	*Kaji*
Help!	*tasukete kudasai*
Hospital	*Byooin*
Police	*Keisatsu*

Pharmacy	*Kusuriya*

BASIC VOCABULARY

address	*jusho*
airport	*kuko, hikojoo (not much used)*
American	*Amerika-jin*
arrival (time, place)	*toochaku (jikan, basho)*
ashtray	*haizara*
bank	*ginko*
bad	*warui*
bad (don't do it)	*dame!*
bath (public)	*ofuro (sento)*
bay	*wan (Tokyo-wan)*
beautiful	*utsukushi*
beer	*biiru*
beyond	*saki*
big	*ookii*
book	*hon*
boy (child)	*onako, (otokonoko)*
bridge	*hashi*
building	*biru*
bus (stop)	*basu (tei, basu no teiryujo)*
bus terminal	*(basu taminaru)*
castle	*shiro*
cheap	*yasui*
cigarettes	*tabako*
closed (window, door)	*shimatte iru*
closed (shop)	*heiten desu*
cold (things and weather)	*tsumetai, samui*
cold (chilly)	*kaze*
cool	*suzushii*
difficult	*muzukashii*
dentist	*shikai*
doctor	*oisha-san (polite)*
do you have?	*ga arimasu ka?*
drink	*nomu*

east	*higashi*	man	*otoko no hito*
eat	*taberu*	map	*chizu*
English (person)	*Eigo* (*Eikoku-jin*) or (*Igirisu-jin*, which is *more popular*]	maybe	*tabun*
		Mr., Ms.	*...san*
		money	*okane*
entrance	*iriguchi*	morning	*asa*
evening (this)	*ban* (*konban*)	name	*namae*
exit	*deguchi*	newspaper	*shinbun*
expensive	*takai*	night	*yoru*
far	*toi*	no	*iie*
		no (don't have)	*nai, (ga nai)*
flower (arranging)	*hana* (*ikebana*)	north	*kita*
		OK	*daijobu*
French	*Furansu*	open (shops)	*kaiten desu*
French person	*Furansu-jin*	park	*koen*
free time	*hima*	photograph	*shashin*
garden (home)	*niwa*	please (take it)	*dozo*
garden (traditional)	*teien*	please (do it)	*kudasai*
German person	*Doitsu-jin*	police (box)	*keisatsu* (*koban*)
girl (child)	*josei* (*onna-no-ko*)	porter	*adaboo* (now rarely used)
good	*ii* or *yoi*		
harbor	*minato*	post office	*yubin-kyoku*
help, please (emergency)	*tasuke te kudasai*	right (direction)	*migi*
		river	*kawa* (or *gawa* when in combination with certain other sounds)
here	*koko*		
hospital	*byoin*		
hot	*atsui*	road	*michi* or *dori*
hotel	*hoteru*	show me please	*misete*
how many?	*ikutsu desu-ka?*	show me please (lit. teach me)	*misete kudasai* *oshiete kudasai*
how much?	*ikura desu-ka?*		
I	*Watashi wa*	shopping center	*shoppingu senta*
inn (Japanese)	*ryokan*	shrine	*jinja*
information office	*annaijo*	sick	*byooki*
interpreter	*tsuuyaku*	sometimes	*toki-doki*
island	*shima* (or *jima* when in combination with certain sounds)	sorry	*sumimasen*
		south	*minami*
		spa	*onsen*
Lake	*mizuumi* or *ko*, ie. *Biwa-ko*	station	*eki*
		stop it!	*yamete kudasai*
left (direction)	*hidari*	street	*tori* (or *dori* when in combination with certain other sounds)
little	*chiisai*		

subway (station)	*chikatetsu (...no eki)*
taxi (stand)	*takushi (noriba)*
tea (Japanese black, ceremony)	*cha (ocha, kocha, cha-no-yu)*
telephone (number)	*denwa (bango)*
temple	*(o) tera*
this	*kono*
this thing	*kore*
that	*sono*
that thing	*are*
there (over there)	*osoko*
ticket	*kippu*
timetable	*jikokuhyo*
today	*kyo*
tomorrow	*ashita*
tourist home	*minshuku*
town	*machi*
toilet	*toirei, otearai, benjo*
train (station)	*densha (eki)*
train (long distance)	*ressha*
trolley	*densha* or *romen densha*
understand?	*wakarimasu-ka?*
don't understand	*wakarimasen*
village	*mura*
visa	*sashoo* or *bisa*
warm	*atatakai*
water	*mizu*
what is this?	*kore wa nan desu-ka?*
what time is it?	*nan-ji desu-ka?*
when?	*itsu?*
where?	*doko?*
weather (good, bad)	*tenki (ii..., warui)*
west	*nishi*
wind	*kaze*
woman	*onna no hito*
yes	*hai*
you	*anata wa*
youth hostel	*yusu hosuteru*

WRITTEN LANGUAGE

The Japanese have the highest literacy rate (98%) in the world, and they have maintained this statistic for over a century. To master their own language, they must learn 4 ways to write Japanese: *Kanji, hiragana, katakana,* and *romanji. Kanji* are Chinese character/pictographs that were adopted by the Japanese in the 5th century. There are over 40,000 and to read a newspaper, over 2,000 must be recognized. A classically educated, older Japanese person can write perfectly proper *kanji* that may be unrecognizable by a modern college graduate. some *kanji* can have 10 differnet pronunciations depending upon context and meaning. Chinese and Japanese can read each other's languages when written in *kanji* although they cannot speak it. *Hiragana* is a cursive, phonetic syllabary of the 50 sounds of the Japanese language. It is used to connect *kanji* and to write Japanese words phonetically. Often, *hiragana* is used to write the names of train stations. *Katakana,* like *hiragana,* is a syllabary of the 50 sounds of Japanese, but its characters are more square than those of *hiragana,* somewhat like printing as opposed to writing. *Katakana* is used to write foreign words in Japanese. In short, *kanji* is visual, a direct relationship of symbol to word, where *hiragana* and *katakana* are phonetic. Thankfully, the Japanese also use the Roman alphabet (*ramanji*). Japanese words can be rendered or at least approximated in *romanji.* Most Japanese can read and write both script and printing in *romanji.* Railway stations in large cities usually have their names rendered in *romanji. Romanji* is often-times coupled with any of the other 3 writing systems. *Kanji* obviously takes years of study, but *hiragana* and *katakana* can be mastered in a few weeks. The following *Kanji* may be useful:

train	列車
station	駅
entrance	入口
exit	出口
bank	銀行
men's toilet	紳士 (用)
women's toilet	婦人 (用)

HIRAGANA
(FOR JAPANESE WORDS & NAMES OF TRAIN STATIONS)

ば pa	ば ba	だ da	ざ za	が ga		ん n	わ wa	ら ra	や ya	ま ma	は ha	な na	た ta	さ sa	か ka	あ a
ぴ pi	び bi	ぢ ji	じ ji	ぎ gi			ゐ i	り ri	(い i)	み mi	ひ hi	に ni	ち chi	し shi	き ki	い i
ぷ pu	ぶ bu	づ zu	ず zu	ぐ gu			う u	る ru	ゆ yu	む mu	ふ fu	ぬ nu	つ tsu	す su	く ku	う u
ぺ pe	べ be	で de	ぜ ze	げ ge			ゑ e	れ re	(え e)	め me	へ he	ね ne	て te	せ se	け ke	え e
ぽ po	ぼ bo	ど do	ぞ zo	ご go			を wo	ろ ro	よ yo	も mo	ほ ho	の no	と to	そ so	こ ko	お o

ぴゃ pya	びゃ bya	ぢゃ ja	じゃ ja	ぎゃ gya		りゃ rya	みゃ mya	ひゃ hya	にゃ nya	ちゃ cha	しゃ sha	きゃ kya
ぴゅ pyu	びゅ byu	ぢゅ ju	じゅ ju	ぎゅ gyu		りゅ ryu	みゅ myu	ひゅ hyu	にゅ nyu	ちゅ chu	しゅ shu	きゅ kyu
ぴょ pyo	びょ byo	ぢょ jo	じょ jo	ぎょ gyo		りょ ryo	みょ myo	ひょ hyo	にょ nyo	ちょ cho	しょ sho	きょ kyo

KATAKANA
(FOR WRITING FOREIGN WORDS)

パ pa	バ ba	ダ da	ザ za	ガ ga		ン n	ワ wa	ラ ra	ヤ ya	マ ma	ハ ha	ナ na	タ ta	サ sa	カ ka	ア a
ピ pi	ビ bi	ヂ ji	ジ ji	ギ gi			ヰ* i	リ ri	(イ i)	ミ mi	ヒ hi	ニ ni	チ chi	シ shi	キ ki	イ i
プ pu	ブ bu	ヅ zu	ズ zu	グ gu			ウ u	ル ru	ユ yu	ム mu	フ fu	ヌ nu	ツ tsu	ス su	ク ku	ウ u
ペ pe	ベ be	デ de	ゼ ze	ゲ ge			エ e	レ re	(エ e)	メ me	ヘ he	ネ ne	テ te	セ se	ケ ke	エ e
ポ po	ボ bo	ド do	ゾ zo	ゴ go			ヲ wo	ロ ro	ヨ yo	モ mo	ホ ho	ノ no	ト to	ソ so	コ ko	オ o

ピャ pya	ビャ bya	ヂャ ja	ジャ ja	ギャ gya		リャ rya	ミャ mya	ヒャ hya	ニャ nya	チャ cha	シャ sha	キャ kya
ピュ pyu	ビュ byu	ヂュ ju	ジュ ju	ギュ gyu		リュ ryu	ミュ myu	ヒュ hyu	ニュ nyu	チュ chu	シュ shu	キュ kyu
ピョ pyo	ビョ byo	ヂョ jo	ジョ jo	ギョ gyo		リョ ryo	ミョ myo	ヒョ hyo	ニョ nyo	チョ cho	ショ sho	キョ kyo

NOTES

BOOKLIST

Abesehsera, Michael. *Zen Macrobiotic Cooking.* New York: Avon, 1968. Recipes of life, philosophy and cooking.

Abe, Kobo. *The Ruined Map.* Also, *The Woman in the Dunes.* Tokyo: Tuttle, 1970. Contemporary, stunning fiction by one of Japan's literary superstars.

Adams, T.F. M. and N. Kobayashi. *The World of Japanese Business.* New York: Kodansha. Tips to foreign businessmen on how the world of finance and commerce operates in Japan.

Bauer, Helen and Sherwin Carlquist. *Japanese Festivals.* Garden City, N.Y.: Doubleday. A fully descriptive book on festivals with a complete calendar of events.

Benedict, Ruth. *The Chrysanthemum and the Sword.* Boston: Houghton Mifflin, 1946. *The* text for many years on the Japanese and their ways. Excellent reference book to begin studies of Japan.

Bergamini, Joseph. *Japan's Imperial Conspiracy.* New York: Morrow, 1971. A highly controversial historical work implicating the present emperor of Japan in the plotting, organizing and carrying out of Japan's activities in WW11. The myth of Hirohito as only a mild-mannered marine biologist is destroyed. One of the most amazing labors of research in modern history. Startlingly real in its descriptions. Almost an unmentionable work in Japan.

Bird, Isabella. *Unbeaten Tracks in Japan.* 1881. Reprint. Rutland, Vermont: Tuttle. This Victorian woman leads her readers through the then, outback Japan.

Bowers, Faubion. *Japanese Theatre.* Rutland, Vermont: Tuttle, 1974. History, development and modern performances of Kabuki, Bunraku and Kyogen. Illustrated.

Buck, Pearl. *The People of Japan.* New York: Simon and Schuster, 1966. This old Asia hand brings her special insight to bear on the social life and attitudes of Japanese life.

Calvocoressi, Peter and Guy Wint. *Total War.* New York: Pantheon, 1972. World War Two is divided into the European and Pacific theaters with a view on the interrelationship. In many ways a factual account, but heavily biased towards the United Kingdom's efforts in the war.

Carpenter, Frances. *People From the Sky.* Illus. Betty Fraser. New York: Doubleday, 1972. Tales and legends of the Ainu. Sensitive and informative with excellent illustrations.

Condon, Camy and Kimiko Nagasawa. *Eating Cheap in Japan.* Tokyo: Shufunotomo, 1072. A food and reference guide for the *gaijin* in Japan. Lists almost all the foods that you will encounter while in Japan along with basic ingredients and color photos. A must to familiarize yourself with Japanese cuisine.

Condon, Camy and Kimiko Nagasawa. *Kites, Crackers and Craftsmen.* Tokyo: Shufunotomo, 1974. A pocket guide full of maps, addresses and photos of Tokyo's folk craft artists. An excellent (incidental) guide for shopping for handcrafted items in Tokyo.

Condon, John and Keisuke Kurata. *What's Japanese About Japan.* Tokyo: Shufunomoto, 1974. Looks at the peculiarities, idiosyncracies and social attitudes of modern Japan. Covers everything from types of laughter to how to sit on a crowded train. Complete with photos, this book is a delightful social commentary.

DeGaris, Frederick. *Their Japan.* Yokohama: Yoshikawa Betendori, 1936. A semi-guide, social commentary and encyclopedia brimming with little known facts and tidbits.

DeMente, Boye. *Bachelor's Japan.* Rutland, Vermont: Tuttle, 1962. Somewhat dated and definitely chauvinistic, this book in DeMente's words is "...dedicated to the women who make Japan a man's paradise..." DeMente has published a number of books on Japan and "things Japanese."

DeMente, Boye. *P's and Cues for Travelers in Japan.* Tokyo: Shufunotomo, 1974. A useful, easily readable book on how to get along in Japan. At times dated, but still useful.

Diaries of Court Ladies of Japan. New York: AMS Press, 1970. Court intrigues, love affairs and the day to day lifestyle of Japan' nobility from times past are subjectively reported by these ladies literati.

Doi, Takeo. *The Anatomy of Dependence.* Trans. John Bester. Tokyo: Kodansha International, 1973. Dr. Doi is a Japanese psychiatrist who has written a work that will leave an impact on Western psychiatric thinking for years to come. An overview of Japanese personality development as it relates to parents, the family, the group and society at large.

Dorson, Richard. *Folk Legends of Japan.* Rutland, Vermont: Tuttle, 1962. An illustrated collection of Japan's best known folk legends. Historical references accompany particular legends.

Gakken Co. Ltd.: *Japanese for Beginners.* Tokyo: Gakken Co., 1973. Also *Japanese for Today.* The basic language texts for beginners which include colloquial Japanese so you can understand the man on the street.

Haga, Hideo. *Japanese Folk Festivals Illustrated.* Trans. Fanny Mayer. Tokyo: Miura Printing Co., 1970. A survey of Japan's folk festivals ranging from Okinawa to Hokkaido. Excellent color photos.

Halloran, Richard. *Japan: Images and Realities.* Rutland, Vermont: Tuttle, 1969.

Hearn, Lafcadio. *Japan: An Interpretation.* Also, *In Ghostly Japan.* Rutland, Vermont: Tuttle, 1955. This turn-of-the-century writer presents a lasting, sensitive view of Japan's history and social development leading up to and including Japan's re-emergence into the community of nations after the Meiji Restoration. The pages glisten with respect for a land and people that Hearn came to love.

Hioshi, Hajime. *Japan—A Country Founded by Mother.* New York: Columbia University Club, 1937. A pre-war, sociological view of Japan.

Intercontinental Marketing Corp. *Asian Sources.* Tokyo: International Marketing Corp. Magazines on how to order and import sporting goods, novelties, toys, hardware, garments, electronics, watches and other items.

International Marketing Corp. "Guide to Japan's Business and Technical Periodicals." Tokyo: Intercontinental Marketing Corp. Journals, magazines and newspapers covering everything from the paper pulp industry to medical products of Japan.

Itoh, Joan. *Rice Paddy Gourmet.* Tokyo: Japan Times, 1976. A cookbook for the expatriot who intends on staying in Japan. Recipes are garnished with tales from the back country of Japan.

Japan Culture Institute. *A Hundred Things Japanese.* Tokyo: Japan Culture Institute, 1975. A compilation of 100 essays by international travelers, foreign residents and Japanese about the customs and ways of modern Japan.

Japan Publications Trading Co. *Teriyaki and Sushi.* Tokyo: Japan Publications Trading Co., 1963. Also, *Tempura and Sukiyaki,* 1961. Basic books on how to prepare everyday, inexpensive Japanese foods.

Jorden, Eleanor. *Beginning Japanese. Parts I and II.* New Haven, Conn: Yale University Press, 1963. Along with 35 accompanying language tapes the best self teaching language course available.

Kawasaki, Ichiro. *Japan Unmasked.* Rutland, Vermont: Tuttle, 1969. With a quality rare in Japan, especially coming from a diplomat, Mr. Kawasaki gives a candid view of the effect that WWII had on the Japanese, both positively and negatively.

Kenny, Don. *A Guide to Kyogen.* Tokyo: Hinoki Shoten, 1968. A compilation of Kyogen plays. Short, funny and to the point.

Kikuchi, Sadao. *Japanese Arts—What and Where.* Tokyo: Japan Travel Bureau. A compendium of art works with photographs.

Kirkup, James. *Heaven, Hell and Hara-Kiri.* London: Angus and Robertson, 1974. Entertaining and informative essays on Japanese culture and life.

Kohno, Sadako. *Home Style Japanese Cooking in Pictures.* Tokyo: Shufunotomo, 1977. Best basic see and do cookbook on everyday Japanese food and party menus.

Lee, Sherman. *A History of Far Eastern Art.* New York: Abrams, 1973. One of the best known and most authoritative introductory texts on Oriental art.

Leiter, Samuel. *Kabuki Encyclopedia.* Westport, Connecticut: Greenwood Press, 1979. All you ever wanted to know about Kabuki. An English language adaptation of the Japanese original, *Kabuki Jiten.*

Maloney, Don. *Japan: It's Not All Raw Fish.* Also, *Son of Raw Fish.* Tokyo: The Japan Times, 1975-1977. Hilarious collection of "Never the twain...?", a weekly column in the Japan Times. A *gaijin* businessman tells what it's really like to live in Japan.

Manchester, William. *Goodbye Darkness.* New York: Dell, 1982. An autobiographical view of a marine coming of age surrounded by the horrors of WWII in the Pacific. This well known historical author vividly portrays the feelings of the times.

Mikes, George. *Land of the Rising Yen.* London: Andre Deutch, 1970.

Mishima, Yukio. *After the Banquet.* Trans. Donald Keene. New York: Alfred A. Knopf, 1963. Mishima is considered with good reason to be one of the greatest modern novelists in Japan. His death by *hara-kiri* was his I at the end of the sentence of his life.

Mizutani, Osamu and Nobuko Mizutani. *Nihongo Notes.* Vol. I, II, III. Tokyo: Japan Times, 1977, 1979, 1980. A compilation of the column appearing in the Japan Times of the same name. Oftentimes hilarious and penetrating views of how the Japanese use their language to communicate along with the nuances not generally found in "language books."

Nagels. *Encyclopedia Guide, Hapa Japan*. New York: Masson. Excellent resource book for travel through Japan. Gives the nuts and bolts of touring but since it is an encyclopedia, it is at times lifeless and dry.

Ohsawa, George. *Book of Judgement*. Los Angeles: The Ohsawa Foundation, 1966. Yin and yang, faith, illness, the wonders of eastern medicine, the horrors of western medicine are all judged, exonerated or condemned by this "fire and brinstone" preacher of foods.

Ono, Hideichi. *Everyday Expressions in Japanese*. Tokyo: Hokuseido Press, 1963. A small and highly useful paperback book that gives the basics for communication in Japanese.

Ozaki, Robert. *The Japanese*. Rutland, Vermont: Tuttle, 1978. A collection of 11 informal essays that give a clear and precise picture of how Japan has developed socially over the centuries. Casts much light on how Japan has become a leading industrial nation and at the same time has retained much of its cultural past.

Papinot, E. *Historical and Geographical Index of Japan*. Ann Arbor, Michigan: Overbeck Co., 1948. A summary of events, customs and historical personages of Japan. Non critical history in alphabetical order. A good fingertip guide for a short summary of facts.

Pearce, Jean. *How to Get Things Done in Japan*. Vol. I, II. Tokyo: The Japan Times, 1975, 1976. Jean Pearce digs into her 12 years of experience writing an advice column in the Japan Times to cast a light on almost every question, confusion or source of information that a foreigner in Japan might possibly come across.

Pearce, Jean. *Footloose in Tokyo*. New York: Weatherhill, 1976. This long term Tokyo resident and columnist for the Japan Times leads you to every station on the Yamanote Line as it loops around Tokyo. Complete with maps and historical references, this paperback is excellent for both the long term resident and itinerant traveler in Tokyo.

Reischauer, Edwin. *The Japanese*. Rutland, Vermont: Tuttle, 1977. Mr. Reischauer was the post WWII US Ambassador General to Japan. His understanding of the Japanese is fathomless, and this deep intimate knowledge of a people that he came to admire is excellently portrayed on every page of his book.

Richie, Donald. *The Inland Sea*. New York: Weatherhill, 1971. An insightful, sensitive and

subjective travelogue by a long term resident of Japan.

Roberts, Lawrence. *The Connoisseur's Guide to Japanese Museums*. Rutland, Vermont: Tuttle.

Rudofsky, Bernard. *The Kimono Mind*. Tokyo: Tuttle, 1965. Historical and social travelogue filled with little known facts and tidbits.

Rudzinski, Russ. *Japanese Country Cookbook*. Concord, California: Nitty Gritty, 1969. A down home, easy to follow cookbook on the basic dishes in Japanese cooking.

Saint-Gilles, Amaury. *Earth 'n Fire*. Tokyo: Shufunotomo, 1978. An excellent introduction to pottery and ceramics in Japan. Color photos, area maps and commentary are included, along with a handful of tips on touring Japan.

Sakade, Florence (editor et al). *A Guide to Reading and Writing Japanese*. Rutland, Vermont:Tuttle, 1959. The book of the "approved" (*"toyo"*) *kanji* that all Japanese learn in school.

Saito, R. *Japanese Coiffure*. Tokyo: Japanese Board of Tourism, 1939. An historical survey of Japanese hairstyles complete with illustrations and photographs. Most hairdos are by and large no longer visible in Japan, except on the few remaining *geisha*.

Seward, Jack. *Japanese in Action*. New York: Weatherhill, 1968. Ostensibly a language book, but much more. The Japanese people and their ways are revealed through the nuances of their language. Hilarious easy reading, fun and educational.

Shurtleff, William and Akiko Aoyagi. *The Book of Kudzu*. Also, *The Book of Tofu*. Brookline, Massachusetts: Autumn Press, 1977, 1975. The basic texts in English. Everything from how to grow soybeans to whipping up a tofu cheesecake pie.

Shurtleff Willian and Akiko Aoyagi. *The Book of Miso*. New York: Ballantine Books, 1981. Over 600 pages of recipes, body chemistry, history, *miso* making and much, much more. A good view of one of the world's future proteins.

Simpson, Colin. *The Country Upstairs*. London: Angus and Robertson, 1966. An insightful interpretation of the Japanese and their ways by this famous Australian writer.

Skidmore, Eliza. *Jinriksha Days in Japan*. New York: Harper Bros., 1891. A delightful Victorian lady's view of traveling in Japan at the turn of the century. Amazing how some things have changed radically while many have remained the same.

Suzuki, D.T. *Manual of Zen Buddhism*. New York: Grove Press, 1964. An authoritative, scholarly work on Zen. Considered *the* text for an introduction to Zen, but very slow reading.

Tempel, Egon. *New Japanese Architecture*. New York: Praeger.

Tsuji, Shizuo. *Japanese Cooking a Simple Art*. Tokyo: Kodansha, 1980. Specializes in Zen cookery. A compendium of the traditional cooking methods. More like an encyclopedia including how to keep you knives sharp. Most recipes are too difficult for the amateur to prepare, but an excellent history of purist Japanese cooking.

Tuttle, Charles. *Incredible Japan*. Illus. Masakasu Kuwata. Rutland, Vermont: Tuttle, 1975. A "comic book" by the publisher himself. A lighthearted, but insightful look at Japanese customs and peculiarities.

Van de Wetering, Janwillem. *The Empty Mirror*. Boston: Houghton Mifflin, 1974. The personal experiences of a spiritual wanderer in a Zen Buddhist monastery. Enlightening in numerous ways.

Woodcock, George. *Asia, Gods and Cities*. London: Faber and Faber, 1966.

GLOSSARY

Ainu—some of the original settlers of Japan. Said to be of Caucasian stock because of their round eyes, hairy bodies and naturally wavy hair. Now only a handful of pure bloods remain in far northern Hokkaido.

akachochin—the common man's drinking and food bar. Easily spotted by the giant red (*aka*) (*chochin*) at the doorway.

Amaterasu—the Sun Goddess. One of the Shinto deities. Enshrined at the Grand Shrines of Ise and the first of the Imperial Family to which all succeeding emperors and empresses traced their lineage.

anagama—single chambered pottery kilns.

ayu—a Japanese fresh water game fish very much like a trout.

baiu (plum rains)—six weeks of drizzling rain from early June to mid-July centered in the Kanto district. Great for wet field rice farmers, but an unbelievably muggy time of year for city dwellers.

bangasa—oiled paper umbrellas.

bento—a boxed lunch which usually contains rice and fish. Often sold at train stations.

bonkei—the art of miniaturizing landscapes on trays.

bonsai—the gardener's art of miniaturizing trees and shrubs.

Bosatsu—the Japanese name for Buddha.

bosozoku—hot rod or motorcycle gangs. Usually benign, travelling in packs and making a general hullabaloo.

bunraku—classical Japanese puppet theatre, very similar to Kabuki. The puppets are ⅔ life-sized and are manipulated at times by three puppet masters.

bushido—the "Way of the Warrior." The code of ethics followed by the *samurai.*

byoin—hospital.

champon—Chinese noodles usually served with vegetables. A specialty of Nagasaki.

chanoyu—the tea ceremony.

Daibutsu—"Giant Buddha." Two famous bronze Buddhas are found in Japan. The more elegant of the two is at Kamakura and the other, larger one is located at Nara's Taoidoji Temple.

daikon—Japanese white radishes usually ground and served with many dishes or sliced and made into pickles.

daimyo—the warlords of Japan that ruled the fiefdoms granted them by the *shogun.*

daruma—folk art dolls that are round at the base and designed so that if they are knocked over, they will right themselves. When purchasing one a wish is made and one eye is painted in. If the wish comes true the other eye is then painted in.

dengaku—ancient Japanese courtly dances that inspired *Noh* drama and can still be seen at shrine festivals.

depato—a Japanese department store.

deshi—a Zen pupil.

dojo—the name of a school for martial arts.

donjon—the central main building of a Japanese castle.

Ebisu—the god of prosperity.

eki—train station.

emeshi—Ainu elders.

eta (*buraku-min*)—the little publicized untouchable caste of Japan. Traditionally held menial jobs, usually dealing with animals and leather. They are looked down upon by the Japanese society and few can marry out of their stigmatized class although "officially" they no longer exist.

fundoshi—traditional underwear; a loincloth with strings attached.

furoshiki—a bolt of cloth (i m sq.) traditionally used to wrap bundles. Many are made of cotton and have elaborate stencil dye patterns. They make excellent souvenirs.

futon—a thick quilt used as bedding. Easily rolled and tucked away during the daytime. The stuffing ranges from traditional rice hulls to foam rubber.

futsu—basic train that stops at all stations.

gaijin—the universal term used by a Japanese for a foreigner (e.g. *gaijin-san,* Mr. or Mrs. Foreigner).

geisha—translates as "refined person." These women study the arts of dance and music and perform privately or at *geisha* parties for patrons. Few women in Japan become *geisha* today as jobs can be easily had in other professions. The *geisha* does not dispense sexual favors as part of her normal job, but is there to comfort and entertain her guests.

geta — traditional wooden thongs worn by the Japanese, especially when on vacation.

gyoji — the referee at a Sumo bout.

Hachiman — the god of war. Believed to be the son of Empress Jingo who carried him in her womb for over two years while at war with Korea in the 2nd century.

haiku — seventeen syllable impressionistic poems. The greatest *haiku* poet was Basho.

hama — a beach.

harigai — belly talk often used to save face; say one thing but mean another.

hashi — common chopsticks made of unlacquered wood and found in most inexpensive restaurants.

hibachi — charcoal brazier of iron or ceramics traditionally used as a heater in winter.

Hidari, Jingoro — a master artist best known for his rendition of the "Sleeping Cat" of Nikko. Hidari means "left." This artist was called by this name because another artist of the time was so envious of Hidari's talents that he cut off his right hand. Undaunted, Hidari Jingoro created masterful works with his left hand.

hina — special courtly dolls given to Japanese girls who display them at the Hina Matsuri (Festival) on May 3-4.

hinoki — Japanese cypress. The best is often used in shrine architecture.

Honen — founder of the Jodo sect of Buddhism.

honne — a Japanese person's private "face." What they really think.

ikebana — the art of flower arranging.

irori — traditional open fireplaces in a lowered section of a floor in the middle of a room.

itoko — blind women soothsayers said to be mediums to the spirit world and who perform their services at festivals, especially throughout Tohoku.

Izanagi and Izanami — brother and sister lover gods that created the islands of Japan when they descended to earth at Amanohashidate.

Izumo-O-Kuni — a priestess from the Izumo Shrine who is believed to be the founder of Kabuki.

Jimmu Tenno — the first semi-mythical emperor of Japan. Traditionally said to have ascended to the Japanese throne in 660 B.C., but a more accurate date places the ascension at 100 A.D.

jinja — a Shinto shrine easily spotted by a *torii* gate at the entrance way.

JNR — Japan National Railroad.

JNTO — Japan National Tourist Organization. Indispensable for giving travelers much needed information, especially the TIC (Tourist Information Center) branch offices in Kyoto, Tokyo and Narita Airport.

jomon — earliest type of pottery found in Japan (8000 B.C.) recognizable by the rope marks impressed into it that were used to give it shape.

joruri — the ballad plot of *bunraku* puppet plays.

JTB — Japan Tourist Bureau. Oftentimes but not always the staffs speak foreign languages. Used to make every manner of ticket purchase and reservation. Offices are found everywhere throughout Japan.

ka — a mosquito by any other name is still a nuisance.

Kabuki — classical Japanese drama that evolved from *Noh*. Usually performed by an all male cast in elaborate costumes using stylized movements portrayed through dances and songs. They can be tragedies or comedies.

kagura — ancient sacred dances imported from India and preserved now only in Japan where they are performed at special shrine festivals.

kama boko — processed fish with a pink coating usually found in *soba*.

kami — loosely defined as a god in Shintoism. A spirit. Can be anything from an exalted ancestor to a natural occurence like Mt. Fuji.

kami kaze — "divine wind." The name given to the typhoon that sunk Kublai Khan's invading armada of Japan in the 13th century. Also the name given to the Japanese suicide pilots of WWII in their effort to duplicate this fortuitous storm from the gods.

kampo yaku — Chinese homeopathic medicine.

Kannon — the goddess of mercy. Many renditions of this Buddhist goddess are found throughout Japan. Sometimes she has hundreds of arms or she takes the form of a "madonna" with a babe in arms. She was revered by the secret Christians during the Tokugawa Era as the manifestation of the Holy Virgin Mary.

katana — a Japanese sword.

katsuobushi — dried bonito. Very hard and grated as a seasoning into many dishes.

kawa or *gawa* — a river.

ki — the will of a martial artist that is considered with equal importance as physical strength, especially in the martial art of *aikido*.

kissaten — coffee shop.

koan—a meditative question technique of Zen.

koban—a police box usually found on a corner. The police inside are very familiar with their neighborhoods and are extremely helpful with giving information.

Kobo Daishi—the most famous Buddhist priest/ saint who preached during the 800s. He established the Shingon Sect and the 88 Temples of Shikoku. Many miracles are attributed to this holy man and myths and legends sing his praises.

koi—giant paper carp that Japanese families fly from their rooftops. The *koi* honor the sons of the family with the largest at the top of the pole for the first born son and smaller ones below it for the other sons in descending order of birth.

Kojiki—the oldest of the ancient Shinto scriptures that relate the mythical beginnings of Japan. Compiled in 700 A.D.

kokeshi—round headed, cylindrical wooden dolls. A favorite folk toy of the Japanese.

kokujin—a black or brown skinned person.

konyoku—mixed bathing, quickly giving way to new puritanical ideals spreading throughout Japan.

kotan—Ainu villages.

kotatsu—a low table covered by a quilt with a heating element underneath. Used in winter to keep warm.

koto—a stringed instrument played oftentimes by a geisha.

Kyogen—classical Japanese farce drama performed during the interludes of *Noh* plays.

kyoiku mama—a Japanese mother who is neurotically overconnected with the education of her children.

kyuko—an ordinary express train that is faster than a *futsu* and stops only at certain stations.

marimo—spherical green barometric duckweed found in Lake Akan in Hokkaido.

matsuri—a festival.

Meiji Emperor—ushered in the Meiji Restoration of the 1860's whereby Japan was roused from its long dormancy and feudalism and entered into the modern age.

meshi—the all important business card. Exchanged almost instantly upon meeting. You are almost a non-person without one.

miko—temple maidens who perform at festivals and serve as temple clerks throughout the year.

mikoshi—portable shrines displayed by being carried or wheeled about at a festival so that the enshrined gods can "see" their constituents.

minshuku—a Japanese style tourist home run by a family. The best and most authentic accomodation for a budget traveler.

miso—a type of boullion made from fermented soybeans and used as a stock in soups and the base of many dishes.

mochi—glutinous, pounded rice served as a sweet often on auspicious occasions and holidays.

mondo—a question and answer technique used by Zen masters.

moningu sabisu—"morning service." A light breakfast included with the price of a cup of coffee at many *kissaten* (coffee shops). Usually served only until 1000.

mura—a village.

natzu kashi—homesick.

Nichiren—founder of the Nichiren sect of Buddhism.

Nihongi—classic Japanese epic histories dating from 700 A.D.

Nippon or Nihon—the Japanese name for themselves in use today. Translates as "Land of the Rising Sun."

noborigama—multiple chambered pottery kilns, usually built in a step sequence on a slope.

Noh—classical Japanese drama performed on a stark stage with few props. The plot of this Zen inspired drama is moved along by a chorus.

norikae—to change (make connections) on buses, trains, etc.

nusa or *gohei*—small papers (at one time cloth) given as an offering at Shinto shrines and seen festooned to trees, shrubs or any likely spot all over the shrine compound.

obasan—grandmother type (old woman).

oden—boiled food sold from carts. Usually eggs, fish and vegetables in a tangy soy soup.

ofuro—a Japanese bath. Taken daily by most Japanese with strict etiquette and decorum maintained.

omen—masks made of wood or more commonly of papier mache.

omiai—arranged marriage. Almost unheard of in modern day Japan but can still occur in rural areas.

omikuji—prayer papers sold at Buddhist temples. Thousands are seen festooned to trees, shrubs or any likely spot on the temple grounds.

omiyaki—an almost socially mandatory souvenir brought home to members of the family by a traveling Japanese.

onnagata—the male actors in a Kabuki play who perform the roles of women.

onsen—mineral spas, usually surrounded by various guest accommodations. The waters of the *onsen* are believed to be beneficial to many ailments and their mineral compositions range from simple sulphur springs to radioactive elements.

oshibori—napkin sized wet cloths found in restaurants. Served cold in summer and hot in winter.

otera—a Buddhist temple. Usually much more ornate than a Shinto Shrine (*jinja*).

pinku saron—guzzle and grab joints. Seedier hostess bars where you pay an entrance fee and are allowed (30 minutes most often) to drink and fondle as much as you can get your hands on.

Ring of Fire—a geological circle of volcanoes in the Pacific, ranging from the Americas to Japan.

romaji—Roman alphabet familiar to most Japanese and used to name main rail and subway stations.

ronin—masterless samurai. The tale of the "47 Ronin" who gave their lives to the honor of their lord is one of the best loved tales in all of Japan.

roshii—a Zen master.

ryokan—a Japanese style inn. Many individual *ryokan* have been accommodating travelers for hundreds of years.

Saicho—founder of the Tendai sect of Buddhism.

sake—potent rice wine served warm in thimble-sized containers.

sakura—cherry blossoms. Many festivals center around these short lived blossoms that move in a pink and white wave from Okinawa to Hokkaido as spring spreads through Japan.

samurai—the warrior class of Japan. Functioned as soldiers for the warlords and were allowed to wear two swords as a sign of their caste.

sangaku—ancient Japanese courtly ballads that inspired *Noh* drama and are still performed at certain shrine festivals.

satori—the Zen concept of enlightenment or nirvana.

sento—public baths found in all cities and towns.

seiza—the lotus position assumed by Zen monks while meditating.

seppuku—more popularly known as *hari kari* (belly cutting), this is the ritualized suicide of Japan.

shakuhachi—a Japanese flute with a deep soulful sound.

shinai—a bamboo sword used to practice *kendo* (sword fighting).

shinkansen—the speedy (200 km/hrs+) bullet train.

Shinran—founder of the Shinshu sect of Buddhism.

Shinto—the indigenous religion of Japan where living and even inanimate objects are believed to have a soul. Ancestor worship and purity are two of the basic tenets. State Shinto, prevalent from Emperor Meiji to the end of WWII, was a bastardized form which made the Emperor an omnipotent living god. Shinto in Japan is called *Kami-No-Machi* (The Way of the Gods).

shogun—"Barbarian Quelling Great General." *Sei-i-Tai Shogun*. The military ruler of Japan to whom all *daimyo* and *samurai* owed allegiance.

shoji—sliding screens used to separate rooms or open out into gardens.

shojin yori—vegetarian meals usually served at Buddhist temples.

shuyuken—a special money saving excursion train ticket.

Suijin—a male water deity especially important to farmers.

sukiya—a tea house where *chanoyu* (tea ceremony) is performed.

sumi—black ink paintings applied with a brush.

sumo—Japanese wrestling.

Susawano—Shinto god known as the Impetuous Male or God of Storms. Born spontaneously from Izanagi's nose when he washed his face in the sea.

tabi—split toed (big toe) Japanese socks worn with *geta*.

tachi-mi-seki—a one act, inexpensive ticket to get a sampling of a Kabuki performance. Literally, a "stand and see" ticket.

takenokozoku—"bamboo sprout gangs." Teenagers in brilliant costumes seen dancing in the fashionable areas of Tokyo.

takenoma—a special alcove considered the most beautiful spot in a Japanese home. Often it is fashioned from the most exquisite wood available and houses a *kakemono* (picture scroll) and an *ikebana* (flower arrangement) suggestive of the season. An honored guest is usually seated facing the *takenoma*.

Takigi Noh—Noh performances that are held at an outdoor stage, usually in the precincts of a shrine and lighted by blazing torches.

tako—colorful Japanese kites.

takoyaki—stall foods. Fried dough balls surrounding bits of octopus and seasonings.

tatamae—the Japanese public "face." How you act in society at large.

tatami—tight woven matting used as a floor covering. Shoes are never worn when one enters a *tatami* covered room.

tenugi—a small bath towel provided at many *sento* and *onsen*.

TIC—Tourist Information Center. These are the most useful branch of JNTO (Japan National Tourist Organization) for the foreign visitor to Japan. There are three operating in the country at Narita Airport and downtown Tokyo and Kyoto. Helpful in 1001 ways.

todai—a light house.

tofu—a curd made from soybeans used in numerous dishes. Very high in protein. A food source of the future.

togarashi—herbs found on almost every table and customarily added to *soba*.

tokkuyu—a limited express train that stops at only one or two major stations en route.

tokoroten—clear noodles that resemble plastic which are made from sea grass. Tasteless but believed to be good for the digestive tract.

Tokugawa Ieyasu—the military leader of Japan who controlled the nation at the turn of the 16th century. The word *shogun* is synonymous with this man. The Tokugawa Era begun by him lasted from 1600 until the Black Ships of Commodore Perry arrived in the 1850s. Feudal Japan with the *samurai* and *bushido* was at its zenith during this time.

torii—the gate at the entrance of a Shinto shrine.

toshiya—an archery contest.

Toyotomi, Hideyoshi—began the unification of Japan just prior to Tokugawa Ieyasu, but died before he became *shogun* in an ill-fated campaign to conquer Korea.

turuko—Turkish baths where prostitutes are available. Should not in any way be confused with an *onsen*.

tsunami—tidal waves, usually following sea centered earthquakes.

ukai—a unique type of fishing employing trained birds (cormorants) who bob for fish and bring them to the surface in their pouch-like necks.

Ukiyo-e—colorful wood block prints that oftentimes portrayed the scenes in the lives of ordinary people.

unagi-no-nedoko—literally "eel's bedrooms." Long narrow shops found in Kyoto selling traditional wares made on the premises by the artists.

Wa—early Chinese name for Japan.

wakame—edible seaweed served in many dishes and always found in *miso shiro* (soup).

warabashi—elegant lacquered chop sticks found in homes and better restaurants. Designed to be washed and used again.

"We Japanese"—the self touted Japanese view of themselves as being different from the remainder of mankind. This can either take the form of intense xenophobia or quaint and curious customs.

yabusame—horse back archery performed at shrine festivals by men dressed in *samurai* costumes.

yaki—the general suffix added to a word which means pottery, e.g. *Arita-yaki*.

yakuza—Japanese organized crime, in many ways like the "mafia."

yamabushi—mystical, ascetic mountain priests who preside over numerous festivals, especially in the Tohoku district.

Yamato—the traditional name of Japan (means Mountain Road, a euphemism for conquest).

yayoi—a type of pottery dating from 300 B.C. and found in the Tokyo area. Generally considered the herald of Japanese "civilization."

yokozuma—*sumo* grand champions.

yukata—a lounging or casual wear robe made of thin cotton for summer, and thick lined cotton for winter.

zabuton—small cushions used to sit on, usually in *tatami* areas.

INDEX

Joe Bisignani was born in Dunmore, a small mining community in the foothills of the Pocono Mountains of N.E. Pennsylvania. His enchantment with travel began at an early age when he would accompany his dad, a long distance trucker, to the terminal where he'd hear the adventurous tales of the truckers that always seemed to happen "down the road." Like many of the "ramblin' generation" of the '60s, Joe traveled throughout North America, mostly by thumb. In 1968 he landed in Alaska where he fought forest fires for the Bureau of Land Management and later built line cabins for some untamable trappers. In 1969 he graduated from Penn State University with a degree in English and a teaching certificate. While at PSU, he met and married his wife Marlene. After teaching high school in Scranton, Pennsylvania and in ghetto schools in Philadelphia, Joe hit the road again, this time heading south and extensively touring Mexico and Latin America. In 1974 Joe and Marlene migrated to Australia where they resumed teaching in the Blue Mountains of New South Wales. Their daughter Sandra was born there in 1976. With Australia as their new home and travel base, the Bisignanis toured Oceania and Australia. Since 1979 when Joe joined the Moon Publications team, he has spent the greatest share of his time researching, traveling in and writing about Japan.

GORDY OHLIGER — THE ILLUSTRATOR, HAS LONG BEEN A STUDENT OF THE ORIENTAL; HIS ART, ATTITUDE, SIMPLE HOME IN THE WOODS, AND STUDY OF AIKIDO ATTEST TO HIS EASTERN WAYS.

HE EARNED A B.F.A. FROM ART CENTER COLLEGE OF DESIGN AND HAS BEEN REPRESENTED BY GALLERIES IN THE SAN FRANCISCO / MARIN AREA AND IN NORTHERN CALIFORNIA WHERE HE RESIDES.

THESE SUMI-E WERE DONE WITH THE STONE AND INK THAT HIS FATHER BROUGHT HIM FROM JAPAN SOME TWENTY YEARS AGO.

South Pacific Handbook by David Stanley

A rugged companion volume to Moon Publication's *INDONESIA HANDBOOK* this compact budget guide to 29 territories is the first of its kind to survey the geography, climate, cultures and customs of the immense area of Oceania. Its 578 compact pages tells you how to catch a ride on yachts through the South Seas, backpack into the wilderness plateaus of Fiji, enjoy the cosmopolitan French life of New Caledonia, experience awesome Bora Bora by rented bicycle, live the life of a beachcomber in Tonga, dive on an eerie sunken Japanese war fleet in the Truk lagoon. Learn how to live in remote villages, witness the weaving of a 'fine mat' under a Samoan *fale,* travel in your own canoe or raft 100 km down the mighty Sepik River of New Guinea. No other travel book covers such a phenomenal expanse of the earth's surface. This Handbook contains 162 illustrations with explanatory captions, 160 photos, a bibliography, glossary, and extensive index. Smyth sewn, 187 mm x 130 mm (7-1/8'' x 5-3/8'').

ALASKA-YUKON HANDBOOK
by DAVID STANLEY

Retrace the route of early explorers and gold rush stampeders through a land of incomparable beauty. Tour the great wilderness ranges and wildlife parks of the North. Backpack across tundra to snowcapped peaks; stand high above the largest glaciers on earth; run mighty rivers. In addition to thousands of specific tips on Alaska and Yukon, this comprehensive guidebook includes detailed coverage of Seattle and British Columbia. *Alaska-Yukon Handbook* is the only travel guide which brings this whole spectacular region within reach of everyone. 244 pages, 70 maps, 37 color photos, 76 black and white photos, 84 illustrations, booklist, glossary, index. Available June 1983.

INDONESIA HANDBOOK
BY BILL DALTON *2nd. ed.*

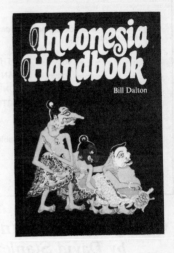

A companion guide to *South Pacific Handbook*, this traveler's pocket encyclopedia scans island-by-island Indonesia's history, ethnology, art forms, geography, climate, flora and fauna. This gypsy's guide outlines the cheapest places to eat and sleep; ancient ruins and historical sites; wildlife and nature reserves; spiritual centers; arts and crafts workshops; folk theater and dance venues; money-making and money-saving tips; mountain treks, caving, surfing, and scuba-diving locales; river travel, plus notes on sailing Indonesian waters, slow boat, bus, horse and foot connections through the cities, mountains, beaches and villages of the largest archipelago in the world.

READERS' QUESTIONNAIRE

(send to Moon Publications, P.O. Box 1696 Chico CA 95927 USA)

Name and address (optional): _____

_____

Country of origin: _____

Education: high school □   college □   post grad □

Occupation: _____

Income: under $10,000 □   under $20,000 □   over $30,000 □

Name of this book: _____

Reason for travel: business □   pleasure □   business and pleasure □
research and education □

Port of entry _____

How do you travel? independent □   package tour □   educational tour □
other _____

_____

Length of trip? 1-2 weeks □   one month □   longer _____

Do you travel with children? _____

Do you travel alone? _____

What do you like about this book? _____

_____

What don't you like about this book? _____

_____

How can we improve this book? _____

_____

Was this book easy to use? _____

_____

Comments and suggestions: _____

_____

_____